A Gentle Introduction to Stata

Revised Sixth Edition

A Gentle Introduction to Stata

Revised Sixth Edition

ALAN C. ACOCK
Oregon State University

A Stata Press Publication
StataCorp LLC
College Station, Texas

Published by Stata Press, 4905 Lakeway Drive, College Station, Texas 77845
Typeset in LaTeX 2_ε
Printed in the United States of America

10 9 8 7 6 5 4 3 2 1

Print ISBN-10: 1-59718-367-9
Print ISBN-13: 978-1-59718-367-3
ePub ISBN-10: 1-59718-368-7
ePub ISBN-13: 978-1-59718-368-0

Library of Congress Control Number: 2022949742

Contents

Figures

Tables

Boxed tips

Preface

This book was written with a particular reader in mind. This reader is learning social statistics and needs to learn Stata but has no prior experience with other statistical software packages. When I learned Stata, I found there were no books written explicitly for this type of reader. There are certainly excellent books on Stata, but they assume extensive prior experience with other packages, such as SAS or IBM SPSS Statistics; they also assume a fairly advanced working knowledge of statistics. These books moved quickly to advanced topics and left my intended reader in the dust. Readers who have more background in statistical software and statistics will be able to read chapters quickly and even skip sections. My goal is to move the true beginner to a level of competence using Stata.

With this target reader in mind, I make far more use of the menus and dialog boxes in Stata's interface than do other books about Stata. Advanced users may not see the value in using the interface, and the more people learn about Stata, the less they will rely on the interface. Also, even when you are using the interface, it is still important to save a record of the sequence of commands you run. Although I rely on the commands much more than the dialog boxes in the interface in my own work, I still find value in the interface. The dialog boxes in the interface include many options that I might not have known or might have forgotten.

To illustrate the interface as well as graphics, I have included more than 100 figures, many of which show dialog boxes. I present many tables and extensive Stata "results" as they appear on the screen. I interpret these results substantively in the belief that beginning Stata users need to learn more than just how to produce the results—users also need to be able to interpret them.

I have tried to use real data. There are a few examples where it is much easier to illustrate a point with hypothetical data, but for the most part, I use data that are in the public domain. For example, I use the General Social Surveys for 2002 and 2006 (Smith et al. 2015) in many chapters, as well as the National Survey of Youth, 1997 (Bureau of Labor Statistics, U.S. Department of Labor 2015). I have simplified the files by dropping many of the variables in the original datasets, but I have kept all the observations. I have tried to use examples from several social-science fields, and I have included a few extra variables in several datasets so that instructors, as well as readers, can make additional examples and exercises that are tailored to their disciplines. People who are used to working with statistics books that have contrived data with just a few observations, presumably so work can be done by hand, may be surprised to see more than 1,000 observations in this book's datasets. Working with these files provides better experience for other real-world data analysis. If you have your own data and the dataset has a variety of variables, you may want to use your data instead of the data provided with this book.

The exercises use the same datasets as the rest of the book. Several of the exercises require some data management prior to fitting a model because I believe that learning data management requires practice and cannot be isolated in a single chapter or single set of exercises.

This book takes the student through much of what is done in introductory and intermediate statistics courses. It covers descriptive statistics, charts, graphs, tests of significance for simple tables, tests for one and two variables, correlation and regression, analysis of variance, multiple regression, logistic regression, reliability, factor analysis, and path analysis. There are chapters on constructing scales to measure variables and on using multiple imputation for working with missing values.

By combining this coverage with an introduction to creating and managing a dataset, the book will prepare students to go even further on their own or with additional resources. More advanced statistical analysis using Stata is often even simpler from a programming point of view than what we will cover here. If an intermediate course goes beyond what we do with logistic regression to multinomial logistic regression, for example, the programming is simple enough. The `logit` command can simply be replaced with the `mlogit` command. The added complexity of these advanced statistics is the statistics themselves and not the Stata commands that implement them. Therefore, although more advanced statistics are not included in this book, the reader who learns these statistics will be more than able to learn the corresponding Stata commands from the Stata documentation and help system.

Two new chapters were added in the fifth edition. Chapter 15 introduces multilevel analysis for longitudinal and panel models. This chapter touches only on the capabilities of multilevel analysis using Stata, but it provides a starting point. Chapter 16 covers item response theory (IRT), which was added in Stata 14. IRT offers an advanced approach to measurement that has many advantages over the use of summated scales, which are discussed in chapters 3 and 12.

In the sixth edition, an extension to the discussion of using the `sem` command (structural equation modeling) to fit regression models to account for missing values was added. This also includes using auxiliary variables to help justify the missing-at-random assumption.

The revised sixth edition has been updated to Stata 17, including Stata command syntax, updated output, and all screenshots of Stata's interface. Discussion and examples include new features added to Stata since Stata 15, including the new `table` command, the `collect` suite of commands for creating, customizing, and exporting tables, and the use of transparencies in graphs.

I assume that the reader is running Stata 17, or a later version, on a Windows-based PC. Stata works equally as well on Mac and on Unix systems. Readers who are running Stata on one of those systems will have to make a few minor adjustments to some of the examples in this book. I will note some Mac-specific differences when they are important.

Corvallis, OR
November 2022

Alan C. Acock

Acknowledgments

I acknowledge the support of the Stata staff who have worked with me on this project. Special thanks goes to Lisa Gilmore, the Stata Press production manager, and David Culwell, the Stata Press technical editor.

Stata has many outstanding technical support people. I was lucky to have Kristin MacDonald be assigned the task of technical support for the sixth edition. After I made an initial draft of changes and additions to this edition, Kristin found many small (and some not-so-small) errors. She is a great statistician, and Stata and I are most fortunate to benefit from her expertise.

The revised sixth edition greatly benefited from Stata's Gabriela Ortiz, who carefully reviewed and suggested revisions to incorporate discussions of new Stata features.

I thank my students who have tested my ideas for the book. They are too numerous to mention, but this and earlier editions have benefited from suggestions by recent graduate students, including Shauna Tominey, Oregon State University; Rob Duncan, Purdue University; Isaac Washburn, Oklahoma State University; and Frank Snyder, Central Michigan University.

I also thank Richard Williams, University of Notre Dame, for sharing a critically important suggestion of Paul Allison, University of Pennsylvania, on how to incorporate auxiliary variables in `sem` commands.

My education benefited from the knowledge of many, but I would like to acknowledge two of my former professors who were especially important. Henry (Bud) Kass, one of my undergraduate professors, was a role model for how to work with students; he encouraged me to pursue my graduate education. Louis Gray, one of my graduate school professors, taught me the power of quantitative analysis and shared his enthusiasm for research.

Finally, I thank my wife, Toni Acock, for her support and for her tolerance of my endless excuses for why I could not do things. She had to pick up many tasks I should have done, and she usually smiled when told it was because I had to finish this book.

Support materials for the book

Stata 17 comes in several varieties. Stata/BE is the least expensive version. It can do everything that we cover in this book, and it has a great price for students. Stata/BE is limited to 2,048 variables but theoretically can handle over 2 billion observations (limited only by the capability of your computer). Large datasets such as longitudinal data can have more than 2,048 variables. Stata/SE can handle 32,767 variables. Stata/MP can handle 120,000 variables and even more observations. Stata/SE and Stata/MP have additional benefits for people who work with gigantic datasets. All Stata versions have a complete set of commands, so you do not have to buy additional add-on modules.

All the datasets and do-files for this book are available for you to download. In the Command window in Stata, type

```
. net from https://www.stata-press.com/data/agis6r/
```

After pressing the Enter key, type

```
. net get agis6r
```

Downloading data will store the data in the folder that appears at the bottom of the Stata screen (under the Command window). You might want to make a separate folder for each major project you do. In this book, we assume that you store your data in the `C:\Data` directory (Windows) or the `/Users/username/Data` folder (Mac). You can change your working folder within Stata by clicking on File ▷ Change working directory.... Stata will retrieve and save your data to this folder.

You will learn about do-files as you work your way through the book. Do-files are text files that contain sets of Stata commands. They contain scripts that can be used to manage data and run a series of commands for statistics and graphics. They are especially useful because you can save them and then rerun them at a later date when you need to run the same series of commands again. They can also serve as a template for when you want to run similar commands on new problems. When you run the `net get` command, you will get a complete set of do-files that reproduce nearly all the results for each chapter, `chapter1.do` to `chapter16.do`.

If you are working on a lab computer that erases anything you download once you shut down the computer, you can still get these do-files whenever you want. For example, if you are doing a logistic regression and want to open the do-file for that chapter, you could run the following command in your Command window:

```
. copy https://www.stata-press.com/data/agis6r/chapter11.do .
```

The `copy` command copies a file from one location to another, in this case from a website into our current working directory (the working directory is shown at the bottom of the Stata screen). At the end of the command, the dot that appears after the space indicates that you want to store `chapter11.do` into your current working directory. You need to have both the space and the dot for this command to work correctly. You could then open `chapter11.do` in your Do-file Editor or run the command `doedit chapter11`. Try this to see how it works.

If your lab computer erases everything you do when your session ends, you can still get the datasets for the book on the fly, whenever you need them. You can directly get whatever specific dataset is mentioned in the book. For example, if you wanted to analyze a dataset called `firstsurvey.dta`, you could enter the command

```
. use https://www.stata-press.com/data/agis6r/firstsurvey
```

Adding the extension `.dta` is optional because this is the default name for Stata datasets. If you already have a dataset open, you will first need to run the command `clear`. I include the command to get the data directly the first time a new dataset is being used in the book. For example, to describe a dataset, you type

```
. describe
```

but I will show

```
. use https://www.statapress.com/data/agis6r/nameofdataset
. describe
```

If you already have the dataset open, you can ignore the first command to get it.

Some datasets are automatically included when Stata is installed. You can open these by entering

```
. sysuse filename
```

For example, the file `cancer.dta` is one of the many files automatically installed. To open this file, you would type the following in the Command window:

```
. sysuse cancer.dta
```

Although this book introduces you to how you can use Stata, it is only an introduction. When Stata is installed on a computer, over 17,000 pages of documentation are included covering every Stata command in detail. The documentation includes examples of many specialized options that are available for each command. One of the first commands we will introduce is `summarize`. This is a very useful command that gives you summary statistical information about variables such as their means and standard deviations. If you want to know more about this or any command, enter `help` *commandname*.

```
. help summarize
```

Stata opens a Viewer window with a short description of what the command does. If you click on the blue `View complete PDF manual entry` link in the upper left corner of this window, Stata opens a PDF file giving you everything about what the `summarize` command can do, including multiple examples with real data. You will find the `help` facility a great way to extend your knowledge, and I know much of what I know about Stata was from using this feature. Try to run this `help summarize` command to see how this works. This support is available for every Stata command.

1 Getting started

1.1 Conventions

Listed below are the conventions that are used throughout the book. I thought it might be convenient to list them all in one place should you want to refer to them quickly.

Typewriter font. I use this font when something would be meaningful to Stata as input. I also use it to indicate Stata output.

I use a typewriter font to indicate the text to type in the Command window. Because Stata commands do not have any special characters at the end, any punctuation mark at the end of a command in this book is not part of the command. Sometimes, to be consistent with Stata manuals, I will put a command on a line by itself with the dot preceding it, as in

```
. sysuse cancer, clear
```

All of Stata's dialog boxes generate commands, which will be displayed in the History window and in the Results window. In the Results window, each command will be preceded by the dot prompt. If you make a point of looking at the command Stata prints each time you use the dialog boxes, you will quickly learn the commands. I may include the equivalent command in the text after explaining how to navigate to it through the dialog boxes.

Why do we show the dot prompt with these commands?

When we show a listing of Stata commands, we place a dot and a space in front of each command. When you enter these commands in the Command window, you enter the command itself and not the dot prompt or space. We include these because Stata always shows commands this way in the Results window. Stata manuals and many other books about Stata follow this convention.

When you type a Stata command in the Command window, you execute the command when you press the Enter key. The command may wrap onto more than one line, but if you press the Enter key in the middle of entering a command, Stata will interpret that as the end of the command and will probably generate an error. The rule is that you should just keep typing when entering a command in the Command window, no matter how long the command is. Press Enter only when you want to execute the command.

I also use the typewriter font for variable names, for names of datasets, and to show Stata's output. In general, I use the typewriter font whenever the text is something that can be typed into Stata or when the text is something that Stata might print as output. This approach may seem cumbersome now, but you will catch on quickly.

Folder names, filenames, and filename extensions, as in "The `survey.dta` file is in the `C:\data` directory (or folder)", are also denoted in the typewriter font. Stata assumes that `.dta` will be the extension, so you can use just the filename without an extension, if you prefer.

Sans serif font. I use this font to indicate menu items (in conjunction with the ▷ symbol), button names, dialog-box tab names, and particular keys:

- Menu items, such as "Select Data ▷ Data utilities ▷ Rename groups of variables from the Stata menu" (see figure 1.1).

Figure 1.1. Stata menu

- Buttons that can be clicked on, as in "Remember, if you are working on a dialog box, it will now be up to you to click on OK or Submit, whichever you prefer."
- Keys on your keyboard, as in "The Page Up and Page Down keys will move you backward and forward through the commands in the History window." Some functions require the use of the Shift, Ctrl, or Alt key, which will be held down while the second key is pressed. For example, Alt+f will open the File menu.

Slant font. I use this font for dialog-box titles and when I talk about labeled elements of a dialog box, with both items capitalized as they are on the dialog box.

Italics font. I use this font when I refer to a word that is to be replaced.

Quotes. I use double quotes when I am talking about labels in a general way, but I will use the typewriter font to indicate a specific label in a dataset. For example, if we decided to label the variable `age` "Age at first birth", we would enter `Age at first birth` in the textbox.

Capitalization. Stata is case sensitive, so `summarize` is a Stata command, whereas `Summarize` is not and will generate an error if you use it. Stata also recognizes capitalization in variable names, so `agegroup`, `Agegroup`, and `AgeGroup` will be three different variables. Although you can certainly use capital letters in variable names, you will probably find yourself making more typographical errors if you do. I have found that using all lowercase letters when creating variable names is usually the best practice.

I will capitalize the names of the various Stata windows, but I do not set them off by using a different font. For example, we will type commands in the Command window and look at the output in the Results window.

Setting how much output is in the Results window

The default size for the scrollback buffer size for the Results window is 200 kilobytes, approximately 200,000 characters. If you have many results being displayed in the Results window, the default is to drop the oldest lines once you use up the 200 kilobyte buffer. If you want to be able to scroll back further, you can make the buffer size larger, up to 2,000 kilobytes. Select Edit ▷ Preferences ▷ General preferences... and click on the Results tab. Stata for Mac users can make this change by selecting Stata ▷ Preferences ▷ General preferences... and clicking on the Windows tab. You might change the scrollback buffer size from the default 200 kilobytes to 500 kilobytes. This change will not take effect until you restart Stata.

Stata for Unix users cannot make this change from the *Preferences* dialog box; they must type the command `set scrollbufsize 500000` directly in the Command window.

Typing the command sets the scrollback buffer size in bytes by default, whereas using the menu method sets the size in kilobytes.

1.2   Introduction

The best way to learn data analysis is to actually do it with real data. These days, doing statistics means doing statistics with a computer and a software package. There is no other software package that can match the internal consistency of Stata, which makes it easy to learn and a joy to use. Stata empowers users more effectively than any other statistical package.

Work along with the book

> Although it is not necessary, you will probably find it helpful to have Stata running while you read this book so that you can follow along and experiment for yourself. Having your hands on a keyboard and replicating the instructions in this book will make the lessons that much more effective, but more importantly, you will get in the habit of just trying something new when you think of it and seeing what happens. In the end, experimentation is how you will really learn how Stata works. The other great advantage to following along is that you can save the examples we do for future use.

Stata is a powerful tool for analyzing data. Stata makes statistics and data analysis fun because it does so much of the tedious work for you. A new Stata user should start by using the dialog boxes. As you learn more about Stata, you will be able to do more sophisticated analyses with Stata commands. Learning Stata well now is an investment that will pay off in saved time later. Stata is constantly being extended with new capabilities, which you can install using the Internet from within Stata. Stata is a program that grows with you.

Stata is a command-driven program. It has a remarkably simple command structure that you use to tell it what you want it to do. You can use a dialog box to generate the commands (this is a great way to learn the commands or prompt yourself if you do not remember one exactly), or you can enter commands directly. If you enter the `summarize` command, you will get a summary of all the variables in your dataset (mean, standard deviation, number of observations, minimum value, and maximum value). Enter the command `tabulate gender`, and Stata will make a frequency distribution of the variable called `gender`, showing you the number and percentage of men and women in your dataset. After you have used Stata for a while, you may want to skip the dialog box and enter these commands directly. When you are just beginning, however, it is easy to be overwhelmed by all the commands available in Stata. If you were learning a foreign language, you would have no choice but to memorize hundreds of common words right away. This is not necessary when you are learning Stata because the dialog boxes are so easy to use.

Searching for help

Stata can help when you want to find out how to do something. You can use the `search` command along with a keyword. For example, you believe that a t test is what you want to use to compare two means. Enter `search t test`; Stata searches its own resources and others that it finds on the Internet. The first entry of the results is

```
[R]    ttest . . . . . . . . . . . . . . . t tests (mean-comparison tests)
       (help ttest)
```

The `[R]` at the beginning of the line means that details and examples can be found in the *Stata Base Reference Manual*. Click on the blue `ttest` to go to the help file for the `ttest` command. If you think this help is too cryptic, repeat the `search t test` command and look farther down the list. Scroll past the lines starting with `Video`, and look for the lines starting with `FAQ` (frequently asked questions). One of these is "What statistical analysis should I use?" Click on the blue URL to go to a UCLA webpage that will help you decide whether the t test is the best choice for what you are doing. You might click on some of the other resources to see how much support you get from a wide variety of resources.

When using the `search` command, you need to pick a keyword that Stata knows. You might have to try different keywords before you get one that works. Searching these Internet locations is a remarkable capability of Stata. If you are reading this book and want to know more about a command, the online help is the first place to start. Suppose that we are discussing the `summarize` command and you want to know more options for this command. Type `help summarize` and you will get an informative help screen. To obtain complete information for a command, you should see the PDF documentation. The PDF documentation can be opened from the Stata menu by selecting Help ▷ PDF documentation. Bookmarks to all the Stata manuals are available; expand the top-level bookmark for each manual to see bookmarks to sections therein.

Stata has done a lot to make the dialog boxes as friendly as possible so that you feel confident using them. The dialog boxes often show many options, which control the results that are shown and how they are displayed. You will discover that the dialog boxes have default values that are often all you need, so you may be able to do a great deal of work without specifying any options.

As we progress, you will be doing more complex analyses. You can do these using the dialog boxes, but Stata lets you create files that contain a series of commands you can run all at once. These files, called do-files, are essential once you have many commands to run. You can reopen the do-file a week or even several months later and repeat exactly what you did. Keeping a record of what you do is essential; otherwise, you will not be able to replicate results of elaborate analyses. Fortunately, Stata makes this easy.

You will learn more about replicating results in chapter 4. The do-files that reproduce most of the tables, graphs, and statistics for each chapter are available on the webpage for this book; see *Support materials for the book* for instructions on how to download the do-files.

Because Stata is so powerful and easy to use, I may include some analyses that are not covered in your statistics textbook. If you come to a procedure that you have not already learned in your statistics text, give it a try. If it seems too daunting, you can skip that section and move on. On the other hand, if your statistics textbook covers a procedure that I omit, you might search the dialog boxes yourself. Chances are that you will find it there.

Depending on your needs, you might want to skip around in the book. Most people tend to learn best when they need to know something, so skipping around to the things you do not know may be the best use of the book and your time. Some topics, though, require prior knowledge of other topics, so if you are new to Stata, you may find it best to work through the first four chapters carefully and in order. After that, you will be able to skip around more freely as your needs or interests demand.

1.3   The Stata screen

When you open Stata, you will see a screen that looks something like figure 1.2.

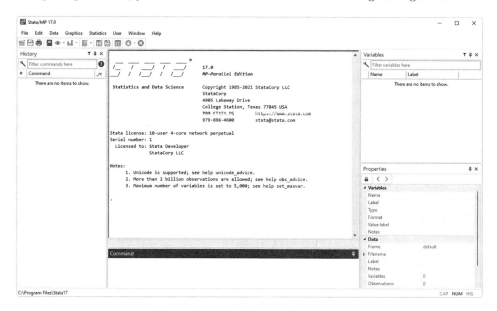

Figure 1.2. Stata's opening screen

You can rearrange the windows to look the way you want them, although many users are happy with the default layout. If you are satisfied with the defaults, you might skip the next couple paragraphs and come back to them if you change your mind later. Many experienced Stata users have particular ways to arrange these screens. Feel free to experiment with the layout.

Selecting Edit ▷ Preferences gives you several options. One thing you might want to do is change the size of the buffer for the Results window. The factory default of 200 kilobytes may be too small to be able to scroll through all your results. To change the size of the buffer, select Edit ▷ Preferences ▷ General preferences... and then click on the tab labeled Results. Depending on how much memory your computer has available, you might want to raise the default value to as much as 500 kilobytes. You can resize the Stata interface as you would any other Windows product. There are other options you can try under Results and each of the other tabs. It is nice to personalize your interface in a way that is attractive to you. I will use the generic "factory settings" for this book, however. If you make several changes and want to return to the starting point, select Edit ▷ Preferences ▷ Load preference set ▷ Factory window settings. If you are using Stata for Mac, select Stata ▷ Preferences ▷ Manage preferences ▷ Factory settings.

When you open a file that contains Stata data, which we will call a Stata dataset, a list of the variables will appear in the Variables window. The Variables window reports the name of the variable (for example, abortion) and a label for the variable (for example, Attitude toward abortion). Other information about the variable is shown in the Properties window, such as the type of variable (for example, float) and the format of the variable (for example, %8.0g). For now, just consider the name and label. You can vary the width of each column in the Variables window by placing your cursor on the vertical line between the name and label, clicking on it, and then dragging your cursor to the right or left.

When Stata executes a command, it prints the results or output in the Results window. First, it prints the command preceded by a . (dot) prompt, and then it prints the output. The commands you run are also listed in the History window. If you click on one of the commands listed in the History window, it will appear in the Command window. If you double-click on one of the commands listed in the History window, it will be executed. You will then see the command and its output, if any, in the Results window.

When you are not using the dialog boxes, you enter commands in the Command window. You can use the Page Up and Page Down keys on your keyboard to recall commands from the History window. On a Mac that does not have the Page Up and Page Down keys, you can use the fn key with the arrow up or arrow down key. You can also edit commands that appear in the Command window. I will illustrate all these methods in the coming chapters.

The bar at the bottom of the screen, called the status bar, displays the current working directory (folder). (Note that this status bar looks slightly different on a Mac.) This directory may be different on different computers depending on how Stata was installed. The working directory is where Stata will look for a file or save a file unless you specify the full path to a different directory that contains the file. Stata recognizes the tilde to represent your home directory. If you have a project and want to store all files related to that project in a particular directory, say, `C:\data\thesis`, you could enter the command `cd C:\data\thesis`. This command assumes that this directory already exists on your computer.

To change the working directory, you can either use the `cd` command or select File ▷ Change working directory... and click on the directory of choice. It is helpful to have a working directory for each project. On a Mac, if you cannot remember where you saved a file containing data, you can click on the magnifying glass in the upper-right corner of the Mac screen to search the name of the file and then click on the file to open it. If you already have a dataset open, you may need to type the `clear` command in the Command window first.

Stata has the usual Windows title bar across the top, on the right side of which are the three buttons (in order from left to right) to minimize, to expand to full-screen mode, and to close the program. Immediately below the Stata title bar is the menu bar, where the names of the menus appear. Some of the menu items (File, Edit, and Window) will look familiar because they are used in other programs. The Data, Graphics, and Statistics menus are specific to Stata, but their names provide a good idea of what you will find under them.

Figures 1.3 and 1.4 show the Stata toolbar as it appears in Windows and Mac, respectively. The icons provide alternate ways to perform some of the actions you would normally do with the menus. If you hold the cursor over any of these icons for a couple of seconds, a brief description of the function appears. For a complete list of the toolbar icons and their functions, see the *Getting Started with Stata* manual.

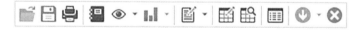

Figure 1.3. The toolbar in Stata for Windows

Figure 1.4. The toolbar in Stata for Mac

1.4   Using an existing dataset

Chapter 2 discusses how to create your own dataset, save it, and use it again. You will also learn how to use datasets that are on the Internet. For now, we will use a simple dataset that came with Stata. Although we could use the dialog box to do this, we will enter a simple command. Click once in the Command window to put the cursor there, and then type the command `sysuse cancer, clear`; the Command window should look like the one in figure 1.5.

Figure 1.5. Stata command to open `cancer.dta`

The `sysuse` command we just used will find the sample dataset on your computer by name alone, without the extension; in this case, the dataset name is `cancer`, and the file that is found is actually called `cancer.dta`. The `cancer` dataset was installed with Stata. This particular dataset has 48 observations and 8 variables related to a cancer treatment.

What if you forget the command `sysuse`? You could open a file that comes with Stata by using the menu File ▷ Example datasets.... A new window opens in which you click on *Example datasets installed with Stata*. The next window then lists all the datasets that come with Stata. You can click on `use` to open the dataset.

Now that we have some data read into Stata, type `describe` in the Command window. That is it: just type `describe` and press the Enter key. `describe` will yield a brief description of the contents of the dataset.

```
. describe
Contains data from C:\Program Files\Stata17\ado\base/c/cancer.dta
  Observations:           48                Patient survival in drug trial
     Variables:            8                3 Mar 2020 16:09
```

Variable name	Storage type	Display format	Value label	Variable label
studytime	byte	%8.0g		Months to death or end of exp.
died	byte	%8.0g	diedlbl	Patient died
drug	byte	%8.0g	type	Drug type
age	byte	%8.0g		Patient's age at start of exp.
_st	byte	%8.0g		1 if record is to be used; 0 otherwise
_d	byte	%8.0g		1 if failure; 0 if censored
_t	byte	%10.0g		Analysis time when record ends
_t0	byte	%10.0g		Analysis time when record begins

```
Sorted by:
```

The description includes a lot of information: the full name of the file, `cancer.dta` (including the path entered to read the file); the number of observations (48); the number

of variables (8); a brief description of the dataset (*Patient survival in drug trial*); and
the date and time the file was last saved. The body of the table displayed shows the
names of the variables on the far left and the labels attached to them on the far right.
We will discuss the middle columns later.

Now that you have opened `cancer.dta`, note that the Variables window lists the
eight variables `studytime`, `died`, `drug`, `age`, `_st` `_d`, `_t`, and `_t0`.

Internet access to datasets

Stata can use data stored on the Internet just as easily as data stored on your
computer. For example, if you do not have the dataset named `cancer.dta`
installed on your computer, you could load the data by typing `webuse cancer`.
However, you are not limited to data stored at the Stata website. Typing `use`
`https://stats.oarc.ucla.edu/stat/data/hsb2` will open a dataset stored at
the UCLA website.

Stata does not discard changes to the dataset currently in memory unless
you tell it to do so. That is, if you have a dataset in memory and you have
modified it, you will receive an error message if you try to load another dataset.
You need to save the dataset in memory, type the `clear` command to discard the
changes, or type the `clear` option of the `use` command to discard the changes.
You can then load the new dataset.

Stata provides all the datasets for every example in its manuals. For example, click on File ▷ Example datasets.... A new window opens in which you click
on Stata 17 manual datasets. There you might click on *Base Reference Manual*
[R]; scroll down to `correlate`, and click on `use` to open any of the datasets or
`describe` to see what variables are in the dataset.

1.5 An example of a short Stata session

If you do not have `cancer.dta` loaded, type the command `sysuse cancer`. We will
execute a basic Stata analysis command. Type `summarize` in the Command window
and then press Enter.

Rather than typing in the command directly, you could use the dialog box by selecting Data ▷ Describe data ▷ Summary statistics to open the corresponding dialog box.
Simply clicking on the OK button located at the bottom of the dialog box will produce
the `summarize` command we just entered. Because we did not enter any variables in the
dialog box, Stata assumed that we wanted to summarize all the variables in the dataset.

You might want to select specific variables to summarize instead of summarizing
them all. Open the dialog box again and click on the pulldown menu within the *Variables*

box, located at the top of the dialog box, to display a list of variables. Clicking on a variable name will add it to the list in the box. Dialog boxes allow you to enter a variable more than once, in which case the variable will appear in the output more than once. You can also type variable names in the *Variables* box. Figure 1.6 shows the dialog box with the drop-down variable list displaying the variables in your dataset:

Figure 1.6. The `summarize` dialog box

In the bottom left corner of the dialog box, there are three icons: ?, C, and ⌧. The ? icon gives us a help screen explaining the various options. The explanations are brief, but there are examples at the bottom of the Viewer window. The C icon resets the dialog box. Just to the right of the C icon is an icon that looks like two pages. If you click on this icon, the command is copied to the Clipboard.

If you enter the `summarize` command directly in the Command window, simply follow it with the names of the variables for which you want summary statistics. For example, typing `summarize studytime age` will display only statistics for the two variables named `studytime` and `age`.

In the Results window, the `summarize` command will display the number of observations (also called cases or *N*), the mean, the standard deviation, the minimum value, and the maximum value for each variable.

```
. summarize
```

Variable	Obs	Mean	Std. dev.	Min	Max
studytime	48	15.5	10.25629	1	39
died	48	.6458333	.4833211	0	1
drug	48	1.875	.8410986	1	3
age	48	55.875	5.659205	47	67
_st	48	1	0	1	1
_d	48	.6458333	.4833211	0	1
_t	48	15.5	10.25629	1	39
_t0	48	0	0	0	0

The first line of output displays the dot prompt followed by the command. After that, the output appears as a table. As you can see, there are 48 observations in this dataset. *Observations* is a generic term. These could be called participants, patients, subjects, organizations, cities, or countries depending on your field of study. In Stata, each row of data in a dataset is called an observation. The average, or mean, age is 55.875 years with a standard deviation of 5.659,[1] and the subjects are all between 47 (the minimum) and 67 (the maximum) years old.

If you have computed means and standard deviations by hand, you know how long this can take. Stata's virtually instant statistical analysis is what makes Stata so valuable. It takes time and skill to set up a dataset so that you can use Stata to analyze it, but once you learn how to set up a dataset (chapter 2), you will be able to compute a wide variety of statistics in little time.

We will do one more thing in this Stata session: we will make the histogram for the age variable, shown in figure 1.7.

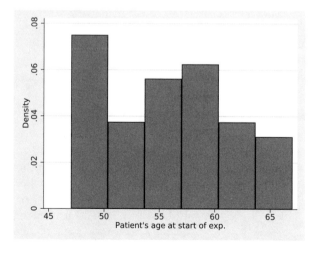

Figure 1.7. Histogram of age

---

1. I may round numbers in the text to fewer digits than shown in the output unless it would make finding the corresponding number in the output difficult.

A histogram is just a graph that shows the distribution of a variable, such as `age`, that takes on many values.

Simple graphs are simple to create. Just type the command `histogram age` in the Command window, and Stata will produce a histogram using reasonable assumptions. I will show you how to use the dialog boxes for more complicated graphs shortly.

At first glance, you may be happy with this graph. Stata used a formula to determine that six bars should be displayed, and this is reasonable. However, Stata starts the lowest bar (called a bin) at 47 years old, and each bin is 3.33 years wide (this information is displayed in the Results window) even though we are not accustomed to measuring years in thirds of a year. Also notice that the vertical axis measures density, but we might prefer that it measure the frequency, that is, the number of people represented by each bar.

Using the dialog box can help us customize our histogram. Let's open the `histogram` dialog box shown in figure 1.8 by selecting Graphics ▷ Histogram from the menu bar.

Figure 1.8. The `histogram` dialog box

Let's quickly go over the parts of the dialog box. There is a textbox labeled *Variable* with a pulldown menu. As we saw on the `summarize` dialog, you can pull down the list of variables and click on a variable name to enter it in the box, or you can type the variable's name yourself. Only one variable can be used for a histogram, and here we want to use `age`. If we stop here and click on OK, we will have re-created the histogram shown in figure 1.7.

There are two radio buttons visible to the right of the *Variable* box: one labeled *Data are continuous* (which is shown selected in figure 1.8) and one labeled *Data are discrete*. Radio buttons indicate mutually exclusive items—you can choose only one of them.

Here we are treating `age` as if it were continuous, so make sure that the corresponding radio button is selected. On the right side of the Main tab is a section labeled *Y axis*. Click on the radio button for *Frequency* so that the histogram shows the frequency of each interval. In the section labeled *Bins*, check the box labeled *Width of bins* and type 2.5 in the textbox that becomes active (because the variable is `age`, the 2.5 indicates 2.5 years). Also check the box labeled *Lower limit of first bin* and type 45, which will be the smallest age represented by the bar on the left.

The dialog box shows a sequence of tabs just under its title bar, as shown in figure 1.9. Different categories of options will be grouped together, and you make a different set of options visible by clicking on each tab. The options you have set on the current tab will not be canceled by clicking on another tab.

Figure 1.9. The tabs on the `histogram` dialog box

Graphs are usually clearer when there is a title of some sort, so click on the Titles tab and add a title. Here we type `Age distribution of participants in cancer study` in the *Title* box. Let's add the text `Data: Sample cancer dataset` to the *Note* box so that we know which dataset we used for this graph. Your dialog box should look like figure 1.10.

Figure 1.10. The Titles tab of the `histogram` dialog box

Now click on the Overall tab. Let's select *s1 monochrome* from the pulldown menu on the *Scheme* box. Schemes are basically templates that determine the standard attributes of a graph, such as colors, fonts, and size; which elements will be shown; and more.

From the **Legend** tab, under the *Legend behavior* section, click on the radio button for *Show legend*. Whether a legend will be displayed is determined by the scheme that is being used, and if we were to leave *Default* checked, our histogram might have a legend or it might not, depending on the scheme. Choosing *Show legend* or *Hide legend* overrides the scheme, and our selection will always be honored.

Now that we have made these changes, click on **Submit** instead of **OK** to generate the histogram shown in figure 1.11. The dialog box does not close. To close the dialog box, click on the **X** (close) button in the upper right corner, but we are not ready to do that yet.

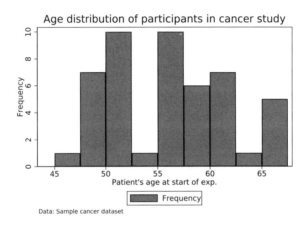

Figure 1.11. First attempt at an improved histogram

If you look at the complex command that the dialog box generated, you will see why even experienced Stata programmers will often rely on the dialog box to create graph commands. In reading this command, you will want to ignore the opening dot (Stata prints this in front of commands in the Results window, but the dot is not part of the command and you do not type it). Stata prints the > sign at the start of the second and third line, which might be confusing. Stata uses the **Enter** key to submit a command. Because of this, Stata sees the entire command as one line. To print the entire line in the confines of the Results window, Stata inserts the > for a line break. If you wanted to enter this command in the Command window, you would simply type the entire thing without the > and let Stata do the wrapping as needed in the Command window. Never press the **Enter** key until you have entered the entire command.

```
. histogram age, width(2.5) start(45) frequency
> title(Age distribution of participants in cancer study)
> note(Data: Sample cancer dataset) legend(on) scheme(s1mono)
(bin=9, start=45, width=2.5)
```

Clearing the Results window: The cls command

As you run commands, the results are displayed in the Results window. There may be times when you want to clear the Results window, so that, for example, seeing the top of the results of a command is easier, especially if your commands and results are lengthy. You can type the `cls` command (with no options) to clear the Results window.

It is much more convenient to use the dialog box to generate that command than to try to remember all its parts and the rules of their use. If you do want to enter a long command in the Command window, remember to type it as one line. Whenever you press **Enter**, Stata assumes that you have finished the command and are ready to submit it for processing.

When to use **Submit** and when to use **OK**

Stata's dialogs give you two ways to run a command: by clicking on **OK** or by clicking on **Submit**. If you click on **OK**, Stata creates the command from your selections, runs the command, and closes the dialog box. This is just what you want for most tasks. At times, though, you know you will want to make minor adjustments to get things just right, so Stata provides the **Submit** button, which still runs the command but leaves the dialog open. This way, you can go back to the dialog box and make changes without having to reopen the dialog box.

The resulting histogram in figure 1.11 is an improvement, but we might want fewer bins. Here we are making small changes to a Stata command, then looking at the results, and then trying again. The **Submit** button is useful for this kind of interactive, iterative work. If the dialog box is hidden, we can use the **Alt+Tab** (Windows) or **Cmd+Tab** (Mac) key combination to move through Stata's windows until the one we want is on top again.

Instead of a width of 2.5 years, let's use 5 years, which is a more common way to group ages. If you clicked on **OK** instead of on **Submit**, you need to reopen the `histogram` dialog box as you did before. When you return to a dialog that you have already used in the current Stata session, the dialog box reappears with the last values still there. So all you need to do is change **2.5** to **5** in the *Width of bins* box on the **Main** tab and click on **Submit**. The result is shown in figure 1.12.

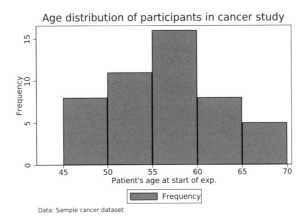

Figure 1.12. Final histogram of `age`

Notice how different the three graphs appear. You need to use judgment to pick the best combination and avoid using graphs that misrepresent the distribution. A good graph will give the reader a true picture of the distribution, but a poor graph may be quite deceptive. When people say that you can lie with statistics, they are often thinking about graphs that do not provide a fair picture of a distribution or a relationship. Can you think of any more improvements? The legend at the bottom center of the graph is unnecessary. You might want to go back to the dialog box, click on the Legend tab, and click on *Hide legend* to turn off the legend.

To finish our first Stata session, we need to close Stata. Do this with File ▷ Exit. If you are using Stata for Mac, select Stata ▷ Quit Stata.

1.6 Video aids to learning Stata

Many Stata users have put videos online that explain aspects of Stata. You can find these videos by searching YouTube or Googling, for example, "video tutorial Stata *t* test". Stata has also produced an excellent set of tutorials, which you can find at https://www.stata.com/links/video-tutorials/. Most of these tutorials are specific and short. At this point, it would be good to view the tutorials listed under *Stata basics*. I will mention a few specific tutorials as we go through the book, but you should look for a tutorial whenever something is not clear or you want to go beyond what is covered in the text.

1.7 Summary

We covered the following topics in this chapter:

- The font and punctuation conventions I will use throughout the book

- The Stata interface and how you can customize it

- How to open a sample Stata dataset

- The parts of a dialog box and the use of the OK and Submit buttons

- How to summarize the variables

- How to create and modify a simple histogram

1.8 Exercises

Some of these exercises involve little or no writing; they are simply things you can do to make sure you understand the material. Other exercises may require a written answer.

1. You can copy and paste text to and from Stata as you wish. You should try highlighting some text in Stata's Results window, copying it to the Clipboard, and pasting it into another program, such as your word processor. To copy highlighted text, you can use the Edit ▷ Copy menu or, as indicated on the menu, Ctrl+c. You will probably need to change the font to a monospaced font (for example, Courier), and you may need to reduce its font size (for example, to 9 point) after pasting it to prevent the lines from wrapping. You may wish to experiment with copying Stata output into your word processor now so that you know which font size and typeface work best. It may help to use a wider margin, such as 1 inch, on each side.

2. After you highlight material in the Results window, right-click on it. You can copy this output in several formats, including Copy, Copy table (only works with some commands), Copy table as HTML, and Copy as picture (copies a graphic image of what you highlighted). The Copy option works nicely, but you will need to use a monospaced font, such as Courier, and may need to use a smaller font size when you paste it into your word processing document. The Copy table option is limited because it only works with a few commands. The Copy table as HTML option will create a table that looks like what you would see on a webpage. Using Microsoft Word, you can edit the table by making columns wider or narrower and by aligning the columns so that each number has the same number of decimal places. Just copy the tabular results and not the command when using the HTML option. The Copy as picture option works nicely in Windows, but you cannot edit it in Word because it is a graphic image. In Word, you can resize the image.

Run the `summarize` command and copy the results to a Word document by using each of the options. Highlight the table. Right-click on it and then select the option you want. Switch to your word processor. Press Ctrl+v to paste what you copied. In your word processor, make the table as nice as you can by adjusting the font, font size, margins, etc.

3. Stata has posted all the datasets from its manuals that were used to illustrate how to do procedures. You can access the manual datasets from within Stata by going to the File ▷ Example datasets... menu, which will open a Viewer window. Click on *Stata 17 manual datasets* and then click on *User's Guide [U]*.

   The Viewer window works much like a web browser, so you can click on any of the links in the list of datasets. Scroll down to chapter 26, and select the `use` link for `censusfv.dta`, which opens a dataset that is used for chapter 26 of the *User's Guide*. Run two commands, `describe` and `summarize`. What is the variable `divorcert` and what is the mean (average) divorce rate for the 50 states?

4. Open `cancer.dta`. Create histograms for `age` using bin widths of 1, 3, and 5. Use the right mouse button to copy each graph to the Clipboard, and then paste it into your word processor. Does the overall shape of the histogram change as the bins get wider? How?

5. Stata has several video tutorials on using Stata. Go to https://www.stata.com/links/video-tutorials/. Click on Stata basics ▷ Tour of the Stata 17 interface. Each video is just a couple of minutes. It would be helpful to view the videos that correspond to topics covered in this book. You can also find many videos on the Stata YouTube channel, https://www.youtube.com/user/statacorp.

2   Entering data

2.1   Creating a dataset

In this chapter, you will learn how to create a dataset. Data entry and verification can be tedious, but these tasks are essential for you to get accurate data. More than one analysis has turned out wrong because of errors in the data.

In the first chapter, you worked with some sample datasets. Most of the analyses in this book use datasets that have already been created for you and are available on the book's webpage, or they may already be installed on your computer. If you cannot wait to get started analyzing data, you can come back to this chapter when you need to create a dataset. You should look through the sections in this chapter that deal with documenting and labeling your data because not all prepared datasets will be well documented or labeled.

The ability to create and manage a dataset is invaluable. People who know how to create a dataset are valued members of any research team. For small projects, collecting, entering, and managing the data can be straightforward. For large, complex studies that extend over many years, managing the data and the documentation can be as complex as any of the analyses that may be conducted.

Stata, like most other statistical software, almost always requires data that are set in a grid, like a table, with rows and columns. Each row contains data for an observation (which is often a subject or a participant in your study), and each column contains the measurement of some variable of interest about the observation, such as age. This system will be familiar to you if you have used a spreadsheet.

Variables and items

In working with questionnaire data, an item from the questionnaire almost always corresponds to a variable in the dataset. So if you ask for a respondent's age, then you will have a variable called `age`. Some questionnaire items are designed to be combined to make scales or composite measures of some sort, and new variables will be created to contain those items, but there is no single item corresponding to the scale or construct on the questionnaire. A questionnaire may also have an item where the respondent is asked to "mark all that apply", and commonly there is a variable for each category that could be marked under that item. The terms *item* and *variable* are often used interchangeably, but they are not synonyms. An item always refers to one question. A variable may be the score on an item or a composite score based on several items.

There is more to a dataset than just a table of numbers. Datasets usually contain labels that help the researcher use the data more easily and efficiently. In a dataset, the columns correspond to variables, and variables must be named. We can also attach to each variable a descriptive label, which will often appear in the output of statistical procedures. Because most data will be numbers, we can also attach value labels to the numbers to clarify what the numbers mean.

It is extremely helpful to pick descriptive names for each variable. For example, you might call a variable that contains people's responses to a question about their state's schools q23, but it is often better to use a more descriptive name, such as `schools`. If there were two questions about schools, you might want to name them `schools1` and `schools2` rather than q23a and q23b. If a set of items are to be combined into scales and are not intended to be used alone, you may want to use names that correspond to the questionnaire items for the original variables and reserve the descriptive names for the composite scores. This is useful with complex datasets where several people will be using the same dataset. Each user will know that q23a refers to question 23a, whereas "friendly" names like `schools1` may make sense to one user but not to another user.

There are a few variable names that Stata reserves: _all, _cons, _N, using, with, etc. For example, Stata uses the variable name _N to always be the size of your sample and uses the variable name _cons to refer to the constant (intercept). See [U] **11.3 Naming conventions** for the complete list of reserved names.

No matter what the logic of your naming, try to keep names short. You will probably have to type them often, and shorter names offer fewer opportunities for typing errors.

A respondent's age can be named `age` or `age_of_respondent` (note that no blank spaces are allowed in a name).

Even with relatively descriptive variable names, it is usually helpful to attach a longer and, one hopes, more descriptive label to each variable. We call these *variable labels* to distinguish them from *variable names*. For example, you might want to further describe the variable `schools` with the label "Public school rating". The variable label gives us a clearer understanding of the data stored in that variable.

For some variables, the meaning of the values in the data is obvious. If you measure people's height in inches, then when you see the values, it is clear what they mean. For other variables, the meaning of the values needs to be specified with a value label. Most of us have run across questions that ask us if we "Strongly agree", "Agree", "Disagree", or "Strongly disagree", or that ask us to answer some question with "Yes" or "No". This sort of data is usually coded as numbers, such as 1 for "Yes" and 2 for "No", and it can make understanding tables of data much easier if you create *value labels* to be displayed in the output in addition to (or instead of) the numbers.

If your project is just a short homework assignment, you could consider skipping the labeling (though your instructor would no doubt appreciate anything that makes your work easier to understand). For any serious work though, clear labeling will make your work much easier in the long run. Remember, we need a variable name, a descriptive label for the variable, and sometimes labels for the values the variable can have.

2.2   An example questionnaire

We have discussed datasets in general, so now let's create one. Suppose that we conducted a survey of 20 people and asked each of them six questions, which are shown in the example questionnaire in figure 2.1.

What is your gender?
  __ Male   __ Female
How many years of education have you completed?
    __ 0–8   __ 9
    __ 10   __ 11
    __ 12   __ 13
    __ 14   __ 15
    __ 16   __ 17
    __ 18   __ 19
    __ 20 or more
How would you rate public schools in your state?
    __ Very poor   __ Poor
    __ Okay   __ Good
    __ Very good
How would you rate public schools in the community you lived in as a teenager?
    __ Very poor   __ Poor
    __ Okay   __ Good
    __ Very good
How would you rate the severity of prison sentences of criminals?
    __ Much too lenient   __ Somewhat too lenient
    __ About right   __ Somewhat too harsh
    __ Much too harsh
How liberal or conservative are you?
    __ Very liberal   __ Somewhat liberal
    __ Moderate   __ Somewhat conservative
    __ Very conservative

Figure 2.1. Example questionnaire

Our task is to convert the questionnaire's answers into a dataset that we can use with Stata.

2.3 Developing a coding system

Statistics is most often done with numbers, so we need to have a numeric coding system for the answers to the questions. Stata can use numbers or words. For example, we could type `Female` if a respondent checked "Female". However, it is usually better to use some sort of numeric coding, so you might type 1 if the respondent checked "Male" on the questionnaire and 2 if the respondent checked "Female". We will need to assign a number to enter for each possible response for each of the items on the survey.

You will also need a short variable name for the variable that will contain the data for each item. Variable names can contain uppercase and lowercase letters, numerals, and the underscore character, and they can be up to 32 characters long. No blank spaces are allowed in variable names. The variable name `mother age` would be interpreted as two variables, `mother` and `age`. Generally, you should keep your variable names to 10 characters or fewer, but 8 or fewer is best. Variable names should start with a letter.

If appropriate, you should explain the relationship between any numeric codes and the responses as they appeared on the questionnaire. For an example, see the example codebook (not to be confused with the Stata command `codebook`, which we will use later) for our questionnaire in table 2.1.

Table 2.1. Example codebook

Question	Variable name	Value labels	Code
Identification number			
	id	Record in order	1 to 20
What is your gender?			
	gender	Male	1
		Female	2
		No answer	−9
How many years of education have you completed?			
	education	0–8	8
		9–20	9 to 20
		No answer	−9
Rate public schools in your state.			
	sch_st	Very poor	1
		Poor	2
		Okay	3
		Good	4
		Very good	5
		No answer	−9
Rate public schools in the community you lived in as a teenager.			
	sch_com	Very poor	1
		Poor	2
		Okay	3
		Good	4
		Very good	5
		No answer	−9
Rate severity of prison sentences of criminals. They are ...			
	prison	Much too lenient	1
		Too lenient	2
		About right	3
		Too harsh	4
		Much too harsh	5
		No answer	−9
How liberal or conservative are you?			
	conserv	Very liberal	1
		Liberal	2
		Moderate	3
		Conservative	4
		Very conservative	5
		No answer	−9

A codebook translates the numeric codes in your dataset back into the questions you asked your participants and the choices you gave them for answers. Regardless of whether you gather data with a computer-aided interviewing system or with paper questionnaires, the codebook is essential to help make sense of your data and your analyses. If you do not have a codebook, you might not realize that everyone with eight or fewer years of education is coded the same way, with an 8. That may have an impact on how you use that variable in later analyses.

We have added an `id` variable to identify each respondent. In simple cases, we just number the questionnaires sequentially. If we have a sample of 5,000 people, we will number the questionnaires from 1 to 5,000, write the identification number on the original questionnaire, and record it in the dataset. If we discover a problem in our dataset (for example, somebody with a coded value of 3 for `gender`), we can go back to the questionnaire and determine what the correct value should be. Some researchers will eventually destroy the link between the ID and the questionnaire as a way to protect human participants. It is good to keep the original questionnaires in a safe place that is locked and accessible only by members of the research team.

Some data will be missing—people may refuse to answer certain questions, interviewers forget to ask questions, equipment fails; the reasons are many, and we need a code to indicate that data are missing. If we know why the answer is missing, we will record the reason too, so we may want to use different codes that correspond to different reasons the data are missing.

On surveys, respondents may refuse to answer, may not express an opinion, or may not have been asked a particular question because of the answer to an earlier question. Here we might code "invalid skip" (interviewer error) as -5, "valid skip" (not applicable to this respondent) as -4, "refused to answer" as -3, "don't know" as -2, and "missing for any other reason" as -1. For example, adolescent boys should not be asked when they had their first menstrual period, so we would type -4 for that question if the respondent is male. We should pick values that can never be a valid response. In chapter 3, we will redefine these values to Stata's missing-value codes. In this chapter, we will use only one missing-value code, -9.

We will be entering the data manually, so after we administered the questionnaire to our sample of 20 people, we prepared a coding sheet that will be used to enter the data. The coding sheet originates from the days when data were entered by professional keypunch operators, but it can still be useful or necessary. When you create a coding sheet, you are converting the data from the format used on the questionnaire to the format that will actually be stored in the computer (a table of numbers). The more the format of the questionnaire differs from a table of numbers, the more likely it is that a coding sheet will help prevent errors.

There are other reasons you may want to use a coding sheet. For example, your questionnaire may include confidential information that should be shown to as few people as possible; also, if there are many open-ended questions for which extended answers were collected but will not be entered, working from the original questionnaire can be unwieldy.

In general, if you transcribe the data from the questionnaire to the coding sheet, you will need to decide which responses go in which columns. Deciding this will reduce errors from those who perform the data entry, who may not have the information needed to make those decisions properly.

Whether you enter the data directly from the questionnaire or create a coding sheet will depend largely on the study and on the resources that are available to you. Some experience with data entry is valuable because it will give you a better sense of the problems you may encounter, whether you or someone else enters the data. For our example questionnaire, we have created a coding sheet, shown in table 2.2.

Table 2.2. Example coding sheet

id	gender	education	sch_st	sch_com	prison	conserv
1	2	15	4	5	4	2
2	1	12	2	3	1	5
3	1	16	3	4	3	2
4	1	8	-9	1	-9	5
5	2	12	3	3	3	3
6	2	18	4	5	5	1
7	1	17	3	4	2	4
8	2	14	2	3	1	5
9	2	16	5	5	4	1
10	1	20	4	4	5	2
11	1	12	2	2	1	5
12	2	11	-9	1	1	3
13	2	18	5	5	-9	-9
14	1	16	5	5	5	1
15	2	16	5	5	4	2
16	1	17	4	3	4	3
17	1	12	2	2	-9	1
18	2	12	2	2	2	2
19	2	14	4	5	4	4
20	1	13	3	3	5	5

Because we are not reproducing the 20 questionnaires in this book, it may be helpful to examine how we entered the data from one of them. We will use the ninth questionnaire. We have assigned an id of 9, as shown in the first column. Reading from left to right, for gender, we have recorded a 2 to indicate a woman, and for education, we have recorded a response of 16 years. This woman rates schools in her state and in the community in which she lived as a teenager as very good, which we can see from the 5s in the fourth and fifth columns. She thinks prison sentences are too harsh and she considers herself to be very liberal (4 and 1 in the sixth and seventh columns, respectively).

2.4   Entering data using the Data Editor

Stata has a Data Editor, shown in figure 2.2, in which we can enter our data from the coding sheet in table 2.2. The Data Editor provides an interface that is similar to that of a spreadsheet, but it has some features that are particularly suited to creating a Stata dataset.

Figure 2.2. The Data Editor

Before we begin, let's type the command `clear` in the Command window. This step will give us a fresh Data Editor in which to enter data. To open the Data Editor in edit mode, type `edit` in the Command window. Alternatively, click on the icon on the toolbar that looks like a spreadsheet with a pencil pointing to it (see figure 2.3) or click on Data ▷ Data Editor ▷ Data Editor (Edit). The Data Editor in edit mode is a convenient way to enter or change data, but if you just want to see the data, you should use the Data Editor in browse mode. The icon for the Data Editor (Browse) is just to the right of the icon for the Data Editor (Edit); it is a spreadsheet with a magnifying glass on top (see figure 2.3). You can also type the command `browse` in the Command window.

Figure 2.3. Data Editor (Edit) and Data Editor (Browse) icons on the toolbar

Data are entered in the white columns, just as in other spreadsheets. Let's enter the data for the first respondent from the coding sheet in table 2.2. In the first cell under the first column, enter the identification number, which is a `1` for the first observation. Press the Tab key to move one cell to the right, and enter the value for the person's gender, which is a `2` for the first observation. Keep entering the values and pressing Tab until you have entered all the values for the first participant. Now you can press the Enter key, which will move the cursor to the second row of the Data Editor (Edit), and then press the Home key, which will move the cursor to the first column of this row. You can proceed to enter the rest of the data. The Tab key is smart, so after you enter the last value for the second row of data, pressing Tab will move the cursor to the first column of the third row. However, before doing this it would be good to enter more informative variable names to replace the default names of `var1`, `var2`, etc. To change a variable's name, click anywhere in the column for that variable or click on its name in the Variables pane at the top right of the Data Editor, for example, `var1`. Then in the Properties pane at the lower right of the Data Editor, change *Name* from `var1` to `id`. The name can be up to 32 characters, but it is usually best to keep the name short. Stata is case sensitive, so it is best to use lowercase names. By using lowercase names, you will not have to remember what case to use because the names will all be lowercase. From the Properties pane, we can also change the variable's label to be "Respondent's identification" by typing this text in the *Label* box. Our Data Editor (Edit) will look like figure 2.4.

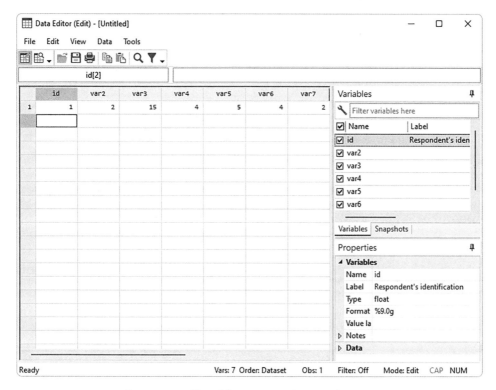

Figure 2.4. Variable name and variable label

Once we click outside the changed field in the Properties pane or press Enter, we
will see the new variable name displayed. Change each of the remaining generic variable
names to rename and label them as listed in table 2.3.

Table 2.3. New variable names and labels

Generic variable name	New variable name	Variable label
var2	gender	Participant's gender
var3	education	Years of education
var4	sch_st	Ratings of schools in your state
var5	sch_com	Ratings of schools in your community of origin
var6	prison	Ratings of prison sentences
var7	conserv	Conservatism/liberalism

As well as allowing us to specify the variable name and variable label, the Properties pane includes a place to specify the format of the variable. The current format is %9.0g, which is the default format for numeric data in the Data Editor. This format instructs Stata to try to print numbers within nine columns. Stata will adjust the format if you enter a number wider than nine columns.

I typed the letter l for the number 1

A common mistake is to type a letter instead of a numeric value, such as typing the letter l rather than the number 1 or simply pressing the wrong key. When this happens for the first value you enter for a variable, Stata will make the variable a "string" variable, meaning that it is no longer a numeric variable. When this happens for a subsequent value you enter for a variable, Stata will display an error message. If you made the mistake of inputting a variable as a string variable instead of a numeric variable, you need to correct this. Simply changing the letter to a number will not work because a string variable may include numbers, such as a variable for a street address. Stata will still think it is a string variable. There is a simple command to force Stata to change the variable from a string variable back to a numeric variable: destring *varlist*, replace. For example, to change the variable id from string to numeric, you would type destring id, replace.

If you have string data (that is, data that contain letters or symbols), you will see a format that looks like %9s, which indicates a variable that is a string (the s) with nine characters. For more detailed information about formats, see the *Stata Data Management Reference Manual*, which is available under Help ▷ PDF documentation. Some people like to enter string data where they enter yes or no, male or female, and so on. It is usually best here to simply enter numbers; I will show how to add value labels for the numbers in the next section. Entering numbers will benefit you later because some Stata commands work fine with string variables, but many of them require numeric values. After entering the rest of your data, the Data Editor (Edit) should now look like figure 2.5.

Figure 2.5. Data Editor with a complete dataset

2.4.1   Value labels

It would be nice to have labels for the values on most of these variables. For example, we would like `gender` labeled, so a code of 1 was labeled "Male" and a code of 2 was labeled "Female". We would not want to label values for `id` or `education`, but the rest of them should have value labels. In Stata, labeling values is a two-step process.

1. First, we define a label and give it a nickname. Some defined labels may apply to just one variable, such as `gender`, but other defined labels may apply to multiple variables that share identical value labels, such as `sch_st` and `sch_com`.

2. Second, we assign the defined label to each variable. You may not appreciate this being a two-step process with a small dataset, but in a major study, this is a valuable feature of Stata. For example, you might have 30 variables that are all coded as 1 for yes and 2 for no. You could define one value label and give it a nickname of `agree`. Then we could apply this defined label to each of the 30 variables.

2.5   The Variables Manager

We could use the Data Editor to define and apply value labels, but we will use another feature of Stata, the Variables Manager. You can open the Variables Manager by clicking on Data ▷ Variables Manager. The Stata for Windows toolbar has an icon for the Variables Manager, as shown in figure 2.6.

Figure 2.6. The Variables Manager icon on the Stata toolbar

Let's open the Variables Manager and define a value label for gender. We could have entered the variable names and variable labels here, but that was simple enough in the Data Editor. The Variables Manager is a convenient place to make any changes we might want. For example, when we click on gender, the Variable properties pane on the right shows whatever information we already have for the variable: its name, label, type, format, value label, and notes.

For the moment, we will use the Variables Manager to define the value labels. Click on the Manage... button next to the *Value label* field, which opens a new dialog box called *Manage value labels*; see figure 2.7. Because we have no value labels yet, nothing is listed. Click on Create label, and the *Create label* dialog box opens as shown in figure 2.7. For *Label name*, type sex. Notice that this is not the name of the variable but a nickname for the set of labels we will use for the variable. For *Value*, type 1; tab to *Label* and type Male; and then click on Add. Next type 2 under *Value*; tab to *Label* and type Female; and then click on Add. Figure 2.7 shows the Variables Manager and what we have done so far.

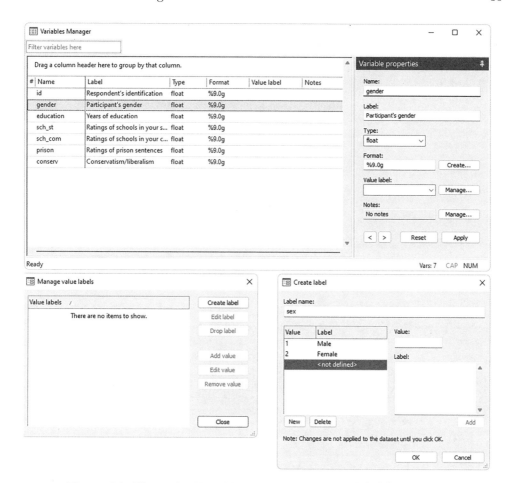

Figure 2.7. Using the Variables Manager to add a label for `gender`

Because we have no more values, click on **OK** to close the *Create label* dialog box and add the label `sex` to the *Manage value labels* dialog box. Now click on the **Close** button of the *Manage value labels* dialog box to return to the Variables Manager. In the Variable properties pane, we can click on the drop-down menu for *Value label* and select our label of `sex`. Then click on **Apply**. You will notice that the value label for `gender` is now `sex` in the list of variables on the left.

Let's define three more value labels. We do not need to click on a variable. We can simply click on the Manage... button next to *Value label*, and then click on Create label, which opens the *Create label* dialog box. Let's make a label nickname of `rating` that we will apply to `sch_st` and `sch_com`. For *Value*, type 1; tab to *Label* and type `Very poor`; and then click on Add. Repeat this step to add the following values and labels for the `rating` value label:

Value	Label
2	Poor
3	Okay
4	Good
5	Very good
-9	Missing

This label needs to have a final value of -9 with the label "Missing" because not everybody answered the relevant items. Click on OK in the *Create label* dialog box.

Repeat these steps, starting by clicking on Create label, and create value labels named `harsh` and `conserv` with the following values and labels:

Label name	Value	Label
harsh	1	Much too lenient
	2	Too lenient
	3	About right
	4	Too harsh
	5	Much too harsh
	-9	Missing
conserv	1	Very liberal
	2	Liberal
	3	Moderate
	4	Conservative
	5	Very conservative
	-9	Missing

Once you have finished creating the last value label, click on Close in the *Manage value labels* dialog box. Now we are back to the Variables Manager. Here we can click on `sch_st`, and then click on the drop-down menu next to *Value label*. We select our just created nickname, `rating`. Clicking on Apply will assign this set of value labels to the `sch_st` variable. We can repeat this for `sch_com` because that variable uses the same set of value labels, that is, `rating`.

Now click on **prison**, and then click on the drop-down menu next to *Value label*. Select the nickname **harsh**. Clicking on **Apply** will assign this set of values labels to the **prison** variable. Repeat these steps to assign the nickname **conserv** to the **conserv** variable.

Going through a series of dialog boxes can be confusing. You should experiment with these dialog boxes until you are confident in using them. Try to change some of the value labels, for example, use the *Edit label* dialog box that appears as an option when you click on the **Manage**... button next to *Value label* in the Variable properties pane. Fortunately, working with value labels is the most confusing part of data management that we will cover. If you can get comfortable with this, the rest of the material on data management will be less confusing. The key to remember is that you use the *Value label* dialog box to define a nickname (**sex**, **harsh**, **rating**, **conserv**) for sets of value labels. Then you apply these sets to the appropriate variables. As you do this, Stata will issue the commands you created, and they will appear in the Results window. Study these commands to see what is involved, and as you get more experience, you will use the commands directly. Here are the commands we generated using the Variables Manager:

```
. label define sex 1 "Male" 2 "Female"
. label values gender sex
. label define rating 1 "Very poor" 2 "Poor" 3 "Okay" 4 "Good" 5 "Very good"
> -9 "Missing"
. label define harsh 1 "Much too lenient" 2 "Too lenient" 3 "About right"
> 4 "Too harsh" 5 "Much too harsh" -9 "Missing"
. label define conserv 1 "Very liberal" 2 "Liberal" 3 "Moderate"
> 4 "Conservative" 5 "Very conservative"
. label values sch_st rating
. label values sch_com rating
. label values prison harsh
. label values conserv conserv
```

We will see how to enter these commands in a do-file in chapter 4. A brief explanation of commands may help now. The **label define** command says that we are going to define some value labels. Then we have a nickname (**sex**, **harsh**, **rating**, **conserv**). After the nickname, we have the values followed by their labels. We put quotes around each of the labels. After we have defined the sets of labels, the **label values** command applies these sets of labels to the variables. For example, the command **label values gender sex** means to apply value labels to the **gender** variable and use the set of value labels that have the nickname of **sex**.

What happened to the Variables Manager? It now looks like figure 2.8:

Figure 2.8. Variables Manager with value labels added

We can use the Variables Manager in more ways. Let's add a note to the variable conserv. We want to make sure anyone using our dataset knows that this is a single-item measure and not a scale of conservatism or liberalism that is based on a series of items. First, highlight the conserv variable by clicking on it. Next click on the Manage... button next to *Notes* in the Variable properties pane. A dialog box opens telling us that there are no items (notes) to show, so we click on Add. Enter This is a single-item measure and click on Submit. Click on Close to close this dialog box.

There are several reasons for applying a note to a variable. When several people are working on a large dataset and making changes, it is nice to have a record of those changes. For example, you might find that both observation 222 and observation 318 were coded with an out-of-range value, say, 8 on sch_com. You check the original questionnaires they answered and find that observation 222 should have been coded as a 4 and observation 318 should have been coded a missing value of -9. You could attach a note that "Observation 222 changed to 4 and 318 changed to -9 on 6/7/2012." You can have several notes assigned to each variable.

Another thing you might want to do is add a note to the entire dataset, not just to a specific variable. If you right-click on any variable, a drop-down menu appears with several useful options including *Manage notes for dataset...*. When you click on this option, you get a dialog box that looks just like the one of *Notes for variable*, but it is for *Notes for data*. You can click on Add and then type These data were collected in January of 2012. Now click on Submit and then Close to close the dialog box. Dataset notes can be very useful for keeping track of general changes in the dataset. For example, if Aidan merged some new variables from a different dataset into this dataset, it would be good to know what dataset was merged and when.

To see how the notes look in output, enter two commands.[1] First, type `describe` in the Command window, and then type `notes`.

```
. describe

Contains data
 Observations:               20
    Variables:                7
                                               (_dta has notes)

Variable      Storage   Display   Value
    name         type    format   label    Variable label

id            float     %9.0g              Respondent's identification
gender        float     %9.0g     sex      Participant's gender
education     float     %9.0g              Years of education
sch_st        float     %9.0g     rating   Ratings of schools in your state
sch_com       float     %9.0g     rating   Ratings of schools in your
                                             community of origin
prison        float     %16.0g    harsh    Ratings of prison sentences
conserv       float     %17.0g    conserv  * Conservatism/liberalism
                                           * indicated variables have notes

Sorted by:

. notes

_dta:
  1.  These data were collected in January of 2012
conserv:
  1.  This is a single-item measure
```

The `describe` command gives us a nice description of the dataset including the number of observations, the number of variables, the date the dataset was originally constructed (displayed once the dataset is saved), and a comment that `_dta has notes`. An asterisk appears by the variable label for `conserv` in the list of variables, and a note at the bottom of the list tells us that an asterisk means there is a note attached to that variable. The `notes` command has one note for the dataset and one note for the `conserv` variable. When a large group of researchers is working on a large and complex research project, the use of notes is extremely important.

There are still other things we can do with the Variables Manager. Suppose that we have a large dataset with 1,500 variables. We are looking for a variable and cannot remember its exact name, but we remember that it starts with the letters `so`. We can click on *Name*—the title of the column that includes all the variable names—to sort our variable list alphabetically. (Sorting our variable list in the Variables Manager does not change the order in which the variables are stored.) An alphabetical listing can help us find all the variables beginning with `so` very quickly. We find the variable; it is `soc_sat1`. If we want that variable included in a Stata command, such as `summarize`, we could type `summarize` in the Command window, and then right-click in the Variables Manager and choose *Send varlist to Command window*.

---

1. If you have not already entered the data, added the labels, and added the notes, you can open an already completed dataset with `use https://www.stata-press.com/data/agis6r/firstsurvey`.

Still using this large dataset, we remember that a particular set of five variables we want were coded as `yes_no` variables. We could click on *Value label*—the title of that column—to sort the variables by value labels. Instead of searching through 1,500 variables in the large dataset, we might have just 20 or 30 variables coded with the `yes_no` nickname. If we then remember that the variable we want is one of several that start with the variable label of "Peer", we could click on *Label* at the top of its column to sort the variables by variable labels.

At this point, we probably should restore the order of the variables as they are in the dataset. To return to the order of the variables in the dataset, click on the hash mark (#), which is to the left of the *Name* title. You should experiment with other features in the Variables Manager.

2.6   The Data Editor (Browse) view

In section 2.4, we entered data using the Data Editor in edit mode. Now that the data have been entered, we want to check our work. We can use the Data Editor in browse mode to do this. The purpose of using the Data Editor in browse mode is to look at data without altering it.

Type `browse` in the Command window to open the Data Editor (Browse). In the Data Editor window that opens, you see the numeric data where you did not add value labels, but for all the variables to which you did assign value labels, you now see the value label of each person, as shown in figure 2.9.

Figure 2.9. Dataset shown in the Data Editor (Browse) mode

Viewing the data in Data Editor (Browse) mode can be quite helpful. For example, person 11 has an ID of 11, is male, has 12 years of education, rates the schools in his state as poor, rates the schools in his community of origin as poor, feels that prison sentences are much too lenient, and considers himself to be very conservative. By seeing it laid out this way, you do not have to remember how each variable was coded. However, if you want to see just numeric values using the Data Editor (Edit), then you need to type the `edit, nolabel` command in the Command window. If you want to see just numeric values using the Data Editor (Browse), then you need to type the `browse, nolabel` command. Some researchers, when working on a small dataset, combine variables or change a variable and instantly see what happens in Browse mode. With a large dataset, this ability is usually not useful.

2.7   Saving your dataset

If you look at the Results window in Stata, you can see that the dialog box has done a lot of the work for you. The Results window shows that a lot of commands have been run to label the variables. These commands also appear in the History window. The Variables window lists all your variables. We have now created our first dataset.

Until now, Stata has been working with our data in memory, and we still need to save the dataset as a file, which we can do from the File ▷ Save as... menu. Doing this will open the familiar dialog box where we can choose where we would like to save our file. Once the data have been saved to a file, we can exit Stata or use another dataset and not lose our changes.

Notice that Stata will give the file the .dta extension if you do not specify one. You must use this extension, because it identifies the file as a Stata dataset. You can give it any first name you want, but do not change the extension. Let's call this file firstsurvey and let Stata add the .dta extension for us. If you look in the Results window, you will see that Stata has printed something like this:

```
. save "C:\data\firstsurvey.dta"
file C:\data\firstsurvey.dta saved
```

It is a good idea to make sure that you spelled the name correctly and that you saved the file into the directory you intended. Note the quotation marks around the filename. If you type a save command in the Command window, you must use the quotes around the filename if the name contains a space; however, if you always use the quotes around the filename, you will never get an error, whether or not the name contains a space.

Saving data and different versions of Stata

This book is written for users of Stata 17 and later. Stata is careful so that new versions can read data files that were saved using earlier versions of Stata. For example, if you were using an older version of Stata and upgraded, your new version should be able to read datasets you stored when you were using the older version. Stata is backward compatible in this sense.

Stata is not always forward compatible. If a person has an older version of Stata and needs to use a dataset you created in Stata 17, you can use the command saveold and the option version(#), where the # may be 13, 12, or 11. For example, to save a file named great.dta to your working directory so a person who has Stata 11 could read it, you would run

```
. saveold great.dta, version(11)
```

If you want to save it to a different directory, you would run

```
. saveold "/your directory/great.dta", version(11)
```

Stata 14, Stata 15, and Stata 16 can read Stata 17 datasets, so unless you are working with a dataset with more than 32,767 variables, you can use save instead of saveold; see help saveold for complete details.

In this book, we will work with one dataset at a time.[2] When you open a new dataset, Stata will first clear the current one from memory. Stata knows when you have changed your data and will prompt you if you attempt to replace unsaved data with new data. It is, however, a good idea to get in the habit of saving before reading new data.

A Stata dataset contains more than just the numbers, as we have seen in the work we have done so far. A Stata dataset contains the following information:

- Numerical data

- Variable names

- Variable labels

- Missing values

- Formats for printing data

- A dataset label

- Notes

- A sort order and the names of the sort variables

To see all the things you can insert into a dataset, type the commands `help label` and `help notes`. If the dataset has been sorted (observations arranged in ascending order based on the values of a variable), that information is also stored.

We have now created our first dataset and saved it to disk, so let's close Stata by selecting File ▷ Exit.

2.8   Checking the data

We have created a dataset, and now we want to check the work we did defining the dataset. Checking the accuracy of our data entry is also our first statistical look at the data. To open the dataset, use the File ▷ Open... menu. Locate `firstsurvey.dta`, which we saved in the preceding section, and click on Open.

Let's run a couple of commands that will characterize the dataset and the data stored in it in slightly different ways. We created a codebook to use when creating our dataset. Stata provides a convenient way to reproduce much of that information, which is useful if you want to check that you entered the information correctly. It is also useful if you share the dataset with someone who does not have access to the original codebook. Use the Data ▷ Describe data ▷ Describe data contents (codebook) menu to open the `codebook` dialog box. You can specify variables for the codebook entry you

---

2. Beginning in Stata 16, you can have multiple datasets in memory; type `help frames` to learn about this feature.

want, or you can get a complete codebook by not specifying any variables. Try it first without specifying any variables.

Let's look at the codebook entry for `gender` as Stata produced it. For this example, you can either scroll back in the Results window or use the Data ▷ Describe data ▷ Describe data contents (codebook) menu and type `gender` in the *Variables* box, as I have done in the examples that follow.

```
. codebook gender

gender                                                        Participant's gender

                    Type: Numeric (float)
                   Label: sex
                   Range: [1,2]                       Units: 1
           Unique values: 2                         Missing .: 0/20

              Tabulation: Freq.   Numeric  Label
                             10          1  Male
                             10          2  Female
```

The first line lists the variable name, `gender`, and the variable label, `Participant's gender`. Next the type of the variable, which is `Numeric (float)`, is shown. The value-label mapping associated with this variable is `sex`. The range of this variable (shown as the lowest value and then the highest value) is from 1 to 2, there are two unique values, and there are 0 missing values in the 20 cases. This information is followed by a table showing the frequencies, values, and labels. We have 10 cases with a value of 1, labeled `Male`, and 10 cases with a value of 2, labeled `Female`.

Using `codebook` is an excellent way to check your categorical variables, such as `gender` and `prison`. If, in the tabulation, you saw three values for `gender` or six values for `prison`, you would know that there are errors in the data. Looking at these kinds of summaries of your variables will often help you detect data-entry errors, which is why it is crucial to review your data after entry.

Let's also look at the display for `education`:

```
. codebook education

education                                                      Years of education

                    Type: Numeric (float)
                   Range: [8,20]                       Units: 1
           Unique values: 10                         Missing .: 0/20

                    Mean:   14.45
                Std. dev.: 2.94645

             Percentiles:      10%      25%      50%      75%      90%
                              11.5       12     14.5     16.5       18
```

Because this variable takes on more values, Stata does not tabulate the individual values. Instead, Stata displays the range (8 to 20) along with the mean, which is 14.45, and the standard deviation, which is 2.95. It also gives the percentiles. The 50th percentile is usually called the median, and here the median is 14.5.

In the `codebook` dialog box, if we leave the box where we enter variables blank, then `codebook` will give us a detailed codebook for every variable in the dataset. This detailed codebook can be combined with other options. By clicking on the **Options** tab, we can ask to include any notes that are attached to variables. Clicking on *Report potential problems in dataset* can be informative. Using this option, we might be told that `sch_st`, `sch_com`, and `conserv` have incomplete value labels. Why would this happen? If we did not assign a value label to the value of −9 for these variables, this option would inform us that there is a value that does not have an assigned value label. We will learn about how to manage missing values in the next chapter.

Sometimes we just want a brief summary of variables like we would get using the `describe` command. Enter `codebook, compact` in the Command window or click on *Display compact report on the variables* on the **Options** tab of the `codebook` dialog box. This option gives you seven columns of information including the variable name, the number of observations, the number of unique values the variable has in your data, the mean for the item, the minimum and maximum values, and the variable label. A variation of the `codebook, compact` command includes one or more variable names in the command, for example, `codebook gender, compact`. This gives you the same information as the `codebook, compact` command, but only for the variable(s) you specify. The `compact` option cannot be combined with the other options.

Alternatively, we could simply use the `describe` command. Enter the command in the Command window, or use the Data ▷ Describe data ▷ Describe data in memory or in a file menu, which will display the dialog box in figure 2.10.

Figure 2.10. The `describe` dialog box

If you do not list any variables in the *Variables* box, all the variables will be included, as shown in the following output:

```
. describe

Contains data from C:\data\firstsurvey.dta
 Observations:           20
    Variables:            7                    15 Jun 2022 15:32
                                               (_dta has notes)
─────────────────────────────────────────────────────────────────────────
Variable      Storage   Display   Value
    name         type    format   label       Variable label
─────────────────────────────────────────────────────────────────────────
id            float     %9.0g                 Respondent's identification
gender        float     %9.0g     sex         Participant's gender
education     float     %9.0g                 Years of education
sch_st        float     %9.0g     rating      Ratings of schools in your state
sch_com       float     %9.0g     rating      Ratings of schools in your
                                                community of origin
prison        float     %16.0g    harsh       Ratings of prison sentences
conserv       float     %17.0g    conserv   * Conservatism/liberalism
                                            * indicated variables have notes
─────────────────────────────────────────────────────────────────────────

Sorted by:
```

As we can see by examining the output, the path to the data file is shown (directory and filename), as are the number of observations, the number of variables, and the last date and time the file was written (called a *timestamp*). We can attach a label to a dataset, too, and if we had done so, it would have been shown above the timestamp. Below the information that summarizes the dataset is information on each variable: its name, its storage type (there are several types of numbers and strings), the format Stata uses when printing values for the variable, the value-label mapping associated with it, and the variable label. This is clearly not as complete a description of each variable as that provided by codebook, but it is often just what you want.

Working with Excel, SAS, and SPSS files

Many researchers use Microsoft Excel to create and store datasets. Typically, the variable names are placed in the first row. Because storing an Excel file like this has no information about variable labels, value labels, or missing values, you will not be able to retrieve that information when you transform the dataset from Excel format to Stata format. If you have coded variables as text in the Excel file by entering the labels "female" and "male" in your Excel file, Stata will read these as string variables. If you entered them as numeric variables such as 0 for male and 1 for female, you will need to add the value labels once they are in Stata.

Stata can both import and export Excel datasets including variable names that you put in the first row of the Excel file. We will illustrate both importing and exporting Excel files using a Stata dataset, `auto.dta`. First, we open `auto.dta`, which comes with Stata, by typing the command

```
. sysuse auto, clear
```

Second, select File ▷ Export ▷ Data to Excel spreadsheet (*.xls; *.xlsx). In the dialog box that opens, click on Save as.... This takes you to a second dialog box where you can enter the name of the Excel file, say, `auto.xlsx`, specify the location where you want to store the Excel file, and select the file format. Clicking on Save adds the path and filename to the *Excel filename* box and takes you to the first dialog box. Here we click on the box for *Save variable names to first row in Excel file*. We then click on OK to save the file.

To import an Excel file named, for example, `auto.xlsx`, you select File ▷ Import ▷ Excel spreadsheet (*.xls; *.xlsx). In the dialog box that opens, click on Browse..., go where you have stored the Excel file, and double-click on the filename. This opens the dialog box shown below. The complete path and Excel filename will be listed in the *Excel file* box. Click on the *Import first row as variable names* box. Although the variable names were stored in lowercase in the Excel file, we use the drop-down menu under *Variable case* to select *Lower* anyway. Many people use uppercase or mixed-case variable names in Excel spreadsheets, but it is usually better to use lowercase variable names in Stata. Here is how our dialog box should look; we can now click on OK.

Working with Excel, SAS, and SPSS files, continued

Some considerations are needed when transferring data. Statistical software datasets may include a lot more information than just the raw data. Datasets may include the name of each variable, labels for each variable, labels for possible values on variables, and information about what is recorded when there is a missing value. For example, a dataset might include a variable called `momrace`, which has a variable label of `Mother's racial or ethnic identity`, with values of 1–5 indicating a particular identity such as Hispanic, Asian, etc., and when a person refuses to answer the question, a number 9 is used to signify that the value is missing. When doing a transfer, you want to keep all of this information. Both SAS and SPSS are widely used for research, and you need a way to transfer data from Stata to one of them or from one of them to Stata. This can be a bit tricky because Stata, SPSS, and SAS periodically release new versions and the storage format and Stata 15 may not be readable by the older version of SAS or SPSS. This can also be a problem if you are working with a colleague who uses an older version of Stata. If your colleague runs an older version of Stata, you need to be able to save your dataset in a compatible version before your colleague can use the data. To save your data to an older version of Stata, you can click on File ▷ Save as... and click on the file format option you want. The default shows up as `Stata Data (*.dta)`, but you can change this to `Stata 13 Data (*.dta)` or to `Stata 12/11 Data (*.dta)`.

Working with Excel, SAS, and SPSS files, continued

If somebody is using SPSS, there are two ways to share this data with a Stata user. The simplest method would be to read the SPSS file directly into Stata with `import spss`; IBM SPSS Statistics files version 16 and higher are supported. The other method would be to save the SPSS data file as a Stata data file. Depending on what release of SPSS is being used, the save file will likely be in an older format of Stata datasets. That is okay because Stata is backward compatible. This means that the current version of Stata can read data that are stored in any of the older Stata formats. Once you open and save the dataset as a `Stata dataset` (`*.dta`), it will be stored in the current version. If you make changes and want to share them with your colleague, you may need to save the Stata dataset in the older version that SPSS can read.

At the time of this writing, when SPSS exports the data in a format that is readable by Stata, it does so in an inefficient way. With a large dataset transferred this way, you should run the `compress` command once you open the dataset the first time. In the Command window run

```
. compress
```

The `compress` command goes through each variable and stores it the most compact format it can without losing any precision.

SAS has a special data format for sharing data that is called an XPORT file. Stata can export a dataset to both the SAS XPORT Version 5 and the SAS XPORT Version 8 Transport format using File ▷ Export ▷ SAS XPORT Version 5 (*.xpt) and File ▷ Export ▷ SAS XPORT Version 8 (*.v8xpt). Similarly, SAS can save its data in the SAS XPORT format. Then, Stata can read the XPORT file using File ▷ Import ▷ SAS XPORT Version 5 (*.xpt) or File ▷ Import ▷ SAS XPORT Version 8 (*.v8xpt), depending on the format of the file. Additionally, you can use `import sas` to import SAS data from version 7 or higher into Stata.

When you import data from Excel, SPSS, or SAS, it is good to make sure that all variable names are lowercase. Suppose you have imported a dataset from SPSS where the first variable is ID and the last variable is ZODIAC. Once you open the dataset in Stata, enter the following in the Command window:

```
. rename ID-ZODIAC, lower
```

This will make all the variable names lowercase. The new Stata dataset will have the variables `id-zodiac`. You always need to inspect any transferred dataset because some features may not be available in one or the other formats. For example, Stata has a very detailed capability for labeling missing values that allows you to distinguish between many possible reasons a value might be missing. Other software that cannot do this will not be able to make so many distinctions.

2.9   Summary

We covered the following topics in this chapter:

- How to create a codebook for a questionnaire

- How to develop a system for coding the data

- How to enter the data into a Stata dataset

- How to add variable names and variable labels to a dataset

- How to create value-label mappings and associate them with variables

2.10   Exercises

1. From the coding sheet shown in table 2.2, translate the numeric codes back into the answers given on the questionnaire by using the codebook in table 2.1.

2. Using the Variables Manager, attach a note that provides a descriptive label to the dataset you created in this chapter. What command is printed in the Results window by the dialog box? Then run the `notes` command from the Command window. See if you can use the Variables Manager to remove the note. What are the advantages of keeping a note for a dataset inside the dataset?

3. Using the Variables Manager, attach a note for each variable you created in this chapter. What command is printed in the Results window when you do this? Then run the `notes` command from the Command window. See if you can use the Variables Manager to remove the notes. What are the advantages of keeping notes for variables inside the dataset?

4. Run the command to create a compact codebook from the Command window. Interpret what the codebook shows for `gender`, `education`, and `conserv`.

5. Administer your own small questionnaire to students in your class. Enter the data into a Stata dataset, and label the variables and values. Be sure to have at least 15 people complete your questionnaire, but do not try to enter data for a very large group of people.

6. Create a codebook for your dataset from the previous exercise that includes notes and any possible problems Stata can identify about your dataset. What command appears in the Results window when you do this?

7. What is the value of using a two-step process for creating value labels? When is this process especially helpful?

3 Preparing data for analysis

3.1 Introduction

Most of the time spent on any research project is spent preparing for analysis. Exactly how much time will depend on the data. If you collect and enter your own data, most of the actual time you spend on the project will not be analyzing the data; it will be getting the data ready to analyze. If you are performing secondary analysis and are using well-prepared data, you may spend substantially less time preparing the data.

Stata has an entire reference manual on data management, the *Data Management Reference Manual*. We will cover only a few of Stata's capabilities for managing data. Some of the data management tasks required for a project you will be able to anticipate and plan, but others will just arise as you progress through a project, and you will need to deal with them on the spot. If your data are always going to be prepared for you and you will use Stata only for statistics and graphs, then you might skip this chapter.

This chapter covers the basics for preparing data for analysis. However, if you want to learn more, there is a remarkably accessible book on data management, Michael Mitchell's (2020) *Data Management Using Stata: A Practical Handbook*. This was published by Stata Press and is a must read for those who want advanced expertise in this area. Data management is a highly prized skill set by members of any research team.

3.2   Planning your work

The data we will be using are from the U.S. Department of Labor, Bureau of Labor Statistics, National Longitudinal Survey of Youth, 1997 (NLSY97) (Bureau of Labor Statistics, U.S. Department of Labor 2015). I selected a set of four items to measure how adolescents feel about their mothers and another set of four parallel items to measure how adolescents feel about their fathers. I used an extraction program available from https://www.bls.gov/nls/nlsdata.htm and extracted a Stata dictionary that contains a series of commands for constructing the Stata dataset, which we will use along with the raw data in plain text. I created a dataset called `relate.dta`. In this chapter, you will learn how to work with this dataset to create two variables, Youth Perception of Mother and Youth Perception of Father.

What is a Stata dictionary file?

A Stata dictionary file is a special file that contains Stata commands and raw data in plain text. We will not cover this type of file here, but we use this format to import the raw data into a Stata dataset. Selecting File ▷ Import ▷ Text data in fixed format with a dictionary opens a window with a blank box for the *Dictionary filename* and a blank box for the *Text dataset filename*. Because the raw data and the commands to create the Stata file are both in the dictionary file, we can simply enter the name of the dictionary file there and leave the *Text dataset filename* empty. The name of the file is `relate.dct`. If we did not have this file stored in the working directory, we could click on Browse... to help us search for it. The extension `.dct` is always used for a dictionary file. Clicking on OK imports the data into Stata. We can then save it using the name `relate.dta`. The dictionary provides the variable names and variable labels. Had the variable labels not been included in the dictionary, we would have created them prior to saving the dataset. If you need to create a dictionary file yourself, you can learn how to do that in the *Stata Data Management Reference Manual*.

It is a good idea to make an outline of the steps we need to take to go from data collection to analysis. The outline should include what needs to be done to collect or obtain the data, enter (or read) and label the data, make any necessary changes to the data prior to analysis, create any composite variables, and create an analysis-ready version (or versions) of the dataset.

An outline serves two vital functions: it provides direction so we do not lose our way in what can often be a complicated process with many details and it provides us with a set of benchmarks for measuring progress. For a large project, do not underestimate the benefit to measuring progress because it is the key to successful project management.

Our project outline, which is for a simple project on which only one person is working, is shown in table 3.1.

Table 3.1. Sample project task outline

○ Consult NLSY97 documentation (see appendix 9 [PDF], page 23, available at https: //www.nlsinfo.org/sites/default/files/attachments/12125/app9pdf.pdf) to determine which variables are needed.

○ Download the data that are in the dictionary file and the codebook. (This was done for you as `relate.dct` and `relate.cdb`.)

○ Create a basic Stata dataset. (This was done for you as `relate.dta`.)

○ Create variable and value labels.

○ Generate tables for variables to compare against the codebook to check for errors.

○ Convert missing-value codes to Stata missing values.

○ Reverse code those variables that need it; verify.

○ Copy variables not reversed to named variables; verify.

○ Create the scale variable.

○ Save the analysis-ready copy of the dataset.

This is a pretty skeletal outline, but it is a fine start for a small project like this. The larger the project, the more detail needed for the outline. Now that we have the NLSY97-supplied codebook to look at, we can fill in some more details on our outline.

First, we will run a `describe` command on the dataset we created, `relate.dta`. Remember that you can download `relate.dta` and other datasets used in this book from the book's webpage. Alternatively, you can open the file `relate.dta` by typing the command

```
. use https://www.stata-press.com/data/agis6r/relate
```

Notice that `relate.dta` has capitalized all the letters in variable names. A widely utilized Stata convention is to use lowercase letters. By conforming to this convention, we do not need to worry about whether the case is upper or lower because the default is almost always lowercase. To change all the variable names in this dataset, we can run a single command. Where the first variable is named R0000100, and the last variable is R3828700, all we need to do is run

```
. rename R0000100-R3828700, lower
```

Now, we can run the command `describe r3483600 r3483700 r3483800 r3483900`, and then we can get more information by running the command `codebook, compact`. For the `codebook`, we do not list the variables because the dataset includes only a few variables. Thus, we use the following command to produce a description of the data:

```
. describe r3483600 r3483700 r3483800 r3483900
```

Variable name	Storage type	Display format	Value label	Variable label
r3483600	float	%9.0g		MOTH PRAISES R DOING WELL 1999
r3483700	float	%9.0g		MOTH CRITICIZE RS IDEAS 1999
r3483800	float	%9.0g		MOTH HELPS R WITH WHAT IMPT TO R 1999
r3483900	float	%9.0g		MOTH BLAMES R FOR PROBS 1999

```
. codebook, compact
```

Variable	Obs	Unique	Mean	Min	Max	Label
r0000100	8984	8984	4504.302	1	9022	PUBID - YTH ID CODE 1997
r3483600	8984	9	-.5638914	-5	4	MOTH PRAISES R DOING WELL 1999
r3483700	8984	9	-1.425312	-5	4	MOTH CRITICIZE RS IDEAS 1999
r3483800	8984	9	-.5893811	-5	4	MOTH HELPS R WITH WHAT IMPT TO...
r3483900	8984	9	-1.769813	-5	4	MOTH BLAMES R FOR PROBS 1999
r3485200	8984	9	-1.535508	-5	4	FATH PRAISES R DO WELL 1999
r3485300	8984	9	-2.143143	-5	4	FATH CRITICIZE IDEAS 1999
r3485400	8984	9	-1.586487	-5	4	FATH HELP WITH WHAT IMPT TO R ...
r3485500	8984	9	-2.388023	-5	4	FATH BLAME R FOR PROBS 1999
r3828100	8984	8	15.02538	-5	20	SYMBOL!KEY!AGE 1999
r3828700	8984	3	.9319902	-5	2	SYMBOL!KEY!SEX 1999

These variable names are not helpful, so we might want to change them later. For example, we may rename r3483600 to mompraise. The variable labels make sense, but notice that there are no value labels listed under the column labeled value label in the results of the describe command. codebook, compact gives us a bit more information. We see there are 8,984 observations, we see a mean for each item, and we see the minimum (−5) and maximum value (4) reported for the items. Still, without value labels, we do not know what these values mean.

Let's read the codebook that we downloaded at the same time we downloaded this dataset. So you do not need to go through the process of getting the codebook from the NLS website, the part we use is called relate.cdb. You can open this file by pointing your web browser to https://www.stata-press.com/data/agis6r/relate.cdb. Table 3.2 shows what the downloaded codebook looks like for the r3483600 variable.

Table 3.2. NLSY97 sample codebook entries

```
r34836.00    [YSAQ-022]                              Survey Year: 1999

             MOTHER PRAISES R FOR DOING WELL

How often does she praise you for doing well?

      118       0 NEVER
      235       1 RARELY
      917       2 SOMETIMES
     1546       3 USUALLY
     1701       4 ALWAYS
    -------
     4517

Refusal(-1)          20
Don't Know(-2)        3
TOTAL =========>   4540   VALID SKIP(-4)   3669   NON-INTERVIEW(-5)   775
```

We can see that a code of 0 means never, a code of 1 means rarely, etc. We need to make value labels so that the data will have nice value labels like these. Also notice that there are different missing values. The codebook uses -1 for refusal, -2 for don't know,-4 for valid skip, and -5 for noninterview. But there is no -3 code. Searching the documentation, we learn that this code was used when there was an interviewer mistake or an "invalid skip". We did not have any of these for this item, but we might for others. The "don't know" responses are people who should have answered the question but instead they said that they did not know what they thought or that they had no opinion. By contrast, notice there are 3,669 valid skips representing people who were not asked the question for some reason. We need to check this out, and reading the documentation, we learn that these people were not asked because they were more than 14 years old, and only youth 12–14 were asked this series of questions. Finally, 775 youth were not interviewed. We need to check this out as well. These are 1999 data, the third year the data were collected, and the researchers were unable to locate these youth, or they refused to participate in the third year of data collection. In any event, we need to define missing values in a way that keeps track of these distinctions.

How does the Stata dataset look compared with the codebook that we downloaded? We can run the command `codebook` to see. Let's restrict it to just the variable `r3483600` by entering the command `codebook r3483600` in the Command window. The problem with the data is apparent when we look at the codebook: the absence of value labels makes our actual data uninterpretable.

```
. codebook r3483600
```

r3483600	MOTH PRAISES R DOING WELL 1999

```
            Type: Numeric (float)
           Range: [-5,4]                      Units: 1
   Unique values: 9                       Missing .: 0/8,984
      Tabulation: Freq.  Value
                    775  -5
                  3,669  -4
                      3  -2
                     20  -1
                    118   0
                    235   1
                    917   2
                  1,546   3
                  1,701   4
```

Before we add value labels to make our codebook look more like the codebook we downloaded, we need to replace the numeric missing values (-5, -4, -3, -2, and -1) with values that Stata recognizes as representing missing values. Stata recognizes up to 27 different missing values for each variable: . (a dot), .a, .b, ..., .z. Note that a missing value will be larger than any numeric value. When there is only one type of missing value, as discussed in chapter 2, we could change all numeric codes of -9 to . (a dot).

Because we have five different types of missing values, we will replace -5 with .a (read as dot-a), -4 with .b, -3 with .c, -2 with .d, and -1 with .e. Stata uses a command called `mvdecode` (missing-value decode) to do this. Because all items involve the same decoding replacements, we can do this with the following command:

```
. mvdecode _all, mv(-5=.a\-4=.b\-3=.c\-2=.d\-1=.e)
    r3483600: 4467 missing values generated
    r3483700: 4469 missing values generated
    r3483800: 4468 missing values generated
    r3483900: 4470 missing values generated
    r3485200: 5608 missing values generated
    r3485300: 5611 missing values generated
    r3485400: 5610 missing values generated
    r3485500: 5611 missing values generated
    r3828100: 775 missing values generated
    r3828700: 775 missing values generated
```

We use `_all` to tell Stata to do the missing-value decoding for all variables. If we wanted to decode only select variables, we would instead type for example `mvdecode r3483600 r3828700`. Some datasets might use different missing values for different variables, which would require several `mvdecode` commands. For example, a value of -1 might be a legitimate answer for some items and for these items a value of 999 might be used for `Refusal`. Each replacement above is separated by a backslash (\). The results appear right below the `mvdecode` command and tell us how many missing values are generated for each variable. For example, `r3483600` has 4,467 missing values generated (775 replace the −5, 3,669 replace the −4, 3 replace the −2, and 20 replace the −1).

Stata and capitalization

Stata commands and options are all lowercase. Because Stata is case sensitive, if you typed a command, say, `Summarize` instead of `summarize`, or an option in uppercase, the word would be meaningless to Stata. For some reason, many national datasets put everything in capital letters. When we get an email message with a lot of capitalization, this does not make us happy; it makes us think the sender is yelling at us and it is hard to read. Other researchers mix the case in names using such names as `MyID` or `MOMfeels`. They might have an item named `MomFeels` and a scale named `MOMFEELS`. Switching case can be confusing, and if you make a mistake, say, you enter `MyId` instead of `MyID`, you will get an error message. Many experienced Stata users use lowercase for variable names and nicknames for value labels. If you do this consistently, you never have to worry about shifting from lowercase to uppercase. Many users capitalize the first word in the label assigned to a value, such as "Very strongly". This capitalization helps make output more readable, and you never have to type these labels again once the dataset is created.

Stata's `rename` command can change the case of any or all variables in a dataset. Suppose that we have five variables in a dataset—ID, Age, `WaistSize`, Ed, and `MOMFEELS`—and want to make all of these lowercase. We type `rename ID-MOMFEELS, lower` in the Command window and press Enter. Regardless of how the variable names used case originally, they will all now be lowercase. We could select Data ▷ Data utilities ▷ Rename groups of variables. Then we can click on *Change the case on groups of variable names*, enter our list of variables, click on *Lowercase variable names*, and then click on OK.

3.3   Creating value labels

Now let's add value labels, including labels for the five types of missing values. To do this, we will open the Variables Manager by selecting Data ▷ Variables Manager or by typing `varmanage`. Click on `r3483600` to highlight the variable. Click on Manage... next to *Value label* on the Variable properties pane. This opens the *Manage value labels* dialog box, where we click on Create label. A new *Create label* dialog box opens. In the *Create label* dialog box, enter `often` for *Label name*; enter 0 for *Value*; enter `Never` for *Label*; and then click on Add. Repeat this step where *Value* is 1 and *Label* is `Rarely`, *Value* is 2 and *Label* is `Sometimes`, *Value* is 3 and *Label* is `Usually`, *Value* is 4 and *Label* is `Always`, *Value* is `.a` and *Label* is `Noninterview`, *Value* is `.b` and *Label* is `Valid skip`, *Value* is `.c` and *Label* is `Invalid skip`, *Value* is `.d` and *Label* is `Don't know`, and *Value* is `.e` and *Label* is `Refusal`. At this point, our three windows appear as figure 3.1:

Figure 3.1. The Variables Manager

From here, we can click on OK to close the *Create label* dialog box and then click on Close in the *Manage value labels* dialog box. We now need to assign our value label, often, to the appropriate variables. In the Variables Manager, we can click on each of the variables. By doing this, all properties of the variable are shown in the Variable properties pane. We will click on r3483600. The *Value label* in the Variable properties pane is shown as a blank because we have not yet assigned the value label often to this variable. Click on the drop-down menu for *Value label* and select often, and then click on Apply. After we have repeated this for all eight variables, the Variables Manager appears as figure 3.2:

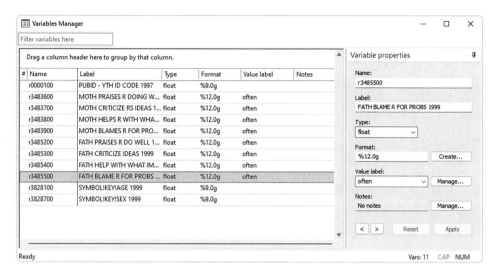

Figure 3.2. The Variables Manager with value labels assigned

Notice that each of the appropriate variables now shows that the value label nick-named `often` is assigned to it. At some point, you might want to remove a value label. For example, you might accidentally have applied the `often` value label to `r3828100`, the age of the observation. To drop the value label, you click on the variable, erase the label `often`, and then click on Apply.

The variable labels (remember, we can create or change variable names, variable labels, and value labels) are okay as they are, but let's change the case so that it does not look like somebody is screaming at us. We also might make them simpler. For instance, the label of `PUBID - YTH ID CODE 1997` for variable `r0000100` could be improved. Because once entered, we never have to type a variable label again, we will use capitalization rules for a normal sentence. We will make a few minor word changes as well. In doing this, we want to keep the labels reasonably short.

In our Variables Manager, we can click on a variable, say, `r3483600`, and then in the *Label* field of the Variable properties pane, change `MOTH PRAISES R DOING WELL 1999` to `Mother praises child for doing well`. Click on Apply and the label for this variable in the *Label* column is immediately changed. Using the Variables Manager, change the variable labels for the other seven variables as indicated in the commands below.

```
. label variable r3483700 "Mother criticizes child's ideas"
. label variable r3483800 "Mother helps child with what is important to child"
. label variable r3483900 "Mother blames child for problems"
. label variable r3485200 "Father praises child for doing well"
. label variable r3485300 "Father criticizes child's ideas"
. label variable r3485400 "Father helps child with what is important to child"
. label variable r3485500 "Father blames child for problems"
```

Do these changes help? Let's do a codebook for **r3483600** and see how it compares with the codebook that appeared in table 3.2.

```
. codebook r3483600
```

r3483600			Mother praises child for doing well

```
                Type: Numeric (float)
               Label: often

               Range: [0,4]                         Units: 1
       Unique values: 5                         Missing .: 0/8,984
     Unique mv codes: 4                        Missing .*: 4,467/8,984

         Tabulation: Freq.    Numeric  Label
                      118          0   Never
                      235          1   Rarely
                      917          2   Sometimes
                    1,546          3   Usually
                    1,701          4   Always
                      775         .a   Noninterview
                    3,669         .b   Valid skip
                        3         .d   Don't know
                       20         .e   Refusal
```

3.4   Reverse-code variables

We have two items for the mother and two for the father that are stated negatively, so we should reverse code these. **r3483700** refers to the mother criticizing the adolescent, and **r3485300** refers to the father criticizing the adolescent. **r3483900** and **r3485500** refer to the mother and father blaming the adolescent for problems. For these items, an adolescent who reports that this always happens would mean that the adolescent had a low rating of his or her parent. We always want a higher score to signify more of the variable. A score of 0 for never blames the child on this pair of items should be the highest score on these items (4), and a response of always blames the child should be the worst response and would have the lowest score (0).

It is good to organize all the variables that need reverse coding into groups based on their coding scheme. It is important to create new variables instead of reversing the originals. This step ensures that we have the original information if any questions arise about what we have done. I recommend that you write things out before you start working, as I have done in table 3.3.

Table 3.3. Reverse-coding plan

Old value	New value
0	4
1	3
2	2
3	1
4	0

For a small dataset like the one we are using, writing it out may seem like overkill. When you are involved in a large-scale project, the experience you gain from working out how to organize these matters on small datasets will serve you well, particularly if you need to assign tasks to several people and try to keep them straight.

There are several ways to do this recoding, but let's use `recode` right now. Select Data ▷ Create or change data ▷ Other variable-transformation commands ▷ Recode categorical variable.

The `recode` command and its dialog box are straightforward. We provide the name of the variable to be recoded and then give at least one rule for how it should be recoded. Recoding rules are enclosed in parentheses, with an old value (or values) listed on the left, followed by an equal sign, and then the new value. The simplest kind of rule lists one value on either side of the equal sign. So for example, the first recoding rule we would use to reverse code our variables would be `(0=4)`.

More on recoding rules

More than one value can be listed on the left side of the equal sign, as in `(1 2 3=0)`, which would recode values of 1, 2, and 3 as 0. Occasionally, you may want to collapse just one end of a scale, as with `(5/max=5)`, which recodes everything from 5 up, but not including the missing values, as 5. You might use this to collapse the highest income categories into one category, for example. There is also a corresponding version to recode from the smallest value up to some value. For example, you might use `(min/8=8)` to recode the values for highest attained grade in school if you wanted everybody with fewer than nine years of education coded the same way.

When you use `recode`, you can choose to recode the existing variables or create new variables that have the new coding scheme. I strongly recommend creating new variables. The dialog boxes shown in figures 3.3 and 3.4 show how to do this for all four variables being recoded. Figure 3.3 shows the original variables on the Main tab.

Figure 3.3. `recode`: specifying recode rules on the Main tab

Figure 3.4 shows the names of the new variables to be created on the Options tab.

Figure 3.4. `recode`: specifying new variable names on the Options tab

The variables for mothers begin with mom, and the variables for fathers begin with dad. Adding an r at the end of each variable reminds you that they are reverse coded. Stata will pair up the names, starting with the first name in each list, and recode according to the rules stated. We must have the same number of variable names in each list. After you click on OK, the output from the selections shown in figures 3.3 and 3.4 is

```
. recode r3483700 r3483900 r3485300 r3485500 (0=4) (1=3) (2=2) (3=1) (4=0),
> generate(momcritr momblamer dadcritr dadblamer)
(3230 differences between r3483700 and momcritr)
(4037 differences between r3483900 and momblamer)
(2562 differences between r3485300 and dadcritr)
(3070 differences between r3485500 and dadblamer)
```

The output above shows how Stata presents output that is too long to fit on one line: it moves down a line and inserts a > character at the beginning of the new line. This differentiates command-continuation text from the output of the command. If you are trying to use the command in output as a model for typing a new command, you should not type the > character.

The recode command labels the variables it creates. The text is generic, so we may wish to replace it. For example, the momcritr variable was labeled with the text

```
RECODE of r3483700 (Mother criticizes child's ideas)
```

This text tells us the original variable name (and its label in parentheses), but it does not tell us how it was recoded. It may be worth the additional effort to create more explicit variable labels. We can do this with the Variables Manager. If you want to try entering the commands directly, they are

```
. label variable momcritr "Mother criticizes child's ideas, reverses r3483700"
. label variable momblamer "Mother blames child for problems, reverses r3483900"
. label variable dadcritr "Father criticizes child's ideas, reverses r3485300"
. label variable dadblamer "Father blames child for problems, reverses r3485500"
```

The recode command is useful. You can specify missing values either as original values or as new values, and you can create a value label as part of the recode command. You can also recode a range (say, from 1 to 5) easily, which is useful for recoding things like ages into age groups. If the resulting values are easily listed (most often integers, but they could be noninteger values), it is worth thinking about using the recode command. See the *Stata Data Management Reference Manual* entry for recode or type help recode in Stata for more information.

Whenever we generate a new variable, we should always check to make sure we did what we wanted to do. We can quickly check by running a cross-tabulation (see chapter 6) of the old variable and the new variable. We will do this for r3483700 and momcritr. Although we will learn a lot more about the tabulate command later, for now we can just run the command to create a cross-tabulation in the Command window:

```
. tabulate momcritr r3483700
```

Mother criticizes child's ideas, reverses r3483700	Mother criticizes child's ideas					Total
	0	1	2	3	4	
0	0	0	0	0	145	145
1	0	0	0	324	0	324
2	0	0	1,285	0	0	1,285
3	0	1,654	0	0	0	1,654
4	1,107	0	0	0	0	1,107
Total	1,107	1,654	1,285	324	145	4,515

Here the first variable after `tabulate`, that is, `momcritr`, appears as the row variable and the second variable, `r3483700`, appears as the column variable. We see only the numeric values, 0, 1, 2, 3, and 4 for `r3483700`, but we know from our codebook that "Never" is 0, "Rarely" is 1, "Sometimes" is 2, "Usually" is 3, and "Always" is 4. However, we see, for example, that the 1,107 people who had a 0 on `r3483700` now have a 4. Why is this? We need value labels for our new variable, `momcritr`. We cannot assign the value label nicknamed `often` to `momcritr` because we have reversed the numbering. We need a new label where 4 is `Never`, 3 is `Rarely`, 2 is `Sometimes`, 1 is `Usually`, and 0 is `Always`.

We could use the Variables Manager to do this like we did to create the value label `often`. We would just give it another name, such as `often_r`, where the `r` stands for reverse order. You can use the Variables Manager, but you might want to type the command in the Command window:

```
. label define often_r 4 "Never" 3 "Rarely" 2 "Sometimes" 1 "Usually" 0 "Always"
> .a "Noninterview" .b "Valid skip" .c "Invalid skip" .d "Don't know"
> .e "Refusal"
```

As we have noted, when a line is too long to fit in the Command window, it just wraps around, but when it appears in the Results window, it has separate lines with `>` signifying that the lines are tied. In the Command window, you would not type the dot prompt (`.`) or the greater than signs (`>`).

Finally, we need to assign this nickname, `often_r`, to the new variables. We can do this with the Variables Manager or by using the following `label values` command:

```
. label values momcritr momblamer dadcritr dadblamer often_r
```

After the `label values` command, we list the variable names that share the same set of value labels, and at the end we have the nickname for that set of value labels, `often_r`.

3.5   Creating and modifying variables

There are several commands that are used in creating, replacing, and modifying variables. Useful commands include **generate**, **egen** (short for extended generate), **rename**, and **clonevar**. Suppose that we want to change the positive items so that their names make more sense to us. A simple way to do this is to make the new variables be clones. The **clonevar** *newname* = *oldname* command does this. **clonevar** has a couple of advantages: the actual command is simple, it keeps the missing values coded the same way as they were in the old variable, and it keeps the same value labels. We could run the following commands from the Command window:

```
. clonevar mompraise = r3483600
. clonevar momhelp = r3483800
. clonevar dadpraise = r3485200
. clonevar dadhelp = r3485400
```

Let's do this for the other three variables in the dataset: identification number, age, and gender.

```
. clonevar id = r0000100
. clonevar sex = r3828700
. clonevar age = r3828100
```

You can open the dialog box for **generate** by selecting Data ▷ Create or change data ▷ Create new variable. The **generate** command does much the same thing as the **clonevar** command, but it does not transfer value labels. It does transfer the missing-value codes we used: **.a**, **.b**, **.c**, **.d**, and **.e**. If we wanted to run the **generate** command directly without using the dialog box, we would type the following commands. (Do not type these commands now because we already created the new variables by using the **clonevar** command.)

```
. generate mompraise = r3483600
. generate momhelp = r3483800
. generate dadpraise = r3485200
. generate dadhelp = r3485400
. generate id = r0000100
. generate sex = r3828700
. generate age = r3828100
```

The **generate** command can also be used to create new variables by using an arithmetic expression. Table 3.4 shows the arithmetic symbols that can be used in these expressions.

Table 3.4. Arithmetic symbols

Symbol	Operation	Example
+	Addition	`mscore + fscore + sibscore`
−	Subtraction	`balance - expenses - penalty`
*	Multiplication	`income * .75`
/	Division	`expenses/income`
^	Exponentiation (x^2)	`x^2`

Attempts to do arithmetic with missing values will lead to missing values. So in the addition example in table 3.4, if `sibscore` were missing (say, it was a single-child household), the whole sum in the example would be set to missing for that observation. From the Command window, type `help generate` to see several more examples of what can be done with the `generate` command. If you ever have trouble finding a dialog box but you know the command name, you can open the help file first. The upper right corner of a help file opened in the Viewer window will show a Dialog menu. Select the command name from the drop-down menu, and the dialog box for that command will open.

For more complicated expressions, order of operations can be important, and you can use parentheses to control the order in which things are done. Parentheses contain expressions too, and those are calculated before the expressions outside of parentheses. Parentheses are never wrong. They might be unnecessary to get Stata to calculate the correct value, but they are not wrong. If you think they make an expression easier to read or understand, use as many as you need.

Fortunately, the rules are pretty simple. Stata reads expressions from left to right, and the order in which Stata calculates things inside expressions is to

1. Do everything in parentheses. If one set of parentheses contains another set, do the inside set first.

2. Exponentiate (raise to a power).

3. Multiply and divide.

4. Add and subtract.

Let's go step by step through an example:

```
. generate example = weight/.45*(5+1/age^2)
```

When Stata looks at the expression to the right of the equal sign, it notices the parentheses (priority #1) and looks inside them. There it sees that it first has to square `age` (priority #2), then divide 1 by the result (priority #3), and then add 5 to that result (priority #4). Once it is done with all the stuff in parentheses, it starts reading from left to right, so it divides `weight` by 0.45 and then multiplies the result by the final value it got from calculating what was inside parentheses. That final value is put into a variable called `example`.

Stata does not care about spaces in expressions, but they can help readability. So for example, instead of typing something like we just did, we can use some spaces to make the meaning clearer, as in

```
. generate example = weight/.45 * (5 + 1/age^2)
```

If we wanted to be even more explicit, it would not be wrong to type

```
. generate example = (weight/.45) * (5 + 1/(age^2))
```

Let's take another look at reverse coding. We already reverse-coded variables by using a set of explicit rules like (0=4), but we could accomplish the same thing using arithmetic. Because this is a relatively simple problem, we will use it to introduce some of the things you may need to be concerned about with more complex problems.

Reversing a scale is swapping the ends of the scale around. The scale is 0 to 4, so we can swap the ends around by subtracting the current value from 4. If the original value is 4 and we subtract it from 4, we have made it a 0, which is the rule we specified with `recode`. If the original value is 0 and we subtract it from 4, we have made it a 4, which is the rule we specified with `recode`.

This scale starts at 0, so to reverse it, you just subtract each value from the largest value in the scale, in this case, 4. So if our scale were 0 to 6, we would subtract each value from 6; if it were 0 to 3, we would subtract from 3. If the scale started at 1 instead of 0, we would need to add 1 to the largest value before subtracting. So for a 1 to 5 scale, we would subtract from 6 ($6 - 1 = 5$ and $6 - 5 = 1$); for a 1 to 3 scale, we would subtract from 4 ($4 - 3 = 1$ and $4 - 1 = 3$).

What we have said so far is correct, as far as it goes, but we are not taking into account missing values or their codes. The missing values are coded in this dataset as -1 to -5, and if you subtract those from 4 along with the item responses that are not missing-value codes, we will end up with $4 - (-1) = 5$ to $4 - (-5) = 9$. So we must first convert the missing-value codes to Stata's missing-value code (`.`) and then do the arithmetic to reverse the scale.

Many researchers would code the values 1–5 rather than 0–4. To reverse a scale that starts at 1 and goes to 5, you need to subtract the current value from 1 more than the maximum value. Thus you would use $6 - variable$. If the variable's current value is 5, then $6 - 5 = 1$.

Let's try this example. We have already run the `mvdecode` command on our variables, so let's reverse code `r3485300` and call it `facritr`. We will use the `generate` dialog box to create the variable. Select Data ▷ Create or change data ▷ Create new variable, type `facritr` for the *Variable name*, and type 4 - `r3485300` in the *Specify a value or an expression* box. Figure 3.5 shows the completed dialog box.

Figure 3.5. The `generate` dialog box

Here is the output of the `generate` command:

```
. generate facritr = 4 - r3485300
(5,611 missing values generated)
```

Whenever you see that missing values are generated (there are 5,611 of them in this example!), it is a good idea to make sure you know why they are missing. These variables have only a small set of values they can take, so we can compare the original variable with the new variable in a table and see what got turned into what. Select Statistics ▷ Summaries, tables, and tests ▷ Frequency tables ▷ Two-way table with measures of association, which will bring up the dialog shown in figure 3.6.

Figure 3.6. Two-way tabulation dialog box

Here we select `facritr` as the *Row variable* and `r3485300` as the *Column variable*. We also check two of the options boxes: Because we are interested in the actual values the variables take, select the option to suppress the value labels (*Suppress value labels*). We are also interested in the missing values, so we check the box to have them included in the table (*Treat missing values like other values*).

```
. tabulate facritr r3485300, miss nolabel
```

	Father criticizes child's ideas					
facritr	0	1	2	3	4	Total
0	0	0	0	0	117	117
1	0	0	0	247	0	247
2	0	0	811	0	0	811
3	0	1,078	0	0	0	1,078
4	1,120	0	0	0	0	1,120
.	0	0	0	0	0	5,611
Total	1,120	1,078	811	247	117	8,984

	Father criticizes child's ideas				
facritr	.a	.b	.d	.e	Total
0	0	0	0	0	117
1	0	0	0	0	247
2	0	0	0	0	811
3	0	0	0	0	1,078
4	0	0	0	0	1,120
.	775	4,816	4	16	5,611
Total	775	4,816	4	16	8,984

From the table generated, we can see that everything happened as anticipated. Those adolescents who had a score of 0 on the original variable (the column with a 0 at the top) now have a score of 4 on the new variable. There are 1,120 of these observations. We need to check the other combinations, as well. Also the missing-value codes were all transferred to the new variable, but we lost the distinctions between the different reasons an answer is missing. The new variable, `facritr`, is a reverse coding of our old variable, r3485300.

3.6   Creating scales

We are finally ready to calculate our scales. We will construct two scale variables: one for the adolescent's perception of his or her mother and one for the adolescent's perception of his or her father. With four items, each scored from 0 to 4, the scores could range from 0 to 16 points. Higher scores indicate a more positive relationship with the parent.

At first glance, this assertion is straightforward. We just add the variables together:

```
. generate ymomrelate = mompraise + momcritr + momhelp + momblamer
. generate ydadrelate = dadpraise + dadcritr + dadhelp + dadblamer
```

Before we settle on this, we should understand what will happen for missing values, and we should check through the documentation to find out what Stata does about missing values. The first thing to do is to determine how many observations have one, two, three, or all four of the items answered, that is, not missing. This need introduces a new command, `egen` (short for extended generate). Selecting Data ▷ Create or change data ▷ Create new variable (extended) opens the `egen` dialog box, shown in figure 3.7.

Figure 3.7. The Main tab for the egen dialog box

As you can see, the dialog box allows us to enter the name of the variable to be created, which we will call mommissing because this will tell us how many of the items about mothers that each adolescent missed answering. The next step is to select the function from the alphabetical list. In this case, we want to look among the row functions for one that will count missing values, which appears as *Row number of missing*. Last, we enter the items about the mother in the box provided. These selections produce

```
. egen float mommissing = rowmiss(mompraise momcritr momhelp momblamer)
```

Beyond egen

We have seen how **generate** and **egen** cover a wide variety of functions. You can always type **help generate** or **help egen** to see a description of all the available functions. Sometimes this is not enough. Nicholas J. Cox, a Stata user, wrote in 2000, with subsequent revisions, a command called **egenmore**, which adds many more functions that are helpful for data management. You can type **ssc install egenmore, replace** in your Command window to install these added capabilities. The **replace** option will check for updates Cox has added if **egenmore** is already installed on your machine. If you now enter **help egenmore**, you will get a description of all the capabilities Cox has added.

If we look at a tabulation of the mommissing variable, the rows will be numbered 0–4, and each entry will indicate how many observations have that many missing values. For example, there are 4,510 observations for which all four items were answered (no

missing values), 6 for which there are three items answered (one missing value), 2 for
which there are two items answered (two missing values), and 4,466 for which there
are no items answered. Our table does not include a row for 3 because there are no
observations in our example that have three missing values.

```
. tabulate mommissing
  mommissing |      Freq.     Percent        Cum.
-------------+-----------------------------------
           0 |      4,510       50.20       50.20
           1 |          6        0.07       50.27
           2 |          2        0.02       50.29
           4 |      4,466       49.71      100.00
-------------+-----------------------------------
       Total |      8,984      100.00
```

We can see that there are a total of eight observations for which there are some, but
not complete, data. There should be little doubt about what to do for the 4,510 cases
with complete information, as well as for the 4,466 with no information (all missing).
The problem with using the sum of the items as our score on ymomrelate is that the
eight observations with partial data will be dropped, that is, given a value of missing.

There are several solutions. We might decide to compute the mean of the items
that are answered. We can do this with the egen dialog box; select Data ▷ Create or
change data ▷ Create new variable (extended) to display the egen dialog box displayed
in figure 3.7. This time, call the new variable mommeana and pick *Row mean* from the
list of egen functions. This function generates a mean of the items that were answered,
regardless of how many were answered, as long as at least one item was answered. If we
tabulate mommeana, we have 4,518 observations, meaning that everybody who answered
at least one item has a mean of the items they answered.

Another solution is to have some minimum number of items, say, 75% or 80% of
them. We might include only people who answered at least three of the items. These
people would have fewer than two missing items. We can go back to the dialog box for
egen and rename the variable we are computing to mommeanb. The by/if/in tab allows
us to stipulate the condition that mommissing < 2, as shown in figure 3.8.

Figure 3.8. The by/if/in tab for the egen dialog box

The Stata command this dialog box generates is

```
. egen float mommeanb = rowmean(mompraise momcritr momhelp momblamer)
> if mommissing < 2
```

This command creates a variable, mommeanb, that is the mean of the items for each observation that has at least three of the four items answered. Doing a tabulation on this shows that there are 4,516 observations with a valid score. This command allows us to keep the six cases that answered all but one of the items and drop the two cases that were missing more than one item.

Deciding among different ways to do something

When you need to decide among different ways of performing a data management task—which is what we have been doing this whole chapter—it is usually better to choose based on how easy it will be for someone to read and understand the record rather than based on the number of commands it takes or based on some notion of computer efficiency. For example, computing the row mean has a major advantage over computing the sum of items. The mean is on the same 0–4 scale that the items have, and this often makes more sense than a scale that has a different range. For example, if you had nine items that ranged from 1 for `strongly agree` to 5 for `strongly disagree`, a mean of 4 would tell you that the person has averaged `agree` over the set of items. This might be easier to understand than a total or sum score of 36 on a scale that ranges from 9 (one on each item) to 45 (five on each item).

3.7   Saving some of your data

Occasionally, you will want to save only part of your data. You may wish to save only some variables, or you may wish to save only some observations. Perhaps you have created variables that you needed as part of a calculation but do not need to save, or perhaps you wish to work only with the created scales and not the original items. You might want to drop some observations based on some characteristic, such as gender or parent's educational level or geographic area.

To drop a variable from your dataset, you can use the Variables Manager. Right-click on the variable name. A drop-down menu appears in which you can select *Drop selected variables*. When you do this, as a safety check, Stata asks you to confirm that you want to drop the variable. Suppose that we want to drop all the original variables, `r0000100`–`r3828700`, because we have given all of them a new name that is easier to understand. We could click on `r0000100` to highlight it, and then press Shift+Down arrow to highlight the rest of the variables that we want to drop. Right-click on the highlighted variables and select *Drop selected variables* to drop the set of variables. The command produced by this example is

```
. drop r0000100 r3483600 r3483700 r3483800 r3483900 r3485200 r3485300 r3485400
> r3485500 r3828100 r3828700
```

Sometimes it is more efficient to indicate the variables you want to keep rather than the variables you want to drop. In the Variables Manager, right-clicking gives us the *Keep only selected variables* choice. If we only wanted to keep a few variables, this might be a bit easier to do. We would highlight the ones we wanted to keep before clicking *Keep only selected variables*.

Sometimes we want to drop or keep selected observations rather than variables. For example, we might want to drop children who are under 12 or keep children if they are in an honors program. Similarly, we might want to keep people who are African American or drop people who are not African American. When we have an enormous dataset, we might want to keep the first 500 observations for preliminary analysis. We can use the same `drop` and `keep` commands we used for variables. Instead of using the Variables Manager, we can enter the commands directly, but rather than using `drop` *varlist*, we follow the syntax of `drop if` *exp* or `drop in` *range*. Here are a few examples:

```
. drop if age < 12
. drop if age > 17 & gender == 1
. keep if age >= 12 & age < 18 & gender == 1
. keep in 1/500
```

The first command, `drop if age < 12`, drops any observation who is under age 12. The second command drops any observation who is over age 17 and whose gender is coded as a 1. The double equal signs are read as "is", that is, `gender` is 1. If you wrote `gender = 1` here, it would create an error. The statement `gender = 1` would naturally tell Stata you want to assign a value of 1 on `gender` to everybody. We do not want to do this! We want to drop people if their `gender` "is" 1. Stata uses two equal signs, `==`, to say this statement. Notice the use of the ampersand, `&`, rather than typing `and`. If you used the word `and` instead of the symbol `&`, you would get an error message. The third example keeps people who are age 12 or over (`>=`) and are under age 18 (`<`) and have a `gender` that is coded as 1. The last example keeps only observations 1 to 500. The `/` sign can be read as "to".

3.8 Summary

This chapter has covered a lot of ground. You may need to refer to this chapter when you are creating your own datasets. We have covered how to label variables and create value labels for each possible response to an item. In explaining how to create a scale, we covered reverse-coding items that were stated negatively and creating and modifying items. We also covered how to create a scale and work with missing values, especially where some people who have missing values are included in the scale and some are excluded. Finally, we covered how to save parts of a file, whether the parts were selected items or selected observations.

In the next chapter, we will look at how to create a file containing Stata commands that can be run as a group. The book's webpage has such a command file for chapter 3 (`chapter3.do`). By recording all the commands into a program, we have a record of what we did, and we can rerun it or modify it in the future. We will also see how to record both output and commands in files.

3.9   Exercises

1. Open `relate.dta`. The R3828700 variable represents the gender of the adolescent and is coded as a 1 for males and 2 for females. There are 775 people who are missing because they dropped out of the study after a previous wave of data collection. These people have a missing value on R3828700 of -5. Run a tabulation on R3828700. Then modify the variable so that the code of -5 will be recognized by Stata as a missing value. Label the variable so that a 1 is male and a 2 is female. Finally, run another tabulation and compare this with your first tabulation.

2. Open `relate.dta`. Using the R3483600 variable, repeat the process you did for the first exercise. Go to the webpage for the book and examine the dictionary file `relate.dct` to see how this variable is coded. Modify the missing values so that -5 is .a, -4 is .b, -3 is .c, -2 is .d, and -1 is .e. Then label the values for the variable and run a tabulation.

3. Using the result of the second exercise, run the command `numlabel, add`. Repeat the tabulation of R3483600, and compare it with the tabulation for the second exercise. Next run the command `numlabel, remove`. Finally, repeat the tabulation, but add the `missing` option; that is, insert a comma and the word "missing" at the end of the command. Why is it good to include this option when you are screening your data?

4. `relate.dta` is data from the third year of a long-term study. Because of this, some of the youth who were adolescents the first year (1997) are more than 18 years old. Assign a missing value on R3828100 (age) for those with a code of -5. Drop observations that are 18 or older. Keep only R0000100, R3483600, R3483800, R3485200, R3485400, and R3828700. Save this as a dataset called `positive.dta`.

5. Using `positive.dta`, assign missing values to four of the variables: R3483600, R3483800, R3485200, and R3485400. Copy these four variables to four new variables called `mompraise`, `momhelp`, `dadpraise`, and `dadhelp`, respectively.

6. Create a scale called `parents` of how youth relate to their parents using the four items (R3483600, R3483800, R3485200, and R3485400). Do this separately for boys (if R3828700 == 1) and girls (if R3828700 == 2). Use the `rowmean()` function to create your scale. Do a tabulation of `parents`.

4 Working with commands, do-files, and results

4.1   Introduction

Throughout this book, I am illustrating how to use the menus and dialog boxes, but underneath the menus and dialogs is a set of commands. Learning to work with the commands lets you get the most out of Stata, and this is true of any statistical software. Even the official Stata documentation is organized by command name, as illustrated by the *Stata Base Reference Manual*, which has more than 3,000 pages explaining Stata commands.

With the logical organization of the menu system, you may wonder why you need to even think about the underlying commands. There are several reasons: Entering commands can be quicker than going through the menus. More importantly, you can put the commands into files that are called *do-files*, allowing for easy repetition of a series of commands. These do-files allow you to replicate your work, something you should always ensure you can do. When you collaborate with co-workers, they can use your do-file as a way to follow exactly what you did. It is hard enough to remember all the commands you create in a session, and if there is a delay between work sessions, it is impossible to remember all those commands. Even when you are using the menu system, it is useful to save the commands generated from the menus into a do-file, and Stata has a way to facilitate saving these commands; we will soon learn how to do this.

What is a command? What is a do-file?

A command instructs Stata to do something, such as construct a graph, a frequency tabulation, or a table of correlations. A do-file is a collection of commands. "Do-file" is a good name because it is so descriptive: the series of commands in the file tells Stata what to "do". A simple do-file might open a dataset, summarize the variables, create a codebook, and then do a frequency tabulation of the categorical variables. A do-file can include all the commands you use to label variables and values; it can recode variables, average variables, and define how you treat missing values. Such a do-file might be only a few lines long, but complicated do-files can be thousands of lines long.

4.2 How Stata commands are constructed

Stata has many commands. Here are some of the commands covered in this book:

`list`	List values of variables
`summarize`	Summary statistics
`describe`	Describe data in memory or in file
`codebook`	Describe data contents
`tabulate`	Tables of frequencies
`generate`	Create or change contents of variable
`egen`	Extensions to generate
`correlate`	Correlations (covariances) of variables or coefficients
`ttest`	Mean-comparison tests
`anova`	Analysis of variance and covariance
`regress`	Linear regression
`logit`	Logistic regression, reporting coefficients
`factor`	Factor analysis
`alpha`	Compute interitem correlations (covariances) and Cronbach's alpha
`graph`	The graph command

Stata has a remarkably simple command structure. Stata commands are all lowercase. Virtually all Stata commands take the following form: *command varlist* if/in, *options*. The *command* is the name of the command, such as `summarize`, `generate`, or `tabulate`. The *varlist* is the list of variables used in the command. For many commands, listing no variables means that the command will be run on all variables. If we said `summarize`, Stata would summarize all the variables in the dataset. If we said `summarize age education`, Stata would summarize just the `age` and `education` variables. The variable list could include one variable or many variables. After the variable list come the `if` and `in` qualifiers regarding what will be included in the particular analysis. Suppose that we have a variable called `male`. A code of `1` means that the participant is a male, and a code of 0 means that the participant is female. We want to restrict the analysis to males. To restrict the analysis, we would say if `male == 1`. Here we use two equal signs, which is the Stata equivalent to the verb "is". So the command means "if male is coded with a value of 1". Why the two equal signs? The statement `male = 1` literally means that the variable called `male` is a constant value of 1, but males are coded as 1 and females are coded as 0 on this variable. Sometimes, we want to run a command on a subset of observations, so we use the `in` qualifier. For example, we might have the command `summarize age education in 1/200`, which would summarize `age` and `education` in the first 200 observations.

Each command has a set of *options* that control what is done and how the results are presented. The options vary from command to command. One option for the `summarize` command is to obtain detailed results, summarizing the variables in more ways. If we wanted to do a detailed summary of scores on age and years of education for adult males, the command would be

```
. summarize age education if male == 1 & age > 17, detail
```

The command structure is fairly simple, which is helpful for us because it is absolutely rigid. This example used the ampersand (&), not the word "and". If we had entered the word "and", we would have received an error message. The ampersand is an example of a logical operator; see table 4.1 for the logical operators available in Stata.

Here are more examples with `if` statements:

```
. summarize age education if sex == 0
. summarize age education if sex == 1 & age > 64
. summarize age sex if sex == 0 & age > 64 & education == 12
```

Note that the double equal signs (==) and greater than signs (>) shown above are relational operators; see table 4.1 for the relational operators available in Stata.

When you have missing values stored as . or .a, .b, etc., you need to be careful about using the `if` qualifier. Stata stores missing values internally as huge numbers that are bigger than any value in your dataset. If you had missing data coded as . or .a and entered the command `summarize age if age > 64`, you would include people who had missing values. The correct format would be

```
. summarize age if age > 64 & !missing(age)
```

`!missing(age)` at the end of the command specifies to include only observations that do not have missing values for `age`; that is, the exclamation point (!) means "not". This is also an example of a logical operator. Table 4.1 shows the relational and logical operators available in Stata.

Table 4.1. Relational and logical operators used by Stata

| Relational operators | | Logical operators | |
Symbol	Meaning	Symbol	Meaning
==	is or is equal to	&	and
!= or ~=	is not or is not equal to	|	or
>	is greater than	!	not
>=	is greater than or equal to		
<	is less than		
<=	is less than or equal to		

The `in` qualifier specifies that you will perform the analysis on a subset of cases based on their order in the dataset. If we had 10,000 participants in a national survey and we wanted to list the values in the dataset for `age`, `education`, and `sex`, this list would go on for screen after screen after screen, which would be a waste of time. We might want to list the data on `age`, `education`, and `sex` for just the first 20 observations by using `in 1/20`. The 1 is where Stata should start (called the first case), the "/" is read as "to", and the 20 is the last case listed. Thus `in 1/20` tells Stata to do the command for the cases numbered from 1 to 20, or for the first 20 cases. The full command is

```
. list age education sex in 1/20
```

Listing just a few cases is usually all you need to check for logical errors. Most Stata dialog boxes include an if/in tab for restricting data.

If your dataset contains few variables, it may be easier to just leave the Data Editor (Browse) open with the data while you are typing your commands instead of running a listing. Any changes made by your commands will appear immediately in the Data Editor (Browse). You can open the Data Editor (Browse) by typing the `browse` command or the `browse, nolabel` command in the Command window or by clicking on the toolbar icon that looks like a spreadsheet with a magnifying glass (see figure 2.3).

The final feature in a Stata command is a list of options. You must enter a comma before you enter the options. As you learn more about Stata, the options become increasingly important. If you do not list any options, Stata gives you what it considers to be basic results. Often these basic results are all you will want. The options let you ask for special results or formatting. For example, in a graph, you might want to add a title. In frequency tabulation, you might want to include cases that have missing values. One of the best reasons for using dialog boxes is that you can discover options that can help you tailor your results to your personal taste. Dialog boxes either include an **Options** tab or have the options as boxes that you can check on the **Main** tab. The most common mistake a beginner makes when typing commands directly in the Command window is leaving the comma out before specifying the options.

Here are a few Stata commands and the results they produce. You can enter these commands in the Command window to follow along.

```
. use http://www.stata-press.com/data/agis6r/firstsurvey_chapter4
. summarize
```

Variable	Obs	Mean	Std. dev.	Min	Max
id	20	10.5	5.91608	1	20
gender	20	1.5	.5129892	1	2
education	20	14.45	2.946452	8	20
sch_st	18	3.444444	1.149026	2	5
sch_com	20	3.5	1.395481	1	5
prison	17	3.176471	1.550617	1	5
conserv	19	2.947368	1.544657	1	5

This `summarize` command does not include a variable list, so Stata will summarize all variables in the dataset. It has no `if`/`in` restrictions and no options, so Stata summarizes all the variables, giving us the number of observations with no missing values, the mean, the standard deviation, and the minimum and maximum values. The statistics for the `id` variable are not useful, but it is easier to get these results for all variables than it is to list all the variables in a variable list, dropping only `id`.

We can add the `detail` option to our command to give more detailed information. Do this for just one variable.

```
. summarize education, detail
```

                        Years of education

	Percentiles	Smallest		
1%	8	8		
5%	9.5	11		
10%	11.5	12	Obs	20
25%	12	12	Sum of wgt.	20
50%	14.5		Mean	14.45
		Largest	Std. dev.	2.946452
75%	16.5	17		
90%	18	18	Variance	8.681579
95%	19	18	Skewness	-.1636124
99%	20	20	Kurtosis	2.522208

As expected, this method gives us more information. The 50% value is the median, which is 14.5. We also get the values corresponding to other percentiles, the variance, a measure of skewness, and a measure of kurtosis (we will discuss skewness and kurtosis later).

Next we will use the `list` command. Here are four commands you can enter, one at a time, to get three different listings:

```
. list gender education prison in 1/5
```

	gender	educat~n	prison
1.	Female	15	Too long
2.	Male	12	Much too lenient
3.	Male	16	About right
4.	Male	8	.
5.	Female	12	About right

```
. list gender education prison in 1/5, nolabel
```

	gender	educat~n	prison
1.	2	15	4
2.	1	12	1
3.	1	16	3
4.	1	8	.
5.	2	12	3

```
. numlabel _all, add
. list gender education prison in 1/5
```

	gender	educat~n	prison
1.	2. Female	15	4. Too long
2.	1. Male	12	1. Much too lenient
3.	1. Male	16	3. About right
4.	1. Male	8	.
5.	2. Female	12	3. About right

The first command shows the first five cases. Notice that the `education` variable appears at the top of its column as `educat~n`. We can use names with more than eight characters, but some Stata results will show only eight characters. For names with more than eight characters, Stata will keep the first six characters and the last character and insert the tilde (~) between them. Because we assigned value labels to `gender` and `prison`, the value labels are printed in the list. However, notice that the numerical values are omitted.

The second command adds the `nolabel` option, which gives us a listing with the numerical values we used for coding but not the labels. The next command, `numlabel _all, add`, adds a numeric value to each label for all variables (the `_all` tells Stata to apply this command to all variables). If we wanted to remove the values later, we would enter `numlabel _all, remove`. Finally, the last listing gives us both the values and the labels for each variable.

4.3   Creating a do-file

You may be asking yourself how you will ever learn to use all the options and qualifiers. One way is to read the Stata documentation, but it is often easier to use the menus and record the command in a do-file. Stata has a simple text editor called the Do-file Editor in which you can enter a series of commands. You can run all the commands in this file or just some of them. You can then edit, save, and open the commands in a do-file at a later date. Saving these do-files means not only that you can replicate what you did and make any needed adjustments but also that you will develop templates you can draw on when you want to do a similar analysis. To open the Do-file Editor window, use Window ▷ Do-file Editor ▷ New Do-file Editor. You can also open the Do-file Editor by clicking on the toolbar icon that looks like a notepad; see figure 4.1 for the icon in Stata for Windows.

Figure 4.1. The Do-file Editor icon on the Stata menu

Stata allows you to have multiple do-files open at once, but we will use only one do-file in this book. When you gain confidence using Stata, the ability to have several do-files open simultaneously is a useful feature. You might use one do-file primarily for data management purposes; you might use another for general analysis of the data; you might use a third for analyzing a subset of the data. You might even work on a couple of different projects in one session. Using multiple do-files in a session is sort of like juggling balls: some of us are better at it than others. For now, one Do-file Editor window is all we need. A blank do-file appears in figure 4.2.

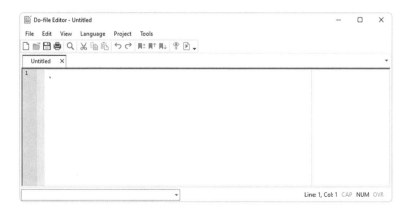

Figure 4.2. The Do-file Editor of Stata for Windows

When you click on another window, the Do-file Editor can be hidden by it. You can bring the Do-file Editor to the front again by clicking on it in the system toolbar or by using the Alt+Tab key combination to move through the open windows until the Do-file Editor is highlighted. You can avoid having the window disappear by arranging your desktop so that other windows do not overlap with the Do-file Editor window. If you have two monitors, it is convenient to have the main Stata window on one monitor and the Do-file Editor on the other monitor.

The Do-file Editor lacks special features, such as underlining or the special fonts you would get with a word processor such as MS Word. Word processors add a lot of hidden features that would be confusing to Stata. The Do-file Editor is a plain-text editor. It does, however, have some nice features for writing a do-file. As you can see in figure 4.3, the toolbar has many features that you would expect in an editor.

Figure 4.3. The Do-file Editor toolbar of Stata for Windows

The first 10 icons on the left are fairly standard. The first four icons let you open a new do-file, open an existing do-file, save your file, and print the file. The fifth icon allows you to perform a search, although most people prefer to use Ctrl+f to perform a search. The next three icons will cut, copy, and paste, although most people prefer to use Ctrl+x, Ctrl+c, and Ctrl+v (Cmd+x, Cmd+c, and Cmd+v for Macs), respectively. The curved arrows provide undo and redo functions, like a word processor. The next three icons have to do with bookmarks, marking lines in a file you are editing so you can easily jump back to them later. The second from last icon will show content of the file in a Viewer window. Finally, the last icon runs either your entire do-file or the part of your do-file that you have selected. This is the key icon for running your do-file. You select lines of code in the same way you would in a word processor, by highlighting them. If you want to select a section of several lines, you do not need to highlight all the lines completely; you can highlight some of each line. Here is an example where we want to run two commands, `describe` and `summarize`. In figure 4.4, we have selected only part of the `describe` command but all the `summarize` command.

```
1    * selecting text.do
2    version 17
3    use firstsurvey_chapter4
4    describe
5    summarize
```

Figure 4.4. Highlighting in the Do-file Editor

The Do-file Editor automatically numbers your lines. Only the number 1 for the first line appeared in figure 4.2 because the rest of the file is blank. In long do-files, the line numbers help you find your way around. In the lower right, the Do-file Editor also gives the exact location of the cursor, such as "Line: 1, Col: 0" (again, see figure 4.2).

I recommend that you include the name of the file as a comment in the first line of the do-file. Placing an asterisk (*) at the beginning of the line marks the text as a comment that Stata prints but does not interpret. I include this line because my do-file will have the name of the file that created the output so that I know where to find the file if I need to change something later on. Let's type * `my_first.do` at the top of our blank do-file.

Another way of adding comments, especially long comments, to a file is by typing /* just before the comment and */ right after the comment. Anything between the /* and */ will be treated as a comment. Figure 4.5 shows what we will use in our example do-file. This type of long comment is helpful for organizing a long do-file into sections with a new comment explaining the purpose of each new section.

We will now add our first command, `version 17`. This command can be important because it will execute the commands as they were written in Stata 17. Stata is continually being improved, and updates may include changes to the commands that you are using. By including the version number you are using when you create the do-file, you ensure that everything will work as intended even when you are using future versions of Stata. This is called version control. It is how Stata maintains compatibility when new versions add new capabilities.

Notice that the comments appear in the Do-file Editor in a green font. This makes them easy to find in a long do-file. Stata commands appear in a bold blue font.

Next we need to open the dataset. In our do-file, we type

```
. use firstsurvey_chapter4.dta, clear
```

Stata automatically looks in our working directory for this file. If we already have a dataset open, the `clear` option will clear those data from Stata's memory. If we had a dataset open with changes made to the data and we did not include the `clear` option with our `use` command, Stata would issue a warning because it does not want us to accidentally clear an active dataset before we save our changes.

You do not have to store your data and do-files in the working directory. You can create a separate directory for each project, or you can use an external flash drive. To open a dataset that is not saved in the working directory, you must specify the full path in your command. Say that our dataset, `firstsurvey_chapter4.dta`, was saved to an external flash drive in a folder called `first project`. We would type

```
. use "E:\first project\firstsurvey_chapter4.dta", clear
```

The quotation marks are required if your folder name or filename contains embedded spaces like the space in `first project` above.

The folder path will vary for Mac and Unix. For example on a Mac if your file is in the `Documents` folder, you would type

```
. use "Users/username/Documents/firstsurvey_chapter4.dta", clear
```

After using Stata for some time, it is usually best to organize your folders in such a way that each project has a separate folder creating a good work flow. Scott Long has written a wonderful book called *The Workflow of Data Analysis Using Stata* (2009), which is available from Stata Press at https://www.stata-press.com/books/workflow-data-analysis-stata. You should read this book if you plan to be involved in a series of major projects using Stata.

The next two commands we need to type are `describe` and `summarize`, which will describe the dataset and then perform a summary of the variables, giving us the number of observations, mean, standard deviation, minimum value, and maximum value. Unless there are too many variables in your dataset, these are good commands to include at the beginning of your do-file.

If you are wondering how Stata knows when it is done with one command and ready to start another, the answer lies with the Enter key. Every time you press the Enter key, Stata assumes you are either done or starting a new command. Having a hard return between them makes `describe` and `summarize` two separate operations. All programs have some way to designate the end of a command. SAS, for example, ends each procedure with a semicolon. The semicolon in SAS is the same as the Enter key in Stata.

In general, one line equals one command in a do-file. This is a great way to distinguish one command from another as long as each command is short enough to fit on one line. One line equals one command. What happens when you have a long command that extends for more than one line? Stata needs a way to know that when you press the Enter key, you are not really done with the command. The solution is to put `///` at the end of a line. This tells Stata that the next line is a continuation of the previous one. We illustrate the use of `///` in the `graph pie` commands shown in figure 4.5. (We will cover these commands in the next chapter. For now, just enter them into the Do-file Editor.)

If you are using dialog boxes to create your commands, you can click on the Copy button in the bottom left corner to copy the command and then press Ctrl+v in the Do-file Editor to paste the command into your do-file.

You must remember to save your do-file. You do this much like you would save a file in any other program; that is, click on File ▷ Save as.... Then you can type the name of the file; in our example, we are using `my_first.do`. You can also browse to find the project folder where you want to save the file, such as `E:\first project`. Until you have more experience, it is probably best to store your do-files and your data in the same folder.

Figure 4.5 shows our do-file, `my_first.do`, as it appears in the Do-file Editor. Notice that when we saved the do-file, the filename now appears at the top of the Editor.

```
* my_first.do
/*==============================================================
This is my first do-file. It uses the dataset called
firstsurvey_chapter4.dta. The commands in this do-file
summarize the variables in the dataset and then create a
pie chart. The data are in the current working directory.
==============================================================*/
version 17
use firstsurvey_chapter4.dta, clear
describe
summarize
graph pie, over(prison) title(Length of Prison Sentences)    ///
    note(firstsurvey_chapter4.dta) plabel(_all name)
graph pie, over(prison) title(Length of Prison Sentences)    ///
    note(firstsurvey_chapter4.dta) plabel(_all name) scheme(s2mono)
```

Figure 4.5. Commands in the Do-file Editor window of Stata for Mac

Are you convinced that you should keep a do-file? I hope so. Imagine that one month from now, you decide to create a pie chart for another variable, `conserv`, from `firstsurvey_chapter4.dta`. You can open the `my_first.do` file and replace `over(prison)` with `over(conserv)`. Click on the icon to run the do-file, and you are done.

As things get more complex, having a set of do-files that perform certain tasks becomes extremely valuable. One thing you might do is create an MS Excel spreadsheet to keep a record of the do-files you create. You might have three columns: the name and path of the do-file, the dataset it uses, and a brief statement of the purpose of each do-file. Eventually, you will have 30 or more do-files, and you can scan this listing to find one that is close to what you plan to do next to serve as a template. If you start doing several major projects, you probably should have a spreadsheet like this for each of the projects.

Stata do-files for this book

The webpage for this book, https://www.stata-press.com/data/agis6r/, has do-files for each chapter along with the datasets used. You can copy the do-files and datasets to your computer and reproduce the results in this book. These do-files may also be useful as templates when you do your own work because they can be modified as you need. You will have to change the paths in these files to the paths where you have stored your data unless you have stored the data in your current working directory, `C:\Users\`*username*`\Documents`. You could also change the current working directory. If you stored the data files in `C:\Users\`*username*`\Documents\agis6r`, you could enter the command `cd "C:\Users\`*username*`\Documents\agis6r"` to make that the current working directory. Then to open a file for Stata to use, you would simply type `use` *filename*, where *filename* is the name of the data file you want to use.

If you are working on a lab computer that erases anything you download after you shut down the computer, you can still get these do-files on the fly. For example, if you wanted to open the do-file for this chapter, you would run

```
. copy https://www.stata-press.com/data/agis6r/chapter4.do .
```

The `copy` command copies a file from one location to another, in this case from a website into our current working directory. At the end of the command, the dot that appears after the space indicates that you want to store `chapter4.do` into your current working directory. You need to have both the space and the dot for this command to work correctly. You could then open `chapter4.do` in your Do-file Editor or type the command `doedit chapter4`.

4.4   Copying your results to a word processor

Many people start using Stata to do their homework for a class in statistical methodology. In those cases, the datasets are often fully prepared, and you will not need to keep a record of how the data were created, how you labeled variables, how you recoded some items and dealt with missing values, or how you produced your results. In fact, many of the analyses will have short results. You can export these results to a Word document, a PDF file, an Excel file, or an HTML file with Stata's reproducible reporting features. With the `dyndoc` and `markdown` commands, you can create HTML and Word documents with Stata output and graphs, as well as Markdown-formatted text. The `putdocx`, `putpdf`, and `putexcel` commands create Word documents, PDF files, and Excel files with formatted text, Stata graphs, and tables with Stata results. All of these commands allow you to create a complete document with Stata results and the accompanying narrative and to reproduce the document as needed.

In some cases, you may prefer to simply save your results by highlighting the text that you want to save in the Results window, right-clicking on the highlighted text, and then selecting Copy from the menu (or using Ctrl+c after you have highlighted the text to copy). You can then paste the text into your favorite word processor. It is a good idea to include the commands that are in the Results window, because these give you a record of what you did. Except when there is no data manipulation, commands like these are no substitute for a do-file that includes everything you did in preparing the data.

When you copy results from Stata's Results window to your word processor, the format may look like a hopeless mess because Stata output is formatted using a fixed-width font; when you paste your results, things will likely not line up properly. The simplest solution to this alignment problem is to change the font and probably the font size, depending on your margins. I usually use the Courier or Courier New font at 9 point. Sometimes the lines may still wraparound, and you may need to widen the margins. Most Stata results will fit nicely if you have 1-inch margins and a 9- or 10-point Courier font. With most word processors, you change the font of the lines that contain the results by highlighting the lines you want to change and then selecting the Courier font and the 9-point font size.

Saving tabular output

If you want to export a table of results, you have a couple of options. The `etable` command can be used to create tables of estimation results and export them to Microsoft Word, Microsoft Excel, PDF, HTML, LaTeX, or Markdown files. If you are creating a tabulation or other table of summary statistics, you can compute these statistics using the `table` command. Immediately after `table`, you can use the `collect export` command to export the table to Microsoft Word, Microsoft Excel, PDF, HTML, LaTeX, or Markdown files. For even more customized tables, the `collect` suite of commands can be used to create an array of tables with summary statistics, estimation results, and any other returned result. You can customize the layout, headers, labels, formatting of results, and several other aspects of the table. If there is a particular style you would like to use for several tables, you can save it and easily apply it to multiple tables. Once you have finalized your table, you can then use `collect export` to export the table to Microsoft Word, Microsoft Excel, PDF, HTML, LaTeX, or Markdown. To learn more, you can type `help tables intro`. If you would like to include these customized tables in a more complete document, the `putdocx`, `putpdf`, and `putexcel` suites of commands allow you to do so; see the respective help file for more information.

As you progress in your class or as you start to use Stata in your own research, you will find that copying and pasting is really not up to the task of creating a record of your work. For more complex work, you will want to use log files, which we will now discuss.

4.5   Logging your command file

Stata can write a copy of everything that is sent to the Results window into a file. The file is called a *log file*. When you start logging, you can create a new file, or you can add on to the end of an existing log. You can temporarily suspend logging at any time and then restart it again. If you do not have a running Stata session, start one now, and let's take a look at output logs.

We can open a log by selecting File ▷ Log ▷ Begin..., which will bring up the file selector window. Navigate to the directory in which we want to keep our log, and then enter a name (or select one from the list). By default, Stata will save this log using a markup language called Stata Markup and Control Language (SMCL) that only Stata can read in a Viewer or Results window. The log will have a *filename*.smcl name, where .smcl is the extension. It looks nice in Stata but in another application, although it is a text file, the SMCL tags will be displayed because the word processor or other text editors will not understand them.

The other file format is called "log", which is a simple text file that your word processor can read. We need to pick the option of having a log file rather than a SMCL file from the dialog box. At the bottom of the *Save* dialog box, we can specify *Save as type*. From the pulldown menu, select *Log (*.log)* for the type. Like the Results window, the .log format uses a fixed-width format, and if you insert this file into a word processor, you need to make sure that the font is fixed width (for example, Courier) and the font size is small enough (for example, 9 point). Make sure to select a location where you can find this log file. We can insert this log into an open file in our word processor, or we can open the log file itself in our word processor. Because the extension will be .log, when we open it into a word processor, we need to make sure that the word processor is not just looking for certain other extensions. For example, in MS Word, you would need to browse for the log file where the type is *.* rather than *.docx.

If you are using MS Word as your word processor, you have two options when working with a .log file. You can open it as a new document in Word as long as you remember to change the file type from *.docx to *.* or show all. If you do this, the Word document will have a fixed font. You may need to change the font size, say, to 9 point, or make the margins wider. If you have an existing Word document, you need to use the Insert option rather than the Open option, and insert the text where you want it.

Open a new log file called `results.log`. Make sure to specify that it is a log file rather than a SMCL file. Then run a `summarize` command on the file. Now open the log by selecting File ▷ Log ▷ View..., which will show us the basic information about our file, where it is stored, and the date and time it was created, and will give the results of our summary in a Viewer. When we go back to our Command window, the Viewer will seem to disappear, but it will be on the taskbar at the bottom of our screen. We can click on it to open it again.

Run a few more commands, such as a tabulation and a graph. Now select the Viewer from the Windows toolbar, and the Viewer returns, but it goes only as far as the original summarize command. However, at the top of the Viewer window is a Refresh button.[1] Clicking on this button will update the Viewer to include the tabulate and the graph commands. What happened to the graph? Unfortunately, the log does not include the graphic output in the log file.

Experienced users use log files a lot. For beginners, log files may not be necessary. Also, if you make a lot of mistakes and need to run each command several times before you get it just right, the log will have all the bad output that you do not want, along with the good output that you do want. You might want to pause the log file while you try out a command or do-file. Then when you have the command the way you want it, you can restart the log to minimize the bad output. To do this, select File ▷ Log ▷ Suspend or Resume, respectively.

A strength of using log files is that they provide a record of both your commands and your results. The commands precede each result, so you can immediately see what you did. A major limitation of the log file is that it does not save graphic output, such as the pie chart we did in this chapter. Graphs need to be saved by right-clicking within the graph and then choosing an option, whether you want to save it (select Save as...) or copy it (select Copy) so you can paste it into your word processor.

4.6 Summary

Let's review what you have learned in this chapter:

- How to open a Do-file Editor and copy commands from the Results window

- How to use the dialog boxes in Stata to generate Stata commands and then copy these to the Do-file Editor

- How to string a series of commands together in the Do-file Editor and add comments to this file

- How to run an individual command and groups of commands from the Do-file Editor

- How to save your do-file and retrieve it for later analysis

- How to cut and paste between Stata and a word processor, like Word

- How to create and view a log file

This is a lot of new knowledge for you to absorb. Never feel bad if you need to review this material because you forgot a step along the way. Even as you gain experience with Stata, this chapter will be a handy resource.

---

1. Stata for Mac users can click on View ▷ Viewer ▷ Reload or use the keyboard shortcut Cmd+R.

This chapter focused on the mechanics of using the Do-file Editor, writing a simple do-file, and saving your results. As you go through the following chapters, you will learn how to write more complex do-files and do more complex data management.

The rest of the book will focus on performing graphic and statistical analysis, building on what we have done so far. Most people learning a statistics program want to learn how to do analyses rather than what we have done so far. Still, what we have done so far sets the groundwork for doing the analyses. Chapter 5 will go over graphic presentations and descriptive statistics.

4.7   Exercises

1. Open `firstsurvey_chapter4.dta` by selecting File ▷ Open.... Open a Do-file Editor, and copy into the Editor the command that opened the dataset. Open the dialog box to summarize the dataset, run the `summarize` command for all the variables, and copy this command from the Results window into the Do-file Editor. Save this do-file as `4-1.do` in a place where you can find it.

2. Open the do-file you created in the first exercise, and add appropriate comments. Save the new do-file under the name `4-2.do`.

3. Open the file `4-2.do`. Put your cursor in the Do-file Editor just below the command that opened the dataset and above the command that summarized the variables (you will need to insert a new line to do this). Type the `describe` command in the Do-file Editor. Add a command at the bottom of the file that gives you the median score on education. Save the new do-file under the name `4-3.do`.

4. Open `4-3.do`, run the `describe` command and the command that gave you the median score on education, highlight the results, paste the results into your word processor, and change the font so that it looks nice.

5. Open `4-3.do`. Open a log file with the log file type. Call the file `4results.log`. Run the entire `4-3.do` file, and exit Stata. Open a new session in your word processor, and open your log file into this session. Format it appropriately.

5   Descriptive statistics and graphs for one variable

5.1   Descriptive statistics and graphs

The most basic use of statistics is to provide descriptive statistics and graphs for individual variables. Advanced statistics and graph presentation can disentangle complex relationships between groups of variables, but for many purposes, simple descriptive statistics and graphs are exactly what is needed. Virtually every issue of a major city newspaper will have many descriptive statistics, and most issues will have one or more graphs. One article might report the percentage of teenagers who smoke cigarettes. Another article might report the average value of new homes. Each spring, there will be one or more articles estimating the average salary new college graduates will earn.

If you are working in a position related to public health, economics, or any of the social sciences, you will be a regular consumer of descriptive statistics, and many of you will be producers of these statistics. A parole office may need a graph showing trends in different types of offenses. A public health agency may need to demonstrate the need for more programs focused on sexually transmitted diseases: How much of a problem are sexually transmitted diseases? Is the problem getting worse or better?

Our society depends more and more on descriptive statistics. Policy makers are reluctant to make decisions without knowing the appropriate descriptive statistics. Social programs need to justify themselves to survive, much less to grow, and descriptive statistics and graphs are critical parts of this justification. In this chapter, you will learn how to produce these statistics and graphs using Stata.

5.2   Where is the center of a distribution?

Descriptive statistics are used to describe distributions. Three measures of central tendency describe the middle of the distribution: mean, median, and mode. The term "average" in statistics is typically defined as a synonym of the mean. Occasionally, this term is used to refer to the other measures of central tendency (the median and mode). When you read a newspaper article, it may say that the average family in a community has two children (this is probably the median, but it could be the mode) or that the average income in the community is $55,218 (also probably the median, but it could be the mean). The article might say that the average SAT score at your university is 1840 (probably the mean). It might say that the average person in a community has a high school diploma (this could be the mean, median, or mode). It is important to know when each central tendency measurement is appropriate.

The mode is the value or the category that occurs most often. We might say that the mode for political party in a parliament is the Labor Party. This would be the mode if there were more members of the parliament who were in the Labor Party than members of any other party. If we said the mode was 17 for age of high school seniors, this means that there are more high school seniors who are 17 than there are seniors who are any other age. This would be a reasonable measure of central tendency because most high school seniors are 17 years old. The mode represents the average in the sense of being the most typical value or category. If there is not a category or value that characterizes a distribution clearly, the mode is not descriptive of the central tendency of a distribution. For example, the heights of eighth-grade class members would not have a descriptive mode because each adolescent might be a different height, and there is no single height that is typical of eighth graders.

When you have unordered categorical variables, such as gender, marital status, or race/ethnicity, the mode is the only measure of central tendency. Even here, the mode is helpful only if one category is much more common than the others. If 79% of the adults in a community are married, saying that the modal marital status is married is a fair description of the typical member of the community. However, if 52% of adults in a community are female and 48% are male, it does not make much sense to say that the modal gender is female because there are nearly as many men as there are women.

The median is the value or the category that divides a distribution into two parts. Half the observations will have a higher value and half will have a lower value than the median. The median can be applied to categories that are ordered (political liberalism, religiosity, job satisfaction) or to quantitative variables (age, education, income). If we said that the median household income of a community is $55,218, we mean that half the households in that community have an income more than $55,218 and half the households have an income less than $55,218. When we used the `summarize, detail` command in chapter 4, we saw that Stata refers to the median as the 50th percentile.

The median is not influenced by extreme cases. If Bill Gates moved to this community, his multibillion dollar income would not influence the median. He would simply be in the half of the distribution that made more than the median income. Because of this property, the median is sometimes used with quantitative variables that are skewed (a distribution is skewed if it trails off in one direction or the other). Income trails off at the high end because relatively few people have huge incomes.

The median is occasionally used with variables that are ordered categories. When there are relatively few ordered categories, there may not be a category that has exactly half the cases above it and half below it. You might ask people about their marital satisfaction and give them response options of a) very dissatisfied, b) somewhat dissatisfied, c) neither satisfied nor dissatisfied, d) somewhat satisfied, and e) very satisfied. Because we usually code numbers rather than letters, we might code very dissatisfied as 1, somewhat dissatisfied as 2, neither satisfied nor dissatisfied as 3, somewhat satisfied as 4, and very satisfied as 5. The median satisfaction for men might be in the category we coded with a 4, somewhat satisfied. The median satisfaction for women might be 3, neither satisfied nor dissatisfied.

More often, researchers compute the mean for variables like this, and the mean for men might be 4.21 compared with 3.74 for women. These values indicate that men are, on average, a little above the somewhat-satisfied level and women are a little bit below the somewhat-satisfied level.

The mean is what lay people usually think of when they hear the word "average". It is the value every case would be, if every case had the same value. It is a fulcrum point that considers both the number of cases above and below it and how far they are above or below it. Although Bill Gates would scarcely change the median income of a community, his moving to a small town would raise the mean by a lot. Some people use M (recommended by the American Psychological Association) to represent the mean, and others use $\overline{X}$ (recommended by most statisticians). The formula for the mean is

$$\overline{X} = \frac{\Sigma X}{n}$$

In plain English, this says the mean is the sum of all the values, ΣX (pronounced sigma X or sum of X), divided by the number of observations, n. For example, if you had five college women who weighed 120, 110, 160, 140, and 210 pounds, respectively, the mean would be

$$\overline{X} = \frac{120 + 110 + 160 + 140 + 210}{5} = 148$$

From now on, we will use M instead of $\overline{X}$ to represent the mean.

What measure of central tendency should you use? This decision depends on the level of measurement you have, how your variable is distributed, and what you are trying to show (see table 5.1).

Table 5.1. Level of measurement and choice of average

Level of measurement	Mode	Median	Mean
Categorical, no order (nominal, e.g., gender)	Yes	No	No
Categorical, ordered (ordinal, e.g., social support)	Yes	Yes	Yes*
Quantitative (interval or ratio, e.g., age)	Yes	Yes	Yes

*Many researchers use the mean when there are several ordered categories.

- When you have categories with no order (gender, religion), you can use only the mode. The mode for religion in Saudi Arabia, for example, is "Muslim". Unordered categorical variables are called *nominal-level variables*.

- When you have ordered categories (religiosity, marital satisfaction), the median is often recommended. Such variables are often labeled as ordinal measures. You might read that the median religiosity response in Chicago is "somewhat religious". Ordered categories can be ordered along some dimension, such as low to high or negative to positive. When there are several categories, many researchers treat them as quantitative variables and use the mean. If religiosity has seven ordinal categories from 1 for not religious at all to 7 for extremely religious, you might use the mean by treating these numbers from 1 to 7 as if they are an interval-level measure. You might say that the mean is 3.4, for example.

- When you have quantitative data (meaningful numbers), you can use the mean, median, or mode. Quantitative data are often called *interval-level variables*. You will usually use the mean. If, however, the variable is extremely skewed, you would use the median.

Suppose that we want an average value for the number of children in households that have at least one child. The distribution is highly skewed in a positive direction because it trails off on the positive tail (see figure 5.1).

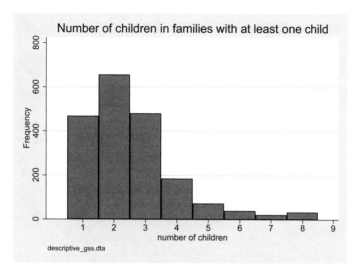

Figure 5.1. How many children do families have?

In this distribution, the mode is 2, the median (Mdn) is 2, and the mean (M) is 2.5. Notice how the small number of families with a lot of children drew the mean toward the tail but did not influence either the mode or the median. When a distribution is skewed, the mean will be bigger or smaller than the median, depending on the direction the distribution trails off.

There are two specialized averages you could use. The harmonic mean is useful when you want to average rates. Suppose that you go on a 60-mile bicycle ride where the first half of the course is a major hill climb and the second half of the course is a major descent. You might average just 5 miles per hour for the first half and then average 25 miles per hour for the second half of the ride. If we call your rate a, the harmonic mean (H) is

$$H = \frac{n}{\frac{1}{a_1} + \frac{1}{a_2} + \cdots + \frac{1}{a_k}}$$

$$= \frac{2}{\frac{1}{5} + \frac{1}{25}}$$

$$= 8.33$$

This harmonic mean of $H = 8.33$ miles per hour is a much better estimate of your average speed for the 60-mile ride than the arithmetic mean, which would be $(5+25)/2 = 15$ miles per hour.

The geometric mean is useful when you have a growth process where the growth is at a constant rate. This happens with population size or annual income, such as having your income grow at a rate of 3% per year. If you made 52,500 in 2000 and made 73,500 in 2010, what did you make in 2005? The arithmetic mean $(52500 + 73500)/2 = 63000$ exaggerates your income in 2005. The geometric mean (G) is

$$G = \sqrt[n]{a_1 \times a_2 \times \cdots \times a_n}$$

$$= \sqrt{52500 \times 73500}$$

$$= 62118.84$$

where $G = \$62{,}118.84$ is a much better estimate of your 2005 income.

The Stata command `ameans` *varlist* computes the arithmetic mean, the geometric mean, and the harmonic mean.

5.3   How dispersed is the distribution?

Besides describing the central tendency or average value in a distribution, descriptive statistics describe the variability or dispersion of observations. Are they concentrated in the middle? Do they trail off in one direction? Are they widely dispersed? Some suburbs are extremely homogeneous with rows of houses that are similar in style and value. These communities are highly concentrated around the average on a range of variables (income, education, ethnic background). Other communities are heterogeneous, and although they may have the same average values as the first community, they differ by having a mix of people who range widely on income, education, and ethnic background. This means that to understand a distribution, we need to know how it is distributed as well as its average value.

When there are only a few values or categories, we can use a frequency distribution (tabulation) to describe the variable. This distribution shows each value or category and how many people have that value or fall into that category. Stata calls this a tabulation. We can also use graphs to describe the dispersion of a distribution. When there are only a few categories being shown, the most common graphs to use are pie charts and bar charts.

When a variable is quantitative, we will usually want one number to represent the dispersion in the same way that we use one number to represent the central tendency. The standard deviation (SD) is used, especially with variables that have many possible values.

There are three parts of the SAT test: reading, writing, and math. Each of these parts will have a score between 200 and 800. If we just consider the reading and math sections of the SAT, the maximum possible score would be 1600. Let's assume that the total score on the math and reading sections has a mean of 1000 ($M = 1000$) and an SD of 100 (SD $= 100$). How can we interpret the mean and SD? Nearly all the students (about 95% of a normal distribution) are within two SDs of the mean and so they would have scores between 800 and 1200 on the combined math and reading sections.[1] This is the tall, but skinny, distribution in figure 5.2. If another school has the identical mean ($M = 1000$) but has an SD of 200, then nearly all the students had scores between 600 and 1400. The dispersion is much greater at the second school than at the first. We can see this in a graph of the two schools (figure 5.2). These two schools would have very different students even though the mean is identical. The smaller the SD, the more homogeneous the distribution is. From the graph, you can see how students at the first school are much more clustered around the mean ($M = 1000$) than are the students at the second school. The greater the SD, the more heterogeneous the distribution is.

Figure 5.2. Distributions with same $M = 1000$ but SDs $= 100$ or 200

Both distributions in figure 5.2 are normal and have identical means of 1000 ($M = 1000$). The distribution that is tightly packed around the mean has an SD of 100 (SD $= 100$). The distribution that is more dispersed, the distribution that is low and wide in the figure, has an SD of 200 (SD $= 200$).

Skewness is known as the third moment of the distribution. A positive value indicates a positive skew, and I mentioned that income is often used as an example because there are relatively few people who have enormous incomes. A negative value indicates a negative skew. An example of a negatively skewed variable would be marital satisfaction. Surveys show that most married people are satisfied or very satisfied, few people are dissatisfied, and even fewer are very dissatisfied. Neither of the distributions in figure 5.2 is skewed. Both are symmetrical around their respective means.

Kurtosis is known as the fourth moment of the distribution. A distribution with high kurtosis tends to have a bigger peak value than a normal distribution. Correspondingly, a low kurtosis goes with a distribution that is too flat to be a normal distribution. The value of kurtosis for a normal distribution is 3. Some programs (both SAS and IBM SPSS Statistics, for example) subtract 3 from the kurtosis to center it on zero,

---

1. The numbers used do not include the writing part of the SAT.

and some statistics books may use this approach, but Stata uses the correct formula. If you are reporting the kurtosis in a field where either SAS or IBM SPSS Statistics is a widely used program, you need to know that for Stata a kurtosis of 3 indicates a normal distribution. In such fields, you might report the value of kurtosis minus 3 to be consistent with common practice in that field. When you report a value of kurtosis minus 3, a kurtosis with an absolute value greater than 10 is problematic.

5.4   Statistics and graphs—unordered categories

About all we can do to summarize a categorical variable that is unordered is to report the mode and show a frequency distribution or a graph (pie chart or bar chart). In this chapter, you will use a dataset, `descriptive_gss.dta` (Smith et al. 2015), that includes three categorical, unordered variables. `sex`, `marital`, and `polviews` are nominal-level variables. The variable `sex` is coded as `male` or `female`, `marital` is coded by marital status, and `polviews` is coded by political view. There is no order to `sex` in that being coded `male` or `female` does not make one higher or lower on `sex`. Similarly, there is no order to `marital` in that having a particular status (that is, never married, married, separated, divorced, or widowed) does not make one higher or lower on marital status. These are just different statuses.

We can use the `tabulate` command to get frequency distributions for `sex`, `marital`, and `polviews`. We could type `tabulate sex`, then `tabulate marital`, and then `tabulate polviews`. However, Stata has another command named `tab1` that will repeatedly issue the `tabulate` command on each of the specified variables: `tab1 sex marital polviews`. This is so simple that you probably want to enter it directly, but if you want to use the dialog box, select Statistics ▷ Summaries, tables, and tests ▷ Frequency tables ▷ Multiple one-way tables; see figure 5.3. Be sure to select Multiple one-way tables rather than One-way table.

Figure 5.3. Dialog box for frequency tabulation

Tabulating a series of variables and including missing values

There are three variations of the `tabulate` command. `tabulate`, followed by one variable name, produces a one-way table of frequency counts for the values of that variable. To do a tabulation of a variable, say, `educ`, the command is `tabulate educ`.

The `tab1` command, as mentioned above, takes a list of variable names and issues the `tabulate` command separately for each of them. Suppose that you want to do a tabulation on `educ`, `sex`, and `polviews`, and you want to do this using one command. You would use `tab1 educ sex polviews`. Sometimes you might want to have the tabulation show missing values. To do this, add the `missing` option. To do a tabulation of the three variables in one command and show the missing values, the command is `tab1 educ sex polviews, missing`.

`tabulate`, followed by two variable names, produces a two-way table of frequency counts for the combinations of values of those variables. The `tab2` command takes a list of variable names and issues the `tabulate` command separately for each possible pair of variable names.

Using the dialog box, we enter the variables sex, marital, and polviews. Clicking on OK produces the following result:

```
. use https://www.stata-press.com/data/agis6r/descriptive_gss, clear
. tab1 sex marital polviews
-> tabulation of sex
```

respondents sex	Freq.	Percent	Cum.
male	1,228	44.41	44.41
female	1,537	55.59	100.00
Total	2,765	100.00	

```
-> tabulation of marital
```

marital status	Freq.	Percent	Cum.
married	1,269	45.90	45.90
widowed	247	8.93	54.83
divorced	445	16.09	70.92
separated	96	3.47	74.39
never married	708	25.61	100.00
Total	2,765	100.00	

```
-> tabulation of polviews
```

think of self as liberal or conservative	Freq.	Percent	Cum.
extremely liberal	47	3.53	3.53
liberal	143	10.74	14.27
slightly liberal	159	11.95	26.22
moderate	522	39.22	65.44
slghtly conservative	209	15.70	81.14
conservative	210	15.78	96.92
extrmly conservative	41	3.08	100.00
Total	1,331	100.00	

The first tabulations for sex and marital tell us a lot. Some 55.6% of our sample of 2,765 adults comprises women, and 44.4% comprises men. We have 1,537 women and 1,228 men. For the marital variable, 45.9% (1,269) of adults are married. This is a clear mode because this marital status is so much more frequent than any of the other statuses. By contrast, the mode for sex is not as predominant a category.

A Stata user, Ben Jann, in 2007, with subsequent revisions wrote a command called fre, which provides more details than tab1. To install the fre command, type search fre. A new Viewer window will open with a list of all packages with the keyword "fre". You can scroll through these to find the command fre, or you can press Ctrl+f on Windows or Cmd+f on Mac, type fre in the resulting box, and then press Enter until you find the command fre. Click on the link, and in the new window, click on the click here to install link, which will install the fre ado-file and help file. Because you know the name of the command, you could install the command more simply by typing `ssc install fre` in the Command window. This will automatically install the command.

Entering the command shown below gives us the result we had before, but the `fre` results are more useful if there are missing values. In this dataset, there are 1,434 people who were not asked—or at least did not report—their political views. The `fre` command provides the percentage of the total sample who selected each category (18.88% picked moderate). We usually do not want to use the percentages in this column because we are interested in the percentage of the valid responses. The valid responses are those 1,331 survey participants who answered the item. The column labeled `Valid` shows us that 39.22% of those valid responses picked the moderate category. The last column on the right is labeled `Cum.`, which is the cumulative percentage for the valid responses. We see that 65.44% of the participants picked moderate or more liberal responses, but only 14.27% picked the liberal or the extremely liberal categories. One of the nicest features of the `fre` command is the way it provides both the value label and the numeric value in one table. Being able to see the label and value together is quite useful when you are recoding or creating a scale. Comparing the `fre` results with the `tab1` results above, we see that the variable label is easier to read with the `fre` command.

```
. fre sex marital polviews
```
sex — respondents sex

		Freq.	Percent	Valid	Cum.
Valid	1 male	1228	44.41	44.41	44.41
	2 female	1537	55.59	55.59	100.00
	Total	2765	100.00	100.00	

marital — marital status

		Freq.	Percent	Valid	Cum.
Valid	1 married	1269	45.90	45.90	45.90
	2 widowed	247	8.93	8.93	54.83
	3 divorced	445	16.09	16.09	70.92
	4 separated	96	3.47	3.47	74.39
	5 never married	708	25.61	25.61	100.00
	Total	2765	100.00	100.00	

polviews — think of self as liberal or conservative

		Freq.	Percent	Valid	Cum.
Valid	1 extremely liberal	47	1.70	3.53	3.53
	2 liberal	143	5.17	10.74	14.27
	3 slightly liberal	159	5.75	11.95	26.22
	4 moderate	522	18.88	39.22	65.44
	5 slghtly conservative	209	7.56	15.70	81.14
	6 conservative	210	7.59	15.78	96.92
	7 extrmly conservative	41	1.48	3.08	100.00
	Total	1331	48.14	100.00	
Missing	.	1434	51.86		
Total		2765	100.00		

Obtaining both numbers and value labels

Before doing the tabulations, you might want to type the command `numlabel _all, add`. After you enter this command, whenever you type the `tabulate` command, Stata reports both the numbers you use for coding the data (1, 2, 3, 4, and 5) and the value labels (married, widowed, divorced, separated, and never married). Later, if you do not want to include both of these, you can drop the numerical values by using the command `numlabel _all, remove`. Practice using these commands as an exercise on your own.

The tables with both numbers and value labels may not look great, so you may want two tables for each variable, with one showing the value labels without the numeric codes and the other showing the numeric codes without the value labels. The default gives you the value labels. On the dialog box, there is an option to *Display numeric codes rather than value labels*. This option produces the numeric values without the value labels. If you want both the numeric values and the value labels using official Stata commands, you need to run either the `numlabel` command or run the `tab1` command twice—once with *Display numeric codes rather than value labels* checked and once with it not checked. It is probably simpler just to run Ben Jann's `fre` command once you have installed it.

In chapter 4, we created a pie chart. Here we will create a pie chart for marital status. Select Graphics ▷ Pie chart and look at the Main tab. If this dialog still has information entered from a previous pie chart, you should click on the ↻ (reset) icon in the lower left of the view screen to clear the dialog box. Type `marital` as the *Category variable*. This uses the categories we want to show as pieces of the pie. Leave the *Variable: (optional)* box blank. Under the Titles tab, enter a nice title in the *Title* box and the name of the dataset we used as a *Note*. Under the Options tab, click on *Order by this variable* and type `marital`. Also check *Exclude observations with missing values (casewise deletion)* because we do not want these, if there are any, to appear as a separate piece of the pie. The dialog box for the Options tab is shown in figure 5.4.

Figure 5.4. The **Options** tab for pie charts (by category)

The initial pie chart (figure 5.5) provides a visual display of the distribution of marital statuses in the United States. The size of each piece of the pie is proportional to the percentage of the people in that status. This pie chart shows that the most common status of adults is married.

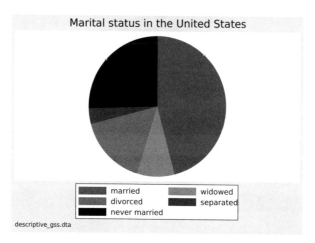

Figure 5.5. Pie charts of marital status in the United States

It is possible to improve the default pie chart. The default pie chart is a bit hard to read because it assumes you want each slice a different color, and this will not work well when printing in black and white. Because many publications require black and white printing, we should edit the pie chart. From our dialog box for the pie chart, we could click on the Overall tab, from which we could select *s2 monochrome* from the drop-down *Scheme* list. However, there are several other ways we can improve this pie chart, so let's switch to using the Graph Editor.

Stata's Graph Editor will allow us to easily make numerous changes to the pie chart. To open the Graph Editor from the Graph window, click on the icon with the bar chart and the pencil labeled "Start Graph Editor". (Click on this same icon from the Graph Editor window, and the Graph Editor will close.) You can also open the Graph Editor by right-clicking on the pie chart (Graph window) and selecting Start Graph Editor or in Windows, by selecting File ▷ Start Graph Editor from the Graph window. When you first open the Graph Editor, your screen appears like figure 5.6.

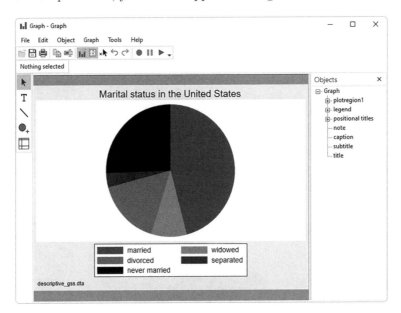

Figure 5.6. The Graph Editor opening screen

Suppose we want to draw attention to the percentage of adults who are divorced. We can do this by using the "tools" in the toolbar on the left. Click on the arrow (Pointer tool) at the top of the toolbar. Now double-click on the piece of pie that represents the divorced adults; doing so opens the dialog box shown in figure 5.7.

Figure 5.7. Pie slice properties dialog box

Here we can change the current color, `Grayscale 8`, to a wide variety of monochrome or color options using the *Color* dropdown menu. To draw attention to the piece of the pie for divorced adults, we will check the *Explode slice* box. We then click on OK.

Now suppose we want to add a subtitle of "A lot of adults are divorced". We can double-click on *subtitle* in the Object Browser, which is on the right side of the Graph Editor. Doing this opens a dialog box in which we can enter the subtitle. We can also change properties for the titles, such as font size. We add the subtitle and then click on OK. From our `fre` command that we previously ran, we saw that 16.09% of adults were divorced. The pie chart shows this as the proportion of the pie, but we could add some text for completeness. Click on the "T" (Add text tool) in the left-hand toolbar, and click approximately where you want to add the text. Let's add "16% are divorced" and then click on OK. Next, click on the Pointer tool, and then click on the new text to move it exactly where you want it.

We may want to make one more change. Notice that the labels in the legend are all lowercased (married, widowed, etc.). Let's capitalize the first letter of each label. Double-click on *married* in the legend, and in the dialog box that opens, change the text to `Married`, and click on OK. Repeat this process for the other names.

Figure 5.8 shows the enhanced version of our pie chart. The Graph Editor has many features. The best way to discover them is to try the different options, some of which are quite sophisticated. On the right side of the top toolbar, you will find icons that let you record a series of changes in one graph that can be played back on a different graph.

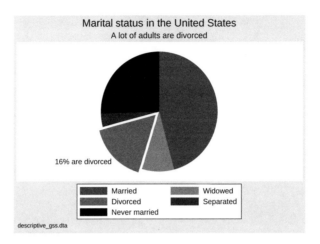

Figure 5.8. Final pie chart of marital status

A bar chart is more attractive than a pie chart for many applications. Instead of selecting **Bar Chart** from the **Graphics** menu, select **Histogram**. Here we are creating a bar chart rather than a histogram, but this is the best way to produce a high-quality bar chart using Stata.

On the **Main** tab, type `marital` in the *Variable* box. Click on the button next to *Data are discrete*. In the section labeled *Y axis*, click on the button next to *Percent*. The trick to making this a bar chart is to click on *Bar properties* in the lower left of the **Main** tab. This opens another dialog box where the default is to have no gap between the bars. Change this to a gap of **10**, which sets the gap between bars to 10 percent of the width of a bar. Click on **Accept**. If you switch to the **Titles** tab, you can enter a title, such as `Marital status in the United States`. Next switch to the **X axis** tab and click on **Major tick/label properties**. This opens another dialog box where you select the **Labels** tab and check the box for *Use value labels*. Sometimes the value labels are too wide to fit under each bar. You may need to create new value labels that are shorter. If they are just a little bit too wide, you can change the angle. Click on *Angle* and select *45 degrees* from the drop-down menu. Click on **Accept**. Finally, switch back to the **Main** tab. In the lower right corner of the dialog box, click on *Add height labels to bars*. Because we are reporting percentages, this option will show the percentage in each marital status at the top of each bar. The **Main** tab is shown in figure 5.9.

Figure 5.9. Using the `histogram` dialog box to make a bar chart

Figure 5.10 shows the resulting bar chart, which has the percentage in each status at the top of each bar. Married is the most common status, but never married is second. This dataset includes people who are 18 and older, and it is likely that many of those in the never-married status are between 18 and 30.

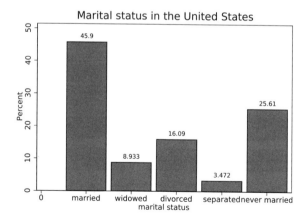

Figure 5.10. Bar chart of marital status of U.S. adults

Sometimes you may have a larger number of categories. When this happens, Stata's default will show only a limited number of value labels, so some of the bars will be unlabeled. If you want to label all of them, you need to go to the **X axis** tab and click on **Major tick/label** properties to open the dialog box we opened before. On the **Rule** tab, click on *Suggest # of ticks* and enter the number of bars in the box by *Ticks*. Another issue can arise if you have value labels that are no longer used. For the `polviews` variable, we could use seven ticks because there are seven categories for `polviews`. However, our missing category includes people who had originally been coded as 0 na for not applicable. They were not asked this question for some reason. If you create a bar chart for `polviews`, you will need to change the value label or make a new set of value labels that does not have this option.

5.5   Statistics and graphs—ordered categories and variables

When our categories are ordered, we can use the median to measure the central tendency. When there are only a couple of categories, however, the median does not work well. Here is an example where there are several categories for the `polviews` variable, which asks people their political views on a seven-point scale from extremely liberal to extremely conservative. We might want to report the median or mean and the SD. We have done a `summarize` and a `tabulate` before using the dialog system, so this time we will just enter the commands directly: `tab1 polviews` and `summarize polviews, detail`. Before you run these commands, make sure that you run the command `numlabel _all, add` so that both the numbers and the value labels are shown.

```
. numlabel _all, add

. tab1 polviews

-> tabulation of polviews
```

think of self as liberal or conservative	Freq.	Percent	Cum.
1. extremely liberal	47	3.53	3.53
2. liberal	143	10.74	14.27
3. slightly liberal	159	11.95	26.22
4. moderate	522	39.22	65.44
5. slghtly conservative	209	15.70	81.14
6. conservative	210	15.78	96.92
7. extrmly conservative	41	3.08	100.00
Total	1,331	100.00	

```
. summarize polviews, detail
```

think of self as liberal or conservative

	Percentiles	Smallest		
1%	1	1		
5%	2	1		
10%	2	1	Obs	1,331
25%	3	1	Sum of wgt.	1,331
50%	4		Mean	4.124718
		Largest	Std. dev.	1.385016
75%	5	7		
90%	6	7	Variance	1.918268
95%	6	7	Skewness	-.1509408
99%	7	7	Kurtosis	2.693351

The frequency distribution produced by `tab1` is probably the most useful way to describe the distribution of an ordered categorical variable. We can see that it is fairly symmetrically distributed around the mode of moderate, with somewhat more people describing themselves as conservative rather than liberal.

Although the tabulation gives us a good description of the distribution, we often will not have the space in a report to show this level of detail. The median is provided by the `summarize` command, which shows that the 50th percentile occurs at the value of 4, so the Mdn is 4, corresponding to a political moderate. Even though these are ordinal categories, many researchers would report the mean. The mean assumes that the quantitative values, 1–7, are interval-level measures. However, the mean ($M = 4.12$) is usually a good measure of central tendency. The mean reflects the distribution somewhat more accurately here than does the median because the mean shows that the average response is a bit more to the conservative end than to the liberal. We know that the mean is a bit more conservative because the higher numeric score on `polviews` corresponds to more conservative views. You should be able to see this from reading the frequency distribution carefully. Although this variable is clearly ordinal, many researchers treat variables like this as if they were interval and rely on the mean as a measure of central tendency. If you are in doubt, it may be a good idea to report both the median and the mean.

Here is how you can create a histogram showing the distribution of political views. Type the command

```
. histogram polviews, discrete percent
> title(Political views in the United States) subtitle(by adult population)
> note(General Social Survey 2002) xtitle(Political conservatism) scheme(s1mono)
```

Remember, this is the way Stata writes it in the Results window. You do not need to type the . or the >. In a do-file, you would actually need to use the ///, preceded by a space at the end of each but the last line, so Stata will know the three lines are all one command. You would write this command in the Do-file Editor as

```
histogram polviews, discrete percent ///
    title(Political Views in the United States) subtitle(by adult population) ///
    note(General Social Survey 2002) xtitle(Political conservatism) scheme(s1mono)
```

Like most graph commands, this is an example of a complicated command that can be easily produced using the dialog box. Commands for making graphs can get complicated, so it is usually best to use the dialog box with graphs.

Select Graphics ▷ Histogram. On the Main tab, select `polviews` from the *Variable* list, and click on the button by *Data are discrete*. Go to the X axis tab, and enter the title you want to appear on the x axis (the x axis is the horizontal axis of the graph). Go back to the Main tab and click on the radio button by *Percent*. If you want your graph to appear without colors, you can pick a monochrome scheme. On the Overall tab, select `s1 monochrome` from the *Scheme* list. Finally, go to the Titles tab; enter the title, subtitle, and notes that you want to appear on the graph. Click on OK. The example graph appears in figure 5.11.

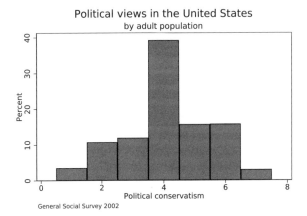

Figure 5.11. Histogram of political views of U.S. adults

This histogram allows the reader to quickly get a good sense of the distribution. In 2002, moderate was the overwhelming choice of adults in the United States. The bars on the right (conservative) are a bit higher than the bars on the left, which indicates a tendency for people to be conservative ($M = 4.12$, Mdn $= 4$, Mode $= 4$, SD $= 1.39$).

Some researchers, when making a graph to show the distribution of an ordinal variable, are reluctant to have the bars for each value touch. Also some like to have the labels posted on the x axis, rather than the coded values. These options and more can be customized in the dialog box.

5.6   Statistics and graphs—quantitative variables

We will study three variables: `age`, `educ`, and `wwwhr` (hours spent on the Internet). Two types of useful graphs are the already familiar histogram and a new graph called the *box plot*. We will usually use the mean or median to measure the central tendency for quantitative variables. The SD is the most widely used measure of dispersion, but a statistic called the *interquartile range* is used by the box plots that are presented below.

Let's start with `wwwhr`, hours spent in the last week on the Internet. These data were collected in 2002, and by now, the hours have probably increased a lot.

Computing descriptive statistics for quantitative variables is easy. Let's skip the dialog box and just enter the command:

```
. summarize wwwhr, detail

                        www hours per week

            Percentiles      Smallest
     1%          0               0
     5%          0               0
    10%          0               0          Obs              1,574
    25%          1               0          Sum of wgt.      1,574

    50%          3                          Mean          5.907878
                              Largest       Std. dev.     8.866734
    75%          7              60
    90%         15              64          Variance      78.61897
    95%         21             100          Skewness      3.997908
    99%         40             112          Kurtosis      30.39248
```

This output says that the average person spent a mean of 5.91 hours on the Internet in the week before the survey was taken. The median is 3 hours. Because the mean is greater than the median when a distribution is positively skewed, we can assume that the distribution is positively skewed (trails off on the right side). A positively skewed distribution makes sense because the value for hours on the Internet cannot be less than zero, but we all know a few people who spend many hours on the web. The SD is 8.87 hours, which tells us that the time on the web varies widely. For a normally distributed variable, about two-thirds of the cases are within one SD of the mean (−2.96 hours and 14.77 hours) and 95% will be within two SDs of the mean (−11.83 hours and 23.64 hours). Clearly, this does not make any sense because you cannot use the Internet fewer than zero hours a week. Still, this information suggests that there is a lot of variation in how much time people spend on the web.

The skewness is 4.00, which means that the distribution has a positive skew (greater than zero), and the kurtosis is 30.39, which is huge compared with 3.0 for a normal distribution. Remember that a kurtosis greater than 10 is problematic; a kurtosis over 20 is very serious. This result suggests that there is a big clump of cases concentrated in one part of the distribution. Can you guess where this concentration was in 2002?

Stata can test for normality based on skewness and kurtosis. For most applications, this test is of limited utility. It is extremely sensitive to small departures from normality when you have a large sample, and it is insensitive to large departures when you have a small sample. The problem is that, when we do inferential statistics, the lack of normality is much more problematic with small samples (where the test lacks power) than it is with large samples (where the test usually finds a significant departure from normality, even for a small departure).

To run the test for normality based on skewness and kurtosis, we can use the dialog box by selecting Statistics ▷ Summaries, tables, and tests ▷ Distributional plots and tests ▷ Skewness and kurtosis normality tests. Once the dialog box is open, enter the variable wwwhr and click on OK. Unlike with the complex graph commands, with statistical tests it is often easier to enter the command in the Command window (unless you cannot remember it). The command is simply sktest wwwhr.

```
. sktest wwwhr
Skewness and kurtosis tests for normality
                                                            ——— Joint test ———
      Variable |      Obs   Pr(skewness)   Pr(kurtosis)   Adj chi2(2)  Prob>chi2
─────────────────────────────────────────────────────────────────────────────
         wwwhr |    1,574         0.0000         0.0000       1060.97     0.0000
```

These results show that, based on skewness, the probability that `wwwhr` is normal is 0.000 and, based on kurtosis, the probability that `wwwhr` is normal is also 0.000. Anytime either probability is less than 0.05, we say that there is a statistically significant lack of normality. Testing for normality based on skewness and kurtosis jointly, Stata reports a probability of 0.000, which reaffirms our concern. It is best to report this as $\Pr < 0.001$ rather than as $\Pr = 0.000$. This test computes a statistic called chi-squared (χ^2).

We need to be quite thoughtful when using `sktest`. When we have a large sample, this command is quite powerful, meaning that it will show even a small departure from normality to be statistically significant. However, when we have a large sample, the assumption of normality is less crucial than it is with a small sample. With a small sample, the `sktest` command may fail to show a substantial departure from normality to be significant because the test has very little power for a small sample. Unfortunately, the violation of the assumption of normality is most important when the sample size is small. So it is a catch-22: `sktest` may show an unimportant violation to be significant for a large sample but fail to show an important violation to be significant for a small sample. This is why we need to look at the actual size of the skewness and kurtosis as a measure, as well as a histogram, and not depend just on the significance test.

When we are describing several variables in a report, space constraints usually limit us to reporting the mean, median, and standard deviation. You can read these numbers along with the measure of skewness and kurtosis and have a reasonable notion of what each of the distributions looks like. However, it is possible to describe `wwwhr` nicely with a few graphs. We will use the `s1mono` scheme for the remaining graphs. First, we will create a histogram by using the dialog box described in section 5.5. Or for a basic histogram (shown in figure 5.12), we could enter

```
. histogram wwwhr, frequency
(bin=31, start=0, width=3.6129032)
```

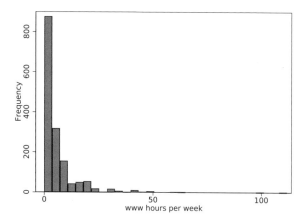

Figure 5.12. Histogram of time spent on the Internet

This simple command does not include all the nice labeling features you can get using the dialog box, but it gives us a quick view of the distribution. This graph includes a few outliers (observations with extreme scores) who surf the Internet more than 25 hours a week. Providing space in the histogram for the handful of people using the Internet between 25 hours and 150 hours takes up most of the graph, and we do not get enough detail for the smaller number of hours that characterizes most of our web users.

We will get around this problem by creating a histogram for a subset of people who use the web fewer than 25 hours a week, and we will do a separate histogram for women and for men. You can get these histograms using the dialog box by inserting the restriction wwwhr < 25 in the *If: (expression)* box under the if/in tab and by clicking on *Draw subgraphs for unique values of variables* and then inserting the sex variable under the By tab. Here is the command we could enter directly:

```
. histogram wwwhr if wwwhr < 25, frequency by(sex)
```

Notice that the frequency by(sex) part of the command appears after the comma. The new histograms appear in figure 5.13.

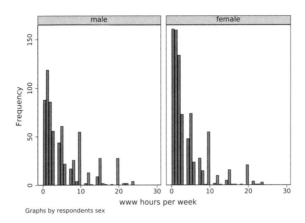

Figure 5.13. Histogram of time spent on the Internet (fewer than 25 hours a week, by gender)

By using the interface, we could improve the format of figure 5.13 by adding titles, and we might want to report the results by using percentages rather than frequencies. We also could experiment with different widths of the bars. Still, figure 5.13 shows that the distribution is far from normal, as the measures of skewness and kurtosis suggested. By creating the histogram separately for women and men, we can see that at the time these data were collected in 2002, far more women were in the lowest interval. Although we do not have more recent data, it would be interesting to compare these data from 2002 with a current histogram. Both of these distributions are surely quite different today, and the gender differences of 2002 may no longer be present.

We could also open the Graph Editor by right-clicking on the graph we just created. It is often easier to make changes using the Graph Editor than to work with the command. The advantage of working with the command is that we have a record of what we did. We might want to replace `male` and `female` with `Men` and `Women`. To do this in the Graph Editor, just click on the headers and change the text in the appropriate boxes. You probably can think of additional changes that would make the graph nicer.

When you want to compare your distribution on a variable with how a normal distribution would be, you can click on an option for Stata to draw how a normal distribution would look right on top of this histogram. We will not show an illustration of this, but all you need to do is open the Density plots tab for the `histogram` dialog box and check the box that says *Add normal-density plot*. This is left for you to do on your own. There is another option on the dialog box for adding a kernel density plot. This is an estimate of the most likely population distribution for a continuous variable that would account for this sample distribution. This will smooth out some of the bars that are extremely high or low because of variation from one sample to the next.

To get the descriptive statistics for men and women separately (but not restricted to those using the web fewer than 25 hours a week), we need a new command:

```
. by sex, sort: summarize wwwhr
```

We can do this from the `summarize` dialog box by checking *Repeat command by groups* and entering `sex` under the by/if/in tab. This command will sort the dataset by `sex` and then summarize separately for women and men.

Another way to obtain a statistical summary of the `wwwhr` variable is to use the `table` command. Select Statistics ▷ Summaries, tables, and tests ▷ Tables of frequencies, summaries, and command results to open the dialog box. For purposes here, we are going to type the command in the Command window, and after exporting the results, we will display them in figure 5.14.

We ask for the mean, median, SD, interquartile range, skewness, kurtosis, and coefficient of variation. The first set of parentheses indicates that we want the levels of sex placed on the rows of the table. The second set of parentheses indicates that we want the results (mean, median, etc.) on the columns. The command is as follows:

```
. table (sex) (result), statistic(mean wwwhr) statistic(p50 wwwhr)
> statistic(sd wwwhr) statistic(iqr wwwhr) statistic(skewness wwwhr)
> statistic(kurtosis wwwhr) statistic(cv wwwhr)
```

We can easily export this table to Microsoft Word, Microsoft Excel, PDF, HTML, LATEX, SMCL, or Markdown. We use the `collect export` command and simply provide a filename with the appropriate suffix for the document type:

```
. collect export wwwhr.docx
```

We used the `.docx` suffix to export this table to a Microsoft Word file. In the Results window, you will see a link to the file. Figure 5.14 shows the file produced.

	Mean	50th percentile	Standard deviation	Interquartile range	Skewness	Kurtosis	Coefficient of variation
respondents sex							
male	7.106892	4	9.98914	9	3.608189	25.2577	1.405557
female	4.920046	2	7.688655	4	4.409274	36.78389	1.56272
Total	5.907878	3	8.866734	6	3.997908	30.39248	1.500832

Figure 5.14. Microsoft Word file showing results of the `table` command

In addition to skewness and kurtosis, we selected two additional statistics I have not yet introduced. The coefficient of relative variation (CV) is simply the SD divided by the mean (that is, $CV = SD/M$). This statistic is sometimes used to compare SDs for variables that are measured on different scales, such as income measured in dollars and education measured in years. The interquartile range is the difference between the value of the 75th percentile and the value of the 25th percentile. This range covers the middle 50% of the observations.

Men, on average, spent far more time using the Internet in 2002 than did women. Because the means are bigger than the medians, we can assume that the distributions are positively skewed (as was evident in the histograms we did). Men are a bit more variable than women because their SD is somewhat greater. Both distributions are skewed and have heavy kurtosis. The CV is 1.41 for men and 1.56 for women. Women have slightly greater variance relative to their mean than men do (based on comparing the CV values), even though the actual SD is bigger for men. Finally, the interquartile range of 9 for men is more than double the interquartile range of 4 for women. Thus the middle 50% of men are more dispersed than the middle 50% of women. Comparing the CVs suggests the opposite finding to comparing interquartile ranges. Because the scale (hours of using the Internet) is the same, we would not rely on the CV.

A horizontal or vertical box plot is an alternative way of showing the distribution of a quantitative variable such as wwwhr. Select Graphics ▷ Box plot. Here we will use four of the tabs: Main, Categories, if/in, and Titles. Under the Main tab, check the radio button by *Horizontal* to make the box plot horizontal, and enter the name of our variable, wwwhr. Under the Categories tab, check *Group 1* and enter the *Grouping variable*, that is, sex. This will create separate box plots for women and for men. We could have additional grouping variables, but these plots can get complicated. If we wanted a box plot that included both women and men, we would leave this tab blank. Under the if/in tab, we need to make a command so that the plots are shown only for those who spend fewer than 25 hours a week on the web. In the *If: (expression)* box, we type wwwhr < 25. Finally, under the Titles tab, enter the title and any subtitles or notes we want to appear on the chart. Here is command generated from the dialog box and the resulting graph appears in figure 5.15.

```
. graph hbox wwwhr if wwwhr < 25, over(sex)
> title(Hours spent on the Internet) subtitle(by gender)
> note(descriptive_gss.dta)
```

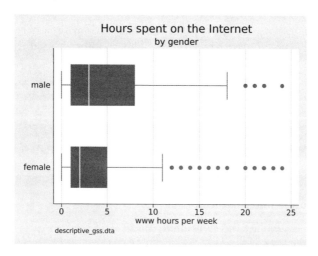

Figure 5.15. Box plot of time spent on the Internet (fewer than 25 hours a week, by gender)

Histograms may be easier to explain to a lay audience than box plots. For a nontechnical group, histograms are usually a better choice. Many statisticians like box plots better because they show more information about the distribution. The white vertical line in the dark-gray boxes is the median. For women, you can see that the median is about 2 hours per week, and for men, about 4 hours per week.

The left and right sides of the dark-gray box are the 25th and 75th percentiles, respectively. Within this dark gray box area are half of the people. This box is much wider for men than it is for women, showing how men are more variable than women. Lines extend from the edge of the dark-gray box 1.5 box lengths, or until they reach the largest or smallest cases. Beyond this, there are some dots representing outliers, or extreme values.

5.7   Summary

After four chapters about how to set up files and manage them, I hope you enjoyed getting to a substantive chapter showing you some of the output produced with Stata. We are just beginning to see the power of Stata, but you can already summarize variables and create several types of attractive graphs. This chapter covered the following topics:

- How to compute measures of central tendency (averages), including the mean, median, and mode

- When to use the different measures of central tendency based on level of measurement, distribution characteristics, and your purposes

- How to describe the dispersion of a distribution by using

  - Statistics (standard deviations)

  - Tables (frequency distributions)

  - Graphs (pie charts, bar charts, histograms, and box plots)

- How to use Stata to give you these results for nominal-, ordinal-, and interval-level variables

- How to use Stata's Graph Editor

We have only scratched the surface of graph capabilities offered by Stata. We will cover a few more types of graphs in later chapters. In addition to the *Stata Graphics Reference Manual*, you should see *A Visual Guide to Stata Graphics, Fourth Edition* by Michael Mitchell (2022), which is available from Stata Press. Mitchell's book offers many examples of graphs and charts along with the Stata code that produced them. Readers can adapt the code to produce the graph they want. Stata's own video tutorials, https://www.stata.com/links/video-tutorials/, are also helpful.

5.8   Exercises

1. Open `descriptive_gss.dta` and do a detailed summary of the variable `hrs1` (hours worked last week). Also create a histogram of the variable. Interpret the mean and median. Looking at the histogram, explain why the skewness value is close to zero. What does the value of kurtosis tell us? Looking at the histogram, explain why the kurtosis is a positive value.

2. Open `descriptive_gss.dta` and do a detailed summary of the variable `satjob7` (job satisfaction). Type the command `numlabel satjob7, add`, and then do a tabulation of `satjob7`. Interpret the mean and median values. Why would some researchers report the median? Why would other researchers report the mean?

3. Open `descriptive_gss.dta` and do a tabulation of `deckids` (who makes decisions about how to bring up children). Do this using the by/if/in tab to select by `sex`. Create and interpret a bar chart by using the `histogram` dialog box. Why would it make no sense to report the mean, median, or standard deviation for `deckids`? Use Stata's Graph Editor to make the bar chart look as nice as you can.

4. Open `descriptive_gss.dta` and do a tabulation of `strsswrk` (job is rarely stressful) and a detailed summary. Do this using the by/if/in tab to select by `sex`. Create and interpret a histogram, using the By tab to do this for males and females. In the Main tab, be sure to select the option *Data are discrete*. Carefully label your histogram to show value labels and the percentage in each response category. Each histogram should be similar to figure 5.11. Interpret the median and mean for men and women.

5. Open `descriptive_gss.dta` and do a tabulation of `trustpeo`, `wantbest`, `advantge`, and `goodlife`. Use the `table` command to produce a table that summarizes descriptive statistics for this set of variables by gender. Include the median, mean, standard deviation, and count for each variable. Interpret the means by using the variable labels you get with the tabulation command.

6. Open `descriptive_gss.dta` and do a tabulation of `polviews`. Create a bar chart for this variable showing the percentage of people who are in each of the seven categories. Next create a chart that has labels at a 45-degree angle for each of the bars. Finally, change the chart by using the X axis tab's Minor tick/label properties and Major tick/label properties (using the *Custom* option) so that the histogram does not have a null category and all the categories are labeled. Compare this final figure with figure 5.11.

7. Open `descriptive_gss.dta`. In figure 5.15, we created a box plot for the hours women and men spend surfing the Internet. First, create a similar box plot for `hrs1` (hours worked last week). Now add a second grouping variable, `marital`. Using this graph, give a detailed interpretation of how marital status and gender are related to hours a person works for pay.

8. Open `descriptive_gss.dta`. Execute the following commands for `educ` and compare the two sets of results. What problem are you illustrating here?

```
. summarize educ, detail
. sktest educ
. histogram educ
. preserve
. sample 10, count
. summarize educ, detail
. sktest educ
. histogram educ
. restore
```

9. Open `descriptive_gss.dta`. Construct a graph showing two histograms, one for women and one for men for the `educ` variable. Use the Graph Editor to improve the appearance of the graph by adding an overall title and making other changes you can think of. Is this graph helpful for comparing the educational achievement of women and men? How so?

10. Repeat all parts of exercise 9, but construct a box plot instead of histograms.

11. Repeat exercise 10 using the `table` command, and ask for the mean, median, standard deviation, skewness, kurtosis, and interquartile range. Interpret each of these statistics to compare the women and men, and explain how the differences are reflected (or not) in the graphs done in exercises 9 and 10.

6 Statistics and graphs for two categorical variables

6.1 Relationship between categorical variables

Chapter 5 focused on describing single variables. Even there, it was impossible to resist some comparisons, and we ended by examining the relationship between gender and hours per week spent using the web. Some research simply requires a description of the variables, one at a time. You do a survey for your agency and make up a table with the means and standard deviations for all the quantitative variables. You might include frequency distributions and bar charts for each key categorical variable. This information is sometimes the extent of statistical research your reader will want. However, the more you work on your survey, the more you will start wondering about possible relationships.

- Do women who are drug dependent use different drugs from those used by drug-dependent men?

- Are women more likely to be liberal than men?

- Is there a relationship between religiosity and support for increased spending on public health?

You know you are "getting it" as a researcher when it is hard for you to look at a set of questions without wondering about possible relationships. Understanding these relationships is often crucial to making policy decisions. If 70% of the nonmanagement employees at a retail chain are women, but only 20% of the management employees are women, there is a relationship between gender and management status that disadvantages women.

In this chapter, you will learn how to describe relationships between categorical variables. How do you define these relationships? What are some pitfalls that lead to misinterpretations? In this chapter, the statistical sophistication you will need increases, but there is one guiding principle to remember: the best statistics are the simplest statistics you can use—as long as they are not too simple to reflect the inherent complexity of what you are describing.

6.2 Cross-tabulation

Cross-tabulation is a technical term for a table that has rows representing one categorical variable and columns representing another. These tables are sometimes called contingency tables because the category a person is in on one of the variables is contingent on the category the person is in on the other variable. For example, the category people are in on whether they support a particular public health care reform may be contingent on their gender. If you have one variable that depends on the other, you usually put the dependent variable as the column variable and the independent variable as the row variable. This layout is certainly not necessary, and several statistics books do just the opposite. That is, they put the dependent variable as the row variable and the independent variable as the column variable.

Let's start with a basic cross-tabulation of whether a person says abortion is okay for any reason and their gender. Say you decide that whether a person accepts abortion for any reason is more likely if the person is a woman because a woman has more at stake when she is pregnant than does her partner. Therefore, whether a person accepts abortion will be the dependent variable, and gender will be the independent variable.

We will use `gss2006_chapter6.dta`, which contains selected variables from the 2006 General Social Survey (Smith et al. 2015), and we will use the cross-tabulation command, `tabulate`, with two categorical variables, `sex` and `abany`. To open the dialog box for `tabulate`, select Statistics ▷ Summaries, tables, and tests ▷ Frequency tables ▷ Two-way table with measures of association. This dialog box is shown in figure 6.1.

Figure 6.1. The Main tab for creating a cross-tabulation

If we had three variables and wanted to see all possible two-by-two tables (`vara` with `varb`, `vara` with `varc`, and `varb` with `varc`), we could have selected instead Statistics ▷ Summaries, tables, and tests ▷ Frequency tables ▷ All possible two-way tables. With our current data, we continue with the dialog box in figure 6.1 and select `sex`, the independent variable, as the *Row variable* and `abany`, the dependent variable, as the *Column variable*. We are assuming that `abany` is the variable that depends on `sex`. Also check the box on the right side under *Cell contents* for the *Within-row relative frequencies* option. This option tells Stata to compute the percentages so that each row adds up to 100%. Here are the resulting command and results:

```
. tabulate sex abany, row
```

```
+----------------+
| Key            |
|----------------|
|   frequency    |
| row percentage |
+----------------+
```

	ABORTION IF WOMAN WANTS FOR ANY REASON		
GENDER	YES	NO	Total
MALE	350	478	828
	42.27	57.73	100.00
FEMALE	434	677	1,111
	39.06	60.94	100.00
Total	784	1,155	1,939
	40.43	59.57	100.00

Independent and dependent variables

Many beginning researchers get these terms confused. The easiest way to remember which is which is that the dependent variable "depends" on the independent variable. In this example, whether a person accepts abortion for any reason depends on whether the person is a man or a woman. By contrast, it would make no sense to say that whether a person is a man or a woman depends on whether they accept abortion for any reason.

Many researchers call the dependent variable an "outcome" and the independent variable the "predictor". In this example, sex is the predictor because it predicts the outcome, abany.

It may be hard or impossible to always know that one variable is independent and the other variable is dependent. This is because the variables may influence each other. Imagine that one variable is your belief that eating meat is a health risk (there could be four categories: strongly agree, agree, disagree, or strongly disagree). Then imagine that the other variable is whether you eat meat or not. It might seem easy to say that your belief is the independent variable and your behavior is the dependent variable. That is, whether you eat meat or not depends on whether you believe doing so is a health risk. But try to think of the influence going the other way. A person may stop eating meat because of a commitment to animal rights issues. Not eating meat over several years leads to look for other justifications, and they develop a belief that eating meat is a health risk. For them, the belief depends on their prior behavior.

There is no easy solution when we have trouble deciding which is the independent variable. Sometimes, we can depend on time ordering. Whichever came first is the independent variable. Other times, we are simply forced to say that the variables are associated without identifying which one is the independent variable and which is the dependent variable.

The independent variable sex forms the rows with labels of MALE and FEMALE. The dependent variable abany, accepting abortion under any circumstance, appears as the columns labeled YES and NO. The column on the far right gives us the total for each row. Notice that there are 828 males, 350 of whom find abortion for any reason to be acceptable, compared with 1,111 females, 434 of whom say abortion is acceptable for any reason. These frequencies are the top number in each cell of the table.

The frequencies at the top of each cell are hard to interpret because each row and each column has a different number of observations. One way to interpret a table is to use the percentage, which takes into account the number of observations within each category of the independent variable (predictor). The percentages appear just below the frequencies in each cell. Notice that the percentages add up to 100% for each row. Overall, 40.43%

of the people said "yes", abortion is acceptable for any reason, and 59.57% said "no". However, men were relatively more likely (42.27%) than women (39.06%) to report that abortion is okay, regardless of the reason. We get these percentages because we told Stata to give us the *Within-row relative frequencies*, which in the command is the `row` option.

Thus men are more likely to report accepting abortion under any circumstance. We compute percentages on the rows of the independent variable and make comparisons up and down the columns of the dependent variable. Thus we say that 42.27% of the men compared with 39.06% of the women accept abortion under any circumstance. This is a small difference, but interestingly, it is in the opposite direction from what we expected.

6.3 Chi-squared test

The difference between women and men seems small, but could we have obtained this difference by chance? Or is the difference statistically significant? Remember, when you have a large sample like this one, a difference may be statistically significant even if it is small.

If we had just a handful of women and men in our sample, there would be a good chance of observing this much difference just by chance. With such a large sample, even a small difference like this might be statistically significant. We use a chi-squared (χ^2) statistic to test the likelihood that our results occurred by chance. If it is extremely unlikely to get this much difference between men and women in a sample of this size by chance, you can be confident that there was a real difference between women and men, but you still need to look at the percentages to decide whether the statistically significant difference is substantial enough to be important.

The chi-squared test compares the frequency in each cell with what you would expect the frequency to be if there were no relationship. The expected frequency for a cell depends on how many people are in the row and how many are in the column. For example, if we asked a small high school group if they accept abortion for any reason, we might have only 10 males and 10 females. Then we would expect far fewer people in each cell than in this example, where we have 828 men and 1,111 women.

In the cross-tabulation, there were many options on the dialog box (see figure 6.1). To obtain the chi-squared statistic, check the box on the left side for *Pearson's chi-squared*. Also check the box for *Expected frequencies* that appears in the right column on the dialog box. The resulting table has three numbers in each cell. The first number in each cell is the frequency, the second number is the expected frequency if there were no relationship, and the third number is the percentage of the row total. We would not usually ask for the expected frequency, but now you know it is one of Stata's capabilities. The resulting command now has three options: `chi2 expected row`. Here is the command and the output it produces:

```
. tabulate sex abany, chi2 expected row
```

```
Key

   frequency
expected frequency
  row percentage
```

	ABORTION IF WOMAN WANTS FOR ANY REASON		
GENDER	YES	NO	Total
MALE	350	478	828
	334.8	493.2	828.0
	42.27	57.73	100.00
FEMALE	434	677	1,111
	449.2	661.8	1,111.0
	39.06	60.94	100.00
Total	784	1,155	1,939
	784.0	1,155.0	1,939.0
	40.43	59.57	100.00

```
          Pearson chi2(1) =    2.0254   Pr = 0.155
```

In the top left cell of the table, we can see that we have 350 men who accept abortion for any reason, but we would expect to have only 334.8 men here by chance. By contrast, we have 434 women who accept abortion for any reason, but we would expect to have 449.2. Thus we have $350 - 334.8 = 15.2$ more men accepting abortion than we would expect by chance and $434 - 449.2 = -15.2$ fewer women than we would expect. Stata uses a function of this information to compute chi-squared.

At the bottom of the table, Stata reports `Pearson chi2(1) = 2.0254` and `Pr = 0.155`, which would be written as $\chi^2(1, N = 1939) = 2.0254$; p not significant. Here we have one degree of freedom. The sample size of $N = 1939$ appears in the lower right part of the table. We usually round the chi-squared value to two decimal places, so 2.0254 becomes 2.03. Stata reports an estimate of the probability to three decimal places. We can report this, or we can use a convention found in most statistics books of reporting the probability as less than 0.05, less than 0.01, or less than 0.001. Because $p = 0.155$ is greater than 0.05, we say p not significant. What would happen if the probability were $p = 0.0004$? Stata would round this to $p = 0.000$. We would not report $p = 0.000$ but instead would report $p < 0.001$.

To summarize what we have done in this section, we can say that men are more likely to report accepting abortion for any reason than are women. In the sample of 1,939 people, 42.3% of the men say that they accept abortion for any reason compared with just 39.1% of the women. This relationship between gender and acceptance of abortion is not statistically significant.

6.3.1   Degrees of freedom

Because I assume that you have a statistics book explaining the necessary formulas, I have not gone into detail. Stata will compute the chi-squared, the number of degrees of freedom, and the probability of getting your observed result by chance.

You can determine the number of degrees of freedom yourself. The degrees of freedom refers to how many pieces of independent information you have. In a 2×2 table, like the one we have been analyzing, the value of any given cell can be any number between 0 and the smaller of the number of observations in the row and the number of observations in the column. For example, the upper left cell (350) could be anything between 0 and 784. Let's use the observed value of 350 for the upper left cell. Now how many other cells are free to vary? By subtraction, you can determine that 434 people must be in the female/yes cell because $784 - 350 = 434$. Similarly, 478 observations must be in the male/no cell ($828 - 350 = 478$), and 677 observations must be in the female/no cell ($1111 - 434 = 677$). Thus with four cells, only one of these is free, and we can say that the table has 1 degree of freedom. We can generalize this to larger tables where degrees of freedom $= (R - 1)(C - 1)$, where R is the number of rows and C is the number of columns. If we had a 3×3 table instead of a 2×2 table, we would have $(3-1)(3-1) = 4$ degrees of freedom.

6.3.2   Probability tables

Many experienced Stata users have made their own commands that might be helpful to you. Philip Ender made a series of commands that display probability tables for various tests. The `search` command finds user-contributed ado-files and lets you install them on your machine. Typing the command `search chitable`[1] produces the results shown in figure 6.2.

---

1. You cannot install this community-contributed command by typing `ssc install chitable`, because the `ssc` command is limited to installing and uninstalling community-contributed commands that are located within the Statistical Software Components (SSC) Archive or often called the Boston College Archive at http://www.repec.org. Although the SSC Archive is by far the dominant depository of community-contributed Stata commands, it does not include all community-contributed commands.

Updating community-contributed commands

Stata will prompt you when you need to update Stata files, and you should do this when prompted. Community-contributed commands such as `fre` or `chitable` may be revised by their authors. You will not be prompted to update these, so you need to remember to do this, say, once a month. The command you type in the Command window is

```
. ado update, update
```

This command will list any community-contributed commands you have installed and then update any of them that have changed.

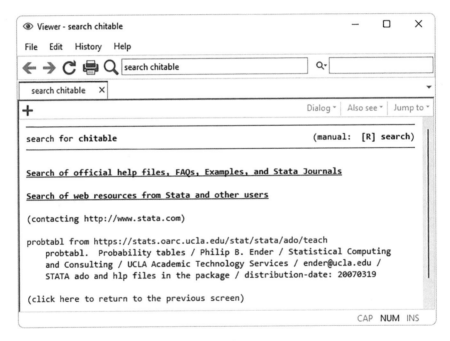

Figure 6.2. Results of `search chitable`

From here, click on the blue web link

```
probtabl from https://stats.oarc.ucla.edu/stat/stata/ado/teach
```

This link takes you to another screen where you can click on the blue link labeled `click here to install`. Once you have done this, anytime you want to see a chi-squared table, you merely type the command `chitable`. This installation also gives you other probability tables that we will use elsewhere in this book, including *t*-test tables (`ttable`) and *F*-test tables (`ftable`). Simply entering `chitable` is a lot more convenient than having to look up a probability in a textbook. Try it now.

```
. chitable

      Critical Values of Chi-square
df    .50    .25    .10    .05   .025    .01    .001
 1    0.45   1.32   2.71   3.84   5.02   6.63   10.83
 2    1.39   2.77   4.61   5.99   7.38   9.21   13.82
 3    2.37   4.11   6.25   7.81   9.35  11.34   16.27
 4    3.36   5.39   7.78   9.49  11.14  13.28   18.47
 5    4.35   6.63   9.24  11.07  12.83  15.09   20.52
 6    5.35   7.84  10.64  12.59  14.45  16.81   22.46
 7    6.35   9.04  12.02  14.07  16.01  18.48   24.32
 8    7.34  10.22  13.36  15.51  17.53  20.09   26.12
 9    8.34  11.39  14.68  16.92  19.02  21.67   27.88
10    9.34  12.55  15.99  18.31  20.48  23.21   29.59
11   10.34  13.70  17.28  19.68  21.92  24.72   31.26
12   11.34  14.85  18.55  21.03  23.34  26.22   32.91
13   12.34  15.98  19.81  22.36  24.74  27.69   34.53
14   13.34  17.12  21.06  23.68  26.12  29.14   36.12
15   14.34  18.25  22.31  25.00  27.49  30.58   37.70
16   15.34  19.37  23.54  26.30  28.85  32.00   39.25
17   16.34  20.49  24.77  27.59  30.19  33.41   40.79
18   17.34  21.60  25.99  28.87  31.53  34.81   42.31
19   18.34  22.72  27.20  30.14  32.85  36.19   43.82
20   19.34  23.83  28.41  31.41  34.17  37.57   45.31
21   20.34  24.93  29.62  32.67  35.48  38.93   46.80
22   21.34  26.04  30.81  33.92  36.78  40.29   48.27
23   22.34  27.14  32.01  35.17  38.08  41.64   49.73
24   23.34  28.24  33.20  36.42  39.36  42.98   51.18
25   24.34  29.34  34.38  37.65  40.65  44.31   52.62
26   25.34  30.43  35.56  38.89  41.92  45.64   54.05
27   26.34  31.53  36.74  40.11  43.19  46.96   55.48
28   27.34  32.62  37.92  41.34  44.46  48.28   56.89
29   28.34  33.71  39.09  42.56  45.72  49.59   58.30
30   29.34  34.80  40.26  43.77  46.98  50.89   59.70
35   34.34  40.22  46.06  49.80  53.20  57.34   66.62
40   39.34  45.62  51.81  55.76  59.34  63.09   73.40
45   44.34  50.98  57.51  61.66  65.41  69.96   80.08
50   49.33  56.33  63.17  67.50  71.42  76.15   86.66
55   54.33  61.66  68.80  73.31  77.38  82.29   93.17
60   59.33  66.98  74.40  79.08  83.30  88.38   99.61
65   64.33  72.28  79.97  84.82  89.18  94.42  105.99
70   69.33  77.58  85.53  90.53  95.02 100.43  112.32
75   74.33  82.86  91.06  96.22 100.84 106.39  118.60
     (output omitted)
100   99.33 109.14 118.50 124.34 129.56 135.81  149.45
```

In a `chitable`, the first row shows the significance levels. The first column shows the degrees of freedom. You can see that with 1 degree of freedom, you need a chi-squared value of 3.84 to be significant at the 0.05 level. If you had 4 degrees of freedom, you would need a chi-squared of 9.49 to be significant at the 0.05 level. You might try the other commands for the other tables. If you have ever had to search for one of these tables in a textbook, you will appreciate the convenience of these commands.

Reporting chi-squared results

How do we report the significance level of chi-squared? How do we report that chi-squared varies somewhat from one field to another? A safe way to report the significance is as $p < 0.05$, $p < 0.01$, or $p < 0.001$. Suppose that we had a chi-squared of 10.05 with 1 degree of freedom and $p = 0.002$. This is less than 0.01 but not less than 0.001. We would say that $\chi^2(1) = 10.05$, $p < 0.01$. Notice that we put the degrees of freedom in parentheses. Some disciplines would also like you to list the sample size, for example, $\chi^2(1, N = 435) = 10.05$, $p < 0.01$. Still other disciplines would rather you report the probability value, for example, $p = 0.002$.

Reporting the probability value has the advantage of providing more-detailed information. For example, one result might have a $p = 0.052$ and another might have a $p = 0.451$. The first of these is almost statistically significant and is an unlikely result if the null hypothesis of no relationship is correct. The second of these is just about what you would expect to get by chance flipping a coin. Saying that both of these have the same classification of p not significant conceals the clear difference between these two results.

6.4   Percentages and measures of association

We have already discussed the use of percentages. These are often the easiest and best way to describe a relationship between two variables. In our last example, the percentage of men who said abortion was okay for any reason was slightly greater than, although not statistically significantly greater than, the percentage of women who said abortion was okay for any reason. Percentages often tell us what we want to know. There are other ways of describing an association called measures of association; they try to summarize the strength of a relationship with a number.

The value of chi-squared depends on two things. First, the stronger the association between the variables, the bigger chi-squared will be. Second, because we have more confidence in our results when we have larger samples, then the more cases we have, the bigger chi-squared will be. In fact, for a given relationship expressed in percentages, chi-squared is a function of sample size. If you had the same relationship as in our example but, instead of having 1,939 observations, you had 19,390 (10 times as many), then chi-squared would be 20.254, also 10 times as big. There would still be 1 degree of freedom, but here the results would be statistically significant, $p < 0.001$. With large samples, researchers sometimes misinterpret a statistically significant chi-squared value as indicating a strong relationship. With a large sample, even a weak relationship can be statistically significant. This makes sense because with a large sample we have the power to detect even small effects.

One way to minimize this potential misinterpretation is to divide chi-squared by the maximum value it could be for a table of a particular shape and number of observations. This is simple in the case of 2×2 tables, such as the one we are using. The maximum value of chi-squared for a 2×2 table is the sample size, N. Thus in our example, if the relationship were as strong as possible, chi-squared would be 1,939. Our chi-squared of 2.03 is tiny in comparison. The coefficient ϕ (phi) is defined as the positive or negative square root of the quantity chi-squared divided by N:

$$\phi = \sqrt{\frac{\chi^2}{N}}$$

Stata uses a different formula for calculating the value of ϕ. Stata's formula produces a positive or negative value directly, depending on the arrangement of rows and columns; see the box on page 134. A ϕ with an absolute value from 0.0 to 0.19 is considered weak, from 0.20 to 0.49 is considered moderate, and from 0.50 and above is considered strong. In our example, $\phi = 0.03$, which we would thus describe as a weak relationship, meaning that the strength of the relationship is weak regardless of whether it is statistically significant. This is an important distinction between the strength of the relationship (some call this substantive or practical significance) and statistical significance. So long as the same distribution based on percentages describes a table, ϕ will have the same value whether we have 194 observations, 1,939 observations, or 19,390 observations.

Because both Cramér's V and ϕ are the square root of chi-squared divided by its maximum possible value and because ϕ can be thought of as a special case of V, Stata simply has an option to compute Cramér's V. However, if you have a 2×2 table, you should call this measure of association ϕ to avoid confusion and recognize that it may be either a positive or negative value. On the dialog box for doing the cross-tabulation with measures of association, simply check *Cramér's V* under the list of *Test statistics*. This results in the command `tabulate sex abany, chi2 row V`. If you type this command directly into the Command window, remember to capitalize the `V`; this is a rare example where you must use an uppercase letter in Stata.

The ability to have a positive or negative ϕ does not extend to larger tables where Cramér's V is the appropriate measure of association. The maximum value chi-squared can obtain for a larger table is N times the smaller of $R - 1$ or $C - 1$, where R is the number of rows and C is the number of columns in the table. For these tables, we report the positive square root of the ratio of chi-squared to its maximum positive value and call it V:

$$V = \sqrt{\frac{\chi^2}{N \times \min(R - 1, C - 1)}}$$

Why can ϕ be negative?

Stata uses a special formula for calculating ϕ, and this formula gives us the positive or negative sign for ϕ directly. The formulas that Stata uses is

$$\phi = \frac{n_{11}n_{22} - n_{12}n_{21}}{\sqrt{n_{1.}n_{2.}n_{.1}n_{.2}}}$$

Let's look at how this formula applies to a sample table. In the following table, the first subscript is the row and the second subscript is the column. Hence, n_{11} is the number of cases in row 1, column 1, and n_{21} is the number of cases in row 2, column 1. A dot is used to refer to all cases in both rows or both columns. Thus $n_{1.}$ is the number of people who are in row 1 summed over both columns; it is the row total. Similarly, $n_{.1}$ is the column total for the first column. Here is how this looks in a 2×2 table:

	column		
row	1	2	Total
1	n_{11}	n_{12}	$n_{1.}$
2	n_{21}	n_{22}	$n_{2.}$
Total	$n_{.1}$	$n_{.2}$	$n_{..}$

Applying the above formula to a simple table, we obtain $\phi = -0.3333$ (reported in the table as Cramér's V):

	column		
row	1	2	Total
1	10	20	30
2	20	10	30
Total	30	30	60

```
Pearson chi2(1) =   6.6667    Pr = 0.010
     Cramér's V =  -0.3333
```

However, if we rearrange the rows and columns, we obtain $\phi = 0.3333$. Here are the rearranged table and results:

	column		
row	1	2	Total
1	20	10	30
2	10	20	30
Total	30	30	60

```
Pearson chi2(1) =   6.6667    Pr = 0.010
     Cramér's V =   0.3333
```

For most 2×2 tables, we do not care about how the rows and columns are arranged and so use only the positive value of V and ϕ.

6.5 Odds ratios when dependent variable has two categories

Odds ratios (ORs) are useful when the dependent variable has just two categories. We define ORs by using the independent variable. What are the odds that a man will say that abortion is okay for any reason? What are the odds a woman will say that abortion is okay for any reason? Let's look at our cross-tabulation, where I have added letter labels for each cell:

```
. tabulate sex abany

              |  ABORTION IF WOMAN
              | WANTS FOR ANY REASON
     GENDER   |     YES          NO |    Total
--------------+----------------------+----------
       MALE   |   350 (a)     478 (b) |      828
     FEMALE   |   434 (c)     677 (d) |    1,111
--------------+----------------------+----------
      Total   |     784        1,155 |    1,939
```

We know that 350 men say abortion is okay for any reason and 478 do not, so the odds are $a/b = 350/478 = 0.73$. What about women? The odds for a woman supporting abortion for any reason are $c/d = 434/677 = 0.64$. The real question is the difference between men and women. We could say simply that the odds of a man supporting abortion are higher, 0.73, than a woman supporting abortion, 0.64. Alternatively, we can calculate an OR. This is the odds of a man supporting abortion divided by the odds of a woman supporting abortion. It is call the OR because it is the ratio of two odds.

$$OR = \frac{a/b}{c/d} = \frac{350/478}{434/677} = 1.14$$

The OR for men compared with women is (approximately) $0.73/0.64 = 1.14$. Thus the odds of a man supporting abortion for any reason are greater than the odds of a woman supporting abortion for any reason. How much greater? When an OR is greater than 1, we calculate $100 \times (OR - 1.00) = (1.14 - 1.00) = 14\%$. The odds of a man supporting abortion are 14% greater than the odds of a woman supporting abortion.

We could reverse this and calculate the OR with the odds for women in the numerator:

$$OR = \frac{c/d}{a/b} = \frac{434/677}{350/478} = 0.88$$

The OR for women compared with men is (approximately) $0.64/0.73 = 0.88$. When the OR is less than 1, we calculate $100 \times (1.00 - OR) = 100 \times (1 - 0.88) = 12\%$. The odds of a woman supporting abortion are 12% lower than the odds of a man supporting abortion.

Sometimes an OR can be calculated for a 2×2 table and provide much more useful information than a measure of association such as ϕ. Here is an illustration of how ϕ can be very misleading. Utts (2014) reports a table showing the relationship between men taking a daily dose of aspirin and having a heart attack. This was originally reported by the Steering Committee of the Physicians' Health Study Research Group and involved a 5-year trial that followed 22,071 male physicians between 40 and 84 years of age who were randomly assigned to either take an aspirin every day or take a placebo pill. We will use `chapter6_aspirin.dta` for our example. Our command and the results are

```
. use https://www.stata-press.com/data/agis6r/chapter6_aspirin
. tabulate aspirin heartattack, chi2 row V
```

```
  ┌──────────────────┐
  │ Key              │
  ├──────────────────┤
  │     frequency    │
  │  row percentage  │
  └──────────────────┘
```

	Heart Attack		
Condition	No Attack	Attack	Total
Placebo	10,845	189	11,034
	98.29	1.71	100.00
Aspirin	10,933	104	11,037
	99.06	0.94	100.00
Total	21,778	293	22,071
	98.67	1.33	100.00

```
          Pearson chi2(1) =  25.0139   Pr = 0.000
              Cramér's V =  -0.0337
```

The results are inconsistent. Notice that the Pearson chi2(1) = 25.01, $p < 0.001$, so the results are highly significant. A problem with this finding is that even a small effect will be significant when we have a large sample, and 22,071 men is definitely a large sample. This is one reason why it is always good to look into other measures of effect size when doing a chi-squared test of significance. We see that Cramér's V (or ϕ) is just -0.03, which suggests a weak relationship. Stata and other statistics software packages report a value for ϕ that can be the positive or negative square root of chi-squared over N and thus have a potential range of -1.0 to $+1.0$. In our example, we coded the aspirin group as 1 and the control group as 0, and those who had a heart attack as 1 and those who did not as 0. With this coding, the negative ϕ indicates that being in the aspirin group (coded 1) is negatively related to being in the heart attack group (coded 1). If we had coded the variables differently, the sign would have been positive.

ORs are also quite useful when interpreting the effect size shown in the above cross-tabulation, but they lead to a very different conclusion. The odds of a man in the aspirin group having a heart attack are $104/10933 = 0.0095$. The odds of a man in the placebo group having a heart attack are $189/10845 = 0.0174$. The OR of a man in the aspirin group having a heart attack compared with a man in the placebo group is the ratio OR $= (a/b)/(c/d) = 0.0095/0.0174 = 0.546$. Because the OR is less than 1.00, we subtract it from 1.00, $100 \times (1.0 - 0.546) = 45.4\%$. Thus we can say that the odds of a man having a heart attack in a 5-year period are reduced by 45.4% if he takes an aspirin every day. This is an important finding that has influenced medical care even though the measure of association is only -0.034. The ϕ coefficient can be very misleading, especially when one outcome (having a heart attack) is a rare event.

Millions of people have been advised to take a daily small aspirin by their physician because of the OR $= 0.546$ and not because the $\phi = -0.034$.

What else can we use to aid our interpretation of this table? The percentage in each cell can be quite useful. The table shows that 1.71% of the men who took the placebo had a heart attack within 5 years, but only 0.94% of the men who took aspirin every day had a heart attack within 5 years. Comparing these percentages, we see that $1.71/0.94 = 1.81$. Thus men who were in the placebo group were 1.81 times as likely to have a heart attack than men in the aspirin group. Alternatively, we could say that $0.94/1.71 = 0.54$, or men taking aspirin were about half as likely to have a heart attack than men taking a placebo.

What is the best way to describe the results? The results of this study indicate that adult males taking a daily dosage of aspirin are significantly less likely to have a heart attack than men who take a placebo pill. Although a heart attack is a rare event for either the treatment or the control group, occurring in only 1.33% of the men, those taking the placebo were 1.81 times as likely to have an attack. The OR $= 0.55$ indicates that the odds of a man taking aspirin daily having a heart attack are 45% lower than if he took a placebo.

6.6   Ordered categorical variables

The example we have covered involves two unordered categorical variables (nominal level). Sometimes the categorical variables have an underlying order. For example, we might be interested in the relationship between health (`health`) and happiness (`happy`) from `gss2006_chapter6.dta`, which contains selected variables from the 2006 General Social Survey. Are people who are healthier also happier? When the question is asked this way, `health` is the independent variable because being happy is said to depend on your health.

$$\text{health} \rightarrow \text{happy}$$

Another researcher might reverse this premise and argue that the happier a person is then the more likely he or she is to rate everything, including his or her own health, as better than people who are unhappy. If this is your argument, then happiness is the independent variable and health depends on how happy you are.

$$\text{health} \leftarrow \text{happy}$$

A third researcher may simply say that the two variables are related without claiming the direction of the relationship. We say that happiness and health are reciprocally related. In other words, the happier you are, the more positive you will report your health to be, and the healthier you are, the happier you will report being.

$$\text{health} \leftrightarrow \text{happy}$$

The example above uses a double-headed arrow, meaning that happiness leads to better perceived health and better perceived health leads to happiness. Because both variables depend on each other, there is no single variable that we can call independent or dependent. This probably makes sense. We have all known people who are happy and see the world through rose-colored lenses, where they rate nearly everything positively. They are likely to rate their health as positive. We have also known people for whom their health has a big influence on their happiness. If they have a health condition that varies, then when they are feeling relatively well they will report being happy, and when they are feeling bad they will report being unhappy.

If there is no clear independent or dependent variable, it is usually best to make the row variable the one with the most categories. Running the command `codebook happy health` shows that `health` has four categories (EXCELLENT, GOOD, FAIR, and POOR) and `happy` has just three categories (VERY HAPPY, PRETTY HAPPY, and NOT TOO HAPPY). So we will make `health` the row variable and `happy` the column variable.

Select Statistics ▷ Summaries, tables, and tests ▷ Frequency tables ▷ Two-way table with measures of association. The resulting dialog box is the same as the one in figure 6.1. We need to enter the names of the variables and the options we want. Enter `health` for the row variable and `happy` for the column variable. We pick both *Within-column relative frequencies* and *Within-row relative frequencies*. Also check *Pearson's chi-squared*, *Goodman and Kruskal's gamma*, *Kendall's tau-b*, and *Cramér's V* to obtain these statistics. Here are the command and results that are produced:

```
. use https://www.stata-press.com/data/agis6r/gss2006_chapter6
(General Social Surveys, 1972-2006 [Cumulative File], Dataset 0001)

. tabulate health happy, chi2 column gamma row taub V
```

Key
frequency
row percentage
column percentage

CONDITION OF HEALTH	GENERAL HAPPINESS			Total
	VERY HAPP	PRETTY HA	NOT TOO H	
EXCELLENT	271	247	33	551
	49.18	44.83	5.99	100.00
	42.74	22.50	12.50	27.61
GOOD	261	567	103	931
	28.03	60.90	11.06	100.00
	41.17	51.64	39.02	46.64
FAIR	82	231	92	405
	20.25	57.04	22.72	100.00
	12.93	21.04	34.85	20.29
POOR	20	53	36	109
	18.35	48.62	33.03	100.00
	3.15	4.83	13.64	5.46
Total	634	1,098	264	1,996
	31.76	55.01	13.23	100.00
	100.00	100.00	100.00	100.00

```
         Pearson chi2(6) = 182.1737   Pr = 0.000
             Cramér's V =   0.2136
                  gamma =   0.3917   ASE = 0.030
        Kendall's tau-b =   0.2492   ASE = 0.020
```

Stata makes some compromises in making this table. If a value label is too big to fit, Stata simply truncates the label. You might need to do a codebook on your variables to make sure you have the labels correct. In this table, the value label "very happy" appears as VERY HAPP, and "not too happy" appears as NOT TOO H. If you were preparing this table for a report or publication, you would want to edit it so that it has proper labels.

Just like with unordered categories, we use chi-squared to test the significance of the relationship. The relationship between perceived health and happiness is statistically significant: $\chi^2(6, N = 1996) = 182.17$, $p < 0.001$.

The percentages are also useful. Here we will pick one variable, health, arbitrarily as the independent variable. The box just above the table tells us that the row percentages are the second number in each cell. Only 18.35% of those with poor health said they are very happy, compared with 49.18% of those in excellent health. Similarly, only 5.99% of those in excellent health said they were not too happy, but 33.03% of those in poor health said they were not too happy.

If you decide to treat happiness as the independent variable, you would say that 42.74% of those who were very happy reported being in excellent health, compared with just 12.50% of those who were not too happy. Analyzing the percentages provides far richer information about the relationship than a measure of association can provide. However, researchers often want the simplicity of having a number that summarizes the strength of the association, and this is exactly why we have measures of association.

Cramér's V can be used as a measure of association, but it does not use the ordered nature of the variables. Both gamma (γ) and tau-b (τ_b) are measures of association for ordinal data. Both of these involve the notion of concordance. If one person is happier than another, we would expect that person to report being in better health. We call this "concordance". If a person has worse health, we expect this person to be less happy. This is what we mean when we say that health and happiness are positively related. Gamma and tau-b differ in how they treat people who are tied on one or the other variable, but both measures are bigger when there is a predominance of concordant pairs. Because of the way it is computed, gamma tends to be bigger than tau-b, and tau-b is closer to what you would get if you treated the variables as interval level and computed a correlation coefficient. Values of tau-b less than 0.2 signify a weak relationship. Values between 0.2 and 0.49 indicate a moderate relationship. Values of 0.5 and higher indicate a strong relationship. Stata tells us that tau-b is 0.25, so we can say the relationship is moderate. After we study the percentages, they seem consistent with this judgment provided by tau-b.

The chi-squared test is an appropriate test for the significance of Cramér's V. Stata does not provide a significance level of gamma or tau-b, but it does provide an asymptotic standard error (ASE) for each. The asymptotic standard error for tau-b is ASE = 0.020. If you divide tau-b by this estimated standard error, you get the z-test value. For our example, $z = 0.249/0.020 = 12.45$. $|z| \geq 1.96$ is significant at the $p < 0.05$ level, $|z| \geq 2.60$ is significant at the 0.01 level, and $|z| \geq 3.32$ is significant at the 0.001 level. Considering these levels, we can say that our tau-b = 0.25, $z = 12.45$, $p < 0.001$, meaning that there is a moderate relationship and that it is statistically significant. A note of caution: Because these are asymptotic standard errors, they are only good estimates when you have a large sample.

6.7 Interactive tables

If you are reading a report, you might find a cross-tabulation where the authors did not compute percentages, did not compute chi-squared, or did not compute any measures of association. Here is an example of a table showing the cross-tabulation of sex and abany (abortion is okay for any reason). We have been using data from the 2006 General Social Survey, but this table is from the 2002 General Social Survey. Let's say that you come across this table and want to study its contents to see if there is a statistically significant relationship and how strong the association is. The author may have presented this table to show that men are less supportive of abortion than women, and you want to make sure the author has interpreted the table correctly.

```
. use http://www.stata-press.com/data/agis6r/gss2002_chapter6
. tabulate sex abany
```

| | Abortion if woman wants for any reason | | |
Respondent sex	yes	no	Total
male	215	269	484
female	172	244	416
Total	387	513	900

If you do not have access to the author's actual data, you need to enter the table into Stata. You can enter the raw numbers in the cells of the table, and Stata will compute percentages, chi-squared, and measures of association.

Select Statistics ▷ Summaries, tables, and tests ▷ Frequency tables ▷ Table calculator to open a dialog box in which you enter the frequencies in each cell. The format for doing this is rigid. Enter each row of cells, separating the rows with a backslash, \. Enter only the cell values and not the totals in the margins of the table. This entry format is illustrated in figure 6.3. You need to check the table Stata analyzes to make sure that you entered it correctly. Check the boxes to request chi-squared and within-row relative frequencies. Because this is not ordinal data, the only measure of association you request is Cramér's V.

Figure 6.3. Entering data for a table

If you click on Submit in this dialog box, you obtain the same results as if you had entered all the data in a big dataset.

```
. tabi 215 269\172 244, chi2 row V
```

```
┌──────────────────────┐
│ Key                  │
├──────────────────────┤
│       frequency      │
│    row percentage    │
└──────────────────────┘

                    col
       row │         1          2 │     Total
───────────┼──────────────────────┼──────────
         1 │       215        269 │       484
           │     44.42      55.58 │    100.00
───────────┼──────────────────────┼──────────
         2 │       172        244 │       416
           │     41.35      58.65 │    100.00
───────────┼──────────────────────┼──────────
     Total │       387        513 │       900
           │     43.00      57.00 │    100.00

         Pearson chi2(1) =    0.8633   Pr = 0.353
             Cramér's V =    0.0310
```

These results indicate that the author overstated his findings. The results are not statistically significant; $p = 0.353$ and Cramér's V is 0.03. A slightly higher percentage of men in the 2002 sample said that abortion was acceptable for any reason (44.42%) compared with women (41.35%), but this difference is not statistically significant.

6.8   Tables—linking categorical and quantitative variables

Many research questions can be answered by tables that mix a categorical variable and a quantitative variable. We may want to compare income for people from different racial groups. A study may need to compare the length of incarceration for men and for women sentenced for the same crime. A drug company may want to compare the time it takes for its drug to take effect with the time it takes another drug.

Here we switch back to 2006 General Social Survey, `gss2006_chapter6.dta`. We will use `hrs1`, hours a person worked last week, as our quantitative variable and compare men with women. Our hypothesis is that men spend more time working for pay each week than do women. We will use a formal test of significance in the next chapter, but here we will just show a table of the relationship. Select Statistics ▷ Summaries, tables, and tests ▷ Tables of frequencies, summaries, and command results to get to the dialog box in figure 6.4.

Figure 6.4. Summarizing a quantitative variable by categories of a categorical variable

In the **Main** tab, under *Row variables*, select `sex` to get categories of sex on the rows of the table. Then select the **Statistics** tab; here we will create three statistics. First, click on **Create...**, select the *Summary statistics* radio button on the left side, and select the variable `hrs1`. This will give us the mean of `hrs1`, but you will see that we can request other summary statistics. Click on **Accept**. Second, we will request the standard deviation. Click on **Create...**, select the *Summary statistics* radio button, and in the *Summary statistics* box on the right-hand side, scroll down to select the *Standard deviation (sd)*. Select the variable `hrs1` and click on **Accept**. Third, we will repeat the process for the count. Click on **Create...**, select the *Summary statistics* radio button, and select *Number of nonmissing values (count)* from the *Summary statistics* box. Select the variable `hrs1` and click on **Accept**. In the `table` dialog box, we see three statistics defined. Click on **Submit** so that we can return to this dialog box at a later time. The resulting command is

```
. table (sex) () (), statistic(mean hrs1) statistic(sd hrs1)
> statistic(count hrs1)
```

	Mean	Standard deviation	Number of nonmissing values
GENDER			
MALE	44.87671	14.27598	1,387
FEMALE	39.2034	13.60452	1,352
Total	42.07631	14.23166	2,739

This table shows that the week before the survey, men spent on average more than 6 hours working for pay than did women: 45 hours for men versus 39 for women.

Now suppose that you want to see the effect of marital status and gender on hours spent working for pay. Go back to the dialog box, and select `marital` under *Column variables* on the **Main** tab. If you want to suppress the totals, you can select the *None* radio button under *Marginal totals*. The command for this is

```
table (sex) (marital) (), nototals statistic(mean hrs1) ///
        statistic(sd hrs1) statistic(count hrs1)
```

I omitted the results here.

These summary tables are useful, but to communicate to a lay audience, a graph often works best. We can create a bar chart showing the mean number of hours worked by gender and by marital status. We created one type of bar chart in chapter 5, where we used the dialog box for a histogram to create the bar chart. Now we are doing a bar chart for a summary statistic, mean hours worked, over a pair of categorical variables, `sex` and `marital`. To do this, access the dialog box for a bar chart by selecting **Graphics** ▷ **Bar chart**. Under the **Main** tab, make sure that the first statistic is checked, and, by default, this is the mean. To the right of this, under *Variables*, type `hrs1` to make the graph show the mean hours worked. Next click on the **Categories** tab. Check *Group 1* and type `sex` as the *Grouping variable*. Check *Group 2* and type `marital` as the *Grouping variable*. There is a button labeled **Properties** to the right of where you entered `sex`. Click on this button and change the *Angle* to *45 degrees*. Click on **Accept**.

It would be nice to have the actual mean values for hours worked at the top of each bar, so switch to the **Bars** tab, and click on the radio button for *Label with bar height*. If we stop here, the numerical labels will have too many decimal places to look nice. We can fix these by making the numerical labels have a fixed format. Click on the **Properties** button in the section labeled *Bar labels*, and type the value `%9.1f` in the *Format* box. The *Bar label properties* dialog box is shown in figure 6.5.

Figure 6.5. The *Bar label properties* dialog box

This effort produces a nice bar chart, but there are some things we can still improve. The marital status labels are too wide and run into each other. The label of the hours worked for pay could also be better. Open the Graph Editor and change the font of the labels of marital status and gender to size small. Then add the title `Hours worked last week` and the subtitle `by sex and marital status`. Your final bar chart is shown in figure 6.6.

Figure 6.6. Bar graph summarizing a quantitative variable by categories of a categorical variable

6.9   Power analysis when using a chi-squared test of significance

Power analysis is discussed in more detail in chapter 7, but I will introduce it briefly here. Power is the ability to do what you want to do. In statistics, power means how likely you are to get a statistically significant result for your chi-squared test if the relationship in the population is strong enough for you to consider it important. One characteristic of chi-squared tests that sometimes leads to misinterpretation is that for a given relationship in terms of percentages, the value of chi-squared varies directly with the sample size. We can illustrate this variation by taking a 10% sample of `gss2006_chapter6.dta` and doing a cross-tabulation of health and gender. There are two steps to taking a 10% sample. The first step is to set an arbitrary value for the seed. The value of the seed controls where the random process starts the generation of our 10% subsample. By specifying a specific value, we ensure that we will get the same 10% sample if we repeat this process at a later time. The second step is to take the random sample. Here are the two commands needed for these steps:

```
. set seed 219
. sample 10
```

I have already done these steps and saved the results as a new dataset,
gss2006_chapter6_10percent.dta, which we will now use to do our tabulation.

```
. use https://www.stata-press.com/data/agis6r/gss2006_chapter6_10percent
(General Social Surveys, 1972-2006 [Cumulative File], Dataset 0001)
. tabulate sex health, lrchi2 row
```

```
┌─────────────────┐
│      Key        │
├─────────────────┤
│   frequency     │
│  row percentage │
└─────────────────┘
```

| | | CONDITION OF HEALTH | | | |
Gender	EXCELLENT	GOOD	FAIR	POOR	Total
MALE	48	82	32	4	166
	28.92	49.40	19.28	2.41	100.00
FEMALE	44	98	43	14	199
	22.11	49.25	21.61	7.04	100.00
Total	92	180	75	18	365
	25.21	49.32	20.55	4.93	100.00

```
         Likelihood-ratio chi2(3) =   6.1135   Pr = 0.106
```

These results are not significant, chi-squared(3) = 6.114, ns. We used what is called
the likelihood-ratio chi-squared with the lrchi2 option in the command. This variation
on how chi-squared is estimated is very similar to what we would have obtained using
the chi2 option, but we need to use the likelihood-ratio chi-squared to do our power
analysis. If we look at the percentages, it seems that relatively fewer women, 22.1%,
say their health is excellent than do men, 28.9%. Also women are more likely to rate
their health as fair or poor. Let's assume these percentages are the true values in the
population. If that were the case, how much power do we have to get a significant
chi-squared with this sample size of $N = 365$?

Philip Ender at UCLA wrote a useful command, chi2power,[2] that can help us. You
can install this command by typing search chi2power and following the instructions.
The chi2power command is run immediately after the tab command that included
the option to get a likelihood-ratio chi-squared, lrchi2. Here is the command and the
results:

---

2. Many community-contributed commands can be installed from the Boston University Statistical
   Software Components (SSC) Archive. Community-contributed commands stored at SSC can be installed directly, for example, ssc install fre. At the time of this writing, the chi2power command
   is not stored at SSC, so you need to first run a search for it to find where it is located.

```
. chi2power, startf(1) endf(10) incr(1)

alpha = .05
sample size factor = 1.00 power = 0.5265 for n = 365
sample size factor = 2.00 power = 0.8476 for n = 730
sample size factor = 3.00 power = 0.9623 for n = 1095
sample size factor = 4.00 power = 0.9922 for n = 1460
sample size factor = 5.00 power = 0.9986 for n = 1825
sample size factor = 6.00 power = 0.9998 for n = 2190
sample size factor = 7.00 power = 1.0000 for n = 2555
sample size factor = 8.00 power = 1.0000 for n = 2920
sample size factor = 9.00 power = 1.0000 for n = 3285
sample size factor = 10.00 power = 1.0000 for n = 3650
```

In the `chi2power` command, the first option, `startf(1)`, asks Stata for the power of the current sample size, that is, $N = 365$. The `endf(10)` option asks Stata to do a power analysis where the percentage in each cell is the same but where there are up to 10 times as many observations (3,650). The `incr(1)` option asks Stata to do this for increments of a factor of 1. That is, 1 times the starting sample size, 2 times the starting sample size, up to 10 times the starting sample size. We assume we are using an alpha equal to 0.05.

The results show that for the sample-size factor of 1.0 of our current sample size of $N = 365$, we have a power of 0.527. This means that if the percentage distribution we observed were true in the population, we would obtain a statistically significant chi-squared just $100 \times 0.527 = 52.7\%$ of the time. If these percentages represent what we consider an important or interesting gender difference (women rating their health worse than men), then we would be doomed to failure with a sample of 365. If we had a sample that was four times bigger, making $N = 1,460$, we would have power of 0.992. Meaning that 99.2% of the time, we would get a sample of 1,460 people in which the chi-squared was significant, but the other 0.8% of the time, we would get a chi-squared that was not statistically significant.

Statisticians usually say that the power should be greater than 0.80, and in many fields, they say it should be greater than 0.90. The results of the `chi2power` command show that we would need 730 observations to have a power greater than 0.80 and 1,095 observations to have a power greater than 0.90.

Why is this important? If you are requesting a grant to support collecting data to test your hypothesis that women rate their health worse than men do, the funders want to be reasonably confident that you will find significant results when there is a substantively significant relationship. If you proposed to collect data on 500 people, you would have inadequate power to get a statistically significant result. The funders would not want to fund you because you would be asking for too little. By contrast, this sort of power analysis may show that you are collecting data from more people than necessary to have good power. Asking for support to collect data on 2,000 observations would be unnecessary and an inefficient investment of the funders' money. This type of power analysis is difficult to implement because the researcher needs to specify what result would be the smallest result that would be substantively important. It is often very difficult to do this, especially with larger tables.

6.10   Summary

Cross-tabulations are extremely useful ways of presenting data, whether the data are categorical variables or a combination of categorical and quantitative variables. This chapter has covered a lot of material. We have learned

- How to examine the relationship between categorical variables

- How to develop cross-tabulations

- How to perform a chi-squared test of significance

- How to use percentages and compute appropriate measures of association for unordered and ordered cross-tabulations

- What the odds ratio is

- How to use an interactive table calculator

- How to extend tables to link categorical variables with quantitative variables

- How a bar graph can show how means on a quantitative variable differ across groups on a categorical variable

Stata has many capabilities for dealing with categorical variables that we have not covered. Still, think about what you have learned in this chapter. Policies are made and changed because of highly skilled presentations. Imagine your ability to make a presentation to a research group or to a policy group. Now you can "show them the numbers" and do so effectively. Much of what you have learned would have been impossible without statistical software. The next chapter will continue to show how Stata helps us analyze the relationship between pairs of variables. It will focus on quantitative outcome variables and categorical predictors and move beyond the point biserial correlation.

6.11   Exercises

1. Open `gss2006_chapter6.dta`, do a `codebook` on `pornlaw`, and then do a cross-tabulation of this with `sex`. Which variable is the independent variable? Which variable will you put on the row, and how will you do the percentages? If you were preparing a document, how would you change the labels of the response options for `pornlaw`?

2. Based on the first exercise, what is the chi-squared value? How would you report the chi-squared and the level of significance? What is the value of Cramér's V, and how strong of an association does this show? Finally, interpret the percentages to answer the question of how much women and men differ in their attitude about legalizing pornography.

3. Open `gss2006_chapter6.dta` and do a cross-tabulation of `pres00` (whom you voted for in 2000) and `pres04` (whom you voted for in 2004). From the dialog box, check the option to include missing values. Do a `codebook` on both variables, and then use the by/if/in tab in the `tabulate` dialog box to repeat the table just for those who voted for Gore or Bush in 2000 and for Kerry or Bush in 2004. Treat the 2000 vote as the independent variable. Is there a significant relationship between how people voted in 2000 and 2004? Interpret the percentages and phi, as well as the statistical significance.

4. Open `gss2006_chapter6.dta` and do a cross-tabulation of `polviews` and `premarsx`. Treating `polviews` as the independent variable, compute percentages on the rows. Because these are ordinal variables, compute gamma and tau-b. Is there a significant relationship between political views and conservatism? Interpret the relationship using gamma and tau-b. Interpret the relationship using the percentages.

5. In exercise 4, Stata reports that there is 18 degrees of freedom. How does it get this number?

6. Open `gss2002_chapter6.dta`. Create a table showing the mean hours worked in the last week (`hrs1`) for each level of political views (`polviews`). In your table, include the standard deviation for hours and the frequency of observations. What do the means suggest about people who are extreme in their views (in either direction)?

7. Based on exercise 6, create a bar chart showing the relationship between hours worked in the last week and political views.

8. You are given the following dataset:

RESPONDENT	FEELINGS ABOUT PORNOGRAPHY LAWS			
S SEX	ILLEGAL T	ILLEGAL U	LEGAL	Total
MALE	234	568	38	840
FEMALE	541	557	29	1,127
Total	775	1,125	67	1,967

Calculate the chi-squared test of significance, percentages, and Cramér's V using the `tabi` command. Interpret Cramér's V.

9. Examine the relationship between gender and self-reported health condition using `gss2006_chapter6.dta`. Recode the `health` variable so `EXCELLENT` and `GOOD` are combined into a new category labeled `satisfactory`, and `FAIR` and `POOR` are combined into a new category labeled `unsatisfactory`. Call the new variable `health2` and label the variable "Is your health satisfactory?" Conduct a chi-squared analysis along with Cramér's V (ϕ). Calculate the odds ratio. Write a short paragraph on how you would report these analyses.

7 Tests for one or two means

7.1   Introduction to tests for one or two means

Imagine that you are in the public relations department for a small liberal arts college. The mean score for the math and reading sections on the SAT at your college is $M = 1180$.[1] Suppose that the mean for all small liberal arts colleges in the United States is $\mu = 1080$. We use M to refer to the mean of a sample and μ, pronounced "mu", to refer to the mean of a population. For our purposes, we are treating the students at your college as the sample and all students at small liberal arts colleges in the United States as the population. Say that our supervisor asked if we could demonstrate that our

---

1. The scores used do not include the writing part of the SAT.

151

college is more selective than its peer institutions. Could this difference, our $M = 1180$, and the mean for all colleges, $\mu = 1080$, occur just by chance?

Suppose that last year, our Boys and Girls Club had 30% of the children drop out of programs before the programs were completed. We have a new program that we believe does a better job of minimizing the dropout rate. However, 25% of the children still drop out before the new program is completed. Because a smaller percentage of children drop out, this is better, but is this enough difference to be statistically significant?

These two examples illustrate a one-sample test where we have one sample (students at our college or the children in the new Boys and Girls Club program), and we want to compare our sample mean with a population value (the mean SAT score for all liberal arts colleges or the mean dropout rate for all programs at our Boys and Girls Club).

At other times, we may have two groups or samples. For example, we have a program that is designed to improve reading readiness among preschool children. We might have 100 children in our preschool and randomly assign half of them to this new program and the other half to a traditional approach. Those in the new program are in the treatment group (because they get the new program), and those in the old program are in the control group (because they did not get the new program). If the new program is effective, the children in the treatment group will score higher on a reading-readiness scale than the children in the control group. Let's say that, on a 0–100 point scale, the 50 children randomly assigned to the control group have a mean of $M = 71.3$ and a standard deviation of SD $= 10.4$. Those in the treatment group, who were exposed to the new program, have $M = 82.5$ and SD $= 9.9$. It sounds like the program helped. The children in the treatment group have a mean that is more than one standard deviation higher than that of the students in the control group. This sounds like a big improvement, but is this statistically significant? Here we have a problem for a two-group or two-sample t test.

We have a 20-item scale that measures the importance of voting. Each item is scored from 1, signifying that voting is not important, to 5, signifying that voting is very important. Thus the possible range for the total score on our 20-item scale is from 20 (all items answered with a 1, indicating that voting is not important) to 100 (all items answered with a 5, signifying that voting is very important). We hypothesize that minority groups will have a lower mean than will whites. Can we justify this hypothesis? Perhaps the lower mean results because minority groups have experienced a history of their votes not counting or because of the perception that their vote does not matter in the final outcome. To do an experiment with a treatment and control group, we would need to randomly assign people to minority status or majority status. Because we cannot do this, we can use a random sample of 200 people from the community. If this sample is random for the community, it is a random sample for any subgroup. Let's say that 70 minority community members are in our sample, and they have a mean importance of voting score of $M = 68.9$. The 130 white community members in our sample have a mean importance of voting score of $M = 83.5$. This is what we hypothesized would happen. A two-sample t test will tell us if this difference is statistically significant.

Sometimes researchers use a two-sample t test even when they do not have random assignment to a treatment or control group or when they do not have random sampling. You might want to know if a highly developed recreation program at a full-care retirement center leads to lower depression among center members. Your community might have two full-care retirement centers, one with a highly developed recreation program and the other without such a program. We could do a two-sample test to see whether the residents in the center with the highly developed recreation program had a lower mean score on depression.

Can you see the problems with the above example? First, without randomization to the two centers, we do not know whether the recreation program makes the difference or if people who are more prone to be depressed selected the center that does not offer much recreation. A second problem is that the programs being compared may be different in many respects other than our focus. A center that can afford a highly developed recreation program may have, for example, better food, more spacious accommodations, and better-trained staff. Even if we have randomization, we want the groups to differ only on the issue we are testing. More-advanced procedures, such as analysis of covariance and multiple regression, can help control for other differences between the groups being compared, but a two-sample t test is limited in this regard without randomization or random sampling.

Random sample and randomization

It is easy to confuse random sample and randomization. A random sample refers to how we select the people in our study. Once we have our sample, randomization is sometimes used to randomly assign our sample to groups. Some examples will better illustrate the distinction between the terms:

Random sample without randomization. We obtain a list of all housing units that have a water connection from our city's utility department. We randomly sample 500 of these houses.

Randomization without a random sample. We solicit volunteers for an experiment. After 100 people volunteer, we randomly assign 50 of them to the treatment group and 50 to the control group. We randomized the assignment, but we did not start with a random sample. Because we did not start with a random sample, we could have a *sample selection bias* problem because volunteers are often much more motivated to do well than the rest of the population.

Randomization with a random sample. Obtaining a list of all students enrolled in our university, we randomly sample 100 of these students. Next we randomly assign 50 of them to the treatment group and 50 to the control group.

7.2 Randomization

How can we select the people we want to randomly assign to the treatment group
and the control group? There are two types of random selection. One is done with
replacement, and one is done without replacement. When we sample with replacement,
each observation has the same chance of being selected. However, the same observation
may be selected more than once. Suppose that you have 100 people and want to do
random sampling with replacement. You randomly pick one case, say, Mary. She has
a 1/100 probability of being selected. If you put her back in the pool (replacement)
before selecting your second case, whomever you select will have the same 1/100 chance
of being selected. However, you may sample Mary again doing it this way.

Many statistical tests assume sampling with replacement, but in practice, we rarely
do this. We usually sample without replacement. This means that the first person would
have a 1/100 chance of being selected, but the second person would have a 1/99 chance
of being selected. This method violates the assumption that each observation has the
same chance of being selected. Sampling without replacement is the most practical way
to do it. If we have 100 people and want 50 of them in the control group and 50 in
the treatment group, we can sample 50 people without replacement (this gives us 50
different people) and put them in the control group. Then we put the other 50 people
in the treatment group. If we had sampled with replacement, the 50 people we sampled
might actually be only 40 different people, with a few of them selected twice or even
three times.

Sampling without replacement is a simple task in Stata. If you have $N = 20$ observations, you would number these from 1 to 20. Then you would enter the command
`sample 10, count` to select 10 observations randomly but without replacement. These
10 people would go into your treatment group, and the other 10 would go into your
control group. Here is the set of commands:

```
clear
set obs 20
generate id = _n
list
set seed 220
sample 10, count
list
```

The first command clears any data we have in memory. You should save anything
you were doing before entering this command. The second command, `set obs 20`,
tells Stata that you want to have 20 observations in your dataset. The next command,
`generate id = _n`, will generate a new variable called `id`, which will be numbered
from 1 to the number of observations in your dataset, in this case, 20. The underscore n
(`_n`) is a reserved name in Stata that refers to the observation number. This command
generates a new variable, `id`, which is the same as the observation number, 1, 2, 3, ...,
20. You can see this in the first listing below. We then use the command `set seed 220`,
where the number 220 is arbitrary. This is not necessary, but by doing this, we will be
able to reproduce our results. When you set the seed at a particular value, every time

you run this set of commands, you will get the same result. Without setting the seed at a specific value, we would get a different result every time we ran the set of commands. Finally, we take the sample using the command `sample 10, count` and show a listing of the 10 cases that Stata selected at random without replacement. These cases would go into the control group, and the other 10 would go into the treatment group. Thus observations numbered 2, 8, 13, 7, 16, 14, 18, 17, 3, and 15 (as shown below with the `list` command) go into the control group, and the other 10 observations go into the treatment group. By doing this, any differences between the groups that are not due to the treatment are random differences.

```
. clear
. set obs 20
Number of observations (_N) was 0, now 20.
. generate id = _n
. list
```

	id
1.	1
2.	2
3.	3
4.	4
5.	5
6.	6
7.	7
8.	8
9.	9
10.	10
11.	11
12.	12
13.	13
14.	14
15.	15
16.	16
17.	17
18.	18
19.	19
20.	20

```
. set seed 220
. sample 10, count
(10 observations deleted)
```

```
. list
```

	id
1.	2
2.	8
3.	13
4.	7
5.	16
6.	14
7.	18
8.	17
9.	3
10.	15

7.3   Random sampling

The process of selecting a random sample is similar. Suppose that you had 20,000 students in your university. Assume that each student has a unique identification number. You would have a Stata dataset with these numbers. Assume too that you need a sample of $N = 500$ students. You would simply set the seed at some arbitrary value, such as 3 with the command `set seed 3`, and then run the command `sample 500, count`. You could then list these ID numbers to see your sample.

If we have a target sample of 500, we can expect that several of our initial list of $N = 500$ either will not be located or will refuse to participate. Therefore, we should draw a second sample of, say, $N = 300$, and go down this list as we need replacements.

7.4   Hypotheses

Before we can run a z test or a t test, we need to have two hypotheses: a null hypothesis (H_0) and an alternative hypothesis (H_a). I will mention these briefly because they are covered in all statistics texts.

Although one-tailed tests are appropriate if we can categorically exclude negative findings (results in the opposite direction of our hypothesis), we will rarely be this confident in the direction of the results.   Most statisticians report two-tailed tests routinely and make note that the direction of results is what they expected. Other statisticians rely on a one-tailed test when they have a clear prediction of the direction. For example, if they have a new drug that should reduce the level of cholesterol, they might use a one-tailed test because they have a clear directional hypothesis. If, however, this new drug increased the level of cholesterol, then they would fail to reject the null hypothesis without having to do a test of significance. A two-tailed test is always more conservative than a one-tailed test, so the tendency to rely on two-tailed tests can be viewed as a conservative approach to statistical significance.

Thoughts on the p = 0.05 significance level

For over 100 years, the 0.05 p-value (sometimes the 0.01 or 0.001 p-value) has been used to make a binary decision to reject the null hypothesis. There are many ways this has been misinterpreted. Greenland et al. (2016) list 35 common misinterpretations. The American Statistical Association published a statement on interpreting p-values (Wasserstein and Lazar 2016).

A p-value is the probability that your data are incompatible with a statistical model as specified by the null hypothesis. We state a null hypothesis listing a value we are testing. However, the statistical model includes all the assumptions from our study design, sampling design, validity of our measure, size of our sample, and assumptions specific to the test statistic. If our data are improbable given this statistical model, the improbability may be because any of these assumptions are problematic. Thus, a low p-value is partial evidence to reject the specified null hypothesis value. After all, the low p-value could be for any number of the assumptions of the statistical model.

A low p-value does not mean the finding is practically significant. Even a trivial effect will be significant if you have a large enough sample. At the same time, if your sample is too small, you will find a strong effect that is not statistically significant. Some researchers lack transparency in their reporting. They "cherry-pick" a few results from a large set of tests. For example, if you correlate 20 variables with one another (resulting in 190 tests of significance) and report only the correlations that are "statistically significant", you are "cherry-picking" results.

There is nothing objective about picking any particular p-value for making a binary decision. We have long used the 0.05 level because we learned this in our introductory training. We learned it this way because our instructors learned it this way. Following tradition, results in this book are often presented as being statistically significant or not based on this criterion. Even so, readers should use caution when interpreting and presenting their own results. Today, many researchers report the p-value for the incompatibility of our data with the specified statistical model (p equal to 0.038, 0.190, or whatever) rather than making a binary decision to reject or fail to reject the null hypothesis.

Stata reports both one- and two-tailed significance for all the tests covered in this chapter. For more-advanced procedures, such as those based on regression, Stata reports only two-tailed significance. It is easy to convert two-tailed significance to one-tailed significance. If something has a probability of 0.1 using a two-tailed test, its probability would be 0.05 using a one-tailed test—we simply cut the two-tailed probability in half.

7.5   One-sample test of a proportion

Let's use items from the 2002 General Social Survey dataset `gss2002_chapter7.dta`
(Smith et al. 2015) to test how adults feel about school prayer. An existing variable,
`prayer`, is coded 1 if the person favors school prayer and 2 if the person does not. We
must recode the variable `prayer` into a new variable, `schpray`, so that a person has a
score of 1 if he or she supports school prayer and a score of 0 if he or she does not. We
can use Stata's `recode` command to accomplish this. We will do a cross-tabulation as
well to make sure we did not make a mistake:

```
. use https://www.stata-press.com/data/agis6r/gss2002_chapter7
. recode prayer (1 = 1 Approve) (2 = 0 Disapprove), gen(schpray)
. tabulate schpray prayer, missing
```

Stata will not let you accidentally write over an existing variable, so if you try to
create a variable that already exists, Stata will issue an error message. When we give
`schpray` a score of 1 for those adults who favor school prayer and a score of 0 for those
who oppose it, Stata can compute and test proportions correctly. If we ran a proportions
test on the `prayer` variable, we would get an error message saying that `prayer` is not a
0/1 variable.

Although we can speculate that most people oppose school prayer, that is, have a
score of 0 on `schpray`, let's take a conservative track and use a two-tailed hypothesis:

Alternative hypothesis H_a: proportion $\neq 0.5$

Null hypothesis H_0: proportion $= 0.5$

The null hypothesis, proportion $= 0.5$, uses a value of 0.5 because this represents
what the proportion would be if there were no preference for or against school prayer.

Open the appropriate dialog box by selecting Statistics ▷ Summaries, tables, and tests
▷ Classical tests of hypotheses ▷ Proportion test. On the Main tab, select *One-sample*, if it
is not already selected, in the *Tests of proportions* section. Enter the `schpray` variable
and the hypothesized proportion for the null hypothesis, 0.5, and click on OK. The
resulting command and results are

```
. prtest schpray == 0.5
One-sample test of proportion                Number of obs    =      859
```

Variable	Mean	Std. err.		[95% conf. interval]	
schpray	.3969732	.0166937		.3642542	.4296923

```
      p = proportion(schpray)                              z =  -6.0392
HO: p = 0.5
      Ha: p < 0.5                Ha: p != 0.5                Ha: p > 0.5
  Pr(Z < z) = 0.0000        Pr(|Z| > |z|) = 0.0000        Pr(Z > z) = 1.0000
```

Let's go over these results and see what we need. All the results in this chapter use this general format for output, so it is worth the effort to review it closely. The first line is the Stata command. The second line indicates that this is a one-sample test of a proportion, the variable is schpray, and we have $N = 859$ observations. The table gives a mean, $M = 0.397$, and standard error, 0.017. Because we recoded schpray as a dummy variable, where a 1 signifies that the person supports school prayer and a 0 signifies that the person does not, the mean has a special interpretation. The mean is simply the proportion of people coded 1. (This is true only of 0/1 variables and would not work if we had used the original variable, prayer.) Thus 0.397, or 39.7%, of the people in the survey say that they support school prayer. The 95% confidence interval tells us that we can be 95% confident that the interval 0.364 to 0.430 includes adults who support school prayer. Using percentages, we could say that we are 95% confident that the interval of 36.4% to 43.0% contains the true percentage of adults who support school prayer.

Below the table, we can see the null hypothesis that the proportion is exactly 0.5, that is, HO: p = 0.5. Also just below the table but to the far right is the computed z test, $z = -6.039$.

Below the null hypothesis are three results that depend on how we stated the alternative hypothesis. Here we used a two-tailed alternative hypothesis, and this result appears in the middle group. Stata's Ha: p != 0.5 is equivalent to stating the alternative hypothesis, H_a: proportion $\neq$ 0.5. Because Stata results are plain text, Stata uses != in place of $\neq$. Stata programmers use an exclamation mark (programmers often call this a "bang") to mean "not", so != literally means "not equal". Below the alternative hypothesis is the probability that the null hypothesis is true: Pr(|Z| > |z|) = 0.0000. The p-value = 0.0000 does not mean that there is no probability that the null hypothesis is true, just that the probability is all zeros to four decimal places. If p-value = 0.00002, this is rounded to 0.0000 in Stata output. A p-value = 0.0000 is usually reported as a significance level of $p < 0.001$. This finding is highly statistically significant and allows us to reject the null hypothesis. Fewer than 1 time in 1,000 would we obtain these results by chance if the null hypothesis were true.

We would write our results as follows: 39.7% of the sample support school prayer. With a $z = -6.039$, we can reject the null hypothesis that proportion is 0.5 at the $p < 0.001$ level. The 39.7% is in the direction expected, namely, that fewer than half of the adult population supported school prayer in 2002.

On the left side of the output is a one-tailed alternative hypothesis, `Ha: p < 0.5`. If another researcher thought that only a minority supported school prayer and could rule out the possibility that the support was in the opposite direction, then the researcher would have this as a one-tailed alternative hypothesis, and it would be statistically significant with a $p < 0.001$.

On the right side of the output is a one-tailed alternative hypothesis, `Ha: p > 0.5`. This means the researcher thought that most adults favored school prayer, and the researcher (incorrectly) ruled out the possibility that the support could be the other way. The results show that we cannot reject the null hypothesis. When we observe only 39.7% of our sample supporting school prayer, we clearly have not received a significant result that most adults supported school prayer in 2002.

Distinguishing between two p-values

In testing proportions, we have two different p-values. Do not let this confuse you. One p-value is the proportion of the sample coded 1. In this example, this is the proportion that supports school prayer, 0.397 or 39.7%.

The second p-value is the level of significance. In this example, $p < 0.001$ refers to the probability that we would obtain this result by chance if the null hypothesis were true. Because we would get our result fewer than 1 time in 1,000 by chance, $p < 0.001$, we can reject the null hypothesis. Many researchers will reject a null hypothesis whenever the probability of the results is less than 0.05, that is, $p < 0.05$.

Proportions and percentages

Often we report proportions as percentages because many readers are more comfortable trying to understand percentages than proportions. Stata, however, requires us to use proportions. As you may recall, the conversion is simple. We divide a percentage by 100 to get a proportion, so 78.9% corresponds to a proportion of 0.789. Similarly, we multiply a proportion by 100 to get a percentage, so a proportion of 0.258 corresponds to a percentage of 25.8%.

7.6   Two-sample test of a proportion

Sometimes a researcher wants to compare a proportion across two samples. For example, you might have an experiment testing a new drug (wide.dta). You randomly assign 40 study participants so that 20 are in a treatment group receiving the drug and 20 are in a control group receiving a sugar pill. You record whether the person is cured by assigning a 1 to those who were cured and a 0 to those who were not. Here are the data:

```
. use https://www.stata-press.com/data/agis6r/wide, clear
. list
```

	treat	control
1.	1	1
2.	0	0
3.	1	0
4.	1	0
5.	1	0
6.	1	1
7.	1	1
8.	0	0
9.	1	0
10.	1	0
11.	1	0
12.	1	1
13.	1	1
14.	0	1
15.	1	1
16.	1	0
17.	0	0
18.	1	0
19.	0	0
20.	1	0

In the treatment group, we have 15 of the 20 people, or 0.75, cured; that is, they have a score of 1. In the control group, just 7 of the 20 people, or 0.35, are cured. Before proceeding, we need a null and an alternative hypothesis. The null hypothesis is that the two groups have the same proportion cured. The alternative hypothesis is that the proportions are unequal, and therefore, the difference between them will not equal zero: $p_{(\text{treat})} - p_{(\text{control})} \neq 0$. Your statistics book may state the alternative hypothesis as $p_{(\text{treat})} \neq p_{(\text{control})}$. The two ways of stating the alternative hypothesis are equivalent. They are both two-tailed tests because we are saying that the proportions cured in the two groups are not equal. We could argue for a one-tailed test that the proportion in the treatment group is higher, but this means that we need to rule out the possibility that it could be lower. The null hypothesis is that the two proportions are equal; hence, there is no difference between them: $p_{(\text{treat})} - p_{(\text{control})} = 0$.

Alternative hypothesis H_a: $p_{(\text{treat})} - p_{(\text{control})} \neq 0$

Null hypothesis H_0: $p_{(\text{treat})} - p_{(\text{control})} = 0$

These are independent samples, and the data for the two groups are entered as two variables. To open the dialog box for this test, select Statistics ▷ Summaries, tables, and tests ▷ Classical tests of hypotheses ▷ Proportion test. Because we have two samples, those participants in the treatment condition and those participants in the control condition, we select *Two-sample using variables* in the *Tests of proportions* section of the Main tab. Type treat in the box for the *First variable*, and type control in the box for the *Second variable*. That is all there is to it, and our results are

```
. prtest treat == control
Two-sample test of proportions                    treat: Number of obs =      20
                                                control: Number of obs =      20
```

Variable	Mean	Std. err.	z	P>|z|	[95% conf. interval]
treat	.75	.0968246			.5602273 .9397727
control	.35	.1066536			.1409627 .5590373
diff	.4	.1440486			.1176699 .6823301
	under H0:	.1573213	2.54	0.011	

```
           diff = prop(treat) - prop(control)                        z =    2.5426
     H0: diff = 0

   Ha: diff < 0                      Ha: diff != 0                   Ha: diff > 0
 Pr(Z < z) = 0.9945           Pr(|Z| > |z|) = 0.0110           Pr(Z > z) = 0.0055
```

These results have a layout that is similar to that of the one-sample proportion test. The difference is that we now have two groups, so we get statistical information for each group. Under Mean is the proportion of 1 codes in each group. We have 0.75 (75%) of the treatment group coded as cured, compared with just 0.35 (35%) of the control group. The difference between the treatment-group mean and the control-group mean is 0.40; that is, $0.75 - 0.35 = 0.40$. This appears in the table as the variable diff with the mean of 0.4.

Directly below the table is the null hypothesis that the difference in the proportion cured in the two groups is 0, and to the right is the computed z test, z = 2.5426. Below this are the three hypotheses we might have selected. Using a two-tailed approach, we can say that $z = 2.54$, $p < 0.05$. If we had a one-tailed test that the treatment-group proportion was greater than the control-group proportion, our z would still be 2.54, but our p would be $p < 0.01$. This one-tailed test has a p-value, 0.0055, that is exactly one-half of the two-tailed p-value. If someone had hypothesized that the treatment-group success would have a lower proportion than the control group, then he or she would have the results on the far left. Here the results would not be significant because the $p = 0.9945$ is far greater than the required $p < 0.05$.

This difference-of-proportions test requires data to be entered in what is called a wide format. Each group (treatment and control) is treated as a variable with the scores on the outcome variable coded under each group, as illustrated in the listing that appeared above. Data in statistics books and related exercises often present the scores this way.

When dealing with survey data, it is common to use what is called a long format in which one variable is a grouping variable of whether someone is in the treatment group, coded 1, or the control group, coded 0. The second variable is the score on the dependent variable, which is also a binary variable coded as 1 if the person is cured and 0 if the person is not cured. This appears in the following long-format listing (long.dta).

```
. use https://www.stata-press.com/data/agis6r/long, clear
. list
```

	group	cure
1.	1	1
2.	1	0
3.	1	1
4.	1	1
5.	1	1
6.	1	1
7.	1	1
8.	1	0
9.	1	1
10.	1	1
11.	1	1
12.	1	1
13.	1	1
14.	1	0
15.	1	1
(output omitted)		
36.	0	0
37.	0	0
38.	0	0
39.	0	0
40.	0	0

When your data are entered this way, you need to use a different test for the difference of proportions. Select Statistics ▷ Summaries, tables, and tests ▷ Classical tests of hypotheses ▷ Proportion test like we did before, but this time we select *Two-sample using groups* in the *Tests of proportions* section. Type cure under *Variable name* (the dependent variable) and group under *Group variable name* (the independent variable). Click on OK to obtain the following results:

```
. prtest cure, by(group)
Two-sample test of proportions                    0: Number of obs =        20
                                                  1: Number of obs =        20
```

Group	Mean	Std. err.	z	P>|z|	[95% conf. interval]	
0	.35	.1066536			.1409627	.5590373
1	.75	.0968246			.5602273	.9397727
diff	-.4	.1440486			-.6823301	-.1176699
	under H0:	.1573213	-2.54	0.011		

```
        diff = prop(0) - prop(1)                              z =  -2.5426
  H0: diff = 0

  Ha: diff < 0                 Ha: diff != 0                  Ha: diff > 0
Pr(Z < z) = 0.0055      Pr(|Z| > |z|) = 0.0110           Pr(Z > z) = 0.9945
```

Here we have two means: one for the group coded 0 of 0.35 and one for the group coded 1 of 0.75. These are, of course, the means for our control group and our treatment group, respectively. Below this is a row labeled `diff`, the difference in proportions, which has a value of -0.40 because the mean of the group coded as 1 is subtracted from the mean of the group coded as 0. Be careful interpreting the sign of this difference. Here a negative value means that the treatment group is higher than the control group: 0.75 versus 0.35. The z test for this difference is $z = -2.54$. This is the same absolute value that we had with the test for the wide format, but the sign is reversed. Be careful interpreting this sign just like with interpreting the difference. It happens to be negative because we are subtracting the group coded as 1 from the group coded as 0.

We can interpret these results, including the negative sign on the z test, as follows. The control group has a mean of 0.35 (35% of participants were cured), and the treatment group has a mean of 0.75 (75% of the participants were cured). The $z = -2.54$, $p < 0.05$ indicates that the control group had a significantly lower success rate than the treatment group. Pay close attention to the way the difference of proportions was computed so that you interpret the sign of the z test correctly.

This long form is widely used in surveys. For example, in the General Social Survey 2002 data (`gss2002_chapter7.dta`), there is an item, `abany`, asking if abortion is okay anytime. The response option is binary, namely, `yes` or `no`. If we wanted to see whether more women said yes than did men, we could use a difference-of-proportions test. The grouping variable would be `sex`, and the dependent variable would be `abany`. First, we must see how they are coded. To do this, we run the command `codebook abany sex`. We see that `abany` is coded as a 1 for yes and 2 for no. We must recode `abany` and make a new variable coded 0 for no and 1 for yes. We do not need to change the coding of `sex`. The independent variable has to be binary (just two values), but does not have to be coded as 0,1. Try this and do the difference of proportions test.

7.7 One-sample test of means

You can do z tests for one-sample tests of means, or you can do t tests. We will cover only the use of t tests because these are by far the most widely used. A z test is appropriate when you know the population variance (which it is highly unusual to know). Unless you have a small sample, both tests yield similar results.

Several decades ago, social theorists thought that the workweek for full-time employees would get shorter and shorter. This has happened in many countries but does not seem to be happening in the United States. A full-time workweek is defined as 40 hours. Among those who say they work full time, do they work more or less than 40 hours? The General Social Survey dataset (**gss2002_chapter7.dta**) has a variable called **hrs1**, which represents the reported hours in the workweeks of the survey participants. The null hypothesis is that the mean will be 40 hours. The alternative hypothesis is that the mean will not be 40 hours. Using a two-tailed hypothesis, you can say

Alternative hypothesis H_a: $\mu_{\text{(hours)}} \neq 40$

Null hypothesis H_0: $\mu_{\text{(hours)}} = 40$

Notice that we are using the Greek letter, μ, to refer to the population mean in both the alternative and the null hypotheses. To open the dialog box for this test, select Statistics ▷ Summaries, tables, and tests ▷ Classical tests of hypotheses ▷ t test (mean-comparison test). In the resulting dialog box, select *One-sample* if it is not already selected in the *t tests* section of the Main tab. Enter **hrs1** (outcome variable) under the *Variable name* and 40 (hypothesized mean for the null hypothesis) under the *Hypothesized mean*.

Because we are interested in how many hours full-time employees work, we should eliminate part-time workers. To do this, click on the by/if/in tab, and type **wrkstat == 1** as the *If: (expression)*. The variable **wrkstat** is coded as 1 if a person works full time (you can run a **codebook wrkstat** to see the frequency distribution). The resulting by/if/in tab is shown in figure 7.1.

Figure 7.1. Restrict observations to those who score 1 on `wrkstat`

Clicking on OK produces the following command and results:

```
. ttest hrs1 == 40 if wrkstat == 1

One-sample t test
```

Variable	Obs	Mean	Std. err.	Std. dev.	[95% conf. interval]
hrs1	1,419	45.97111	.3156328	11.88977	45.35195 46.59026

```
      mean = mean(hrs1)                                              t =   18.9179
H0: mean = 40                                      Degrees of freedom =       1418

   Ha: mean < 40              Ha: mean != 40                  Ha: mean > 40
 Pr(T < t) = 1.0000       Pr(|T| > |t|) = 0.0000          Pr(T > t) = 0.0000
```

From these results, we can see that the mean for the variable `hrs1` is $M = 45.97$ hours, and the standard deviation is SD = 11.89 hours. Because we are using a two-tailed test, we can look at the center column under the table to see that, for $t = 18.92$, $p < 0.001$. Thus full-time workers work significantly more than the traditional 40-hour workweek. In fact, they worked about 6 hours more than this standard on average in 2002. Remember, 2002 was a year of relatively full employment.

When we report a t test, we need to also report degrees of freedom. Look closely at the results above. The number of observations is 1,419, but the degrees of freedom is 1,418 (found just below the $t = 18.92$). For a one-sample t test, the degrees of freedom is always $N - 1$. If we report the degrees of freedom as 1,418, a reader will also know that the sample size is one more than this, or 1,419.

Different specialty areas report one-sample t tests slightly differently. The format I recommend is $t(1418) = 18.918$, $p < 0.001$. This is read as saying that t with 1,418 degrees of freedom is 18.918, p is less than 0.001. The results show that the average full-time employee worked significantly more than the standard 40-hour week.

Degrees of freedom

The idea of degrees of freedom was discussed in chapter 6 on cross-tabulations. For t tests, the degrees of freedom is a little different. Your statistics book will cover this in detail, but here we will present just a simple illustration. Suppose that we have four cases with $M = 10$. The first three of the four cases have scores of 8, 12, and 12. Is the fourth case free? Because the mean of the four cases is 10, the sum of the four cases must be 40. Because $40 - 8 - 12 - 12 = 8$, the fourth case must be 8. It is not free. In this sense, we can say that a one-sample test of means has $N - 1$ degrees of freedom.

Those who like to use confidence intervals can see these in the results. Stata gives us a 95% confidence interval of 45.4 hours to 46.6 hours. The confidence interval is more informative than the t test. We are 95% confident that the interval of 45.4 to 46.6 hours contains the mean number of hours full-time employees report working in a week. Because the value specified in the null hypothesis, $\mu = 40$, is not included in this interval, we know the results are statistically significant. The confidence interval also focuses our attention on the number of hours and helps us understand the substantive significance (importance), as well as the statistical significance.

7.8   Two-sample test of group means

A researcher says that men make more money than women because men work more hours a week. The argument is that a lot of women work part-time jobs, and these neither pay as well nor offer opportunities for advancement. What happens if we only consider people who say they work full time? Do men still make more than women when both the men and the women are working full time?

The General Social Survey 2002 dataset (`gss2002_chapter7.dta`) has a question asking about the respondent's income, variable `rincom98`. Like many surveys, the General Social Survey does not report the actual income but reports income in categories (for example, under \$1,000, \$1,000 to 2,999). Run a `tabulate` command to see the coding the surveyors used. For some reason, they have not defined a score coded as 24 as a "missing value", but this is what a code of 24 represents. Even with highly respected national datasets like the General Social Survey, you need to check for coding errors. A code of 24 was assigned to people who did not report their income. Many researchers have used `rincom98` as it is coded (I hope after defining a code of 24 as a missing value). However, this coding is problematic because the intervals are not equal. The first interval, under $1,000, is $1,000 wide, but the second interval, $1,000 to $2,999, is nearly $2,000 wide. Some intervals are as much as $10,000 wide.

Before we can compare the means for women and men, we need to recode the `rincom98` variable. We could recode it by using the dialog box as described in section 3.4, but let's type the commands instead. You could enter the following commands in the Command window, one by one. A much better approach would be to enter them into a do-file so that we can easily modify or reproduce the routine later if we need to. Remember that we should add some comments at the top of the do-file that include the name of the file and its purpose. To run the `tabulate` commands in this example, you must use Stata/MP or Stata/SE because the number of columns exceeds the 20-column limit of `tabulate` in Stata/BE. If you do not want to enter all of these commands yourself, then you could open the do-file for chapter 7, that is, `chapter7.do`, and copy them from that. Go to File ▷ Open... and find where it is stored on your computer. It will be in the folder where you stored the datasets. Alternatively, you could open a dataset where the recoding has already been done, `gss2002_chapter7b.dta`.

```
* recode income.do       (sample do-file)
* This is a short do-file that recodes income. It does a
* tabulation to see how income is coded (tab rincom98). People
* given a value of 24 are recoded as missing (mvdecode rincom98,
* mv(24)). We generate a new variable called inc that is equal to the
* old variable, rincom98. We recode each interval with its
* midpoint. We do a cross-tabulation of the new and old income
* variables as a check.
version 17
tabulate rincom98, missing
mvdecode rincom98, mv(24)
generate inc = rincom98
replace inc = 500    if rincom98 == 1
replace inc = 2500   if rincom98 == 2
replace inc = 3500   if rincom98 == 3
replace inc = 4500   if rincom98 == 4
replace inc = 5500   if rincom98 == 5
replace inc = 6500   if rincom98 == 6
replace inc = 7500   if rincom98 == 7
replace inc = 9000   if rincom98 == 8
replace inc = 11250 if rincom98 == 9
replace inc = 13250 if rincom98 == 10
replace inc = 16250 if rincom98 == 11
replace inc = 18750 if rincom98 == 12
replace inc = 21250 if rincom98 == 13
replace inc = 23750 if rincom98 == 14
replace inc = 27500 if rincom98 == 15
replace inc = 32500 if rincom98 == 16
replace inc = 37500 if rincom98 == 17
replace inc = 45000 if rincom98 == 18
replace inc = 55000 if rincom98 == 19
replace inc = 67500 if rincom98 == 20
replace inc = 82500 if rincom98 == 21
replace inc = 100000 if rincom98 == 22
replace inc = 110000 if rincom98 == 23
tabulate inc rincom98, missing
```

There are several lines commenting on what the do-file will do.   The first line after
the `version` command runs a tabulation (`tabulate`), including missing values. The
results help us understand how the variable was coded. The next line makes the code of
24 into a missing value so that anybody who has a score on `rincom98` of 24 is defined as
having missing values (`mvdecode`). The next line generates (`generate`) a new variable
called `inc` that is equal to the old variable `rincom98`. Following this command is a series
of commands to replace (`replace`) each interval with the value of its midpoint. Thus a
code of 8 for `rincom98` is given a value of 9000 on `inc`. The final command does a cross-
tabulation (`tabulate`) of the two variables to check for coding errors. Economists and
demographers may not be happy with this coding system. Those who have a `rincom98`
code of 1 may include people who lost a fortune, so substituting a value of 500 may
not be ideal. The commands make no adjustment for these possible negative incomes.
Those who have a code of 23 include people who make \$110,000 but also may include
people who make \$1,000,000 or more. We hope that there are relatively few such cases
at either end of the distribution, so the values we use here are reasonable.

Now that we have income measured in dollars, we are ready to compare the income
of women and men who work full time by using a two-sample t test. Open the dialog
box by selecting Statistics ▷ Summaries, tables, and tests ▷ Classical tests of hypotheses ▷ t
test (mean-comparison test). In this dialog box, select *Two-sample using groups* in the t
tests section of the Main tab because the data are arranged in the common long format.
Type `inc` (outcome variable) as the *Variable name* and `sex` as the *Group variable name*.
This dialog box is shown in figure 7.2.

Figure 7.2. Two-sample t test using groups dialog box

Statistics books discuss assumptions for doing this t test, one of which is that the variance of the outcome variable, inc, is equal for both categories of the grouping variable, sex. That is, the variance in income is the same for women as it is for men. If we believed that the variances were unequal, we could click on the *Unequal variances* box, and Stata would automatically adjust everything accordingly.

We can click on **Submit** at the bottom of the dialog box at this point, and we will find a huge difference between women and men, with men making much more on average than women. However, remember that we only wanted to include people who work full time. To implement this restriction, click on the by/if/in tab in the dialog box. In the *Restrict observations* section, type wrkstat == 1 (remember to use the double equal signs) in the *If: (expression)* box. Here are the results:

```
. ttest inc if wrkstat == 1, by(sex)

Two-sample t test with equal variances
```

Group	Obs	Mean	Std. err.	Std. dev.	[95% conf. interval]	
male	671	44567.81	1054.665	27319.7	42496.96	46638.66
female	589	33081.07	895.9353	21743.74	31321.45	34840.69
Combined	1,260	39198.21	718.7267	25512.27	37788.18	40608.25
diff		11486.74	1404.217		8731.874	14241.61

```
    diff = mean(male) - mean(female)                           t =    8.1802
HO: diff = 0                                 Degrees of freedom =      1258

    Ha: diff < 0                 Ha: diff != 0                 Ha: diff > 0
 Pr(T < t) = 1.0000        Pr(|T| > |t|) = 0.0000        Pr(T > t) = 0.0000
```

The layout of these results is similar to what we had for the one-sample t test. Using a two-tailed hypothesis (center column, below the main table), we see that the t = 8.1802 has a $p < 0.001$ ($p = 0.0000$). The $N = 671$ men who work full time have an average income of just under $44,568, compared with just over $33,081 for the $N = 589$ women who are employed full time. Notice that the degrees of freedom, 1,258, is two fewer than the total number of observations, 1,260, because we used two means and lost one degree of freedom for each of them. For this two-sample t test, we have $N - 2$ degrees of freedom. A good layout for reporting a two-sample t test is $t(1258) = 8.18$, $p < 0.001$.

Is this result substantively significant? This question is pretty easy to answer because we all understand income. Men make about $11,487 more on average than do women, and this is true even though both our men and our women are working full time. It is sometimes helpful to compare the difference of means with the standard deviations. The $11,487 difference of means is roughly one-half of a standard deviation if we use the average of the two standard deviations as a guide. A difference of less than 0.2 standard deviations is considered a weak effect, a difference of 0.2 to 0.49 is considered a moderate effect, and a difference of 0.5 or more is considered a strong effect. If your statistics book covers the delta statistic, δ, you can get a precise number, but here we have just eyeballed the difference.

So far, we have been using the group-comparison t test, which assumes that the data are in the long format. The dependent variable `inc` is coded with the income of each participant. `inc` is compared across groups by `sex`, which is coded 1 for each participant who is a man and 2 for each participant who is a woman. If the data were arranged in the wide format, we would still have two variables, but they would be different. One variable would be the income for each man and would have 671 entries; the other variable would be the income for each woman and would have 589 entries. This would look like the wide format shown previously for comparing proportions, except that the variables would be called `maleinc` and `femaleinc`.

When our data are in a wide format, we again select Statistics ▷ Summaries, tables, and tests ▷ Classical tests of hypotheses ▷ t test (mean-comparison test) to open the dialog box; however, we now select *Two-sample using variables* in the t tests section of the Main tab. We simply enter the names of the two variables, `maleinc` and `femaleinc`. The resulting command would be `ttest maleinc == femaleinc, unpaired`. I cannot illustrate this process here because the data are in the long format. If you are interested, you can use Stata's `reshape` command to convert between formats; see `help reshape`.

Effect size

There are several effect-size coefficients that are used to measure the strength of the difference between means. It is especially important to report the effect size when you have a large sample because even a substantively trivial difference of means can be statistically significant with a large sample. It is also important to specify the specific measure of effect size you are using. You could report R^2 as a measure of how much variance in the dependent variable is explained by the difference between the two groups. For our example, how much variance in income does gender explain. Although Stata does not report this R^2 for an independent t test automatically, you can compute it knowing just the sample size and the t value. In the case of an independent t test, $r^2 = t^2/(t^2 + df)$. We can compute this with Stata's hand calculator:

```
. display "r-squared = " 8.1802^2/(8.1802^2 + 1258)
r-squared = .05050561
```

It is useful to remember this formula because many authors fail to report any measure of effect size and just report the t value and sample size. With this formula, you can quickly calculate the value of r^2.[4] Thus, a person's gender explains just 5.1% of the variance in their reported income.

---

4. After we cover regression, you will see that it can duplicate the results of a t test. If you are already familiar with regression, this r^2 measure of the effect size and the other result of a t test are computed when you run the command `regress inc i.sex if wrkstat==1`.

Effect size, continued

People often report r rather than r^2. Because our independent variable, `sex`, is categorical and our dependent variable, `inc`, is quantitative, this correlation is technically called a point-biserial r. Cohen's d and Hedges's g are also widely used measures of effect size. Both Cohen's d and Hedges's g estimate the separation of the two distributions in terms of standard deviation units. If d or $g = 1.0$, then the means of the two distributions would be separated by one standard deviation. In our example, the mean income for men is a little over \$44,000 and just over \$33,000 for women; thus, men make about \$11,000 more than women, on average. The standard deviation for men is a bit larger than for women, \$27,319.70 versus \$21,743.74. Just looking at these numbers, we can see that men's earnings are a bit less than half a standard deviation higher than women's earnings.

Cohen's d and Hedges's g make slightly different estimates of the pooled standard deviation. In both cases, the coefficient is simply the ratio of the difference between the means over the pooled estimate. For large samples, both measures will be very close to each other. For smaller samples, Hedges's g will be somewhat smaller. It is recommended that you use Hedges's g for small samples and either measure for large samples.

We can use the `esize twosample` command to calculate Cohen's d, Hedges's g, and the point-biserial r. We again use `if wrkstat==1` because we restrict our sample to men and women who are working outside the home.

```
. esize twosample inc if wrkstat==1, by(sex) cohensd hedgesg pbcorr
Effect size based on mean comparison

                                     Obs per group:
                                          male =        671
                                        female =        589

        Effect size  │   Estimate    [95% conf. interval]

           Cohen's d │   .4618797    .3496624    .5739179
         Hedges's g  │   .4616043    .3494539    .5735757
   Point-biserial r  │   .2247338    .1719972    .2754888
```

Cohen's d and Hedges's g are both 0.46. Thus, the mean of the distribution of income for men is almost half a standard deviation higher than the mean of the distribution of income for women. Cohen (1988) suggested that a value of 0.20 is a small effect, a value of 0.50 is a medium effect, and a value of 0.80 or more is a large effect. Our observed values of 0.46 is therefore close to a medium effect.

Effect size, continued

Cohen (1988) suggested that a point-biserial r of 0.10 or lower indicates a small effect size. A value between 0.10 and 0.30 indicates a medium effect size, and a value larger than 0.50 indicates a strong effect size. Our point-biserial $r = 0.22$ indicates a medium effect of gender on earnings.

If you have a t test where you do not assume equal variances (see section 7.8.1), you can estimate the effect size by simply adding the option unequal to the end of the esize command.

If you read an article and they report the result of a t test but not the effect size, Stata has an immediate form for calculating the effect size: esizei *#obs1 #mean1 #sd1 #obs2 #mean2 #sd2*, cohensd hedgesg pbcorr. Suppose they say the mean income for men is \$50,000, SD = \$25,000, and the mean for women is \$45,000, SD = \$24,000. They also say their study surveyed 200 men and 250 women. What is the effect size?

```
. esizei 200 50000 25000 250 45000 24000, cohensd hedgesg pbcorr
Effect size based on mean comparison

                                    Obs per group:
                                       Group 1 =          200
                                       Group 2 =          250

          Effect size  │   Estimate     [95% conf. interval]
          ─────────────┼──────────────────────────────────────
            Cohen's d  │   .2045053      .017972      .3908115
           Hedges's g  │   .2041627     .0179419      .3901569
      Point-biserial r │   .1013219     .0089499       .191044
```

An example of a difference between groups with a larger effect size comes when we restrict our sample to individuals whose parents have no more than a high school education.

```
. ttest inc if wrkstat==1 & paeduc<=12 & maeduc<=12, by(sex)
```

Two-sample t test with equal variances

Group	Obs	Mean	Std. err.	Std. dev.	[95% conf. interval]	
male	281	43579.18	1454.339	24379.16	40716.36	46442.01
female	235	30192.55	1221.461	18724.64	27786.09	32599.02
Combined	516	37482.56	1010.58	22955.96	35497.19	39467.92
diff		13386.63	1943.497		9568.453	17204.8

$$\text{diff} = \text{mean}(\text{male}) - \text{mean}(\text{female}) \qquad\qquad t = 6.8879$$
$$\text{H0: diff} = 0 \qquad\qquad \text{Degrees of freedom} = 514$$

Ha: diff < 0	Ha: diff != 0	Ha: diff > 0
$Pr(T < t) = 1.0000$	$Pr(|T| > |t|) = 0.0000$	$Pr(T > t) = 0.0000$

```
. esize twosample inc if wrkstat==1 & paeduc<=12 & maeduc<=12, by(sex)
> cohensd hedgesg pbcorr
```

Effect size based on mean comparison

```
                              Obs per group:
                                      male =       281
                                    female =       235
```

Effect size	Estimate	[95% conf. interval]	
Cohen's d	.6088707	.431381	.785793
Hedges's g	.6079817	.4307512	.7846457
Point-biserial r	.2906929	.2104296	.3650358

These results show that there is a significant difference ($t = 6.89; p < 0.001$) with males having a much higher mean income, \$43,579.18, than the mean income for females, \$30,192.55. The effect-size values now fall in the medium-size range with Cohen's d being 0.609. Thus, mean income for males is 0.609 standard deviations larger than income for females in this group.

How confident are we in these findings? Do you see any problems with the assumptions underlying this t test? One assumption is that the variances of the two groups are equal. Our t test results show that the standard deviation for the males is \$24,379 compared with \$18,725 for females. This does seem like a substantial difference, but a t test is robust against small violations, especially when the N's of each group are similar. We can run a test of equal variances as described in the next section. A limitation of the test of equal variances is that the violation is most important when there are small samples, but then the test has insufficient power. The violation is less important when you have fairly large samples like this, but then even a small difference might be statistically significant. Using the unequal variance assumption for the t test, we calculate the degrees of freedom differently, and the t value will vary somewhat ($t = 7.048; p < 0.001$), but the difference of means and effect size measures are identical.

Another assumption of the t test is that the distributions are normally distributed. We could run the `table` command with options for skewness and kurtosis as described in section 5.6, but with these data a histogram with a normal density line added is enough to demonstrate a concern:

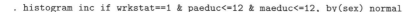

. histogram inc if wrkstat==1 & paeduc<=12 & maeduc<=12, by(sex) normal

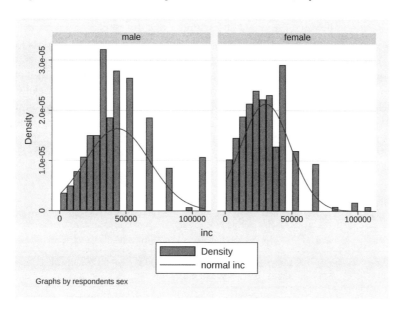

These results show that the distribution for the males has a large number of people in the right tail of the distribution who have large incomes. How serious is this problem? With such a large sample, this assumption is not as problematic as the univariate distributions might suggest. The crucial issue for the t test is the normality of the sampling distribution—the distribution of means or distribution of the difference in means across all possible samples. Regardless of the distribution of the original variables, the sampling distribution of a difference of means will approach a normal distribution as N increases. This is based on the central limit theorem, and it applies except in very unusual distributions that have infinite variance. Of course, if we had a much smaller sample, the normality assumption would be more of a limitation.

Although the t test is widely reported by researchers even when the one distribution or both are nonnormal, it is reasonable to run a nonparametric test such as the median test (see section 7.11.2) because the median test does not assume normality of the distributions. After you read section 7.11.2, you can run that test, and it shows that the medians differ significantly ($\chi^2 = 25.7$; $p < 0.001$). This is a useful check on the results of the t test, and the fact that both tests show significant results adds to our confidence in the finding of a significant difference with a relatively large effect size in the central tendency of the two groups.

7.8.1   Testing for unequal variances

In the dialog box for the group-comparison t test, we did not click on the option that would adjust for unequal variances. If the variances or standard deviations are similar in the two groups, there is no reason to make this adjustment. However, when the variances or standard deviations differ sharply between the two groups, we may want to test whether the difference is significant. Before doing the t test, some researchers will do a test of significance on whether variances are different. This test is problematic because the test of equal variances will show small differences in the variances to be statistically significant in large samples (where the lack of equal variance is less of a problem), but the test will not show large differences to be significant in small samples (where unequal variance is a bigger problem). To open the dialog box, select Statistics ▷ Summaries, tables, and tests ▷ Classical tests of hypotheses ▷ Variance-comparison test. Here we select *Two-sample using groups* in the *Variance-comparison tests* section. We enter our dependent variable, inc, and the grouping variable, sex, just like we did for the t test. We also should use the by/if/in tab to restrict the sample to those who work full time, wrkstat == 1. The command and results are

```
. sdtest inc if wrkstat == 1, by(sex)

Variance ratio test
```

Group	Obs	Mean	Std. err.	Std. dev.	[95% conf. interval]	
male	671	44567.81	1054.665	27319.7	42496.96	46638.66
female	589	33081.07	895.9353	21743.74	31321.45	34840.69
Combined	1,260	39198.21	718.7267	25512.27	37788.18	40608.25

```
       ratio = sd(male) / sd(female)                              f =   1.5786
HO: ratio = 1                                    Degrees of freedom = 670, 588

     Ha: ratio < 1                 Ha: ratio != 1                 Ha: ratio > 1
   Pr(F < f) = 1.0000           2*Pr(F > f) = 0.0000           Pr(F > f) = 0.0000
```

This test produces an F test that tests for a significant difference in the variances (although the output reports only standard deviations). The F test is simply the ratio of the variances of the two groups. Just below the table, we can see on the left side that the null hypothesis is HO: ratio = 1. Below the table on the right side, we see that the f = 1.5786 (note that this is the ratio of the variances, that is, $27319.7^2/21743.74^2$) and we see two degrees of freedom, degrees of freedom = 670, 588. The first number, 670, is the degrees of freedom for males $(N_1 - 1)$, and the second number is the degrees of freedom for females $(N_2 - 1)$. The variance for males is 1.58 times as great as the variance for females. In the middle bottom of the output, we can see the two-tailed alternative hypothesis, Ha: ratio != 1, and a reported probability of 0.0000. Because the F test has two numbers for degrees of freedom, we would report this as $F(670, 588) = 1.58, p < 0.001$.

Although the variances are significantly different, remember that this test is sensitive to large sample sizes, and in such cases, the assumption is less serious. If the groups have roughly similar sample sizes and if the standard deviations are not dramatically different, most researchers choose to ignore this test. If you want to adjust for unequal variances, however, look back at the dialog box for the two-sample t test. All you need to do is check the box for *Unequal variances*. When you get the results, the degrees of freedom are no longer $N - 2$ but are based on a complex formula that Stata will compute for you.

7.9 Repeated-measures t test

The repeated-measures t test goes by many names. Some statistics books call it a repeated-measures t test, some call it a dependent-sample t test, and some call it a paired-sample t test. A repeated-measures t test is used when one group of people is measured at two points. An example would be an experiment in which you measured everybody's weight at the start of the experiment and then measured their weight a second time at the end of the experiment. Did they have a significant loss of weight? As a second example, we may want to know if it helps to retake the GRE. How much better do students perform when they repeat the GRE? We have one group of students, but we measure them twice—once the first time they take the GRE and again the second time they take it. The idea is that we measure the group on a variable, something happens, and then we measure them on that variable a second time. A control group is not needed in this approach because the participants serve as their own control.

An alternative use of the repeated-measures t test is to think of the group as being related people, such as parents. Husbands and wives would be paired. An example would be to compare the time a wife spends on household chores with the time her husband spends on household chores. Here each husband and each wife would have a score on time spent for the wife and a score on time spent for the husband.

Who spends more time on chores—wives or husbands? Here we do not measure time spent on chores twice for the same person, but we measure it twice for each related pair of people. The way the data are organized involves having two scores for each case. With paired data, the case consists of two related people (see `chores.dta`). Here is what five cases (couples) might look like:

```
. use https://www.stata-press.com/data/agis6r/chores, clear
. list
```

	husband	wife
1.	11	31
2.	10	40
3.	21	44
4.	15	36
5.	12	29

We will illustrate the related-sample t test with data from the General Social Survey 2002 dataset `gss2002_chapter7.dta`. Each participant was asked how much education his or her mother and his or her father had completed. This survey is not like the example of mothers and fathers because we have two measures for each participant. We know how much education each person reports for his or her mother and for his or her father. Do these respondents report more education for their mothers or for their fathers? Here we will use a two-tailed test with a null hypothesis that there is no difference on average and an alternative hypothesis that there is a difference:

Alternative hypothesis: H_a: $\mu_{\text{diff}} \neq 0$

Null hypothesis: H_0: $\mu_{\text{diff}} = 0$

Remembering that we use M for a sample mean and μ for a population mean, we express these hypotheses as mean differences in the population (μ_{diff}). To open the dialog box, select Statistics ▷ Summaries, tables, and tests ▷ Classical tests of hypotheses ▷ t test (mean-comparison test). This is the same dialog box that we have been using, but this time we select *Paired* in the *t tests* section. We enter the two variables. It does not really matter which we enter as the *First variable* and which as the *Second variable*, but we need to remember this order because changing the order will reverse the signs on all the differences. Type `paeduc` as the *First variable* and `maeduc` as the *Second variable*. Remember that different statistics books will call this test the repeated-measures *t* test, paired-sample *t* test, or dependent-sample *t* test. All of these tests are the same.

Here are the command and results:

```
. use https://www.stata-press.com/data/agis6r/gss2002_chapter7, clear
. ttest paeduc == maeduc
Paired t test
```

Variable	Obs	Mean	Std. err.	Std. dev.	[95% conf. interval]	
paeduc	1,903	11.42091	.0917118	4.000779	11.24105	11.60078
maeduc	1,903	11.58276	.0781763	3.410314	11.42944	11.73608
diff	1,903	-.1618497	.0729315	3.181518	-.3048838	-.0188156

```
        mean(diff) = mean(paeduc - maeduc)                        t =  -2.2192
    H0: mean(diff) = 0                          Degrees of freedom =      1902

   Ha: mean(diff) < 0             Ha: mean(diff) != 0            Ha: mean(diff) > 0
   Pr(T < t) = 0.0133          Pr(|T| > |t|) = 0.0266            Pr(T > t) = 0.9867
```

Mothers have more education on average than fathers. The mean for mothers is $M = 11.58$ years, compared with $M = 11.42$ years for fathers. Before going further, we need to ask if this difference (father's education − mother's education = −0.16) is important. Because we entered father's education as the first variable and mother's education as the second variable, the negative difference indicates that the mothers had slightly more education than did the fathers. However, 0.16 years of education would amount to $0.16 \times 12 = 1.92$ months of education, which does not sound like an important difference, even though it is statistically significant.

Just below the table, on the left, is the null hypothesis that there is no difference, `H0: mean(diff) = 0`, and on the right is the *t* test, `t = -2.2192`, and its degrees of freedom, 1,902. The middle column under the main table has the alternative hypothesis, namely, that the mean difference is not 0. The $t = -2.22$ has a $p < 0.05$; thus, the difference is statistically significant.

This example illustrates a problem with focusing too much on the tests of significance. With a large sample, almost any difference will be statistically significant; it still may not be important. We have seen that this difference represents fewer than 2 months of education ($M_{\text{diff}} = 1.92$ months), so it might be fair to say that we have a statistically significant difference that is not substantively significant.

7.10   Power analysis

You can think of the power of a test as its ability to do what you want to do. Normally, using your sample, you want to reject the null hypothesis in favor of the alternative hypothesis when the alternative hypothesis is correct in the larger population. If the power of a test is 0.20, this means that you have only a 20% chance of rejecting the null hypothesis when the alternative hypothesis is correct. Before a researcher begins collecting data to do a study, he or she should have a good idea of the power of the tests that will be run. A pharmaceutical company would not want to fund a $1,000,000 study that had only a 20% chance of finding a statistically significant result for a new drug that actually was effective. Nor would a thesis committee want to support such a study. Certainly, you would not want to invest your own time in such a project because it is virtually doomed to failure.

Power analysis can be done a priori, that is, before the study is done, or a posteriori, that is, after the study is done. It makes the most sense to do power analysis before you do the study so that you are confident that your sample size will be sufficient to have adequate power. However, the procedures for doing power analysis can be reversed so that they are done after a study is completed. Doing power analysis a posteriori is controversial but may be appropriate in some cases. Suppose that you read a study that had a very small sample and, in spite of having means that were very different, did not obtain a statistically significant alpha. Was this because the means really were not different in the population as specified by the null hypothesis? Or was this because the means in the population really were different as specified by the alternative hypothesis, but the sample size or alpha level was too small to have a powerful test? A posteriori power analysis could tell you that given the study design, say, a two-sample t test a sample size, say, $n_1 = n_2 = 10$; and an alpha value, say, 0.01, the power was extremely low. This information would help you evaluate the importance of the statistically insignificant finding. With Stata, we can do either an a priori or an a posteriori power analysis.

There are seven things we need to know or estimate to do a power analysis for a *t* test:

1. Is it a repeated or paired *t* test, or are there two independent samples?

2. Is it a one-tailed or two-tailed test?

3. What alpha value is used? Usually, $\alpha = 0.05$.

4. How big of a difference do we need for it to be considered a substantively significant difference? This is called the critical effect size (Cohen 1988).

5. How much power do we need? Usually, a power of 0.80 is minimally adequate for exploratory research, but a power of 0.90 or 0.95 may be required in highly critical areas.

6. If there are two independent samples, what is the ratio of the Ns? (Do we have the same number of participants in each group? Do we have twice as many participants in one group as in the other?)

7. We need an estimate of the standard deviation of the two groups.

We have already covered most of these requirements, but the idea of an effect size is new. The effect size is simply how much difference we need to be able to consider it substantively significant. There are many measures of effect size, depending on what test you are using. We will illustrate effect size with a measure called Cohen's *d* that is used when there are two independent samples. Cohen's *d* is calculated using

$$d = \frac{M_t - M_c}{\text{SD}_{\text{pooled}}}$$

where

$$\text{SD}_{\text{pooled}} = \sqrt{\frac{\text{SD}_t^2(N_t - 1) + \text{SD}_c^2(N_c - 1)}{N_c + N_t - 2}}$$

and where M_t and M_c are the means for the treatment group and the control group, respectively; SD_t^2 and SD_c^2 are the square of the respective standard deviations; and N_t and N_c are the respective sample sizes.

Cohen's *d* tells us how far the two means need to be separated for the results to be substantively significant. Sometimes we do not need the pooled standard deviation that is in the denominator to say a difference is substantively significant. If, in comparing women and men on income, we said the mean for men was \$90,000 and the mean for women was \$50,000, we would all be satisfied that this was a big difference. Other times, our variables are measured in ways where it is hard to compare the two means directly.

Suppose we said that one group had a mean score on depression of 49 and the other group had a mean score of 40. Is this an important difference? One way to judge the difference is in terms of how many standard deviations separate the two groups. This is precisely what Cohen's d does. If we have a mean of 100 in one group and a mean of 115 in another group and the pooled standard deviation is 15, then we would say that the groups are one standard deviation apart. This would be a very big difference. Imagine two people, one with an IQ of 100 and the other with an IQ of 115, where the standard deviation for IQ scores is about 15. These two people are about one standard deviation apart. With an IQ of 100, a person should be able to complete high school without much trouble but might have trouble completing a college degree. The person with an IQ of 115 would be able to complete college without much trouble. A difference of one standard deviation is definitely a big difference.

When Cohen defined his Cohen's d, he said that a $d = 0.2$ would be considered a small effect, a $d = 0.5$ would be a moderate effect, and a $d = 0.8$ would be a large effect. The following three figures give you a visual of these three d values. Figure 7.3(a) has a Cohen's d of 0.2 and shows the distribution of two groups. Clearly, there is a lot of overlap and this is a small effect. Those in the treatment group are the distribution under the solid line and those in the control group are the distribution under the dashed line.

Figure 7.3(b) shows a medium effect, where there is still a lot of overlap. Even in figure 7.3(c), where the effect is described as large, there is a lot of overlap. Indeed, the majority of people under the control-group distribution would also fall under the treatment-group distribution, and vice versa.

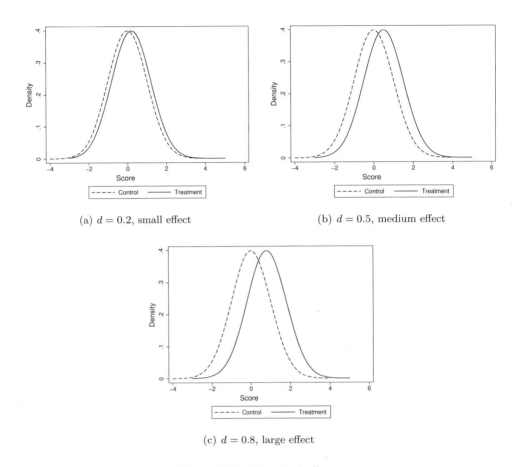

(a) $d = 0.2$, small effect   (b) $d = 0.5$, medium effect

(c) $d = 0.8$, large effect

Figure 7.3. Cohen's d effects

You can see how Cohen's d is important to power. It would take a very large sample to show a statistically significant difference between the two groups if you insist on being able to detect a small effect. It would take a much smaller sample to be able to detect a statistically significant effect for the large effect.

To estimate power, we do not need to first estimate the effect size, but we need to decide whether we want to detect a small, medium, or large effect. If a cost-benefit analysis shows that a small difference would be important, then we need a big enough sample to detect a small effect. If any improvement or any difference between the null and the alternative hypothesis would be important, then a small effect size is what you have. Otherwise, you may only be interested in demonstrating a difference if the effect size is moderate or large. This is a decision you need to make.

Looking at the equation defining Cohen's d, we need to estimate the pooled standard deviation, which is often challenging to do. Suppose that you have an intervention designed to reduce depression. You know that the depression score runs from 0 to 50. Reading literature where this scale has been used, you may find that several authors reported standard deviations for their samples. You could use one of those values as your standard deviation. If you are unable to find a published standard deviation, you might run a pretest on 30 people and compute the standard deviation for this sample. If you cannot do that, you can make an intelligent guess. A good guess would be the interquartile range divided by 1.35, but you are not likely to know the interquartile range. So here is a very crude way to guess what the standard deviation is. We know that 4 standard deviations covers about 95% of a normal distribution. We might think that very few people would score below 5 or above 45 on our 0 to 50 scale of depression. If that is the case, then perhaps about 95% of the people would have a score between 5 and 45. Our guess of the standard deviation would be $(45 - 5)/4 = 10$. Then we can use this value of 10 in our estimation of power.

We also need some way to estimate the means for the two groups. Again, if we have any past research or a pilot study, we might get good estimates of the mean. But let's suppose that we have no available information to help us estimate the means. We can use Cohen's d to give us a difference of means. The difference of means, $(M_c - M_t)/10$, is 0.2 for a small effect size, 0.5 for a medium effect size, and 0.8 for a large effect size. Thus $\text{SD} \times 0.2 = 10 \times 0.2 = 2$ for a small difference of means, $10 \times 0.5 = 5$ for a medium difference of means, and $10 \times 0.8 = 8$ for a large difference of means.

If we want to be able to detect a small difference of means on a depression scale that ranges from 0 to 50, we could pick as examples reasonable values that are 2 points apart, for example, 35 and 37, 30 and 32, or 38 and 40. If we have a large effect size, then we would pick means that are within our scale range and are 8 points apart, such as 30 and 38, 25 and 33, or 35 and 43.

With this background on picking a mean and a standard deviation, we are ready for our power analysis. Here is what we know or assume:

1. Two-sample comparison of means (two independent samples)

2. Two-tailed test

3. $\alpha = 0.05$

4. Small effect size, $M_c = 35$, $M_t = 37$; $\text{SD} = 10$

5. Desired power $= 0.90$

6. $N_c = N_t$, so the ratio is 1

7. SD for both groups approximately 10

To open the *Power, precision, and sample-size analysis* Control Panel, select Statistics ▷ Power, precision, and sample size; see figure 7.4. From this control panel, we can easily open a dialog box to perform power, precision, and sample-size analysis for confidence intervals.

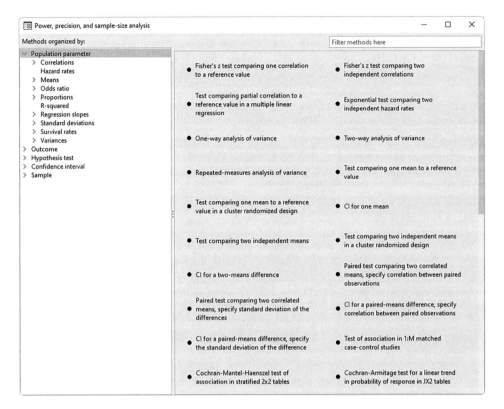

Figure 7.4. *Power, precision, and sample-size analysis* Control Panel

The left pane organizes the methods, and the right pane displays the methods corresponding to the selection in the left pane. Because we are comparing two means from independent samples, we will use the `power twomeans` command. To open the related dialog box, select Population parameter from the left pane, and then select Test comparing two independent means from the right pane.

In the dialog box that opens, confirm that *Total sample size* is selected in the *Compute* menu. We set alpha in the *Significance level* at 0.05. We want to have 90% power so we set the *Power* at 0.90. We assume equal size in both groups, so we set the sample size *Allocation ratio, N2/N1* at 1. If we had more people in one group than in the other group, we would enter the ratio of N2/N1. Because we are interested in detecting a small effect size, Cohen's $d = 0.20$, we need to enter information for the effect size. We expect the standard deviation for both groups to be about 10, so a Cohen's $d = 0.20$ would be a difference of 2. We have decided that the control group mean might be about 35, which would make the other mean 37. These are only guesses; the important thing is that with a small effect size and a standard deviation of 10, the difference between the groups must be 2. Confirm that *Two-sided test* is selected in the *Sides* menu.

With all the specifications we made, our dialog box for **power twomeans** should look like figure 7.5.

Figure 7.5. Power, precision, and sample-size dialog box for comparing two means

The control panel is great, whether you are doing power analysis just once or exploring the effect of making different assumptions. However, the command syntax is also quite simple. You specify **power twomeans** because this is the type of power analysis you are doing. Then you specify the values of the two means. After the comma, you specify the common standard deviation and the power level you want to ensure having. The default is $\alpha = 0.05$, so we do not need to specify this option in our command. If we preferred to use another level, we would simply add the option, say, **alpha(0.001)**. Here are the results of the above dialog box:

```
. power twomeans 35 37, sd(10) power(0.90)

Performing iteration ...

Estimated sample sizes for a two-sample means test
t test assuming sd1 = sd2 = sd
H0: m2 = m1  versus  Ha: m2 != m1

Study parameters:
        alpha =    0.0500
        power =    0.9000
        delta =    2.0000
           m1 =   35.0000
           m2 =   37.0000
           sd =   10.0000

Estimated sample sizes:
            N =    1,054
  N per group =      527
```

We need a large sample of 1,054 participants to have this much power to detect such a small difference with a high level of power. Assumptions are important. Try the same command, but add the option `alpha(0.001)`. Where we needed an $N = 1054$ for the default $\alpha = 0.05$, with $\alpha = 0.001$, we need a much larger sample, $N = 2096$. Try the command again with the default $\alpha = 0.05$ for a power of 0.80 (total $N = 788$). What if you use a power of 0.80 and a moderate effect size of Cohen's $d = 0.3$, resulting in means of 35 and 38 ($N = 352$). It should be apparent that the power analysis is no better than the quality of what you assume and seemingly small differences in assumptions result in widely different total sample-size requirements.

Power analysis is highly dependent on the assumptions you make:

- What is a clinically important difference?

- What is the standard deviation of each group?

- How much power do I want to have?

- What alpha level am I using?

If you make small changes in how you answer any of these questions, you will get very different results. We used an effect size of $d = 0.20$ with an $SD_1 = SD_2 = 10.0$ to select our means of 35 and 37. Try slightly different means, say, 35 and 36 or 35 and 38. These small changes in the minimum difference you consider clinically important make a huge difference in the sample sizes you would need. Increasing your desired power has a similar effect. You can obtain the results by typing

```
power twomeans 35 (36 37 38), sd(10) power(0.80)
```

The positive value of power analysis is it helps us to plan our studies and to justify what we are doing when we are requesting funding for our project. If a funding agency considers a small effect to be substantively important, they will not want to fund us if we have too small of a sample to detect such an effect. On the other hand, if we request funding for a very large sample when we have adequate power for a much smaller sample, the funding agency will not want to waste its money on the excessively large sample.

7.11   Nonparametric alternatives

The examples in this chapter for t tests have assumed that the outcome or dependent variable is measured on at least the interval level. The examples also assumed that both groups have equal variances in their populations and are normally distributed. The tests we have covered are remarkably robust against violations of these assumptions, but sometimes we want to use tests that make less-challenging assumptions. Nonparametric alternatives to conventional t tests are such tests. These tests have some limitations of their own, including being somewhat less powerful than the t test. Here are examples of nonparametric alternatives available in Stata.

7.11.1   Mann–Whitney two-sample rank-sum test

If we assume that we have ordinal measurement rather than interval measurement, we can do the rank-sum test. We can test the hypothesis that two independent samples (that is, unmatched data) are from a population distribution by using the Mann–Whitney two-sample rank-sum test. The rank-sum test works for both ordinal and interval data.

This test involves a simple idea. It combines the two groups into one group and ranks the participants from top to bottom. The highest score gets a rank of N (8,871 in this example), and the lowest score gets a rank of 1. If one group has higher scores than the other group, that group should have a predominance of higher ranks. If girls report that more of their friends smoke, they should have more of the top ranks, and boys should have more of the lower ranks. If girls and boys have the same distribution, then both groups should have about the same number of high ranks and low ranks. In other words, the sum of the girls' ranks should be about the same as the sum of the boys' ranks.

The test computes the sum of ranks for each group and compares this with what we would expect by chance. Using data from the National Longitudinal Survey of Youth 1997 (`nlsy97_chapter7.dta`) (Bureau of Labor Statistics, U.S. Department of Labor 2015), we can compare the answers girls and boys give on how many of their friends smoke. They were asked what percentage of their friends smoke, and they answered in broad categories that were coded 1–5. Treating these categories as ordinal, we can do a rank-sum test. I will not show the dialog box for this, but the command and results are

```
. use https://www.stata-press.com/data/agis6r/nlsy97_chapter7, clear
(National Survey of Youth, 1997, selected variables from first wave)

. ranksum psmoke97, by(gender97)

Two-sample Wilcoxon rank-sum (Mann-Whitney) test
```

gender97	Obs	Rank sum	Expected
1	4540	19130393	20139440
2	4331	20221363	19212316
Combined	8871	39351756	39351756

```
Unadjusted variance     1.454e+10
Adjustment for ties    -7.360e+08

Adjusted variance       1.380e+10

H0: psmoke97(gender97==1) = psmoke97(gender97==2)
        z = -8.589
Prob > |z| = 0.0000
```

This output shows that there is a significant difference of $z = -8.589$. We should also report the medians and means so that the direction of this difference is clear. The rank test compares the entire distribution rather than a particular parameter, such as the mean or median.

7.11.2   Nonparametric alternative: Median test

Sometimes you will want to compare the medians of two groups rather than the means. Whereas the Mann–Whitney rank-sum test compares entire distributions, the median test performs a nonparametric K-sample test on the equality of medians. It tests the null hypothesis that the K samples were drawn from populations with the same medians. In the case of two samples ($K = 2$), a chi-squared statistic is calculated with and without a continuity correction.

Ideally, there would be no ties, and a median could be identified that had exactly 50% of the observations above it and 50% below it. With this example, the dependent variable is on a 1-to-5 scale, and there are many ties; for example, hundreds of students have a score of 2. This means that there is not an equal number of observations that are above and below the median for either group. I will not illustrate the dialog box for this command, but the command and results are

```
. median psmoke97, by(gender97) exact medianties(split)
Median test
   Greater │
  than the │    youth gender 1997
   median  │        1           2  │    Total
───────────┼───────────────────────┼──────────
        no │    2,904       2,470  │    5,374
       yes │    1,636       1,861  │    3,497
───────────┼───────────────────────┼──────────
     Total │    4,540       4,331  │    8,871

              Pearson chi2(1) =  44.6269   Pr = 0.000
               Fisher's exact =             0.000
       1-sided Fisher's exact =             0.000

       Continuity corrected:
              Pearson chi2(1) =  44.3371   Pr = 0.000
```

The median test makes sense for comparing skewed variables, such as income. We would report the example as $\chi^2(1) = 44.63$, $p < 0.001$. If we set up a hypothesis, we would reject the null hypothesis, H_0: $\text{Med}_1 = \text{Med}_2$, in favor of the alternative hypothesis, H_a: $\text{Med}_1 \neq \text{Med}_2$.

7.12   Video tutorial related to this chapter

Stata has video tutorials related to this chapter; see https://www.stata.com/links/ video-tutorials/. The "Tour of effect sizes" video shows how to do what we have covered and provides extensions to what we have done. Many video tutorials on power analysis are also relevant to this chapter. Most of these are short, and the topics are specific. The "Tour of power and sample size" video is a good place to start. If you have a specific question, such as how do you do a power analysis when you have a single sample mean, say, a sample of 50 students from your university that are 35% female, and you want to compare it with the percentage of female students in the entire university, see if you can find a tutorial. Looking down the list of videos on "Power and sample size", you will find "Power calculation for comparing a sample proportion to a reference value using Stata".

7.13   Summary

The tests presented in this chapter are among the most frequently used statistical tests. As you read this chapter, you may have thought of applications in which you can use a t test or a z test for testing individual means and proportions or for testing differences. These are extremely useful tests for people who work in an applied setting and need to make decisions based on statistics. It is becoming a requirement to demonstrate that any new program has advantages over older programs; it is not enough to say that you believe that the new program is better or that you can "see" the difference. You need to find appropriate outcomes, such as reading readiness, retention rate, loss of weight, increased skill, or participant satisfaction. Then you need to show that the new program has a statistically significant influence on the outcomes you select. If you are designing an exercise program for older adults, there is not much reason to implement your program unless you can demonstrate that it has a good retention rate, that participants are satisfied with the program, and that behavioral outcome goals are met.

In this chapter, we discussed statistical significance and substantive significance, both of which are extremely important. If something is not statistically significant, we do not have confidence that there is a real effect or difference; what we observed in our data may be something that could have happened just by chance. There are two major reasons why a result may not be statistically significant. The first is that the result represents a small effect where there is little substantive difference between the groups. The second is that we have designed our study with too few observations to show significance, even when the actual difference is important. Therefore, I introduced the basic Stata commands to estimate the sample size needed to do a study with sufficient power to show that an important result is statistically significant. We only touched the surface of what Stata can do with power analysis, and I encourage you to check the Stata reference manuals for more ways to estimate power and sample-size requirements.

When we have statistical significance, we are confident that what we observed in our data represents a real effect that should not be attributed to chance. It is still essential to evaluate how substantively significant the result is. With a large sample, we may find a statistically significant difference of means when the actual difference is small and substantively insignificant. Finding a significant result begs the question of how important the result is. A statistically significant result may or may not be large enough to be important.

Finally, we learned briefly about nonparametric alternatives to z tests and t tests. These alternatives usually have less power but may be more easily justified in the assumptions they make.

Sometimes we have more than two groups, and the t test is no longer adequate. Chapter 9 discusses analysis of variance (ANOVA), which is an extension of the t test that allows us to work with more than two groups. Before we do analysis of variance, however, we will cover bivariate correlation and regression in chapter 8.

7.14 Exercises

When doing these exercises, you should create a do-file for each assignment; you might name the do-file for the first exercise c7_1.do. Put these do-files in the directory where you are keeping the Stata programs related to this book. Having these do-files will be useful in the future if you need to redo one of these examples or want to do a similar task. For example, you could use the do-file for the second exercise anytime you need to do randomization of participants in a study.

1. According to the registrar's office at your university, 52% of the students are women. You do a web-based survey of attitudes toward student fees supporting the sports program. You have 20 respondents, 14 of whom are men and 6 of whom are women. Is there a gender bias in your sample? To answer this, create a new dataset that has one variable, namely, `sex`. Enter a value of 1 for your first 14 observations (for your 14 males) and a value of 0 for your last 6 observations (for your 6 females). Your data will have one column and 20 rows. Then do a one-sample z test against the null hypothesis that $p = 0.52$. Explain your null hypothesis. Interpret your results.

2. You have 30 volunteers to participate in an exercise program. You want to randomly assign 15 of them to the control group and 15 to the treatment group. You list them by name—the order being arbitrary—and assign numbers from 1 to 30. What are the Stata commands you would use to do the random assignment (randomization without replacement)? Show how you would do this.

3. You learned how to do a random sample without replacement. To do a random sample with replacement, you use the `bsample` command. Repeat exercise 2, but use the command `bsample 15`. Then do a tabulation to see if any observations were selected more than once.

4. Using the approach you used in exercise 1, draw a random sample of 10 students from a large class of 200 students. You use the class roster in which each student has a number from 1 to 200. Show the commands you use, and set the seed at 953. List the numbers for the 10 students you select.

5. Open `nlsy97_chapter7.dta`. A friend says that Hispanic families have more children than do other ethnic groups. Use the variables `hh18_97` (number of children under age 18) and `ethnic97` (0 being non-Hispanic and 1 being Hispanic) to test whether this is true. Are the means different? If the result is statistically significant, how substantively significant is the difference?

6. Use the same variables as exercise 5. Use `summarize`, `detail`, and `tabulate` to check the distribution of `hh18_97`. Do this separately for Hispanics and for non-Hispanics. What are the medians of each group? Run a median test. Is the difference significant? How can you reconcile this with the medians you computed? (Think about ties and the distributions.)

7. You want to compare Democrats and Republicans on their mean scores on abortion rights. From earlier uses of the scale, you know that the mean is somewhere around 50 and the standard deviation is about 15. Select an alpha level and the minimum difference that you would find important. Justify your minimum difference (this is pretty subjective, but you might think in terms of a proportion of a standard deviation difference). How many cases do you need to have 80% power? How many cases do you need to have 90% power? How many cases do you need to have 99% power?

8. A friend believes that women are more likely to feel that abortion is okay under any circumstances than are men because women have more at stake in a decision about whether to have an abortion. Use the General Social Survey 2002 dataset (`gss2002_chapter7.dta`), and test whether there is a significant difference between women and men (`sex`) on whether abortion is acceptable in any case (`abany`).

9. You are planning to evaluate the effectiveness of Overeaters Anonymous to reduce the body mass index (BMI) of participants. You will weigh each person at the start of the intervention and then again after they have participated for 5 weeks. From past research, you expect the average BMI to be 30 prior to the intervention. The standard deviation is about 4. You want to be able to detect a difference if the effect size is medium. How many people do you need to have in your intervention?

10. You are planning to compare how satisfied women and men are with a particular weight loss program. You have 20 items measuring satisfaction and each item is scored from 1 for very dissatisfied to 5 for very satisfied. You are interested in being able to detect a small effect size with alpha = 0.05 and power = 0.90. How big of a sample will you need?

11. A researcher is planning a study of the effectiveness of a new method of teaching a course on statistics. Students in one class get a traditional course, where all the work is done without computers. Students in a different course (new method) do half the work by hand and half using Stata. If you want a moderate effect size, alpha of 0.05, and a power of 0.80, how many students are needed in each class? The final examination is used to evaluate performance, and the mean score has been around 80 with a standard deviation of 10.

12. You are planning an intervention to reduce test-taking anxiety. You have a 100-point scale to measure anxiety and a pretest you did without any intervention had a mean of 70 and a standard deviation of 15. You want to be able to show that a true difference of means between your intervention group and your control group should lower the anxiety by one third of a standard deviation or 5 points. You want a power of 0.80.

   a. How many students do you need in each group (control group and intervention group) using a two-tailed test?

   b. How many using a one-tailed test?

13. Suppose you are doing question 12, it is much more expensive to get measures for the intervention group. Because of the cost of running the intervention, let's say it is two times as expensive to obtain students' scores for the intervention group. How many students do you need in the intervention group? The control group?

   a. For a two-tailed test?

   b. For a one-tailed test?

8 Bivariate correlation and regression

8.1 Introduction to bivariate correlation and regression

Bivariate correlation and regression are used to examine the relationship between two variables. They are usually used with quantitative variables that we assume are measured on the interval level. Some social-science statistics books present correlation first and then regression, whereas others do just the opposite. You need to understand both of these, but which comes first is sort of like asking whether the chicken or the egg came first. In this chapter, I present topics in the following order:

1. Construct a scattergram. This is a graphic representation of the relationship between two variables.

2. Superimpose a regression line. This is a straight line that best describes the linear form of the relationship between two variables.

3. Estimate and interpret a correlation. This tells us the strength of the relationship.

4. Estimate and interpret the regression coefficients. This tells us the functional form of the relationship.

5. Estimate and interpret Spearman's rho as a rank-order correlation for ordinal data.

6. Estimate and interpret the reliability coefficient called alpha. This uses correlation to assess the reliability of a measure.

7. Estimate and interpret kappa as a measure of agreement for categorical data.

In chapter 10, we will expand this process to include multiple correlation and multiple regression. If you have a good understanding of bivariate correlation and regression, you will be ready for chapter 10.

8.2 Scattergrams

Suppose that we are interested in the relationship between an adult man's education and the education his father completed. We believe that the advantages of education are transmitted from one generation to the next. Fathers who have limited education will have sons who have restricted opportunities, and hence they too will have limited education. On the other hand, fathers who have high education will offer their sons opportunities to get more education. When examining a relationship like this, we know that it is not going to be "perfect". We all know adult men who have far more education than their own fathers, and we may know some who have far less.

To understand the relationship between these two variables, let's use the dataset `gss2006_chapter8.dta` (Smith et al. 2015) and create a graph. Because this is a large dataset, a scattergram will have so many dots that it will not make much sense. Suppose that we have 20 father–son dyads that have a father with a score of 15 and a son with a score of 15, but just 1 father–son dyad that has a father with a score of 20 and a son with a score of 10. The 20 dyads and the 1 dyad would each appear as one dot on the graph, creating a visual distortion of the relationship. (We will discuss ways to work around this later.) To manage this problem, limit the scattergram to a random sample of 100 observations by using

```
. use https://www.stata-press.com/data/agis6r/gss2006_chapter8
(General Social Surveys, 1972-2006 [Cumulative File], Dataset 0001)
. sample 100, count
```

How can you get the same result each time?

When you take a random sample of your data for a scattergram or for any other purpose, you may want to make sure you get the same sample if you repeat the process later. Random sampling is done by first generating a *seed* that instructs Stata where to begin the random process. If you have a table of random numbers, generating a seed is equivalent to picking where you will start in the table. By setting the seed at a specific value, you can replicate your results. The easiest way to select your subsample and make sure that you get the same subsample if you repeat the process is with this pair of commands:

```
. set seed 111
. sample 100, count
```

Here I used a seed of 111. You can pick any number, and when you repeat the command using the same number, you will get the same random sample.

Because a father's education comes before his son's, the father's education will be the predictor (the X or independent variable). The son's education will be the outcome (the Y or dependent variable). By convention, a scattergram places the predictor on the horizontal axis and the outcome on the vertical axis.

The interface is helpful when working with scattergrams because scattergrams have so many options that it would be hard to remember them all. Open the dialog box by selecting Graphics ▷ Twoway graph (scatter, line, etc.). The resulting dialog box is shown in figure 8.1.

Figure 8.1. Dialog box for a scattergram

Under the Plots tab, click on Create.... We will use the *Basic plots* and make sure *Scatter* is highlighted. Type `educ` (*Y* variable) and `paeduc` (*X* variable), and click on Accept. This returns you to the main Plots tab. You can add features to the graph by using the other tabs. Click on the if/in tab and type `sex==1` in the *If: (expression)* box, because we want to limit this graph to sons and `sex==1` is the code for males. Click on the Y axis tab and, under *Title*, type `Son's education`. Click on the X axis tab and, under *Title*, type `Father's education`. Using the Titles tab, you can give the graph a title of `Scattergram relating father's education to his son's education` and add a note at the bottom of the graph, `Data source: GSS 2006; random sample of N = 100`. If you click on Submit, you will probably decide the title is too wide for the graph. To make it fit better, you can click on Properties (to the right of the title) in the dialog box and change the *Size* to *Medium*.

Click on Submit. This gives a nice graph, but the *y*-axis title might be too close to the numbers on the *y* axis. If you want to move that title away from the numbers, then go back to the Y axis tab and click on Properties, which is to the right of the title. This gives you several options. Go to the Advanced tab to change the *Inner gap*. Try putting a 5 here. Click on Submit and see how you like the graph.

These dialog boxes are complex, but remember that you are not going to hurt Stata or your data by trying different options. If you do not understand what an option does, just try it and see what happens. You can always return to the default value for the option in the dialog box by clicking on the C icon in the bottom left of the dialog box.

Here is the resulting Stata command. (Notice that in addition to what we have done with the dialog box, I turned the legend off in the Legend tab. The command is listed as you would see it in a do-file with the three forward slashes, ///, used as a line break.) The resulting graph is shown as figure 8.2.

```
twoway (scatter educ paeduc) if sex==1, ytitle(Son's education)        ///
   yscale(titlegap(5)) xtitle(Father's education)                      ///
   title(Scattergram relating father's education to his son's education, ///
   size(medium)) note(Data source: GSS 2006; random sample of N = 100) legend(off)
```

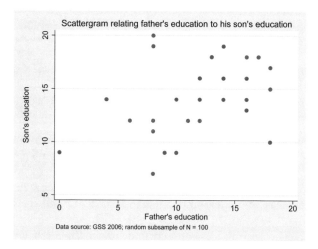

Figure 8.2. Scattergram of son's education on father's education

How do we interpret the resulting scattergram? There is a general pattern that the higher the father's education, the higher his son's education, but there are many exceptions. The data are for the United States. Some countries have a virtual caste system, which permits little opportunity for upward mobility and little risk of downward mobility. In those countries, the scattergram would fall close to a straight line, meaning the father's education largely determined his son's education. In liberal democracies, such as the United States, the relationship is only moderately strong, and there is a lot of room for intergenerational mobility.

Can you think of relationships for which a scattergram would be useful? A gerontologist might want to examine the relationship between a score on the frequency of exercise and the number of accidental falls an older person has had in the last year. Unlike the results in figure 8.2, the older people who exercise more often might have fewer falls. The scatter would start in the upper left and go down if those who exercise more regularly are less prone to accidental falls. An educational psychologist might examine the relationship between parental support and academic performance. All you need is a pair of variables that are interval level or that you are willing to treat as interval level. What happens to the relationship between self-confidence among college students and how long they have been in college? Is the initial level of self-confidence high? Does it drop to a low point during the freshman year, only to gradually increase during the sophomore, junior, and senior years? This is an empirical question whose answer could be illustrated with a scattergram.

Rarely does a scattergram help when you have a very large sample, say, 500 or more observations. However, there is a clever approach in Stata that tries to get around this problem and that works for reasonably sized datasets: the `sunflower` command. Sunflowers are used to represent clusters of observations. Sunflowers vary in the number of "petals" they have. The more petals there are, the more observations are at that particular coordinate point. Even the `sunflower` command is of limited value with really large samples. If you want to try the `sunflower` command, you can enter `help sunflower` to see the various options. When you are in the Viewer window with the help file for the `sunflower` command open, you can select Dialog ▷ sunflower from the menu at the top right corner to open the `sunflower` dialog box. If you have trouble finding a dialog box but you know the name of the command, you can always access the dialog box through the help file in this way.

A more common approach is to add "jitter", which is spherical random noise, to the markers (dots) where there are several observations with the same score on both the X variable and the Y variable. To do this, return to the `twoway` dialog box and click on the Plots tab. Make sure that *Plot 1* is highlighted, and click on *Edit*. Next you will click on Marker properties and click on the Advanced tab. Check the box for *Add jitter to markers* and type 6 for the *Noise factor*. You might want to set the seed at some number, here 222. The resulting command and graph (figure 8.3) are shown below. Notice that this is a more realistic representation of our 100 observations.

```
twoway (scatter educ paeduc, jitter(6) jitterseed(222)) if sex==1,      ///
    ytitle(Son's education) yscale(titlegap(5)) xtitle(Father's education)  ///
    title(Scattergram relating father's education to his son's education,  ///
    size(medium)) note(Data source: GSS 2006; random sample of N = 100) legend(off)
```

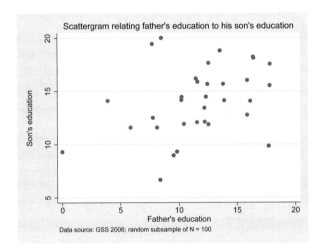

Figure 8.3. Scattergram of son's education on father's education with "jitter"

Predictors and outcomes

Different statistics books and different substantive areas vary in the terms they use for predictors and outcomes. We need to be comfortable with all these different terms. A scattergram is a great place to really understand the terminology because we must have one variable on the horizontal x axis and another variable on the vertical y axis. Sometimes it helps to think of the X variable as a cause and the Y variable as an effect. This works if we can make the statement "X is a cause of Y". It makes sense to say that the father's education is a cause of his son's education rather than the other way around. We say "a" cause rather than "the" cause because many variables will contribute to how much education a son will achieve.

People who are uncomfortable with cause–effect terminology often call the X variable the independent variable and the Y variable the dependent variable. Which variable is dependent? In the scattergram, we would say that the son's education is dependent on his father's education. We would not say that the father's education depends on his son's education. The dependent variable is the Y variable, and the other variable is the X variable or the independent variable—because it does not depend. That is, a father's education does not depend on his son's education.

Other people prefer to think of an outcome variable and a predictor. We do not need to know what causes something, but we can discover what predicts it. The son's education is an outcome, and the father's education is the predictor. Predictors may or may not meet a philosopher's definition of a cause. Couples who fight a lot before they get married are more likely to fight after they are married, so we would say that conflict prior to marriage predicts conflict after marriage. The premarriage conflict is the predictor, and the postmarriage conflict is the outcome.

Many statisticians call all predictors covariates. This terminology avoids making causality claims that would be hard to justify. A father's education is a covariate of his son's education. Other covariates of a son's education would be his mother's education, his family's income, his race/ethnicity, and so on. A number of researchers use a statistical analysis called analysis of covariance. They use the term covariate differently as a continuous independent variable. In using a father's education to predict his son's education, you might need to consider the father's income race/ethnicity as a covariate. They might want to know if the relationship between father's and son's education varied somehow depending on the father's income.

Predictors and outcomes, continued

Sometimes none of these terms makes a lot of sense. Wives who have high marital satisfaction more often have husbands who have high marital satisfaction. Both variables depend on each other and simultaneously influence each other. Sometimes we refer to these kinds of variables as having reciprocal relationships. In such a case, which variable is the X variable and which is the Y variable is arbitrary.

8.3   Plotting the regression line

Later in this chapter, we will learn how to do a regression analysis. For now, I will simply introduce the concept and show how to plot it on the scattergram. The regression line shows the form of the relationship between two variables. Ordinarily, we assume that the relationship is linear. For example, what is the relationship between income and education? To answer this question, we need to know how much income you could expect to make if you had no education (intercept or constant) and then how much more income you can expect for each additional year of education (slope). Suppose that you could expect to make \$10,000 per year, even with no formal education, and for each additional year of education, you could expect to earn another \$3,000. You could write this as an equation

$$\text{Estimated income} = 10000 + 3000(\texttt{educ})$$

where 10000 is the estimated income if you had no education, that is, $\texttt{educ} = 0$. This is called the intercept or constant. The 3000 is how much more you could expect for each additional year of $\texttt{educ}$, and it is called the slope. Thus a person who has 12 years of education would have an estimated income of $10000 + 3000(12) = 46000$ or \$46,000.

A symbolic way of writing a regression equation is

$$\widehat{Y} = a + b(X)$$

where a is the intercept or constant, and b is the slope. The $\widehat{Y}$ (pronounced Y-hat) is the dependent variable ($\texttt{income}$), and the circumflex means that it is estimated (many statistics texts use a ⌢ over the Y for an estimated value). The X is the independent variable ($\texttt{educ}$). Let's use the example relating educational attainment of fathers and sons to see how the regression line appears. We will not get the values of a and b until later, but we will get a graph with the line drawn for us.

Return to your Plots tab, or if you closed the dialog box by clicking on OK instead of Submit, you will need to reopen it by selecting Graphics ▷ Twoway graph (scatter, line, etc.). We already have the information entered for *Plot 1*, the scattergram. Click on *Create....* Previously, we selected *Basic plots* and *Scatter*. This time, we select *Fit plots* and make sure that *Linear prediction* is highlighted. We type $\texttt{educ}$ and $\texttt{paeduc}$ as the

Y variable and X variable, respectively. Click on **Submit**, and the graph appears as shown in figure 8.4.

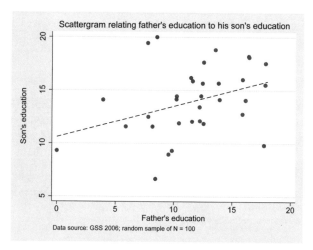

Figure 8.4. Scattergram of son's education on father's education with a regression line

The linear regression line gives you a good sense of the relationship. It shows how the higher the father's education is, the higher his son's education is on average. The observations are not extremely close to the regression line, meaning that there is substantial intergenerational mobility. Sons whose fathers have little education are expected to have more education than their fathers, but sons whose fathers have a lot of education are expected to have a little less education than their fathers. Can you see this in the scattergram? Pick a father who has 5 years of education, $X = 5$. Project a line straight up to the regression line and then straight over to the Y axis, and you can see that we would expect his son to have about $Y = 10$ years of education. Pick a father who has 20 years of education, $X = 20$. Can you see that we would expect his son to have less education than he did?

8.4 An alternative to producing a scattergram, binscatter

Using a scattergram with a large sample is impractical, and taking a subsample of observations or adding the `jitter()` option is an imperfect solution. Michael Stepner (2013) is the author of a community-contributed command, `binscatter`. This command is based on an earlier version by Jessica Laird and developed with guidance from Raj Chetty, John Friedman, and Lazlo Sandor. It produces a remarkably simple solution for conveying a relationship by plotting the mean value of the dependent variable for equal-sized bins on the continuous independent variable. Rather than having hundreds or thousands of dots on the scattergram, we have a small number of means. The set of mean outcome scores for the bins gives a clearer idea of the relationship than does a scatter when there are a large number of observations. We will illustrate this by using a few of the commands borrowed from the `binscatter` help file.

First, you need to install the command, because it is not part of official Stata. In your Command window, type `ssc install binscatter`. This will install the command and the help file. The command can do much more than I illustrate, so you might want to read the help file, `help binscatter`. The help file uses a dataset that is installed with Stata, so you can type

```
. sysuse nlsw88, clear
. keep if age > 34 & age < 45 & race < 3
```

The first command opens the 1988 National Longitudinal Survey of Women. The second command restricts our sample to people who are between ages 35 and 44 and who are either white or black. We want to know the relationship between tenure on a job and a woman's wages. Now type a `scatter` command and a `binscatter` command to see the differences:

Here is the `scatter` command, which creates the graph in figure 8.5.

```
. scatter wage tenure, mcolor(%30)
```

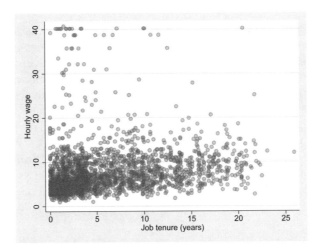

Figure 8.5. Scattergram relating hourly wage to job tenure

We have over 2,000 observations in this dataset. We added the `mcolor(%30)` option to our `scatter` command to make the plotted points transparent. If you are working with the dialog box, you can find this option labeled *Opacity* on the same *Marker properties* dialog box where we found the option for `jitter()`. In our graph, the color of each marker has only 30% opacity, so coordinate points that represent more observations appear darker than those that represent fewer observations. The transparency helps us visualize patterns in relationships when we plot many observations. In this case, there is yet more we could learn about the relationship, especially in the lower left corner of the graph.

The `binscatter` command divides the independent variable, `tenure`, into a series of bins. The default is 20 bins. (If the independent variable has fewer than 20 distinct values, `binscatter` will compute the mean for each value.) `binscatter` then places a dot for the mean on the outcome variable, `wage`, for each bin. Here is the `binscatter` command, followed by the resulting graph in figure 8.6.

```
. binscatter wage tenure
```

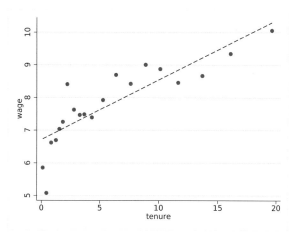

Figure 8.6. Average wage by tenure

As you can see, the `binscatter` command also places a linear regression line on the figure. Unlike the scattergram, the graph created by `binscatter` shows a consistent increase in wages over years. We would have missed this finding completely if we relied on the scattergram. Examining the graph created by `binscatter`, you might say that a curve would fit better. Fitting a curve will be covered in chapter 10, but the option for `binscatter` is `line(qfit)`. We will not show the result, but you can run the command yourself to see how the curve fits.

Can you see an alternative to using a curve? Carefully examining the `binscatter` graph, we see that there is a very rapid increase in wages the first 2 or 3 years. After that, an increase is evident, but the increase is less dramatic. We could use two linear regressions. The point of discontinuity looks to be around 3 years of tenure. Between 0 and 3 years, there is a dramatic increase, but from 3 years to 20 years, there is a much less dramatic increase in wages. Here is the `binscatter` command followed by the resulting graph in figure 8.7. Notice that the `rd(3.0)` option is the point of discontinuity where the rate of growth changes. You might try this option with slightly different values, such as `rd(2.5)`. Do you see if a different possible point of discontinuity produces similar results?

```
. binscatter wage tenure, rd(3.0)
```

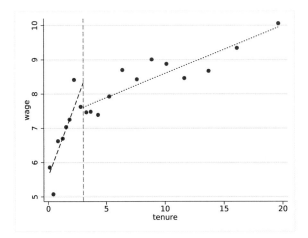

Figure 8.7. Relationship between wages and tenure with a discontinuity in the relationship at 3 years

We might want to see if this relationship varies by race. We may hypothesize that the rate of increase is less dramatic for blacks than it is for whites because of discrimination. We have already restricted our sample to blacks and whites, and we can show a separate result for each group by using

```
. binscatter wage tenure, rd(3.0) by(race)
```

Figure 8.8 shows the result. It appears that both black and white women have a positive relationship between wages and tenure and the discontinuity applies to both groups. The biggest contrast is that black women are systematically paid less than white women regardless of their tenure. The rate of increase does not appear to be greater for whites than it is for blacks, but the main take away is that black women have lower wages regardless of their tenure. In figure 8.8, I used the Graph Editor to slightly modify the graph produced by `binscatter`.

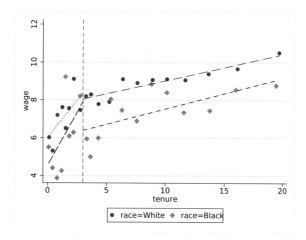

Figure 8.8. Relationship between wages and tenure with a discontinuity in the relationship at 3 years; whites shown with solid lines and blacks shown with dashed lines

8.5   Correlation

Your statistics textbook gives you the formulas for computing correlation, and if you have done a few of these by hand, you will love the ease of using Stata. We will not worry about the formulas. Correlation measures how close the observations are to the regression line. We need to be cautious in interpreting a correlation coefficient. Correlation does not tell us how steep the relationship is; that measure comes from the regression. You may have a steep relationship or an almost flat relationship, and both relationships could have the same correlation. Suppose that the correlation between education and income is $r = 0.3$ for women and $r = 0.5$ for men. Does this mean that education has a bigger payoff for men than it does for women? We really cannot know the answer from the correlation. The correlation tells us almost nothing about the form of the relationship. The fact that the r is larger for men than it is for women is not evidence that men get a bigger payoff from an additional year of education. Only the regression line will tell us that. The $r = 0.5$ for men means that the observations for men are closer to the regression line than are the observations for women ($r = 0.3$) and that the income of men is more predictable than that of women. Correlation also tells us whether the regression line goes up (r will be positive) or down (r will be negative). Strictly speaking, correlation measures the strength of the relationship only for how close the dots are to the regression line.

Bivariate correlation is used by social scientists in many ways. Sometimes we will be interested simply in the correlation between two variables. We might be interested in the relationship between calorie consumption per day and weight loss. If you discover that $r = -0.5$, this would indicate a fairly strong relationship. Generally, a correlation of $|r| = 0.1$ is a weak relationship, $|r| = 0.3$ is a moderate relationship, and $|r| = 0.5$ is a strong relationship. An r of -0.3 and an r of 0.3 are equally strong. The negative correlation means that as X goes up, Y goes down; the positive correlation means that as X goes up, Y goes up.

We might be interested in the relationship between several variables. We could compare three relationships between 1) weight loss and calorie consumption, 2) weight loss and the time spent in daily exercise, and 3) weight loss and the number of days per week a person exercises. We could use the three correlations to see which predictor is more correlated with weight loss.

Suppose that we wanted to create a scale to measure a variable, such as political conservatism. We would use several specific questions and combine them to get a score on the scale. We can compute a correlation matrix of the individual items. All of them should be at least moderately correlated with each other because they were selected to measure the same concept.

When we estimate a correlation, we also need to report its statistical significance level. The test of statistical significance of a correlation depends on the size or substantive significance of a correlation in the sample and depends on the size of the sample. An $r = 0.5$ might be observed in a very small sample, just by chance, even though there were no correlations in the population. On the other hand, an $r = 0.1$, although a weak substantive relationship, might be statistically significant if we had a huge sample.

Statistical and substantive significance

It is easy to confuse statistical significance and substantive significance. Usually, we want to find a correlation that is substantively significant (r is moderate or strong in our sample) and statistically significant (the population correlation is almost certainly not 0). With a very large sample, we can find statistical significance even when $r = 0.1$ or less. What is important about this is that we are confident that the population correlation is not 0 and that it is very small. Some researchers mistakenly assume that a statistically significant correlation automatically means that it is important when it may mean just the opposite—we are confident it is not very important.

With a very small sample, we can find a substantively significant $r = 0.5$ or more that is not statistically significant. Even though we observe a strong relationship in our small sample, we are not justified in generalizing this finding to the population. In fact, we must acknowledge that the correlation in the population might even be 0.

- Substantive significance is based on the size of the correlation.

- Statistical significance is based on the probability that you could get the observed correlation by chance if the population correlation is 0.

Now let's look at an example that we downloaded from the UCLA Stata Portal. As mentioned at the beginning of the book, this portal is an exceptional source of tutorials, including movies on how to use Stata. The data used are from a study called High School and Beyond. Here you will download a part of this dataset used for illustrating how to use Stata to estimate correlations. Go to your command line, and enter the command

    . use https://stats.oarc.ucla.edu/stat/data/hsb2, clear

You will get a message back that you have downloaded 200 cases, and your listing of variables will show the subset of the High School and Beyond dataset. If your computer is not connected to the Internet, you should use one that is connected, download this file, save it to a flash disk, and then transfer it to your computer. This dataset is also available from this book's webpage.

Say that we are interested in the bivariate correlations between `read`, `write`, `math`, and `science` skills for these 200 students. We are also interested in the bivariate relationships between each of these skills and each students' socioeconomic status and between each of these skills and each students' gender. We believe that socioeconomic status is more related to these skills than gender is.

It is reasonable to treat the skills as continuous variables measured at close to the interval level, and some statistics books say that interval-level measurement is a critical assumption. However, it is problematic to treat socioeconomic status and gender as continuous variables. If we run a tabulation of socioeconomic status and gender, `tab1 ses female`, we will see the problem. Socioeconomic status has just three levels (low, middle, and high) and gender has just two levels (male and female). This dataset has all values labeled, so the default tabulation does not show the numbers assigned to these codes. We can run `codebook ses female` and see that `female` is coded 1 for girls and 0 for boys. Similarly, `ses` is coded 1 for low, 2 for middle, and 3 for high. If you have installed the `fre` command using `ssc install fre`, you can use the command `fre female ses` to show both the value labels and the codes, as we discussed in section 5.4. We will compute the correlations anyway and see if they make sense.

Stata has two commands for doing a correlation: `correlate` and `pwcorr`. The `correlate` command runs the correlation using a casewise deletion (some books call this listwise deletion) option. Casewise deletion means that if any observation is missing for any of the variables, even just one variable, the observation will be dropped from the analysis. Many datasets, especially those based on surveys, have many missing values. For example, it is common for about 30% of people to refuse to report their income. Some survey participants will skip a page of questions by mistake. Casewise deletion can introduce serious bias and greatly reduce the working sample size. Casewise deletion is a problem for external validity or the ability to generalize when there are a lot of missing data. Many studies using casewise deletion will end up dropping 30% or more of the observations, and this makes generalizing a problem even though the total sample may have been representative.

The `pwcorr` command uses a pairwise deletion to estimate each correlation based on all the people who answered each pair of items. For example, if Julia has a score on `write` and `read` but nothing else, she will be included in estimating the correlation between `write` and `read`. Pairwise deletion introduces its own problems. Each correlation may be based on a different subsample of observations, namely, those observations who answered both variables in the pair. We might have 500 people who answered both `var1` and `var2`, 400 people who answered both `var1` and `var3`, and 450 people who answered both `var2` and `var3`. Because each correlation is based on a different subsample, under extreme circumstances it is possible to get a set of correlations that would be impossible for a population.

To open the `correlate` dialog box, select Statistics ▷ Summaries, tables, and tests ▷ Summary and descriptive statistics ▷ Correlations and covariances. To open the `pwcorr` dialog box, select Statistics ▷ Summaries, tables, and tests ▷ Summary and descriptive statistics ▷ Pairwise correlations. Because the command is so simple, we can just enter the command directly.

```
. correlate read write math science ses female
(obs=200)

                 |     read    write     math  science      ses   female
-----------------+------------------------------------------------------
            read |   1.0000
           write |   0.5968   1.0000
            math |   0.6623   0.6174   1.0000
         science |   0.6302   0.5704   0.6307   1.0000
             ses |   0.2933   0.2075   0.2725   0.2829   1.0000
          female |  -0.0531   0.2565  -0.0293  -0.1277  -0.1250   1.0000
```

We can read the correlation table going either across the rows or down the columns. The $r = 0.63$ between `science` and `read` indicates that these two skills are strongly related. Having good reading skills is probably helpful to having good science skills. All the skills are weakly to moderately related to socioeconomic status, `ses` ($r = 0.21$ to $r = 0.29$). Having a higher socioeconomic status does result in higher expected scores on all the skills for the 200 adolescents in the sample.

A dichotomous variable, such as gender, that is coded with a 0 for one category (man) and 1 for the other category (woman) is called a dummy variable or indicator variable. Thus `female` is a dummy variable (a useful standard is to name the variable to match the category coded as 1). When you are using a dummy variable, the stronger the correlation is, the greater impact the dummy variable has on the outcome variable. The last row of the correlation matrix shows the correlation between `female` and each skill. The $r = 0.26$ between being a girl and writing skills means that girls (they were coded 1 on `female`) have higher writing skills than boys (they were coded 0 on `female`), and this is almost a moderate relationship. You have probably read that girls are not as skilled in math as are boys. The $r = -0.03$ between `female` and `math` means that in this sample, the girls had just slightly lower scores than boys (remember an $|r| = 0.1$ is weak, so anything close to 0 is very weak). If, instead of having 200 observations, we had 20,000, this small of a correlation would be statistically significant. Still, it is best described as very weak, whether it is statistically significant or not. The math advantage that is widely attributed to boys is very small compared with the writing advantage attributed to girls.

Stata's `correlate` command does not give us the significance of the correlations when using casewise deletion. The `pwcorr` command is a much more general command to estimate correlations because it has several important options that are not available using the `correlate` command. Indeed, the `pwcorr` command can do casewise/listwise deletion as well as pairwise deletion. When you are generating a set of correlations, you usually want to know the significance level, and it would be nice to have an asterisk attached to each correlation that is significant at the 0.05 level. You can use the dialog box Statistics ▷ Summaries, tables, and tests ▷ Summary and descriptive statistics ▷Correlations and covariances for the `correlate` command or Statistics ▷ Summaries, tables, and tests ▷ Summary and descriptive statistics ▷ Pairwise correlations for the `pwcorr` command. You can see additional options on the dialog boxes, but we can also simply enter the command directly. We use the same command as we did for `correlate`, substituting `pwcorr` for `correlate` and adding `listwise`, `sig`, and `star(5)` as options:

```
. pwcorr read write math science socst ses female, listwise sig star(5)
```

	read	write	math	science	socst	ses	female
read	1.0000						
write	0.5968* 0.0000	1.0000					
math	0.6623* 0.0000	0.6174* 0.0000	1.0000				
science	0.6302* 0.0000	0.5704* 0.0000	0.6307* 0.0000	1.0000			
socst	0.6215* 0.0000	0.6048* 0.0000	0.5445* 0.0000	0.4651* 0.0000	1.0000		
ses	0.2933* 0.0000	0.2075* 0.0032	0.2725* 0.0001	0.2829* 0.0000	0.3319* 0.0000	1.0000	
female	-0.0531 0.4553	0.2565* 0.0002	-0.0293 0.6801	-0.1277 0.0714	0.0524 0.4614	-0.1250 0.0778	1.0000

In this table, the listwise correlation between science and reading is $r = 0.63$. The asterisk indicates this is significant at the 0.05 level. Below the correlation is the probability and we can say that the correlation is significant at the $p < 0.001$ level. The reported probability is for a two-tailed test. If you had a one-tailed hypothesis, you could divide the probability in half.

If you want the correlations using pairwise deletion, you would also want to know how many observations were used for estimating each correlation. The command for pairwise deletion that gives you the number of observations, the significance, and an asterisk for correlations significant at the 0.05 level is

```
pwcorr read write math science ses female, obs sig star(5)
```

Notice that the only change was to replace the `listwise` option with the `obs` option.

Multiple-comparison procedures with correlations

When you are estimating several correlations, the reported significance level given by the `sig` option can be misleading. If you made 100 independent estimates of a correlation that was 0 in the population, you would expect to get five significant results by chance (using the 5% level). In this example, we had 21 correlations, and because we are considering all of them, we might want to adjust the probability estimate. One of the ways to adjust the probability estimate in the `pwcorr` command is with the option `bon`, short for the Bonferroni multiple-comparison procedure. You can get this procedure simply by adding the `bon` option at any point after the comma in the `pwcorr` command. The complete command would be (add the `listwise` option if you want to use casewise/listwise deletion)

```
pwcorr read write math science socst ses female, bon obs sig star(5)
```

Without this correction, the correlation between `write` and `ses`, $r = 0.21$, had a $p = 0.0032$ and was significant at the 0.01 level. With the Bonferroni adjustment, the $r = 0.21$ does not change, but the correlation now has a $p = 0.067$ and is no longer statistically significant. (An alternative multiple-comparison procedure uses the `sidak` option, which produces the Šidák-adjusted significance level.) It is difficult to give simple advice on when you should or should not use a multiple-comparison adjustment. If your hypothesis is that a certain pattern of correlations will be significant and this involves the set of all the correlations (here, 21), the multiple-comparison adjustment is appropriate. If your focus is on individual correlations, as it probably is here, then the adjustment is not necessary.

8.6 Regression

Earlier you learned how to plot a regression line on a scattergram. Now we will focus on how to estimate the regression line itself. Suppose that you are interested in the relationship between how many hours per week a person works and how much occupational prestige he or she has. You expect that careers with high occupational prestige require more work rather than less. Therefore, you expect that the more hours respondents work, the more occupational prestige they will have. This is certainly not a perfect relationship, and we have all known people who work many hours, even doing two jobs, who do not have high occupational prestige. We will use the General Social Survey 2006 dataset (`gss2006_chapter8_selected.dta`) for this section. It has variables called `prestg80`, which is a scale of occupational prestige, and `hrs1`, which is the number of hours respondents worked last week in their primary jobs.

Before doing the regression procedure, we should summarize the variables:

```
. use https://www.stata-press.com/data/agis6r/gss2006_chapter8_selected
(General Social Surveys, 1972-2006 [Cumulative File], Dataset 0001)
. summarize prestg80 hrs1
    Variable |        Obs        Mean    Std. dev.        Min         Max
-------------+-----------------------------------------------------------
    prestg80 |      4,270    44.16745    13.99946         17          86
        hrs1 |      2,739    42.07631    14.23166          1          89
```

This summary gives us a sense of the scale of the variables. The independent variable, hrs1, is measured in hours with a mean of $M = 42.08$ hours and a standard deviation of $\mathrm{SD} = 14.23$ hours. The outcome variable, prestg80, has corresponding values of $M = 44.17$ and $\mathrm{SD} = 14.00$. A scattergram does not help because there are so many cases that no pattern is clear. A correlation—pwcorr prestg80 hrs1, obs sig—tells us that $r = 0.16$, $p < 0.001$. We can interpret this as a fairly weak relationship that is statistically significant.

To estimate the regression, open the regress dialog box by selecting Statistics ▷ Linear models and related ▷ Linear regression. This dialog box is shown in figure 8.9.

Figure 8.9. The Model tab of the regress dialog box

Enter the *Dependent variable*, prestg80, and the *Independent variable*, hrs1. Click on the Reporting tab and check *Standardized beta coefficients*. Click on Submit to obtain the following command and results:

```
. regress prestg80 hrs1, beta

      Source |       SS           df       MS      Number of obs   =     2,715
-------------+----------------------------------   F(1, 2713)      =     67.32
       Model |  13125.035          1   13125.035   Prob > F        =    0.0000
    Residual |  528901.224      2,713  194.950691   R-squared       =    0.0242
-------------+----------------------------------   Adj R-squared   =    0.0239
       Total |  542026.259      2,714  199.714908   Root MSE        =    13.962


     prestg80 | Coefficient  Std. err.      t    P>|t|                     Beta
-------------+----------------------------------------------------------------
        hrs1 |   .1546416   .0188468     8.21   0.000                 .1556109
       _cons |   38.14733   .8362129    45.62   0.000                        .
```

Understanding the format of this regression command is important because more-advanced procedures that generalize from this command follow the same command structure. The first variable after the name of the command, that is, `prestg80`, is always the dependent variable. The second variable, `hrs1`, is the independent variable. When we do multiple regression in chapter 10, we will simply add more independent variables. When we do logistic regression in chapter 11, we will simply change the name of the command. After the comma, we have the option `beta`. This will give us beta weights, which are represented as β and will be interpreted below.

The table in the upper left of the output shows the `Source`, `SS`, `df`, and `MS`. This is an analysis of variance (ANOVA) table summarizing the results from an ANOVA perspective (ANOVA is covered in chapter 9), and we will ignore this table for now. In the upper right corner is the number of observations, $N = 2715$, representing the number of people who have been measured on both variables. We also have an F test, which we will cover more fully in the ANOVA chapter. The larger the F ratio is, the greater the significance. Like the t test and chi-squared, F also involves the idea of degrees of freedom. There are two values for the degrees of freedom associated with an F test: the number of predictors (here, 1) and $N - 2$ (here, 2,713). Just below the number of observations are $F(1, 2713) = 67.32$ and the probability level (Prob > $F = 0.0000$). Any probability less than 0.0001 is reported as 0.0000 by Stata. We could write this as $F(1, 2713) = 67.32$, $p < 0.001$. Thus there is a statistically significant relationship between hours worked and the prestige of the job.

Is this relationship strong? We have two values, namely, R^2 and the adjusted R^2, that serve to measure the strength of the relationship. When we are doing bivariate regression, R^2 is simply $r \times r$. Similarly, $r = \sqrt{R^2}$, but we need to decide on the sign of the r-value—whether it is positive or negative. For our model, $R^2 = 0.02$, meaning that the hours worked explain 2% of the variation in the prestige rating. Because of the large sample, this R^2, although obviously weak because it does not explain 98% of the variation in prestige, is still statistically significant. When there are many predictors and a small sample, neither of which apply here, some report the adjusted R^2. The adjusted R^2 removes the part of R^2 that would be expected just by chance. Whenever the adjusted R^2 is substantially smaller than the R^2 because there is a small sample relative to the number of predictors, it is best to report both values.

The root mean squared error, `Root MSE = 13.96`, has a strange name, but it is a useful piece of information. The `summarize` command showed SD = 14.00 for our dependent variable, `prestg80`. The root mean squared error is the standard deviation around the regression line. Recall when we did a plot of a regression line. If the observations are close to this line, the standard deviation around it should be much smaller than the standard deviation around the overall mean. It is not surprising that our R^2 is so small, given that the standard deviation around the regression line, 13.96, is nearly as big as the standard deviation around the mean, 14.00. In other words, the regression line does little to improve our prediction.

The bottom table gives us the regression results. The first column lists the outcome variable, `prestg80`, followed by the predictor, `hrs1`, and the constant, called `_cons`. This last variable is the constant, or intercept. The equation would be written as

$$\text{Estimated prestige} = 38.15 + 0.15(\text{hours})$$

Remember that $M = 44.17$ and SD = 14.00 for prestige. If we did not know how many hours a person worked per week, we might guess that they had a prestige score of 44.17 given that 44.17 is the mean prestige score. The regression equation lets us estimate prestige differently depending on how many hours a person works per week. This equation tell us that a person who worked 0 hours would have a prestige score of 38.15 (the intercept or constant), and for each additional hour he or she worked, the prestige score would go up 0.15. For example, a person who worked 40 hours a week would have a predicted prestige score of (approximately, because we have rounded) $38.15 + 0.15(40) = 44.15$, but a person who worked 60 hours a week would have a predicted prestige score of $38.15 + 0.15(60) = 47.15$. This shows a small payoff in prestige for working longer hours. The payoff is statistically significant but not very big.

The column labeled `Std. err.` is the standard error. The `t` is computed by dividing the regression coefficient by its standard error; for example, $0.1546416/0.0188468 = 8.21$. The `t` is evaluated using $N - 2$ degrees of freedom. We do not need to look up the t-value because Stata reports the probability as 0.000. We would report this as $t(2713) = 8.21$, $p < 0.001$. You often see researchers just report whether an effect is statistically significant but utterly fail to report the strength of the relationship. Calculate a few scenarios like this where you see how the predicted value of the dependent variable varies for a specified difference in the independent variable. A lot of people have 40-hour work weeks. Not many people work 60 hours a week. A difference of 3 points on a prestige scale where a standard deviation is about 14 is a small effect for a 50% difference in the length of the work week. Giving your audience examples like this gives meaning to what might otherwise be dry statistical results.

The final column gives us a beta weight, $\beta = 0.16$. When we have just one predictor, the β weight is always the same as the correlation (this is not the case when there are multiple predictors). The β is a measure of the effect size and is interpreted much like a correlation with $\beta = 0.10$ being weak, 0.30 being moderate, and 0.50 being strong.

Your statistics book may also show you how to do confidence intervals. There are two types of these: a confidence interval around the regression coefficient and a confidence interval around the regression line. Stata gives you the former as an option for regression and the latter as an option for the scattergram. First, let's do the confidence interval around the regression coefficient. Reopen the **regress** dialog box and click on the Reporting tab. This time, make sure that the *Standardized beta coefficients* box is not checked. By unchecking this option, you automatically get the confidence interval in place of β. The command is the same except there is no option.

```
. regress prestg80 hrs1
```

Source	SS	df	MS			
				Number of obs	=	2,715
				F(1, 2713)	=	67.32
Model	13125.035	1	13125.035	Prob > F	=	0.0000
Residual	528901.224	2,713	194.950691	R-squared	=	0.0242
				Adj R-squared	=	0.0239
Total	542026.259	2,714	199.714908	Root MSE	=	13.962

prestg80	Coefficient	Std. err.	t	P>|t|	[95% conf. interval]	
hrs1	.1546416	.0188468	8.21	0.000	.117686	.1915972
_cons	38.14733	.8362129	45.62	0.000	36.50765	39.78701

All of this is identical, except that where we had β, we now have a 95% confidence interval for each regression coefficient. The effect of an additional hour of work on prestige is $b = 0.15$. (Do not confuse $b = 0.15$ with $\beta = 0.16$ from the previous example.) The bs and βs are usually different values. The 95% confidence interval for b has a range from 0.12 to 0.19. Because a value of 0 is not included in the confidence interval (a 0 value signifies no relationship), we know that the slope is statistically significant. It could have been as little as 0.12 or as much as 0.19. We would report this by stating that we are 95% confident that the interval of 0.12 to 0.19 contains the true slope.

The second type of confidence interval is on the overall regression line. We will run into trouble using the regression line to predict cases that are very high or very low on the predictor. Usually, there are just a few people at the tails of the distribution, so we do not have as much information there as we do in the middle. We also get to areas that make no sense or where there is likely a misunderstanding. For example, predicting the occupational prestige of a person who works 0 hours a week makes no sense, but it does not make much more sense to predict it for somebody who works just 1 or 2 hours a week. Similarly, if a person said they worked 140 hours a week, they probably misunderstood the question because hardly anybody actually works 140 hours a week on a regular basis given that there are only 168 hours in a week. That would be 20 hours a day, 7 days a week! On the other hand, there are lots of people who work 30–50 hours a week, and here we have much more information for making a prediction. Thus if we put a band around the regression line to represent our confidence, it would be narrowest near the middle of the distribution on the independent variable and widest at the ends.

This relationship is easy to represent with a graph. If we use the menu system, selecting Graphics ▷ Twoway graph (scatter, line, etc.) opens the dialog box we need. Next click on *Create...*. Then click on *Fit plots* and highlight *Linear prediction w/CI*. Finally, we enter our two variables. The results are shown in figure 8.10.

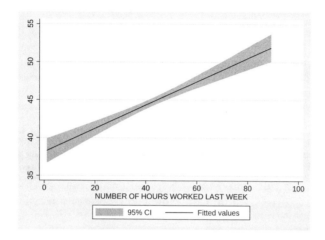

Figure 8.10. Confidence band around regression prediction

8.7 Spearman's rho: Rank-order correlation for ordinal data

Spearman's rho, ρ_s, is the correlation between two variables that are treated as ranks. This procedure converts the variables to ranks (1st, 2nd, ..., nth) before estimating the correlation. For example, if the ages of five observations are 18, 29, 35, 61, and 20, these five participants would be assigned ranks of 1 for 18, 3 for 29, 4 for 35, 5 for 61, and 2 for 20. If we had a measure of liberalism for these five cases, we could convert that to a rank as well. Here are the data (`spearman.dta`) for this simple example:

```
. use https://www.stata-press.com/data/agis6r/spearman, clear
. list
```

	age	liberal	rankage	ranklib
1.	18	90	1	4.5
2.	29	90	3	4.5
3.	35	80	4	2
4.	61	50	5	1
5.	20	89	2	3

Ideally, all the scores (and hence, the ranks) would be unique. Stata will assign an average value when there are ties. The two observations who have a score of 90 on `liberal` occupy the fourth and fifth (highest) rank. Because they are tied, they are both assigned a rank score of 4.5. Computing the correlation between `age` and `liberal` by using the command `corr age liberal`, we obtain an r of -0.97. Computing the correlation between the ranked data by using the command `corr rankage ranklib`, we obtain an r of -0.82. This is lower because the one extreme case (`age = 61`, `liberal = 50`) inflates the Pearson correlation, but this case is not extreme when ranked data are used.

Spearman's rho is a correlation of ranked data. To save the time of converting the variables to ranks and then doing a Pearson's correlation, Stata has a special command: `spearman`. Here we could run the command `spearman age liberal` to yield $\rho_s = -0.82$.

8.8   Power analysis with correlation

Power analysis can be used for a single correlation against a null hypothesis that there is no correlation. First, you need to specify the minimum correlation you would find substantively or practically important. Say you decide that you need power only to detect a population correlation of 0.20. How many observations will you need in your sample?

H_o: There is no correlation in the population.

H_a: There is a population correlation of 0.20.

Power $= 0.80$

$\alpha = 0.05$

Question: How many observations do I need?

Select Statistics ▷ Power, precision, and sample size. In the *Power, precision, and sample-size analysis* Control Panel, expand the Population parameter menu, and select Correlations from the left pane. Then click on Fisher's z test comparing one correlation to a reference value from the right pane. The resulting dialog box appears in figure 8.11.

Figure 8.11. Power, precision, and sample size dialog box for one correlation

Under *Compute*, we select *Sample size* because this is what we want to know. We enter the alpha value of 0.05 as the *Significance level* and 0.8 as the *Power*. Under *Effect size*, we enter 0 as the *Null* value of the population correlation and 0.20 as the *Alternative* value. The resulting command, **power onecorrelation**, displays two parameters: 0 for the null hypothesis and 0.20 for the alternative hypothesis. The power of 0.80 and alpha of 0.05 do not appear because they are the default. Here is the command along with the result:

```
. power onecorrelation 0 0.20

Performing iteration ...

Estimated sample size for a one-sample correlation test
Fisher's z test
H0: r = r0  versus  Ha: r != r0

Study parameters:
        alpha =    0.0500
        power =    0.8000
        delta =    0.2000
           r0 =    0.0000
           ra =    0.2000

Estimated sample size:
            N =       194
```

From these results, we see that we need $N = 194$ observations in our sample to have a power of 0.80 and an alpha of 0.05 and a two-tailed test to detect a population correlation of 0.20 as statistically significant.

We can reverse this process and see what the power is for a given sample size. Suppose a colleague says that she did not find any statistically significant relationship between self-confidence and years of education. She says she has a correlation of $r = 0.40$ from a sample of 15 people, but it was not significant at the $\alpha = 0.05$ level. Did she have sufficient power to say this is a meaningful finding?

We open the same dialog box, but this time we select *Power* under *Compute* and keep the *Significance level* at 0.05. Now we enter 15 as the *Sample size*. We enter 0 for the *Null* hypothesis and 0.40 for the *Alternative* hypothesis under *Effect size*. We keep this as a *Two-sided test*. Try this. What power do you get? What does this mean for how confident we are in her finding?

8.9   Summary

Scattergrams, correlations, and regressions are great ways to evaluate the relationship between two variables.

- The scattergram helps us visualize the relationship between two variables and is usually most helpful when there are relatively few observations.

- The correlation is a measure of the strength of the relationship between two variables. Here it is important to recognize that it measures the strength of a particular form of the relationship. The other examples have used a linear regression line as the form of the relationship. Although it is not covered here, it is possible for regression to have other forms of the relationship.

- The regression analysis tells us the form of the relationship. Using this line, we can estimate how much the dependent variable changes for each unit change in the independent variable.

- The standardized regression coefficient, β, measures the strength of a relationship and is identical to the correlation for bivariate regression.

- You have learned how to compute Spearman's rho for rank-order data, and you now understand its relationship to Pearson's r.

8.10   Exercises

1. Use gss2006_chapter8.dta. Imagine that you heard somebody say that there was no reason to provide more educational opportunities for women because so many of them just stay at home anyway. You have a variable measuring education, educ, and a variable measuring hours worked in the last week, hrs1. Do a

correlation and regression of hours worked in the last week on years of education. Then do this separately for women and for men. Interpret the correlation and the slope for the overall sample and then for women and for men separately. Is there an element of truth to what you heard?

2. Use `gss2006_chapter8.dta`. What is the relationship between the hours a person works and the hours his or her spouse works? Do this for women and for men separately. Compute the correlation, the regression results, and the scattergrams. Interpret each of these. Next test if the correlation is statistically significant and interpret the results.

3. Use `gss2006_chapter8.dta`. Repeat figure 8.2 using your own subsample of 250 observations. Then repeat the figure using a `jitter(3)` option. Compare the two figures. Set your seed at 111.

4. Use `gss2006_chapter8.dta`. Compute the correlations between `happy`, `hapmar`, and `health` by using `correlate` and then again by using `pwcorr`. Why are the results slightly different? Then estimate the correlations by using `pwcorr`, and get the significance level and the number of observations for each case. Finally, repeat the `pwcorr` command so that all the *N*s are the same (that is, there is casewise/listwise deletion).

5. Use `gss2002_chapter8.dta`. There are two variables called `happy7` and `satfam7`. Run the `codebook` command on these variables. Notice how the higher score goes with being unhappy or being dissatisfied. You always want the higher score to mean more of a variable, so generate new variables (`happynew` and `satfamnew`) that reverse these codes so that a score of 1 on `happynew` means very unhappy and a score of 7 means very happy. Similarly, a score of 1 on `satfamnew` means very dissatisfied and a score of 7 means very satisfied. Now do a regression of happiness on family satisfaction with the new variables. How correlated are these variables? Write the regression equation. Interpret the constant and the slope.

6. Use `spearman.dta`. Plot a scattergram, including the regression line for `age` and `liberal`, treating `liberal` as the dependent variable. Repeat this using the variables `rankage` and `ranklib`. Interpret this scattergram to explain why the Spearman's rho is smaller than the Pearson's correlation. Your explanation should involve the idea of one observation being an outlier.

7. Use `depression.dta` from the Stata Press website; that is, type

   ```
   . use https://www.stata-press.com/data/r17/depression
   ```

   From this hypothetical data, you are interested in the relationship between depression (variable `TotalScore`) and age. (This dataset uses capitalization as an aid in reading the total score variable. This is rarely a good idea because it is hard to remember these conventions, and if you always use all lowercase, you do not need to remember when and how you used capitalization. Perhaps better options would be to label the variable `totalscore` or `total_score`.) Are older people more or less depressed?

    a. Type `scatter` and `binscatter` to describe the relationship.

    b. Interpret these results. Why is the `binscatter` graph easier to interpret?

8. You suspect that the relationship may be nonlinear with a gradual increase among those over about 50 years of age.

    a. Type `binscatter` to fit a curve.

    b. Interpret these results and compare them with the graphs created in exercise 7.

9 Analysis of variance

9.1   The logic of one-way analysis of variance

In many research situations, a one-way analysis of variance (ANOVA) is appropriate, most commonly when you have three or more groups or conditions and want to see if they differ significantly on some outcome. This procedure is an extension of the two-sample t test.

You might have two new teaching methods you want to compare with a standard method. If you randomly assign students to three groups (standard method, first new method, and second new method), an ANOVA will show whether at least one of these groups has a significantly different mean. ANOVA is usually a first step. Suppose you find that the three groups differ, but you do not know how they differ. The first new method may be best, the second new method may be second best, and the standard method may

221

be worst. Alternatively, both new methods may be equal but worse than the standard method. When you do an ANOVA and find a statistically significant result, this begs a deeper look to describe exactly what the differences are. These follow-up tests often involve several specific tests (first new method versus standard method, second new method versus standard method, first new method versus second new method). When you do multiple tests like this, you need to make adjustments to the tests because they are not really independent tests, and you need to control for the type I error, α. If you run a single test of significance that is significant at the $\alpha = 0.05$ level, everything is okay. Can you see the problem when you run a series of related significance tests? Imagine running 100 of these tests using purely random data. You would expect about 5% of them to be significant at the 0.05 level, just by chance.

ANOVA is normally used in experiments, but it can also be used with survey data. In a survey, you might want to compare Democrats, Republicans, independents, and noninvolved adults on their attitudes toward stem cell research. There is no way you could do an experimental design because you could not randomly assign people to these different party identifications. However, in a national survey, you could find many people belonging to each group. If your overall sample was random, then each of these subgroups would be a random sample as well. An ANOVA would let you compare the mean score on the value of stem cell research (your outcome variable) across the four political party identifications.

ANOVA makes a few assumptions:

- The outcome variable is quantitative (interval level).

- The errors or residuals are normally distributed. This is problematic if we have a small sample.

- The observations represent a random sample of the population.

- The errors are independent. (We have repeated-measures ANOVA when this assumption is violated.)

- The variance of each group is equal. You can test this assumption.

Sometimes violating these assumptions is more problematic than at other times. For example, unequal variances are worse when the number of observations per group is unequal than when the number of observations is the same across groups.

9.2   ANOVA example

People having different political party identifications may vary in how much they support stem cell research. You might expect Democrats to be more supportive than Republicans, on average. What about people who say they are independents? What about people who are not involved in politics? Stata allows you to do a one-way ANOVA and then do multiple-comparison tests of all pairs of means to answer two questions:

- Are the means equal for all groups? This is a global question answered by ANOVA.

- Are pairs of group means different from one another? Specific tests answer this question.

There are two ways of presenting the data. Most statistics books use what Stata calls a wide format, in which the groups appear as columns and the scores on the dependent variables appear as rows under each column. An example appears in table 9.1.

Table 9.1. Hypothetical data—wide view

	democrat	republican	independent	noninvolved	overall
	9	5	7	5	
	7	9	8	4	
	9	4	6	6	
	6	6	6	4	
	9	3	7	5	
	8	1	7	4	
	9	5	8	6	
	7	9	7	4	
	9	4	8		
	6	6	6		
	9	3	6		
	8	1	7		
			7		
			8		
M	8.00	4.67	7.00	4.75	6.26
SD	1.21	2.61	.78	.88	2.09

Stata can work with data arranged like this, but it is usually easier to enter data in what Stata calls a long format. We could enter the data as shown in table 9.2.

Table 9.2. Hypothetical data—long view

stemcell	partyid
9	1
6	1
6	1
9	1
9	1
7	1
8	1
7	1
9	1
8	1
9	1
9	1
6	2
5	2
4	2
1	2
6	2
4	2
1	2
3	2
5	2
9	2
3	2
9	2
. . .	. . .
5	4

There are 46 observations altogether, and table 9.2 shows 25 of them. We know the party membership of each person by looking at the partyid column. We have coded Democrats with a 1, Republicans with a 2, independents with a 3, and those not involved in politics with a 4. To see the entire dataset, open up partyid.dta and enter the command list, nolabel. This method of entering data is similar to how we enter data for a two-sample t test, with one important exception. This time, we have four groups rather than two groups, and the grouping variable is coded from 1 to 4 instead of from 1 to 2.

We can now use these data (`partyid.dta`) to perform a one-way ANOVA. Select Statistics ▷ Linear models and related ▷ ANOVA/MANOVA ▷ One-way ANOVA to open the dialog box shown in figure 9.1.

Figure 9.1. One-way analysis-of-variance dialog box

Under the Main tab, indicate that the *Response variable* is `stemcell` and the *Factor variable* is `partyid`. Many analysis-of-variance specialists call the response variable the dependent or outcome variable. They call the categorical factor variable the independent, predictor, or grouping variable. In this example, `partyid` is the factor that explains the response, `stemcell`. Stata uses the names *response variable* and *factor variable* to be consistent with the historical traditions of analysis of variance. Many sets of statistical procedures developed historically, in relative isolation, and produced their own names for the same concepts. Remember, the response or dependent variable is quantitative and the independent or factor variable is categorical.

Stata asks if we want multiple-comparison tests, and we can choose from three: *Bonferroni*, *Scheffé*, and *Šidák*. These are three multiple-comparison procedures for doing the follow-up tests that compare each pair of means. A comparison of these three approaches is beyond the purpose of this book. We will focus on the Bonferroni test, so click on *Bonferroni*. Finally, check the box to *Produce summary table* to get the mean and standard deviation on support for stem cell research for members grouped by `partyid`. Here are the results:

```
. use https://www.stata-press.com/data/agis6r/partyid
. oneway stemcell partyid, bonferroni tabulate
```

party identificat ion	Summary of support for stem cell research Mean	Std. dev.	Freq.
democrat	8	1.2060454	12
republica	4.6666667	2.6053558	12
independe	7	.78446454	14
noninvolv	4.75	.88640526	8
Total	6.2608696	2.0916212	46

Analysis of variance

Source	SS	df	MS	F	Prob > F
Between groups	92.7028986	3	30.9009662	12.46	0.0000
Within groups	104.166667	42	2.48015873		
Total	196.869565	45	4.37487923		

Bartlett's equal-variances test: chi2(3) = 20.1167   Prob>chi2 = 0.000

Comparison of support for stem cell research by party identification
(Bonferroni)

Row Mean- Col Mean	democrat	republic	independ
republic	-3.33333 0.000		
independ	-1 0.684	2.33333 0.003	
noninvol	-3.25 0.000	.083333 1.000	-2.25 0.015

This is a lot of output, so we need to go over it carefully. Just below the command is a tabulation showing the mean, standard deviation, and frequency on support for stem cell research by people in each political party. Democrats and independents have relatively high means, $M_{\text{democrat}} = 8.00$ and $M_{\text{independent}} = 7.00$, and Republicans and those who are not involved in politics have relatively low means, $M_{\text{republican}} = 4.67$ and $M_{\text{noninvolved}} = 4.75$. (These are hypothetical data.)

Looking at the standard deviations, we can see a potential problem. In particular, the Republicans have a much larger standard deviation than that of any other group. This could be a problem because we assume that the standard deviations are equal for all groups. Finally, the table gives the frequency of each group. There are relatively fewer noninvolved people than there are people in the other groups, but the differences are not dramatic.

Next in the output is the ANOVA table. This is undoubtedly discussed in your statistics textbook, so we will go over it only briefly. The first column, Source, has two sources. There is variance between the group means, which should be substantial if the groups are really different. There is also variance within groups, which should be relatively small if the groups are different from each other, but should be homogeneous within each group. Think about this a moment. If the groups are really different, their means will be spread out, but within each group the observations will be homogeneous. The column labeled SS is the sum of squared deviations for each source, and when we divide this by the degrees of freedom (labeled df), we get the values in the column labeled MS (mean squares). This label sounds strange if you are not familiar with ANOVA, but it has a simple meaning. The between-group mean square is the estimated population variance based on differences between groups; this should be large when there are significant differences between the groups. The within-group mean square is the estimated population variance based on the distribution within each group; this should be small when most of the differences are between the groups (Agresti 2018). The test statistic, F, is computed by dividing the MS(between) by the MS(within). F is the ratio of two variance estimates. The $F = 30.90/2.48 = 12.46$. This ratio is evaluated using the degrees of freedom. We have 3 degrees of freedom for the numerator (30.90) and 42 degrees of freedom for the denominator (2.48). You can look this up in a table of the F distribution. However, Stata gives you the probability as 0.0000. We would never report a probability as 0.0000 but instead would say $p < 0.001$.

Can Stata give me an F table?

We get the probability directly from the Stata output, so we do not need to look it up in an F table. However, if you ever need to use an F table, you can get one from Stata without having to find the table in a statistics textbook. Type the command search ftable, which opens a window with a link to a webpage. Go to that webpage, and click on install to install several tables. You may have already downloaded these tables when you were obtaining z tests or t tests. From now on, whenever you want an F table, you need only enter the command ftable.

When you download these tables, you also have ttable, ztable, and chitable.

Years ago, these ANOVA tables appeared in many articles. Today, we simplify the presentation. We could summarize the information in the ANOVA table as $F(3, 42) = 12.46$, $p < 0.001$, meaning that there is a statistically significant difference between the means.

Stata computes Bartlett's test for equal variances and tells us that the χ^2 with 3 degrees of freedom is 20.12, $p < 0.001$. (Do not confuse this χ^2 test with the χ^2 test for a frequency table. The χ^2 distribution is used in many tests of significance.) One of the assumptions of ANOVA is that the variances of the outcome variable, stemcell, are equal in all four groups. The data do not meet this assumption. Some researchers discount this test because it will usually not be significant, even when there are substantial differences in variances, if the sample size is small. By contrast, it will usually be significant when there are small differences, if the sample size is large. Because unequal variances are more problematic with small samples, where the test lacks power, and less important with large samples, where the test may have too much power, the Bartlett test is often ignored. Be careful when the variances are substantially different and the Ns are also substantially different: this is a serious problem. One thing we might do is go ahead with our ANOVA but caution readers in our reports that the Bartlett test of equal variances was statistically significant.

Given that the overall F test is statistically significant, we can proceed to compare the means of the groups. This is a multiple comparison involving six tests of significance: Democrat versus Republican, Democrat versus independent, Democrat versus noninvolved, Republican versus independent, Republican versus noninvolved, and independent versus noninvolved. Stata provides three different options for this comparison, but here I consider only the Bonferroni. Multiple comparisons involve complex ideas, and we will mention only the principal issues here. The traditional t test worked fine for comparing two means, but what happens when we need to do six of these tests? Stata does all the adjustments for us, and we can interpret the probabilities Stata reports in the way we always have. Thus if the reported p is less than 0.05, we can report $p < 0.05$ using the Bonferroni multiple-comparison correction.

Below the ANOVA table in our output above is the comparison table for all pairs of means. The first number in each cell is the difference in means (Row Mean - Col Mean). Because political independents had a mean of 7 and Democrats had a mean of 8, the table reports the difference, $7 - 8 = -1$. Independents, on average, have a lower mean score on support for stem cell research. Is this statistically significant? No; the $p = 0.684$ far exceeds a critical level of $p < 0.05$. The noninvolved people and the Republicans have similar means, and the small difference, 0.08, is not statistically significant. However, all the other comparisons are statistically significant. For example, Republican support for stem cell research has a mean that is 3.33 points lower than that of Democrats, $p < 0.001$. One way to read the table is to remember that a negative sign means that the row group mean is lower than the column group mean and that a positive sign means that the row group mean is higher than the column group mean.

How strong is the difference between means? How much of the variance in stemcell is explained by different political party identification? We can compute a measure of association to represent the effect size. Eta-squared (η^2) is a measure of explained variation. Some refer to this as r^2 because it is the ANOVA equivalent of r^2 for correlation and regression. Knowing the political party identification improves our ability to predict the respondent's attitude toward stem cell research. The η^2 or r^2 in the context of ANOVA is the ratio of the between-groups sum of squares to the total sum of squares. The oneway command does not compute this for you, but you can compute it by using the simple division below. Or you could obtain this by using Stata's anova command. For example, you could type anova stemcell partyid and then type the postestimation command estat esize.

$$\eta^2 = r^2 = \frac{\text{Between group SS}}{\text{Total SS}} = \frac{92.703}{196.870} = 0.471$$

Do not forget about Stata's calculator. You can enter `display 92.703/196.870`, and Stata will report back the answer of 0.471. This result means that 47.1% of the variance in attitude toward stem cell research is explained by differences in party identification. Some researchers prefer a different measure that is called ω^2 (pronounced omega-squared), and you will learn how to obtain this later in the chapter.

The `pwmean` command is a way of doing multiple comparisons, which you might find as a useful supplement to the straight ANOVA approach we just covered. `pwmean`'s output includes more information than `oneway`, and it offers a wider variety of multiple-comparison procedures. Your statistics books probably cover several of these procedures but describing them is beyond the scope of this book. There is a brief discussion of each of these procedures in the *Stata Base Reference Manual*. The available multiple-comparison adjustments include the following:

- no adjustment for multiple comparisons; the default

- Bonferroni's method

- Šidák's method

- Scheffé's method

- Tukey's method

- Student–Newman–Keuls' method

- Duncan's method

- Dunnett's method

We will apply `pwmean` to our data on support for use of stem cells to see how much the support varies across our categories of party identification using the same hypothetical data as above. The `pwmean` command has many options and methods for adjusting the error rate. We will use the following command:

```
. pwmean stemcell, over(partyid) effects cimeans mcompare(bonferroni)
Pairwise comparisons of means with equal variances
Over: partyid
```

stemcell	Mean	Std. err.	Unadjusted [95% conf. interval]	
partyid				
democrat	8	.4546206	7.082538	8.917462
republican	4.666667	.4546206	3.749205	5.584128
independent	7	.4208969	6.150596	7.849404
noninvolved	4.75	.5567943	3.626344	5.873656

	Number of comparisons
partyid	6

stemcell	Contrast	Std. err.	Bonferroni t	P>|t|	Bonferroni [95% conf. interval]	
partyid						
republican						
vs						
democrat	-3.333333	.6429306	-5.18	0.000	-5.113618	-1.553048
independent						
vs						
democrat	-1	.6195435	-1.61	0.684	-2.715526	.7155256
noninvolved						
vs						
democrat	-3.25	.7188183	-4.52	0.000	-5.240419	-1.259581
independent						
vs						
republican	2.333333	.6195435	3.77	0.003	.6178077	4.048859
noninvolved						
vs						
republican	.0833333	.7188183	0.12	1.000	-1.907086	2.073753
noninvolved						
vs						
independent	-2.25	.6979785	-3.22	0.015	-4.182714	-.3172864

pwmean speaks for itself. Our dependent variable is support for stem cell research. We are comparing the means over the different party identifications. We want the effects of these differences, such as Democrat versus independent, to see which individual pairs are significantly different. We have also asked for confidence intervals and means for each category by using the cimeans option. Finally, we make our mean comparisons using the Bonferroni adjustment. If we wanted these results without any adjustment for multiple comparisons, we would replace mcompare(bonferroni) with mcompare(noadjust).

The results are different from the ANOVA table in terms of the layout and what is reported. We do not get the traditional ANOVA table with the F test for the overall relationship. We do get the means and standard errors for each category. We now get a confidence interval for each mean. We see that with our four categories of the party identification, we make six comparisons; these six comparisons appear in the bottom table. An advantage of this approach is that along with the contrast and standard error, we now get a Bonferroni adjusted *t*-test value reported with the two-tailed probability. Also we now get a confidence interval for each difference. For example, the `republican vs democrat` row has a difference of −3.33. This number is the result of the Republican mean of 4.67 minus the Democratic mean of 8.00. This difference has a $t = -5.18$ and a $p < 0.001$ using the Bonferroni adjustment. This significance is confirmed because the confidence interval does not include 0.00.

The *Stata Base Reference Manual* has an extensive set of examples illustrating the different options and comparison criteria. `pwmean` is a nice addition to the traditional ANOVA approach.

9.3   ANOVA example with nonexperimental data

You will find several examples of studies like the one we just did in standard statistics textbooks. Our second example uses data from a large survey, the 2006 General Social Survey (Smith et al. 2015) (`gss2006_chapter9.dta`), and examines occupational prestige. For our one-way ANOVA, we will see if people who are more mobile have the benefit of higher occupational prestige. We will compare three groups (the factor or independent variable must be a grouping variable). One group includes people who are living in the same town or city they lived in at the age of 16. We might think that these people have lower occupational prestige, on average, because they did not or could not take advantage of a broader labor market that extended beyond their immediate home city. The second group comprises those who live in a different city but still in the same state they lived in at the age of 16. Because they have a larger labor market, one that includes areas outside of their city of origin, they may have achieved higher prestige. The third group contains those who live in a different state than they lived in at the age of 16. By being able and willing to move this far, they have the largest labor market available to them. We will restrict the age range so that age is not a second factor; the sample is restricted to adults who are between 30 and 59 years of age.

Make sure that you open the *One-way analysis of variance* dialog box shown in figure 9.1. There is another option for analysis of variance and covariance that we will cover later in this chapter. In the **Main** tab, we are asked for a *Response variable*. The dependent variable is `prestg80`, so enter this as the response variable. This is a measure of occupational prestige that was developed in 1980 and applied to the 2006 sample. The dialog box asks for the *Factor variable*, so type `mobile16` (the independent variable). This variable is coded 1 for respondents who still live in the same city they lived in when they were 16; 2 if they live in a different city but still in the same state; and 3 if they live in a different state. Also click on the box by *Produce summary table* to get the means for each group on the factor variable. Finally, click on the box by *Bonferroni* in the section labeled *Multiple-comparison tests*. Because we have three groups, we can use this test to compare all possible pairs of groups, that is, same city to same state, same city to different state, and same state to different state. On the by/if/in tab, we enter the following restriction under *If: (expression)*: age > 29 & age < 60 & wrkstat==1. This restriction limits the sample to those who are 30–59 years old and have a wrkstat of 1, signifying that they work full time. Remember to use the symbol & rather than the word "and".

In our results (shown below), we first get a table of means and standard deviations. The first two means are in the direction predicted, but the third mean is not. Those who live in the same city have a mean of 44.12, those who have moved from the city but are still in the same state have a mean of 48.67, and those who have moved out of the state have a mean of 47.19. The standard deviations are similar (we can use Bartlett's test of equal variances to test this assumption). Also the *N* for each group varies from 269 to 425. Usually, the unequal *N*s are not considered a serious problem unless they are extremely unequal and one or more groups have few observations.

```
. use https://www.stata-press.com/data/agis6r/gss2006_chapter9
(General Social Surveys, 1972-2006 [Cumulative File], Dataset 0001)
. oneway prestg80 mobile16 if age > 29 & age < 60 & wrkstat==1, bonferroni
> tabulate
```

GEOGRAPHIC MOBILITY SINCE AGE 16	Summary of RS OCCUPATIONAL PRESTIGE SCORE (1980)		
	Mean	Std. dev.	Freq.
SAME CITY	44.116162	13.73443	396
SAME ST,D	48.672862	13.002183	269
DIFFERENT	47.185882	13.959368	425
Total	46.437615	13.758919	1,090

Analysis of variance

Source	SS	df	MS	F	Prob > F
Between groups	3716.07404	2	1858.03702	9.98	0.0001
Within groups	202440.184	1087	186.23752		
Total	206156.258	1089	189.307858		

Bartlett's equal-variances test: chi2(2) =   1.6873   Prob>chi2 = 0.430

Comparison of RS OCCUPATIONAL PRESTIGE SCORE (1980)
by GEOGRAPHIC MOBILITY SINCE AGE 16
(Bonferroni)

Row Mean-Col Mean	SAME CIT	SAME ST,
SAME ST,	4.5567	
	0.000	
DIFFEREN	3.06972	-1.48698
	0.004	0.487

We can summarize the second table (the ANOVA table) by writing $F(2, 1087) = 9.98$, $p < 0.001$. Just beneath the ANOVA table is Bartlett's test for equal variances. Because $\chi^2(2) = 1.69$, this finding is not statistically significant ($p = 0.43$). This is good because equal variances is an assumption of ANOVA. The *F* test is an overall test of significance for any differences between the group means. You can have a significant F test when the means are different but in the opposite direction of what you expected.

Now let's perform multiple comparisons using the Bonferroni adjustment. Those adults who moved to a different state scored 3.07 points higher on prestige, on average, than those who stayed in their hometown ($47.19 - 44.12 = 3.07$), $p < 0.01$. Those who moved but stayed in the same state scored 4.55 points higher on the prestige scale ($48.67 - 44.12 = 4.55$), $p < 0.001$. Although these two comparisons are significant, those who moved but stayed in the same state are not significantly different from those who moved to a new state.

We can do a simple one-way bar chart of the means. The command is

```
. graph bar (mean) prestg80 if age > 29 & age < 60 & wrkstat==1, over(mobile16)
```

You can enter this command in the Command window or enter it in a do-file. Alternatively, you could use the dialog box, as discussed in chapter 5. Select Graphics ▷ Bar chart to open the appropriate dialog box. On the Main tab, select *Graph of summary statistics* and *Vertical* in the *Orientation* section. Under *Statistics to plot*, check the first box, select *Mean* from the drop-down menu and, to the right of this, type `prestg80` as the variable. Next go to the Categories tab and check *Group 1*; select `mobile16` as the *Grouping variable*. Finally, open the if/in tab and, under the *If: (expression)*, type `age > 29 & age < 60 & wrkstat==1`.

The resulting bar chart, shown in figure 9.2, provides a visual aid showing that the mean is highest for those with some geographical mobility, that is, who live in the same state but a different city. Although all three means are different in our sample, only two comparisons (staying in your hometown versus moving to a different city within your home state and staying in your hometown versus moving to a different state) reach statistical significance.

Figure 9.2. Bar graph of relationship between prestige and mobility

We can compute $\eta^2 = r^2 = 3716.074/206156.258 = 0.02$, as described in the previous section. Thus even though the overall result is significant and two of the three comparisons are significant in the direction we predicted, the mobility variable does not explain much of the variance in prestige. Why is this? To get an answer, look at the means and standard deviations. In the previous example, the standard deviations for groups tended to be much smaller than the overall standard deviation. This is not the case in this example. The standard deviations for each group are between 13.00 and 13.96, whereas the overall standard deviation is 13.76. Although the means do differ, most of the variance still remains within each group. When the variance within the groups is not substantially smaller than the overall variance, the group differences are not explaining much variance.

9.4   Power analysis for one-way ANOVA

Power analysis can be performed using Stata's `power oneway` command. You can access the control panel for this command by selecting Statistics ▷ Power, precision, and sample size and then clicking on One-way analysis of variance. There are numerous options, so you may want to consult either the help file or the documentation for the command. You can open the help file by typing `help power oneway`; from the help file, you can then click on the `View complete PDF manual entry` link at the top of the help file to open the PDF documentation. Many of the options make you specify assumptions about the actual means of each group and the variance estimates.

One way to do power analysis is to rely on Cohen's f as a measure of effect size. A small effect is an $f = 0.10$, a moderate effect is an $f = 0.25$, and a large effect is an $f = 0.40$ (Cohen 1988). Suppose we are planning a one-way ANOVA and wondered how many observations we would need for different effect sizes, different levels of alpha, and different levels of power. The default alpha is 0.05, and the default power is 0.80. Here is a command that will give us a wide range of sample-size estimates based on these assumed values for effect size of $f = 0.1$, $f = 0.25$, ..., $f = 0.4$. These have the default $\alpha = 0.05$ and a power $= 0.80$; thus the command is as follows:

```
. power oneway, ngroups(3) delta(.1(.05).4)
Estimated sample size for one-way ANOVA
F test for group effect
H0: delta = 0   versus  Ha: delta != 0
```

alpha	power	N	N_per_group	delta	N_g	Var_m	Var_e
.05	.8	969	323	.1	3	.01	1
.05	.8	432	144	.15	3	.0225	1
.05	.8	246	82	.2	3	.04	1
.05	.8	159	53	.25	3	.0625	1
.05	.8	111	37	.3	3	.09	1
.05	.8	84	28	.35	3	.1225	1
.05	.8	66	22	.4	3	.16	1

From these results, we see that if we wanted to detect a very small effect, $f = 0.1$, as statistically significant at the $\alpha = 0.05$ level with a power of 0.80, we would need a total of 969 people in our sample with 323 in each group. However, if we are interested only in detecting an effect size that was at least moderate, $f = 0.25$, then we would need just 159 people with 53 in each group. What happens if we were interested only in detecting a significant result in the case of a large effect size, $f = 0.4$? We would need only 66 cases with 22 in each group. It is always good to run a power analysis before you start your data collection, but you can see how what you specify as a practically significant effect size is crucial to the sample size you will need.

We can expand `power oneway` with even more options. In addition to the effect size, we might want to see what size sample we would need for power values of 0.70, 0.80, and 0.90 and also see how things vary depending on our setting of alpha at 0.05 or 0.01. We would simply add the options `power(.7(.1).9)` and `alpha(.05 .01)`.

```
. power oneway, ngroups(3) delta(.1(.05).4) power(.7(.1).9) alpha(.05 .01)
Estimated sample size for one-way ANOVA
F test for group effect
H0: delta = 0  versus  Ha: delta != 0
```

alpha	power	N	N_per_group	delta	N_g	Var_m	Var_e
.05	.7	774	258	.1	3	.01	1
.05	.8	969	323	.1	3	.01	1
.05	.9	1,269	423	.1	3	.01	1
.01	.7	1,164	388	.1	3	.01	1
.01	.8	1,395	465	.1	3	.01	1
.01	.9	1,749	583	.1	3	.01	1
.05	.7	348	116	.15	3	.0225	1
.05	.8	432	144	.15	3	.0225	1
.05	.9	567	189	.15	3	.0225	1
.01	.7	519	173	.15	3	.0225	1
.01	.8	624	208	.15	3	.0225	1
.01	.9	780	260	.15	3	.0225	1
		(output omitted)					
.05	.7	90	30	.3	3	.09	1
.05	.8	111	37	.3	3	.09	1
.05	.9	144	48	.3	3	.09	1
.01	.7	135	45	.3	3	.09	1
.01	.8	159	53	.3	3	.09	1
.01	.9	201	67	.3	3	.09	1
.05	.7	66	22	.35	3	.1225	1
.05	.8	84	28	.35	3	.1225	1
.05	.9	108	36	.35	3	.1225	1
.01	.7	102	34	.35	3	.1225	1
.01	.8	120	40	.35	3	.1225	1
.01	.9	147	49	.35	3	.1225	1
.05	.7	54	18	.4	3	.16	1
.05	.8	66	22	.4	3	.16	1
.05	.9	84	28	.4	3	.16	1
.01	.7	78	26	.4	3	.16	1
.01	.8	93	31	.4	3	.16	1
.01	.9	114	38	.4	3	.16	1

9.5   A nonparametric alternative to ANOVA

Sometimes treating the outcome variable as a quantitative, interval-level measure is problematic. Many surveys have response options, such as agree, don't know, and disagree. In such cases, we can score these so that 1 is agree, 2 is don't know, and 3 is disagree, and then we can do an ANOVA. However, some researchers might say that the score was only an ordinal-level measure, so we should not use ANOVA. The Kruskal–Wallis rank test lets us compare the median score across the groups. If we are interested in political party identification and differences in support for stem cell research, we might use the Kruskal–Wallis rank test instead of the one-way ANOVA. If we want to use only ordinal information, it may be more appropriate to compare the median rather than the mean.

For this example, we will use `partyid.dta`. To open the dialog box for the Kruskal–Wallis rank test, select Statistics ▷ Nonparametric analysis ▷ Tests of hypotheses ▷ Kruskal-Wallis rank test. In the resulting screen, there are only two options. Type `stemcell` under *Outcome variable* and `partyid` under *Variable defining groups*. As with ANOVA, the variable defining the groups is the independent variable, and the outcome variable is the dependent variable.

```
. use https://www.stata-press.com/data/agis6r/partyid
. kwallis stemcell, by(partyid)
Kruskal–Wallis equality-of-populations rank test
```

partyid	Obs	Rank sum
democrat	12	422.00
republican	12	174.00
independent	14	391.00
noninvolved	8	94.00

```
chi2(3) = 22.115
   Prob = 0.0001
chi2(3) with ties = 22.696
            Prob = 0.0001
```

This test ranks all the observations from the lowest to the highest score. With a scale that ranges from 1 to 9, there are many ties, and the command adjusts for that. If the groups were not different, the rank sum for each group would be the same, assuming an equal number of observations. Notice from the output that the rank sum for Democrats is 422 and for Republicans it is just 174, even though there are 12 observations in each group. This means that Democrats must have higher scores than Republicans. The output gives us two chi-squared tests. Because we have people who are tied on the outcome variable (have the same score on `stemcell`), use the chi-squared with ties: chi-squared(3) = 22.696, $p < 0.001$. Thus there is a highly significant difference between the groups in support for stem cell research.

Because we are treating the data as ordinal, it makes sense to use the median rather than the mean. Now run a `tabstat` to get the median. It is easiest to type the command in the Command window, but if you prefer to use the dialog box, select Statistics ▷ Summaries, tables, and tests ▷ Other tables ▷ Compact table of summary statistics.

```
. tabstat stemcell, statistics(mean median sd) by(partyid)
Summary for variables: stemcell
Group variable: partyid (party identification)
    partyid |     Mean       p50        SD
------------+------------------------------
   democrat |        8       8.5  1.206045
 republican | 4.666667       4.5  2.605356
independent |        7         7  .7844645
noninvolved |     4.75       4.5  .8864053
------------+------------------------------
      Total |  6.26087         6  2.091621
```

We have the same pattern of results we had when we ran an ANOVA on these data. The p50 is the median. Notice that the medians are in the same relationship as the means with Democrats having the highest median, Mdn = 8.5; followed by the independents, Mdn = 7.0; and the Republicans and noninvolved having the lowest, Mdn = 4.5.

There are two graphs we can present to represent this information. We can do a bar chart like the one we did for the ANOVA, only this time we will do it for the median rather than for the mean. Select Graphics ▷ Bar chart to open the appropriate dialog box, or type the command

```
. graph hbar (median) stemcell, over(partyid)
> title(Median stem cell attitude score by party identification)
> ytitle(Median score on stem cell attitude)
```

which produces the graph in figure 9.3.

Figure 9.3. Bar graph of support for stem cell research by political party identification

Because we are working with the median, we can use a box plot. Open the appropriate dialog box by selecting Graphics ▷ Box plot. Under the Main tab, we enter `stemcell` under *Variables*. Switching to the Categories tab, we check the *Group 1* box and enter `partyid` as the variable under *Grouping variable*. Clicking on OK produces the following command and figure 9.4.

```
. graph box stemcell, over(partyid)
```

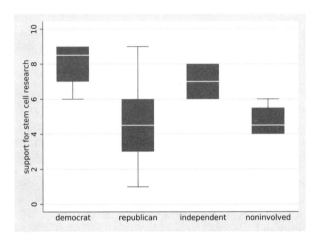

Figure 9.4. Box plot of support for stem cell research by political party identification

This is a much nicer graph than the bar chart because it not only shows the median of each group but also gives us a sense of the within-group variability. With the ANOVA, political party identification explained nearly half (0.471) of the variance in support for stem cell research. This box plot shows that not only are the medians different but also there is little variance within each group, except for the Republicans. (Again, these are hypothetical data.)

9.6   Analysis of covariance

We will discuss analysis of covariance (ANCOVA) as an extension of multiple regression in chapter 10. However, I will present an example of it here because it has a long history as a type of analysis of variance. ANCOVA has a categorical predictor (factor) and a quantitative dependent variable (response) like one-way ANOVA. ANCOVA adds more covariates that are quantitative variables that need to be controlled.

One of the areas in which ANCOVA developed was education, where the researchers could not assign children to classrooms randomly. Researchers needed to adjust for the fact that without random assignment, there might be systematic differences between the classrooms before the experiment started. For instance, one classroom might have students who have better math backgrounds than students in another classroom, so they might seem to do better because they were ahead of the others before the experiment started. We would need to control for initial math skills of students. People who volunteer to participate in a nutrition education course might do better than those in a control group, but this might happen because volunteers tend to be more motivated. We would need to control for the level of motivation. The idea of ANCOVA is to statistically control for group differences that might influence the result when you cannot rule out these possible differences through randomization. We might think of ANCOVA as a design substitute for randomization. Randomization is ideal, but when it is impossible to randomly assign participants to conditions, we can use ANCOVA as a fallback.

I do not mean to sound negative. ANCOVA allows us to make comparisons when we do not have randomization. Researchers often need to study topics for which randomization is out of the question. If we can include the appropriate control variables, ANCOVA does a good job of mitigating the limitations caused by the inability to use randomization.

The one-way ANOVA, with `gss2006_chapter9.dta`, showed that people who moved out of their hometown had higher prestige than people who did not. Perhaps there is a benefit to opening up to a broader labor market among people who move away from their hometown. They advance more because there are more opportunities when they cast their job search more broadly than if they never moved out of their home city. On the other hand, there might be a self-selection bias going on. People who decide to move may be people who have more experience in the first place. A person who is 30 years old may be less likely to have moved out of state than a person who is 40 years old simply because each year adds to the time in which such a move could occur. Also people who are 40 or 50 years old may have higher occupational prestige simply because they have had more time to gain experience. Because age could be related to the chances of a respondent living in the same place that he or she did at age 16 and to a respondent's prestige, we should control for age. Ideally, we would identify several other variables that need to be controlled, but for now we will just use age.

Instead of using the one-way ANOVA dialog box, we need to use the full ANOVA procedure. We have two predictors. The first is `mobile16`, which has three categories: same city, same state–different city, and different state. We are interested in differences in occupational prestige, `prestg80`, based on these fixed mobility categories. The mobility categories are not a random sample of mobility categories, but they are the specific population of categories about which we want to make a statistical inference. There are $k = 3$ groups and we should have 2 degrees of freedom $(k - 1)$. The other variable is `age`. Although `age` can take on several values (30–59 in our example), we do not think of these values as categories because this is just one continuous variable, where the older you get, the higher we think your prestige will be. As a continuous variable, `age` should have 1 degree of freedom.

What are categorical (factor) covariates, and what are continuous covariates?

Whenever we have an intervention, we could think of the intensity of the intervention varying widely. We could think of the intensity as the dosage level, that is, how much of the intervention the participant received. We might be interested in the dosage of a daily aspirin, and our dependent variable could be some measure of a specific side effect. To generalize across the full range of dosage levels, we would need to randomly sample levels of the dosage. One participant might take 10 mg; another, 500 mg; a third, 50 mg; a fourth, 35 mg; a fifth, 325 mg; and so on. If we had 80 participants, each of them might get a different dosage level. Here the dosage is thought of as a continuous covariate. The dosage each participant receives would be a continuous variable. We would want to be able to generalize our findings across a wide range of possible dosage levels.

More often, we think of an intervention as a categorical or factor covariate. One group of 20 participants would all get a daily placebo, a second group of 20 would all get a low dosage of 50 mg, a third group of 20 would all get 325 mg, and a fourth group of 20 would all get 500 mg. Although we would want to randomly assign our 80 people to each of these groups, the groups themselves represent factor covariates of none, low level, moderate level, and high level. We want to generalize to the fixed effects of these specific levels. We are not going to be able to generalize to other levels. We could not say what happens when the dosage is very low rather than low or when it is 400 mg—just what it is at the four categorical covariates in our study.

When we have an intervention and a control group, we think of them as fixed effects. When we are comparing views on stem cell research of Muslims to Catholics to Protestants, we are thinking of these as three categorical covariates. We have a random sample of members of each religion, but the three religions we picked are categorical. We cannot generalize to other religions (Hinduism, Buddhism, Judaism, Taoism, etc.)—just these three. When we have a continuous covariate, we usually think of it as a continuous covariate. In our example, we do not use categorical age groups; everybody can be a different age. We are asking the question of whether prestige goes up or down with age, and if it does, we control for it in estimating the effect of the three fixed mobility categories. The `anova` command identifies a continuous variable with the prefix `c.`, as in `c.age`. If we just enter `age`, then `anova` treats this variable as a categorical covariate. As a categorical covariate, the mean of people who are 30 is compared with the overall mean, the mean of people who are 31 is compared with the overall mean, etc. To do this, treat each possible age as its own categorical covariate.

Let's use the `tabulate` command to obtain the mean prestige for each mobility category and for each year of age:

```
. use https://www.stata-press.com/data/agis6r/gss2006_chapter9
(General Social Surveys, 1972-2006 [Cumulative File], Dataset 0001)
. tabulate mobile16 if age > 29 & age < 60 & wrkstat==1, summarize(prestg80)
```

GEOGRAPHIC MOBILITY SINCE AGE 16	Summary of RS OCCUPATIONAL PRESTIGE SCORE (1980) Mean	Std. dev.	Freq.
SAME CITY	44.116162	13.73443	396
SAME ST,D	48.672862	13.002183	269
DIFFERENT	47.185882	13.959368	425
Total	46.437615	13.758919	1,090

It looks like some mobility (within the state) goes with the highest prestige and no mobility goes with the lowest prestige. These differences are not huge, though, given that the overall standard deviation is 13.76.

Let's see how prestige varies across the age range.

```
. tabulate age if age > 29 & age < 60 & wrkstat==1, summarize(prestg80)
```

AGE OF RESPONDENT	Summary of RS OCCUPATIONAL PRESTIGE SCORE (1980) Mean	Std. dev.	Freq.
30	48.766667	15.6133	60
31	46.860465	13.772957	43
32	43.71875	13.082727	64
33	41.807692	12.929732	52
34	45.761905	13.523831	63
35	46.627451	13.518818	51
36	48.869565	14.200158	69
(output omitted)			
56	47.128205	12.825098	39
57	42.969697	14.08786	33
58	47	15.007315	42
59	45.261905	12.597056	42
Total	46.021537	13.863176	1,718

Looking at the results for `age`, we see a mess. The prestige goes up and down but not consistently up like we speculated. When we do an ANCOVA and treat `age` as a continuous variable, we may expect that it will not be significant because prestige does not seem to go consistently up or down with `age`. Undaunted, we will still add `age` as a covariate so that we can see how this is done.

Stata identifies continuous variables when doing ANOVA by adding `c.` as a prefix to the variable. To add `age` as a continuous covariate, we must type `c.age`. Here are the results if we do not prefix `age` with `c.`:

```
. anova prestg80 mobile16 age if age > 29 & age < 60 & wrkstat==1
                       Number of obs =       1,090     R-squared     =  0.0421
                       Root MSE      =     13.6621     Adj R-squared =  0.0140

          Source | Partial SS          df          MS           F    Prob>F

           Model | 8676.6203           31    279.89098        1.50    0.0396

        mobile16 | 3668.5073            2    1834.2537        9.83    0.0001
             age | 4960.5462           29    171.05332        0.92    0.5943

        Residual | 197479.64        1,058    186.65372

           Total | 206156.26        1,089    189.30786
```

Notice that we have $k-1 = 2$ degrees of freedom for the fixed effects of `mobile16` and the effect of mobility is highly significant, $F(2, 1058) = 9.83$, $p < 0.001$. In sharp contrast, `age`, which has $k-1 = 29$ degrees of freedom for the mobility effects is not significant, $F(29, 1058) = 0.92$, *pns*. The overall `Model`, however, is significant, $F(31, 1058) = 1.50$, $p < 0.05$. This model provides a different prediction for each of the 3 categories of `mobile16` and for each of the 30 categories of `age`.

We now add `c.` to `age` to identify it as a continuous variable.

```
. anova prestg80 mobile16 c.age if age > 29 & age < 60 & wrkstat==1
                       Number of obs =       1,090     R-squared     =  0.0183
                       Root MSE      =     13.6511     Adj R-squared =  0.0156

          Source | Partial SS          df          MS           F    Prob>F

           Model | 3777.3325            3    1259.1108        6.76    0.0002

        mobile16 | 3750.7312            2    1875.3656       10.06    0.0000
             age | 61.258461            1    61.258461        0.33    0.5665

        Residual | 202378.93        1,086     186.3526

           Total | 206156.26        1,089    189.30786
```

The conclusion does not change in this example because `age` does not have a significant effect either way, but in other applications, the difference can be dramatic. Notice that we have just 1 degree of freedom for `age` here, where we had 29 degrees of freedom when `age` was treated as a categorical variable.

In many applications where you do not have a randomized trial, you will need to control for more than one continuous covariate. Depending on what you are studying, you may want to add age, education, ability, and motivation as additional covariates. This is done by simply adding these variables with a `c.` prefix on each of them. Typically, your primary focus is on whether the categorical variable still has a significant effect after these covariates are included. In our example, mobility categories still have a significant effect after we control for age.

Significant covariates can change the result for your categorical variable. If you have two different interventions in two classrooms and have a third classroom as a control group, you would probably adjust for possible differences in ability level of the students and their parents' education. If the difference you observe without these covariates is explainable by these covariates, then the adjusted difference might disappear. One classroom may seem to do better but does not do better when you adjust the means for the covariates. In Stata, estimating the adjusted effects is best handled using the `margins` command, which will give you the estimated mean for each level of your categorical variable for a person who was average (mean) on each of the covariates.

Immediately after running the `anova` command, you type the `margins` command. You can find the dialog box for this command by opening the Postestimation Selector: select Statistics ▷ Postestimation, expand the Marginal effects, estimated means, interactions, ... menu, expand the Marginal means and interaction analysis menu, and then double-click on At sample means. In the dialog box that opens, choose mobile16 from the *Covariate* drop-down menu in *Covariate to compute margins, contrasts, or effects across*. Select *Marginal means of outcome for levels of covariate* from the *Analysis type* drop-down menu. At the bottom of the dialog box, select *Compute estimates at average of estimation sample*. Then click on OK.

```
. margins mobile16, atmeans

Adjusted predictions                              Number of obs = 1,090

Expression: Linear prediction, predict()
At: 1.mobile16 = .3633028 (mean)
    2.mobile16 = .246789  (mean)
    3.mobile16 = .3899083 (mean)
    age        = 43.82294 (mean)
```

	Margin	Delta-method std. err.	t	P>|t|	[95% conf. interval]	
mobile16						
SAME CITY	44.10402	.6863205	64.26	0.000	42.75736	45.45068
SAME ST,DIF..	48.68809	.832746	58.47	0.000	47.05412	50.32206
DIFFERENT S..	47.18756	.6621822	71.26	0.000	45.88826	48.48686

The command shows that the `mobile16` variable is the categorical variable on which we are focused. We want to know the adjusted mean for each level of this categorical variable. This would be extended if we had two or more continuous covariates. The option `atmeans` specifies that the continuous covariate, `age`, is to be fixed at its mean.

This is a very useful result. It estimates what the mean prestige would be for each category of mobility for a person who was average on the covariate `age`. The number of observations is 1,090, which matches our `anova` results, so we know that this includes only the subsample that we analyzed in the ANOVA, namely, people between 30 and 59 who were working full time.

If we wanted to do pairwise tests of significance comparing the `prestg80` score for our three types of `mobile16`, while adjusting for age, we could add the `pwcompare` option to our `margins` command. This command would not show us the adjusted means, but it would show us the difference between the pairs of means.

The mean age for our subsample of people who are over 29 and under 60 and who work full time is 43.82. This is a reasonable way to adjust for a continuous covariate. A person who was average on the covariate but never left his or her hometown would have one estimated mean; a person who was average on the covariate but moved, staying within his or her state, would have a different estimated mean; and a person who was average on the covariate but moved out of state would have a different estimated mean.

What happens if you want to include a covariate that is categorical? We have seen that age was not significant when used as a covariate. We might think that gender may also be an important covariate. Perhaps men are more mobile than women and gender influences occupational prestige. First, let's check on these two possibilities. We do a cross-tabulation of mobility and gender for our subsample.

```
. tabulate mobile16 sex if age > 29 & age < 60 & wrkstat==1, col chi2
```

```
  +------------------+
  | Key              |
  |------------------|
  |     frequency    |
  | column percentage|
  +------------------+
```

GEOGRAPHIC MOBILITY SINCE AGE 16	RESPONDENTS SEX MALE	FEMALE	Total
SAME CITY	188	212	400
	32.36	40.85	36.36
SAME ST,DIF CITY	142	129	271
	24.44	24.86	24.64
DIFFERENT STATE	251	178	429
	43.20	34.30	39.00
Total	581	519	1,100
	100.00	100.00	100.00

```
          Pearson chi2(2) =  11.0260   Pr = 0.004
```

This output does show a significant relationship—chi-squared(2) = 11.03, $p < 0.01$—and notice that 43.2% of men moved to a different state compared with just 34.3% of the women, but 40.9% of the women are in the same city compared with just 32.4% of the men. Our second idea was that there would be gender differences in prestige. We could check that using a t test, but we will go ahead and put it in the `anova`. To do this, we can repeat our first `anova` and simply add the variable for gender, `sex`. It is coded as 1 for male and 2 for female. We will not put a `c.` in front of `sex` because gender is a factor variable and not a continuous variable.

```
. anova prestg80 mobile16 sex c.age if age > 29 & age < 60 & wrkstat==1
                      Number of obs =      1,090    R-squared     =  0.0207
                      Root MSE      =     13.641    Adj R-squared =  0.0171

          Source |  Partial SS          df          MS          F     Prob>F

           Model |  4263.5812            4     1065.8953       5.73   0.0001

        mobile16 |  3917.4313            2     1958.7156      10.53   0.0000
             sex |   486.2487            1      486.2487       2.61   0.1063
             age |  45.250989            1     45.250989       0.24   0.6220

        Residual |  201892.68        1,085      186.0762

           Total |  206156.26        1,089      189.30786
```

We see that our overall model is significant, $F(4, 1085) = 5.73$, $p < 0.001$. Mobility is still significant, $F(2, 1085) = 10.53$, $p < 0.001$. However, neither sex nor age is significant. For gender, we have a significance of $F(1, 1085) = 2.61$, *pns*. For age, we have a significance of $F(1, 1085) = 0.24$, *pns*. So we can conclude that there are significant differences for prestige and these are related to mobility, but neither of the covariates we added is significant.

For illustrative purposes, we will show how to use the margins command to get the adjusted means. We are estimating the mean prestige for each category of mobility, adjusting for gender and age. We will open the margins dialog box again by selecting Statistics ▷ Postestimation, expanding the Marginal effects, estimated means, interactions, ... menu, expanding the Marginal means and interaction analysis menu, and then double-clicking on At sample means. In the dialog box that opens, choose mobile16 from the *Covariate* drop-down menu in *Covariate to compute margins, contrasts, or effects across.* Select *Marginal means of outcome for levels of covariate* from the *Analysis type* drop-down menu. Check the box next to *Interaction analysis with another covariate*, and choose sex from the *Covariate* drop-down menu in this box. At the bottom of the dialog box, select *Compute estimates at average of estimation sample.* The dialog box will look like figure 9.5:

Figure 9.5. The *Main* dialog box under `margins`

We click on OK. Here are the command that is generated and the results:

```
. margins mobile16#sex, atmeans

Adjusted predictions                              Number of obs = 1,090

Expression: Linear prediction, predict()
At: 1.mobile16 = .3633028 (mean)
    2.mobile16 =   .246789 (mean)
    3.mobile16 = .3899083 (mean)
    1.sex      = .5275229 (mean)
    2.sex      = .4724771 (mean)
    age        = 43.82294 (mean)
```

	Margin	Delta-method std. err.	t	P>|t|	[95% conf. interval]
mobile16#sex					
SAME CITY # MALE	43.39188	.8151133	53.23	0.000	41.7925 44.99126
SAME CITY # FEMALE	44.73797	.7900194	56.63	0.000	43.18783 46.28811
SAME ST,DIF.. # MALE	48.04545	.9222139	52.10	0.000	46.23592 49.85497
SAME ST,DIF.. # FEMALE	49.39154	.9390421	52.60	0.000	47.54899 51.23408
DIFFERENT S.. # MALE	46.62672	.7471295	62.41	0.000	45.16074 48.0927
DIFFERENT S.. # FEMALE	47.97281	.8208526	58.44	0.000	46.36217 49.58344

Additional specifications to the `margins` command are straightforward. We still have the `atmeans` option, specifying that `age` be set at its mean, but now we specify `mobile16#sex` to request that the adjusted means be reported for each combination of `mobile16` and `sex`. Therefore, we get separate estimated means for males and females. Both of these results have `age` set to the overall mean of 43.82.

It made sense to set the continuous variable, `age`, at its mean as a way of controlling for age. It would not make sense to set the categorical variable, `sex`, at its mean. People are either male or female. These are fixed categories. Setting `sex` at its mean for our subpopulation (the mean happens to be 1.47) would not be meaningful. What is a 1.47 sex?

The estimated means still appear under the column labeled `Margin`. The first two rows are for men in the same town, 43.39, and women in the same town, 44.74. The next two rows are for men and women in the same state but different towns. The last two rows are for men and women in different states. It is interesting how occupational prestige for women in this age group who work full time has the same pattern but is slightly higher than the corresponding occupational prestige of men.

Using adjusted means can be very informative. Consider the effects of family structure (married, divorced, never married) on child outcomes. Generally, children living in families with married parents have better outcomes. This could be tested using a one-way ANOVA, where each outcome was a dependent variable and the three family types were a categorical independent variable. You might ask whether the differences have to do with marital status or whether they are dependent on other covariates. Never-married parents tend to have much lower income and somewhat lower maternal education than do married parents. Divorced parents tend to have much lower income than do married parents. These income and educational differences may be what is influencing child outcomes rather than just the family structure. Acock and Demo (1994) did a series of ANOVAs for different child outcomes using family structure as a categorical variable and adding income, education, and several other covariates. They found that for many of the outcomes, the advantage of the married parents structure was greatly reduced when controlling for the covariates.

In this example, some of the covariates of marital status may be intervening variables. Lower income or a change in school following a divorce may be mechanisms whereby divorce creates problems for child well-being. We could say that marital status is the driver variable and covariates such as income and school quality are variables that mediate the effect of divorce on child well-being (see section 13.4).

Estimating the effect size and omega-squared, ω^2

There are four closely related measures of effect size for analysis of variance. These are eta-squared (η^2), omega-squared (ω^2), epsilon-squared (ϵ^2), and Cohen's f. When you have two or more independent factors, you also have a corresponding partial measure of the effect size for each factor. The eta-squared value is simply the sum of squares for the model, divided by the total sum of squares. A problem with this is that when you add a factor, the model sum of squares will increase just by chance. Both omega-squared and epsilon-squared are adjustments for the model complexity. All of these coefficients can be interpreted as the proportion of the variance explained by the model or for the partial coefficients by each individual factor. The eta-squared will be a biased estimator. The relationship of positive values for the coefficients will be that $\omega^2 \leq \epsilon^2 \leq \eta^2$. Cohen (1988) suggests that a value of eta-squared of 0.01 is a small effect, 0.06 is a medium effect, and 0.14 is a large effect. Both epsilon-squared and omega-squared will be somewhat smaller and in fact may be negative when the factor or model explains less than a chance amount.

Stata provides the eta-squared and partial eta-squared by the command `estat esize`:

```
. estat esize
Effect sizes for linear models
```

Source	Eta-squared	df	[95% conf. interval]	
Model	.0206813	4	.005142	.0371681
mobile16	.0190342	2	.0055725	.0369944
sex	.0024027	1	.	.0116359
age	.0002241	1	.	.005375

```
Note: Eta-squared values for individual model terms are partial.
```

The overall model explains just 2% of the variation in `prestige80`. The partial eta-squared values show 1.9% of the variation in `prestige80` is explained by mobility after removing the variation explained by sex and age. Based on Cohen's suggestion, this represents a small effect for mobility and for the overall model.

Estimating the effect size and omega-squared, ω^2, continued

We obtain omega-squared by adding the option `omega`:

```
. estat esize, omega
Effect sizes for linear models
```

Source	Omega-squared	df
Model	.0170555	4
mobile16	.0172104	2
sex	.0014819	1
age	-.0006967	1

```
Note: Omega-squared values for individual
      model terms are partial.
```

The epsilon-squared is obtained by adding the option epsilon:

```
. estat esize, epsilon
Effect sizes for linear models
```

Source	Epsilon-squared	df
Model	.0170709	4
mobile16	.017226	2
sex	.0014832	1
age	-.0006974	1

```
Note: Epsilon-squared values for individual
      model terms are partial.
```

9.7 Two-way ANOVA

Stata has enormous capacity for estimating a wide range of ANOVA models; we are only touching on a few of the ways Stata can fit ANOVA models here. One important extension of one-way ANOVA is two-way ANOVA, where we have two categorical predictors. For our example, we will use `gss2006_chapter9_2way.dta` to predict how many hours a person watches TV, `tvhours`, our dependent variable. We think this varies by marital status, `married` (coded 0 if a person is not married and 1 if a person is married), and work status, `workfull` (coded 0 if a person is not working full time and 1 if a person is working full time). We believe that people who work full time and people who are married will watch fewer hours of TV. Before doing the two-way ANOVA, let's check the mean number of hours of TV that married people watch compared with the number of hours that people who are not married watch and the corresponding mean number for people who work full time compared with the number for those who do not work. We do this with the following `tabulate` commands:

```
. use https://www.stata-press.com/data/agis6r/gss2006_chapter9_2way, clear
(General Social Surveys, 1972-2006 [Cumulative File], Dataset 0001)
```

`. tabulate married, summarize(tvhours)`

Are you married or not?	Summary of HOURS PER DAY WATCHING TV		
	Mean	Std. dev.	Freq.
Not Marri	3.2383268	2.5831093	1,028
Married	2.611691	1.8652487	958
Total	2.9360524	2.2864047	1,986

`. tabulate workfull, summarize(tvhours)`

Does R work full time or not	Summary of HOURS PER DAY WATCHING TV		
	Mean	Std. dev.	Freq.
Not Full	3.4610778	2.5842414	1,002
Full-time	2.4010152	1.784816	985
Total	2.9355813	2.2859255	1,987

It looks like we might be on to something. Those working full time average 2.40 hours a day watching TV compared with 3.46 hours for people who do not work full time. Those who are married watch TV 2.61 hours per day compared with 3.24 hours per day for those who are not married.

To do a two-way ANOVA, we can open the anova dialog box by clicking on Statistics ▷ Linear models and related ▷ ANOVA/MANOVA ▷ Analysis of variance and covariance. In the dialog box, we enter tvhours as our *Dependent variable*. For *Model*, we simply list our two categorical variables, workfull and married. We are asking for partial sum of squares. Here are the command and results:

`. anova tvhours workfull married`

	Number of obs =	1,986	R-squared	= 0.0701
	Root MSE =	2.2059	Adj R-squared =	0.0692

Source	Partial SS	df	MS	F	Prob>F
Model	727.59783	2	363.79892	74.76	0.0000
workfull	532.87817	1	532.87817	109.51	0.0000
married	170.13923	1	170.13923	34.96	0.0000
Residual	9649.2808	1,983	4.8660014		
Total	10376.879	1,985	5.2276467		

Both workfull, $F(1,1983) = 109.51$, $p < 0.001$, and married, $F(1,1983) = 34.96$, $p < 0.001$, are statistically significant. The $R^2 = 0.07$ means that we can explain just 7% of the variance. If you now use the estat esize, omega command, you can see that both workfull and married have fairly small effect sizes, so the relationships are significant but somewhat weak. The omega-squared for workfull is 0.05 and the omega-squared for married is 0.02. Both of these results are considered small to medium effects.

Imagine that you think the effect of working full time may be different if you are not married than if you are married. You think that people who are not married watch a lot more TV if they do not work full time than if they do work full time. You think this difference will be less for people who are married because of marital obligations they have. This is the basis of what is called a statistical interaction. We can look at the combination of means to get a sense of this. We run a `tabulate` listing both of our predictors.

```
. tabulate workfull married, summarize(tvhours)
  Means, Standard Deviations and Frequencies of HOURS PER DAY WATCHING TV

  Does R |
work full | Are you married or
 time or  |       not?
    not   | Not Marri    Married |     Total
----------+----------------------+----------
 Not Full | 3.8215613  3.0431034 | 3.4610778
          | 2.8497018  2.1664723 | 2.5842414
          |       538        464 |      1002
----------+----------------------+----------
Full-time | 2.5979592  2.2064777 | 2.4014228
          | 2.0761564  1.4163199 | 1.7856777
          |       490        494 |       984
----------+----------------------+----------
    Total | 3.2383268   2.611691 | 2.9360524
          | 2.5831093  1.8652487 | 2.2864047
          |      1028        958 |      1986
```

It looks like you were right! An unmarried person who is not working full time watches over one more hour a day of TV than an unmarried person who is working; the means are 3.82 compared with 2.60 hours, a difference of 1.22 hours a day. By contrast, the difference is about half as much for those who are married; the means are 3.04 compared with 2.21, a difference of just 0.83 hours a day. This means that the effect of one variable, work status, on the dependent variable is different for different levels of the other variable, marital status. If you are married, the effect of work status on TV watching is weaker than if you are not married.

Two-way ANOVA lets us test this very easily. We open the `anova` dialog box again. This time under the *Model*, we enter `workfull married workfull#married`. Stata interprets `workfull#married` as telling it to multiply these two variables and use the product terms for testing the interaction. You might click on Examples... in the dialog box to see how you can do even more complicated models and how there are shortcuts beyond what we have used here. Here are the results:

```
. anova tvhours workfull married workfull#married
                        Number of obs =      1,986    R-squared     =  0.0719
                        Root MSE      =    2.20434    Adj R-squared =  0.0705

              Source |    Partial SS         df         MS         F      Prob>F

               Model |    746.1336            3     248.7112     51.18    0.0000

            workfull |    525.37818           1     525.37818   108.12    0.0000
             married |    169.42138           1     169.42138    34.87    0.0000
    workfull#married |    18.535767           1     18.535767     3.81    0.0509

            Residual |    9630.745        1,982     4.8591045

               Total |    10376.879       1,985     5.2276467
```

These results show not only that workfull and married influence TV watching,
which we saw before, but also that there is a marginally significant interaction,
workfull#married, $F(1, 1982) = 3.81$, $p = 0.0509$. The tabulation we did aids our
interpretation. After running this ANOVA, we probably should use a postestimation
command, like margins, to estimate these means because it also provides confidence
intervals for each of the means. Select Statistics ▷ Postestimation, expand the Marginal
effects, estimated means, interactions, ... menu, and then double-click on Custom and
high-dimensional analyses. Under the Main tab, all we need to do is enter our three predictors, workfull, married, and workfull#married, in the space under *Factor terms
to compute margins for*. Here are the results:

```
. margins workfull married workfull#married
Predictive margins                                   Number of obs = 1,986
Expression: Linear prediction, predict()
```

	Margin	Delta-method std. err.	t	P>|t|	[95% conf. interval]	
workfull						
Not Full	3.446051	.0696898	49.45	0.000	3.309378	3.582724
Full-time	2.409118	.070326	34.26	0.000	2.271197	2.547038
married						
Not Married	3.215305	.0688002	46.73	0.000	3.080377	3.350234
Married	2.628582	.071277	36.88	0.000	2.488796	2.768368
workfull# married						
Not Full # Not Married	3.821561	.0950357	40.21	0.000	3.635181	4.007942
Not Full # Married	3.043103	.1023338	29.74	0.000	2.84241	3.243797
Full-time # Not Married	2.597959	.0995818	26.09	0.000	2.402663	2.793255
Full-time # Married	2.206478	.0991778	22.25	0.000	2.011974	2.400982

Although the R^2 is small and the partial or semipartial R^2s for `workfull`, `married`, and `workfull#married` are even smaller, the means show what many would consider a substantively important effect. It is probably better to look at these means than simply rely on the measures of effect size.

If you are really good with numbers, the results of the `margins` command are all you need. We can see that `workfull` is associated with fewer hours watching TV (2.409 versus 3.446 under the `Margin` column). We see that those who are married also watch less TV. The interaction of working full time and marriage is hard to understand if we just look at these numbers. Fortunately, this is exactly where a graph is useful.

We have three factors in our ANOVA: `workfull`, `married`, and their interaction, `workfull#married`. We can produce three graphs. The first graph we create is the effect of `workfull` to visually display the difference in hours watching TV. We rerun the `margins` command, this time with only the `workfull` variable. (We include the `quietly` prefix because we do not want to see these results again.) Then we run `marginsplot`, which creates the graph in figure 9.6.

```
. quietly: margins workfull

. marginsplot
```

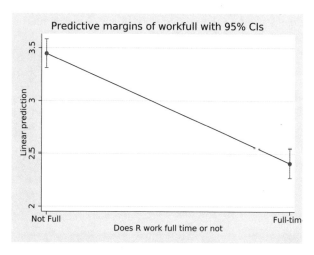

Figure 9.6. Hours of TV watching by whether the person works full time

Figure 9.6 might be improved with some judicious editing, but it is nice this way. What would you change with the Graph Editor? I would change the y-axis title from "Linear prediction" to "Hours watching TV", a more appropriate title. After examining all three graphs we will produce, I would change the range on the y axis to be consistent. The graph shows the difference in hours TV was watched and includes a 95% confidence interval. If we do not want this confidence interval, we simply add the `noci` option as we do in the next two graphs. To display whether the person is married, we use the following command, which creates figure 9.7:

```
. quietly: margins married
. marginsplot, noci
```

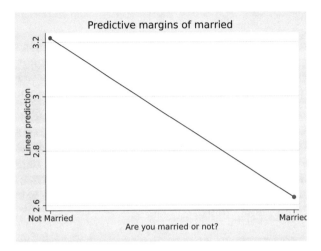

Figure 9.7. Hours of TV watching by whether the person is married

This graph makes it clear that married people watch fewer hours of TV than people who are not married. The real value of the `marginsplot` command is evident in the next example, which creates the graph in figure 9.8, when we plot the interaction between working full time and marital status:

```
. quietly: margins workfull#married
. marginsplot, noci
```

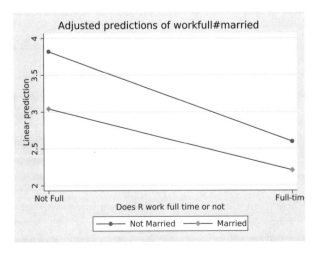

Figure 9.8. Hours of TV watching by whether the person is married and whether the person works full time

Many readers of reports will find a graph like this more understandable than the table of `workfull#married` marginal means. This shows that married people watch fewer hours of TV regardless of their work status, $p < 0.001$ (from the `anova` command output). Those who work full time also watch fewer hours of TV regardless of their marital status ($p < 0.001$). The marginally significant interaction of marital status and work status, $p < 0.10$, is reflected in the lines not being parallel. Those who do not work full time have a greater gap in hours watching TV that depends on their marital status and those who work full time have less of a gap. In cases of extreme interaction, the lines might even cross over.

9.8 Repeated-measures design

Chapter 7 included a section on repeated-measures t tests. These tests were useful when you had a before–after design in which participants were measured before an intervention and then the same participants were measured again after the intervention. We use repeated-measures ANOVA when there are more than two measurements. For example, we might want to know if the effect of the intervention was enduring. With only before and after measurements, we do not know what happens in the weeks or months following the experiment. We might have three time points, namely, pretest (before the intervention), posttest (shortly after the intervention is completed), and follow-up (another measurement a couple of months later). Students can think of many subjects where the follow-up measure would be revealing. They would have scored poorly on the final examination if they took it before taking the class. They would score much better when they took the final examination after taking the course. However, they might score poorly again if they took the same test again a few months after completing the course. This is a special problem with courses that emphasize memorization. A repeated-measures ANOVA allows us to test what happens over time.

A critical assumption of the F test when doing ANOVA is that the observations are independent. This makes sense when comparing several groups; the people in one group are independent of the people in the other group. This is not a reasonable assumption when you have repeated measures on the same set of people. For example, if Alexander, Matthew, Emma, Abigail, and Jacob are each measured on their attitude toward people who are obese before an intervention, after an intervention, and three months after the intervention, each of the three measures are likely to be correlated. If Jacob is the most prejudiced at the start, the researcher hopes his prejudice will be reduced, but he is still likely to be more prejudiced than the others. If Abigail is the least prejudiced initially, she is likely to be one of the less prejudiced at each of the four measurement points. This is what we mean by a lack of independence. The scores will be somewhat homogeneous within each person. That is, three scores for the same person will be more similar than three randomly selected scores.

The way a repeated-measures ANOVA adjusts for this lack of independence is to adjust the degrees of freedom using three different strategies. The Box conservative approach is a lower bound on the adjustment. It makes it hardest to obtain statistical significance. The Greenhouse–Geisser adjustment is somewhat less conservative, but it still may have a conservative bias. The Huynh–Feldt approach is the least conservative.

There are alternatives to a repeated-measures ANOVA that go beyond the scope of this chapter. One alternative is to do a multivariate ANOVA, which Stata implements with the `manova` command. A second alternative is to do a mixed-model approach, as done with the `mixed` command. Both of these methods are beyond the scope of this chapter. We will see how to do a repeated-measures ANOVA with the caution that this does not work on a very large sample and the other approaches not covered in this book may be more appropriate.

Here are some hypothetical data for students in a small class as the data might be presented in a textbook (`wide9.dta`).

```
. use https://www.stata-press.com/data/agis6r/wide9, clear
. list
```

	id	test1	test2	test3
1.	1	55	85	80
2.	2	65	90	85
3.	3	34	70	71
4.	4	55	75	65
5.	5	61	59	65
6.	6	79	94	85
7.	7	63	59	59
8.	8	45	65	50
9.	9	54	70	60
10.	10	69	90	82

Stata refers to this arrangement as a *wide* layout of the data, but Stata prefers a *long* arrangement. You could make this conversion by hand with a small dataset like this, but it is easier to use the `reshape` command. Many find this command confusing, and I will illustrate only this one application of it. A detailed explanation appears at https://stats.oarc.ucla.edu/stata/modules/reshaping-data-wide-to-long/. For our purposes, the command to reshape the data into a long format is as follows:

```
reshape long test, i(id) j(time)
```

This looks strange until we analyze what is being done. The `reshape long` part lets Stata know that we want to change from the wide layout to a long layout. This is followed by a variable name, `test`, that is not a variable name in the wide dataset. However, `test` is the prefix for each of the three measures: `test1`, `test2`, and `test3`. If we had used names like `pretest`, `posttest`, and `followup`, we would have needed to rename the variables so that they would have the same stubname and then a number. We can do this by opening the Data Editor, double-clicking on the variable name we want to change, and then changing the name in the Properties pane. We could also do this by opening the Variables Manager, clicking on the variable name, changing the name in the Variable properties pane, and clicking on the Apply button. Performing the changes in the Data Editor or the Variables Manager generates the commands `rename pretest test1`, `rename posttest test2`, and `rename followup test3`.

After the comma in the `reshape` command are two required options. (Stata calls everything after the comma an option, even if it is required for a particular purpose.) The `i(id)` option will always be the ID number for each observation. The parentheses would contain whatever variable name was used to identify the individual observations. Here we use `id`, but another dataset might use a different name, such as `ident` or `case` (if you do not have an identification variable, run the command `gen id = _n` before using the `reshape` command). The `j(time)` option refers to the time of the measurement. This option creates a new variable, `time`, that is scored a 1 if the score is for `test1`, a 2 for `test2`, or a 3 for `test3`. The choice of the name `time` is arbitrary. Here are the command and its results:

```
. reshape long test, i(id) j(time)
(j = 1 2 3)
Data                                    Wide   ->   Long

Number of observations                   10   ->   30
Number of variables                       4   ->   3
j variable (3 values)                         ->   time
xij variables:
                        test1 test2 test3   ->   test

. list

        id   time   test

  1.     1      1     55
  2.     1      2     85
  3.     1      3     80
  4.     2      1     65
  5.     2      2     90

  6.     2      3     85
  7.     3      1     34
  8.     3      2     70
  9.     3      3     71
 10.     4      1     55

 11.     4      2     75
 12.     4      3     65
 13.     5      1     61
 14.     5      2     59
        (output omitted )
 26.     9      2     70
 27.     9      3     60
 28.    10      1     69
 29.    10      2     90
 30.    10      3     82
```

Alternatively, you can enter the data yourself in the long format. `id` is repeated three times for each observation, corresponding to the times 1, 2, and 3 that appear under `time`. The last column is the variable stub `test` with 55 being how person 1, `id` = 1, did on `test1` at `time` = 1; 85 being how person 1 did at time 2; and 80 being how person 1 did at time 3. You can see how the long format appears as a wide format to check that you have either entered the data correctly or done the `reshape` command correctly. In this example, the command to type is `tabdisp id time, cellvar(test)`.

With the data in the long format, we can first see how much we have violated the assumption of independence. The intraclass correlation coefficient (ICC), which is often called rho-sub-i, ρ_I, is a measure of the lack of independence. The variance in our three sets of test scores can be thought of as consisting of two components. There is the difference between the people because some people tend to consistently score high or consistently score low. There is also the difference within individual people, which represents the variance from one test to another for each person. If all the variability is between people, then each person would score the same at each testing and there would be complete dependence. If I know how Jacob or Abigail, or anybody else, scored at one point, I would know exactly how he or she scored at each other point. We can run a command to obtain the ICC or ρ_I when the data are in the long form. Without showing the dialog box, here are the commands and output:[1]

```
. xtset id
Panel variable: id (balanced)
. xtreg test
Random-effects GLS regression            Number of obs      =          30
Group variable: id                       Number of groups   =          10
R-squared:                               Obs per group:
    Within  = 0.0000                                         min =        3
    Between = 0.0000                                         avg =      3.0
    Overall = 0.0000                                         max =        3
                                         Wald chi2(0)       =          .
corr(u_i, X) = 0 (assumed)               Prob > chi2        =          .
```

test	Coefficient	Std. err.	z	P>|z|	[95% conf. interval]	
_cons	67.96667	3.510988	19.36	0.000	61.08526	74.84808

sigma_u	8.8746414	
sigma_e	11.555662	
rho	.37099391	(fraction of variance due to u_i)

`xtreg` is one of several xt commands. This group of Stata commands is appropriate for panel data like our example above, where the scores for each person are measured at three separate times. Prior to using `xtreg`, we must declare our data to be panel data arranged in long form. We do this with the `xtset` command. In our example, variable `id` identifies the observations (people) that have repeated measures. Each person was measured at three different times. Depending on what is repeated, the variable could have different names, for example, `xtset case`, `xtset school`, or `xtset clinic`.

---

1. We can also use the `icc` command (see `help icc` for details) to compute intraclass correlation. If you type `icc test id`, the same ICC of 0.371 is reported as the Individual ICC.

The `xtreg` command estimates our intraclass correlation. The variable `test` is our dependent variable. The variable name `test` is the common stem of the three variables we had (`test1`, `test2`, and `test3`) when the data were in the wide format.

We see from the `xtreg` results that `rho = 0.371`. This is called either the ICC or the ρ_I, depending on your area of specialty. This would be considered a substantial lack of independence. Whenever the ICC is 0.05 or more, we need to make some adjustment. Many researchers would make an adjustment regardless of the size of the ICC because some dependency is expected as part of the research design that involves repeated measures on the same observations.

Here are the Stata command to do our repeated-measures ANOVA and the results:

```
. anova test id time, repeated(time)
                      Number of obs =        30    R-squared     =  0.8284
                      Root MSE      =   7.56233    Adj R-squared =  0.7235

       Source |  Partial SS        df        MS           F     Prob>F

        Model |   4969.5667        11    451.77879       7.90   0.0001

           id |     3328.3          9    369.81111       6.47   0.0004
         time |   1641.2667         2    820.63333      14.35   0.0002

     Residual |     1029.4         18    57.188889

        Total |   5998.9667        29    206.86092

Between-subjects error term:  id
                    Levels:   10        (9 df)
        Lowest b.s.e. variable:  id
Repeated variable: time
                             Huynh-Feldt epsilon         =  0.7848
                             Greenhouse-Geisser epsilon  =  0.6969
                             Box's conservative epsilon  =  0.5000

                                   ---------- Prob > F ----------
       Source |     df      F     Regular     H-F       G-G       Box

         time |      2    14.35   0.0002    0.0007    0.0012    0.0043
     Residual |     18
```

In this command, we list the dependent variable, `test`; the grouping variable, `id`, because the repeated measures are repeated for each person; and the `time` variable. We included the `repeated(time)` option to make this repeated over `time`.

The top part of the results shows a traditional ANOVA table. We do not make much use of this information. The $R^2 = 0.828$ is misleading because this applies to the `Model`, which includes both the differences between individuals and the differences across time. We are only interested in the differences across time, which we must compute by hand. The R^2 for `time` is the partial sum of squares for `time` divided by the total sum of squares. Hence, R^2 for `time` is $1641.267/5998.967 = 0.274$.

To test our significance, we need to use the table at the bottom of the results. The Huynh–Feldt epsilon will adjust the degrees of freedom by multiplying it by 0.785, the Greenhouse–Geisser will multiply it by 0.697, and Box's conservative approach would multiply it by 0.500 to estimate the probability of the F. Our $F = 14.35$ for our unadjusted degrees of freedom of 2 and 18. You can see that by using this degrees of freedom, our $p < 0.001$ as it is for using the Huynh–Feldt adjustment. For the Greenhouse–Geisser adjustment, the $p < 0.01$, and this is also true by using Box's conservative adjustment. In this case, all our results are significant, but whether we report it as $p < 0.001$ or $p < 0.01$ will be determined by our choice of adjustment. Because there is no definitive best choice, it may be best to report the p for all three adjustment methods. Box's approach is generally considered to be too conservative.

These results show that the scores do change significantly over time and the results are substantial in terms of R^2 and the effect size. However, this does not tell us exactly what the effects are. To get that, we need to run the `margins` command immediately after running the `anova` command:

```
. margins time

Predictive margins                                      Number of obs = 30
Expression: Linear prediction, predict()

                    Delta-method
            Margin   std. err.       t     P>|t|     [95% conf. interval]

      time
         1       58     2.39142    24.25   0.000     52.97581    63.02419
         2     75.7     2.39142    31.65   0.000     70.67581    80.72419
         3     70.2     2.39142    29.35   0.000     65.17581    75.22419
```

9.9 Intraclass correlation—measuring agreement

The intraclass correlation coefficient, ICC or ρ_I, can be used as a measurement of agreement. When we have just two measures, we may be tempted to measure agreement using a simple correlation coefficient. We might have just a before and an after measure, or we might have a measure on two related people, say, a husband and his wife or a mother and her child. It is a mistake to use a simple correlation coefficient to measure agreement. Consider data reflecting how liberal a mother and her child are. If each child scored 2 points higher than the mother on a 1 to 10 scale of liberalism, then they clearly would not agree, but the correlation would be 1.0. The regression equation, `kidscore` $= 2 + 1$(`momscore`), would fit perfectly, yielding an $R^2 = 1.0$, even though each child scored 2 points higher than his or her mother. If each child scored two times the mother's score, the equation `kidscore` $= 0 + 2$(`momscore`) would fit perfectly. In either of these examples, we would say that there was agreement, and the $R^2 = 1.0$ would be inappropriate as a measure of agreement.

The ICC will only be 1.0 if there is perfect agreement. We will illustrate it with an example from dynamics. The ICC is a better measure of agreement than the correlation, but in this example, we have three scores rather than two and agreement is across all three scores.

We randomly assign three people to each of 10 groups and have them discuss reforming Medicare. After 30 minutes of discussing the issue, each person completes a questionnaire that includes a scale measuring attitude toward welfare reform. Assume that one member out of both groups 3 and 7 got sick, so we would have only two scores for each group 3 and 7 on their attitudes toward reforming Medicare. You enter your data using the long format, and the data look like this (`intraclass.dta`):

```
. use https://www.stata-press.com/data/agis6r/intraclass, clear
(Intraclass Correlation Data)

. list
```

	medicare	group
1.	21	1
2.	22	1
3.	22	1
4.	17	2
5.	16	2
6.	15	2
7.	15	3
8.	16	3
9.	18	4
10.	19	4
11.	20	4
12.	12	5
13.	12	5
14.	14	5
15.	14	6
16.	21	6
17.	24	6
18.	23	7
19.	22	7
20.	26	8
(output omitted)		
26.	35	10
27.	33	10
28.	45	10

The groups, numbered 1 to 10, each appear three times, with the exception of groups 3 and 7 (because one member in each group got sick and did not complete the questionnaire). The three people in the first group have scores of 21, 22, and 22. The order of members is arbitrary in this example. If the group process leads to agreement among group members, we would expect the variance within each group to be small—all of them would have similar scores. By contrast, we would expect there to be considerable variance across groups. Compare the three people in group 1 with the three people in group 2, and you can see that most of the variance is between groups. If everybody within each group agrees with his or her group members and all the differences are between groups, then the intraclass correlation will be 1.0.

In section 9.8, we illustrated the commands to declare data to be panel and to produce the ICC once the data are in the long format. We can use the same statistic as our measure of agreement. Here are the commands and results:

```
. xtset group
Panel variable: group (unbalanced)
. xtreg medicare
Random-effects GLS regression              Number of obs      =          28
Group variable: group                      Number of groups   =          10

R-squared:                                 Obs per group:
     Within  = 0.0000                                    min =           2
     Between = 0.0000                                    avg =         2.8
     Overall = 0.0000                                    max =           3

                                           Wald chi2(0)       =           .
corr(u_i, X) = 0 (assumed)                 Prob > chi2        =           .
```

medicare	Coefficient	Std. err.	z	P>|z|	[95% conf. interval]
_cons	21.38081	2.214351	9.66	0.000	17.04077 25.72086
sigma_u	6.7602232				
sigma_e	2.9907264				
rho	.83631742	(fraction of variance due to u_i)			

In this example, the **xtset** command specified **group** as our unit of observation. The **xtreg** command specified **medicare** as our dependent variable. Each group is one observation that has three repeated scores for the three people in each group. Notice that in section 9.9, we used **id** as the unit of observation with three repeated tests for each individual. Here we use **group** as the unit of observation with three scores for the group members.

Stata reports that the ICC is 0.836, which reflects an extremely high level of agreement. Many studies have reported correlations as measures of agreement when the ICC would be more appropriate. Sometimes researchers say a correlation is a reliable measure because when a scale is given to the same people on two occasions, we get a high correlation. This is not an appropriate measure of agreement, and the ICC should be reported instead.

9.10   Power analysis with ANOVA

Stata's **power** command can be very useful when you are designing a study. The **power** command has a wide range of capabilities for analyzing power in ANOVA studies, and we will illustrate only some of the basic applications. The capabilities are fully described in the *Stata Power, Precision, and Sample-Size Reference Manual*.

We have already seen one example of power analysis for one-way ANOVA models in section 9.4. In this section, we will examine another example for one-way ANOVA and then extend this and perform power analysis for two-way ANOVA. Finally, we will perform power analysis for a repeated-measures ANOVA example.

9.10.1   Power analysis for one-way ANOVA

Imagine you are designing a study in which you will randomly assign women with chronic back pain to one of three conditions. Condition A uses the current, best practice treatment. Condition B uses an alternative holistic treatment. Condition C tells the women to rest and take it easy. You want to do a one-way ANOVA to see if the condition matters. How many participants will you need in your study? Let's say it is practical for you to have at least 60 participants with 20 randomly assigned to each of the three groups or conditions. However, you are writing a grant proposal to fund this project, and you could have a lot more participants if needed to have a good study. What does it mean to have a good study? One key ingredient is that your study will have the power necessary to show a significant result given that the true condition is substantively and clinically important. You need a measure of the effect size you consider important to help you decide what would be a clinically important result.

We could enter the means and standard deviations for each group, but we do not usually know them. One solution is to use a general measure of effect size used in ANOVA. We have already discussed Cohen's f statistic for power analysis in section 9.4, where we indicated that $f = 0.10$ represents a small effect, $f = 0.25$ represents a medium effect, and $f = 0.40$ represents a strong effect.

You will need a much larger sample size for power to detect a small effect than you would need for power to detect a large effect. Let's say you want power to detect a medium effect. You decide that you need to have a power of 0.80 to detect a medium effect size of 0.25 with an alpha of 0.05. The power of 80% means that if you replicated this study an infinite number of times, 80% of the studies would obtain a statistically significant result at the $p < 0.05$ level when the true effect size was $f = 0.25$. You would still be taking a gamble, because you had the bad fortune of having one of the 20% of studies that did not obtain a significant result even though there was a true difference at the effect-size level. However, greater certainty, such as a power of 0.90, might make the study cost prohibitive. Many researchers and funding agencies are satisfied to have a power of 0.80.

We will use the `power oneway` command to see what happens to the effect size we can detect with different N's. We will let the total N vary from 40 to 500 in increments of 20, that is, 40, 60, 80, ..., 500. We will specify a power of 0.80, an alpha of 0.05, and the three conditions or groups. We will ask for a graph and a table. Here is our command with the resulting table and graph (figure 9.9):

```
. power oneway, n(40(20)500) power(0.80) alpha(0.05) ngroups(3) graph table
Performing iteration ...
Estimated between-group variance for one-way ANOVA
F test for group effect
H0: delta = 0  versus  Ha: delta != 0
```

alpha	power	N	N_per_group	delta	N_g	Var_m	Var_e
.05	.8	40	13	.5185	3	.2688	1
.05	.8	60	20	.4115	3	.1693	1
.05	.8	80	26	.3586	3	.1286	1
.05	.8	100	33	.3169	3	.1004	1
.05	.8	120	40	.287	3	.08238	1
.05	.8	140	46	.2672	3	.07139	1
.05	.8	160	53	.2485	3	.06177	1
.05	.8	180	60	.2333	3	.05444	1
.05	.8	200	66	.2223	3	.04942	1
.05	.8	220	73	.2112	3	.04461	1
.05	.8	240	80	.2016	3	.04066	1
.05	.8	260	86	.1944	3	.03779	1
.05	.8	280	93	.1868	3	.03491	1
.05	.8	300	100	.1801	3	.03244	1
.05	.8	320	106	.1749	3	.03059	1
.05	.8	340	113	.1693	3	.02868	1
.05	.8	360	120	.1643	3	.02699	1
.05	.8	380	126	.1603	3	.02569	1
.05	.8	400	133	.156	3	.02433	1
.05	.8	420	140	.152	3	.02311	1
.05	.8	440	146	.1488	3	.02215	1
.05	.8	460	153	.1454	3	.02113	1
.05	.8	480	160	.1421	3	.0202	1
.05	.8	500	166	.1395	3	.01946	1

Figure 9.9. Effect size for power of 0.80, alpha of 0.05 for N's from 40 to 500

If we look at the graph (the effect size is labeled σ), we can see that our original hope of doing this study with an $N = 60$ was off the mark. We now know why a funding agency would not want to fund such a study with an $N = 60$, because it would require a much greater effect size than the minimum effect size, $f = 0.25$, for which we said it would be clinically important to have a power of 0.80 with an alpha of 0.05. Based on the graph, it appears that we need about 160 observations overall with about 53 in each of our three groups. If we want a more precise way to pick our needed sample size, we can look at the tabular results. There we see that we would have a power of 0.80 to detect an effect size of 0.25 (column labeled `delta`) if we had just under 160 participants with 53 in each group. We could hone it down even more precisely by varying the total N from 150 to 170 in increments of 1.

```
power oneway, n(150(1)170) power(0.80) alpha(0.05) ngroups(3) graph table
```

Try this command and see why we would decide on $N = 159$ with 53 participants in each group.

What if we said only a large effect size would have clinical importance, $f = 0.40$? Looking at our tabular results, we see that we would need only about 60 study participants, with 20 in each group. We can also see what would happen if we insisted on detecting a small effect size. We would need a huge sample to obtain an effect size of $f = 0.10$ with an alpha of 0.05 and a power of 0.80. From the table above, we see that not even 500 participants would be enough. If we were to again type

```
power oneway, n(500(20)1000) power(0.80) alpha(0.05) ngroups(3) graph table
```

we would see that we would need about 980 participants with 326 in each group. You can imagine that when even a small effect has important clinical implications, many research studies have samples that are too small to be effective. In that case, we do not know whether a lack of significance is because the effect is unimportant or if it is because the study design is underpowered.

9.10.2   Power analysis for two-way ANOVA

Let's extend our one-way example to a two-way ANOVA. Our one-way example was restricted to women. Let's see if there is also a gender difference. With a two-way ANOVA, we have three interests: 1) whether the three conditions make a difference; 2) whether being a woman or a man makes a difference; and 3) whether there is a gender x condition interaction.

For the condition difference (three columns in the two-way ANOVA), we will use the 0.80 for our power, 0.05 for our alpha, and 0.25 for our effect size. Our data now have two rows, one for women and one for men. To run the `power twoway` command, we will need to add the number of rows, `nrows(2)`, and specify that we want the results for the condition effect in the three columns, `factor(column)`. Here is our command for the condition difference and the table and graph (figure 9.10) it produces:

```
. power twoway, nrows(2) ncols(3) power(0.80) n(100(20)300) factor(column)
> graph table

Performing iteration ...

Estimated column variance for two-way ANOVA
F test for column effect
H0: delta = 0  versus  Ha: delta != 0
```

alpha	power	N	N_per_cell	delta	N_r	N_c	Var_c	Var_e
.05	.8	100	16	.3221	2	3	.1038	1
.05	.8	120	20	.2871	2	3	.08244	1
.05	.8	140	23	.2673	2	3	.07143	1
.05	.8	160	26	.251	2	3	.06301	1
.05	.8	180	30	.2334	2	3	.05446	1
.05	.8	200	33	.2223	2	3	.04943	1
.05	.8	220	36	.2127	2	3	.04525	1
.05	.8	240	40	.2017	2	3	.04066	1
.05	.8	260	43	.1944	2	3	.03779	1
.05	.8	280	46	.1879	2	3	.0353	1
.05	.8	300	50	.1801	2	3	.03245	1

Figure 9.10. Effect size for power of 0.80 with two rows in each of the three columns for N's from 100 to 300

These results are virtually the same as we had for the columns in the one-way ANOVA. In the results, the only difference is that we need 26 people in each cell.

If we were testing for gender differences, we would simply use the option `factor(row)`:

```
power twoway, nrows(2) ncols(3) power(0.8) n(100(10)300) factor(row) graph ///
    table
```

Detecting a row effect of gender would require about 130 observations.

If we were testing for an interaction of condition x row, we would use the option `factor(rowcol)`:

```
power twoway, nrows(2) ncols(3) power(0.8) n(100(10)300) factor(rowcol)    ///
      graph table
```

Detecting a medium interaction effect of $f = 0.25$ would require about 160 observations. Each of these `power` commands show that having around 160 participants in our study will work fine.

9.10.3 Power analysis for repeated-measures ANOVA

This time we are going to think about designing a different study. Suppose we are interested in how maternal stress varies depending on the age of a mother's oldest child. We will select three fixed ages for the oldest child. We will have one group of mothers, but we will measure their stress at four points. The first time is when the oldest child is 10. The second time is when the oldest child turns 13. The third time is when the oldest child turns 16. Finally, the fourth time is when the oldest child turns 19. Our question is whether maternal stress is consistent or varies depending on the age of the mother's oldest child. Our hypothesis is that a mother's stress does vary with the age of the oldest child and our null hypothesis is that it does not. We want to use the 0.05 alpha level of significance. We want to have a power of 0.80. How big of a sample do we need?

We know we cannot treat this as a one-way ANOVA because we do not have four independent samples. The issue is that a mother's maternal stress at one point is likely to strongly correlate with her maternal stress at another point. To allow for this lack of independence, we need to make some estimate of the correlation. Let's pick a value of $r = 0.6$. If you have no basis for estimating the correlation, you might try to repeat the analysis using different values to see how much difference that makes. You could run a simple pilot test with a few mothers to get a reasonable value for this correlation. The $r = 0.60$ was picked because we expect there to be a strong correlation between measures of the maternal stress. We might find this value through a literature review, or we may have to just make a guess. We decide that a small effect size of $f = 0.10$ is unlikely to be clinically important, but a moderate effect size of $f = 0.25$ would be important. This decision on the size of effect size can sometimes be justified by reference to literature in the field. We will be interested in how many mothers we need in our sample to have a power of 0.80 with an alpha of 0.05, four repeated measurements, and a correlation between measurements of $r = 0.60$ to detect an effect size of 0.25. Here are the command, table, and graph (figure 9.11):

```
. power repeated, n(100(10)300) power(0.80) alpha(0.05) corr(0.60) nrepeated(4)
> ngroups(1) graph table
```

Performing iteration ...

Estimated within-subject variance for repeated-measures ANOVA
F test for within subject with Greenhouse-Geisser correction
H0: delta = 0 versus Ha: delta != 0

alpha	power	N	N_per_group	delta	N_g	N_rep	Var_w
.05	.8	100	100	.3324	1	4	.01105
.05	.8	110	110	.3167	1	4	.01003
.05	.8	120	120	.3031	1	4	.00919
.05	.8	130	130	.2911	1	4	.00847
.05	.8	140	140	.2804	1	4	.00786
.05	.8	150	150	.2708	1	4	.00733
.05	.8	160	160	.2621	1	4	.00687
.05	.8	170	170	.2542	1	4	.00646
.05	.8	180	180	.247	1	4	.0061
.05	.8	190	190	.2404	1	4	.00578
.05	.8	200	200	.2342	1	4	.00549
.05	.8	210	210	.2286	1	4	.00522
.05	.8	220	220	.2233	1	4	.00499
.05	.8	230	230	.2183	1	4	.00477
.05	.8	240	240	.2137	1	4	.00457
.05	.8	250	250	.2094	1	4	.00438
.05	.8	260	260	.2053	1	4	.00421
.05	.8	270	270	.2014	1	4	.00406
.05	.8	280	280	.1978	1	4	.00391
.05	.8	290	290	.1943	1	4	.00378
.05	.8	300	300	.1911	1	4	.00365

Var_we	Var_e	corr
.1	1	.6
.1	1	.6
.1	1	.6
.1	1	.6
.1	1	.6
.1	1	.6
.1	1	.6
.1	1	.6
.1	1	.6
.1	1	.6
.1	1	.6
.1	1	.6
.1	1	.6
.1	1	.6
.1	1	.6
.1	1	.6
.1	1	.6
.1	1	.6
.1	1	.6
.1	1	.6
.1	1	.6

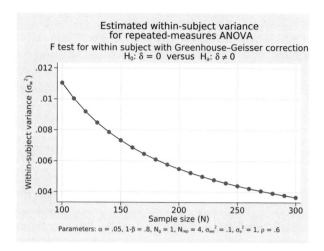

Figure 9.11. Effect size for power of 0.80, alpha of 0.05, four repeated measurements, and a 0.60 correlation between measurements for N's from 100 to 300

We decided to try sample sizes of between 100 and 300 in increments of 10. If this does not work, we could quickly try a larger or smaller set of sample sizes. We added the `corr(0.60)` option because our measures are not going to be independent; we indicated that we have 4 repeated measurements with the `nrepeated(4)` option and just one group of mothers with the `ngroups(1)` option.

It looks like we need about 170 mothers in our sample. We could rerun the command changing `n(100(10)300)` to `n(160(1)180)` to get a more precise estimate of the sample size required. You can see how important it is to pick the appropriate minimum effect size that would be clinically important. If you insist on being able to demonstrate a small effect size, you may need to have an impractically large sample size. If you pick a large effect size, you may find you need a very small sample, but you run a very high risk of not finding a true moderate effect to be significant.

9.10.4 Summary of power analysis for ANOVA

We have just scratched the surface of the capabilities of the **power** command when used with ANOVA. You can see how useful this is for studies involving ANOVA. When you propose to do a study and are requesting funding for your research, you need to justify your cost, and your sample size is usually a critical factor in your cost—more people means more money. A funding agency would have no reason to fund you if you requested money for a far larger sample than you need to find an appropriate effect size. At the same time, a funding agency would have no reason to fund you if you requested less money for a sample that was too small to have a good chance, say, a power of 0.80, of demonstrating a clinically worthwhile result when one existed in the population.

The menu system offers all the power analysis features we have covered as well as some options not covered. You can explore these additional options by selecting Statistics ▷ Power, precision, and sample size. In the control panel that opens, expand the menu Population parameter ▷ Means ▷ ANOVA (multiple means) from the left pane. Here one-way ANOVA, two-way ANOVA, and repeated-measures ANOVA are listed. These methods are explained in the online video tutorials at https://www.stata.com/links/video-tutorials/ on power analysis.

9.11 Summary

ANOVA is an extremely complex and powerful approach to analyzing data. We have only touched the surface of ANOVA here. Stata offers a powerful collection of advanced procedures that extend traditional ANOVA. In this chapter, you have learned how to

- Conduct a one-way ANOVA as an extension of the independent t test to three or more groups

- Use nonparametric alternatives to ANOVA for comparing distributions or comparing medians when you have three or more groups

- Control for a covariate through ANCOVA when you do not have randomization but know how the groups differ on background variables

- Use a two-way ANOVA for situations in which you have two categorical predictors that might or might not interact with one another

- Graph interaction effects for a two-way ANOVA

- Perform a repeated-measures ANOVA as an extension of the dependent/paired t test for when you have three or more measurements on each subject

- Calculate the intraclass correlation coefficient to measure agreement or homogeneity within groups

The next chapter presents multiple regression. Many of the models we have fit within an ANOVA framework can be done equally well or better within a multiple-regression format. Multiple regression is an extremely general approach to data analysis.

9.12 Exercises

1. Suppose that you have five people in condition A, five in condition B, and five in condition C. On your outcome variable, the five people in condition A have scores of 9, 8, 6, 9, and 5. The five in condition B have scores of 5, 9, 6, 4, and 8. The five in condition C have scores of 2, 5, 3, 4, and 6. Show how you would enter these data using a wide format. Show how you would enter them using a long format.

2. Using the data in the long format from exercise 1, do an ANOVA. Compare the means and the standard deviations. What does the F test tell us? Use `pwmean` to conduct multiple-comparison tests. What do the results tell us?

3. Use `gss2002_chapter9.dta`. Does the time an adult female watches TV (`tvhours`) vary depending on her marital status (`marital`)? Do a one-way ANOVA, including a tabulation of means; do a Bonferroni multiple-comparison test; and then present a bar chart showing the means for hours spent watching TV by marital status. Carefully interpret the results. Can you explain the pattern of means and the differences of means? Do a tabulation of your dependent variable, and see if you find a problem with the distribution.

4. Use `gss2002_chapter9.dta`. Does the time an adult watches TV (`tvhours`) depend on his or her political party identification (`partyid`)? Do a tabulation of `partyid`. Drop the 48 people who are Other party. Combine the strong Democrats, not strong Democrats, and independent near Democrats into one group and label it Democrats. Combine the strong Republicans, not strong Republicans, and independent near Republicans into one group and label it Republicans. Keep the independents as a separate group. Now do a one-way ANOVA with a tabulation and Bonferroni test to answer the question of whether how much time adults spend watching TV depends on their political party identification. Carefully interpret the results.

5. Use `gss2002_chapter9.dta`. Repeat exercise 3 using the Kruskal–Wallis rank test and a box plot. Interpret the results, and compare them with the results in exercise 3.

6. Use `nlsy97_selected_variables.dta`. A person is interested in the relationship between having fun with your family (`fun97`) and associating with peers who volunteer (`pvol97`). She thinks adolescents who frequently have fun with their families will associate with peers who volunteer. The fun-with-family variable is a count of the number of days a week an adolescent has fun with his or her family. Although this is a quantitative variable, treat this as eight categories, 0–7 days per week. Because of possible differences between younger and older adolescents, control for age (`age97`). Do an analysis of covariance, and compute adjusted means. Present a table showing both adjusted and unadjusted means. Interpret the results.

7. Use `partyid.dta`. Do a two-way ANOVA to see if there is 1) a significant difference in support for stem cell research (`stemcell`) by political party identification (`partyid`), 2) a significant difference in support by gender, and 3) a significant interaction between gender and party identification. Construct a two-way overlay graph to show the interaction and interpret it.

8. In exercise 1, you entered data for five people in each of three conditions, A, B, and C, in a wide format. Now use these same data but assume that five people were measured at three times where A is a pretest measure of the dependent variable

before an intervention of some program, B is a posttest measure of the dependent variable at the conclusion of the intervention, and C is a follow-up measure 30 days after the completion of the intervention. Because you are treating this as a repeated-measures ANOVA, you need to add a variable named `id`, numbered 1–5 for the five people. You also need to label the three measures with a common stem. Let's use `time1`, `time2`, and `time3` to replace A, B, and C as labels. Use the `reshape` command to transform the data from the wide to the long format. Do a repeated-measures ANOVA and interpret the result.

9. You have 5 two-parent families, each of which has two adolescent children. You want to know if the parents agree more with each other about the risks of premarital sex or if the siblings agree more. The scores for the five sets of parents are (9, 3) (5, 5) (4, 2) (6, 7) (8, 10). The scores for the five sets of siblings are (9, 8) (7, 4) (8, 10) (3, 2) (8, 8). Enter these data in a long format, and compute the intraclass correlation for parents and the intraclass correlation for siblings. Which set of pairs has greater agreement regarding the risks of premarital sex?

10 Multiple regression

10.1   Introduction to multiple regression

Multiple regression is an extension of bivariate correlation and regression that opens a huge variety of new applications. Multiple regression and its extensions provide the core statistical technique for most publications in social-science research journals. Stata is an exceptional tool for doing multiple regression because regression applications are at the heart of the original conceptualization and subsequent development of Stata. In this chapter, I introduce multiple regression and regression diagnostics. In the following chapter, I will introduce logistic regression.

10.2   What is multiple regression?

In bivariate regression, you had one outcome variable and one predictor. Multiple regression expands on this by allowing any number of predictors. Allowing many predictors makes sense because few outcomes have just one cause. Why do some people have more income than others? Clearly, education is an important predictor, but education is only part of the story. Some people inherit great wealth and would have substantial income whether or not they had any education. The incomes people have tend to increase as they get older, at least up to some age where their incomes may begin to decline. The careers people select will influence their incomes. A person's work ethic may also be important because those who work harder may earn more income. There are many more variables that influence a person's income, for example, race, gender, and marital status. You need more than one variable to adequately predict and understand the variation in income.

Predicting and explaining income can be even more complicated than having multiple predictors. Some of the predictors may interact such that combinations of independent variables have unique effects. For example, a physician with a strong work ethic may make much more than a physician who is lazy. By contrast, an assembly-line worker who has a strong work ethic has little advantage over an assembly-line worker who is working only at the minimum required work rate. Hence, the effect of work ethic on income can vary depending on occupation. Similarly, the effect of education on income may be different for women and men. Clearly, social science requires a statistical strategy that allows you to study many variables working simultaneously to produce an outcome; multiple regression provides that strategy.

In this chapter, we will use data from a 2004 survey of Oregon residents, called `ops2004.dta`. There is a series of 11 items with views on how concerned the person is about different environmental issues, such as pesticides, noise pollution, food contamination, air quality, and water quality. Using the alpha reliability procedures and factor analysis that are covered in chapter 12, I constructed a scale called `env_con` that has a strong alpha of 0.89. This will serve as our dependent variable; it is the outcome we want to predict.

Say that you are interested in several independent variables (predictors). These might include variables related to the person's health, education, income, and community identification. For example, we might expect people who have higher education and community identification to score higher on concern for environmental issues. Perhaps the expectation is less clear for how a person's health or income will be related to concerns for the environment, but we think they both might be important. Clearly, we have left out some important predictors, but these predictors will be sufficient to show how multiple regression analysis is done using Stata.

10.3 The basic multiple regression command

Select Statistics ▷ Linear models and related, and you will see a long list of regression-related commands. Stata gives us more options than I could possibly cover in this book. In this chapter, we focus on the Statistics ▷ Linear models and related ▷ Linear regression menu item. The basic dialog box for linear regression asks for the dependent variable in one box and a list of our independent variables in another box. Type env_con as the dependent variable, and then type the following independent variables: educat (years of education), inc (annual income in dollars), com3 (identification with the community), hlthprob (health problems), and epht3 (impact of the environment on the person's own health). The resulting dialog box looks like figure 10.1.

Figure 10.1. The Model tab for multiple regression

The by/if/in tab lets you fit the regression model by some grouping variable (you might estimate it separately for women and men), restrict your analysis to cases if a condition is met (you might limit it to people 18–40 years old), or apply your regression model to a subset of observations. We will go over the Weights tab and the SE/Robust tab later. The Reporting tab has several options for what is reported. Click on that tab, and check the option to show *Standardized beta coefficients*.

These dialog box options produce the simple command regress env_con educat inc com3 hlthprob epht3, beta. The syntax of this command is simple, and unless you want special options, you can just enter the command directly in the Command window. The command name, regress, is followed by the dependent variable, env_con, and then a list of the independent variables. After the comma comes the only option you are using, namely, beta. Here are the results:

```
. regress env_con educat inc com3 hlthprob epht3, beta

      Source |       SS           df       MS      Number of obs   =      3,769
-------------+----------------------------------   F(5, 3763)      =     320.15
       Model |  647.67793          5  129.535586   Prob > F        =     0.0000
    Residual |   1522.5587      3,763  .404612995   R-squared       =     0.2984
-------------+----------------------------------   Adj R-squared   =     0.2975
       Total |  2170.23663      3,768  .575965136   Root MSE        =     .63609

------------------------------------------------------------------------------
     env_con | Coefficient  Std. err.      t    P>|t|                      Beta
-------------+----------------------------------------------------------------
      educat |   .0011841    .004077     0.29   0.772                  .0044584
         inc |   5.51e-08   3.62e-07     0.15   0.879                  .0023317
        com3 |  -.0503162   .0092717    -5.43   0.000                 -.074352
    hlthprob |   .2974034   .0248129    11.99   0.000                  .172927
       epht3 |   .4020741    .012687    31.69   0.000                  .4575999
       _cons |   1.273655   .0651735    19.54   0.000                         .
------------------------------------------------------------------------------
```

The results have three sections. The upper left block of results is similar to what you saw in chapter 9 on analysis of variance. This time, the source called Model refers to the regression model rather than to the between-group source. The regression model consists of the set of all five predictors. The source called Residual corresponds to the error component in analysis of variance. You have 5 degrees of freedom for the model. The degrees of freedom will always be k, the number of predictors (here educat, inc, com3, hlthprob, and epht3) in the model.

The analysis of variance does not show the F ratio like the tables in chapter 9. The F appears in the block of results in the upper right section. The output says F(5, 3763) = 320.15. The F of 320.15 is the ratio of the mean square for the model to the mean square for the residual. It is $129.535586/0.404612995 = 320.15$ in this example. The degrees of freedom for the numerator (Model) is 5, and for the denominator (Residual) it is 3,763. The probability of this F ratio appears just below the F value, Prob > F = 0.0000. When this probability is less than 0.05, you can say $p < 0.05$; when it is less than 0.01, you can say $p < 0.01$; and when it is less than 0.001, you can say $p < 0.001$. In a report, you would write this as $F(5, 3763) = 320.15$, $p < 0.001$. There is a highly significant relationship between environmental concerns and the set of five predictors.

How well does the model fit the data? This question is usually answered by reporting R^2. The regression model explains 29.8% of the variance in environmental concerns. Stata reports this as R-squared = 0.2984. In bivariate regression, the r^2 measured how close the observations were to the straight line used to make the prediction. With multiple regression, you use the capital R^2, which measures how close the observations are to the predicted value, based on the set of predictors. What is a weak or a strong value for R^2 varies by the topic being explained. If you are in a fairly exploratory area, an R^2 near 0.3 is considered reasonably good. A rule of thumb some researchers use is that an R^2 less than 0.1 is weak, between 0.1 to 0.2 is moderate, and greater than 0.3 is strong. Be careful in applying this rule of thumb because some areas of research require higher values and others allow lower values. You might report our results as showing that we can explain 29.8% of the variance in environmental concern using our set of predictors, and this is a moderate-to-strong relationship.

On a small sample with several predictors, the value of R^2 can exaggerate the strength of the relationship. Each time you add a variable, you expect to increase R^2 just by chance. R^2 cannot get smaller as you add variables. When you have many predictors and a small sample, you may get a big R^2 just by chance. To offset this bias, some researchers report the adjusted R^2. This will be smaller than the R^2 because it attempts to remove the chance effects. When you have a large sample and relatively few predictors, R^2 and the adjusted R^2 will be similar, and you might report just the R^2. However, when there is a substantial difference between the two, you should report both values.

Across the bottom of the results is a block that has six columns containing the key regression results. A formal multiple regression equation is written as

$$\widehat{Y} = b_0 + b_1 X_1 + b_2 X_2 + \cdots + b_k X_k$$

$\widehat{Y}$ is the predicted value of the dependent variable. b_0 is the intercept or constant. Stata calls b_0 the _cons, which is an abbreviation for the constant. You can think of this as the base prediction of Y when all the X variables are fixed at zero. b_1 is the regression coefficient for the effect of X_1, b_2 is the regression coefficient for the effect of X_2, and b_k is the regression coefficient for the last X variable. You might see these coefficients called *unstandardized regression coefficients*. You can get the values for the equation from the output (see table 10.1).

Table 10.1. Regression equation and Stata output

Name in the regression equation	Stata name	Stata results: Unstandardized coefficient
b_0	_cons	1.274
b_1	educat	0.001
b_2	inc	5.51e–08
b_3	com3	−0.050
b_4	hlthprob	0.297
b_5	epht3	0.402

You can input this information into the equation, calculating the estimated value of the dependent variable:

$$\widehat{\texttt{env\_con}} = 1.274 + 0.001(\texttt{educat}) + 0.000(\texttt{inc}) - 0.050(\texttt{com3})$$
$$+ 0.297(\texttt{hlthprob}) + 0.402(\texttt{epht3})$$

The regression results next give a standard error, t-value, and $P > |t|$ for each regression coefficient. If you divide each regression coefficient by its standard error, you obtain the t-value that is used to test the significance of the coefficient. Each of the t ratios has $N - k - 1$ degrees of freedom. Subtract one degree of freedom for each of the $k = 5$ predictors and another degree for the constant. From the upper right corner of the results, you can see that there are 3,769 observations, and from the analysis of variance table, you can see that there are 3,763 degrees of freedom for the residual. If you forget the $N - k - 1$ rule for degrees of freedom, you can use the number of degrees of freedom for the residual in the analysis of variance table. You might want to include the degrees of freedom in your report, but you do not need to look up the probability in a table of t-values because Stata gives you a two-tailed probability. For example, you might write that $b_5 = 0.402$, $p < 0.001$. In some fields, you would write $b_5 = 0.402$, $t(3763) = 31.69$, $p < 0.001$.

The unstandardized regression coefficients have a simple interpretation. They tell you how much the dependent variable changes for a unit change in the independent variable. For example, a 1-unit change in com3, identification with the community, produces a 0.05-unit decrease in env_con, environmental concern, holding all other variables constant. Without studying the range and distribution of each of the variables, it is hard to compare the unstandardized coefficients to see which variable is more or less important. The problem is that each variable can be measured on a different scale.

Here we measured income using dollars, and this makes it hard to interpret the b-value as a measure of the effect of income. After all, a \$1.00 change in your annual income is something you might not even notice, and this change surely would not have much of an effect on anything. This is reflected in $b_{\text{inc}} = 5.51\text{e–}08$, which is a tiny value. (If you have not seen this format for numbers, it is a part of scientific notation, which is used for tiny numbers. The e–08 tells us to move the decimal place eight places to the left. Thus this number is 0.0000000551.) If we had used the natural logarithm of income or if we had measured income in 1,000s of dollars or even 10,000s of dollars, we would have obtained a different value. When you use income as a predictor, it is common to use a natural logarithm or measure income in 10,000s of dollars, where an income of 47,312 would be represented as 4.7312.

In our command above, we included the option to get beta weights (β). Beta weights are more easily compared because they are based on standardizing all variables to have a mean of 0 and a standard deviation of 1. These beta weights are interpreted similarly to how you interpret correlations in that $\beta < 0.20$ is considered a weak effect, β between 0.2 and 0.5 is considered a moderate effect, and $\beta > 0.5$ is considered a strong effect. The beta weights tell you that education, income, and community identity all have a weak effect, and of these, only community identity is statistically significant, $p < 0.001$. Having a health problem in the family, hlthprob, has a beta weight that is still weak, $\beta = 0.173$, but it is statistically significant, $p < 0.001$. Having environmental health concerns, epht3, has $\beta = 0.458$, $p < 0.001$, which is a moderate-to-strong effect.

You might summarize this regression analysis as follows: A model including education, income, community identity, environmental health concerns, and health problems in the family explains 29.8% of the variance in environmental concerns of adults in Oregon, $F(5, 3763) = 320.15$, $p < 0.001$. Neither education nor income has a statistically significant effect. Community identity has a weak but statistically significant effect, $\beta = -0.074$, $p < 0.001$. The two health variables are the strongest predictors in this group: having a health problem in the family has $\beta = 0.173$, $p < 0.001$, and having environmental health concerns has $\beta = 0.458$, $p < 0.001$.

If you do not want beta weights, you would simply rerun the regression without the `beta` option. Without the `beta` option, you get a confidence interval for each unstandardized regression coefficient. If you have an analysis where your primary interest is in the unstandardized coefficients, confidence intervals are a useful extension on the simple tests of significance.

10.4   Increment in R-squared: Semipartial correlations

Beta weights are widely used for measuring the effect sizes of different variables. Because it is based on standardized variables, a beta weight tells you how much of a standard deviation the dependent variable changes for each standard deviation change in the independent variable. Except for special circumstances, beta weights range from -1 to $+1$, with a zero meaning that there is no relationship. Sometimes the interpretation of beta weights is problematic. If you have a categorical variable like gender, the interpretation is unclear. What does it mean to say that as you go up one standard deviation on gender, you go up β standard deviations on the dependent variable? Also, when you are comparing groups, the beta weights can be misleading. If you compare regression models predicting income for women and for men, the beta weights would be confounded with real differences in variance between women and men in the standardization of all variables.

Another approach to comparing the importance of variables is to see how much each variable increases R^2 if the variable is entered last. Effectively, this approach fits the model with all the variables except for the one you are interested in. You obtain an R^2 value for this model. Then you fit the model a second time, including the variable in which you are interested. This will have a larger R^2, and the difference between the two R^2 values will tell you how much the variable increases R^2. This increment is how much of the variance is uniquely explained by the independent variable you are interested in, controlling for all the other independent variables. This increment is often called simply an *increment* in R^2, which is a very descriptive name. Some people call it a *part-correlation square* because it measures the part that is uniquely explained by the variable. Others call it a *semipartial* R^2. Another way to compare variables is using what is called a *partial correlation*; we will not cover that here because it has less-desirable properties for comparing the relative importance of each variable.

Estimating the increment in R^2 would be a tedious process because you would have to fit the model twice for every independent variable and compute each of these differences. In this example, we would have to run 10 regression models. Fortunately, there is a Stata command, `pcorr`, that automatically does this and gives us the partial and semipartial correlations for each variable controlling for all the other variables. Select Statistics ▷ Summaries, tables, and tests ▷ Summary and descriptive statistics ▷ Partial correlations to open the `pcorr` dialog box.

In the dialog box, we enter our dependent variable in the box labeled *Display partial and semipartial correlation coefficient of variable*. Then we enter our list of independent variables in the box labeled *Against variables*. Figure 10.2 displays our updated dialog box:

Figure 10.2. The Main tab of the pcorr dialog box

Here are the command and results:

```
. pcorr env_con educat inc com3 hlthprob epht3
(obs=3769)
```

Partial and semipartial correlations of env_con with

Variable	Partial corr.	Semipartial corr.	Partial corr.^2	Semipartial corr.^2	Significance value
educat	0.0047	0.0040	0.0000	0.0000	0.7715
inc	0.0025	0.0021	0.0000	0.0000	0.8788
com3	-0.0881	-0.0741	0.0078	0.0055	0.0000
hlthprob	0.1918	0.1637	0.0368	0.0268	0.0000
epht3	0.4590	0.4327	0.2107	0.1873	0.0000

Here you are interested only in the column labeled Semipartial corr.^2, semipartial R^2, which shows how much each variable contributes uniquely. The concern for environmental health problems has an increment to R^2 of 0.1873, $p < 0.001$. Although two other variables have statistically significant effects, this is the only variable that has a substantial increment to R^2. The semipartial R^2 is a conservative estimate of the effect of each variable because it measures only how much the R^2 increases when that variable is entered after all the other variables are already in the model. You might notice that the sum of the semipartial R^2s is just 0.220 even though the model R^2 is 0.298. This happens because some of the predictors are explaining the same part of the variance in the dependent variable, and whatever is shared with other predictors is not unique. The semipartial R^2 estimates only the unique effect of each predictor.

10.5   Is the dependent variable normally distributed?

Now let's examine the distribution of the dependent variable. Many applied researchers believe that multiple regression assumes the dependent variable is normally distributed. Actually, the assumption is that the residuals (error term) are normally distributed; this will be discussed in section 10.6. If the dependent variable has a highly skewed distribution or is bimodal, the residuals may not be normally distributed unless we have independent variables that predict this pattern. If we do not have independent variables that predict this pattern, the residuals may also be skewed. Because we make the assumption that the residuals are normally distributed, it would be helpful to understand the distribution of the dependent variable and consider whether we have predictors to explain any skewness and other nonnormalities. This section shows how to examine the distribution of the dependent variable.

Let's create a histogram on `env_con`:

```
. histogram env_con, frequency normal kdensity
```

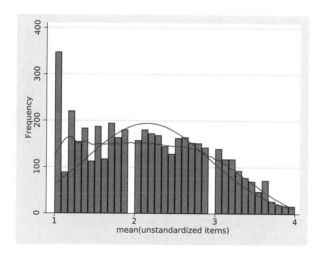

Figure 10.3. Histogram of dependent variable, `env_con`

Three distributions are represented in figure 10.3. The bars represent the actual distribution, which does not look too bad except for the big bunch of low scores (there are 348 people who have the minimum possible score of 1.0 on the environmental concerns scale). The smooth, bell-shaped curve represents how the data would be distributed if they were normal.

The other curve, called a kdensity curve, is a bit hard to see in figure 10.3. The kdensity curve is an estimation of how the population data would look given our sample data. The actual data from the histogram, the normal curve, and the kdensity curve are similar beyond a value of about 1.5–1.8. At the center of the distribution, the data and the kdensity curve are a little flatter than a normal curve. We have too few cases in the middle of the distribution to call it normal. The real problem, however, is on the left side of the distribution, where we have too many people who have a mean score of less than about 1.5. The scale ranged from 1 to 4, and a mean score of 1.5 or less means that the person has very little environmental concern.

An alternative plot is the hanging rootogram (`ssc install hangroot`). Once the `hangroot` command is installed, we simply enter `hangroot env_con, bar`. This produces the graph in figure 10.4.

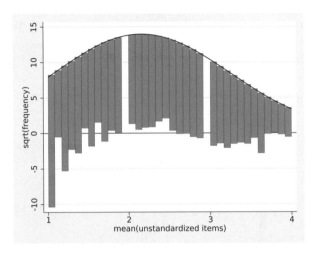

Figure 10.4. Hanging rootogram of dependent variable, `env_con`

This hanging rootogram has a smooth curve representing how the data would be distributed if it were normal. When a bar descends below the horizontal line, there are too many observations at this value compared with a normal distribution. At a value of 1, the bar drops far below the horizontal line, and the bars are all below the line from a value of about 1.5 and lower. There are a few values toward the middle of the distribution that do not drop down to the horizontal line; there are not enough values in this area of the distribution.

The hanging rootogram is sometimes easier to read than a histogram, in part, because the vertical axis is the square root of the frequency rather than the actual frequency. This makes it much easier to see deviations from normality in the tails where there are usually relatively few observations. John Tukey suggested this type of graph, and Maarten L. Buis, a Stata user, wrote the `hangroot` command in 2010.

We can evaluate the normality of our dependent variable by using two additional statistics that are known as skewness and kurtosis. We learned earlier about the `detail` option to the `summarize` command; this option provides these statistics. Just use the `summarize` command with the `detail` option now.

```
. summarize env_con, detail
                    mean(unstandardized items)
```

	Percentiles	Smallest		
1%	1	1		
5%	1	1		
10%	1.181818	1	Obs	4,506
25%	1.5	1	Sum of wgt.	4,506
50%	2.1		Mean	2.157595
		Largest	Std. dev.	.7705153
75%	2.727273	4		
90%	3.2	4	Variance	.5936939
95%	3.454545	4	Skewness	.2302043
99%	3.818182	4	Kurtosis	2.059664

In the lower right column, you find skewness of 0.23 and kurtosis of 2.06. Skewness is a measure of whether a distribution trails off in one direction or another. env_con is positively skewed because there are a lot of people who have a low level of environmental concern, but there are relatively fewer people who have a high level of environmental concern. A normal distribution has skewness of 0. If the skewness is greater than 0 (as with env_con), the distribution is positively skewed; if the skewness is less than 0, the distribution is negatively skewed.

Kurtosis measures the thickness of the tails of a distribution. If you look at our histogram, you see that the tail to the left of the mean is a little too thick and the tail to the right of the mean is way too thick to be normally distributed. When a distribution has a problem with kurtosis indicated by thick tails, it will also have too few cases in the middle of the distribution. By contrast, when a distribution has a problem with kurtosis indicated by thin tails, it will also have too many cases in the middle of the distribution (peaked) for it to be normally distributed; this would happen for a variable in which most people were very close to the mean value.

A normal distribution will have a kurtosis of 3.00. A value of less than 3.00 means that the tails are too thick (hence, too flat in the middle), and a value of greater than 3.00 means that the tails are too thin (hence, too peaked in the middle). The kurtosis is 2.06 for env_con, meaning that the tails are too thick; you could tell that by looking at the histogram. Some statistical software, such as SAS or IBM SPSS Statistics, reports a value for kurtosis that is the actual value of kurtosis minus three so that a normal distribution would have a value of 0. Stata does not do this, so the correct value for a normal distribution in Stata is 3.00. You need to be careful when writing a report that will be read by people who rely on other programs that may have kurtosis of 0 for a normal distribution.

The `summarize` command does not give you the significance of the skewness or kurtosis coefficients. To get the significances, you need to run a command that you enter directly:

```
. sktest env_con

Skewness and kurtosis tests for normality
                                                            ─── Joint test ───
        Variable |    Obs   Pr(skewness)   Pr(kurtosis)   Adj chi2(2)  Prob>chi2
─────────────────┼────────────────────────────────────────────────────────────
         env_con |  4,506      0.0000         0.0000        631.52       0.0000
```

Combining this result with the results from the `summarize` command, we would say that skewness = 0.23, $p < 0.001$, and kurtosis = 2.06, $p < 0.001$. Both of these tested jointly have a $p < 0.001$. Hence, the distribution is not normal, the skewness tells us the distribution has a positive skew, and the kurtosis tells us the tails are too thick.

10.6   Are the residuals normally distributed?

An important assumption of regression is that the residuals are normally distributed. At a risk of oversimplification, this means that we are as likely to overestimate a person's score as we are to underestimate their score, and we should have relatively few cases that are extremely overestimated or underestimated.

We could examine the residual to see if it is normally distributed. Following the `regress` command that we ran on page 276, we can obtain the residual values by running the `predict` command with the `residual` option. This command generates a new variable that we have called `res`, which includes the residual value for each observation. We then run a `summarize` command to obtain the skewness and kurtosis. Here are our results:

```
. regress env_con educat inc com3 hlthprob epht3, beta
  (output omitted )

. predict res, residuals
(739 missing values generated)

. summarize res, detail

                            Residuals
─────────────────────────────────────────────────────────────
        Percentiles      Smallest
 1%    -1.357709        -1.944407
 5%     -.9625443       -1.914089
10%     -.7994747       -1.852046    Obs              3,769
25%     -.483786        -1.849233    Sum of wgt.      3,769

50%     -.0352801                    Mean          3.51e-10
                         Largest     Std. dev.      .6356698
75%     .4719241         1.762432
90%     .8467105         1.940851    Variance       .4040761
95%     1.05727          1.951321    Skewness       .0997807
99%     1.425768         2.247876    Kurtosis       2.592773
```

We see that the skewness of 0.10 is close to the value of 0.00 for a normal distribution. The kurtosis of 2.593 a bit low compared with the value of 3.00 for a normal distribution (remember SAS and SPSS subtract 3.0 from the kurtosis). If we wanted to test the significance of the skewness and kurtosis, we would type

```
. sktest res
Skewness and kurtosis tests for normality
                                                  ────── Joint test ──────
     Variable |    Obs   Pr(skewness)   Pr(kurtosis)   Adj chi2(2)  Prob>chi2
──────────────┼───────────────────────────────────────────────────────────
          res |   3,769       0.0124         0.0000        41.53      0.0000
```

Both the skewness and the kurtosis are significantly different from what they would be if our residuals were normally distributed. However, we have a very large sample, and this large sample N not only contributes to the tests being statistically significant, but also limits the concern we have about violating the normality of residuals assumption. You should use this test of a normal residual cautiously because it tends to result in a significant test when there is only a small departure of normality for a large sample where there is considerable robustness against violating the normality assumption. By contrast, when you have a smaller sample, say, under 100 observations, the violation of normality is more serious, but this test may have insufficient power to detect the departure from normality.

Assumptions about the distribution of the residual become more difficult when we add the fact that this distribution should be about the same for any value or combination of values for the predictors. Imagine predicting income from a person's education. With a low education, we would predict a low income. As a person goes up the scale on education, we would predict higher income. However, for those with 16 or more years of education, there is a huge range in income. Some may be in low-paying service positions, and others may be in extremely high-paying positions. If we plotted a scattergram with the regression line drawn through it, we might expect the variance around the line to increase as education increases. This effect is illustrated in figure 10.5.

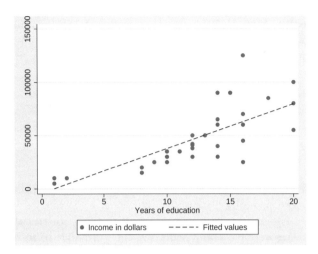

Figure 10.5. Heteroskedasticity of residuals

This figure shows that the residual values are not normally distributed for each value of education (think of a vertical slice at a particular value of education); they are not equally likely to be above or below the predicted value for a particular value of education. Additionally, figure 10.5 shows that the variance of the residual values increases as education increases. That is, if you consider people who have less than about 12 years of education, there is little variance in the residuals. For any particular value of education up to about 12 years, a vertical slice has little variance with all the residuals closely packed together. By contrast, if you look at people who have more than 12 years of education, say, those with 16 years of education, a vertical slice of the residuals has a lot of variance. The residual values in this case range from far below the predicted value to far above it. The way the variance of the residual increases as years of education increases is called heteroskedasticity of residuals. When there is heteroskedasticity as shown in this example, we cannot predict income well for higher values of education. When we have heteroskedasticity of the residuals, an R^2 value is misleading. We can explain a lot of the variance in income attributable to education up to about 12 years of education. For values of education up to 12 years, the overall R^2 underestimates the explained variance. For education above 12 years, the overall R^2 overestimates how much variance we can explain.

When we have multiple regression, it is difficult to do a graph like this because we have several predictors. The solution is to look at the distribution of residuals for different predicted values. That is, when we predict a small score on environmental concern, are the residuals distributed about the same as they are when we predict a high score?

Stata has several options to view distributions of residuals. Selecting Statistics ▷ Linear models and related ▷ Regression diagnostics ▷ Residual-versus-fitted plot opens a dialog box for the residual-versus-fitted value plot. There are no details to provide on the Main tab. Let's go to the Y axis tab, click on Reference lines, and check the box for *Add lines to graph at specified y-axis values*. Enter a value of 0 in the box below your check mark. This makes a residual of 0, a perfect prediction, that is, the reference line. The resulting command is `rvfplot, yline(0)`. We could use the other tabs to make the graph more appealing, but for now, we click on OK. Figure 10.6 shows the results.

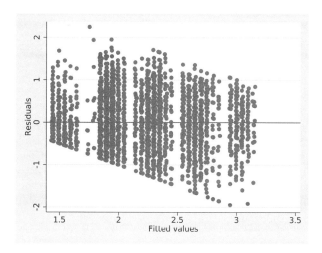

Figure 10.6. Residual-versus-fitted plot

This graph is a bit hard to read. Ideally, the observations would be normally distributed for any fitted values (*x* axis) about the reference line (residual of 0 on *y* axis). Where the fitted values are low, the residuals tend to be mostly positive, and where the fitted values are high, the residuals tend to be mostly negative.

A residual-versus-predicted plot, similar to the plot in figure 10.6, makes the most sense when the dependent variable takes on a larger range of values. In those situations, it may show that there is increasing or decreasing error variance as the predicted value gets larger. With our current example, where the dependent variables are between 1 and 4, it makes the problem clear but does not suggest any solution.

Sometimes it is easier to visualize how the residuals are distributed by doing a graph of the actual score of `env_con` on a predicted value for this score. It is easiest to show how to do this using the commands. Before doing that, however, we might want to draw a sample of the data. Because this is a very large dataset, there will be so many dots in a graph that it will be hard to read and many of the dots will be right on top of each other. To make the graph easier to read, we will include a step to sample 100 observations. Here are the commands:

```
. regress env_con educat inc com3 hlthprob epht3, beta
. predict envhat
. preserve
. set seed 515
. sample 100, count
. twoway (scatter env_con envhat) (lfit env_con envhat)
. restore
```

This series of commands does the regression first. The next line, `predict envhat`, will predict a score on `env_con` for each person based on the regression equation. Here the new variable is called `envhat`, but you can use any name because the default is to predict the score based on the regression equation. Before we take a sample of 100 observations, we enter the command `preserve`, which allows us to `restore` the dataset back to its original size. The fourth line, `set seed 515` provides a fixed start for the random sampling so that we can repeat what we did and get the same results. The command `sample 100, count` will draw a random sample of 100 cases. We are doing this to make the graph easier to read. We might want to save our data before doing this because once we drop all but 100 people, they are gone. If you save the sample of 100 observations, make sure you give the file a different name. (Using the `preserve` and `restore` commands is a simpler way to preserve the full dataset.) The next line is a `twoway` graph, as we have done before. The first section does a scattergram of `env_con` on `envhat`, and the second section does a linear regression line, regressing `env_con` on `envhat`. The final line has the command `restore`, which returns the complete dataset. The resulting graph is shown in figure 10.7, where I have used the Graph Editor to relabel some parts of the figure.

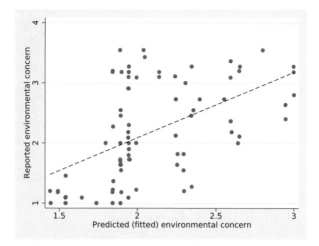

Figure 10.7. Actual value of environmental concern regressed on the predicted value

A perfect fit would mean that all the values were on the line. Examining this graph, we can see that there are roughly the same number of actual scores above and below the line for all values that are predicted when the estimated value is between approximately 1.8 and 2.6. There is a problem for extremely low predicted values (below approximately 1.8) and extremely high predicted values (at approximately 3). In both cases, the predicted values are underestimated.

In creating figure 10.7, we took a random sample of 100 observations. You might run these commands without this restriction, where the graph would have dots everywhere, and it would be hard to make any sense out of it. A serious limitation of taking a relatively small sample as we did is that you might get a very different figure using a different value for the seed. Before you draw any strong conclusions about there being a problem, it would be good to run the commands a couple of times using different seeds.

Is there anything we can do when we have concerns about the distribution of the residuals? One solution is to run a robust regression. A robust regression uses what is known as a sandwich estimator to estimate the standard errors. The command is

```
regress env_con educat inc com3 hlthprob epht3, vce(robust)
```

The vce(robust) option tells Stata to estimate the variance–covariance matrix of the errors in a way that does not assume normality. This will yield identical parameter estimates for the b's, β's, and R^2, but somewhat different t-values for testing their significance. It is important to emphasize that only the standard errors and resulting t-values will change, so violating normality of residuals' direct impact is on tests of significance.

Another alternative when you are concerned about the distribution of the residuals is to use a bootstrap estimation of the standard errors. This will draw several random samples with replacement (we will use 1,000 here) from your dataset. The regression will be estimated for each of these samples. Stata then examines the distribution of each parameter, for example, the b for `educat`, across the 1,000 results and then Stata uses the variance of that distribution to estimate a standard error. The `regress` command with bootstrap estimation of the standard errors is

```
regress env_con educat inc com3 hlthprob epht3, vce(bootstrap, reps(1000))
```

As with the robust estimator, the only thing that changes is the standard errors and hence the t-values. The `vce(bootstrap, reps(1000))` option may sound like it would take forever to run, but with modern computers and the efficient programming behind Stata commands, this command runs quickly.

10.7   Regression diagnostic statistics

Stata has a strong set of regression diagnostic tools. We will cover only a few of them. Enter the command `help regress postestimation`, and you will see a basic list of what we cover as well as several other regression diagnostic tools that are beyond the scope of this book.

10.7.1   Outliers and influential cases

When we are doing regression diagnostics, one major interest is finding outliers. These are cases with extreme values, and they can have an extreme effect on an analysis. One way to think of outliers is to identify those cases that the regression equation has the most trouble predicting; these are the cases that are farthest from the predicted values. These cases are of special interest for several reasons. You might want to examine them to see if there was a coding error by comparing your data with the original questionnaires. If you can contact these people, you might want to do a qualitative interview to better understand why the variables you thought would predict their scores failed. You may discover factors that you had not anticipated, and this could guide future research.

To find the cases we cannot predict, use postestimation commands. Select Statistics ▷ Postestimation, expand the Predictions menu, and then double-click on Predictions and their SEs, leverage statistics, distance statistics, etc. to open the dialog box to predict the estimated value, `yhat`; the residual, `residual`; and the standardized residual, `rstandard`. We could also enter the following series of commands directly:

```
. use https://www.stata-press.com/data/agis6r/ops2004, clear
. regress env_con educat inc com3 hlthprob epht3, beta
. predict yhat
. predict residual, residuals
. predict rstandard, rstandard
. list respnum env_con yhat residual rstandard
> if abs(rstandard) > 2.58 & !missing(rstandard)
```

The first prediction command, `predict yhat`, will predict the estimated score based on the regression. This has no option after a comma because the estimated score is the default prediction and the variable name, `yhat`, could be any name we choose. The next command, `predict residual, residuals`, will predict the residual, or $Y - \widehat{Y}$, giving us a raw or unstandardized measure of how far the estimated value, `yhat`, is from the person's actual score on the environmental-concern outcome. The `residual` option tells Stata to predict this residual value. The last prediction command, `predict rstandard, rstandard`, tells Stata to estimate the standardized residual for each observation and to create a new variable called `rstandard`. This is a z score that we can use to test how bad our prediction is for each case. We usually will be interested in our "bad" predictions, because these are the residual outliers. The `list` command lists all cases that have a standardized residual—that is, z score—whose size is greater than 2.58 (we include the restriction that `rstandard` is also less than "`.`"). We picked 2.58 because this corresponds to the two-tailed 0.01 level of significance. In other words, we would expect residuals this large in either direction less than 1% of the time by chance. Here are the results of this string of commands:

```
. use https://www.stata-press.com/data/agis6r/ops2004, clear

. regress env_con educat inc com3 hlthprob epht3, beta
```

Source	SS	df	MS		Number of obs	=	3,769
					F(5, 3763)	=	320.15
Model	647.67793	5	129.535586		Prob > F	=	0.0000
Residual	1522.5587	3,763	.404612995		R-squared	=	0.2984
					Adj R-squared	=	0.2975
Total	2170.23663	3,768	.575965136		Root MSE	=	.63609

env_con	Coefficient	Std. err.	t	P>|t|	Beta
educat	.0011841	.004077	0.29	0.772	.0044584
inc	5.51e-08	3.62e-07	0.15	0.879	.0023317
com3	-.0503162	.0092717	-5.43	0.000	-.074352
hlthprob	.2974034	.0248129	11.99	0.000	.172927
epht3	.4020741	.012687	31.69	0.000	.4575999
_cons	1.273655	.0651735	19.54	0.000	.

```
. predict yhat
(option xb assumed; fitted values)
(738 missing values generated)

. predict residual, residuals
(739 missing values generated)

. predict rstandard, rstandard
(739 missing values generated)
```

```
. list respnum env_con yhat residual rstandard
> if abs(rstandard) > 2.58 & !missing(rstandard)
```

	respnum	env_con	yhat	residual	rstandard
65.	100072	1	2.944407	-1.944407	-3.060185
170.	100189	1	2.660943	-1.660942	-2.616319
323.	100370	1	2.644924	-1.644924	-2.589258
539.	100626	1	2.646108	-1.646108	-2.591119
800.	100928	1	2.646784	-1.646784	-2.5918
803.	100931	3.545455	1.889344	1.656111	2.604731
	(output omitted)				
3743.	200712	1	2.852046	-1.852046	-2.918959
3745.	200716	3.7	1.937568	1.762432	2.772711
3762.	200743	4	2.333803	1.666197	2.624323
3795.	200785	4	1.752124	2.247876	3.542243
4117.	201350	3.636364	1.992138	1.644226	2.586329
4147.	201423	4	2.290355	1.709645	2.690599
4172.	201472	1	2.757992	-1.757992	-2.767844
4348.	201767	1	2.652623	-1.652623	-2.600933

Remember this listing only shows the cases that have the worst fit because we show only those with a standardized residual z score of $|2.58|$ or larger. In this dataset, **respnum** is the identification number of the participant. Participant 100072 had an actual mean score of 1 for the scale. This is the lowest possible score, yet we predicted that this person would have a score of 2.94. The residual is -1.94, indicating how much less environmentally concerned this person is than we predicted. The z score is -3.06. Toward the bottom of the listing, participant 200785 had a score of 4, indicating that he or she was at the high point on our scale of environmental concern. However, we predicted that this person would have a score of 1.75, and the z score is 3.54. We might look at the questionnaires for these two people to see if there was a miscoding. If the coding was correct, we might try to contact these participants to find out other variables we need to add to the regression equation. Unstructured interviews with participants that have extreme outliers can be helpful. We may find that those who have positive outliers are politically liberal and those who have negative outliers are politically conservative. Then we could add a variable measuring liberalism as a predictor. Correlating **rstandard** with other possible predictors would also be helpful. A variable that is highly correlated with **rstandard** helps explain the variance in our outcome that is not already explained by the predictors in our model.

10.7.2 Influential observations: DFbeta

Stata offers several measures of the influence each observation has. DFbeta (the **dfbeta** command) is the most direct of these. It indicates the difference between each of the regression coefficients when an observation is included and when it is excluded. You could think of this as redoing the regression model, omitting just one observation at a time and seeing how much difference omitting each observation makes. A value of DFbeta $> 2/\sqrt{N}$ indicates that an observation has a large influence.

To open the `dfbeta` dialog box, select Statistics ▷ Postestimation, expand the Specification, diagnostic, and goodness-of-fit analysis menu, and then double-click on DFBETA influence statistics. However, it is easier to type the one-word command, `dfbeta`, in the Command window:

```
. dfbeta

Generating DFBETA variables ...

(739 missing values generated)
    _dfbeta_1: DFBETA educat
(739 missing values generated)
    _dfbeta_2: DFBETA inc
(739 missing values generated)
    _dfbeta_3: DFBETA com3
(739 missing values generated)
    _dfbeta_4: DFBETA hlthprob
(739 missing values generated)
    _dfbeta_5: DFBETA epht3
```

These results show that Stata created five new variables. `_dfbeta_1` has a DFbeta score for each person on the education variable; `_dfbeta_2` does this for the income variable; `_dfbeta_3` does this for the community identity variable; `_dfbeta_4` does this for health problems; and `_dfbeta_5` does this for environmental-specific health concerns.

We could then list cases that have relatively large values of DFbeta, using the formula DFbeta $= 2/\sqrt{3769} = 0.03$ as our cutoff because we have $N = 3769$ observations in our regression analysis. For example, if we wanted to know problematic observations for the `educat` variable, the `list` command would be

```
list respnum rstandard _dfbeta_1 if abs(_dfbeta_1) > 2/sqrt(3769) &  ///
    !missing(_dfbeta_1)
```

I do not show the results of this command here. This `list` command, however, has a few features you might note. We use the absolute value function, `abs(_dfbeta_1)`. We also include a simple formula, `2/sqrt(3769)`, where 3,769 is the sample size in our regression. This listing is just for the `educat` variable. `dfbeta` gives us information on how much each observation influences each parameter estimate. This is more specific information than that provided by the standardized residual. If there are a few observations that have a large influence on the results, we might see if they were miscoded. If possible, we might interview the individuals to see why they picked the answers they did and how they interpreted the item.

10.7.3 Combinations of variables may cause problems

Collinearity and multicollinearity can be a problem in multiple regression. If two independent variables are highly correlated implicitly, it is difficult to know how important each of them is as a predictor. Multicollinearity happens when a combination of variables makes one or more of the variables largely or completely redundant. Figure 10.8 shows how this can happen with just two predictors, X1 and X2, which are trying to predict a dependent variable, Y. The figure on the left shows that areas a and c represent the portion of Y that is explained by X1, and areas b and c represent the portion of Y that is explained by X2. Because X1 and X2 overlap a little bit (are correlated), the area c cannot be distributed to either X1 or X2. Still, there is a lot of variance in both predictors that is not overlapping, and we can get a good estimate of the unique effect of X1, namely, area a, and the unique effect of X2, namely, area b. Earlier in this chapter, we referred to the areas represented by a and b as the semipartial R^2s.

The figure on the right shows what happens when the two predictors are more correlated and, hence, overlap more. Together, X1 and X2 are explaining much of the variance of Y, but the unique effects represented by areas a and b are relatively small. You can imagine that as X1 and X2 become almost perfectly correlated, the areas a and b all but disappear while the confounded area c increases. This example illustrates what could happen with just two predictors. You can imagine what could happen in multiple regression when there are many predictors that are correlated with each other. The more correlated the predictors, the more they overlap and, hence, the more difficult it is to identify their independent effects. In such situations, you can have multicollinearity in which one or more of the predictors are virtually redundant.

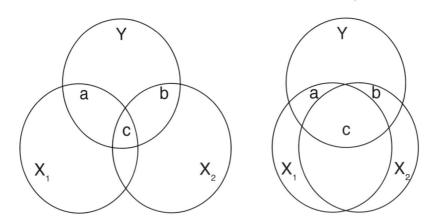

Figure 10.8. Collinearity

Stata can compute a variance inflation factor to assess the extent to which multicollinearity is a problem for each independent variable. This is computed by running the command `estat vif` after the regression. Here are the results for our example:

```
. estat vif
    Variable │        VIF        1/VIF
─────────────┼─────────────────────────
      educat │       1.26     0.791143
         inc │       1.25     0.797304
       epht3 │       1.12     0.894240
    hlthprob │       1.12     0.895659
        com3 │       1.01     0.993215
─────────────┼─────────────────────────
    Mean VIF │       1.15
```

This command computes both the variance inflation factor (VIF) and its reciprocal (1/VIF). Statisticians usually look at the VIF. If this is more than 10 for any variable, a multicollinearity problem may exist, and you may need to consider making an adjustment to your model. None of the variables has a problem using this criterion. If the average VIF is substantially greater than 1.00, there still could be a problem. Here the mean VIF is 1.15, and this is not a problem.

The value of 1/VIF may have a more intuitive interpretation than the VIF. If we regress educat on inc, epht3, hlthprob, and com3, we get an R^2 of 0.21. This means that there is an overlap of education with all the other predictors of 21% of the variance in education. Alternatively, $1 - 0.21 = 0.79$, or 79% of the variance in education is not overlapping, that is, it is not explained by the other predictors. Thus 79% of the variance in educat is available to give us an estimate of the independent effect of education on environmental concern, controlling for the other predictors. Some people call 1/VIF the tolerance. It is 1.00 minus the R^2 you obtain if you regress an independent variable on the set of other independent variables. It tells how much of the variance in the independent variable is available to predict the outcome variable independently. When VIF = 10, this means that only 10% of the variance in an independent variable is really available after you adjust for the other predictors. When VIF > 10 or 1/VIF < 0.10, there may be a multicollinearity problem.

When you have a problem with multicollinearity, consider these solutions. Dropping a variable often helps. If two variables both have a high VIF value, try dropping one of them and repeating the analysis. Dropping a variable that has a high VIF value is not as much of a problem as you might suspect; a variable that has more than 90% of its variance confounded with the other predictors probably does not explain much uniquely because it has little unique variance itself. Sometimes there are several closely related variables. For example, you might have a series of items involving concerns people have about global warming. Rather than trying to include all of these individual items, you might create a scale that combines them into one variable.

Multicollinearity sometimes shows up in what may seem like strange parameter estimates. Normally, the standardized βs should not be outside the range of -1 to $+1$. Yet you might have one variable that has $\beta = 2.14$ and a closely related variable that has $\beta = -1.56$. Sometimes these βs will be excessively large, but neither of them will be statistically significant. You almost certainly have a multicollinearity problem when this happens. If you drop either variable, the remaining variable may have a β that is within the normal range and is statistically significant.

10.8   Weighted data

Regression allows us to weight our cases. Many large datasets will use what is known as a weighted sample. Researchers want to have an adequate number of observations of groups that otherwise would be a small subsample. One survey of a community that is mostly Caucasians may oversample Hispanics and African Americans. Another survey might oversample people who are cohabiting or people who have a disability. If you want to take a subsample of people who are disabled, cohabiting, Hispanic, or African American, this oversampling is critically important, because it means that your subsample will be large enough for meaningful analysis. However, if you want to generalize to the entire population, you will need to adjust for this oversampling.

Many surveys provide a weight that tells you how many people each respondent represents, based on the sample design. This sampling fraction is simply the population N for the group, say, the number of African Americans in the United States, divided by the sample n for African Americans in your sample. Other surveys provide a proportional weight so that if you oversampled African Americans by a factor of two (that is, an African American was twice as likely to be sampled as anyone else), then each African American would have a weight value of 0.5 when you tried to generalize to the entire population.

When using a weighted sample, you need to consult the documentation on the survey to know what weight variable to use. The Oregon sample we have been using has both types of weights. We can list these for the first five observations:

```
. list finalwt finalwt2 in 1/5
```

	finalwt	finalwt2
1.	969.7892	1.602893
2.	384.8077	.6360203
3.	91.07467	.1505306
4.	5000	8.264132
5.	27.0839	.044765

With complex weighting, we can have different weights for each person. The first observation in the Oregon sample represents 969.79 Oregonians, and the fifth observation represents just 27.08 Oregonians, as indicated by the scores they have for the variable finalwt. The sum of all the finalwt scores will be close to the population of Oregon.

The probability weights represented by finalwt2 accomplish the same thing for the sample. A person who is in a highly oversampled group (say, Native Americans) will have a finalwt2 score of less than 1.00. A person who is not oversampled because we know we will have plenty of them (say, Caucasian males) in our sample will have a finalwt2 score of more than 1.00. The sum of all the finalwt2 scores will approximate the total sample size.

Weighting is complicated and beyond the scope of this book. Consult the documentation for the dataset you are using to find out the right weight variable to use. Stata can adjust for different kinds of weights, but here we will use what Stata calls `pweights`. In the dialog box for multiple regression, you will find a tab called **Weights**. Click on this tab, and select *Sampling weights* (this is the name Stata's interface uses for what Stata calls `pweights`). Then all you need to do is enter the name of the weight variable; here use `finalwt`. The command and results are as follows:

```
. regress env_con educat inc com3 hlthprob epht3 [pweight=finalwt], beta
(sum of wgt is 2,316,709.257443)
Linear regression                               Number of obs   =       3,769
                                                F(5, 3763)      =      120.73
                                                Prob > F        =      0.0000
                                                R-squared       =      0.3073
                                                Root MSE        =      .60771
```

env_con	Coefficient	Robust std. err.	t	P>|t|	Beta
educat	.0077949	.0071749	1.09	0.277	.0303352
inc	1.64e-07	5.96e-07	0.28	0.783	.0076229
com3	-.0467495	.0181525	-2.58	0.010	-.0694139
hlthprob	.2687916	.0449038	5.99	0.000	.1620468
epht3	.4099326	.0226743	18.08	0.000	.4702973
_cons	1.202771	.1182412	10.17	0.000	.

When you do a weighted regression this way, Stata automatically uses the robust regression—whether you ask for it or not—because weighted data require robust standard errors. The results of this robust regression have important differences from the original regression. Because it is robust regression, we do not get the ANOVA table and cannot get an adjusted R^2. Because we used a weighted sample, we get a line saying that the `sum of wgt is 2,316,709.257443`. This is the approximate total adult population of Oregon at the time of this survey. It is good to check this value, which should be the total population size if you use this type of weight or the total sample size if you use the proportional weight.

The number of observations is 3,769, and this is the actual size of the sample used for tests of significance. We should check this to make sure that we did the weighting correctly. If we had used the other weight, `finalwt2`, the line would read `sum of wgt is 3,829.118`; this value is close to the actual sample size we have of 3,769. The Oregon Survey includes 4,508 observations. Because regression uses casewise deletion, we have only 3,769 observations with valid scores on all the variables used in the regression. Because the sum of the weights for the observations with incomplete data is not equal to the actual number of observations with incomplete data, the sum of the weights for the complete data will not be identical to 3,769.

You may have observed that many of the results are different from the unweighted results. For example, the F value is 120.73 compared with 320.15 for the unweighted sample. This difference is partly due to the weighting and partly due to using robust regression. The parameter estimates of the coefficients and the βs are different, as are the standard errors and t tests. When the weighted sample gives different results, this means that the weighting is important. Imagine that the authors of the study decided they needed many Native Americans, so they oversampled Native Americans by a factor of 10. This means that each Native American would count 10 times as much in the unweighted sample as he or she would if you wanted to generalize the overall population. If the relationship between the variables were somehow different for Native Americans than for other groups, these differences would be overrepresented by a factor of 10. Weighting makes every case accurately represent its proportion of the population.

10.9 Categorical predictors and hierarchical regression

Smoking by adolescents is a major health problem. We will examine this problem by using `nlsy97_selected_variables.dta` (Bureau of Labor Statistics, U.S. Department of Labor 2015) as a way of illustrating what can be done with categorical predictors. Let's pick a fairly simple model to illustrate the use of categorical variables. Say that we think smoking behavior depends on the adolescent's age (a continuous variable), gender (a dichotomous variable), peer influence (a continuous variable), and race/ethnicity (a multicategory nominal variable). Let's also say that we think of these variables as being hierarchical. Start with age and gender and see how much they explain. Then, add peer influence and see how much it adds. Finally, add race/ethnicity to see if it has a unique effect above, beyond what is explained by age, gender, and peer influence.

```
. use https://www.stata-press.com/data/agis6r/nlsy97_selected_variables.dta, clear
(National Survey of Youth, 1997, selected variables from first wave)
```

When we are working with categorical predictors, it is important to distinguish between dichotomous predictors, such as gender, and multicategorical predictors, such as race, for which there are more than two categories. When we have a dichotomous predictor, we can create an indicator variable coded 0 for one gender, say, females, and 1 for the other gender, males. We can then enter this as a predictor in a regression model. We can do this by using the `recode` command; select Data ▷ Create or change data ▷ Other variable-transformation commands ▷ Recode categorical variable. In the *Variables* box, type `gender97` because this is the name of the variable for gender in our dataset. Because males are coded as 1 and females as 2, we need to recode. An indicator or dummy variable is a 0/1 variable, where a 1 indicates the presence of the characteristic and a 0 indicates its absence. Click on the Options tab, and check *Generate new variables*. Name the variable `male` because that is the category we will code as 1. If we had named the variable `female`, we would code females as 1. The choice is arbitrary and only changes the sign of the regression coefficient. Returning to the Main tab, enter the *Required* rule: (1 = 1 Male) (2 = 0 Female). The command and results are as follows:

```
. recode gender97 (1 = 1 Male) (2 = 0 Female), generate(male)
(4,385 differences between gender97 and male)
```

Coding values and names used for categorical variables

The conventions for coding categorical variables precede the widespread use of multiple regression. Conventions are slow to change, and we usually need to recode categorical variables before doing regressions. Most surveys code dichotomous response items using codes of 1 and 2 for `yes/no`, `male/female`, and `agree/disagree` items. We need to convert these to codes of 0 and 1. With more than two category response options for categorical variables (for example, religion or marital status), we need to recode the variable into a series of dichotomous variables, each of which is coded as 0 or 1. I explain how to do this in the text, but there is some inconsistency in names used for these recoded variables.

A common name for a 0/1 variable is *dummy variable*. Others call these variables *factor variables* or *indicator variables*, and still others call them *binary variables*. You should use whatever naming convention is standard for your content area. Here I will use these names interchangeably.

When we pick a name for one of these variables, it is useful to pick a name representing the category coded as 1. If we code women with 1 and men with 0, we would call the variable `female`. Calling the variable `gender` would be less clear when we interpret results. If whites are coded 1 and nonwhites are coded 0, it would make sense to call the variable `white`. Which category is coded 1 and which is coded 0 is arbitrary and affects only the sign of the coefficient. A positive sign signifies that the category coded 1 is higher on the dependent variable, and a negative sign signifies that it is lower on the dependent variable.

We must always check our changes, so enter a cross tabulation, `tab2 gender97 male, missing`, to verify that we did not make a mistake. Once we have an indicator variable, we can enter it in the regression as a predictor just like any other variable. The unstandardized regression coefficient tells us the change in the outcome for a 1-unit change in the predictor. Because a 1-unit change in the predictor, `male`, constitutes being a male rather than being a female, the regression coefficient is simply the difference in means on the dependent variable for males and females, controlling for other variables. Although this regression coefficient is easy to interpret, many researchers also report the βs. These make a lot of sense for a continuous variable; that is, a 1-standard-deviation change in the independent variable produces a β-standard-deviation change in the dependent variable. However, the βs are of dubious value for an indicator variable. It does not make sense for an indicator variable to vary by degree. Going from 0 for female to 1 for male makes sense, but going up or down one standard deviation on gender does not make much sense.

Using dummy variables is more complex when there are more than two possible scores. Consider race: We might want a variable to represent differences between Caucasians, African Americans, Hispanic Americans, and others. We might code a variable

race as 1 for Caucasian, 2 for African American, 3 for Hispanic American, and 4 for
other. This variable, race, is a nominal-level categorical variable, and it makes no sense
to think of a code of 4 being higher or lower than a code of 1 or 2 or 3. These are simply
nominal categories and the order is meaningless. To represent these four racial or ethnic
groups, we need three indicator variables. In general, when there are k categories, we
need $k - 1$ indicator variables.

How does this work? First, choose one category that serves as a reference group. It
makes sense to pick the group we want to compare with other groups. In this example,
it would make sense to pick Caucasian as our reference group. This is a large enough
group to give us a good estimate of its value, and we will probably often want to compare
other groups with Caucasians. It would make little sense to pick the "other" group as
the reference category because this is a combination of several different ethnicities and
races (for example, Pacific Islander and Native American). Also, there are relatively
few observations in the "other" category.

Next generate three dummy or indicator variables (aa, hispanic, and other), allowing us to uniquely identify each person's race/ethnicity. A score of 1 on other means
that the person is in the "other" category. A score of 1 on hispanic means that the
person is Hispanic. A score of 1 on aa means that the person is African American. You
may be wondering how we know that a person is Caucasian. A Caucasian person will
have a score of 0 on aa, 0 on hispanic, and 0 on other.

The dataset used two questions to measure race/ethnicity. This is done to more
accurately represent Hispanics, who may be of any race. The first item asks respondents
if they are Hispanic. If they say no, they are then asked their race. The coding is fairly
complicated, and here are the Stata commands used.

```
. generate race=race97
. replace race=1 if race97==1 & ethnic97==0
. replace race=2 if race97==2 & ethnic97==0
. replace race=3 if ethnic97==1
. replace race=4 if (race97==4 | race97==5) & ethnic97==0
. tab2 race race97 ethnic97
. recode race (2 = 1 African_American) (1 3/4 = 0 Other), generate(aa)
. recode race (3 = 1 Hispanic) (1/2 4 = 0 Other), generate(hispanic)
. recode race (4 = 1 Other_race) (1/3 = 0 W_AA_H), generate(other)
. tab1 aa hispanic other
```

The first line creates a new variable, race, which is equal to the old variable, race97.
We never want to change the original variable. We then change the code of race based
on the codes the person had on two variables, his or her original race97 variable and his
or her ethnicity, ethnic97. You can type the command codebook race97 ethnic97
to see how these were coded. For example, we make race=1 if the person had a code of
1 on race97 and a code of 0 on ethnic97. We use the command tab2 race race97
ethnic97 to check that we have done this correctly. We then use the recode command
to generate the three dummy variables. Finally, we do frequency tabulations for the
three dummy variables. Here only African Americans will have a code of 1 on aa, only
Hispanics will have a code of 1 on hispanic, only others will have a code of 1 on other,
and only Caucasians will have a code of 0 on all three indicator variables.

Now we are ready to do the multiple regression. In this example, we will enter the variables in blocks. The first block is estimated by using

```
. regress smday97 age97 male
> if !missing(smday97, age97, male, psmoke97, aa, hispanic, other), beta
```

Source	SS	df	MS		Number of obs	=	3,467
					F(2, 3464)	=	94.68
Model	22864.9705	2	11432.4853		Prob > F	=	0.0000
Residual	418279.523	3,464	120.75044		R-squared	=	0.0518
					Adj R-squared	=	0.0513
Total	441144.493	3,466	127.277696		Root MSE	=	10.989

smday97	Coefficient	Std. err.	t	P>|t|			Beta
age97	1.838514	.1337569	13.75	0.000			.2274106
male	.2707643	.3735982	0.72	0.469			.0119908
_cons	-20.33657	1.995249	-10.19	0.000			.

We have a special qualification on who is included in this regression with the `if` qualifier. By inserting `if !missing(smday97, age97, male, psmoke97, aa, hispanic, other)`, we exclude people who did not answer all the items. If we did not exclude these people, the number of observations for each regression might differ. When you put this qualification with a command, there are a couple of things to remember: 1) `!missing` means "not missing"; programmers like to use the exclamation mark to signify "not". 2) You must insert the commas between variable names in this particular function; this is inconsistent with how Stata normally lists variables (without commas) but is necessary because `missing()` is a Stata function, not a command.

The $R^2 = 0.05$, $F(2, 3464) = 94.68$, $p < 0.001$. Although age and gender explain just a little bit of the variance in adolescent smoking behavior, their joint effect is statistically significant. How important is age as a predictor? For each year an adolescent gets older, he or she smokes an expected 1.84 more days per month. This is highly significant: $t(3464) = 13.75$, $p < 0.001$. This seems like a substantial increase in smoking behavior. However, $\beta = 0.23$ suggests that this is not a strong effect. What about gender—is it important? Because we coded males as 1 and females as 0, the coefficient 0.27 for `male` indicates that males smoke an average of 0.27 more days per month than females do, controlling for age. This difference does not seem great, and it is not significant. The β is very weak, $\beta = 0.01$, but we will not try to interpret β because gender is a categorical variable.

The next regression equation adds peer influence. Repeat the command, but add the variable psmoke97, which represents the percentage of peers who smoke. The command and results are

```
. regress smday97 age97 male psmoke97
> if !missing(smday97, age97, male, psmoke97, aa, hispanic, other), beta
      Source |       SS           df       MS      Number of obs   =     3,467
-------------+----------------------------------   F(3, 3463)      =    134.24
       Model |  45956.7038          3  15318.9013   Prob > F        =    0.0000
    Residual |  395187.789      3,463  114.117179   R-squared       =    0.1042
-------------+----------------------------------   Adj R-squared   =    0.1034
       Total |  441144.493      3,466  127.277696   Root MSE        =    10.683

     smday97 | Coefficient  Std. err.      t    P>|t|                      Beta
-------------+----------------------------------------------------------------
       age97 |   1.286699   .1356942     9.48   0.000                  .1591551
        male |   .9523383   .3663385     2.60   0.009                  .0421741
    psmoke97 |   2.250031   .1581743    14.23   0.000                  .2406996
       _cons |  -19.47606   1.940615   -10.04   0.000                         .
```

This new model explains 10% of the variance in smoking behavior: $R^2 = 0.10$, $F(3, 3463) = 134.24$, $p < 0.001$. Does psmoke97 make a unique contribution? There are two ways of getting an answer. First, we can see that the regression coefficient of 2.25 is significant: $t(3463) = 14.23$, $p < 0.001$, and $\beta = 0.24$.

A second way of testing the unique effect of adding psmoke97 is to use the pcorr command, as follows:

```
. pcorr smday97 age97 male psmoke97
> if !missing(smday97, age97, male, psmoke97, aa, hispanic, other)
(obs=3467)
Partial and semipartial correlations of smday97 with
```

Variable	Partial corr.	Semipartial corr.	Partial corr.^2	Semipartial corr.^2	Significance value
age97	0.1591	0.1525	0.0253	0.0233	0.0000
male	0.0441	0.0418	0.0019	0.0017	0.0094
psmoke97	0.2350	0.2288	0.0552	0.0523	0.0000

So we can say that the influence of peer smoking adds 5% to the explained variance because the semipartial $R^2 = 0.05$, $p < 0.001$. The significance level is reported as a probability without any test statistic. There are two ways of obtaining the test statistic. Most statistics books show how to do an F test for adding a single variable (or set of variables). More simply, because we are interested in the contribution of a single added variable, the t test Stata reports for psmoke97 will be the same as the square root of the F test. We could say that the semipartial $R^2 = 0.05$, $t(3463) = 14.23$, $p < 0.001$. This t-value was reported in the previous regression command.

The next model we want to fit includes race/ethnicity. We can fit this by simply adding the variables `aa`, `hispanic`, and `other` to the regression command. Here are the command and its results:

```
. regress smday97 age97 male psmoke97 aa hispanic other
> if !missing(smday97, age97, male, psmoke97, aa, hispanic, other), beta
```

Source	SS	df	MS		Number of obs	=	3,467
					F(6, 3460)	=	90.57
Model	59879.4994	6	9979.91657		Prob > F	=	0.0000
Residual	381264.994	3,460	110.192195		R-squared	=	0.1357
					Adj R-squared	=	0.1342
Total	441144.493	3,466	127.277696		Root MSE	=	10.497

smday97	Coefficient	Std. err.	t	P>|t|	Beta
age97	1.308304	.1333711	9.81	0.000	.1618275
male	1.058956	.3601243	2.94	0.003	.0468957
psmoke97	2.173683	.1557058	13.96	0.000	.2325322
aa	-4.676358	.4592876	-10.18	0.000	-.1674716
hispanic	-3.223299	.4638056	-6.95	0.000	-.1144606
other	.3825068	1.143897	0.33	0.738	.0053334
_cons	-18.01775	1.911984	-9.42	0.000	.

When we add the set of three indicator variables that collectively represent race and ethnicity, we increase our R^2 to 0.14, $F(6, 3460) = 90.57$, $p < 0.001$. This represents a $0.1357 - 0.1042 = 0.0315$, or 3.2%, increase in R^2 when we add the set of three indicator variables that represent race/ethnicity.

The t tests for `aa` and `hispanic` are statistically significant, and the t test for `other` is not. This shows that both African Americans and Hispanics smoke fewer days per month than do Caucasians. If we want to know whether the set of three indicators is statistically significant (this refers to the three variables simultaneously and tests the significance of the combined race/ethnicity variable), we can type the following test command immediately after the regression and before doing another multiple regression (because it uses the most recent results):

```
. test aa hispanic other
( 1)  aa = 0
( 2)  hispanic = 0
( 3)  other = 0

      F( 3, 3460) =    42.12
           Prob > F =    0.0000
```

This `test` command is both simple and powerful. It does a test that three null hypotheses are all true. It is testing that the effect of `aa` is 0, of `hispanic` is 0, and of `other` is 0. It gives us $F(3, 3460) = 42.12$, $p < 0.001$. Thus we can say that the effect of race/ethnicity is weak because it adds just 3.2% to the explained variance, but it is statistically significant. If you paid careful attention to the unstandardized regression coefficients, you may object to the statement that the effect is weak. Uniquely explaining 3.2% of the variance sounds weak, which is why we described it this way. However, $b = -4.68$ for African Americans, and this means that they are expected to smoke almost five fewer days per month than Caucasians. If you think this is a substantial difference, you might want to focus on this difference rather than the explained variance.

More on testing a set of parameter estimates

We have seen one important use for the `test` command, namely, testing a set of indicator variables (`aa`, `hispanic`, `other`) that collectively define another variable (race/ethnicity). There are many other uses for this command. You may want to test whether a set of control variables is significant. When you have interaction terms, you may want to test a set of them. The test is always done in the context of the multiple regression most recently estimated. In this example, if we ran the command `test age97 male`, we would get a different result from when we entered these two variables by themselves. This is because we are testing whether these two variables are simultaneously significant, controlling for all the other variables that are in the model.

There is a useful command called `nestreg`. The procedures we have been using here involve nested regressions. The regressions are nested in the sense that the first regression is nested in the second regression because all the predictors in the first regression are included in the second. Likewise, the second regression is nested in the third regression, and so on. Some people call this hierarchical regression. If you call it hierarchical regression, you should not confuse it with hierarchical linear modeling, which is the name of a program that does multilevel analysis or mixed regression, which is related to the command in Stata called `mixed`. Nested regression is used where we have blocks of variables that we want to enter in a sequence, each step adding another block. Our method, using a series of regressions followed by the `test` command, is extremely powerful and flexible. However, the `nestreg` command was created to automate this process.

To use the `nestreg` command, you add the `nestreg:` prefix (the colon must be included) to the regression command. You then write a `regress` command, but put each block of predictors in parentheses. Here we have three blocks of predictors: (`age97 male`), (`psmoke97`), and (`aa hispanic other`). The usual options for the `regress` command are available. We selected the option to produce the beta weights.

```
. nestreg: regress smday97 (age97 male) (psmoke97) (aa hispanic other), beta
Block 1: age97 male
```

Source	SS	df	MS		Number of obs	=	3,467
					F(2, 3464)	=	94.68
Model	22864.9705	2	11432.4853		Prob > F	=	0.0000
Residual	418279.523	3,464	120.75044		R-squared	=	0.0518
					Adj R-squared	=	0.0513
Total	441144.493	3,466	127.277696		Root MSE	=	10.989

smday97	Coefficient	Std. err.	t	P>|t|	Beta
age97	1.838514	.1337569	13.75	0.000	.2274106
male	.2707643	.3735982	0.72	0.469	.0119908
_cons	-20.33657	1.995249	-10.19	0.000	.

```
Block 2: psmoke97
```

Source	SS	df	MS		Number of obs	=	3,467
					F(3, 3463)	=	134.24
Model	45956.7038	3	15318.9013		Prob > F	=	0.0000
Residual	395187.789	3,463	114.117179		R-squared	=	0.1042
					Adj R-squared	=	0.1034
Total	441144.493	3,466	127.277696		Root MSE	=	10.683

smday97	Coefficient	Std. err.	t	P>|t|	Beta
age97	1.286699	.1356942	9.48	0.000	.1591551
male	.9523383	.3663385	2.60	0.009	.0421741
psmoke97	2.250031	.1581743	14.23	0.000	.2406996
_cons	-19.47606	1.940615	-10.04	0.000	.

```
Block 3: aa hispanic other
```

Source	SS	df	MS		Number of obs	=	3,467
					F(6, 3460)	=	90.57
Model	59879.4994	6	9979.91657		Prob > F	=	0.0000
Residual	381204.994	3,460	110.192195		R-squared	=	0.1357
					Adj R-squared	=	0.1342
Total	441144.493	3,466	127.277696		Root MSE	=	10.497

smday97	Coefficient	Std. err.	t	P>|t|	Beta
age97	1.308304	.1333711	9.81	0.000	.1618275
male	1.058956	.3601243	2.94	0.003	.0468957
psmoke97	2.173683	.1557058	13.96	0.000	.2325322
aa	-4.676358	.4592876	-10.18	0.000	-.1674716
hispanic	-3.223299	.4638056	-6.95	0.000	-.1144606
other	.3825068	1.143897	0.33	0.738	.0053334
_cons	-18.01775	1.911984	-9.42	0.000	.

Block	F	Block df	Residual df	Pr > F	R2	Change in R2
1	94.68	2	3464	0.0000	0.0518	
2	202.35	1	3463	0.0000	0.1042	0.0523
3	42.12	3	3460	0.0000	0.1357	0.0316

This command will run the three regressions, and report increments in R^2 and whether these are statistically significant. A special strength of this command is that it works with many types of nested models, as you can see by typing `help nestreg`. The `nestreg` command is hard to find under the menu system. You find it at Statistics ▷ Other ▷ Nested model statistics. In addition to working with our multiple regression example, the dialog box provides a way of evaluating nested models by using 18 specialized extensions of multiple regression, such as logistic regression.

The results show the three regressions we ran earlier—calling them `Block 1`, `Block 2`, and `Block 3`—and list the variables added with each block. After the last block is entered, there is a summary table showing the change in R^2 for the block along with its significance. For example, the second block added the variable `psmoke97`. This block increased the R^2 by 0.0523, from 0.0518 to 0.1042. This increment in R^2 is significant, $F(1, 3463) = 202.35$, $p < 0.001$. The significance of $R^2 = 0.104$ at this stage is taken from the `Block 2` regression, $F(3, 3463) = 134.24$, $p < 0.001$. Avoid confusing the F test for the increment in R^2 from the summary table and the F test for the R^2 itself from the regression for the block. Adding the race/ethnicity variables to the model in `Block 3` increased R^2 by 0.032, and this is significant, $F(3, 3460) = 42.12$, $p < 0.001$. So, too, is the final $R^2 = 0.136$, $F(6, 3460) = 90.57$, $p < 0.001$.

Tabular presentation of hierarchical regression models

You may find it helpful to have a table showing the results of your nested (hierarchical) regressions. The table should show b's, standard errors, and standardized betas for each model you fit. You should also include R^2 for each model and the F test of the change in the R^2. In many fields, it is conventional to show the significance of regression coefficients by using asterisks. One asterisk is used for parameter estimates that are significant at the 0.05 level, two asterisks for parameters significant at the 0.01 level, and three asterisks for parameters significant at the 0.001 level. Some fields—for example, psychology through the American Psychological Association—have recommended tables that only report the coefficients for the variables that are added at each step. This approach ignores the fact that the coefficients for the variables from previous blocks will change when the new block of variables is added. This can become misleading because a variable in block 1 may be significant at that step, but it may become insignificant when subsequent blocks are added. A detailed example of a summary table format for nested regression is shown at https://www.ncfr.org/jmf/submit-jmf/format-jmf-tables.

Nested regression is commonly used to estimate the effect of personality characteristics or individual beliefs after you have controlled for background variables. If you want to know whether motivation was important to career advancement, you would do a multiple regression entering background variables first and then adding motivation as a final step. For example, you might enter gender, race, and parents' education in the first step as background variables over which the individual has no control; then enter achievement variables, such as education, in a second step; and finally, enter motivation. If motivation makes a significant increase in R^2 in the final step, then you have a much better test of the importance of motivation than if you had just done a correlation of career achievement and motivation without entering the control variables first.

10.10   A shortcut for working with a categorical variable

In the previous analysis, we did a regression of smday97 on age97, male, psmoke97, aa, hispanic, and other. The last three are our race/ethnicity variables, where we used Caucasian as our reference group and created dummy variables for African Americans, Hispanics, and others. Stata calls race or ethnicity a factor variable. There is a much easier way of working with factor variables than generating multiple dummy variables. There are also advantages to treating categorical variables as factor variables, but you need to understand how they work.

Stata treats categorical variables, regardless of the number of categories, as factor variables. Gender is a two-level factor variable. Our race/ethnicity variable is a four-level factor variable. Stata then has an elegant way of producing the dummy variables for us and entering them in a regression analysis. Using this feature makes the most sense when the first category is a good reference category and when you want to use all the categories. If you put i. as a stub in front of a categorical variable, Stata will make the first category the reference category and then generate a dummy variable for each of the remaining categories. Here are two regression results. The first uses the dummy variables as we named them before and the second uses the factor-variable feature.

```
. regress smday97 age97 male psmoke97 aa hispanic other

      Source |       SS           df       MS      Number of obs   =     3,467
-------------+----------------------------------   F(6, 3460)      =     90.57
       Model |  59879.4994          6  9979.91657   Prob > F        =    0.0000
    Residual |  381264.994      3,460  110.192195   R-squared       =    0.1357
-------------+----------------------------------   Adj R-squared   =    0.1342
       Total |  441144.493      3,466  127.277696   Root MSE        =    10.497

     smday97 | Coefficient  Std. err.      t    P>|t|     [95% conf. interval]
-------------+----------------------------------------------------------------
       age97 |   1.308304   .1333711     9.81   0.000     1.04681    1.569798
        male |   1.058956   .3601243     2.94   0.003    .3528779    1.765033
    psmoke97 |   2.173683   .1557058    13.96   0.000    1.868399    2.478968
          aa |  -4.676358   .4592876   -10.18   0.000    -5.57686   -3.775856
    hispanic |  -3.223299   .4638056    -6.95   0.000   -4.132659   -2.313938
       other |   .3825068   1.143897     0.33   0.738   -1.860274    2.625288
       _cons |  -18.01775   1.911984    -9.42   0.000   -21.76648   -14.26902
```

```
. regress smday97 age97 male psmoke97 i.race

      Source |       SS           df       MS      Number of obs   =     3,467
-------------+----------------------------------   F(6, 3460)      =     90.57
       Model |  59879.4994          6  9979.91657   Prob > F        =    0.0000
    Residual |  381264.994      3,460  110.192195   R-squared       =    0.1357
-------------+----------------------------------   Adj R-squared   =    0.1342
       Total |  441144.493      3,466  127.277696   Root MSE        =    10.497

     smday97 | Coefficient  Std. err.      t    P>|t|     [95% conf. interval]
-------------+----------------------------------------------------------------
       age97 |   1.308304   .1333711     9.81   0.000     1.04681    1.569798
        male |   1.058956   .3601243     2.94   0.003    .3528779    1.765033
    psmoke97 |   2.173683   .1557058    13.96   0.000    1.868399    2.478968
             |
        race |
          2  |  -4.676358   .4592876   -10.18   0.000    -5.57686   -3.775856
          3  |  -3.223299   .4638056    -6.95   0.000   -4.132659   -2.313938
          4  |   .3825068   1.143897     0.33   0.738   -1.860274    2.625288
             |
       _cons |  -18.01775   1.911984    -9.42   0.000   -21.76648   -14.26902
```

Notice that under `race` in the second result, we have three categories that are labeled 2, 3, and 4. Category 2 is the second category and corresponds to the `aa` category in the first results. Similarly, category 3 matches the `hispanic` category, and category 4 matches the `other` category.

This method saves us the work of having to generate the dummy variables, but it has the possible disadvantage of not having clear labels for the resulting categories. It is easy to remember that `aa` is African American, `hispanic` is Hispanic, and `other` is other races. It is harder to remember which category coincides with 2, 3, or 4. Still, if you have several categorical variables, you can save a lot of recoding time by using the factor-variable feature. It is possible to change the reference category or what Stata refers to as the `baselevel`. If we want to make Hispanics the reference category, we could type

```
regress smday97 age97 male psmoke97 ib3.race
```

where the `ib3.` makes category 3 the base. If we wanted African Americans to be the reference category, we would use `ib2.race`. Rarely would we want the last category to be the reference category, but if we did, we would use `ib(last).race`.

10.11 Fundamentals of interaction

In many situations, the effect of one variable depends on where you are on another variable. For example, there is a well-established relationship between education and income. The more education you have, the more income you can expect, on average. There is also an established relationship between gender and income. Men, on average, make more money than do women. With this in mind, we could do a regression of income on both education and gender to see how much of a unique effect each predictor has. There is, however, an important relationship that we could miss by doing this. In addition to the possibility of men making more money than women, the payoff men get for each additional year of education may be greater than the payoff women receive. Thus men are advantaged in two ways. First, they make more money on average, and second, they get a greater return on their education. This second issue is what we mean by interaction. That is, the effect of education on income depends on your gender—stronger effect for men, weaker effect for women. How can we test this relationship using multiple regression?

As an example here, we will fit two models. The first model includes just education and gender as predictors, or main effects, to distinguish them from interaction effects. The second model adds the interaction between education and gender. Let's use c10interaction.dta, a dataset with hypothetical data. The first model is fit using regress inc educ male, where inc is income measured in thousands of dollars, educ is education measured in years, and male represents gender, with men coded 1 and women coded 0. Here are the command and results:

```
. use https://www.stata-press.com/data/agis6r/c10interaction, clear
. regress inc educ male, beta
```

Source	SS	df	MS		Number of obs	=	120
					F(2, 117)	=	37.19
Model	100464.105	2	50232.0527		Prob > F	=	0.0000
Residual	158015.895	117	1350.5632		R-squared	=	0.3887
					Adj R-squared	=	0.3782
Total	258480	119	2172.10084		Root MSE	=	36.75

inc	Coefficient	Std. err.	t	P>|t|	Beta
educ	8.045694	1.008586	7.98	0.000	.5775017
male	19.04991	6.719787	2.83	0.005	.2052297
_cons	-42.54411	14.2919	-2.98	0.004	.

We can explain 38.87% of the variance in income with education and gender, $F(2, 117) = 37.19$, $p < 0.001$, and both education and gender are significant in the ways we anticipated. Each additional year of education yields an expected increase in income of \$8,046, and men expect to make \$19,050 more than women. (Remember, these are hypothetical data!)

We can make a graph of this relationship. First, generate a predicted income for women as a new variable and a predicted income for men as a new variable. Just after the regression, type the following commands:

```
. predict incfnoi if male==0
. predict incmnoi if male==1
```

The first command generates a predicted value for income for women (male==0), and the second command does the same for men. Then do an overlaid two-way graph by using the dialog box we discussed earlier in the book. The graph command used to produce figure 10.9 is long:

```
. twoway (connected incmnoi educ if male == 1, lcolor(black) lpattern(dot)
> msymbol(diamond) msize(large)) (connected incfno educ if male == 0,
> lcolor(black) lpattern(solid) msymbol(circle) msize(large)),
> ytitle(Income in thousands) xtitle(Education) legend(order(1 "Men" 2 "Women"))
```

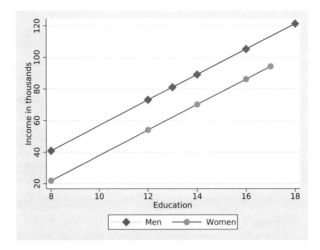

Figure 10.9. Education and gender predicting income, no interaction

There is one line for the education-to-income relationship for men (the higher line) and another line for women. This shows a strong positive connection between education and income, as well as a big gender gap. We use this model that includes just the main effects and has both lines parallel because it is the best model, as long as we assume that the gender gap is constant. If the size of the gender gap increases with increasing age, this model would not be able to show that.

Testing for interaction takes us a huge step further. When we test for interaction, we want to see if the slopes are different. In other words, we want to see if the slope between education and income is different and perhaps steeper for men than it is for women. You may be thinking that the graph shows the lines to be parallel, but this is because we set up the equation without an interaction term; without the interaction term, Stata gives us the best parallel lines. To see if the lines really should not have this restriction, we add an interaction term. We get the interaction term as the product of gender and education.

There are two ways to include an interaction term as the product of gender and education. One way is to use the **generate** command, for example,

```
generate ed_male = educ*male
```

where **ed_male** is the interaction term. Then we would refit the model by adding the interaction term:

```
regress inc educ male ed_male, beta
```

A better way to include an interaction term is to use factor-variable notation. This produces identical parameter estimates, but has two advantages. First, you do not need to generate the interaction or product term, `ed_male`, before running the regression. This is a small advantage in this example, but in more complex models, it can save considerable time. The second, and more important advantage, is that some postestimation commands (for example, `margins` and `marginsplot`) require that you used the factor-variable notation. For a categorical variable like gender, we insert `i.` at the front of the variable name, `i.male`. For a continuous variable, like education, we insert `c.` at the front of the name of the variable, `c.educ`. Stata uses the `##` notation to indicate a product of variables. Thus we can write a command that includes both the main effects of gender and education and the interaction between gender and education as follows:

```
regress inc i.male##c.educ, beta
```

With the `##` notation, Stata knows to include both `male` and `educ` along with their product. Thus this command is equivalent to the command in the above paragraph, `regress inc educ male ed_male, beta`. Here are the results:

```
. regress inc i.male##c.educ, beta
```

Source	SS	df	MS		Number of obs	=	120
					F(3, 116)	=	34.89
Model	122604.719	3	40868.2397		Prob > F	=	0.0000
Residual	135875.281	116	1171.33863		R-squared	=	0.4743
					Adj R-squared	=	0.4607
Total	258480	119	2172.10084		Root MSE	=	34.225

inc	Coefficient	Std. err.	t	P>|t|		Beta
1.male	-91.88539	26.27242	-3.50	0.001		-.9899052
educ	3.602369	1.388076	2.60	0.011		.2585699
male#c.educ						
1	8.196446	1.885263	4.35	0.000		1.287508
_cons	16.84834	19.07279	0.88	0.379		.

These results show that we can explain 47.43% of the variance, $F(3, 116) = 34.89$, $p < 0.001$, in income after we add the effect of the interaction of education and gender. This is an increase of 8.56% in the explained variance we had when we did not include the interaction. Is the interaction significant? In the result, we see that `male#c.educ`, the interaction, has a $t = 4.35$, $p < 0.001$ so we know the interaction is significant. (The output does not include the `i.` at the start of the categorical variable, but it is implied.) We could also get this increase in explained variance increase by using `pcorr` for the semipartial R^2 or by using `nestreg: regress inc (educ i.male) (i.male#c.educ), beta`.

Centering quantitative predictors before computing interaction terms

Although we have not done it here, some researchers choose to center quantitative independent variables, such as education, before computing the interaction terms. The interaction term is the product of the centered variables, but the interaction term will not be centered itself. Centering involves subtracting the mean from each observation. If the mean of education were 12 years, centered education would be `generate c_educ = educ - 12`. A better way to do this is to summarize the variable first. Stata then saves the mean to many decimal places in memory as a variable called `r(mean)`. We would use two commands: `summarize educ` and then `generate educ_c = educ - r(mean)`. If you plan to center many variables, you may want to install the community-contributed command `center` (type `search center` or `ssc install center`). Ben Jann wrote this command in 2004, with subsequent revisions. Once it is installed, you can type `center educ` to automatically create a new variable named `c_educ`.

If you center these variables, the mean has a value of 0. Because the intercept is the estimated value when the predictors are 0, the intercept is the estimated value when the centered variable is at its mean. This often makes more sense, especially when a value of 0 for the uncentered variable is a rare event, like it is in the example of years of education. The centered education variable becomes a measure of how far a person is above or below average on years of education rather than how many years of education they have had. This centering can help you interpret the intercept.

Interpreting the interaction term (`i.male#c.educ`) and the main effects (`educ`, `male`) is tricky when the interaction is significant. Just glancing at them seems to suggest ridiculous relationships. The -91.89 for the `male` variable might look like men make significantly less income than do women, but we cannot interpret it this way in the presence of interaction. We need to make a separate equation for each level of the categorical variable. Thus we need to make an equation for men and a separate equation for women. This is not hard to do; just remember that women have a score of 0 on two variables: `male` and `ed_male` (educ $\times$ 0 $= 0$). For men, by substituting a value of 1 for the `male` variable, the equation simplifies to

$$\widehat{\text{inc}} = (16.85 - 91.89) + (3.60 + 8.20)\text{educ}$$
$$\widehat{\text{inc}} = -75.04 + 11.80(\text{educ})$$

For women, by substituting a value of 0 for the `male` variable, the equation simplifies to

$$\widehat{\text{inc}} = 16.85 + 3.60(\text{educ})$$

Here the payoff of one additional year of education for men is \$11,800 compared with just \$3,600 for women. The adjusted constant or intercept for men of $-\$75,040$ does not make much sense. In the data, the lowest education is 8 years, and the constant refers to a person who has no education. Do not interpret an intercept that is out of the range of the data.

A nice way to see how the interaction works is with a graph. In this example, we are interested in how the relationship between income and education varies by gender. We want to see if the numerical results shown above really show a substantively important difference in this relationship. We will use two commands to do this. The `margins` command is run first to find out what the estimated income is for specific years of education for women and for men. Let's do this by specifying that education years will have values of 8 years, 10 years, 12 years, 14 years, 16 years, and 18 years. The `margins` has the categorical variable, `male`, listed immediately following the command. Then after the command, we specify the specific values for the continuous variable, `educ`. Here are the command and results:

```
. margins male, at(educ=(8 10 12 14 16 18))
Adjusted predictions                          Number of obs = 120
Model VCE: OLS
Expression: Linear prediction, predict()
1._at: educ =  8
2._at: educ = 10
3._at: educ = 12
4._at: educ = 14
5._at: educ = 16
6._at: educ = 18
```

	Margin	Delta-method std. err.	t	P>|t|	[95% conf. interval]	
_at#male						
1 0	45.66729	8.66112	5.27	0.000	28.51285	62.82173
1 1	19.35346	8.545103	2.26	0.025	2.42881	36.27812
2 0	52.87203	6.431252	8.22	0.000	40.13412	65.60003
2 1	42.95109	6.496577	6.61	0.000	30.0838	55.81838
3 0	60.07676	4.808436	12.49	0.000	50.55305	69.60048
3 1	66.54872	4.940843	13.47	0.000	56.76276	76.33468
4 0	67.2815	4.505014	14.93	0.000	58.35875	76.20425
4 1	90.14635	4.431483	20.34	0.000	81.36924	98.92346
5 0	74.48624	5.734395	12.99	0.000	63.12855	85.84393
5 1	113.744	5.280516	21.54	0.000	103.2853	124.2027
6 0	81.69097	7.802914	10.47	0.000	66.23632	97.14563
6 1	137.3416	7.01066	19.59	0.000	123.4561	151.2271

The first part of the results show that we picked 6 values for education, where the first value represents 8 years and the sixth value represents 18 years. The second part shows the estimated incomes for each value when `male` equals a value of 0 (woman) and when it equals a value of 1 (man).

Next we want to plot the estimated values of income on education separately for women and men. We simply type `marginsplot, noci`. We added the `noci` option to the `marginsplot` command because we did not want confidence intervals. If you retype this command without the option, you will see that the confidence interval is widest at the extremes (8 years of education and 18 years of education) in the resulting graph; see figure 10.10. (Note that I have made some minor enhancements to the figure with the Graph Editor.)

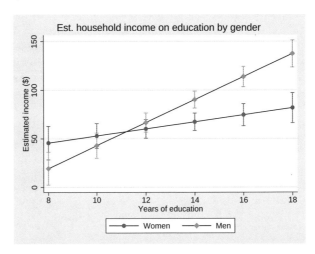

Figure 10.10. Education and gender predicting income, with interaction term

Figure 10.10 shows that at low levels of education, men are estimated (using a linear model) to make less than women, but at higher levels of education, the men make much more than women. It shows that the rate of increase in income for additional years of education is much steeper for men than it is for women. Remember that we are using hypothetical data.

Do not compare correlations across populations

We have found a significant interaction showing that women are relatively disadvantaged in the relationship between education and income. We did this by examining the unstandardized slopes, which showed that the payoff for an additional year of education was \$11,800 for men, compared with \$3,600 for women. If these were actual data, this would be compelling evidence of a gross inequity. Some researchers compare standardized beta weights or correlations to make this argument, but this is a serious mistake. The standardized beta weights depend on the form of the relationship (shown with the unstandardized slopes in figure 10.10) and the differences in variance. Unless the men and women have identical variances, comparing the correlations or beta weights can yield misleading results. Correlation is a measure of fit or the clustering of the observations around the regression line. You can have a steep slope like that for men, but the observations may be widely distributed around this, leading to a small correlation. Similarly, you can have a much flatter slope, like that for women, but the observations may be closely packed around the slope, leading to a high correlation. Whether the correlation between education and income is higher or lower for women than it is for men measures how closely the observations are to the estimated values. How steep the slopes are, measured by the unstandardized regression coefficients as we have done, measures the form of the relationship.

10.12 Nonlinear relations

We have been assuming that the relationship between each independent variable and our dependent variable is linear and thereby described by a straight line. This is often an adequate assumption, even when it is not the best possible model. Many relationships have a curve. You could think of one example as a decreasing marginal utility. If the income of the average college student goes up or down \$10,000 per year, this represents a big change in their resources and will influence many outcome variables. What about the average billionaire? As their income goes up or down \$10,000 per year, they are unlikely to notice the change and the change will not influence any outcomes. Figure 10.11(A) shows such a relationship. Note the following equation:

$$\widehat{y} = 0.10 \;+\; \underset{\text{linear}}{0.122x} \;-\; \underset{\text{quadratic}}{0.006x^2}$$

We fit this by adding a quadratic term, x^2. The $0.122x$ is the linear component and has a positive slope, but the $-0.006x^2$ has a negative slope. The positive component is pushing the estimated value of y up and the negative quadratic is pushing the estimated value of y down. Because the -0.006 is a much smaller value than the 0.122, the positive linear push dominates initially. Although the -0.006 is a small value, it is multiplied by x^2 rather than by x. Because x changes arithmetically, x^2 changes geometrically and the quadratic component will eventually bring the estimated value of y down. We can illustrate this using different values of x. Because x increases from 0 to 10, the estimated value of y increases from 0.91 to 1.53; after that, additional increases in x actually lead to a lowering of the estimated value of y.

Value of x	Value of x^2	Estimated value of y using $y = 0.910 + 0.122x - 0.006x^2$
0	0	0.91
10	100	1.53
20	400	0.95
30	900	-0.83
40	1600	-3.81
50	2500	-7.99

Sometimes we need a model that allows a positive relationship for part of the range of the independent variable and a negative relationship for the rest of the range. How often do a husband and wife have conflict? If they have conflict all the time, they will be unhappy. However, one theory argues that couples that never or rarely have conflict are also unhappy and those who have a moderate degree of conflict are the happiest. Figure 10.11(B) shows such a relationship. Notice that the positive linear component is pushing the estimated value of y, happiness, up and that the negative quadratic component is pushing the estimated value of y down. Within the range of the data, the value of x^2 becomes so great that the initially small quadratic component effect reverses the effect of the linear component.

Figure 10.11 illustrates some of the models that can be fit by adding a quadratic term to our regression model. We have discussed the first two models, which are examples of a positive linear component and a negative quadratic component. The `regress` command provides the best estimates of the linear and quadratic parameters for all of these curves. Figure 10.11(C) is labeled decreasing decay. Here a negative effect begins being quite strong but then levels out for high values of x. Notice figure 10.11(C) is obtained by having a negative value for the linear component, x, and a very small positive value for the quadratic component, x^2. Can you think of an example where this would apply? Suppose you were studying infant mortality (y) at the nation level and your independent variable is the gross national product (GNP). Countries with the lowest GNP would have a high rate of infant mortality, but this would drop quickly in countries with somewhat higher GNP's. However, at some point, a further increase in GNP would not lead to a substantial reduction in infant mortality. There would be a leveling off of infant mortality for nations that have higher GNP's.

When using a quadratic, you never want to make an inference that goes beyond your range of the independent variable. What would happen if the x axis were extended farther to the right? The small positive quadratic component would push up more and more, and you would get something like figure 10.11(D), a U curve. Imaging a group of patients who have headache pain (y), you administered varying dosages of a pain medicine (x). Initially, you have a large drop in the pain, but as you increase the dosage, the benefit diminishes. You know you have a model like that in figure 10.11(C) or 10.11(D) when you have a negative linear coefficient and a positive quadratic component. The distinction between models like those in figures 10.11(C) and 10.11(D) is often difficult to distinguish without creating a graph.

Figure 10.11(E) shows an example of accelerating growth. Both the linear and the quadratic components are positive. The linear component is fairly small meaning that at the lower range of the x variable, the estimate y value is increasing only slightly. The positive quadratic term is being added to this effect as an extra push to a higher estimated value of y.

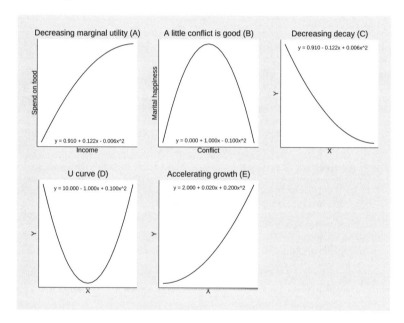

Figure 10.11. Five quadratic curves

10.12.1   Fitting a quadratic model

Consider the relationship between the log of your wages and your total years of experience. We believe that the more years of experience you have, the greater the log of your wages. Let's use data that come from Stata:

```
. use https://www.stata-press.com/data/r17/regsmpl, clear
(NLS Women 14-26 in 1968)
```

We run a linear regression and obtain the following results:

```
. regress ln_wage ttl_exp, beta
```

Source	SS	df	MS		
Model	1150.37005	1	1150.37005
Residual	5371.51384	28,532	.188262787
Total	6521.88388	28,533	.228573367

	Number of obs	=	28,534
	F(1, 28532)	=	6110.45
	Prob > F	=	0.0000
	R-squared	=	0.1764
	Adj R-squared	=	0.1764
	Root MSE	=	.43389

ln_wage	Coefficient	Std. err.	t	P>|t|	Beta
ttl_exp	.0431613	.0005522	78.17	0.000	.4199835
_cons	1.406646	.0042866	328.15	0.000	.

We can represent these results as a graph (figure 10.12) by typing

```
. twoway lfit ln_wage ttl_exp
```

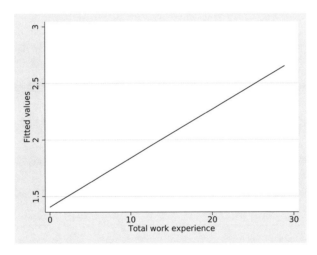

Figure 10.12. Graph of quadratic model

Figure 10.12 shows a moderately strong relationship between the total years of work experience and the estimated log wage. Do you see a problem? With many occupational positions, there is a top wage, so after several years, your wage rate may not increase or may only increase very gradually. We expect that wages will increase fairly rapidly the first several years and then level off in latter years. We can get a feel of whether this is correct using the `binscatter` command that we discussed in section 8.4.

```
. binscatter ln_wage ttl_exp
```

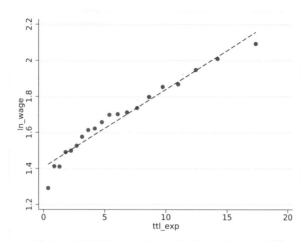

Figure 10.13. `binscatter` representation of nonlinear relationship between the log of wages and total years of experience

How does adding a quadratic component represent this? We expect the linear component to be positive because initially there is a regular increase in your wage rate, but we expect diminishing returns for additional years, especially after you have worked for many years. Therefore, we expect the linear component to be positive and the quadratic component to have a small, but significant, negative effect. We can handle the quadratic term the same way we could handle the interaction term. We could generate a new variable by multiplying the variables together, for example,

```
generate ttl_sq = ttl_exp*ttl_exp
```

and then adding the new term to the regression model:

```
regress ln_wage ttl_exp ttl_sq, beta
```

As with the interaction term, we have a better alternative. We can use the factor-variable notation for the continuous variable. Stata lets us use this special notation to indicate that a variable is continuous. We will use the `##` notation like we did with an interaction term, `c.ttl_exp##c.ttl_exp`. This notation keeps the main effect of total experience, `ttl_exp`, and it adds the product term to the model, `ttl_exp*ttl_exp`. This method is better than generating the squared term in a separate step because postestimation commands will behave properly. The double hash marks, `##`, along with the `c.` prefixes (for continuous independent variables) tell Stata to include both the linear component of `ttl_exp` and the quadratic component `ttl_exp2`.

Here are the command and results:

```
. regress ln_wage c.ttl_exp##c.ttl_exp, beta
```

Source	SS	df	MS		
Model	1184.57867	2	592.289333		
Residual	5337.30522	28,531	.187070387		
Total	6521.88388	28,533	.228573367		

	Number of obs	=	28,534
	F(2, 28531)	=	3166.13
	Prob > F	=	0.0000
	R-squared	=	0.1816
	Adj R-squared	=	0.1816
	Root MSE	=	.43252

ln_wage	Coefficient	Std. err.	t	P>|t|	Beta
ttl_exp	.0660334	.0017787	37.12	0.000	.6425416
c.ttl_exp# c.ttl_exp	-.0013929	.000103	-13.52	0.000	-.2340455
_cons	1.348441	.0060651	222.33	0.000	.

These results are exactly the same as we would have obtained by using the `generate` command to create the `ttl_sq` variable.

Just like with interaction terms, we can use the `margins` and `marginsplot` commands to graph these nonlinear results. This time we just have one predictor so we must set representative values for it. Running the `fre ttl_exp` (or `tab ttl_exp`) command, we find that experience ranges from 0 years to 28.885 years. Let's specify values from 0 to 28 years in increments of 2.

```
. margins, at(ttl_exp = (0(2)28))
```

Adjusted predictions   Number of obs = 28,534
Model VCE: OLS

Expression: Linear prediction, predict()
1._at: ttl_exp =   0
2._at: ttl_exp =   2
3._at: ttl_exp =   4
4._at: ttl_exp =   6
5._at: ttl_exp =   8
6._at: ttl_exp = 10
7._at: ttl_exp = 12
8._at: ttl_exp = 14
9._at: ttl_exp = 16
10._at: ttl_exp = 18
11._at: ttl_exp = 20
12._at: ttl_exp = 22
13._at: ttl_exp = 24
14._at: ttl_exp = 26
15._at: ttl_exp = 28

		Delta-method				
	Margin	std. err.	t	P>|t|	[95% conf.	interval]
_at						
1	1.348441	.0060651	222.33	0.000	1.336553	1.360329
2	1.474936	.0037037	398.24	0.000	1.467676	1.482195
3	1.590288	.0029503	539.03	0.000	1.584505	1.59607
4	1.694497	.0033365	507.87	0.000	1.687957	1.701036
5	1.787563	.0038029	470.06	0.000	1.780109	1.795016
6	1.869485	.0040283	464.08	0.000	1.861589	1.877381
7	1.940265	.0042471	456.84	0.000	1.93194	1.948589
8	1.999901	.0050573	395.45	0.000	1.989989	2.009814
9	2.048394	.0069713	293.83	0.000	2.03473	2.062059
10	2.085745	.0100468	207.60	0.000	2.066052	2.105437
11	2.111952	.0141597	149.15	0.000	2.084198	2.139705
12	2.127016	.0192161	110.69	0.000	2.089351	2.16468
13	2.130936	.0251649	84.68	0.000	2.081612	2.180261
14	2.123714	.0319792	66.41	0.000	2.061033	2.186395
15	2.105348	.039644	53.11	0.000	2.027644	2.183053

In this `margins` command, we use a shortcut, 0(2)28, meaning to start at a value of 0 and increment it by 2 until you get to 28 (that is, 0 2 4 6 8 ... 28). This will give us an estimate value of the log of income for 15 different values on total years of experience.

We now run the `marginsplot` command, which produces figure 10.14.

```
. marginsplot
```

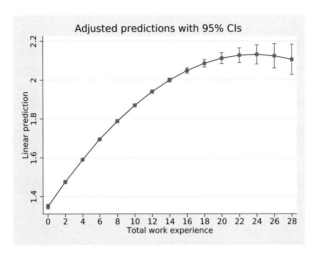

Figure 10.14. Quadratic model of relationship between total experience and log of income

The linear component is 0.066, and it is significant, $t = 37.12$, $p < 0.000$. The quadratic component, -0.001, is significant, $t = -13.52$, $p < 0.001$. We can interpret these results in terms of their significance and the fact that they are in the predicted direction, that is, positive for the linear component and negative for the quadratic component. Caution is needed for interpreting the coefficients beyond noting their direction and significance. Converting to standardized β values will not simplify the interpretation.

There is no single slope coefficient that describes the relationship like we had without the quadratic term. We cannot make a meaningful statement about the effect of a one-unit difference in experience on wages using the linear component or the quadratic component individually. Examining figure 10.14, we see that going from 0 to 1 year of work experience has a steep increase in the wages, going from 22 to 23 years has almost no increase in estimated wages, and going from 26 to 28 years of experience actually results in a slight decrease in estimated wages. We should be cautious about the 26 to 28 difference because this is at the upper end of the range of our independent variable and we have relatively few observations at that part of the distribution. You can see this in the confidence interval Stata constructed for each estimated value.

It can be shown that the linear slope, $B = 0.066$, is actually the tangent of the curve at a value of 0.0 on total years of experience. This may or may not be of much interest, but it is critical to not represent this as the difference in y for a unit difference in x because this only applies at a value of 0 on the x variable. It is important to show a figure so the reader can see the big picture.

There are interpretations you can make based on the coefficients that are useful. The intercept (_cons) is simply the estimated value of y when x is 0, and this is the same whether we have a linear or a quadratic model. The linear slope is the tangent of the curve when $x = 0$. In our example, the tangent of the curve for the ln_wage variable is 0.066 when you have zero total work experience. What else can we say? The curve is flat (the tangent to the curve being 0) at a value of $-B_1/2B_2$. For our example, the curve is flat at $-0.0660334/\{2(-0.0013929)\} = 23.704$ total years of experience. (It is important to keep all the decimal places you have in calculating this value and to use the unstandardized coefficients.) You can verify that the curve is flat in this area by observing where the tangent of the curve approaches 0 in figure 10.14.

10.12.2 Centering when using a quadratic term

Often, it is useful to center the independent variable to provide a more reasonable value for the linear component. We center a variable by subtracting the mean of the variable from each score. We use this centered variable to generate the squared value. We covered centering a bit more when we introduced interaction models. Here is what we do for now by replacing the uncentered total experience variable, ttl_exp, with its centered value, cttl_exp:

```
. summarize ttl_exp

    Variable |        Obs        Mean    Std. dev.         Min         Max

     ttl_exp |     28,534    6.215316    4.652117           0    28.88461

. generate cttl_exp = ttl_exp - 6.215

. regress ln_wage c.cttl_exp##c.cttl_exp, beta
```

Source	SS	df	MS		
				Number of obs	=	28,534
				F(2, 28531)	=	3166.13
Model	1184.57867	2	592.289333	Prob > F	=	0.0000
Residual	5337.30522	28,531	.187070387	R-squared	=	0.1816
				Adj R-squared	=	0.1816
Total	6521.88388	28,533	.228573367	Root MSE	=	.43252

ln_wage	Coefficient	Std. err.	t	P>|t|	Beta
cttl_exp	.0487197	.0006869	70.92	0.000	.4740703
c.cttl_exp# c.cttl_exp	-.0013929	.000103	-13.52	0.000	-.0903913
_cons	1.705036	.0033948	502.25	0.000	.

The intercept, _cons = 1.705, is the estimated log income when cttl_exp = 0 that is at the mean on experience, which is 6.215 years. At this point, with 6.215 years of experience, the tangent is 0.0487, notably less steep than when we did not center experience. We will generate our figure to show the centered experience results using the following commands:

```
. margins, at(cttl_exp = (-6(2)22))
. marginsplot
```

The figure corresponding to the centered solution appears in figure 10.15. This is the same shape as in figure 10.14, where the total experience was not centered except for the shift in the x variable due to subtracting the mean (6.215) from each person's score on `ttl_exp`. Thus instead of ranging from 0 years of experience to 28 years, it ranges from −6 years of experience to 22 years. The only added value of this approach, which is the linear component—now 0.049—is the instantaneous rate of change for a person with an average amount of experience, that is, with 6.215 years of experience.

Figure 10.15. Quadratic model relating log of income to total experience where experience is centered

Centering is important for independent variables where a value of zero may not be meaningful. For example, we would not be interested in a person who had zero years of education compared with a person who has an average amount of education. We would not be interested in the instantaneous rate of change for a person who had a graduate record examination of zero because that is not even a possible value. Other examples where a zero value is probably not meaningful and you should center include body mass index, weight, depression measured on a 30–75 point scale, and age in subsample of retired people. In each instance, a value of zero is neither useful nor meaningful. Nobody has a body mass index of zero or weight zero. No retired person has an age of zero and nobody has a score of zero on a scale that ranges from 30–75. With centering the independent variable, the size of the linear component still needs to be interpreted with care, but it is often more useful than using uncentered data. With a centered independent variable, the linear component represents the instantaneous rate of change for the person who has an average score on the independent variable.

10.12.3   Do we need to add a quadratic component?

The possible answers to this question are yes, no, or maybe. Consider our example of predicting a person's wage based on their total years of work experience. Figure 10.16 shows the result for both the linear model and the quadratic model.

```
. twoway (lfit ln_wage ttl_exp) (qfit ln_wage ttl_exp)
```

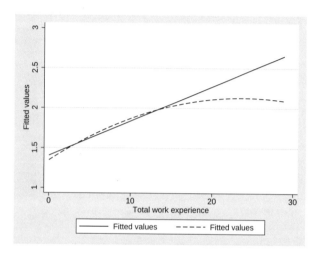

Figure 10.16. Comparison of linear and quadratic models

Examining figure 10.16, if you are interested in people with fewer than about 15 years of work experience, the linear model and the quadratic model are nearly indistinguishable. The linear model, being simpler, might be preferred. For people with more than 15 years of total work experience, the alternative models are different. The downward trend in the quadratic model indicates that it may be important to think of the wage benefit of increasing experience as leveling off. Sometimes the linear component works nearly as well as a quadratic model or at least does so over a range of the x variable. Science always favors the simplest solution that works, so the linear model may be preferred at least for a partial range of the independent variable.

Let's use the `nestreg` command to determine if adding the quadratic term strengthens R^2 and whether the improvement is statistically significant.

We open the dialog box for the `nestreg` command by selecting Statistics ▷ Other ▷ Nested model statistics. In the *Dependent variable* box, type `ln_wage`. In the *Command* box, select `regress`. Under *Blocks*, click on Add..., select `ttl_exp` in the resulting *Term 1* dialog box, and then click on OK. Again, click on Add... but this time specify the interaction `c.ttl_exp#c.ttl_exp` and then click on OK. Then click on OK in the `nestreg` dialog box. Alternatively, you could type the command directly. Here are the command and results:

```
. nestreg: regress ln_wage (ttl_exp) (c.ttl_exp#c.ttl_exp)
```
Block 1: ttl_exp

Source	SS	df	MS
Model	1150.37005	1	1150.37005
Residual	5371.51384	28,532	.188262787
Total	6521.88388	28,533	.228573367

Number of obs	= 28,534
F(1, 28532)	= 6110.45
Prob > F	= 0.0000
R-squared	= 0.1764
Adj R-squared	= 0.1764
Root MSE	= .43389

ln_wage	Coefficient	Std. err.	t	P>|t|	[95% conf. interval]	
ttl_exp	.0431613	.0005522	78.17	0.000	.042079	.0442435
_cons	1.406646	.0042866	328.15	0.000	1.398244	1.415048

Block 2: c.ttl_exp#c.ttl_exp

Source	SS	df	MS
Model	1184.57867	2	592.289333
Residual	5337.30522	28,531	.187070387
Total	6521.88388	28,533	.228573367

Number of obs	= 28,534
F(2, 28531)	= 3166.13
Prob > F	= 0.0000
R-squared	= 0.1816
Adj R-squared	= 0.1816
Root MSE	= .43252

ln_wage	Coefficient	Std. err.	t	P>|t|	[95% conf. interval]	
ttl_exp	.0660334	.0017787	37.12	0.000	.0625471	.0695197
c.ttl_exp# c.ttl_exp	−.0013929	.000103	−13.52	0.000	−.0015948	−.001191
_cons	1.348441	.0060651	222.33	0.000	1.336553	1.360329

Block	F	df	Block Residual df	Pr > F	R2	Change in R2
1	6110.45	1	28532	0.0000	0.1764	
2	182.86	1	28531	0.0000	0.1816	0.0052

The "Block 1" result replicates our linear regression solution. The "Block 2" result replicates our results for the quadratic model that includes both `ttl_exp` and `ttl_sq`. The key results are in the bottom table. "Block 1" has an $F(1, 28532) = 6110.45$, $p < 0.001$, and an $R^2 = 0.176$. "Block 2", for which we add the quadratic component, increases the R^2 by just 0.005 to a total $R^2 = 0.182$. The increase in R^2 of 0.005 is small, but it is statistically significant, $F(1, 28531) = 182.86$, $p < 0.001$.

Is our answer to the question posed in this section "yes", "no", or "maybe"? Based on the test of significance, the answer is yes. The quadratic model significantly improves our explanatory power. However, we need considerable caution with this result and should acknowledge that the improvement, while it should not be attributed to chance, is quite small. We should examine our graphs to further note the quadratic effect that applies mostly latter in a person's career. Although the curvature is interesting, the tiny increase in the R^2 is likely because only a small portion (less than 5%) of the total sample have scores on `ttl_exp` of more than 20 years.

10.13 Power analysis in multiple regression

When you are designing a study that will use multiple regression, it is often difficult to know how large a sample you will need. If you need only a sample of 100 to test your multiple regression equation for significance, then you would waste a lot of money collecting a sample of 1,000. Vice versa, if you sampled 100 people when you really needed 1,000 to have sufficient power to test your hypothesis, then you would likely fail. When a funding agency is deciding on what grant proposals to fund, they expect you to show that your sample size is large enough to have sufficient power to find a practically significant result is statistically significant, but not a larger and more expensive sample than is needed.

The first thing you need to decide before doing a power analysis is what value is the minimum R^2 you believe would be practically important. You can do this by going through the relevant literature to see what is a reasonable minimum value. That is, what is the minimum proportion of the variation of the dependent variable that you need to explain to be practically significant. The smaller this value, the bigger of a sample you will need to find a statistically significant result.

If you cannot find a minimum R^2 based on your review of the literature, you can use general guidelines. Dattalo (2008) presents a table (10.2) showing what is generally recognized as a small, moderate, and large R^2. These are general recommendations, and your particular study area may use different values.

Table 10.2. Effect size and R^2

Effect size	R^2
Small	0.02
Medium	0.13
Large	0.26

These numbers may sound small, but remember that they are squared values. The corresponding Rs are 0.14, 0.36, and 0.51.

Suppose you have five independent variables to predict a student's college GPA:

- GPA in high school
- Gender
- Race/ethnicity (white versus nonwhite)
- Father's education
- Mother's education

How large of a sample will you need to see whether your model explains a practically or substantively significant portion of the variance in college GPAs. We will assume you want an $\diamond = 0.05$. Suppose we are interested only in a strong effect size for our model, so we will set $R^2 = 0.26$. We need to also specify that our model includes five independent variables. How much power do we need to be confident that we will find a large R^2 when the relationship in the population is this strong. In many fields where we are doing exploratory research, we are happy with a power of 0.80. In areas where there is a history of significant results, many researchers will specify a power of 0.90. Because there is a lot of research to suggest that these five independent variables should have a strong effect, we will choose a power of 0.90.

Select Statistics ▷ Power, precision, and sample size. When the control panel opens, select Regression slopes ▷ Multiple linear regression from the panel on the left. From the panel on the right, select R-squared test of all coefficients in a multiple linear regression. See figure 10.17 for reference.

Figure 10.17. Power, precision, and sample-size analysis Control Panel

This opens a dialog box (figure 10.18) where we want to *Compute* the `Sample size`, when the *Significance level* is set to `0.05`, the `Power` is set at `0.90`, the *R-squared of tested model* is set at `0.26`, and the *Number of tested covariates* is set at `5`.

Figure 10.18. Power analysis for an R^2

Clicking on OK, we obtain these results:

```
. power rsquared 0.26, power(0.90) ntested(5)
Performing iteration ...
Estimated sample size for multiple linear regression
F test for R2 testing all coefficients
H0: R2_T = 0  versus  Ha: R2_T != 0
Study parameters:
        alpha =      0.0500
        power =      0.9000
        delta =      0.3514
         R2_T =      0.2600
      ntested =           5
Estimated sample size:
            N =          53
```

We want to verify that the study parameters are what we intended. For an $R^2 = 0.26$, Stata computes the effect size, delta $= 0.3514$. Sometimes called f^2 rather than delta, it is $R^2/(1 - R^2)$ or $0.26/(1 - 0.26)$. We need only a sample of $N = 53$. This is really important to know because it is telling us a large sample of hundreds of students would waste resources and money because that would not be necessary to have sufficient power. We would need a much larger sample than $N = 53$ to have 90% power to find a significant result if the R^2 were a lot smaller. Try some values of R^2 such as 0.13 and

0.02 to see how the needed sample size goes up with a smaller R^2. For example, with the minimum $R^2 = 0.02$ (corresponding to a small effect in table 10.2), you will find you would need $N = 813$. This illustrates that we can detect a statistically significant R^2 based on a very large sample even though it is a very small effect and of little practical significance.

A second place where a power analysis is useful is testing the effect of adding a subset of additional independent variables. Let's say we want to see whether mother's education and father's education are significant and important when added to our first three independent variables. We need to assume how much variance the initial set of independent variables, GPA in high school, gender, and race/ethnicity explain. Let's say after reviewing the literature, we believe they will have an R^2 of 0.30 (this is an educated guess because we cannot actually know the R^2 before collecting any data). We go through the same process in the menus to open the *Power and sample-size analysis* control panel, but this time we select the R-squared test of a subset of coefficients in a multiple linear regression option. We are estimating the sample size, using the 0.05 significance level, and a power of 0.90. In the box for *Effect size*, we enter an R^2 of 0.30 for the *Reduced model* (the three initial independent variables) and 0.40 for the *Full model*, where we have added mother's education and father's education. This means we expect mother's education and father's education to increase R^2 by 0.10. Finally, we are testing for two added covariates and controlling for the three initial covariates. Figure 10.19 shows the completed dialog menu.

Figure 10.19. Power analysis for R^2 test, subset of coefficients

The resulting command and results are as follows:

```
. power rsquared 0.30 0.40, power(0.9) ntested(2) ncontrol(3)

Performing iteration ...

Estimated sample size for multiple linear regression
F test for R2 testing subset of coefficients
H0: R2_F = R2_R  versus  Ha: R2_F != R2_R

Study parameters:
        alpha =     0.0500
        power =     0.9000
        delta =     0.1667
         R2_R =     0.3000
         R2_F =     0.4000
      R2_diff =     0.1000
     ncontrol =          3
      ntested =          2

Estimated sample size:
            N =         80
```

Thus, we need a sample size of $N = 80$ to detect an increase of the R^2 to 0.40 when adding the mother's and father's education, assuming a model with the first three variables has an $R^2 = 0.30$.

Instead of computing sample size, we might know the number of people that we could include in a sample, but we first want to make sure that we would have enough power to detect the effect size we are interested in. In this case, the process can be reversed in that you can use the **power rsquared** command to see how much power you get with a specific sample size. Suppose you want to use the same set of five independent variables to model college GPA. We know that we can collect a sample of $N = 50$ students. Does this give us sufficient power to detect a medium, but real, effect in the population? If the true population explained variance were 0.13 (a medium effect in table 10.2), how much power did we have to show a statistically significant result given their sample of 50 observations?

```
. power rsquared 0.13, n(50) ntested(5)

Estimated power for multiple linear regression
F test for R2 testing all coefficients
H0: R2_T = 0  versus  Ha: R2_T != 0

Study parameters:
        alpha =     0.0500
            N =         50
        delta =     0.1494
         R2_T =     0.1300
      ntested =          5

Estimated power:
        power =     0.4745
```

This shows that with a sample of $N = 50$, we have very little power to demonstrate that a true medium effect of $R^2 = 0.13$ is statistically significant. We have as much power, 0.4745, as a coin toss! How much power would we have to detect a small effect size of 0.02. You can run the command to verify that the power would be 0.0935.

Clearly, the design to use a sample of $N = 50$ will have inadequate power to detect a medium effect size and virtually no power to detect a small effect size.

This use of power analysis retrospectively is highly controversial. Staying with the last example, suppose you find an $R^2 = 0.13$ with an $N = 50$ in your study, and it is not significant. If you have done an analysis and not obtained a significant result, running this analysis after the fact is essentially saying you have a poorly designed study. You should have done the power analysis prospectively. One possible use of a retrospective power analysis is as a critical review of existing literature that has indicated a variable is not significant based on an inadequate sample size. You could argue that the variable may or may not have a medium effect but that the study was poorly set up to test for this.

10.14 Summary

Multiple regression is an extremely powerful and general strategy for analyzing data. We have covered several applications of multiple regression and diagnostic strategies. These provide you with a strong base, and Stata has almost unlimited ways of extending what you have learned. Here are the main topics we covered in chapter 10:

- What multiple regression can do, and how it is an extension of the bivariate correlation and regression we covered in chapter 8

- The basic command for doing multiple regression, including the option for standardized beta weights

- How we measure the unique effects of a variable, controlling for a set of other variables, which included a discussion of semipartial correlation and the increment in R^2

- Diagnostics of the dependent variable and how we test for normality of the error term

- Diagnostics for the distribution of residuals or errors in prediction

- Diagnostics to find outlier observations that have too much influence and may involve a coding error

- Collinearity and multicollinearity, along with how to evaluate the seriousness of the problem and what to do about it

- How to use weighted samples where different observations have different probabilities of being included, such as when there is oversampling of certain groups and we want to generalize to the entire population

- How to work with categorical predictors with just two categories and with more than two categories

- How to work with nested (hierarchical) regression in which we enter blocks of variables at a time

- How to work with interaction between a continuous variable and a categorical variable

If you are a Stata beginner, you may be amazed by the number of things you can do with regression and by what we have covered in this chapter. If you are an experienced user, I have only whetted your appetite. The next chapter, on logistic regression, includes several references that you should pursue if you want to know more about Stata's capabilities for multiple regression. Stata has special techniques for working with different types of outcome variables, for working with panel data, and for working with multilevel data where subgroups of observations share common values on some variables.

The next chapter is the first extension of multiple regression. I will cover the case in which there is a binary outcome because this happens often. You will have data with which you want to predict whether a couple will get divorced, whether a business will survive its first year, whether a patient recovers, whether an adolescent reports having considered suicide, whether a bill will become a law, or something similar. In each case, the outcome will be either a success or a failure. Then we will learn how to predict a success or a failure.

10.15 Exercises

1. Use `gss2002_chapter10.dta` (Smith et al. 2015). You are interested in how many hours a person works per week. You think that men work more hours, older people work fewer hours, and people who are self-employed work the most hours. The GSS has the needed measures, `sex`, `age`, `wrkslf`, and `hrs1` (hours worked last week). Recode `sex` and `wrkslf` into dummy variables, and then do a regression of hours worked on the predictors. Write out a prediction equation showing the β. What are the predicted hours worked for a female who is 20 years old and works for herself? How much variance is explained and is this statistically significant?

2. Use `census.dta`. The variable `tworace` is the percentage of people in each state and the District of Columbia who report being a combination of two or more races. Predict this by using the percentage of the state that is white (`white`), the median household income (`hhinc`), and the percentage with a BA degree or more education (`ba`). Predict the estimated value, calling it `yhat`. Predict the standardized residual, calling it `rstandard`. Plot a scattergram like the one in figure 10.5. Do a listing of states that have a standardized residual of more than 1.96. Interpret the graph and the standardized residual list.

3. Use `census.dta`. Repeat the regression in exercise 2. Compute the DFbeta score for each predictor, and list the states that have relatively large DFbeta values on any of the predictors. Explain why the problematic states are problematic.

4. Use `gss2002_chapter10.dta`. Suppose that you want to know if a man's socioeconomic status depends more on his father's or his mother's socioeconomic status. Run a regression (use `sei`, `pasei`, and `masei`), and control for how many hours a week the man works (`hrs1`). Do a test to see if `pasei` and `masei` are equal. Create a graph similar to that in figure 10.7, and carefully interpret it for the distribution of residuals.

5. Use `gss2002_chapter10.dta`. You are interested in predicting the socioeconomic status of adults. You are interested in whether conservative political views predict higher socioeconomic status uniquely, after you have included background and achievement variables. The socioeconomic variable is `sei`. Do a nested regression. In the first block, enter gender (you will need to recode the variable `sex` into a dummy variable, `male`), mother's education (`maeduc`), father's education (`paeduc`), mother's socioeconomic index (`masei`), and father's socioeconomic index (`pasei`). In the second block, enter education (`educ`). In the third block, add conservative political views (`polviews`). Carefully interpret the results. Create a table summarizing the results.

6. Use `c10interaction.dta`. Repeat the interaction analysis presented in the text, but first center education and generate the interaction term to be male times the centered score on education. Centering involves subtracting the mean from each observation. You can either use the `summarize` command to get the mean for education and then subtract this from each score or type `search center` and install the ado-file called `center`. Type `center educ` to generate a new variable called `c_educ`. Then generate the interaction term with the command `generate educc_male = c_educ*male`. After running the regression (`regress inc male c_educ educc_male`) and creating a two-way overlay graph, compare the results with those in the text. Why is the intercept so different? Hint: The intercept is when the predictors are zero—think about what a value of zero on a centered variable is.

7. Repeat exercise 6 using the `i.`, `c.`, and `#` factor-variable operators. You do not need to do the graph, just type the commands, and show how the results match the results in exercise 6.

8. You want to do a study of sleep problems of college students. You have a scale measuring sleep problems. You think the following are all predictors: 1) use of social drugs (yes/no), 2) frequency of use of social drugs (0–30 times a month), 3) hours worked for pay, 4) stress about academic performance, and 5) stress about social relationships. How big of a sample do you need if you are interested in showing that these variables have a moderate effect on sleep problems? You need to justify the R^2 value you use along with the alpha and power.

9. Suppose that the study described in exercise 8 was conducted and the $R^2 = 0.20$. You think these predictors are important, but another predictor should have been financial stress. You think financial stress would explain at least an additional 5% of variance. You are interested in showing that such an increase would be

statistically significant. Setting your alpha and power, what sample size will you need?

10. You are going to do the study described in exercise 9, but just as you are starting, you find an article that already did it. Using a sample of 75 people, the researchers found that financial stress did increase the R^2 by 6%, but it was not a significant increase. How much power did they have? Why is this a problem?

11. In section 8.4, we used `nlsw88.dta`, which is installed with Stata. We again load this dataset by typing `sysuse nlsw88`. We will also again drop people who are under 35 or over 45 and keep only blacks and whites by keeping only people who had a code of less than 3 on the variable `race`. We will use the `binscatter` command. If you did not install this command in section 8.4, type `ssc install binscatter`.

   a. Type `binscatter wage tenure`, and then type `binscatter wage tenure, line(qfit)`.

   b. Does it look like a quadratic component is needed?

   c. Use the `nestreg` prefix command to test whether adding the quadratic term improves the fit.

12. Repeat the previous exercise using `nlsw88.dta` but this time center `tenure`.

   a. What is different?

   b. What is the same?

   c. Carefully interpret the linear effect.

11   Logistic regression

11.1   Introduction to logistic regression

The regression models that we covered in chapter 10 focused on quantitative outcome variables that had an underlying continuum. There are important applications of regression in which the outcome is binary—something either does or does not happen and we want to know why. Here are a few examples:

- A woman is diagnosed as having breast cancer

- A person is hired

- A married couple get divorced

- A new faculty member earns tenure

- A participant in a study drops out of the program

- A candidate is elected

We could quickly generate many more examples where something either does or does not happen. Binary outcomes were fine as predictors in chapter 10, but now we are interested in them as dependent variables. Logistic regression is a special type of regression that is used for binary-outcome variables.

11.2 An example

One of the best predictors of marital stability is the amount of positive feedback a spouse gives her or his partner.

- You observe 20 couples in a decision-making task for 10 minutes.

- You do this 1 week prior to their marriage and record the number of positive responses each of them makes about the other. An example would be "you have a good idea" or "you really understand my goals".

- You look just at the positive comments made by the husband and call these `positives`.

- You wait 5 years and see whether they get divorced. You call this `divorce`.

- You assign a code of 1 to those couples who get divorced and a code of 0 to those who do not.

- The resulting dataset has just two variables and is called `divorce.dta`.

The following is a list of the data in `divorce.dta`:

```
. use https://www.stata-press.com/data/agis6r/divorce
. list divorce positives
```

	divorce	positi~s
1.	0	10
2.	0	8
3.	0	9
4.	0	7
5.	0	8
6.	0	5
7.	0	9
8.	0	6
9.	0	8
10.	0	7
11.	1	1
12.	1	1
13.	1	3
14.	1	1
15.	1	4
16.	1	5
17.	1	6
18.	1	3
19.	1	2
20.	1	0

If we graph this relationship (see figure 11.1), it looks strange because the outcome variable, `divorce`, has just two possible values. (The graph has been enhanced by using the Graph Editor, but the basic command is `scatter divorce positives`.)

Figure 11.1. Positive feedback and divorce

A couple with a very low rating, say, 0–4 on `positives`, is almost certain to have a score of 1 on `divorce`. With a score of 7–10, a couple is almost certain to not get divorced, that is, to score 0 on `divorce`. A couple somewhere in the middle on `positives`, with a score of 5 or 6, may or may not get divorced. This is the zone of transition. It would not make sense to use a straight line as a prediction rule like we did with bivariate regression.

If we use logistic regression to predict the probability of a divorce based on the husband's rating on giving positive feedback prior to the marriage (we will soon learn how to do this), we get a predicted probability of divorce based on the score a husband has for `positives`. This conforms to what is sometimes called an *S*-curve as shown in figure 11.2.

Figure 11.2. Predicted probability of positive feedback and divorce

Now this graph makes sense; it is a nonlinear relationship. The probability of divorce is nonlinearly related to the number of positive responses of the husband. If he gives relatively few positive responses, the probability of a divorce is very high; if he gives a lot of positive feedback, the probability of divorce is very low. Those husbands who are somewhere in the middle on positive feedback are the hardest to predict a divorce outcome for. This is exactly what we would expect and what our figure illustrates.

To fit a model like this, we do not estimate the probability directly. Instead, we estimate something called a logit. When the logit is linearly related to the predictor, the probability conforms to an *S*-curve like the one in figure 11.2. The reason we go through the trouble of computing a logit for each observation and using that in the logistic regression as the dependent variable is that the logit can be predicted by using a linear model. Notice that the probability of getting a divorce varies from 0 to 1, but, in fact, the logit ranges from about −10 to about 10 in this example. Although the probability of divorce is not linearly related to `positives`, the logit is. The relationship between the positive feedback the husband gives and the logit of the `divorce` variable is shown in figure 11.3.

Figure 11.3. Predicted probability of positive feedback and logit of divorce

From a statistical point of view, figure 11.3 predicting the logit of divorce is equivalent to figure 11.2 predicting the probability of divorce.

Before logistic regression was available, people did ordinary least-squares (OLS) regression, as described in chapter 10, when there was a binary-outcome variable. One problem with this is that the probability of the outcome being a 1 is much more likely to follow an S-curve than it is to follow a straight line. A second problem is that there is an absolute lower limit of zero and an absolute upper limit of one for a binary variable. If you predict 1 using OLS regression, you are saying that the probability is 1.0. If you predict 0.5, you are saying that the probability is 0.5. What if you are predicting −0.2 or 1.5? These are impossible values, but they can happen using OLS regression. Figure 11.4 shows what would happen using OLS regression because OLS regression has no way of knowing that your outcome cannot be below 0 or above 1.

```
. regress divorce positives

      Source |       SS           df       MS      Number of obs   =        20
-------------+----------------------------------   F(1, 18)        =     42.95
       Model |  3.52343538         1  3.52343538   Prob > F        =    0.0000
    Residual |  1.47656462        18   .082031368  R-squared       =    0.7047
-------------+----------------------------------   Adj R-squared   =    0.6883
       Total |           5        19   .263157895  Root MSE        =    .28641

------------------------------------------------------------------------------
     divorce | Coefficient  Std. err.      t    P>|t|     [95% conf. interval]
-------------+----------------------------------------------------------------
   positives |  -.1381739    .021083    -6.55   0.000    -.1824677   -.0938801
       _cons |   1.211596   .1260582     9.61   0.000     .9467574    1.476434
------------------------------------------------------------------------------

. predict divols
(option xb assumed; fitted values)
```

```
. twoway (scatter divorce positives) (lfit divols positives), scheme(s2mono)
```

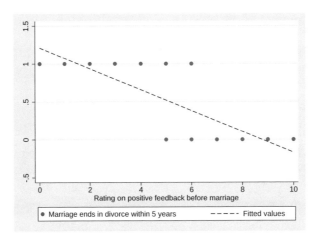

Figure 11.4. Positive feedback and divorce using OLS regression

You can see the problem with using a straight line with OLS regression. A couple with a score of 10 on `positives` would have a probability of getting divorced within 5 years of less than zero. A couple with a score of 0 on `positives` would have a probability of about 1.25. Both of these are impossible values because a probability must not be greater than 1.0 nor less than 0.0. Comparing figure 11.2 and figure 11.4, you can see that a logistic regression approach makes sense for binary-outcome variables.

11.3   What is an odds ratio and a logit?

I will explain odds ratios and logits by using a simple example with hypothetical data, `environ.dta`. Suppose that you are interested in the relationship between environmental support and support for a liberal candidate in a community election. Your survey asks items that you can use to divide your sample into two categories of environmental concern, namely, high or low environmental concern. You also ask participants whether they support a particular liberal candidate, and they either support this candidate or they do not. We have two variables that we will call `environ` (1 means high environmental concern; 0 means low environmental concern) and `libcand` (1 means that they support this liberal candidate; 0 means that they do not). Here is how the relationship between these variables looks:

```
. use https://www.stata-press.com/data/agis6r/environ, clear
. tab2 environ libcand, row
-> tabulation of environ by libcand
```

```
┌─────────────────┐
│ Key             │
├─────────────────┤
│    frequency    │
│  row percentage │
└─────────────────┘
```

Environmental concern: 1 high, 0 low	support liberal candidate: 1 yes, 0 no		Total
	0	1	
0	6	4	10
	60.00	40.00	100.00
1	3	7	10
	30.00	70.00	100.00
Total	9	11	20
	45.00	55.00	100.00

- The probability of supporting a liberal candidate (1 on support liberal) is 11/20, or 0.55.

- The probability of supporting a liberal candidate if you have low environmental concern (1 on support liberal if 0 on environmental concern) is 4/10, or 0.4.

- The probability of supporting a liberal candidate if you have high environmental concern (1 on support liberal if 1 on environmental concern) is 7/10, or 0.7.

From these last two probabilities, we can see that there is a relationship. With only 4 of the 10 people who have a low environmental concern supporting the liberal candidate compared with 7 of the 10 people who have high environmental concern, this looks like a fairly strong difference.

What are the odds of supporting a liberal candidate? The odds are the ratio of those who support the candidate to those who do not.

- The odds of supporting a liberal candidate are $11/9 = 1.22$. This means that there are 1.22 people supporting the liberal candidate for each person who opposes the liberal candidate.

- The odds of supporting a liberal candidate if you have low environmental concern are $4/6 = 0.67$. This means that among those with low environmental concern there are just 0.67 people supporting the liberal candidate for each person who opposes the liberal candidate.

- The odds of supporting a liberal candidate if you have high environmental concern are $7/3 = 2.33$. This indicates that among those with high environmental concern, there are 2.33 people supporting the liberal candidate for each person who opposes the liberal candidate.

11.3.1   The odds ratio

We need a way to combine these two odds, 2.33 and 0.67, into one number. We can take the ratio of the odds. The odds ratio of supporting the liberal candidate is $2.33/0.67 = 3.48$. The odds of supporting a liberal candidate are 3.48 times as great if you have high environmental concern as they are if you have low environmental concern.

The odds ratio gives us useful information for understanding the relationship between environmental concern and support for the liberal candidate. Environmental concern is a strong predictor of this support because the odds of a person high on environmental concern supporting the liberal are 3.48 times as great as the odds of a person with low environmental concern supporting the liberal.

11.3.2   The logit transformation

Odds ratios make a lot of sense for interpreting data, but for our purposes, they have some problems as a score on the dependent variable. The distribution of the odds ratio is far from normal.

An odds ratio of 1.0 means that the odds are equally likely and that the predictor makes no difference. Thus an odds ratio of 1.0 is equivalent to a beta weight of 0.0. If those with and without environmental concerns were equally likely to support the liberal candidate, the odds ratio would be 1.0.

An odds ratio can go from 1.0 to infinity for situations where the odds are greater than 1.0. By contrast, the odds ratio can go from 1.0 to just 0.0 for situations where the odds are less than 1.0. This makes the distribution extremely asymmetrical, which could create estimation problems. On the other hand, if we take the natural logarithm of the odds ratio, it will not have this distributional problem. This logarithm of the odds ratio is the logit:

$$\text{logit} = \ln(\text{odds ratio})$$

Although the probability of something happening makes a lot of sense to most people and the odds ratio also makes sense to most of us, a lot of people have trouble understanding the score for a logit. Because the logistic regression is predicting a logit score, the values of the parameter estimates are difficult to interpret. To get around this problem, we can reverse the transformation process and get coefficients for the odds ratio that are easier to interpret.

11.4 Data used in the rest of the chapter

The National Longitudinal Survey of Youth, 1997 (Bureau of Labor Statistics, U.S. Department of Labor 2015) (`nlsy97_chapter11.dta`) asked a series of questions about drinking behavior among adolescents between the ages of 12 and 16. One question asked how many days, if any, each youth drank alcohol in the past month, `drday97`. We have dichotomized this variable into a binary variable called `drank30` that is coded 1 if the youth reported having had a drink in the past month or 0 if the youth reported not having had a drink in the past month.

Say that we want to see if peer behavior is important and if having regular meals together with the family is important. Our contention is that the greater the percentage of your peers who drink, the more likely you are to drink. By contrast, the more often you have meals together with your family, the less likely you are to drink. Admittedly, having meals together with your family is a limited indicator of parental influence. Because older youth are more likely to drink, we will control for age. We will also control for gender.

```
. use https://www.stata-press.com/data/agis6r/nlsy97_chapter11, clear
(National Survey of Youth, 1997, selected variables from first wave)
```

Predicting a count variable

We have a variable that is a count of the number of days the youth reports drinking in the last month. We have dichotomized this as none or some. This makes sense if we are interested in predicting whether a youth drinks or not. What if we were interested in predicting how often a youth drinks rather than simply whether they did? Certainly, there is a difference between an adolescent who drank once in the last month and an adolescent who drank 30 days in the last month.

Stata has commands for estimating a dependent variable that is a count, although these commands are beyond the scope of this book. Using OLS regression with a count variable can be problematic when the count is of a rare event such as the number of days a youth drank in the past month. The distribution of rare events is skewed and sometimes has a substantial percentage of participants reporting a count of zero.

Here are two things we could do. One is to use what is called *Poisson regression of the count*. Poisson regression is useful for counts that are skewed, with most people doing the behavior rarely or just a few times. A second thing Stata can do is called *zero-inflated Poisson regression*, in which there is not only a skewed distribution but there are more zeros than you would expect with a Poisson distribution. If you asked how many times a female adolescent had a fist fight in the past 30 days, most would say zero times. Zero-inflated Poisson regression simultaneously estimates two regressions, one for the binary result of whether the count is zero and the other for how often the outcome occurred. Different factors may predict the onset of the outcome than would predict the count of the outcome. Long and Freese (2014) have an excellent book that discusses these extensions to what we cover in this chapter.

Interpreting a logistic regression depends on understanding something of the distribution of the variables. First, do a summary of the variables so that we know their means and distributions. If we need to eliminate any observations that did not answer all the items, we drop the cases that have missing values on any of the variables. It would also be important to do a tabulation, although those results are not shown here. The summary of the variables is

```
. summarize drank30 age97 pdrink97 dinner97 male
> if !missing(drank30, age97, pdrink97, dinner97, male)

    Variable │       Obs        Mean    Std. dev.        Min        Max
─────────────┼─────────────────────────────────────────────────────────
     drank30 │     1,654     .382104    .4860487          0          1
       age97 │     1,654    13.67352    .9371347         12         16
    pdrink97 │     1,654    2.108222    1.214858          1          5
    dinner97 │     1,654    4.699516    2.349352          0          7
        male │     1,654    .5405079    .4985071          0          1
```

We see that the mean for **drank30** is 0.382. This means that 38.2% of the students reported drinking at least once a month. Logistic regression also works well even when the outcome is rare, such as whether a person dies after surgery. When the mean is around 0.50, the OLS regression and logistic regression produce consistent results, but when the probability is close to 0 or 1, the logistic regression is especially important.

11.5   Logistic regression

There are two commands for logistic regression: **logit** and **logistic**. The **logit** command gives the regression coefficients to estimate the logit score. The **logistic** command gives us the odds ratios we need to interpret the effect size of the predictors. Select Statistics ▷ Binary outcomes. From here, we can select Logistic regression. Selecting the latter produces the dialog box in figure 11.5.

Figure 11.5. Dialog box for doing logistic regression

This dialog box is pretty straightforward. Type **drank30** as the *Dependent variable* and **age97 male pdrink97 dinner97** as the *Independent variables*. The *Offset variable* is for special purposes and is not discussed here. The option to *Retain perfect predictor variables* should not be checked in most applications. In a rare case where there is a category that has no variation on the outcome variable, Stata drops the predictor.

Checking the *Retain perfect predictor variables* box forces Stata to include the variable, which can lead to instabilities in the estimates. The other tabs have the usual set of options to restrict our sample, weight the observations, or use different estimators.

The only difference between the dialog boxes for logistic regression and for logistic regression with odds ratios is that the default for logistic regression is the estimated regression coefficients and the default for the logistic regression with odds ratios is the odds ratios. Regardless of which dialog box you choose, on the **Reporting** tab, we can specify whether we want the regression coefficients or the odds ratios. The following commands and output show the results of both dialogs. The first results are for the command `logistic`, where we get the odds ratios, and the second results are for the command `logit`, where we get the regression coefficients.

```
. logistic drank30 age97 male pdrink97 dinner97
Logistic regression                                  Number of obs =    1,654
                                                     LR chi2(4)    =    78.01
                                                     Prob > chi2   =   0.0000
Log likelihood = -1061.0474                          Pseudo R2     =   0.0355
```

drank30	Odds ratio	Std. err.	z	P>|z|	[95% conf. interval]	
age97	1.169241	.0684191	2.67	0.008	1.042546	1.311332
male	.9794922	.1046935	-0.19	0.846	.7943646	1.207764
pdrink97	1.329275	.0598174	6.33	0.000	1.217056	1.451841
dinner97	.942086	.0208682	-2.69	0.007	.9020603	.9838878
_cons	.0524677	.0415938	-3.72	0.000	.0110944	.2481314

```
Note: _cons estimates baseline odds.
. logit drank30 age97 male pdrink97 dinner97
Iteration 0:    log likelihood = -1100.0502
Iteration 1:    log likelihood =  -1061.142
Iteration 2:    log likelihood = -1061.0474
Iteration 3:    log likelihood = -1061.0474
Logistic regression                                  Number of obs =    1,654
                                                     LR chi2(4)    =    78.01
                                                     Prob > chi2   =   0.0000
Log likelihood = -1061.0474                          Pseudo R2     =   0.0355
```

drank30	Coefficient	Std. err.	z	P>|z|	[95% conf. interval]	
age97	.1563548	.0585158	2.67	0.008	.0416659	.2710437
male	-.020721	.1068855	-0.19	0.846	-.2302128	.1887708
pdrink97	.2846336	.0450001	6.33	0.000	.1964351	.3728321
dinner97	-.0596587	.022151	-2.69	0.007	-.1030739	-.0162434
_cons	-2.947557	.7927494	-3.72	0.000	-4.501317	-1.393797

Both commands give the same results, except that `logit` gives the coefficients for estimating the logit score and `logistic` gives the odds ratios. The results of the `logit` command show the iterations Stata went through in obtaining its results. Logistic regression relies on maximum likelihood estimation rather than ordinary least squares; this is an iterative approach where various solutions are estimated until the best solution of having the maximum likelihood is found. The results show the number of observations followed by a likelihood-ratio (LR) chi-squared test and something called the pseudo-R^2. In this example, the likelihood-ratio chi-squared(4) = 78.01, $p < 0.001$.

Several statistics are called pseudo-R^2s. The one reported by Stata is the McFadden (1974) pseudo-R^2, and you should indicate this if you report this value. This is not the R^2 we had for multiple regression; it is not explained variance. The logistic regression first fits a model with no predictors, just the intercept. To see this log likelihood, you can type

```
. logit drank30 if !missing(age97, male, pdrink97, dinner97)
Iteration 0:   log likelihood = -1100.0502
Iteration 1:   log likelihood = -1100.0502

Logistic regression                             Number of obs =   1,654
                                                LR chi2(0)    =    0.00
                                                Prob > chi2   =       .
Log likelihood = -1100.0502                     Pseudo R2     = 0.0000
```

drank30	Coefficient	Std. err.	z	P>|z|	[95% conf. interval]	
_cons	-.4806274	.0506039	-9.50	0.000	-.5798091	-.3814456

You will find that the log likelihood with only an intercept is -1100.0502. The maximized log likelihood for the model with all the independent variables is reported in the last iteration, here iteration 3, and is -1061.0474. No other solution would fit better in terms of maximizing the log-likelihood function. The McFadden pseudo-R^2 represents how much larger log likelihood is for the final solution. You could calculate it using Stata's `display` command,

```
. display (-1100.0502 - (-1061.0474))/1100.0502
-.03545547
```

Remember that this is not explained variance. The pseudo R^2 is often a small value, and many researchers do not report it. The biggest mistake is to report it and interpret it as explained variance.

The pseudo-R^2 is low, but the results are important

The R^2 in multiple regression is interpreted as explained variance. This important interpretation is not appropriate for the pseudo-R^2, which can be small even when there is an important finding. The pseudo-R^2 is often quite small, and a small value does not mean individual variables are of little importance. If you are interested in specific effects of individual variables, it is better to rely on odds ratios for interpreting results of logistic regression, and many researchers do not even bother to report the pseudo-R^2. This can be illustrated by a simple example. Open the Stata dataset on low birthweight:

```
. use https://www.stata-press.com/data/r17/lbw, clear
```

Now we can run a logistic regression of low birthweight, low, on whether a mother smokes during pregnancy, smoke. Here are the results:

```
. logit low smoke, or
Iteration 0:   log likelihood =   -117.336
Iteration 1:   log likelihood =  -114.9123
Iteration 2:   log likelihood =  -114.9023
Iteration 3:   log likelihood =  -114.9023
Logistic regression                             Number of obs =       189
                                                LR chi2(1)    =      4.87
                                                Prob > chi2   =    0.0274
Log likelihood = -114.9023                      Pseudo R2     =    0.0207
```

low	Odds ratio	Std. err.	z	P>|z|	[95% conf. interval]
smoke	2.021944	.6462989	2.20	0.028	1.08066 3.783112
_cons	.3372093	.0724103	-5.06	0.000	.2213694 .5136667

```
Note: _cons estimates baseline odds.
```

The pseudo-$R^2 = 0.021$, meaning the log likelihood for the fitted model is 2% larger than for the log likelihood for the intercept-only model. If you are used to relying on R^2 in multiple regression, this is likely discouraging. Remember that the pseudo-R^2 measures the change in the likelihood and does not measure explained variance.

Now look at the odds ratio. This shows that mothers who smoke have 2.02 times greater odds of having a low-birthweight child. This odds ratio is statistically significant and certainly extremely important information in spite of the low pseudo-R^2. At the same time, if the outcome variable is extremely rare, the odds ratio may also be misleading. This is not a problem in this example because almost one-third of the children had low birthweight (summarize low). You can imagine other situations where you had a rare outcome: perhaps, only 1% of the observations were 1, and 99% were 0. In such a case, even doubling the odds would not make the outcome likely.

It is difficult to interpret the regression coefficients for the `logit` command. We can see that both the percentage of peers who drink and the number of dinners a youth has with his or her parents are statistically significant. The peer variable has a positive coefficient, meaning that the more of the youth's peers who drink, the higher the logit for the youth's own drinking. The `dinner97` variable has a negative coefficient, and this is as we expected; that is, having more dinners with your family lowers the logit for drinking. We can also see that age is significant and in the expected direction. Sex, by contrast, is not statistically significant, so there is no statistically significant evidence that male versus female adolescents are more likely to drink.

The first output is for the `logistic` command, which gives us the odds ratios. We need to spend a bit of time interpreting these odds ratios. The variable `age97` has an odds ratio of 1.17, $p < 0.01$. This means that the odds of drinking are multiplied by 1.17 for each additional year of age. When the odds ratio is more than 1, the interpretation can be simplified by subtracting 1 and then multiplying by 100: $(1.17 - 1.00) \times 100 = 17\%$. This means that for each increase of 1 year, there is a 17% increase in the odds of drinking. This is an intuitive interpretation that can be understood by a lay audience. You have probably seen this in the papers without realizing the way it was estimated.

For example, you may have seen that there is a 50% increase in the risk of getting lung cancer if you smoke. People sometimes use the word *risk* instead of saying that there is a 50% increase in the odds of getting cancer. What would you say to a lay audience? Each year older an adolescent gets, the odds of drinking increases by 17%. You need to be careful when you interpret the odds ratio. There is a separate coefficient called the relative-risk ratio, which is discussed in the box a few pages from here about the odds ratio versus the relative-risk ratio. Lay audiences often act as if both of these were the same thing, but they are not and they can be different when the outcome is not a rare event. Odds ratios tell us what happens to the odds of an outcome, whereas risk ratios tell us what happens to their probability.

What happens if you compare a 12-year-old with a 15-year-old? The 15-year-old is 3 years older, so you might be tempted to say that the risk factor is $3 \times 17\% = 51\%$ greater. However, this underestimates the effect. If you are familiar with compound interest, you have already guessed the problem. Each additional year builds on the previous year's compounded rate. To compare a 15-year-old with a 12-year-old, you would first cube the odds ratio, $1.17^3 = 1.60$ (to compare a 16-year-old with a 12-year-old, you would compute $1.17^4 = 1.87$). Thus the odds of drinking for a 15-year-old is $(1.60 - 1.00) \times 100 = 60\%$ greater than that for a 12-year-old. The odds for a 16-year-old is $(1.87 - 1.00) \times 100 = 87\%$ greater than that for a 12-year-old.

When an odds ratio is less than 1.00, you need to change the calculation just a bit. We like to talk of the decrease in the odds ratio, so we need to subtract the odds ratio from 1.00 to find this decrease. Thus for each extra day per week that an adolescent has dinner with his or her family, the odds of drinking are reduced by $(1.00 - 0.94) \times 100 = 6\%$. Consider two adolescents. One has no family dinners, and the other has them every day of the week. Once again, you could be tempted to say that the odds of drinking are now $(7 \times 6\%) = 42\%$ lower. This is just as wrong for odds ratios smaller than one as it is for odds ratios larger than one. Just as before, we must raise the original odds ratio to a power: the odds of drinking for the adolescent who eats at home is $0.94^7 = 0.65$ times as large as the odds of drinking for the adolescent who never eats with his or her family. Again we want to express this as a percentage change. Because the multiplier is less than 1.00, we compute the change as $(1.00 - 0.65) \times 100 = 35\%$, meaning that a youth who has dinner with the family every night of the week has 35% lower odds of drinking than a youth who has no meals with his or her family.

Using Stata as a calculator

When doing logistic regression, we often need to calculate something to help us interpret the results. We just said that $1.17^4 = 1.87$. To get this result, in the Stata Command window, enter `display 1.17^4`, which results in 1.87.

The odds ratios are a transformation of the regression coefficients. The coefficient for `pdrink97` is 0.2846. The odds ratio is defined as $\exp(b)$, which for this example is $\exp(0.2846)$. This means that we exponentiate the coefficient. More simply, we raise the mathematical constant e to the b power, e^b or $e^{0.2846}$ for the `pdrink97` variable. This would be a hard task without a calculator. To do this within Stata, in the Command window, type `display exp(0.2846)`, and 1.33 is displayed as the odds ratio.

It is hard to compare the odds ratio for one variable with the odds ratio for another variable when they are measured on different scales. The `male` variable is binary, going from 0 to 1, and the variable `dinner97` goes from 0 to 7. For binary predictor variables, you can interpret the odds ratios and percentages directly. For variables that are not binary, you need to have some other standard. One solution is to compare specific examples, such as having no dinners with the family versus having seven dinners with them each week. Another solution is to evaluate the effect of a 1-standard-deviation change for variables that are not binary. This way, you could compare a 1-standard-deviation change in dinners per week with a 1-standard-deviation change in peers who drink. When both variables are on the same scale, the comparison makes more sense, and this is exactly what we can do when we use the standard of a 1-standard-deviation change.

Using the 1-standard-deviation change as the basis for interpreting odds ratios and percentage change is a bit tedious if you need to do the calculations by hand. There is a command, `listcoef`, that makes this easy. Although this command is not part of standard Stata, you can do a `search spost` command and install the most recent version of `spost`, which will include `listcoef`. There are several items that appear when you enter `search spost13`. Toward the end of this list of items is a section called `packages found`. Under this heading, go to `spost13_ado`, and click on the link to install it. When you install `spost13_ado`, you will install a series of commands that are useful for interpreting logistic regression. Be sure to install the latest version of this package. To run this command, after doing the logistic regression, enter the command `listcoef, help`. The `help` option gives a brief description of the various values the command estimates. Here are the results:

```
. use https://www.stata-press.com/data/agis6r/nlsy97_chapter11, clear
. listcoef, help
logit (N=1654): Factor change in odds
    Odds of: 1 vs 0
```

	b	z	P>|z|	e^b	e^bStdX	SDofX
age97	0.1564	2.672	0.008	1.169	1.158	0.937
male	-0.0207	-0.194	0.846	0.979	0.990	0.499
pdrink97	0.2846	6.325	0.000	1.329	1.413	1.215
dinner97	-0.0597	-2.693	0.007	0.942	0.869	2.349
constant	-2.9476	-3.718	0.000	.	.	.

```
         b = raw coefficient
         z = z-score for test of b=0
      P>|z| = p-value for z-test
       e^b = exp(b) = factor change in odds for unit increase in X
   e^bStdX = exp(b*SD of X) = change in odds for SD increase in X
     SDofX = standard deviation of X
```

This gives the values of the coefficients (called b), their z scores, and the probabilities. These match what we obtained with the `logit` command. The next column is labeled `e^b` and contains the odds ratios for each predictor. The label may look strange if you are not used to working with logarithms. If you raise the mathematical constant e, which is about 2.718, to the power of the coefficient b, you get the odds ratio. Thus $e^{0.15635} = 1.1692$.

We can interpret the odds ratio for `male` directly because `male` is a binary variable. The other variables are not binary, so we use the next column, which is labeled `e^bStdX` to interpret their odds ratios. This column displays the odds ratio for a 1-standard-deviation change in the predictor. For example, the odds ratio for a 1-standard-deviation change in age is 1.16, and this is substantially smaller than the odds ratio for a 1-standard-deviation change in the percentage of peers who drink, 1.41.

If you prefer to use percentages, you can use the command

```
. listcoef, help percent
logit (N=1654): Percentage change in odds
  Odds of: 1 vs 0
```

	b	z	P>|z|	%	%StdX	SDofX
age97	0.1564	2.672	0.008	16.9	15.8	0.937
male	-0.0207	-0.194	0.846	-2.1	-1.0	0.499
pdrink97	0.2846	6.325	0.000	32.9	41.3	1.215
dinner97	-0.0597	-2.693	0.007	-5.8	-13.1	2.349
constant	-2.9476	-3.718	0.000	.	.	.

```
     b = raw coefficient
     z = z-score for test of b=0
 P>|z| = p-value for z-test
     % = percent change in odds for unit increase in X
 %StdX = percent change in odds for SD increase in X
 SDofX = standard deviation of X
```

For communicating with a lay audience, this last result is remarkably useful. The odds of drinking are just 2.1% lower for males than for females, and this is not statistically significant. Having a 1-standard-deviation-higher percentage of peers who drink increases a youth's odds of drinking by 41.3%, and having dinner with his or her family 1 standard deviation more often reduces the odds by 13.1%. Both of these influences are statistically significant.

It is often helpful to create a graph showing the percentage change in the odds ratio associated with each of the predictors. This could be done with any graphics package, such as PowerPoint. To do this using Stata, we need to create a new dataset, c11barchart.dta. This dataset has just four variables, which we will name age, male, peers, and dinners. There is just one observation, and this is the appropriate percentage change in the odds ratio. For age, peers, and dinners, we enter 15.8, 41.3, and −13.1, respectively, because we are interested in the effects of a 1-standard-deviation change in each of these variables. For male, we enter −2.1 because we are interested in a 1-unit change for this dichotomous variable (female versus male). The Data Editor is shown in figure 11.6.

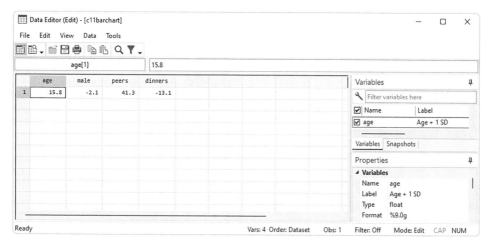

Figure 11.6. The dataset for creating a bar chart, `c11barchart.dta`

To construct a bar chart, you can select Graphics ▷ Bar chart. The resulting command
is

```
. use https://www.stata-press.com/data/agis6r/c11barchart, clear
. graph bar (asis) age male peers dinners, bargap(10)
> blabel(name, position(outside)) ytitle(Percentage change in odds)
> title(Percentage change in odds of drinking by)
> subtitle("age, gender, percent of peers drinking, meals with family")
> legend(off) scheme(s2manual)
```

Note that if your title or subtitle includes commas, as shown in the `subtitle()`
option above, you must enclose the title in quotes. We had Stata put the variable labels
just above or below each bar; we must have very short labels for this to work. Also, on
the Bars tab, we put a *Gap between bars* of 10 that so the bars would be separated a
little bit. The resulting bar chart is shown in figure 11.7.

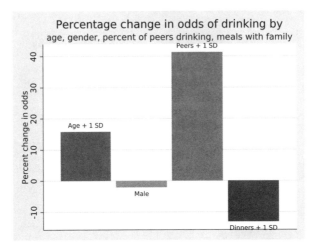

Figure 11.7. Risk factors associated with teen drinking

This bar graph shows that as adolescents get older, there is a substantial increase in the odds of their drinking; that drinking risks are roughly comparable for males and females; that having peers who drink is a substantial risk factor; and that the more the adolescent shares dinners with his or her family, the lower the odds of drinking.

Odds ratio versus relative-risk ratio

In section 11.3, we learned how to compute the odds ratio. There we noted that among the 10 people who favored environmental protection, seven voted liberal and three voted conservative, creating odds of voting liberal of $7/3 = 2.33$. By contrast, the 10 people who did not favor environmental protection had odds of voting liberal of $4/6 = 0.67$. The resulting odds ratio was $2.33/0.67 = 3.48$.

The analogous measure for percentages or probabilities is the relative-risk ratio. There are 7 of 10 (70% or 0.70) pro-environmentalists supporting a liberal candidate. There are 4 of 10 (40% or 0.40) people who are not pro-environment supporting a liberal candidate. The relative risk of supporting a liberal candidate for people who are pro-environment is $0.70/0.40 = 1.75$. People who are not used to odds ratios and popular media such as newspapers often misinterpret the odds ratio as if it were the relative risk. Generally, the odds ratio will be larger than the relative-risk ratio. The difference is small with a rare outcome, but with an outcome like this, there is a substantial difference. Being pro-environment makes the odds of voting for a liberal 3.48 times as great. Being pro-environment increases the risk of voting for a liberal candidate 1.75 times. In this example, there is a 248% increase in the odds of voting liberal if you are pro-environment, but there is only a 75% increase in the risk of voting liberal.

Stata's `logit` and `logistic` commands do not estimate the relative-risk ratio (sometimes called incidence relative risk). However, Joseph Hilbe, a Stata user, wrote a command, `oddsrisk`, in 2008 that converts odds ratios to risk ratios. You can install this command by entering `ssc install oddsrisk`.

The relative risk is appealing, but it should not be used in a study that controls the number of people in each category. For example, you should not use the relative risk if you are comparing 100 stroke victims to 100 people who did not have a stroke on their participation in a rigorous physical activity. By controlling the number of people in each group, you have artificially (nonrandomly) inflated the number of stroke victims because 50% of your sample have had a stroke—a far greater percentage than would be obtained in a representative sample.

11.6   Hypothesis testing

There are many types of hypothesis testing that can be done with logistic regression. I will cover some of them here. As with multiple regression, we have an overall test of the model, tests of each parameter estimate, and the ability to test hypotheses involving combinations of parameters. As noted above, with logistic regression there is a chi-squared test that has k degrees of freedom, where k is the number of predictors. For our current example, the $\chi^2(4) = 78.01$, $p < 0.001$. This tells us only that the overall model has at least one significant predictor.

11.6.1 Testing individual coefficients

There are two tests we can use to test individual parameters, and they often yield slightly different probabilities. The most common is a Wald test, commonly reported in journal articles. The z test in the Stata output is actually the square root of the Wald chi-squared test. Some other statistical packages test individual parameters by using the Wald chi-squared test (evaluated with 1 degree of freedom), but this is identical to the square of the z test in Stata.

Many statisticians prefer the likelihood-ratio chi-squared test to the Wald chi-squared test or the equivalent z test reported by Stata. The likelihood-ratio chi-squared test for each parameter estimate is based on comparing two logistic models, one with the individual variable we want to test included and one without it. The likelihood-ratio test is the difference in the likelihood-ratio chi-squared values for these two models (this appears as LR chi2(1) near the upper right corner of the output). The difference between the two likelihood-ratio chi-squared values is 1 degree of freedom. In standard Stata, the likelihood-ratio test is rather tedious to get. If you want the best possible test of the significance of the effect of age on drinking, with nlsy97_chapter11.dta, you would need to type the command—logistic drank30 male dinner97 pdrink97—and record the chi-squared. Then you would type the command—logistic drank30 age97 male dinner97 pdrink97—and record the chi-squared. The difference between the chi-squared values with 1 degree of freedom would be the best test of the effect of age on drinking.

Stata lets us simplify this process a bit with the following set of commands:

```
. use https://www.stata-press.com/data/agis6r/nlsy97_chapter11, clear
. logistic drank30 male dinner97 pdrink97
. estimates store a
. logistic drank30 age97 male dinner97 pdrink97
. lrtest a
```

The first line runs the logistic regression without including age97. The second line saves all the estimates and stores them in an estimation set labeled a. This estimation set includes the LR chi2(1) value. The third line runs a new logistic regression, this time including age97. The last line, lrtest a, subtracts the chi-squared values and estimates the probability of the chi-squared difference. Although this is not too difficult, doing this process for each of the four predictors would be a bit tedious. An automated approach is available with a command written by user Zhiqiang Wang in 1999 called lrdrop1, which gives the likelihood-ratio test for each parameter estimate, along with some other information we will not discuss (lrdrop1 works with the logit, logistic, and poisson regression commands). Type the command ssc install lrdrop1 to install this command. Immediately after running the full model (with all four predictors), simply type the following command:

```
. lrdrop1
Likelihood Ratio Tests: drop 1 term
logistic regression
number of obs = 1654
-----------------------------------------------------------------
  drank30     Df    Chi2    P>Chi2   -2*log ll  Res. Df   AIC
-----------------------------------------------------------------
Original Model                        2122.09    1649    2132.09
  -age97       1    7.18    0.0074    2129.27    1648    2137.27
  -male        1    0.04    0.8463    2122.13    1648    2130.13
-dinner97      1    7.23    0.0072    2129.33    1648    2137.33
-pdrink97      1   40.62    0.0000    2162.72    1648    2170.72
-----------------------------------------------------------------

Terms dropped one at a time in turn.
```

Here we can see that the likelihood-ratio chi-squared for the age97 variable is $\chi^2(1) = 7.18$, $p < 0.01$. If we take the square root of 7.18, we obtain 2.68, which is close to the square root of the Wald chi-squared, that is, the z test provided by Stata of 2.67. The likelihood-ratio chi-squared and the Wald statistic are not always this close, but the two approaches rarely produce different conclusions. Although the likelihood-ratio test has some technical advantages over the Wald test, the Wald test is usually what people report—perhaps because it is a bit tedious to estimate the likelihood-ratio chi-squared in other statistical packages. If the Wald test and the likelihood-ratio tests differ, the likelihood-ratio test is preferred. These results are identical whether you are testing the regression coefficients with the logit command or the odds ratios with the logistic command. Because this lrdrop1 command is so easy to use and because the likelihood-ratio test is invariant to nonlinear transformations, you may want to report the likelihood-ratio test routinely. When you do so, specify that it is the likelihood-ratio chi-squared test rather than the Wald test.

11.6.2 Testing sets of coefficients

There are three situations for which we would need to test a set of coefficients rather than a single coefficient. These parallel the tests we used for multiple regression in chapter 10.

1. We have a categorical variable that requires several dummies. Suppose that we want to know if marital status has an effect, and we have three dummies representing different marital statuses (divorced or separated, widowed, and never married, with married serving as the reference category). We want to know if marital status is significant, so we need to test the set of coefficients rather than just one coefficient.

2. We want to know if a set of variables is significant. The set might be whether peer and family variables are significant when age and gender are already included in a model to predict drinking behavior. We need to test the combination of coefficients for peer and family rather than testing these individually.

3. We have two variables measured on the same scale, and we want to know if their parameter estimates are equal. Suppose that we want to know if mother's education is more important than father's education as a predictor of whether an adolescent plans to go to college. Both predictors are measured on the same scale (years of education), so we can test whether the mother's education and the father's education have significantly different coefficients.

The first two situations are tested by the hypothesis that all coefficients in the set are zero. For the marital status set, the three simultaneous null hypotheses would be

H_0: Divorce effect = 0

H_0: Widow effect = 0

H_0: Never-married effect = 0

For the peer and family set, the set of two simultaneous null hypotheses would be

H_0: `pdrink97` effect = 0

H_0: `dinner97` effect = 0

We will illustrate how to test for the first two situations with the data we have been using. The full model is

```
. logistic drank30 age97 male pdrink97 dinner97
```

We want to know if `pdrink97` and `dinner97`, as a set, are significant.

There are several ways of testing this. We could run the model twice:

(a) `logistic drank30 age97 male`

(b) `logistic drank30 age97 male pdrink97 dinner97`

We would then see whether the difference of chi-squared values was significant. Because the second model added two variables, we would test the chi-squared with 2 degrees of freedom.

We can alternatively use the `test` command. We run this after we run the full logistic regression. In other words, we run the command `logistic drank30 age97 male pdrink97 dinner97`, and then we run the command `test pdrink97 dinner97`. Here are the results:

```
. test pdrink97 dinner97
 ( 1)   pdrink97 = 0
 ( 2)   dinner97 = 0

        chi2(  2) =     48.85
      Prob > chi2 =     0.0000
```

The variables `pdrink97` and `dinner97`, as a set, are statistically significant, chi-squared(2) = 48.85, $p < 0.001$. We can say that one or both of these variables are statistically significant. When the set of variables is significant, we should always look at the tests for the individual coefficients because this overall test only tells us that at least one of them is significant.

The third situation for testing a set of parameter estimates is to test the equality of parameter estimates for two variables (assuming that both variables are measured on the same scale). We might do a logistic regression and find that both mother's education and father's education are significant predictors of whether an adolescent intends to go to college. However, we may want to know if the mother's education is more or less important than the father's education. Say that we want to test whether the parameter estimates are equal. Our null hypothesis is

H_0: mother's education effect = father's education effect

I will not illustrate this test because it uses a different dataset, but the command is simple. Let's assume that mother's education is represented by the variable `maeduc` and father's education is represented by `faeduc`. The command is `test maeduc=faeduc`.

11.7 Margins: More on interpreting results from logistic regression

This section will stay with the same basic model except we will substitute the variable `black` for the variable `male`. We do this substitution because the effect of gender was not significant, and because we are interested in understanding possible differences between whites and blacks. To keep the example straightforward, we limit our analysis to whites and blacks and exclude other racial and ethnic groups. We first need to generate this new variable:

```
. generate black = race97 - 1
. replace black = . if race97 > 2
```

We also will label our race variable:

```
. label define black 0 "White" 1 "Black"
. label define drank30 0 "No" 1 "Yes"
. label values drank30 drank30
. label values black black
```

We discussed the special notation for factor variables in chapter 10 as used in modeling interaction and with a quadratic term. We can use this notation here as well. We can think of three of our independent variables, `age97`, `pdrink97`, and `dinner97`, as having underlying continuums and hence as continuous variables even though some are measured crudely. However, our variable `black` is strictly categorical because it is coded 1 for blacks and 0 for whites. We can run the logistic regression using the

i. label for this categorical variable, i.black. This produces the same results for the logistic regression as if we had simply used black, but the results will work properly if we follow this command with other postestimation commands. Here are the command and the results:

```
. logit drank30 age97 i.black pdrink97 dinner97
Iteration 0:    log likelihood = -935.86755
Iteration 1:    log likelihood = -901.48553
Iteration 2:    log likelihood = -901.37312
Iteration 3:    log likelihood = -901.37311

Logistic regression                              Number of obs =    1,413
                                                 LR chi2(4)    =    68.99
                                                 Prob > chi2   =   0.0000
Log likelihood = -901.37311                      Pseudo R2     =   0.0369
```

drank30	Coefficient	Std. err.	z	P>|z|	[95% conf. interval]	
age97	.138153	.0635579	2.17	0.030	.0135818	.2627241
black						
Black	-.3804608	.1352133	-2.81	0.005	-.645474	-.1154476
pdrink97	.2822417	.048233	5.85	0.000	.1877067	.3767767
dinner97	-.069024	.0246204	-2.80	0.005	-.1172791	-.0207689
_cons	-2.590308	.8609411	-3.01	0.003	-4.277722	-.9028946

We have already discussed how to interpret these results, but now we are going to consider some new aids. The first margins command that we use below is useful for categorical variables. In our example, the categorical variable is black (see Williams [2012] for an excellent discussion of the margins command or see https://stats.oarc.ucla.edu/stata/dae/logistic-regression/ for applications of this command, including use of interactions). The margins command will tell us the difference in the probability of having drunk in the last 30 days if an individual is black compared with if an individual is white. For this to be meaningful, we need to set the covariates at some meaningful value. We will set them at the mean. So the question we want to answer is as follows: What is the difference between blacks and whites who are average on the other covariates in the probability that they drank in the last 30 days? Here is our command:

```
. margins, dydx(black) atmeans
Conditional marginal effects                    Number of obs = 1,413
Model VCE: OIM

Expression: Pr(drank30), predict()
dy/dx wrt:  1.black
At: age97    = 13.67445 (mean)
    0.black  = .7523001 (mean)
    1.black  = .2476999 (mean)
    pdrink97 = 2.112527 (mean)
    dinner97 = 4.760793 (mean)
```

		Delta-method				
	dy/dx	std. err.	z	P>|z|	[95% conf. interval]	
black						
Black	−.0862436	.0296054	−2.91	0.004	−.144269	−.0282181

```
Note: dy/dx for factor levels is the discrete change from the base level.
```

We specified two options. First, we specified dydx(black) because black is the variable on which we are focused. Second, we specified atmeans because this option will set the covariates at their mean. From the results, we see that age was fixed at 13.674 and so on. The dy/dx value of −0.086 is the difference. Because blacks are coded 1 and whites are coded 0, a hypothetical black adolescent who is average in age, percent of peers who drink, and in how often his or her family eats together will have a probability of drinking in the last 30 days that is 0.086 lower than a hypothetical white adolescent with the same scores on the covariates. An easier way of saying this is that black adolescents who are average on covariates are 8.6% less likely to report having drunk in the last 30 days than white adolescents.

Now we know that the difference between the probability of black adolescents and white adolescents drinking is −0.086 and that this is statistically significant ($z = −2.91$, $p < 0.05$). However, we likely also want to know just what the values of those probabilities are. To obtain this, we run

```
. margins black, atmeans
Adjusted predictions                            Number of obs = 1,413
Model VCE: OIM

Expression: Pr(drank30), predict()
At: age97    = 13.67445 (mean)
    0.black  = .7523001 (mean)
    1.black  = .2476999 (mean)
    pdrink97 = 2.112527 (mean)
    dinner97 = 4.760793 (mean)
```

		Delta-method				
	Margin	std. err.	z	P>|z|	[95% conf. interval]	
black						
White	.393289	.0153725	25.58	0.000	.3631595	.4234186
Black	.3070455	.0252289	12.17	0.000	.2575977	.3564932

In the last 30 days, 30.7% of black youth are estimated to have drunk compared with 39.3% of white youth when all the covariates are set at their mean. The `margins` command with the `dydx(black)` option shows that this difference is statistically significant. Long and Freese (2014) provide extensions to Stata's `margins` command using their own `mtable` command, which was installed when you installed `spost13`. You are referred to their book if you want even more aids to interpreting the results of logistic regression.

Rather than trying to interpret the dy/dx values for quantitative and continuous independent variables, we will use a different option with the `margins` command. Suppose we wanted to understand the relationship between the percentage of friends who drink and whether the adolescent drank in the last 30 days, but we want to control for the other covariates. As before, we will fix the other covariates at their means. This way we can estimate the probability a hypothetical adolescent drank in the last 30 days who is average on all the covariates, except they differ on the percentage of their friends who drank. The `pdrink97` variable was coded 1 for up to 20% of friends, 2 for 20 to 40% of friends, 3 for 40 to 60% of friends, 4 for 60 to 80% of friends, and 5 for 80 to 100% of friends.

In the following command, the `at()` option fixes the other covariates at their means for each value of `pdrink97` from 1 to 5. If we were doing this for a variable that ranged from 0 to 100, we might type `margins, at(var = (0(10)100))`, which would be equivalent to typing `margins, at(var = (0 10 20 30 40 50 60 70 80 90 100))`, meaning every 10 years.

```
. margins, at(pdrink97=(1 2 3 4 5)) atmeans
Adjusted predictions                                      Number of obs = 1,413
Model VCE: OIM
Expression: Pr(drank30), predict()
1._at: age97    = 13.67445 (mean)
       0.black  = .7523001 (mean)
       1.black  = .2476999 (mean)
       pdrink97 =        1
       dinner97 = 4.760793 (mean)
2._at: age97    = 13.67445 (mean)
       0.black  = .7523001 (mean)
       1.black  = .2476999 (mean)
       pdrink97 =        2
       dinner97 = 4.760793 (mean)
3._at: age97    = 13.67445 (mean)
       0.black  = .7523001 (mean)
       1.black  = .2476999 (mean)
       pdrink97 =        3
       dinner97 = 4.760793 (mean)
4._at: age97    = 13.67445 (mean)
       0.black  = .7523001 (mean)
       1.black  = .2476999 (mean)
       pdrink97 =        4
       dinner97 = 4.760793 (mean)
5._at: age97    = 13.67445 (mean)
       0.black  = .7523001 (mean)
       1.black  = .2476999 (mean)
       pdrink97 =        5
       dinner97 = 4.760793 (mean)
```

	Margin	Delta-method std. err.	z	P>|z|	[95% conf. interval]	
_at						
1	.3011665	.0168523	17.87	0.000	.2681367	.3341963
2	.3636614	.0132156	27.52	0.000	.3377592	.3895636
3	.4311242	.0169284	25.47	0.000	.3979451	4643033
4	.501244	.0261244	19.19	0.000	.450041	.5524469
5	.5713148	.0361017	15.83	0.000	.5005567	.6420729

From these results, we see that if our hypothetical average adolescent on the covariates had a code of 1 on `pdrink97`, then we estimate a probability of 0.301 that this adolescent drank in the last 30 days. This estimated probability goes up fairly sharply so that if our hypothetical average adolescent on the covariates was coded 5 on `prink97`, then he or she would have a probability of 0.571 of having drunk in the last 30 days. It would be nice to be able to see a figure showing these results, so after the `margins` command, we can type the `marginsplot`. This graph is shown as figure 11.8 with a few minor changes applied using the Graph Editor:

Figure 11.8. Probability of drinking by percent of friends who drink, controlling for covariates

We have investigated the effects of the variables `black` and `pdrink97` based on the model that we fit by typing `logit drank30 age97 i.black pdrink97 dinner97`.

This model does not allow for the effect of percentage of friends drinking to differ for black and white youth. We can do this if we include an interaction in our model. The command and output are

```
. logit drank30 age97 i.black##c.pdrink97 dinner97

Iteration 0:   log likelihood = -935.86755
Iteration 1:   log likelihood = -898.50967
Iteration 2:   log likelihood = -898.41873
Iteration 3:   log likelihood = -898.41872

Logistic regression                             Number of obs =   1,413
                                                LR chi2(5)    =   74.90
                                                Prob > chi2   =  0.0000
Log likelihood = -898.41872                     Pseudo R2     =  0.0400
```

drank30	Coefficient	Std. err.	z	P>|z|	[95% conf. interval]	
age97	.1256206	.0637992	1.97	0.049	.0005765	.2506648
black						
Black	.185704	.2660364	0.70	0.485	-.3357178	.7071258
pdrink97	.3563796	.0576201	6.18	0.000	.2434464	.4693129
black#						
c.pdrink97						
Black	-.2489923	.102516	-2.43	0.015	-.4499199	-.0480647
dinner97	-.0691665	.024649	-2.81	0.005	-.1174776	-.0208555
_cons	-2.576897	.8617579	-2.99	0.003	-4.265911	-.8878823

The term `i.black##c.pdrink97` tells Stata to include the factor variable `black`, the continuous variable `pdrink97`, and their interaction in the model. The interaction is significant ($z = -2.43$, $p = 0.015$). We can use the `margins` and `marginsplot` commands to investigate how the probability of drinking in the last 30 days changes with the percentage of friends who drink for both black and white youth. We combine elements of our two previous `margins` commands. Again, we use `atmeans` to set other variables to their means. Now, the probability of drinking in the last 30 days is estimated for each level of `pdrink` and of `black`.

```
. margins black,  at(pdrink97=(1 2 3 4 5)) atmeans
Adjusted predictions                                 Number of obs = 1,413
Model VCE: OIM

Expression: Pr(drank30), predict()
1._at: age97    = 13.67445 (mean)
       0.black  = .7523001 (mean)
       1.black  = .2476999 (mean)
       pdrink97 =        1
       dinner97 = 4.760793 (mean)
2._at: age97    = 13.67445 (mean)
       0.black  = .7523001 (mean)
       1.black  = .2476999 (mean)
       pdrink97 =        2
       dinner97 = 4.760793 (mean)
3._at: age97    = 13.67445 (mean)
       0.black  = .7523001 (mean)
       1.black  = .2476999 (mean)
       pdrink97 =        3
       dinner97 = 4.760793 (mean)
4._at: age97    = 13.67445 (mean)
       0.black  = .7523001 (mean)
       1.black  = .2476999 (mean)
       pdrink97 =        4
       dinner97 = 4.760793 (mean)
5._at: age97    = 13.67445 (mean)
       0.black  = .7523001 (mean)
       1.black  = .2476999 (mean)
       pdrink97 =        5
       dinner97 = 4.760793 (mean)
```

	Margin	Delta-method std. err.	z	P>|z|	[95% conf. interval]	
_at#black						
1#White	.30322	.0194871	15.56	0.000	.265026	.3414139
1#Black	.2900174	.0330156	8.78	0.000	.225308	.3547268
2#White	.3832842	.0154657	24.78	0.000	.3529721	.4135963
2#Black	.3126171	.0255099	12.25	0.000	.2626187	.3626156
3#White	.4702223	.0203825	23.07	0.000	.4302733	.5101713
3#Black	.3361442	.0294923	11.40	0.000	.2783404	.393948
4#White	.5590057	.0309363	18.07	0.000	.4983717	.6196397
4#Black	.3605132	.0436407	8.26	0.000	.274979	.4460474
5#White	.6441695	.0406445	15.85	0.000	.5645078	.7238312
5#Black	.3856226	.0623185	6.19	0.000	.2634805	.5077647

We can visualize this interaction (figure 11.9) by typing

```
. marginsplot
Variables that uniquely identify margins: pdrink97 black
```

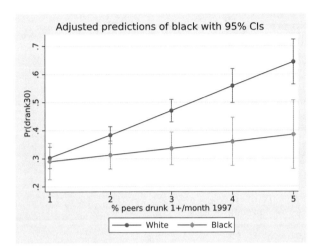

Figure 11.9. Probability of drinking in the last 30 days by percent of friends who drink for both black and white youth

We can make a publication-ready graph using a more complex set of options to go with the `marginsplot` command:

```
. marginsplot, xdimension(pdrink97,
> labels("10%" "20%" "30%" "40%" "50%"))
> plot1opts (msymbol(circle))
> plot2opts (msymbol(diamond_hollow))
> ytitle(Probability of drinking)
> xtitle(Percentage of peers who drink)
> title(Adjusted probability of drinking for Blacks and Whites) scheme(s2mono)
```

This command is not as complicated as it may appear. The first line specifies variables on the x axis. The second line provides the labels for the x axis, so it shows the percentage rather than the coded numbers for `pdrink97`. The next two lines use a solid circle for whites and a hollow diamond for blacks on their respective slopes. The rest of the lines provide the titles for the x axis, the y axis, and the overall title. At the very bottom, `scheme(s2mono)` uses a monochrome style for the graphs. Figure 11.10 shows the resulting graph.

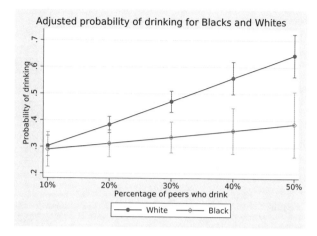

Figure 11.10. Publication-ready graph: Probability of drinking in the last 30 days by percent of friends who drink for both black and white youth

The probability of drinking in the last 30 days increases faster for white adolescents than for black adolescents as the percentage of peers who drink increases.

11.8   Nested logistic regressions

In chapter 10, we discussed nested regression (sometimes called hierarchical regression), where blocks of variables are entered in a planned sequence. The `nestreg` command is extremely general, applicable across a variety of regression models, including logistic, negative binomial, Poisson, probit, ordered logistic, tobit, and others. It also works with the complex sample designs for many regression models. Although most of these models are beyond the scope of this book, I will illustrate how `nestreg` can be generalized with logistic regression.

We have been interested in whether the percentage of an adolescent's peers who drink and the number of days a week the adolescent eats with his or her family influence drinking behavior. In doing this, we controlled for gender and age. We might decide to enter the four predictors in three blocks. In the first block, we enter gender; in the second block, we enter age; and in the third block, we enter dinners with the family and peer drinking. We now apply the format used in chapter 10 for logistic regression to get the following results:

```
. nestreg: logistic drank30 (male) (age97) (dinner97 pdrink97)

Block 1: male

Logistic regression                          Number of obs =  1,654
                                             LR chi2(1)    =   4.37
                                             Prob > chi2   = 0.0365
Log likelihood = -1097.864                   Pseudo R2     = 0.0020
```

drank30	Odds ratio	Std. err.	z	P>|z|	[95% conf. interval]	
male	.8087911	.0820956	-2.09	0.037	.6628816	.9868173
_cons	.6926503	.0510996	-4.98	0.000	.599401	.8004065

Note: _cons estimates baseline odds.

```
Block 2: age97

Logistic regression                          Number of obs =  1,654
                                             LR chi2(2)    =  27.87
                                             Prob > chi2   = 0.0000
Log likelihood = -1086.1173                  Pseudo R2     = 0.0127
```

drank30	Odds ratio	Std. err.	z	P>|z|	[95% conf. interval]	
male	.8304131	.0849837	-1.82	0.069	.6794898	1.014858
age97	1.304566	.0723084	4.80	0.000	1.170271	1.454273
_cons	.0178754	.0137142	-5.25	0.000	.0039738	.080409

Note: _cons estimates baseline odds.

```
Block 3: dinner97 pdrink97

Logistic regression                          Number of obs =  1,654
                                             LR chi2(4)    =  78.01
                                             Prob > chi2   = 0.0000
Log likelihood = -1061.0474                  Pseudo R2     = 0.0355
```

drank30	Odds ratio	Std. err.	z	P>|z|	[95% conf. interval]	
male	.9794922	.1046935	-0.19	0.846	.7943646	1.207764
age97	1.169241	.0684191	2.67	0.008	1.042546	1.311332
dinner97	.942086	.0208682	-2.69	0.007	.9020603	.9838878
pdrink97	1.329275	.0598174	6.33	0.000	1.217056	1.451841
_cons	.0524677	.0415938	-3.72	0.000	.0110944	.2481314

Note: _cons estimates baseline odds.

Block	Wald chi2	df	Pr > F
1	4.37	1	0.0366
2	23.01	1	0.0000
3	48.85	2	0.0000

These results show that each block is statistically significant. Our main interest is in the third block, and we see that adding dinners with your family and peer drinking has $\chi^2(2) = 48.85$, $p < 0.001$. These results duplicate those obtained with the lrtest command. The results do not duplicate those for the first two blocks (age and gender) using the lrtest. Here we are testing if each additional block makes a statistically significant improvement above what was done by the preceding blocks. We would say that "Block 1", `male`, is significant. Gender was not significant in the overall model, controlling for the other three variables, but "Block 1" contains only the variable `male`. "Block 2", `age97`, increases the significance, but it does not control for "Block 3" variables because they have yet to be added to the model.

11.9   Power analysis when doing logistic regression

As with multiple regression, when doing logistic regression, it is helpful to perform a power analysis before beginning a study. Logistic regression, using maximum likelihood estimation tends to require a larger sample size than ordinary least-squares multiple regression. The program will run on a sample that is very small, but it is best to have at least 100 observations when doing a logistic regression for even a simple model. Philip Ender at the University of California–Los Angeles adapted a SAS macro to create a command called `powerlog`. You can type the command `search powerlog` and follow the online instructions to install the command. This command is designed to work either with one continuous predictor or several predictors. We will illustrate it first for one predictor.

Suppose that a researcher wants to know if motivation (the predictor) can predict whether a person stays in a smoking cessation program or drops out. The question is whether a person with higher motivation has a higher rate of retention. Here is what we need to know to run the `powerlog` command:

1. What proportion of people would stay in the program if they had average motivation? Let's say that we found some results for similar programs, and about 70% of the participants stayed in the program and 30% dropped out. We would say the proportion for people with average motivation would be $p_1 = 0.70$.

2. What proportion of people would stay in the program if they were 1-standard-deviation change above average on motivation? We should think in terms of the smallest increase (or decrease) that would be considered important. Let's say that increasing the retention rate from 70% to 75% would be considered important. We would say the proportion of people who are retained for the entire program, if they were 1-standard-deviation change above average on motivation, would be $p_2 = 0.75$.

3. We need to set our alpha level at, say, 0.05.

This is all we need for the command.

```
. powerlog, p1(.70) p2(.75) alpha(.05)
Logistic regression power analysis
One-tailed test: alpha=.05  p1=.7  p2=.75  rsq=0  odds ratio=1.285714285714286

power          n
0.60         204
0.65         233
0.70         266
0.75         303
0.80         348
0.85         404
0.90         481
```

To have a power of 0.90, we would need a sample of 481 people. If we were satisfied with a power of 0.80, we would only need 348 people. Say that a person comes to you and says that she can collect retention data on a sample of 50 people and wants to do this analysis. You must advise her that she has too little power if she is interested in a difference that is this small. She says, What if I am interested in an increase of 0.10, so the retention rate would go from 70% to 80%. If you run the command using p2(80), you will see that she would have 0.80 power with just 89 cases, so you still need to advise her to get a larger sample.

When we are using this command, we set it up as a one-tailed test because we thought about increasing the retention rate. If you want a two-tailed test, where the proportion could go up or down, you could use $\alpha/2 = 0.025$ for your alpha value. You will also notice that we are thinking in terms of proportions rather than odds ratios. The command results report that the odds ratio is 1.286. Do you know how it got this value? For p_1, we had a proportion of 0.70, so the odds were $0.70/0.30 = 2.333$. For p_2, we had a proportion of 0.75, so the odds were $0.75/0.25 = 3.000$. Thus the odds ratio is $3.000/2.333 = 1.286$. This is a good reminder that when we say the odds are 28.6% greater, we are describing the odds and not the proportions, where the corresponding change from 0.70 to 0.75 represents only a 7.1% increase in the proportion.

Sometimes when you are doing a logistic regression, you have several predictors and want to know the power for adding one more predictor. Let's stick with our study of retention. Suppose that in addition to motivation being a predictor of whether a person stays in the smoking cessation program, we expect the following people to be more likely to stay for the entire program: people who are older, people who smoked fewer days in the last month, and people who are more educated. We want to add to this the number of other program participants who are their friends. If you have a group in which several of your friends are participating, you think this will substantially increase your retention rate. What do we need to know to do the power analysis?

- What proportion of people would stay in the program if they had average motivation, age, days smoked in last month, and education? Let's say that we found some results for similar programs, and about 70% of the participants stayed in the program and 30% dropped out. We would say the proportion for people with average scores would be $p_1 = 0.70$.

- What proportion of people would stay in the program if they were 1-standard-deviation change above average on the number of friends they had who were also in the program? Again we should think in terms of the smallest increase (or decrease) that would be considered important. Let's stay with the idea that increasing the retention rate from 70% to 75% would be considered important. We would say the proportion of people who are retained for the entire program, if they were 1-standard-deviation change above average on number of friends also participating, would be $p_2 = 0.75$.

- We need to set our alpha level at, say, 0.05.

- This time we need one additional estimate. When there are multiple variables on the right side of an equation, we need to worry about multicollinearity; thus we need an estimate of how serious the multicollinearity is. This estimate is the proportion of the variance in our new variable, which is the number of friends also participating. The proportion of the variance is explained by the variables already in the model (motivation, age, days smoked in last month, and education). We might find some data where we could do an R^2 for predicting number of friends from motivation, age, days smoked in last month, and education. Let's estimate the $R^2 = 0.30$.

Here are our command and results. We added the `help` option to get an explanation of the terms.

```
. powerlog, p1(.70) p2(.75) alpha(.05) rsq(.30) help
Logistic regression power analysis
One-tailed test: alpha=.05  p1=.7  p2=.75  rsq=.3  odds ratio=1.285714285714286
power         n
0.60         292
0.65         333
0.70         380
0.75         434
0.80         498
0.85         578
0.90         687

Explanation of terms
p1  --  the probability that the response variable equals 1
         when the predictor is at the mean
p2  --  the probability that the response variable equals 1
         when the predictor is one standard deviation above the mean
rsq --  the squared mulitple correlation between the predictor
         variable and all other variables in the model
```

As these results show, if we want a power of 0.90, we will need 687 participants in our study.

What do you do when some of your predictors are categorical, such as race/ethnicity or gender? One possibility is to use the `powerlog` command, but it will only give very approximate results because the command assumes you have continuous and normally distributed predictors.

It is not unusual for people to run a logistic regression command when they have less-than-optimal power. Suppose that you ran this analysis on a sample of just 200 people and all your variables were statistically significant. This can be interpreted two ways. First, you are a big risk taker because you had woefully inadequate power to run this analysis. You were most lucky to find a funding source that would support a study that had inadequate power. Second, you must be a lucky researcher because you did find significant results, and when you find significant results even when you do not have a lot of power, they are still significant.

11.10   Next steps for using logistic regression and its extensions

The University of California–Los Angeles Institute for Digital Research and Education has excellent tutorials related to logistic regression; see https://stats.oarc.ucla.edu/stata/dae/logistic-regression/. At the time of publication of this text, these tutorials are based on older versions of Stata, but they are still useful. Additional online support is available on the Stata website, https://www.stata.com/links/video-tutorials/. There is a three-part series of videos on logistic regression in the "Binary, ordinal, count, and fractional outcomes" section, and each video is only a couple of minutes long.

11.11   Summary

Logistic regression is a powerful data-analysis procedure that on one hand is fairly complicated but on the other hand can be presented to a lay audience in a clear and compelling fashion. Policy makers are likely to understand what odds mean, and they want to know which factors raise the odds of a success and reduce the odds of a failure. Although the language surrounding logistic regression can be intimidating, the results are easy to understand and explain. To continue with the example from this chapter, policy makers are definitely interested in the factors that increase or decrease the odds that an adolescent will drink. With logistic regression, this is exactly the information you can provide.

Some inexperienced researchers, upon learning logistic regression, may use it for too many applications. Logistic regression makes sense whenever you have an outcome that is clearly binary. If you have an outcome that is continuous or a count of how often something happens, you may want to use other procedures. For example, if you have a scale measuring political conservatism, which is what you want to explain, it is probably not wise to dichotomize people into conservative versus liberal categories just so that you can do logistic regression. When you have a continuous variable and you dichotomize it, you lose a lot of variance. The difference between a person who is just a little right of center and a radical conservative is lost if they both go into the same category. In our example, we lost the difference between an adolescent who drank only occasionally and one who drank 30 days a month. This was probably okay because we wanted to find out what explained whether the child drank or did not drink. Therefore, the variance in how often an adolescent drinks was not part of our question.

This chapter covered the following topics that prepare you to do logistic regression:

- Examples of when the technique is appropriate

- Key concepts, including odds, odds ratios, and logit

- How a linear estimation of a logit value corresponds to a nonlinear relationship for the probability of a success

- Two Stata commands, `logit` and `logistic`, that are used for doing logistic regression

- The regression coefficients and the odds ratios

- How to interpret the results for categorical and continuous predictors

- How to associate a percentage change in the odds ratio with each variable and how to summarize this in a bar chart

- Alternatives for hypothesis testing, including two ways to test the significance of each variable's effect and how to test the significance of sets of predictors

Chapters 10 and 11 provided the core techniques used by many social scientists. Although multiple regression and logistic regression are both complex procedures, they can provide informative answers to many research and policy questions. I have covered many useful and powerful methods of data analysis using Stata, and you are prepared for the next steps. Many researchers can do everything they need to do with the techniques we have already covered, but we have tapped only the core capabilities of Stata. An exciting thing about working with Stata is that it is a constantly evolving statistical package, and it is one that few of us will outgrow.

11.12 Exercises

1. Use `severity.dta`, which has three variables. The variable `severity` is whether the person sees prison sentences as too severe (coded 1) or not too severe (coded 0). The variable `conserv` is how liberal the person is, varying from 1 for conservative to 5 for liberal. The variable `gender` is coded 1 for women and 0 for men. Do a logistic regression analysis with `severity` as the dependent variable and `conserv` and `gender` as the independent variables. Carefully interpret your results.

2. Use `gss2002_chapter11.dta` (Smith et al. 2015). What predicts who will support abortion for any reason? Recode `abort12` to be a dummy variable called `abort`. Use the following variables as predictors: `reliten`, `polviews`, `premarsx`, and `sei`. You may want to create new variables for these so that a higher score goes with the

name; for example, `polviews` might be renamed `conservative` because a higher score means more conservative. Do a logistic regression followed by the `listcoef` command. Carefully interpret the results.

3. Using the results from exercise 2, create a bar graph showing the percentage change in odds of supporting abortion for any reason associated with each predictor. Justify using a 1-unit change or a 1-standard-deviation change in the score on each predictor.

4. Using the results from the logistic regression in exercise 2, compute likelihood-ratio chi-squared tests for each predictor, and compare them with the standard z tests in the logistic regression results.

5. In exercise 1, you did a logistic regression using gender and how liberal a person was to predict whether they thought prison sentences were too harsh. Suppose that you think people with more education are likely to feel that sentences are too severe. Do a tabulation on severity to see what proportion overall think sentences are too severe. Then do a power analysis to see how big a sample you would need to have a power of 0.80 to detect whether a 1-standard-deviation increase in education would raise the proportion of people who think sentences are too severe by 0.10 when liberalism and gender are already in the model. You would be adding education as a third predictor. State the information you need and the values you assume. What assumption of the command you used did you violate?

12 Measurement, reliability, and validity

12.1 Overview of reliability and validity

The quality of our measurement is the foundation for all statistical analysis. We must always keep two facts in mind: First, our analysis can be no better than our measurement. If we have poor measurement of our variables, then the relationship we find will be inaccurate and will often underestimate the true strength of the relationship. Second, virtually every variable we measure has some error, and often this error is substantial.

Imagine doing a study of the relationship between postpartum depression and body fat among a group of women two months after childbirth. Suppose that we find a weak relationship, say, $r = 0.10$. Is this because postpartum depression is not strongly related to body fat percentage? Perhaps, but it could be due to poor measurement of depression and body fat. Our depression scale might have an alpha (α) reliability of 0.90, and our measure of body fat percentage might have a test–retest reliability of 0.80. I will explain these measures of reliability later, but both of them indicate that at least some of the variance in our two measures is not related to what we call them but is simply measurement error. Reliability means that our measurement process will produce consistent results.

We also need to worry about validity. Many measures of body fat percentage are not only prone to error, that is, have low reliability, but also are biased. For example, a strong athlete may have a completely wrong estimated fat percentage. An NFL running back may be 5'11" and weigh 235 pounds. An estimator of his body fat—such as the BMI, which uses just height and weight to estimate body fat—might grossly overestimate his percentage of body fat. In his case, his weight is coming from musculature rather than from fat. Just adding his waist size of 32 inches would greatly improve the accuracy of the estimate. This is a problem of validity. The answer we get is off the mark. It may or may not be reliable, but it is not valid.

This chapter discusses what we can do to evaluate the reliability and the validity of our measures. Our discussion is largely limited to what is known as classical measurement theory.

12.2 Constructing a scale

The most typical situation is having a set of k items that measure a concept. We might have 10 items measuring depression, 5 items measuring attitude toward abortion, or 15 items measuring perceived risk of sexually transmitted HIV. How does Stata generate a scale score? Some researchers like to generate the sum of the items. If each of 10 items is on a scale of 1 to 4 (strongly agree, agree, disagree, and strongly disagree), the sum (total score) would range from a minimum of 10 to a maximum of 40. Other researchers like to generate the mean of the items, and in this example, the mean would be between 1 and 4. One advantage of generating the mean is that it is on the same scale as the individual items and hence can be interpreted more easily. For example, a sum of 25 might not have an obvious meaning, but a mean of 2.5 would indicate that the participant was halfway between agree and disagree on the 4-point scale.

The 2006 General Social Survey (Smith et al. 2015) (gss2006_chapter12.dta) asked people a series of seven items, empathy1–empathy7, designed to measure empathy. Each of these was scored from 1 for *Does not describe me very well* to 5 for *Describes me very well*. There was also a category of 8 for *Don't know*, which we treat as a missing value.

```
. use https://www.stata-press.com/data/agis6r/gss2006_chapter12
(General Social Surveys, 1972-2006 [Cumulative File], Dataset 0001)
```

If you run a `tabulate` on the empathy items, you will see that some of the items,
`empathy2`, `empathy4`, and `empathy5`, are worded so that a higher score goes with less
empathy, and the others, `empathy1`, `empathy3`, `empathy6`, and `empathy7`, are worded so
that a higher score goes with more empathy. When we cover factor analysis, we will see
how such an arrangement introduces a methods factor. For now, we will recode the three
negative items so that each item has a higher score indicating greater empathy. Always
coding a scale so that a higher score represents more of whatever is being measured
makes it easier for readers to understand what you are doing. We will again need to
recode our variables by using the `recode` command as follows:

```
. recode empathy2 empathy4 empathy5 (1=5 "Does not describe very well")
> (2=4) (3=3) (4=2) (5=1 "Describes very well"), pre(rev) label(empathy)
```

Because we are recoding three variables with one command, this is a bit more complicated. We are applying value labels to two values, the new value 5 and the new value
1, and we did not bother to make labels for the other values. When we have value labels
in the command, we need to give a nickname for this set of labels. This could be any
value label name we have not used already in a dataset. I chose the `label(empathy)`
option for the nickname. We never overwrite variables but instead generate new variables, and to name those variables, we chose to add a prefix of `rev` to each variable
by using the `pre(rev)` option. Thus our seven variables are now named `empathy1`,
`revempathy2`, `empathy3`, `revempathy4`, `revempathy5`, `empathy6`, and `empathy7`.

12.2.1   Generating a mean score for each person

Stata has a convenient command for generating the mean score for each person. Because
each participant's data are in a row, we want the row mean for the selected items. The
command name is `egen`, which stands for extended generation. We name the new
variable that we want to generate `empathy`, and we make this equal to the row mean
(with the `rowmean()` function) of the listed variables. The variables are listed inside
parentheses and have no commas separating them. Here is the command:

```
. egen empathy = rowmean(empathy1 revempathy2 empathy3 revempathy4 revempathy5
> empathy6 empathy7)
```

One drawback to using the `rowmean()` function is that it simply adds the score on
the items a person answers and divides by the number of items answered. This might
be problematic if there are a number of people who skipped a substantial number of
the items because we just do not know why they skipped them. One solution would
be to generate a score for those people who answered most of the items. You might
simply drop anybody who answered fewer than 75% of the items: 75% of 7 items would
be 5.2 items. Let's round this to 5 items. Anybody who skipped fewer than 3 of the 7
items (0, 1, or 2 responses of the 7 items missing) would be included. To do this, we
need to count the number of items each person missed and then restrict the mean score
on empathy to those who skipped just 0, 1, or 2 items. To do this, we use the `egen`
command with the `rowmiss()` function to generate a variable labeled `miss` that is the

number of the items that have a missing value. We then restrict the `egen` command
with the `rowmean()` function to those for which `miss < 3`.

```
. egen miss = rowmiss(empathy1 revempathy2 empathy3 revempathy4
> revempathy5 empathy6 empathy7)
. egen empathya = rowmean(empathy1 revempathy2 empathy3 revempathy4
> revempathy5 empathy6 empathy7) if miss < 3
```

What about generating a total score?

Although generating a mean score rather than a total score for a scale has clear
advantages, sometimes you may need to generate a total (sum) score. Total
scores can be problematic when there are any missing responses. Stata's `egen`
command with the `rowtotal()` function, as well as other statistical software like
SPSS, generates a total score by assigning a value of 0 to each item a person fails
to answer. Assigning a score of 0 to a missing value makes no sense because this
is not even a possible value for most items. If you don't know whether the person
should have a score of 1, 2, 3, or 4, then assigning a value of 0 is not on the scale
and is simply wrong.

Stata has an option that does not treat missing values as zeros. If you
open the menu Data ▷ Create or change data ▷ Create new variable (extended) and
select `Row total` as the *egen function*, you will find an option not to treat missing
values as zeros. However, if you use this option, Stata will make the total score a
missing value for anybody who does not respond to every single item. You may
be losing data from a lot of participants this way.

What if you are working on a project and the principal investigator insists
on you generating a total score. One solution is to generate the mean score and
then multiply it by the number of items on the scale. You could also do this by
first limiting the score to those people who answered at least 75% of the items as
discussed above. Here is how we would generate a total score for our 7-item scale,
including people who answered at least 75% (5 of 7) of the items.

```
. egen miss = rowmiss(empathy1 revempathy2 empathy3 revempathy4
> revempathy5 empathy6 empathy7)
. egen empathya = rowmean(empathy1 revempathy2 empathy3 revempathy4
> revempathy5 empathy6 empathy7) if miss < 3
. generate empathytotal = empathya * 7
```

This approach assumes that when a person skips an item, then the individuals'
own average score for the answered items is a reasonable substitute value for that
item. Although this is a better guess of the value than assigning an impossible
value of 0, it may not be the best. In chapter 14, I discuss advanced options for
imputing the best value in cases where an item is skipped.

12.3 Reliability

There are four types of reliability, and these are illustrated in Shultz, Whitney, and Zickar [2021].

Table 12.1. Four kinds of reliability and the appropriate statistical measure

Type of reliability	Reliability focus	Name of procedure	Statistical measure
Stability	Changes in participants	Test–retest correlation Test–retest agreement	correlation, r intraclass correlation, ρ_I
Equivalence	Sampling of content domain	Alternate forms	correlation, $r_{xx'}$
Internal consistency	Sampling of content domain	Split-half Alpha reliability	correlation, r_{XaXb} alpha, α
Rater consistency	Interrater agreement	Agreement	kappa, κ

Stability means that if you measure a variable today using a particular scale and then measure it again tomorrow using the same scale, your results will be consistent. For depression, we would expect new mothers who are higher than average on depression today to still be higher than average tomorrow.

Equivalence means that you have two measures of the same variable and they produce consistent results. For example, you might have mothers write an essay on motherhood, and then your coders would rate the essay from 1 to 10 based on indications in the essay that the mother is depressed. Then you might give the new mothers a questionnaire that includes a 20-item scale measuring depression. The alternate forms or alternate measures could be evaluated for reliability by correlating the score on one measure with the score on the other measure.

Internal consistency is widely used with scales that involve several items in the same format. Likert-type items that have responses varying from strongly agree to strongly disagree are one example. A reliability assessment might be done by generating the mean score on the first half of the items and the mean score on the second half and then correlating these two scores. A reliable test would be internally consistent if the score for the first half of the items was highly correlated with the score for the second half of the items. Below we will discuss the coefficient alpha, α, which is a better measure of internal consistency.

Rater consistency is important when you have observers rating a video, observed behavior, essay, or something else where two or more people are rating the same information. Here reliability means that a pair of raters gives consistent results. If a person who wrote an essay is rated high on depression by one rater and low on depression by a second rater, then we have reason to say there is low reliability measured for rater consistency.

12.3.1 Stability and test–retest reliability

A researcher uses the identical measure twice and simply correlates the results. The data (retest.dta) consist of the score at time one, called score1, and the score at time two, called score2.

The test–retest correlation is computed by using the command

```
. use https://www.stata-press.com/data/agis6r/retest.dta, clear
. pwcorr score1 score2, obs sig
```

	score1	score2
score1	1.0000	
	10	
score2	0.7702	1.0000
	0.0091	
	10	10

The option obs reports the number of observations, and the option sig reports the significance level. From the results, we see that there is a high test–retest reliability, $r = 0.77, p < 0.01$. We would expect the correlation to be substantial, say, $r > 0.5$. If the correlation is not substantial, then the measure is not giving reliable results.

Test–retest reliability has some limitations as a measure of reliability. First, distinguishing between a lack of a reliable measure and real change can be difficult. If the length of time between the two measures is very long or if some event related to the concept has occurred between the measurements, there may be real change. In that case, the correlation would be low regardless of the reliability of the true measure. If you have a measure of health risks associated with smoking tobacco, a television special on the topic might air between the first and second measurements. The measure might be reliable, but the correlation could be low if those who viewed the television program changed their beliefs. If you try to minimize the risk of this happening by having the two measurements close together, say, one in the morning and the other in the afternoon, participants may recall their responses and try to be consistent.

A second limitation of using test–retest reliability to measure reliability is that correlation does not measure agreement in a strict sense. If the scores at time one had been 2, 3, 4, 5 and the corresponding scores at time two had been 4, 6, 8, 10, then the regression equation

$$\widehat{Y} = 0 + 2X$$

would have a correlation of $r = 1.0$ because each score at the second measurement is exactly twice the time one score. There is no strict agreement, only relative agreement, with the higher the score at time one being matched to the higher the score at time two.

12.3.2 Equivalence

An alternative approach to reliability uses a different form of the measure for the second measurement. This alternative form has different items and, hence, the issue of participants trying to remember how they answered items the first time is eliminated. The alternative forms can be administered at separate times or one right after the other. The main problem with this approach is that developing two versions of a measure that we can assume are truly equivalent is extremely difficult. With this approach, the correlation, r, between the scores on the two forms is all that is needed to measure reliability. A low correlation means either that the measure is not reliable or that the measures are not truly equivalent.

12.3.3 Split-half and alpha reliability—internal consistency

Instead of developing alternative forms of a measure, one approach is known as split-half reliability. This is easier to use because you only need to have one measurement time. Suppose that you have 10 items. You compute a score for the first five items and a separate score for the last five items. Then you correlate these two scores. There are various ways of splitting the items. A random selection would probably be best. One problem with this approach is that we are using only 5-item measures to estimate the reliability of a 10-item measure. A 10-item measure will be more reliable than a 5-item measure, so our correlation for the two 5-item measures will underestimate the correlation for the 10-item measure. To correct this, we can use the Spearman–Brown prophecy formula (developed by Spearman and Brown independently over a century ago).

The major limitation of split-half reliability is that we could get a different result with each split we make. Using the first half and the second half of the items would yield a different reliability estimate than would using the even versus the odd items or randomly selecting items. Also, if the ordering of items is important, this method could be misleading.

Given these concerns with the split-half correlation, the standard for measuring reliability within classical measurement-theory framework is to use a coefficient called Cronbach's alpha (α). In general, an $\alpha > 0.80$ is considered good reliability, and many researchers feel an $\alpha > 0.70$ is adequate reliability.

There are two widely used interpretations of α. The simplest is that it is the expected value of all corrected split-half correlations. This approach is a simple interpretation. The second interpretation of α is the proportion of the observed variance that represents true variance. If we believe our items are an unbiased sample of items from a domain of possible items and hence that α is valid, we can interpret α as the ratio of the true variance to the total variance (the total variance contains both the true variance and the error variance): $\alpha = \sigma_{\text{true}}^2/(\sigma_{\text{true}}^2 + \sigma_{\text{error}}^2)$. This approach is elegant in that an $\alpha = 0.80$ means that 80% of the variance in the scale represents the true score on the variable, and 20% is random error. However, for this interpretation to be used, we need to assume that the scale is valid. We will discuss validity assessment techniques later in this chapter.

There are two formulas for computing α. One of these uses the covariance matrix, and the other uses the correlation matrix. You can think of the correlation matrix as a special transformation of the covariance matrix, where all the variances are rescaled to be equal and fixed at a value of 1.0. Analyzing the covariance matrix is called the unstandardized approach, and analyzing the correlation matrix is called the standardized approach. If items have similar variances, the two approaches will yield similar results. The unstandardized alpha is more general because it allows for items to have different variances. This can happen where some items have most people giving the same response, say, most people strongly agree to the item. By contrast, other items may have considerable variance with some people strongly agreeing and some people strongly disagreeing. The unstandardized alpha is the default in Stata. This is appropriate when generating a total score or a mean of the items.

However, sometimes people are generating a scale score when items are measured on different scales. One item might have three response options (agree, undecided, and disagree) and another item might have four response options (strongly agree, agree, disagree, and strongly disagree). In this case, it is reasonable to first standardize the items before generating the total or mean score. With standardized variables pooled this way, the standardized alpha would be appropriate.

We now return to using the recoded `gss2006_chapter12.dta`. We will use the dialog box to generate the `alpha` command because there are several options that might be hard to remember if you write the command directly. Open the dialog box by selecting Statistics ▷ Multivariate analysis ▷ Cronbach's alpha. On the Main tab, simply enter the variables, `empathy1 revempathy2 empathy3 revempathy4 revempathy5 empathy6 empathy7`. Under the Options tab, there are several powerful options. The first one takes the sign of each item as is. This makes sense to select because we already reverse-coded the items that were worded negatively. If we do not check this option, Stata will decide if any items should have their signs reversed. The second option will delete cases with missing values on any item. We will not check this option for now. Next we have an option to list individual interitem correlations and covariances. We will not check this option now, but it is useful when combined with selecting a standardized solution to see if there are problematic items, that is, items that have low or negative correlations with the other items.

Next is an option that will generate the scale for us. I already showed you how to generate this score earlier by using the `egen rowmean` command. It is reasonable to check this if you want Stata to generate the mean score for you. But only do this after you are satisfied with your scale and its reliability. If you check this option, there is a box highlighted in which you enter the name of the computed scale score. We check the next option to display item-test and item-rest correlations. We do not check the box to include variable labels, though with big scales this can be useful. We do check the box to require a certain number of items and enter 5. This means that people who answer 5, 6, or 7 of the items will be included, and people who answer fewer than 5 items will be dropped. At the bottom of the dialog box is the option to select a standardized solution. This can be useful when combined with asking for correlations if your reliability is low to see where there is a problem. We will not check this for now. The command and results are as follows:

```
. use https://www.stata-press.com/data/agis6r/gss2006_chapter12, clear
(General Social Surveys, 1972-2006 [Cumulative File], Dataset 0001)
. recode empathy2 empathy4 empathy5 (1=5 "Does not describe very well")
> (2=4) (3=3) (4=2) (5=1 "Describes very well"), pre(rev) label(empathy)
(1027 differences between empathy2 and revempathy2)
(1050 differences between empathy4 and revempathy4)
(1152 differences between empathy5 and revempathy5)
. alpha empathy1 revempathy2 empathy3 revempathy4 revempathy5 empathy6 empathy7,
> asis item min(5)

Test scale = mean(unstandardized items)
```

Item	Obs	Sign	Item-test correlation	Item-rest correlation	Average interitem covariance	alpha
empathy1	1349	+	0.6701	0.5151	.3722749	0.7034
revempathy2	1346	+	0.5957	0.3933	.3954405	0.7332
empathy3	1348	+	0.5733	0.4027	.4118086	0.7281
revempathy4	1349	+	0.6303	0.4474	.3827332	0.7191
revempathy5	1342	+	0.6088	0.4277	.3932707	0.7233
empathy6	1347	+	0.6762	0.5358	.3764256	0.7004
empathy7	1349	+	0.6701	0.5204	.3748609	0.7026
Test scale					.3866902	0.7462

We have selected three options. The `asis` (as is) option means that we do not want Stata to change the signs of any of our variables. We want a display of the item analysis, and we require that there are a minimum of 5 answered items, `min(5)`. The bottom row of the output table, `Test scale`, reports the α for the scale (0.7462). Above this value is the α we would obtain if we dropped each item, one at a time. For example, if we dropped `empathy7`, our α would be 0.7026. Dropping this item would make our scale less reliable. Sometimes you will find an item that, if dropped, would improve α. Carefully used, this information can maximize your α. However, be cautious in doing this because you are capitalizing on chance. Imagine having 100 items and computing α. Then drop one item to increase α and redo the analysis using 99 items. You could continue until you had a very high α with, say, 20 items, but you would have not tested to see if you are capitalizing on chance.

The column labeled `Obs` reports the number of observations. This varies slightly because we used pairwise deletion for people who answered at least 5 of the 7 questions. The column labeled `Sign` contains all plus signs, meaning that all the items are positively related to the scale. If any item had a minus sign in this column, you would need to reverse-code the item or drop it. The `Item-test correlation` column reports the correlation of each item with the total score of the seven items. All of these are strong. Because the total score includes the item, the values in this column are artificially inflated. Therefore, Stata also reports the `Item-rest correlation`. This is the correlation of each item with the total of the other items. For example, the correlation between `empathy1` and the total of the other six items is 0.5151. The correlations are useful, but the most valuable information is in the `alpha` column, where we can see whether each item is useful (dropping it would lower α) or not useful (dropping it would increase α).

Alpha, average correlation, number of items

The unstandardized alpha is a function of the number of items, the mean covariance of the items, and the mean variance of the items. The standardized alpha is a function of just the number of items and their mean correlation. We will have a large α whenever we have either a large average correlation among the items, $\bar{r}$, or a large number of items, k. This can lead to misleading results when you have just a few items that are reasonably consistent or when you have a large number of items that are not consistent.

For example, we might not consider a set of items with an average correlation of $\bar{r} = 0.1$ as having much in common. With a 5-item scale, this results in an alpha of 0.36; with a 20-item scale, the alpha becomes 0.69; and with a 50-item scale, the alpha is 0.85. This shows an important qualification on how we view alpha. A 50-item scale with a reliability of just 0.85 contains items that do not have much in common. Some major scales are like this where they gain consistency from the large number of items and not from the items sharing much common variance.

The opposite happens when we have scales with just a few items. Many large-scale surveys attempt to measure many concepts and have just a few items to measure each of the concepts. If we have an average correlation among items of 0.3, a 3-item scale yields a standardized alpha of just 0.56, whereas a 10-item scale yields an alpha of 0.81. Adding just a few items greatly enhances the reliability of a scale, and 10-item scales should be adequate even if the average correlation is only moderate. At the other extreme, some researchers feel the need to have many items. Increasing our scale from 10 items to 30 items, and measuring one-third as many concepts in the survey as a result, raises the alpha from 0.81 to 0.93. For many applications, this small improvement will not offset the resulting increase in the length of the questionnaire.

12.3.4   Kuder–Richardson reliability for dichotomous items

The equivalent of alpha for items that are dichotomous is the Kuder–Richardson measure of reliability. The dichotomous items need to be coded as a 1 for "Yes" or "Correct" and a 0 for "No" or "Incorrect". This measure is sometimes used with multiple-choice tests where students get each item right or wrong. It is also used when there are simple yes/no response options to the items. You can estimate the Kuder–Richardson reliability coefficient by simply running `alpha` on the set of items about using the web for art that were asked on the 2002 General Social Survey (`kuder-richardson.dta`):

```
. use https://www.stata-press.com/data/agis6r/kuder-richardson, clear
(General Social Surveys, 1972-2006 [Cumulative File], Dataset 0001)
. alpha newartmus1 newartmus2 newartview newartinfo newartmus3, asis item
Test scale = mean(unstandardized items)
```

Item	Obs	Sign	Item-test correlation	Item-rest correlation	Average interitem covariance	alpha
newartmus1	90	+	0.5767	0.3432	.0578652	0.5626
newartmus2	90	+	0.6600	0.3966	.0485019	0.5327
newartview	90	+	0.5948	0.3123	.0563046	0.5784
newartinfo	90	+	0.6420	0.3831	.0506242	0.5404
newartmus3	90	+	0.6423	0.3749	.0506242	0.5448
Test scale					.052784	0.6066

The value of alpha reported by Stata is identical to the value given using the formula for the Kuder–Richardson reliability. The results show that the Kuder–Richardson reliability coefficient is 0.607.

12.3.5   Rater agreement—kappa (κ)

Reliable coding of observational data is often extremely difficult. If you have two people trained to code videotapes of interactions for evidence of conflict, it is hard to have both of them code everything the same way. If your two coders do not agree on how they are coding the observational data, then it is difficult to have much confidence in the analysis based on their coding.

When collecting observational data, we often have two or more raters code their observations, and we measure the reliability of their agreement. We might have two physicians rating the health of the same patients on a 5-point scale. We might have two clinicians identify the mental health condition of patients. A widely used measure of interrater agreement is the coefficient kappa (κ).

Suppose that we are observing people from the press who are asking questions of a political leader. We might have several categories such as

- Friendly questions that the political leader would like to have asked—Do you feel education is important?

- Difficult questions that the political leader would like to have asked—Could you elaborate on the benefits of your plan to reform the Social Security system?

- Unwanted questions that the political leader would not like to have asked—Why did your press secretary resign?

- Extremely unwanted and difficult questions that the political leader would not like to have asked—How can you justify the $125,000 donation you received from the Committee to Promote Higher Pay for Men?

Perhaps at the beginning of the politician's tenure, there is a honeymoon period in which most of the questions are ones the leader wants to answer because they are easy or because they allow the leader to clarify his or her plans. Perhaps later in their tenure, the questions become less desirable from the politician's perspective. You have two coders rate a press conference in which 20 questions were asked, and their hypothetical ratings are in `kappa1.dta`.

We can do a tabulation of these data:

```
. use https://www.stata-press.com/data/agis6r/kappa1, clear
. tabulate coder1 coder2
```

	coder2				
coder1	Easy	Hard want	Unwanted	Very unwa	Total
Easy	5	1	0	0	6
Hard wanted	0	3	0	0	3
Unwanted	1	2	2	0	5
Very unwanted	0	1	1	4	6
Total	6	7	3	4	20

The coders seem to agree on the classification of the friendly questions and the unwanted questions. They seem to have a harder time distinguishing the difficult-but-wanted questions from the difficult-unwanted questions. Ideally, all the observations should fall on the diagonal where coder one and coder two have the same classification of the question.

To estimate κ, we enter the command `kap coder1 coder2`. Note that we typed `kap` and not `kappa`. The latter is only used for data entered in a special way. The output is as follows:

```
. kap coder1 coder2
```

	Expected				
Agreement	agreement	Kappa	Std. err.	Z	Prob>Z
70.00%	24.00%	0.6053	0.1221	4.96	0.0000

We would describe this by writing that the judges agree exactly on the classification 70% of the time, that is, $(5+3+2+4)/20$. The coefficient of agreement is $\kappa = 0.61$, $z = 4.96$, $p < 0.001$, indicating a reasonable level of agreement.

Some people would use the percentage agreement instead of κ, but the percentage agreement exaggerates the amount of agreement because it ignores the agreement we would expect by chance. κ only gives us credit for the extent the agreement exceeds what we would have expected to get by chance alone.

What is a strong kappa?

We would like alpha to be 0.80 or higher for a scale to be considered reliable. The expectations for kappa are different. Because kappa adjusts the percentage agreement for what would be expected by chance, kappa tends to be lower than alpha. Landis and Koch (1977) suggested these guidelines; see also Altman (1991):

Alpha	Strength of agreement
Under 0.20	Poor
0.21 – 0.40	Fair
0.41 – 0.60	Moderate
0.61 – 0.80	Good
0.81 – 1.00	Very good

Thus our $\kappa = 0.605$ is between moderate and good.

If you conceptualize the classes as ordinal, it is possible to estimate a weighted kappa. This $\kappa_{weighted}$ gives partial credit for being close. If the two judges are close, the weighted kappa gives us partial credit. Stata allows us to use the default value for the weights or to enter our own criterion. This is explained in [R] **kappa** with a detailed example. Entering the command `help kap` provides a brief explanation. We will not cover weighted kappa here.

Some researchers can use three raters rather than two, and this offers much more information. With three raters, kappa not only reports the overall κ but also can give us a κ for each category. For example, we may find that the coders have a high level of reliability for coding items that are in the "Easy" or "Hard wanted" categories, but a very low reliability for the "Unwanted" or "Very unwanted" categories. Here we might find that combining the "Unwanted" and "Very unwanted" categories into one category is necessary to have interrater reliability. The extension of kappa to three raters is described in [R] **kappa**.

12.4   Validity

A good measure needs to be reliable, but it also needs to be valid. A valid measure is one that measures what it is supposed to be measuring. A measure of maternal depression may be reliable, meaning it gets consistent results, without being valid. In order to be valid, the measure should have a high score for mothers who actually are depressed and a low score for mothers who are not. A measure is not valid when it is measuring other phenomena. For example, asking a person if they have high anxiety is not an especially valid item to measure depression. A person may have high anxiety just before an examination, but this is different from being depressed. The gist of validity is simply that a measure needs to measure what you are trying to measure and not something else. Assessing validity involves comparing a measure with one or more standards. There are many possible standards, resulting in several types of validity checks.

12.4.1 Expert judgment

In making a scale, you first need to carefully define the content domain of what you are measuring. Once you have done this, you share your items and your definition of the domain with a small group of experts in the field and have them critique each item. This will provide a good measure of content validity if your definition of the content domain and the quality of your experts are both good.

Defining the content domain is often difficult. Suppose that you are measuring self-reported health. What does this include? Does it include mental health? Does it include living a healthy lifestyle? Is it limited to physical health? What about ability to perform activities of daily living? What about flexibility, strength, and endurance? Are you interested in a global rating of health or more specific aspects?

Once you have carefully defined the domain of your concept, your panel of experts can judge whether you have items that represent this domain. Judges may be academic scholars who have published in the area or others who have worked in the field. A psychiatric social worker, a physician, and an academic scholar on health might be good candidates for your panel of experts. In other cases, you might want to include people who are experiencing issues related to your content. A member of a youth gang would be an expert if you were measuring gang-related violence.

One measure of content validity is the content validity ratio (CVR) (Lawshe 1975; Shultz et al. 2021). Judges rate each item as *essential*, *useful*, or *not necessary*. For each item, you compute the CVR by using

$$\text{CVR}_i = \frac{n_e - \frac{N}{2}}{\frac{N}{2}}$$

where n_e is the total number of judges rating item i as *essential*, and N is the number of judges. Assume that you have a 10-item scale and four judges, with three of the four judges rating the first item as *essential*. The CVR_i would be $(3 - 2)/2 = 0.50$. You can keep the items that have a relatively high CVR and drop those that do not. However, a limitation of this is that it is no better than the quality of your definition of your domain and the quality of the judges.

Face validity is a type of content validity, but it does not require expert judgment. People like those who will be measured by your scale can often be most helpful for evaluating face validity. If there are subgroups that might have special understandings (gender, ethnicity, etc.), they should be asked to say whether the items make sense for measuring the variable you are trying to measure. Imagine that you are developing a scale to measure the self-regulation in a group of 8-year-olds. You could ask a small number of 8-year-olds to read each item aloud and explain what the item is trying to say or ask. Then ask each of these 8-year-olds to pick an answer and explain why they picked that answer. You will almost always find that a few of the items are interpreted differently by these 8-year-olds from the way you intended and that the reason they pick an answer is extraneous to what you are measuring.

12.4.2 Criterion-related validity

Criterion-related validity picks one or more criteria or standards for evaluating a scale. The standard may be a concurrent measure or a predictive measure. If you have a 10-item scale of self-reported health, you need to find a standard. This could be a more comprehensive 40-item measure that has been used in the literature but is too long for your purposes. You include both your 10-item measure and the 40-item measure in a pilot survey and correlate the two scale scores. You might also use as a standard a clinical evaluation of the person's health.

Predictive standards are criteria that your measure should predict, and these typically require a time interval. A measure of motivation to achieve given to high school juniors might use grade point averages during their senior year as a criterion. Where correlations are used, a value of 0.30 is considered moderate support, and a correlation of 0.50 is considered strong support.

If you are measuring intention of medical students to work in rural areas, you might wait until the group graduates and see how many of them actually do work in a rural area. This would involve predictive validity. Because working in a rural area is a binary 0/1 variable, you would use logistic regression with your scale score as the predictor. If your scale score is a substantively and statistically significant predictor of whether medical students work in a rural area, then this would be evidence of predictive criterion validity. If you are measuring the commitment to quit smoking, you might use the number of cessation sessions a person attends as your criterion, in which case you would compute a simple correlation.

Criterion-related validity can also be used to evaluate individual items. If you believe the overall scale is valid, you can correlate each item with the total score and drop those that have low correlations with the total score. Stata's command `alpha` with the option `item` provides this information, as was shown in the output on page 387 under the columns labeled `Item-test correlation` and `Item-rest correlation`.

You can also divide the sample into quartiles based on the total score. Then you would compare the top quartile to the bottom quartile on each item by using a *t* test. Try this as an exercise.

12.4.3 Construct validity

The term construct validity is reserved for analyses that involve more than one approach to assessing validity. Some of the analyses that fall under the rubric of construct validity include the following:

- Comparing known groups. A measure of depression might be evaluated by comparing the mean score for a group of people being treated for post-traumatic stress disorder with a group who are not being treated. With two groups, you would use a t test, and with more than two groups, you would use ANOVA.

- Internal consistency. Although I presented alpha reliability as a measure of reliability, it is also reasonable to think of it as tapping validity. If you have a series of items measuring commitment to stop smoking, they should all be internally consistent, as indicated by item-rest correlations and alpha, as well as by comparing the top and bottom quartiles. These techniques were covered in the previous section. If the scale is valid, then $\alpha = 0.80$ signifies that 80% of the variance represents true variance in the variable.

- Correlational analysis. We would expect criterion-related validity to be demonstrated. Better yet, with construct validity we would use multiple criteria. Our motivation scale given in the junior year of high school should predict grade point average in the senior year, college plans, etc. These are known as *convergent* criteria-related validity because we expect these correlations to all be positive. *Divergent* criteria-related validity would identify additional criteria for which we would expect a negative relationship. We would expect our motivational scale score to be negatively related to such criteria as frequency of arrest, use of hard drugs, likelihood of dropping out of high school, and unprotected sexual behavior. With construct validity, we are looking at a pattern of correlations. An extension of this is to use factor analysis (see the next section) and possibly confirmatory factor analysis.

- Qualitative analysis. We should interview people who complete our set of items and ask them to explain each answer they gave. Having a group of fifth-grade students answer questions about how much they like school by using a computer-assisted interview program that includes neat graphics may be measuring how much they like school, but it also may measure how much they like "foolin' around on the computer". Asked why they give a positive response to an item, we might learn that it is because they would rather play on the computer than sit in a class. A surprising number of scales have been developed by academics that have never been evaluated by the target population. We should always evaluate whether the people in our target population are interpreting the items and the options the way we expected.

We can illustrate construct validity using items designed to measure hope in the 2016 General Social Survey, `gss2016_chapter12.dta`. Each of the six hope items is coded from a 1 for definitely false to 8 for definitely true. Sample items ask the participants whether they could think of ways to get themselves out of a jam, whether they are energetically pursuing their goals, whether there are lots of ways around problems they are facing, whether they see themselves as being successful, whether they think of ways to reach their current goals, and whether they are currently meeting their goals. The six hope items were asked of a subsample of the 2016 General Social Survey.

We first run an alpha reliability on the items using the `asis` option that leaves the items as they are originally coded:

```
. use https://www.stata-press.com/data/agis6r/gss2016_chapter12, clear
. alpha hope1-hope6, asis item label generate(hope)
Test scale = mean(unstandardized items)
```

Items	S	it-cor	ir-cor	ii-cov	alpha	Label
hope1	+	0.611	0.466	1.4439	0.843	i could get out of a jam
hope2	+	0.766	0.626	1.189	0.816	i am energetically pursuing my goals
hope3	+	0.719	0.587	1.3138	0.822	there are many ways around problems i face
hope4	+	0.799	0.677	1.155	0.802	i see myself as successful
hope5	+	0.805	0.711	1.2194	0.800	i can think of many ways to reach my current goals
hope6	+	0.782	0.656	1.1828	0.808	i am meeting my current goals
Test scale				1.2507	0.842	mean(unstandardized items)

The `alpha = 0.842` indicates good reliability—the set of 6 items form a consistent scale with all items consistently correlated with the total of the items and none of the items needing to be reverse coded. The `generate(hope)` option created a new variable called `hope` that contains our scale of hope. We will now evaluate our scale of `hope` for validity.

First, we might consider divergent validity by comparing known groups. We hypothesize that there will be a divergence between those who work full or part time and those who do not work. Those who are currently working will score higher on `hope` than people who are not working. We will run the `ttest` command to see whether the means differ significantly and the `esize` command to see what the effect size is. This test does not account for a lack of reliability, but it validates our measure by testing a prediction based on known groups. We will generate a variable called `work` that is coded 1 if a person works full time or part time and coded 0 otherwise.

```
. generate work = 1 if wrkstat <= 2
(1,201 missing values generated)
. replace work = 0 if wrkstat > 2 & !missing(wrkstat)
(1,198 real changes made)
```

Now, we run the `ttest`:

```
. ttest hope, by(work)
Two-sample t test with equal variances
```

Group	Obs	Mean	Std. err.	Std. dev.	[95% conf. interval]	
0	607	5.885146	.0541057	1.333022	5.778888	5.991403
1	838	6.249841	.0383753	1.110897	6.174518	6.325164
Combined	1,445	6.096644	.0321489	1.22208	6.03358	6.159707
diff		-.3646954	.0644468		-.4911148	-.2382759

```
    diff = mean(0) - mean(1)                                  t =  -5.6589
HO: diff = 0                               Degrees of freedom =      1443

    Ha: diff < 0              Ha: diff != 0                Ha: diff > 0
 Pr(T < t) = 0.0000      Pr(|T| > |t|) = 0.0000        Pr(T > t) = 1.0000
. esize twosample hope, by(work)
Effect size based on mean comparison
                                     Obs per group:
                                          work==0 =        607
                                          work==1 =        838
```

Effect size	Estimate	[95% conf. interval]	
Cohen's d	-.3016105	-.4066004	-.1965172
Hedges's g	-.3014537	-.406389	-.196415

These results show that the means differ significantly in the predicted direction ($t = -5.66$, degrees of freedom $= 1443$, $p < 0.001$) and that the effect size is moderate (Cohen's $d = -0.302$). There is divergence between these two groups.

We can assess the convergent and divergent validity of our measure, `hope`, by seeing whether it is positively correlated with variables with which we believe it converges and negatively correlated with variables with which we believe it diverges. We will hypothesize that people who score high on `hope` will be negatively correlated with `cesd1` (the amount of time the individual was depressed in the last week). A test for predicted negative correlation is a test for divergent validity. We would expect that `hope` would be positively correlated with `hapmar` (happiness of marriage), and `health` (health condition), and `coneduc` (level of confidence in education). We use these predicted positive correlations to assess convergent validity. However, `hapmar`, `health`, and `coneduc` are coded so that a higher score is more negative. Therefore, we need to reverse-code them:

```
. recode hapmar (3 = 1 "Not too happy") (1 = 3 "Very happy"), pre(new) label(new)
(774 differences between hapmar and newhapmar)
. recode health (4 = 1 "Poor") (3 = 2 "Fair") (2 = 3 "Good") (1 = 4 "Excellent"),
> pre(new) label(new)
(1885 differences between health and newhealth)
. recode coneduc (3 = 1 "Hardly any") (1 = 3 "A great deal"), pre(new) label(new)
(850 differences between coneduc and newconeduc)
```

To preserve all the observations that have scores on each correlation pair, we will use the `pwcorr` command:

```
. pwcorr hope cesd1 newhapmar newhealth newconeduc, obs sig
                 hope    cesd1 newhap~r newhea~h newcon~c

        hope   1.0000

                 1447

       cesd1  -0.3571   1.0000
               0.0000
                  962      963

   newhapmar   0.2003  -0.3396   1.0000
               0.0000   0.0000
                  603      415     1204

   newhealth   0.4028  -0.3109   0.2117   1.0000
               0.0000   0.0000   0.0000
                  972      962      819     1885

  newconeduc   0.0745  -0.0193   0.0169   0.0993   1.0000
               0.0046   0.5503   0.6318   0.0019
                 1443      960      809      973     1948
```

The first column shows the correlation of the `hope` score with each convergent and each divergent criterion. All the convergent criteria are positively and significantly correlated with scoring higher on `hope`. However, the correlation with confidence in education is small. Health condition has the largest correlation with `hope` (0.403). Nevertheless, all the correlations are positive and statistically significant at the $p < 0.05$ level.

What about the divergent criteria. We predicted that `cesd1` would be negatively correlated with `hope`, and that is exactly what happened. This correlation, -0.357, is significant at the $p < 0.001$ level.

The last step in the evaluation of the validity of our scale involves a qualitative analysis. We cannot do this because we are using secondary analysis and do not have access to the participants in the survey. If we had direct access to the participants, we could do a qualitative analysis of those with very unusual combinations, for example, extremely hopeful but have felt depressed all or almost all the time in the last week. If we were developing this scale from scratch, we should also select a small number of people (5–10) like those we expect to have in our sample and ask them to a) read each item out loud, b) pick their response, and c) explain why they picked that response. This could help us understand if any of the items are misleading.

12.5   Factor analysis

Ideally, a scale measures just one concept. We sometimes ignore this, and the results can be misleading. Imagine that Shanice has a GRE score on the quantitative reasoning part of the examination of 165 (very high),[1] but her score on the verbal reasoning part of the examination is just 140 (low). A second student, Emma, has just the opposite scores, that is, 140 on the quantitative reasoning part and 165 on the verbal reasoning part. Some graduate programs use a single number, the total of the quantitative and verbal sections, to evaluate applications. Using one number, the same 305 total for both Shanice and Emma, can be problematic if they both are applying for a statistics program or for a humanities program. This is because we are combining two distinct dimensions of academic ability—verbal and quantitative achievements. It would make more sense for graduate programs to consider the quantitative and verbal reasoning scores as two separate dimensions with some graduate programs emphasizing one or the other of these.

Some concepts are multidimensional. For example, health might have one dimension for physical health and a separate dimension for psychological health. We would expect these two dimensions of health to be correlated, but the correlation should be small enough that we recognize them as two distinct dimensions of health. In such a case, we might not want to average items. Instead, we might want to make two scales, one for physical health and one for psychological health. Some researchers would ignore our advice to have two scales and simply combine them. If you do this, it would make more sense to call this an index rather than to call it a scale. Ideally, a scale should represent one dimension.

How do we know a set of items represents one dimension? This is where we use factor analysis. If the items represent one dimension, then all of them should be moderately to strongly correlated with each other, and the pattern of correlations should be consistent. If we had a six-item scale, it might look something like table 12.2.

Table 12.2. Correlations you might expect for one factor

	Item 1	Item 2	Item 3	Item 4	Item 5	Item 6
Item 1	1.00					
Item 2	0.60	1.00				
Item 3	0.45	0.40	1.00			
Item 4	0.50	0.55	0.45	1.00		
Item 5	0.70	0.55	0.45	0.40	1.00	
Item 6	0.35	0.40	0.45	0.40	0.35	1.00

---

1. Before August 2011, the GRE scores ranged from 200 to 800 for both the verbal reasoning and the quantitative reasoning sections. Since August 2011, the GRE scores have ranged from 130 to 170 for both sections.

What would happen if we had two dimensions with the first three items representing physical health and the last three items representing psychological health? This scenario is illustrated in table 12.3, where the first three items are highly correlated with each other (top left triangle), the last three items are highly correlated with each other (bottom right triangle), but the two sets of items are only moderately correlated with each other (bottom left rectangle).

Table 12.3. Correlations you might expect for two factors

	Item 1	Item 2	Item 3	Item 4	Item 5	Item 6
Item 1	**1.00**					
Item 2	**0.60**	**1.00**				
Item 3	**0.80**	**0.70**	**1.00**			
Item 4	0.30	0.25	0.35	**1.00**		
Item 5	0.20	0.25	0.25	**0.70**	**1.00**	
Item 6	0.25	0.20	0.15	**0.75**	**0.65**	**1.00**

Factor analysis is a collection of techniques that does an exploratory analysis to see if there are clusters of items that go together. When constructing a scale, you would hope that all the items you include in your scale form one factor or principal component.

There are two types of analysis that are often lumped together under the label of factor analysis. The default is exploratory factor analysis, which Stata calls principal factor analysis. We will use PF to refer to this type of factor analysis. The second type is principal-component factor analysis. We will use PCF to refer to this approach. Each of these procedures has distinct objectives.

PF analysis attempts to identify a small number of latent variables or dimensions that explain the shared variance of a set of measures. If you believe that an attitude toward use of methamphetamines includes a cognitive component (beliefs), an affective component (emotional response, feelings), and a behavioral component (predispositions), you might do a PF analysis of a set of 30 items to see if the items fall into these three dimensions and label each dimension as a latent variable. Here the latent variables explain how you respond to the items. In PF analysis, the variance is partitioned into the shared variance and unique or error variance. The shared variance is how much of the variance in any one item can be explained by the rest of the items. This shared variance is estimated using a multiple R^2. In practical terms, factor analysis analyzes a correlation matrix in which the 1.00s on the diagonal are replaced by the square of the multiple correlation of each item with the rest of the items. PF analysis is not trying to explain all the variance, just the variance that is shared among the set of items.

PCF analysis has a different approach, and its strength is in the area of data reduction. It does not distinguish between the common or shared variance and the unique or error variance. In practical terms, PCF analysis analyzes a correlation matrix in which the 1.00s on the diagonal stay there. It is trying to explain all the variance. PCF analysis is used when developing a scale where one dimension is identified to represent the core of a set of items. If we have 20 items measuring your satisfaction with a drug, and we find that 15 of the items load highly on the first dimension in a PCF analysis, then we may want to use those 15 items in our scale and drop the other 5 items.

Factor analysis has a special vocabulary of its own. The following is a list of some of the most important terminology. You can read this now, but it may be most helpful to refer to it after you have read the section where each term is used.

- Extraction. There are different ways of extracting a solution. This extraction involves analyzing the correlation matrix (sometimes the covariance matrix) to obtain an initial factor solution. The initial factor solution may subsequently be rotated to aid interpretation.

- Eigenvalues. Both PCF analysis and PF analysis produce a value for each factor that is known as the eigenvalue for that factor. In the case of PCF analysis, because all the variance is being explained, the sum of the eigenvalues for all possible components is the number of items. If there are 10 items, the sum of the eigenvalues will be 10. Therefore, a component that has an eigenvalue of less than 1 is not helpful for data reduction because it accounts for less than one item. The factors will be ordered from the most important, which has the largest eigenvalue, to the least important, which has the smallest eigenvalue. In PF analysis, the sum of the eigenvalues will be less than the number of items, and the eigenvalues' interpretation is complex.

- Communality and uniqueness. Communality is how much of each item is explained by the set of factors, and uniqueness (shown in Stata) is how much is unexplained. PF analysis tries to explain the shared variance. PCF analysis tries to explain all the variance, which is why it is ideal for the uniqueness to approach zero. This ideal is rarely achieved in practice but is a caution that PCF may not be appropriate.

- Loadings. Both PCF analysis and PF analysis produce a matrix with the items in the rows and the factors in the columns. The elements of this matrix are called loadings, and they are used to assess how clusters of items are most related to one or another of the factors. If an item has a loading over 0.4 on a factor, it is considered a good indicator of that factor. Many researchers limit themselves to orthogonal rotation. This may be a problem if they conceptualize the factors as correlated. For example, we might have a physical health factor and a mental health factor. Conceptually, these would be correlated.

- Simple structure. This is a pattern of loadings where each item loads strongly on just one factor and a subset of items load strongly on each factor. When an item loads strongly on more than one factor, it is factorially confounded.

- Scree plot. This is a graph showing the eigenvalue for each factor. Its name comes from geology, where scree collects at the bottom of a cliff. It is used to decide how many factors are included by throwing out those that are considered scree.

When doing a PCF analysis, we usually drop factors that have eigenvalues in the neighborhood of 1.0 or smaller.

- Rotation. Neither PF analysis nor PCF analysis has a unique solution without making a series of assumptions. It is often helpful to rotate the initial solution to obtain a solution that is more interpretable.

- Orthogonal versus oblique. Some rotations require that the factors be uncorrelated. These are orthogonal solutions. Other rotations allow the factors to be correlated and are called oblique solutions. There are many options for each type of rotation, and each type of rotation makes different assumptions to obtain identification.

- Factor score. This is a score on each factor. Rather than simply averaging or adding the items that load above some value, such as 0.4, on the factor to get a scale score, a factor score weights each item based on how related it is to the factor. Also the factor score is scaled to have a mean of 0.0 and a variance of 1.0.

Should you use PF analysis or PCF analysis? If you want to explain as much of the variance in a set of items as possible with one dimension, then PCF analysis is reasonable. Use PCF when you have a set of items that you believe all measure one concept. In this situation, you would be interested in the first principal factor. You would want to see if it explained a substantial part of the total variance for the entire set of items, and you would want most of the items to have a loading of 0.4 or above on this factor.

If, on the other hand, you want to identify two or more latent variables that represent interpretable dimensions of some concept, then PF analysis is probably best. For example, you might have 20 items asking about a person's level of alienation. A PF analysis might find that there are subsets of items that fall into different dimensions such as value isolation, powerlessness, and normlessness. With PF analysis, the focus is on finding two or more interpretable dimensions or factors rather than on maximizing the amount of variance that is explained.

In this chapter, we limit our coverage to PCF analysis because it relates to developing a measure of a concept. Using the Stata menu, select Statistics ▷ Multivariate analysis ▷ Factor and principal component analysis. Here you will find several options:

- Factor analysis

- Factor analysis of a correlation matrix

- Principal component analysis (PCA)

- PCA of a correlation or covariance matrix

- Postestimation

We will focus on the first of these, factor analysis. This option allows us to do either PF analysis or PCF analysis. (Be careful not to select Principal component analysis (PCA).) The terminology used in factor analysis is highly specialized, and the same terms can be used differently by different software packages.

The second menu option, Factor analysis of a correlation matrix, allows you to enter a correlation matrix and do the factor analysis of it. This is useful when reading an article that includes a correlation matrix because you do not need the raw data to do the factor analysis; you just need the correlation matrix.

The third and fourth options involve Stata's application of principal component analysis (PCA). We will not consider these options here. The last option, Postestimation, includes things we can do after we obtain the first solution to help us interpret the results, including rotating the solution, creating scree plots, and estimating factor scores.

What's in a name?

Because factor analysis is an area of long-standing specialization, there are many differences of opinion as to what is the best approach to it. Many of these distinctions are not of great importance when we use factor analysis to develop or evaluate a scale. There are many technical terms that you rarely see in other areas of statistics. To make matters especially confusing, different software may use the same name for different procedures. We will only cover the procedures for factor analysis as Stata implements them. But do not be surprised if you hear the same names used differently with other packages.

In Stata, PCF analysis produces the same results as what IBM SPSS Statistics calls principal component analysis. However, what Stata calls principal component analysis (PCA—the third and fourth options in the menu) has important differences. We will use the name PCF analysis to refer to what IBM SPSS Statistics calls principal component analysis.

The default in Stata is to do a PF analysis; in IBM SPSS Statistics, the default is to do a PCF analysis.

12.6 PCF analysis

Here is an example of PCF analysis using 14 items from the 2006 General Social Survey (gss2006_chapter12_selected.dta). There are four options for how Stata extracts factors from your data. Other packages offer more options not available in Stata, but the options in Stata should meet most needs for people developing or evaluating a scale.

We will examine the 14 items from the 2006 General Social Survey that measure desire to invest in different national programs. Our goal is to select items that we can use in a scale. Here is a compact codebook of the items:

```
. use https://www.stata-press.com/data/agis6r/gss2006_chapter12_selected, clear
(General Social Surveys, 1972-2006 [Cumulative File], Dataset 0001)

. codebook natspac natenvir natheal natcity natcrime natdrug nateduc natrace
> natarms natfare natroad natsoc natchld natsci, compact

Variable     Obs Unique     Mean  Min  Max  Label

natspac     1407      3  2.237385    1    3  SPACE EXPLORATION PROGRAM
natenvir    1446      3  1.375519    1    3  IMPROVING  PROTECTING ENVIRONMENT
natheal     1451      3  1.297726    1    3  IMPROVING  PROTECTING NATIONS HE...
natcity     1349      3  1.634544    1    3  SOLVING PROBLEMS OF BIG CITIES
natcrime    1448      3  1.446133    1    3  HALTING RISING CRIME RATE
natdrug     1428      3   1.45028    1    3  DEALING WITH DRUG ADDICTION
nateduc     1462      3  1.317373    1    3  IMPROVING NATIONS EDUCATION SYSTEM
natrace     1348      3  1.780415    1    3  IMPROVING THE CONDITIONS OF BLACKS
natarms     1442      3  2.144938    1    3  MILITARY, ARMAMENTS, AND DEFENSE
natfare     1434      3  2.110879    1    3  WELFARE
natroad     2899      3  1.756468    1    3  HIGHWAYS AND BRIDGES
natsoc      2864      3  1.407472    1    3  SOCIAL SECURITY
natchld     2758      3  1.517041    1    3  ASSISTANCE FOR CHILDCARE
natsci      2786      3  1.688442    1    3  SUPPORTING SCIENTIFIC RESEARCH
```

Running `tabulate` with the `codebook` command or the `fre` command, if you have that command installed, we see that these items have a higher score, implying less support for spending. We can reverse these codes, reverse the corresponding labels, and add a prefix of "`r`" to each variable to remind us that we have reversed them:

```
. recode natspac natenvir natheal natcity natcrime natdrug nateduc natrace
> natarms natfare natroad natsoc natchld natsci
> (1=3 "Too little") (2=2 "About right") (3=1 "Too much"), prefix(r) label(revnat)
(756 differences between natspac and rnatspac)
(1081 differences between natenvir and rnatenvir)
(1169 differences between natheal and rnatheal)
(839 differences between natcity and rnatcity)
(992 differences between natcrime and rnatcrime)
(1027 differences between natdrug and rnatdrug)
(1152 differences between nateduc and rnateduc)
(746 differences between natrace and rnatrace)
(967 differences between natarms and rnatarms)
(919 differences between natfare and rnatfare)
(1392 differences between natroad and rnatroad)
(1973 differences between natsoc and rnatsoc)
(1756 differences between natchld and rnatchld)
(1570 differences between natsci and rnatsci)
```

Now a higher score implies greater support. A researcher may think there is one dimension representing how liberal or conservative a person is regarding government spending. This researcher may feel that a liberal would score high on all of these items (big spenders) and a conservative would score low, meaning that they want to minimize government spending initiatives. Another person may think there are two separate dimensions, one focused on investing in social welfare issues—for example, education, health, welfare, environment—and one focused on investing in the national infrastructure. A third researcher may believe it is more complicated and want to see what dimensions are needed to explain this set of 14 items.

To run a PCF analysis, we select Statistics ▷ Multivariate analysis ▷ Factor and principal component analysis ▷ Factor analysis. The first tab is labeled Model, and here we list our 14 recoded variables. The second tab is labeled Model 2. Here we select *Principal-component factor*. This generates the following results:

```
. factor rnatspac rnatenvir rnatheal rnatcity rnatcrime rnatdrug rnateduc
> rnatrace rnatarms rnatfare rnatroad rnatsoc rnatchld rnatsci, pcf
(obs=1,082)
```

Factor analysis/correlation		Number of obs	=	1,082
Method: principal-component factors		Retained factors	=	4
Rotation: (unrotated)		Number of params	=	50

Factor	Eigenvalue	Difference	Proportion	Cumulative
Factor1	3.00301	1.62066	0.2145	0.2145
Factor2	1.38235	0.12372	0.0987	0.3132
Factor3	1.25863	0.22702	0.0899	0.4031
Factor4	1.03161	0.06974	0.0737	0.4768
Factor5	0.96187	0.05047	0.0687	0.5455
Factor6	0.91140	0.09801	0.0651	0.6106
Factor7	0.81339	0.02930	0.0581	0.6687
Factor8	0.78409	0.05945	0.0560	0.7247
Factor9	0.72464	0.01659	0.0518	0.7765
Factor10	0.70804	0.04088	0.0506	0.8271
Factor11	0.66717	0.06485	0.0477	0.8747
Factor12	0.60231	0.01414	0.0430	0.9178
Factor13	0.58817	0.02484	0.0420	0.9598
Factor14	0.56333	.	0.0402	1.0000

```
LR test: independent vs. saturated:  chi2(91) = 1701.47 Prob>chi2 = 0.0000
Factor loadings (pattern matrix) and unique variances
```

Variable	Factor1	Factor2	Factor3	Factor4	Uniqueness
rnatspac	-0.0405	0.6150	-0.4468	-0.0108	0.4204
rnatenvir	0.5562	0.0698	-0.1925	0.1629	0.6221
rnatheal	0.6298	0.0420	0.0923	0.2638	0.5235
rnatcity	0.5264	-0.0580	-0.0677	-0.4598	0.5036
rnatcrime	0.4533	0.1160	0.5154	-0.4234	0.3361
rnatdrug	0.5381	0.1048	0.3346	-0.2872	0.5051
rnateduc	0.5997	0.0035	0.0425	0.3838	0.4912
rnatrace	0.5921	-0.2286	-0.2660	-0.1885	0.4909
rnatarms	-0.1087	0.4926	0.4682	0.1719	0.4968
rnatfare	0.4725	-0.1726	-0.3547	-0.0629	0.6172
rnatroad	0.1421	0.5022	0.0704	-0.1269	0.7065
rnatsoc	0.4196	-0.1209	0.3374	0.4575	0.4862
rnatchld	0.5369	-0.1049	-0.1130	0.1343	0.6699
rnatsci	0.3057	0.6059	-0.2865	0.0493	0.4549

If these 14 items all fall along one dimension, we would expect the first factor to have a dominant effect. We can assess this by using the Eigenvalues. Remembering that in PCF analysis the total of the eigenvalues for all factors is the number of items, 14 in this case, we can see that the first factor has an eigenvalue of 3.00, and this is 21% of the total possible of 14. By comparison, the second factor has an eigenvalue of just 1.38. It looks like there is a strong first factor.

If you look at the matrix showing the "Factor loadings", you can go down the column labeled `Factor1` to see the loadings for each item on the first factor (component). Notice how many of the items have a loading greater than 0.40. The exceptions are for the space programs, armaments, roads, and science. The rest of the items have strong loadings and include the environment, health, crime, drugs, education, race, welfare, social programs, and children. This seems to be a general liberal spending program, and we could make a scale using these 10 items, dropping the other 4 items.

There is a problem with our results that many researchers ignore. Because PCF analysis is trying to explain all the variance in the items, the uniqueness for each item should approach zero. For example, `rnatchld` has a loading of 0.537 on the first factor and this is considered satisfactory. However, the uniqueness for this item is 0.670. In other words, the set of factors does not explain about two-thirds of the variance in `rnatchld`. This calls to question the use of PCF analysis and suggests that another type of factor analysis would be more appropriate. Although we note this problem with PCF, we will still illustrate PCF because of its wide use in scale construction. You will need to explore the *Stata Multivariate Statistics Reference Manual* to learn about these more advanced options.

Generally, we should consider any factor that has an eigenvalue of more than 1.0. A visual way to examine the eigenvalues is with a scree plot. This is a postestimation command that we run just after doing a factor analysis. Select Statistics ▷ Multivariate analysis ▷ Factor and principal component analysis ▷ Postestimation ▷ Scree plot of eigenvalues. This dialog box gives us a variety of options, but it takes less work to enter the command directly than it does to find the dialog box. The command is `screeplot`, and it produces the graph in figure 12.1.

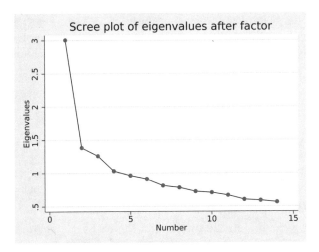

Figure 12.1. Scree plot: National priorities

This scree plot starts leveling off (going across more quickly than it is going down) with the fourth factor. This would suggest that we need three factors, and we could drop the rest of them. Deciding on the number of factors when doing a PCF analysis is not an easy task. We had four factors that had an eigenvalue of more than 1, although the fourth factor was just barely over 1. The scree plot suggests that we might just focus on the first three factors, and the scree plot makes it clear that the first factor is dominant because there is such a big drop-off in the size of the eigenvalue between the first and second factors.

When there is more than one factor, it is usually useful to rotate the initial solution to see if a different solution is easier to interpret. We have two ways of doing this. One is an orthogonal rotation where we force the factors to be uncorrelated with each other. The other is an oblique rotation in which we allow the factors to be correlated. There are multiple options for both types of rotation (15 for orthogonal rotation and 8 more for oblique rotation). I will illustrate just one approach for each type.

12.6.1 Orthogonal rotation: Varimax

Stata has kept the factor analysis solution in memory, so to do an orthogonal rotation, all we need to do is enter the command `rotate` (this is the default rotation). If you forget this command, you can find it under the Statistics ▷ Multivariate analysis ▷ Factor and principal component analysis ▷ Postestimation ▷ Rotate loadings menu. Here is what we obtain:

```
. rotate
Factor analysis/correlation                        Number of obs   =     1,082
    Method: principal-component factors            Retained factors =        4
    Rotation: orthogonal varimax (Kaiser off)      Number of params =       50
```

Factor	Variance	Difference	Proportion	Cumulative
Factor1	1.96564	0.29211	0.1404	0.1404
Factor2	1.67353	0.04093	0.1195	0.2599
Factor3	1.63260	0.22876	0.1166	0.3766
Factor4	1.40384	.	0.1003	0.4768

```
    LR test: independent vs. saturated:  chi2(91) = 1701.47 Prob>chi2 = 0.0000
Rotated factor loadings (pattern matrix) and unique variances
```

Variable	Factor1	Factor2	Factor3	Factor4	Uniqueness
rnatspac	-0.1295	-0.0143	-0.1449	0.7360	0.4204
rnatenvir	0.4623	0.3085	0.0890	0.2471	0.6221
rnatheal	0.6328	0.1374	0.2186	0.0975	0.5235
rnatcity	0.0262	0.4831	0.5052	0.0839	0.5036
rnatcrime	0.0941	-0.0276	0.8066	-0.0599	0.3361
rnatdrug	0.2187	0.0910	0.6618	0.0296	0.5051
rnateduc	0.6899	0.1329	0.0932	0.0808	0.4912
rnatrace	0.2352	0.6335	0.2259	0.0389	0.4909
rnatarms	0.1103	-0.6491	0.1967	0.1763	0.4968
rnatfare	0.2255	0.5642	0.0480	0.1061	0.6172
rnatroad	0.0039	-0.1708	0.2889	0.4252	0.7065
rnatsoc	0.6718	-0.1136	-0.0967	-0.2007	0.4862
rnatchld	0.4475	0.3393	0.1075	0.0559	0.6699
rnatsci	0.1777	0.0334	0.0832	0.7110	0.4549

```
Factor rotation matrix
```

	Factor1	Factor2	Factor3	Factor4
Factor1	0.6858	0.4868	0.5116	0.1758
Factor2	0.0311	-0.4717	0.1951	0.8594
Factor3	0.1676	-0.6530	0.5615	-0.4798
Factor4	0.7075	-0.3379	-0.6204	-0.0190

The second table shows the factor loadings. With a varimax rotation, we can think of the loadings as being the estimated correlation between each item and each factor. For example, the last item, rnatsci has a high correlation with the fourth factor, 0.711. We hope each item has a loading of 0.40 or higher on one factor and a smaller loading on the other factors. We use the items that have relatively large loadings on each factor to decide on what the factor is to be called. Let's work backward, starting with the fourth and weakest factor. It has just two items with high loadings, rnatspac and rnatsci. This factor might be labeled liberal spending support for science as a national priority. Factor3 has three items with loadings higher than 0.4, namely, rnatcity, rnatcrime, and rnatdrug. This might be called a priority on urban problems, although we need to acknowledge that crime and drugs are problems outside of urban places as well. We could call this liberal spending support for urban problems.

`Factor2` has four items with loadings higher than 0.4. Support for minorities (`rnatrace`) and support for welfare programs (`rnatfare`) both have strong positive loadings. By contrast, support for the military (`rnatarms`) has just as strong a loading, but it is negative. This factor seems to be pitting together support for the disadvantaged against support for the military. This might make sense considering the disproportional burden minorities pay for military engagements and how military expenses can drain money from social welfare. The problem with this factor and the third factor is that `rnatcity` loads strongly on both factors. It is compounded. Although Stata distinguishes between these two factors, the public sees both of these as special concerns in urban areas. We could call this factor liberal spending support for the disadvantaged.

`Factor1` is the strongest, and it has five items with loadings greater than 0.4. These involve the environment, health, education, Social Security, and child care. One might think of this as representing a liberal–conservative factor, where liberals want to put a higher spending priority on each of these than do conservatives.

12.6.2   Oblique rotation: Promax

Sometimes it is unreasonable to think that the factors are orthogonal. We could argue that the first factor, which we have labeled liberalism, would be correlated with the second factor, which we have labeled support for the disadvantaged. It is possible through an option for the `rotate` command to do an oblique rotation in which we allow the factors to be correlated. Here we illustrate one of the seven options for oblique rotation. We will do a promax rotation by using the command `rotate, promax`. When we allow the factors to be correlated, it is useful to see how correlated they are. When we run any command in Stata, the program saves some statistics that it does not report in the Results window. These saved statistics can be obtained with the `estat` command. To obtain the correlations between the common factors in an oblique rotation, the command is `estat common`. Here are the results of running these two commands in sequence:

```
. rotate, promax
Factor analysis/correlation                   Number of obs    =      1,082
    Method: principal-component factors        Retained factors =          4
    Rotation: oblique promax (Kaiser off)      Number of params =         50
```

Factor	Variance	Proportion	Rotated factors are correlated
Factor1	2.46691	0.1762	
Factor2	1.99629	0.1426	
Factor3	1.97508	0.1411	
Factor4	1.53936	0.1100	

```
LR test: independent vs. saturated:  chi2(91) = 1701.47 Prob>chi2 = 0.0000
```

Rotated factor loadings (pattern matrix) and unique variances

Variable	Factor1	Factor2	Factor3	Factor4	Uniqueness
rnatspac	-0.1749	-0.0294	-0.2002	0.7787	0.4204
rnatenvir	0.4216	0.2378	-0.0437	0.2156	0.6221
rnatheal	0.6293	0.0361	0.0830	0.0460	0.5235
rnatcity	-0.1558	0.4893	0.5021	0.0281	0.5036
rnatcrime	-0.0338	-0.0575	0.8526	-0.1366	0.3361
rnatdrug	0.1026	0.0462	0.6555	-0.0410	0.5051
rnateduc	0.7179	0.0258	-0.0616	0.0370	0.4912
rnatrace	0.1043	0.6229	0.1546	-0.0083	0.4909
rnatarms	0.1864	-0.7131	0.2047	0.1762	0.4968
rnatfare	0.1329	0.5519	-0.0371	0.0790	0.6172
rnatroad	-0.0535	-0.2080	0.2760	0.4176	0.7065
rnatsoc	0.7637	-0.2163	-0.0129	-0.2463	0.4862
rnatchld	0.4121	0.2818	-0.0035	0.0167	0.6699
rnatsci	0.1175	-0.0307	-0.0209	0.7162	0.4549

Factor rotation matrix

	Factor1	Factor2	Factor3	Factor4
Factor1	0.8518	0.6478	0.6627	0.3341
Factor2	-0.0024	-0.4155	0.2418	0.8357
Factor3	0.1455	-0.5818	0.5015	-0.4341
Factor4	0.5032	-0.2632	-0.5008	-0.0396

. estat common

Correlation matrix of the promax(3) rotated common factors

Factors	Factor1	Factor2	Factor3	Factor4
Factor1	1			
Factor2	.3358	1		
Factor3	.3849	.1688	1	
Factor4	.1995	.1322	.2256	1

We can see that the factors are all positively correlated. The factor loadings can no longer be interpreted as simple correlations like before, but they tend to be "cleaner" than with the oblique rotation. By this I mean that the big loadings tend to be even bigger, and the small loadings tend to be even smaller. This sometimes simplifies the interpretation.

12.7   But we wanted one scale, not four scales

The rotations helped us gain insight into how people cluster different items and helped us recognize that there are some differences between people who would support each of these dimensions. However, we are trying to develop one scale, and we need to select items that represent one dimension. For this, we go back to our original PCF analysis results.

We clearly had one dominant factor as the first principal component, and most of the items loaded strongly on that first component. Indeed, 10 of the 14 items had loadings over 0.4. The items that failed to meet this standard are support for the space program, support for spending on science, support for roads, and support for the military. Space and science are special areas, as are roads and the military. Both liberals and conservatives may support or not support more spending for roads, space, and science. Some liberals may not support spending on the military in general, but many liberals and conservatives support spending to support the soldiers. By contrast, the 10 items with strong loadings on the first factor clearly differentiate liberals and conservatives. We could think of the 10 items as representing a general liberal-to-conservative dimension for federal spending policies.

We need to rerun our PCF analysis, including just the 10 items. Try this as an exercise. When we do this, the eigenvalue for the first factor is 2.941, explaining almost 30% of the variance in the set of 10 items. There are a second and third factor, but the eigenvalue for each of them is just barely over 1. All the items load over 0.4 on the first factor.

Not all researchers use factor analysis when they are constructing a scale. However, if you use this approach and obtain a set of 10 items that have loadings over 0.4 on a first factor, and the first factor has a much larger eigenvalue than the other factors, your results of doing a reliability analysis are almost certainly going to be positive. For these 10 items, the alpha is 0.72 and dropping any of the items would reduce alpha.

12.7.1 Scoring our variable

We have used factor analysis to identify a set of items that load highly on one dimension. We can use the 10 items to construct our scale in one of two ways. One of these is exactly what we did before by using the `egen` command to generate the row mean of the 10 items. We could do that and then do an alpha for the 10 items to estimate the reliability of our scale.

There is a more complex alternative, which is to estimate what is called a factor score. This is a standardized value that has a mean of 0 and a standard deviation of 1. If our variable is normally distributed, about two-thirds of the observations will have a score between −1.0 and +1.0, and about 95% of the observations will have a score between −2.0 and +2.0.

An advantage of a factor score over a mean or total score is that the factor score weights each of the items differently, based on how central it is to the first factor. For example, education has a loading of 0.6, and health has a loading of 0.63. These should be weighted more in the factor score than Social Security, which has a loading of 0.43. By contrast, when we generate a mean or total for the set of items, each item counts as if it were equally central to the concept.

It is easy to estimate a factor score. Using the default options for the command just after doing the PCF analysis, we enter the command `predict libfscore, norotate`, where `libfscore` is the name we are giving the factor score.

Which method is better? There is some controversy about how to best estimate a factor score, so I have simply used the default option, which is a regression-based approach. Although there is some disagreement about the best method, there is rarely a substantive difference in the result.

We should not forget that there is an advantage of a factor score over a mean or total score in that the factor score weights less-central items less and more-central items more, which makes sense. However, this distinction rarely makes a lot of practical difference. The factor score may make a difference if there are some items with very large loadings, say, 0.9, and others with very small loadings, say, 0.2. But we would probably drop the weakest items. When the loadings do not vary a great deal, computing a factor score or a mean/total score will produce comparable results. Here are the commands you would use to compute a factor score and a mean score:

```
. factor rnatenvir rnatheal rnatcity rnatcrime rnatdrug rnateduc rnatrace
> rnatfare rnatsoc rnatchld, pcf

. predict libfscore, norotate

. egen libmean = rowmean(rnatenvir rnatheal rnatcity rnatcrime rnatdrug
> rnateduc rnatrace rnatfare rnatsoc rnatchld)
```

12.8 Summary

This chapter introduced some of the classical procedures for developing a scale. This is an area of social research that often is given too little attention. Without measures that are both reliable and valid, it is impossible for social science to develop. The intent of this chapter was to introduce the most basic ideas for developing a scale and how to execute basic Stata commands that help demonstrate the reliability and validity of a scale. We covered

- How to use the **egen** command to generate a scale score.

- Test–retest reliability.

- How to estimate alpha and how to use it to evaluate the internal consistency standard for a reliable scale. We saw that alpha depends on the average correlation between the items and the number of items in the scale; too few items makes it hard to obtain an adequate alpha, and too many items makes a questionnaire needlessly long. We also covered the Kuder–Richardson reliability coefficient for dichotomous items.

- Kappa as a measure of interrater reliability. We briefly discussed weighted kappa and how kappa can be used when there are three raters.

- Various types of validity, including expert judges, face validity, criterion-related validity, predictive validity, and construct validity.

- Principal factor (PF) analysis and principal-component factor (PCF) analysis, with an example of how to use PCF analysis.

- Key terminology for understanding factor analysis, along with orthogonal and oblique rotations of the PCF analysis solution.

- How to construct a factor score and how this compares with generating a mean score.

12.9 Exercises

1. Use `gss2002_and_2006_chapter12.dta`. Compute a split-half correlation for the 10 items that load most strongly on the first factor in the PCF analysis (section 12.6). Correlate the mean of the first five items and the mean of the second five items. Why does this correlation underestimate the reliability of the 10-item scale?

2. Using the data from above, compute the alpha reliability for this scale. Interpret alpha to decide if this scale is adequate. Interpret the item-test correlations, item-rest correlations, and what happens to alpha if any of the items is dropped. Why is alpha a better measure of reliability for this 10-item scale than the split-half correlation?

3. Using the data from above, do an alpha analysis including all 14 items. Use the values of alpha to drop the worst item and repeat alpha for the remaining 13 items. Repeat this process, dropping an item each time, until there is no item to drop that would increase alpha. Compare this set of items with what the factor analysis indicated was the best set of items.

4. Use `gss2002_and_2006_chapter12.dta`. Do a PCF analysis (section 12.6) of the 10 items that load on the first factor for the spending items. Interpret the results.

5. Using the results from exercise 4, create the factor score for the 10 items and use `egen` to create a mean score for the 10 items. Compare the means and standard deviations of both scores, and explain the differences. What is the correlation between the two scale scores? What does it mean that it is so high? When would it not be so high?

6. Use `gss2002_and_2006_chapter12.dta`. Do a PCF analysis of the 14 items, and construct a factor score. Do a PCF analysis for the 10 items as done above, and construct a factor score. Correlate these two scores, and explain why they are so highly correlated even though they are based on different items.

13 Structural equation modeling and generalized structural equation modeling

The `sem` (structural equation model) and `gsem` (generalized structural equation model) commands extend everything we have covered with regression and factor analysis. These commands are more fully discussed in terms of structural equation modeling (SEM) for continuous outcome variables and growth curve analysis in Acock (2013). In this chapter, we will show how to use the `sem` and `gsem` commands to fit basic regression models and logistic regression models, and we will extend this to an introduction to path analysis including mediation models with direct and indirect effects. We will not cover latent variables, confirmatory factor analysis, or growth curves; see Acock (2013) for more information on these topics.

13.1 Linear regression using sem

The application of `sem` to models that we have been fitting using the `regress` command offers two distinct advantages:

1. Stata's SEM Builder provides a production-quality graphic interface that provides an enhanced way to report your regression results using a figure rather than a table. Many readers find that a figure is a great way to understand what is happening in a regression model and a valuable tool for remembering their work.

2. In the presence of missing data when the missing at random (MAR) assumption and the assumption of multivariate normality are both reasonable, the `sem` command provides a much simpler way of handling missing values than the use of multiple imputation that we will cover in chapter 14. Sometimes called full-information maximum likelihood (FIML), this method uses all available data and is equivalent to multiple imputation when the number of imputed datasets approaches infinity (Graham et al. 2007). Where the `regress` command's default of listwise deletion assumes missing completely at random (MCAR), the FIML approach assumes only MAR.

To show how to use `sem` to represent a basic regression model, we will use data from the Flourishing Families Study (Day and Acock 2013). I have modified the data to simplify the example so generalizations of our findings are problematic; thus our results will not replicate the results obtained by analyzing the unmodified Flourishing Families Study Data. To be in the Flourishing Families Study, the women had to have a child who was approaching adolescence, so this does not represent a nationally representative sample of adult women. We are predicting a mother's body mass index (BMI). Many variables are related to BMI among women. For this example, we have selected five predictors (independent variables). These include the mother's age, the number of children in the household, the natural log of the family income, the mother's education, and how often the family members eat at fast food restaurants. We hypothesize that the BMI is positively associated with age, the number of children, and how often the family eats at fast food restaurants. Conversely, we hypothesize that BMI is negatively associated with the log of household income and the mother's education. If we wanted to use the `regress` command, we would type

```
. use http://www.stata-press.com/data/agis6r/flourishing_bmi.dta
. regress bmi age children income educ quickfood, beta
```

Source	SS	df	MS		
Model	2921.16092	5	584.232183		
Residual	15264.4284	442	34.5349059		
Total	18185.5893	447	40.683645		

	Number of obs	=	448
	F(5, 442)	=	16.92
	Prob > F	=	0.0000
	R-squared	=	0.1606
	Adj R-squared	=	0.1511
	Root MSE	=	5.8766

bmi	Coefficient	Std. err.	t	P>|t|	Beta
age	.0849882	.0471673	1.80	0.072	.085525
children	.6167338	.2881417	2.14	0.033	.0983799
incomeln	-1.750445	.4360436	-4.01	0.000	-.2080029
educ	-.6900809	.2208598	-3.12	0.002	-.1627779
quickfood	.9260216	.2496412	3.71	0.000	.1716324
_cons	37.48497	3.890134	9.64	0.000	.

We obtain an $R^2 = 0.161$, $F(5, 442) = 16.92$, and $p < 0.001$. The p-values are for a two-tailed test. Because our hypotheses are all one-tailed tests and because the sign of the estimated coefficient is in the same direction as our hypotheses, we cut the p-values in half. Thus all the variables have a $p < 0.05$ using a one-tailed test. When using the more conservative two-tailed test, all the variables except for age have a $p < 0.05$, and age is marginally significant, $p < 0.10$. The standardized beta's (β's) are fairly small, but all of them are in the predicted direction.

13.1.1 Using the sem command directly

There are two ways of fitting an SEM model. First, you can run the sem command. Second, Stata has a graphic interface where you can draw the model, and Stata interprets the command based on your drawing to create the command for you. We will first introduce the sem command itself in this section, because it is extremely straightforward in the case of fitting a multiple regression model. After writing the command sem, we enter the dependent variable followed by an arrow and dash pointing toward the dependent variable and then ending with a listing of the independent variables. To fit the regression model in the previous section, we would type

```
sem bmi <- age children incomeln educ quickfood
```

This would give us the unstandardized solution. This command uses maximum likelihood estimation rather than the ordinary least-squares (OLS) estimation used by the regress command. If we wanted a standardized solution with beta weights instead of unstandardized regression coefficients, we would specify the option standardized. Here are the results for a standardized solution:

```
. sem bmi <- age children incomeln educ quickfood, standardized
(32 observations with missing values excluded)
```

Endogenous variables
  Observed: bmi

Exogenous variables
  Observed: age children incomeln educ quickfood

Fitting target model:
Iteration 0:   log likelihood = -5442.1579
Iteration 1:   log likelihood = -5442.1579

Structural equation model   Number of obs = 448
Estimation method: ml

Log likelihood = -5442.1579

Standardized	Coefficient	OIM std. err.	z	P>|z|	[95% conf. interval]	
Structural						
bmi						
age	.085525	.0469395	1.82	0.068	-.0064747	.1775247
children	.0983799	.045372	2.17	0.030	.0094524	.1873074
incomeln	-.2080029	.0503358	-4.13	0.000	-.3066593	-.1093464
educ	-.1627779	.0510614	-3.19	0.001	-.2628563	-.0626995
quickfood	.1716324	.0450981	3.81	0.000	.0832418	.260023
_cons	5.883455	.606841	9.70	0.000	4.694069	7.072842
var(e.bmi)	.8393695	.0304844			.7816981	.9012957

LR test of model vs. saturated: chi2(0) = 0.00   Prob > chi2 = .

Because we specified the standardized option, these coefficients are the standardized beta weights comparable with those we obtained for the regression command and have the same interpretation. The **regress** command tests whether the unstandardized coefficients are different from zero. The **sem** command provides a test for the unstandardized coefficients when we ask for an unstandardized solution and for the standardized coefficients, betas, when we ask for a standardized solution. For technical reasons, the tests for standardized and unstandardized coefficients may differ slightly. In this solution, the $\beta = 0.17$ for **quickfood**. The **sem** command relies on a z test, and the **regress** command relies on a t test. Some other SEM software reports χ^2 values rather than z values for each coefficient. The χ^2 value will be the squared z value, $\chi^2 = z^2$. A nice characteristic of the z value is its sign matches the direction of the coefficient. Although there are 480 observations in our sample, the $N = 448$ because some observations have missing values. The default for **sem** is listwise deletion, as was the case for **regress**.

13.1.2 SEM and working with missing values

The **sem** command has multiple estimation approaches. One of these uses a variation of maximum likelihood estimation that includes observations with missing values. This is implemented by specifying the option **method(mlmv)** (maximum likelihood with missing values) when running a **sem** command. Whenever you have missing values on some or all your variables, the **sem** command can use all the available data as long as certain assumptions are reasonable. This is an effective and relatively simple way of working with missing values and taking advantage of all the data you do have. Chapter 14 presents a different approach to working with missing values based on multiple imputation. That chapter discusses missing values in more detail, is extremely flexible, and offers an approach that can be applied to many Stata estimation commands.

Both maximum likelihood and maximum likelihood with missing-values estimation assume multivariate normality. Estimation is less robust to the assumption of multivariate normality when using the `method(mlmv)` option than when using maximum likelihood estimation with listwise deletion of observations with missing values. Because some of the five variables in our model are not normally distributed, the `method(mlmv)` option needs to be used with caution. The estimation performed when we use the `method(mlmv)` option also assumes that the missing values are MAR. By contrast, when listwise deletion is used we are assuming that missing values are MCAR, and this is a much more restrictive assumption.

It is easy to confuse MAR and MCAR, but MAR is actually a much more realistic assumption. MCAR means exactly what it sounds like, the missing values are MCAR and unrelated to any observed or unobserved variable. This assumption is hard to justify.[1] For example, people who are very low on `educ` may skip items on other variables, or very old people may be more likely to skip some items. Missing values will almost surely be correlated with some variables, making the MCAR assumption unreasonable; therefore, parameters such as beta coefficients from solutions based on listwise deletion will be biased.

Using the `method(mlmv)` option, we can account for some of the missing values because of their relationship to other variables that are already in our model. For example, if we have education in the model, then it may account for some missing values on other variables in the model, such as income. Similarly, if we have age in the model, this may account for the fact that very old people tend to have more missing values. Fortunately, both age and education are in our model, but there could be other variables such as gender that account for missing values even though they are not in our model. We will discuss such auxiliary variables in the next section. MAR assumes that missing values are fully accounted for by other variables. Even when this assumption is a stretch, it is less of a stretch than the MCAR assumption required by listwise deletion.

We fit our multiple regression model to take into account the missing values by adding the option `method(mlmv)`. For a standardized solution, we specify two options, `method(mlmv)` and `standardized`.

---

1. The MCAR assumption is appropriate in some cases such as when you have a missing by design study. For example, if you have a 50-item measure of a psychological construct and a sample of fourth graders, there is a problem. The students may not be able to concentrate through so many items. By design, each student could receive a random sample of 10 items. There would be a massive number of missing values, 80% for each student. However, the missing values would be MCAR.

```
. sem bmi <- age children incomeln educ quickfood, method(mlmv) standardized
note: Missing values found in observed exogenous variables. Using the
      noxconditional behavior. Specify the forcexconditional option to override
      this behavior.
Endogenous variables
  Observed: bmi

Exogenous variables
  Observed: age children incomeln educ quickfood

Fitting saturated model:
Iteration 0:   log likelihood = -5755.9852
Iteration 1:   log likelihood = -5755.3782
Iteration 2:   log likelihood = -5755.3751
Iteration 3:   log likelihood = -5755.3751

Fitting baseline model:
Iteration 0:   log likelihood = -5793.2531
Iteration 1:   log likelihood = -5793.2466
Iteration 2:   log likelihood = -5793.2466

Fitting target model:
Iteration 0:   log likelihood = -5755.3751
Iteration 1:   log likelihood = -5755.3751

Structural equation model                      Number of obs = 480
Estimation method: mlmv

Log likelihood = -5755.3751
```

Standardized	Coefficient	OIM std. err.	z	P>|z|	[95% conf. interval]	
Structural						
bmi						
age	.1025498	.0464111	2.21	0.027	.0115857	.1935139
children	.0761626	.0449013	1.70	0.090	-.0118424	.1641676
incomeln	-.2031064	.0509003	-3.99	0.000	-.3028691	-.1033437
educ	-.174441	.0507598	-3.44	0.001	-.2739285	-.0749536
quickfood	.1560023	.0456212	3.42	0.001	.0665864	.2454182
_cons	5.819998	.6113505	9.52	0.000	4.621773	7.018223
mean(age)	6.689349	.2206699	30.31	0.000	6.256844	7.121854
mean(children)	2.316993	.0876098	26.45	0.000	2.145281	2.488706
mean(incomeln)	11.07493	.3621459	30.58	0.000	10.36514	11.78472
mean(educ)	2.944047	.1058155	27.82	0.000	2.736653	3.151442
mean(quickfood)	1.727495	.0722062	23.92	0.000	1.585973	1.869016
var(e.bmi)	.8477139	.0308644			.7893288	.9104177
var(age)	1	.			.	.
var(children)	1	.			.	.
var(incomeln)	1	.			.	.
var(educ)	1	.			.	.
var(quickfood)	1	.			.	.
cov(age, children)	-.2302454	.0432238	-5.33	0.000	-.3149625	-.1455282
cov(age, incomeln)	.2463728	.043313	5.69	0.000	.161481	.3312647
cov(age,educ)	.3231003	.0408804	7.90	0.000	.2429762	.4032243
cov(age, quickfood)	-.1298331	.0451698	-2.87	0.004	-.2183644	-.0413019
cov(children,						

incomeln)	.0046738	.0460874	0.10	0.919	-.0856559	.0950035
cov(children, educ)	-.1980476	.043919	-4.51	0.000	-.2841273	-.1119679
cov(children, quickfood)	-.0633405	.0454746	-1.39	0.164	-.1524691	.025788
cov(incomeln, educ)	.4756463	.0356959	13.32	0.000	.4056837	.5456089
cov(incomeln, quickfood)	-.3270838	.0410795	-7.96	0.000	-.4075981	-.2465695
cov(educ, quickfood)	-.2109199	.0438928	-4.81	0.000	-.2969482	-.1248916

```
LR test of model vs. saturated: chi2(0) = 0.00          Prob > chi2 = .
```

Because we are using maximum likelihood assuming missing-values (MLMV) estimation instead of the OLS estimation used with the **regress** command, we see a series of iterations. Notice that the number of observations is now 480 instead of the 448 we had with the **regress** command or as the default with the **sem** command. Again, this is because **regress** and **sem** without **method(mlmv)** throw out what we do know about an observation whenever we do not know everything about that observation.

The table in the output displays our solution with the coefficients being beta weights. Because this is a standardized solution, the values labeled covariances are actually the corresponding correlations. For example, **cov(age,children)** is the correlation between **age** and number of children (-0.230).

There is one important regression result that is missing, namely, the R^2. To obtain this, we need to run a second command immediately after the **sem** command. This additional command gives us extended statistics for the equation goodness of fit and hence is called **estat eqgof**.

```
. estat eqgof
Equation-level goodness of fit
```

Dependent variables	Fitted	Variance Predicted	Residual	R-squared	mc	mc2
Observed bmi	40.71618	6.200509	34.51568	.1522861	.3902385	.1522861
Overall				.1522861		

```
mc  = Correlation between dependent variable and its prediction.
mc2 = mc^2 is the Bentler-Raykov squared multiple correlation coefficient.
```

The overall $R^2 = 0.152$ is what we want.

How do the SEM results compare with the OLS regression results? Here is a comparison of the two sets of results from **sem** and the results from the **regress** command:

Table 13.1. Comparison of two sets of results from **sem** and the results from **regress**

Predictor	OLS regression solution			SEM solution without MLMV			SEM solution with MLMV		
	Beta	t-value	p-value	Beta	z-value	p-value	Beta	z-value	p-value
Age	0.086	1.80	0.072	0.086	1.82	0.068	0.103	2.21	0.027
Number of children	0.098	2.14	0.033	0.098	2.17	0.030	0.076	1.70	0.090
Log income	−0.208	−4.01	0.000	−0.208	−4.13	0.000	−0.203	−3.99	0.000
Education	−0.163	−3.12	0.002	−0.163	−3.19	0.001	−0.174	−3.44	0.001
Quick food	0.172	3.71	0.000	0.172	3.81	0.000	0.156	3.42	0.001
Sample size	448			448			480		
R^2	0.161			0.161			0.152		

The OLS regression solution and the SEM solution without MLMV, which uses listwise deletion, are producing the same standardized parameter estimates and R^2's. As noted, the z values are slightly larger than the t-values, and the p-values are slightly smaller. The z tests for the SEM solution are directly testing the standardized solution. The **regress** solution's t tests are testing the significance of the unstandardized B coefficients and do not directly test the significance of the Betas. The **regress** command does not provide such a direct test for the significance of Betas.

What happens with the SEM solution with MLMV estimation? Notice that the R^2 using **sem** with **method(mlmv)** is actually slightly smaller. Using a two-tailed test, we find that the effect of the number of children is no longer significant for this **sem** estimation but that age is now significant. Using all the available information in the SEM solution with MLMV is not cheating if the assumptions are met. The MAR assumption for the SEM solution is more realistic than the MCAR assumption required for listwise deletion to be unbiased. Using **sem** doesn't always make everything more significant simply because the N is larger and it doesn't make all the effects greater. If the assumptions are appropriate, using the SEM result will give an unbiased result. Where the results differ, the `sem` with MLMV result should be preferred if its assumptions are met.

13.1.3 Exploring missing values and auxiliary variables

Although we do not have an explicit test for the MAR assumption, we can add a few auxiliary variables to help us justify this assumption. One type of auxiliary variable is a variable that is correlated with missing values. We can generate a series of indicator variables and see what possible auxiliary variables are correlated with these indicators. Another type of auxiliary variable that can be helpful is any variable that is predictive of the variables in our model even though it is not part of the model itself. Some auxiliary variables will fit both descriptions. We do not have gender in our model, but it is likely a good candidate to be an auxiliary variable. First, gender is likely correlated with missing values because males skip more items than females on most surveys. Thus, including gender as an auxiliary variable will help justify the MAR assumption. Gender may also be a useful auxiliary variable because, although it is not part of our model, it is likely related to some of the variables in our model. For example, gender is likely correlated with income and will help explain the income for those who skipped that item.

It is important to know which variables have missing values and how many missing values occur for each variable. Stata has a command, `misstable summarize`, that is designed to give you this information. To run this command, we simply list all the variables in our model, including the dependent variable. The `method(mlmv)` method considers missing values on all variables in the model, and this includes the dependent variable.

```
. misstable summarize bmi age children incomeln educ quickfood, generate(miss_)
```

					Obs<.	
Variable	Obs=.	Obs>.	Obs<.	Unique values	Min	Max
bmi	23		457	296	15.41407	59.72754
incomeln	5		475	191	5.298317	11.15625
educ	1		479	7	1	7
quickfood	3		477	24	.5	11.5

Remember that Stata treats a missing value as a very large number that is greater than any number in your dataset, so observations who score `<.` have an observed score. This shows that the major culprit in this particular dataset is not income but the BMI measure. A person's BMI was calculated for each person based on their reported height and weight. It appears that 23 people refused to give the needed information for this calculation. Still, there is a substantial range given that the BMI values varied from 15.41 to 59.73 (a value greater than 30.0 is considered obese).

So far, we have used only variables that are already in our model to help justify the MAR assumption. However, it is useful to find auxiliary variables that may help us justify the MAR assumption, although the auxiliary variables are not in the model. To find potential auxiliary variables that help justify the MAR assumption, we need to generate an indicator variable for each variable in our model. This indicator variable will be coded 1 if the model variable has a missing value. The four variables in our model that have missing values are `bmi`, `incomeln`, `educ`, and `quickfood`. Using the option `generate(miss_)` in the command above, we generated an indicator variable for each of these named `miss_bmi`, `miss_incomeln`, `miss_educ`, and `miss_quickfood`. The `miss_` is added as a prefix.

There is a quick way to evaluate this if we have a large dataset with several potential auxiliary variables that might be correlated with missingness. We would simply run the `pwcorr` command with the `sig` option to obtain the correlation between the potential auxiliary variables, the variables in our model, and the missing-values indicator variables (`miss_bmi`, `miss_incomeln`, `miss_educ`, and `miss_quickfood`). Here we would include a few possible auxiliary variables that might be related to missing values. This particular dataset does not include auxiliary variables, but the command would be as follows:

```
pwcorr miss_bmi miss_incomeln miss_educ miss_quickfood age children   ///
    incomeln educ quickfood list of auxiliary variables, sig
```

Any potential auxiliary variables in the resulting correlation matrix that have a significant correlation with the missing-value indicators (`miss_bmi` to `miss_quickfood`) could be used as auxiliary variables because they at least partially explain missingness. Any potential auxiliary variables that are significantly correlated with the variables in our model (`age children incomeln educ quickfood`) could be included in the `sem` command. Incorporating a few of the most highly correlated auxiliary variables, say, four or five auxiliary variables in the `sem` command, can make the MAR assumption much more realistic.

One problem with adding auxiliary variables is to avoid potential auxiliary variables that have substantial missing values themselves. This will add only additional uncertainty to your model.

There are three rules to follow when using the maximum likelihood with missing-values estimation.

1. Generate an indicator variable for each variable in your model to reflect whether an observation has a missing value.

2. Correlate potential auxiliary variables to see whether they predict missing-value indicator variables.

3. Include additional auxiliary variables that are substantially correlated with a person's score on a variable that has missing values.

13.1.4 Getting auxiliary variables into your SEM command

Although we have not identified potential auxiliary variables because of the limited number of variables in this subset of the dataset, we will assume that we found three potential auxiliary variables: gender, minority, and alienation. Let's assume that men, people of minority status, and people who were more alienated had more missing values on one or more of the variables in our model. Because we do not actually have these variables in the subset of the dataset we are using, we cannot fit the model. However, here is how to proceed when you have the auxiliary variables in your data. Incorporating them into our analysis is a bit tricky. We need to allow the auxiliary variables to be correlated with all of our original variables. We can allow them to be correlated with our original variables by regressing the auxiliary variables on the original dependent and independent variables. We can also allow for correlation among the auxiliary variables by allowing their errors to covary. Richard Williams shared a personal communication with Paul Allison that suggested what is likely the best way to do this. Here is the command:

```
sem (bmi <- age children incomeln educ quickfood)         ///
    (gender minority alienation <- bmi age children incomeln  ///
       educ quickfood),                                    ///
    covariance(e.gender*e.minority e.gender*e.alienation   ///
       e.minority*e.alienation)                            ///
    method(mlmv) standardized
```

We are interested only in reporting the results for the first line in this command, that is, the effect of age, children, incomeln, educ, and quickfood on a person's bmi. However, including the additional lines in the command ensures we are using all the available information in the full covariance that includes both the model variables and the auxiliary variables. The line beginning with covariance() provides for the covariance of the residual for gender (e.gender) with the residual for minority. It also allows for covariance between the residuals of gender and alienation and the residuals of minority and alienation. Specifying all these covariances could become lengthy if a large number of auxiliary variables were included. It is recommended to include a limited number of auxiliary variables, say, four to five.

13.2 A quick way to draw a regression model

Now that we have fit an SEM model by using the sem command, we will try an example using the graphic interface called the SEM Builder. This works for any estimation method, but we will illustrate it using the method(ml) option (the default), which uses listwise deletion. Because we are going to use the maximum-likelihood listwise deletion estimator, the results will be closer to those results of the regress command.

Typing the command `sembuilder` in the Command window will open the graphic interface for building `sem` and `gsem` models. Figure 13.1 shows the SEM Builder.

Figure 13.1. SEM Builder

The drawing tools appear on the left side of the Builder. Let's start drawing our model.

Select the third tool up from the bottom, ⯮, of the drawing toolbar. This tool is designed explicitly for drawing regression models. With this tool highlighted, click on the right side of the SEM Builder about halfway from the top and bottom. Doing this opens the dialog box shown in figure 13.2.

Figure 13.2. Regression component dialog box

Notice that we typed `bmi` as the dependent variable, entered the independent variables, and selected `Left` for the direction of the independent variables. When entering the independent variables, be sure that you use the exact names. Now, you can click on `OK` and have the regression drawn without showing the correlations of the independent variables; see figure 13.3.

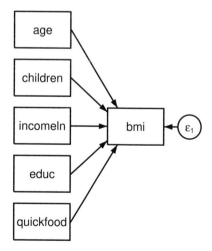

Figure 13.3. Quick drawing of regression model

To fit this model, we select Estimation ▷ Estimate. In the resulting dialog box, check the radio button for *Maximum likelihood* on the Model tab, check the radio button for *Display standardized coefficients and values* on the Reporting tab, and then click on OK. Figure 13.4 shows the results.

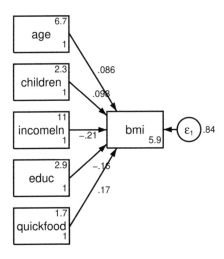

Figure 13.4. Maximum likelihood estimation of model using listwise deletion

Although the diagram does not show the correlations among the independent variables, these correlations are accounted for. If we had selected *Maximum likelihood with missing values*, we would have received a message box saying "Connections implied by your model are not in your diagram: Shall I add them?" We can click on "No" to keep our figure simple. This opens another message box that asks whether we want to see the results anyway, and here we click on "Yes". The correlations will be accounted for but not shown in the figure.

You can continue to make enhancements to the figure using the SEM Builder after you have fit the model.

After you have done this a few times, making a figure like this will be a relatively quick process. Do you see the value of the figure? It is easier for most readers who are not statisticians themselves to interpret a figure than a regression summary table. We see that education and income are both contributing to lower obesity. Obesity is a significant problem for mothers with limited education and low income. There are many reasons for this, such as the elevated cost of a high-quality diet. Eating at fast food restaurants also leads to great risk of obesity. The more often family members eat at fast food restaurants, the higher the mother's estimated BMI. As a writer, I often find it easier to tell my story by using a figure like this than by using a regression summary table.

13.3 The gsem command for logistic regression

To show how to use **gsem** to fit a logistic regression model, we will dichotomize BMI. Rather than trying to predict a BMI for each mother, we can try to predict whether the mother is obese. Here we define obesity as having a BMI score of 30 or more. There are 111 mothers (24.3%) who have a BMI of 30 or more and 346 (75.7%) who have a BMI of less than 30. We can construct a variable called **obese**, which is coded 1 if the mother is obese and 0 if she is not obese.

```
. recode bmi (0/29.999=0) (30/60=1), generate(obese)
```

Alternatively, we could type

```
. generate obese = bmi>=30 & !missing(bmi)
```

13.3.1 Fitting the model using the logit command

In chapter 11, we covered logistic regression, which is appropriate for a binary outcome. We can fit the logistic regression model with the **logistic** command. To help simplify our interpretation, we will obtain odds ratios for a one-unit difference in each variable and for a one standard-deviation difference by using the **listcoef** postestimation command. If you do not already have the community-contributed command **listcoef** installed, type **search spost13** in the Command window. Then click on the **spost13_ado** package and install this package. This command was previously discussed in section 11.5. Here are the results:

```
. logit obese age children incomeln educ quickfood
Iteration 0:   log likelihood = -247.43569
Iteration 1:   log likelihood = -221.17297
Iteration 2:   log likelihood = -220.50785
Iteration 3:   log likelihood = -220.50712
Iteration 4:   log likelihood = -220.50712

Logistic regression                             Number of obs =      448
                                                LR chi2(5)    =    53.86
                                                Prob > chi2   =   0.0000
Log likelihood = -220.50712                     Pseudo R2     =   0.1088
```

obese	Coefficient	Std. err.	z	P>|z|	[95% conf. interval]	
age	.0288883	.0190012	1.52	0.128	-.0083534	.06613
children	.2782205	.1189227	2.34	0.019	.0451362	.5113047
incomeln	-.6097175	.1797268	-3.39	0.001	-.9619756	-.2574595
educ	-.2011274	.0917525	-2.19	0.028	-.3809591	-.0212957
quickfood	.2603238	.108617	2.40	0.017	.0474383	.4732093
_cons	2.301053	1.574824	1.46	0.144	-.7855441	5.387651

```
. listcoef
logit (N=448): Factor change in odds
  Odds of: 1 vs 0
```

	b	z	P>|z|	e^b	e^bStdX	SDofX
age	0.0289	1.520	0.128	1.029	1.204	6.419
children	0.2782	2.340	0.019	1.321	1.327	1.017
incomeln	-0.6097	-3.392	0.001	0.544	0.630	0.758
educ	-0.2011	-2.192	0.028	0.818	0.739	1.505
quickfood	0.2603	2.397	0.017	1.297	1.360	1.182
constant	2.3011	1.461	0.144	.	.	.

Examining the results of the `listcoef` command, we can see that having more children and eating more meals at fast food restaurants is associated with greater odds of obesity. The odds ratio appears in the column labeled `e^b` because the odds ratio is the exponentiated value of the regression coefficient. Having more education and more income is associated with lower odds of obesity. The mother's age and controlling for the other predictors do not have a significant effect. You may want to review chapter 11 to provide a more detailed interpretation.

The `logit` command is a special application of the generalized linear model. We can obtain the same results by using the `glm` command, which requires us to specify the family of our model, `family(binomial)`, and the link function, `link(logit)`. To obtain the odds ratio, we can replay these results by using `glm, eform`. We show this only because the `gsem` command is using the generalized linear model, and we will need to enter both the family and the link function. Here are the `glm` commands and results:

```
. glm obese age children incomeln educ quickfood, family(binomial) link(logit)
Iteration 0:    log likelihood = -220.76408
Iteration 1:    log likelihood = -220.50737
Iteration 2:    log likelihood = -220.50712
Iteration 3:    log likelihood = -220.50712
```

Generalized linear models				Number of obs	=	448
Optimization	: ML			Residual df	=	442
				Scale parameter	=	1
Deviance	=	441.0142362		(1/df) Deviance	=	.9977698
Pearson	=	429.8899828		(1/df) Pearson	=	.9726018
Variance function: V(u) = u*(1-u/1)				[Binomial]		
Link function : g(u) = ln(u/(1-u))				[Logit]		
				AIC	=	1.011192
Log likelihood = -220.5071181				BIC	=	-2257.304

obese	Coefficient	OIM std. err.	z	P>|z|	[95% conf. interval]	
age	.0288883	.0190012	1.52	0.128	-.0083534	.06613
children	.2782205	.1189227	2.34	0.019	.0451362	.5113047
incomeln	-.6097175	.1797268	-3.39	0.001	-.9619756	-.2574595
educ	-.2011274	.0917525	-2.19	0.028	-.3809591	-.0212957
quickfood	.2603238	.108617	2.40	0.017	.0474383	.4732093
_cons	2.301053	1.574824	1.46	0.144	-.7855441	5.387651

```
. glm, eform
```

Generalized linear models				Number of obs	=	448
Optimization	: ML			Residual df	=	442
				Scale parameter	=	1
Deviance	=	441.0142362		(1/df) Deviance	=	.9977698
Pearson	=	429.8899828		(1/df) Pearson	=	.9726018
Variance function: V(u) = u*(1-u/1)				[Binomial]		
Link function : g(u) = ln(u/(1-u))				[Logit]		
				AIC	=	1.011192
Log likelihood = -220.5071181				BIC	=	-2257.304

obese	Odds ratio	OIM std. err.	z	P>|z|	[95% conf. interval]	
age	1.02931	.0195581	1.52	0.128	.9916814	1.068366
children	1.320777	.1570704	2.34	0.019	1.04617	1.667465
incomeln	.5435044	.0976823	-3.39	0.001	.3821372	.7730129
educ	.8178083	.075036	-2.19	0.028	.6832059	.9789295
quickfood	1.29735	.1409143	2.40	0.017	1.048582	1.605137
_cons	9.984695	15.72413	1.46	0.144	.4558716	218.6891

Note: _cons estimates baseline odds.

13.3.2   Fitting the model using the gsem command

We will use the graphic interface to draw the figure in the same way we did before, except this time after typing `sembuilder` we need to click on the top tool, $\overset{G}{\text{SEM}}$, from the drawing toolbar. This is the generalized SEM tool, GSEM, which uses the generalized linear model. This tool allows Stata to work with outcomes that are not continuous. In this example, our outcome is binary but it could be a count of a rare event when using a Poisson model, or it could be a nominal outcome that has more than two possibilities, such as religion (Muslim, Christian, Jewish, Hindu, Other), when using a multinomial model. Although we only illustrate the results of a binary outcome, there are many other options. Table 13.2 shows several of these options. The `gsem` command can also be used with censored, fractional, and survival outcomes.

Table 13.2. Selected families available with `gsem`

Dependent or outcome variable	Traditional command	Selected families	Link function
Continuous	`regress`	`gaussian`	`identity`
Binary	`logit`	`binomial` or `bernoulli`	`logit`
Binary	`probit`	`binomial` or `bernoulli`	`probit`
Multinomial (nominal)	`mlogit`	`multinomial`	`logit`
Ordinal	`ologit`	`ordinal`	`logit`
Ordinal	`oprobit`	`ordinal`	`probit`
Count	`poisson`	`poisson`	`log`
Count	`nbreg`	`nbreg`	`log`
Continuous		`gamma`	`log`

With the GSEM tool selected, click on the add regression tool, ⏵, and then click
on the right side of the SEM Builder about halfway from the top and bottom. In
the dialog box that opens, we again enter **obese** as our *Dependent variable* and **age
children incomeln educ quickfood** as our *Independent variables*. We specify the
family and the link function for our estimation by checking the box for *Make response
generalized* and selecting **Binomial, Logit** in the *Family/Link* box. By doing this, we
are identifying the variable **obese** as being in the **binomial** family and in the **logit**
link. Figure 13.5 is how we represent the model.

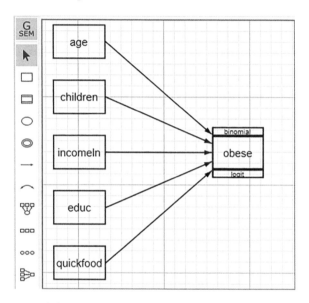

Figure 13.5. A logistic regression model with the outcome, **obese**

With the GSEM logistic regression model, we cannot use the method(mlmv). The default estimator, method(ml), with listwise deletion is our only choice. We can click on Estimation ▷ Estimate and then click on OK. This produces the results in figure 13.6 (I changed the format of the paths to %5.3f):

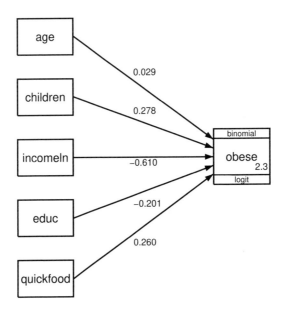

Figure 13.6. Initial results

We now want to add asterisks to indicate the level of significance and odds ratios. To calculate the odds ratios from the gsem results, we need the standard deviations for each independent variable. When running a summarize command to obtain the standard deviations, we need to make sure that we are using listwise deletion. We use the if !missing (not missing) restriction to do this and include all variables in our logistic model. It is necessary to include the comma delimiter between each variable in this list:

```
. summarize age incomeln educ quickfood
> if !missing(age,incomeln,educ,quickfood,obese)
    Variable |        Obs        Mean    Std. dev.         Min         Max
-------------+--------------------------------------------------------------
         age |        448    43.10491    6.418665          27          74
    incomeln |        448    8.403083    .7579329    5.298317    11.15625
        educ |        448    4.430804    1.504546           1           7
   quickfood |        448    2.064174    1.182192          .5        11.5
```

For `age` with a 1-standard-deviation change, 6.419, we obtain the odds ratio for a 1-standard-deviation change by using $e^{(B \times \text{SD})}$ or by typing `display exp(.029*6.419)`. We do this respectively for `age`, `incomeln`, `educ`, and `quickfood` by typing the following `display` commands:

```
. display exp(.029*6.419)
1.2046041

. display exp(.278*1.017)
1.3267416

. display exp(-.610*.758)
.62978298

. display exp(-.201*1.505)
.73896479

. display exp(.260*1.182)
1.359776
```

Thus a 1-standard-deviation difference in `incomeln` is associated with a 47% reduction in the odds of being obese $[(1 - 0.630) \times 100]$.

Note that we did not include `children` in the above calculations. In the case of `children`, a one-unit difference, that is, one additional child, is meaningful and is associated with a 32.1% increase in the odds of obesity $[(1.321 - 1) \times 100]$.

These results differ slightly from those of the `listcoef` command shown in section 13.3.1, which uses more significant digits. We will use the `listcoef` result because of its greater precision.

We can now return to our SEM Builder to insert the odds ratios and notes. For this, select the add text tool, or the large T, which is the second tool up from the bottom of the drawing toolbar. Click on the SEM Builder near where you would like to insert the text and an *Add text* dialog box will open. Add the odds ratios in parentheses for each variable and the notes as shown in figure 13.7. Note that you can use the select tool, or the arrow, to select and move a textbox. You can also use this tool to select the textbox and then change the font size in the Contextual Toolbar at the upper left corner of the Builder. I changed the font size from 9 points to 7 points. You can double-click on a completed textbox to see a dialog box where additional changes to the appearance of the text can be made.

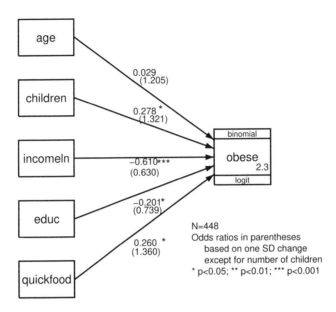

Figure 13.7. Final results for logistic regression

In our final generalized SEM diagram shown in figure 13.7, we see that asterisks show the significance levels. Odds ratios are given in parentheses.

13.4   Path analysis and mediation

Path analysis is an extension of regression where we believe there is a causal order to the variables. In our regression model, we had all the predictors on the left and allowed them to be correlated. Can you see how one of the predictors might actually be an endogenous variable, meaning it depends on the other predictors? Consider the `quickfood` variable. It is reasonable to argue that mothers who have higher income and more education are less likely to have more meals at fast food restaurants. Because of their education, these mothers may be more aware of the health issues associated with eating more meals at fast food restaurants. Mothers from families with more income may be more able to afford options other than eating in fast food restaurants. For simplicity, we will drop the `age` and `children` variables. Figure 13.8 is our model that does not include the `quickfood` variable:

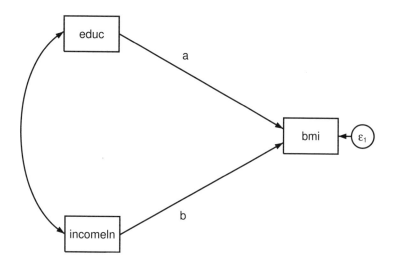

Figure 13.8. BMI predicted without using the `quickfood` variable

When we add the `quickfood` variable, we show it is an intervening mechanism (mediator) between `educ` and `incomeln` on the one hand and `bmi` on the other hand. The underlying argument is that education and income lead to eating fast food less often, and eating fast food less often in turn leads to a lower BMI. This appears in figure 13.9.

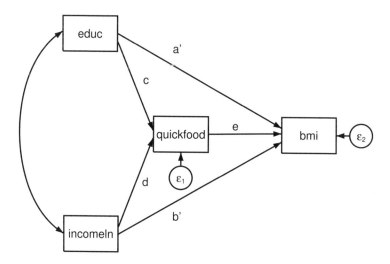

Figure 13.9. A path model with the `quickfood` variable mediating part of the effect of `educ` and `incomeln` on `bmi`

To evaluate whether `quickfood` mediates the influence of `educ` and `incomeln` on `bmi`, we normally fit both of these models.

Figure 13.8 had only two paths with the coefficients `a` and `b`. If these coefficients are not significant, then we would usually not go farther to test for mediation because there was not a significant effect to begin. There are special cases where we have multiple mediators that have the opposite effects. For example, divorce may indirectly harm the well-being of children mediated by a loss of income, but divorce may indirectly benefit the well-being of children by reducing parental conflict.

If `a` in figure 13.8 is significant, but `a'` in figure 13.9 is not significant while `c × e` is significant (indirect effect of `educ` on `bmi` that is mediated by `quickfood`), we say that `quickfood` mediates the effect of education on BMI (full mediation). If `a` in figure 13.8 is significant, and `a'` in figure 13.9 is smaller but also significant while `c × e` is significant, we say that `quickfood` mediates part of the relationship (partial mediation) between education and BMI. Whether there is full mediation or partial mediation, the mediation model has extended our understanding of the relationship between education and BMI. A similar analysis would be done by using `incomeln`.

When you read an article that says income predicts a person's BMI, you should think of possible mediators like we did here when we considered how often the person eats at fast food restaurants. Often there are two or more possible mediators. For example, food that is better for your health may cost more. People with higher income can afford a better diet. You might include dietary variables such as consumption of food that is high in fat. If we had two possible mediators, namely, eating food high in fat and eating at fast food restaurants, both of these or just one of these might be the mediator.

Path models are often called causal models. This is problematic because we are only examining associations and partial associations. A causal argument could be strengthened if we had longitudinal data. For example, we might measure education and income one year, measure the use of fast food restaurants the second year, and then measure BMI the third year. Instead, we measured all three variables simultaneously. When we measure all the variables concurrently, we cannot rule out the possibility that the true model goes in the opposite direction. A mother who has a very high BMI may have had this obesity problem all of her life, and that may have influenced her education level and her income. There is considerable evidence, for example, of discrimination against overweight women in the workforce. In any event, path models never prove anything with certainty, and this is especially true when the variables are measured concurrently. This is an important limitation that we need to keep in mind so that we do not overstate our findings. Used with caution, however, path models can enrich our understanding of influence processes. Path models offer a more elaborate explanation of causal processes and may be consistent or inconsistent with the observed data.

To fit a causal model that involves mediation, it is common to fit the model without the mediator or mediators first. For example, if `a` in figure 13.8 were not significant, then many researchers would not go on because they would conclude there was not a significant effect to be mediated. As noted earlier, there are special cases where this is

not the case. The standardized results for the model that were shown in figure 13.8 are
seen in figure 13.10:

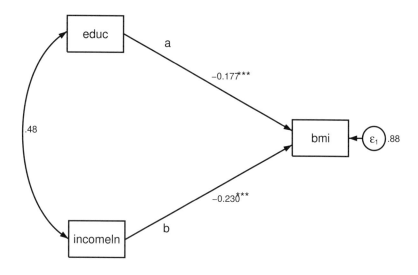

Figure 13.10. Direct effects without the mediator

   We see that both education and income have significant negative effects on BMI. We
meet our first goal of having **a** and **b** both statistically significant. Next we fit the model
that includes the mediation term. In figure 13.11, I had to click on ϵ_1, drag it to the
right, and then click on the path from it to `quickfood` and move the line to improve the
alignment. I also moved the letters to improve their alignment with the standardized
regression coefficients, β's.

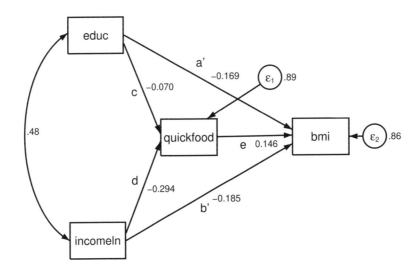

Figure 13.11. Final mediation model

We can obtain the indirect effects by calculating the product of the path coefficients. That is, the indirect effect of education on BMI that is mediated by `quickfood` is $c \times e = -0.070 \times 0.146 = -0.010$, and the indirect effect of income on BMI that is mediated by `quickfood` is $d \times e = -0.294 \times 0.146 = -0.043$. However, this does not tell us whether these indirect effects are statistically significant. We can obtain the indirect effects and their significance by clicking on Estimation ▷ Testing and CIs ▷ Direct and indirect effects. In the resulting dialog box, we select *Decomposition of effects into total, direct, and indirect (teffects)*. We click on *Report standardized effects* and then click on OK. Looking at the Results window, we see a section of `Direct effects`, a second section of `Indirect effects`, and a final section of `Total effects`.

We see that the indirect effect of `educ` through `quickfood` on `bmi` is -0.010 and this is not significant (as a caution, we should note that the test of significance is actually for the unstandardized solution). The indirect effect of `incomeln` through `quickfood` on `bmi` is -0.043 and this is significant, $p = 0.005$. We summarize these results in table 13.3. We include the total effect in the table that is simply the sum of the direct and indirect effects.

Table 13.3. Direct and indirect effects of mother's education and family income on her BMI

Relationship	Direct effect	Indirect effect	Total effect
Education on BMI	-0.169^{***}	-0.010^{ns}	-0.179^{***}
Income on BMI	-0.185^{***}	-0.043^{**}	-0.228^{***}

With these results, we can go back to our question of whether eating in fast food restaurants mediates the effect of education and income on a mother's BMI. Using the rules for whether mediation is partial, full, or insignificant, we will first look at the effects of education on BMI without controlling for `quickfood`. Education has a highly significant direct effect on a mother's BMI without controlling for `quickfood`. The more education she has, the lower her BMI ($\beta = -0.169^{***}$). However, there is no significant indirect effect of education that is mediated by `quickfood` ($\beta = -0.010^{ns}$).

Now consider the effects of income on the mother's BMI. The larger the family income, the lower the mother's BMI, ($\beta = -0.185^{***}$) when we do not control for `quickfood`. There is also a small but statistically significant indirect effect mediated by eating at fast food restaurants ($\beta = -0.043^{*}$). When we compare these results to figure 13.8 where there was no mediation, the direct effect was larger ($\beta = -0.230^{***}$) than the $\beta = -0.185$ we have for figure 13.9. Thus we conclude that there is partial mediation whereby part of the direct effect of income on BMI is mediated by eating at fast food restaurants. Although significant, we should acknowledge that the indirect effect is quite small.

13.5   Conclusions and what is next for the sem command

This chapter has just given you a taste of what the `sem` command can do. If you are fitting more complex path models, you should also read the companion book; see Acock (2013). Nonetheless, what we have covered here is useful for presenting results for regression and logistic regression models that will have greater potential for impact on your reader than would presenting tabular results. Also there are many path models that can enrich a simple regression model by inserting potential mediators. Whenever you add a significant mediator to your model, you are helping explain the influence process. Consider the effects of divorce on child well-being. Generally, we have seen a negative effect where divorce is associated with somewhat worse child well-being. We can add to our understanding by thinking of possible mediators. What happens after divorce that might lead to problems for the children? Perhaps some things happen that will be good for the children.

- Possible adverse mediators

  1. Loss of household income post divorce
  2. Difference in peer group educational aspirations

- Possible positive mediators

  1. Reduced parental conflict
  2. Enhancement in mother–child relationship

How could we put all of these together? Figure 13.12 shows what the model predicts. Divorce is shown to have a direct effect on child well-being, but to also have two negative indirect effects mediated by a loss in income and a difference in the peer group educational aspirations, plus two positive indirect effects that include reduced parental conflict and enhancement of the relationship between the mother and child.

When we have endogenous mediators that do not have a causal relationship specified between them, it is important to consider whether the errors should be correlated. Otherwise, our model will not fit the data very well. For example, a loss of income and a difference in peers may be fully explained by divorce (errors would be zero in this case), but more likely there are other variables that account for these variables and the correlation of the error terms provides for this possibility.

What's next? The `sem` command has so many possibilities that it is hard to provide more than a rudimentary inventory. Acock (2013) discusses many of these extensions. Consider the model in figure 13.12; it is possible for the paths for daughters to be quite different from what they are for sons. Perhaps the mother–child relationship might become stronger for the daughters but not for the sons. Perhaps reduced parental conflict is more important for daughters than it is for sons. The `sem` command allows us to simultaneously fit the model for daughters and sons and test for all possible differences.

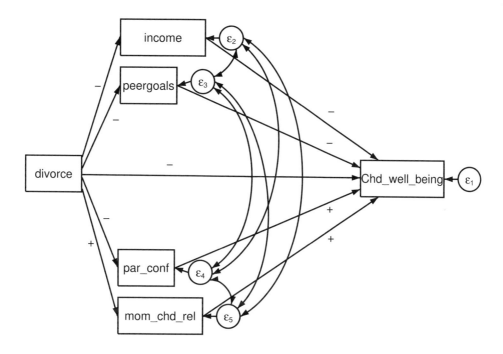

Figure 13.12. More complex path model

We have limited our discussion to observed variables. The `sem` command allows us to work with latent variables, as well as use confirmatory factor analysis models where we specify a specific form for a factor solution. We might be interested in internal and external political efficacy. We would specify observed indicators of each and confirm or disconfirm this model. Extending this, we can combine confirmatory factor analysis and our path models (the structural model) where instead of linking observed variables, we are linking latent variables.

13.6   Exercises

1. You are interested in the socioeconomic status (`sei`) of adult children. You have the following predictors: respondent's gender (`sex`), mother's education (`maeduc`), father's education (`paeduc`), hours worked last week (`hrs1`), and education (`educ`). Using `gss2002_chapter10.dta` (Smith et al. 2015), recode the variable `sex` to be `male` (1 is male; 2 is female).

    a. Fit this model using the `regress` command, and estimate standardized coefficients.

    b. Repeat the previous item, but use the `sem` command and the SEM Builder.

    c. List the commands as you would enter them in a do-file.

2. Use a subset of data from the National Longitudinal Survey (NLS) of women who were aged 14–28 in 1968. You can obtain these data by typing

   ```
   . use https://www.stata-press.com/data/r17/regsmpl.dta
   ```

   Predict wages by using a person's age, their highest grade completed, whether they live in a non-SMSA (rural) area, whether they are from the south, their total years of work experience, and their years at this job.

   a. Fit the regression model using the `regress` command (standardized) and interpret the results.

   b. Fit the regression model using the `sem` command and the SEM Builder, showing the results in a diagram. Interpret these results.

   c. Fit the regression model again using the `method(mlmv)` option of `sem`. Explain what this option does.

3. Redo exercise 2 from chapter 11 using the SEM Builder.

   a. Show your results in the figure and include both the significance level and the odds ratios.

   b. Interpret the results.

4. Open https://stats.oarc.ucla.edu/stata/faq/path-analysis/. This page was developed by the Institute for Digital Research and Education at UCLA. Fit the model using the SEM Builder.

   a. Does math fully mediate, partially mediate, or not significantly mediate the effect reading and writing have on science?

   b. Present a table summarizing your findings.

14 Working with missing values—multiple imputation

14.1 Working with missing values—multiple imputation

Chapter 13 on the `sem` command presented one way to work with missing values using the full-information maximum-likelihood approach based on the maximum likelihood with missing values `method(mlmv)` estimation option. In this chapter, I present a valuable alternative to this, multiple imputation. Many advanced Stata estimation models can use multiple imputation for handling missing values. This chapter shows you how to use multiple imputation but does not go into all the advanced Stata applications that can take advantage of multiple imputation.

14.2   What variables do we include when doing imputations?

Some applied researchers are reluctant to include the main outcome variable from the analysis model when doing multiple imputation. They think including the outcome variable is somehow cheating; they are wrong. When doing multiple imputation, it is important to properly specify the imputation model. If we leave out any relevant variable, we are effectively assuming that the deleted variable is unrelated to the other variables. Because the outcome variable should be related to each of the predictors in the model, leaving the outcome variable out of the imputation will bias correlations to zero.

In addition to the variables in our model and the auxiliary variables, we should include any available variables that would help us predict the score on the variable that has missing values. Of course, this can be a problem if the additional variable has many missing values itself. Here is a checklist:

1. Include all variables in the analysis model, including the dependent variable,

2. Include auxiliary variables that predict patterns of missingness, and

3. Include additional variables that predict a person's score on a variable that has missing values.

Excluding variables from the imputation process is a misspecification of the imputation model. This probably does not matter much when there are few missing values; say, no variable has more than a couple percent of missing values. But it can lead to substantial biases when many missing values exist. This book has not fully addressed the more advanced topic of working with complex sample designs, but in those cases, it would also be important to include sampling characteristics such as weights and strata. The capabilities are fully described in the *Stata Multiple-Imputation Reference Manual*.

Figure 14.1 illustrates the process of multiple imputation. On the left side, we show the imputation model that includes all analysis variables. This includes the outcome variable as well as the covariates. It also may include additional auxiliary variables that either help justify the MAR assumption by explaining who has missing values or help predict those missing values even though the variables are not part of the analysis model. The imputation model is then used to generate a complete dataset. This process is repeated a number of times. With less efficient software and with outdated computers, researchers might have generated as few as five complete datasets. With the efficiency of Stata and with modern computers, it is common to generate 20 to 100 complete datasets. Let's assume you generate 20 complete datasets.

Once the 20 complete datasets have been generated, you begin the analysis stage. The analysis model is run on each of the 20 datasets. The 20 separate results are then pooled, incorporating the variability of the solutions to reflect the uncertainty of the imputation process. This leads to unbiased estimates of the parameters as well as the standard errors.

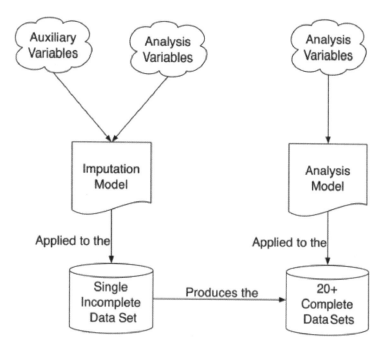

Figure 14.1. Multiple imputation for data analysis (Acock 2012)

All this discussion of what variables to include to properly specify the imputation model needs to be balanced with common sense. First, you probably only want to impute values for variables where a score would be meaningful. It would not make sense to ask men the age they were when they had their first period. Theoretically, you could impute this without bias, but you might want to leave it missing. People who were not asked a question on purpose might be left missing. Many questionnaires use complex skip patterns where you get a different set of questions based on your answers to initial questions. If there were a legitimate skip of an item because it would make no sense to ask it, you probably do not want to impute the missing value.

The advice is to include a lot of variables to ensure proper specification, but this can make matters worse if the included variables are themselves adding a lot of missing values. If you were using education as a variable in your model, but not income, you might say income would be a good additional variable because it would help predict education. However, income might have so many missing values that it will not be helpful. Once you have included a reasonably large number of variables, adding additional variables may not be helpful because of multicollinearity. If you were to put 100 variables in your imputation model, the contribution of many of these variables may be virtually redundant, adding complexity without materially improving the proper specification of your imputation.

14.3   The nature of the problem

Most data that social scientists analyze have missing values. These can occur for many reasons.

- A participant in a randomized trial may decide to withdraw from the study halfway through data collection.

- In a panel study, some participant may have no data at one wave. For example, they were ill when measurement was done halfway through the project. They would have missing values on every item at that wave of the study.

- There are sensitive items that people are reluctant to report, such as criminal behavior. A business may conduct an anonymous survey of employees that includes some questions about employee theft. Although the survey is anonymous, some employees may be reluctant to answer these questions, resent being asked these questions, or even be suspicious of the stated anonymity of their responses.

- About 20–30% of people, when asked their income in national surveys, simply do not give an answer.

- Interviewers sometimes accidentally skip a section of a questionnaire.

- A survey participant simply gets tired of answering questions and turns in a partially complete questionnaire.

- Participants in an experimental condition do poorly on the baseline and decide the intervention is going to be too hard so they drop out.

In the first 12 chapters of this book, we used the default approach to missing values, which drops any participant who does not have complete information on every item used in the analysis. This approach goes by several names, including full case analysis, casewise deletion, or listwise deletion. Perhaps the term listwise deletion is most common in the social sciences. If you use 50 items in an analysis, anybody who did not give a complete answer to all 50 items (the list) is deleted. It is not unusual for this approach to result in 20–50% of the participants being dropped from a complex analysis. This loss of information has two serious implications:

- There will be a substantial loss of power because of the reduced sample size. When doing a power analysis using listwise deletion, you need to take this loss of power into account.

- Listwise deletion can introduce substantial bias. For example, if people who are poorly motivated at the start of an intervention drop out of a study, it will look like the intervention was more successful than it really was.

One alternative to listwise deletion involves substituting the mean on a variable for anybody who does not have a response. This is based on the idea that if you do not know anything about an observation and need to guess a value, the mean is the best guess. This has two serious limitations. People who are average on a variable are often more likely to give an answer than are people who have an extreme value. Income provides a good example of this. People who have extremely low income are hesitant to reveal this. If the average income in a community were $52,500, this would be a terrible estimate for many people who have refused to report their income because they felt that their income was too low. The second problem with mean substitution is that when you give several people the same score on a variable, these people have zero variance on the variable. Sticking with income, if we have 30% of our people not reporting their income and give each of them the same estimated value of $52,500, we will dramatically attenuate the variance on income. Because this makes income a constant for 30% of our sample, there is no explanatory power for 30% of our sample—they all are treated as if they had the same incomes. This artificially reduced variance will seriously bias our parameter estimates. You can imagine the effect this will have on R^2. We will not be able to explain any variance in any outcome for the 30% of the people who have identical estimated incomes. This will attenuate the variance explained by income but can have a complex effect on other variables that have fewer missing values.

14.4 Multiple imputation and its assumptions about the mechanism for missingness

Beginning with Stata 11, there is a comprehensive suite of commands for doing multiple imputation of missing values. These are in addition to the excellent community-contributed commands `ice` (Royston 2004, 2009) and `mim` (Carlin, Galati, and Royston 2008; Royston, Carlin, and White 2009). All of these procedures make an important assumption about the mechanism for missingness but are fairly robust against violations of these assumptions.

When a value is missing, we need to make some assumption about the underlying process that generated this missingness (Rubin 1987). Ideally, the missing value could be missing completely at random (MCAR). Suppose that you have a research team developing a survey that will be given to children in the third grade. Each member of the team is likely to want his or her own set of variables measured. When you get a good measure of each of these variables, your draft questionnaire explodes to 150 items. You are not likely to give a 150-item questionnaire to a third grader; they would skip over many of the items or give answers without reading each of the items carefully. Thoughtful completion of a 150-item questionnaire is just too much to expect of a typical third grader. You decide the most items you can ask a third grader to expect thoughtful responses is 50. What can you do? You could randomly select 50 items from your list of 150 and give them to the first child. Then randomly select a new set of 50 items and give them to the second child. You could use the `sample` command in Stata to randomly generate a different set of 50 items for each participant. Each child would have missing values on 100 of the 150 items, 67% missing values, but these missing values would be MCAR. The process that produced the missingness in this example is unrelated to whether a child was asked any particular item or to how the child might answer any item. Because the process that generated the missingness is completely random, there is no bias introduced in your study.

MCAR is probably unreasonable in most research settings because people with missing values are likely to be different from people without missing values. A second mechanism for missingness occurs whenever the reason for missingness can be explained by variables that are in your analysis. For example, we know that men are less likely to answer items than are women. So long as we have gender in our model, we can explain that part of the differential missingness. The missing data would not be MCAR, but a variable in our analysis would explain the missingness. This missing-value type is called missing at random (MAR).

MAR is not to be confused with MCAR. Many researchers are confused by the name MAR, thinking that it literally means that the missing values are like a random sample of all values, which is not the case. The variables that explain missingness are either included in the model or added as auxiliary variables when imputing missing values. Fortunately, many of our studies include the key variables that predict who will and who will not be as likely to answer individual items. We know that in addition to gender, race/ethnicity and education are related to missingness, and many studies include measures of these variables.

The MAR assumption is more reasonable than you might think. Suppose that you have an intervention that is given at three different levels of intensity: low, medium, and high. Let's imagine an exercise program for people who are obese. Some people who were randomly assigned to the low-intensity condition may decide that the intervention is not likely to be effective because they recognize that not much is happening. They drop out. Conversely, the high intensity of exercise may overwhelm some of the people who were randomly assigned to the high-intensity intervention and they also drop out. Certainly, the dropouts are not MCAR. However, they are MAR because the reason they have missing data, namely, the intensity of the intervention, is a variable that is included in the model.

The key to understanding multiple imputation is that the imputed missing values will not contain any unique information once the variables in the model and the auxiliary variables are allowed to explain the patterns of missing values and predict the score of the missing values. The imputed values for variables with missing values are simply consistent with the observed data. This allows us to use all available information in our analysis.

Unfortunately, there is no test of the validity of the MAR assumption. We may include gender, race/ethnicity, and education as more or less universal mechanism variables. If we know a pretest score and believe people who score poorly on that measure will drop out, we want to include the pretest score even if it is not relevant to our model. The reason we do not have an explicit test of the MAR assumption is that we never know if some additional unobserved variable also provides a mechanism for missingness—because we would not have the variable in our analysis. We can never be certain that we have specified the exact right imputation model.

How can we locate important auxiliary variables? One way is to generate an indicator variable coded as 1 if the value is missing and 0 if the value is present, regardless of what the person's score on the variable might be. This is a new indicator variable, and it may or may not be related to the observed score. It is simply an indicator of missingness. We will have one such indicator variable for each variable that has any missing values. Next we can run a series of logistic regressions, where each of these indicator variables is regressed on a list of potential auxiliary variables. We probably should err on the side of inclusion and might have 10 to 20 candidate auxiliary variables. Any of these candidate auxiliary variables that is significantly related to any of the indicator variables should be included as an auxiliary variable. If a variable has very few missing values, the logistic regressions will encounter estimation problems and will drop some variables and cases. You may want to ignore these results because there are so few missing values on those variables anyway. Doing this makes the MAR assumption reasonable. Extensive studies including simulations have shown that including a reasonable set of auxiliary variables leads to excellent results.

14.5 Multiple imputation

A powerful way of working with missing values involves multiple imputation. The command mi will be illustrated in this chapter. This command involves three straightforward steps:

1. Create m complete datasets by imputing the missing values. Each dataset will have no missing values, but the values imputed for missing values will vary across the m datasets.

2. Do your analysis in each of the m complete datasets.

3. Pool your m solutions to get one solution.

   a. The parameter estimates—for example, regression coefficients—will be the mean of their corresponding values in the m datasets.

   b. The standard errors used for testing significance will combine the standard errors from the m solutions plus the variance of the parameter estimates across the m solutions. If each solution is yielding a very different estimate, this uncertainty is added to the standard errors. Also the degrees of freedom is adjusted based on the number of imputations and proportion of data that have missing values.

Is this cheating? This really is not cheating! The uncertainty caused by missing values comes into the process at multiple points. In generating m complete datasets, each of which will have somewhat different imputed values, the variability of the resulting solutions is added to the estimated standard errors. If the imputations are doing a good job, not much variance will be added. The results report the average relative increase in the variance (RVI) of the estimates (squared standard errors) because of missing values. Because this cannot be done with a single imputation, studies that rely on single imputation will potentially underestimate standard errors and inflate t-values. If the RVI is close to zero, then the imputation will increase power, but power may not increase over listwise deletion if the RVI is substantial. If the imputations are problematic, then considerable variance is added. The imputed values do not contain any additional information than that contained in all the variables in your model and those used as auxiliary variables. The imputed values allow Stata to use all available data. Imagine having 10 waves of data in a study of the transition to adulthood. John participated in all but the third wave because he was sick the day that measurement was taken. It makes no sense to ignore all the information John provides on the other nine waves; that would be a waste of valuable information. Using multiple imputations will usually increase power by using all available data on all participants.

14.6   A detailed example

Stata has a comprehensive set of commands for working with missing values. We will only consider the most general case. The *Stata Multiple-Imputation Reference Manual* provides details on alternatives. The most widely used approach is using multivariate normal regression (MVN). Stata's `mi impute mvn` command implements an iterative Markov chain Monte Carlo method (Schafer 1997) that is known as data augmentation. The MVN method is designed for continuous variables.   Where there are several categorical or count variables, Stata's `mi impute chained` command implements the chained equation approach for imputing missing values (van Buuren, Boshuizen, and Knook 1999) and provides a useful alternative.

The chained equations approach has less theoretical justification than the MVN approach, but it has the advantage of using an appropriate estimator for each imputed variable based on the measurement level and distribution characteristics of the variable, for example, logistic regression, multinomial logistic regression, Poisson regression, negative binomial regression, and others. In practical experience, the final model estimation usually produces similar results whether the `mi impute mvn` command or the `mi impute chained` command is used. This section focuses on the MVN method and is intended to be introductory. Users of multiple imputation are encouraged to consult the *Stata Multiple-Imputation Reference Manual*, which provides a comprehensive treatment on over 350 pages.

We will use a modified version of a dataset, `regsmpl.dta`, that is available from the Stata menu, File ▷ Example datasets... ▷ Stata 17 manual datasets. The modified version we will use, `chapter14_missing.dta`, can be thought of as a nonrandom subsample of `regsmpl.dta`.

We are interested in the natural log of wages (`ln_wagem`). We have as predictors the person's highest grade completed (`gradem`), age (`agem`), total work experience (`ttl_expm`), time in years at his or her present job (`tenurem`), whether they are from a non-SMSA area (`not_smsa`), whether they are from the South (`south`), and whether they are black (`blackm`). The letter `m` has been appended to each variable where there are missing values to distinguish them from the original dataset.

14.6.1 Preliminary analysis

To get an idea of the extent of the problem with `chapter14_missing.dta`, we use the `misstable` command: first, to get a summary of missing values, and second, to get a sense of the pattern of missingness.

```
. use https://www.stata-press.com/data/agis6r/chapter14_missing
(NLS Women 14-26 in 1968)

. misstable summarize ln_wagem gradem agem ttl_expm tenurem not_smsa south blackm
```

Variable	Obs=.	Obs>.	Obs<.	Unique values	Min	Max
ln_wagem	300		1,393	393	.0682788	4.242752
gradem	148		1,545	13	0	18
agem	165		1,528	12	18	30
ttl_expm	206		1,487	>500	.0833333	15.53846
tenurem	200		1,493	74	0	15.5
blackm	99		1,594	2	0	1

This is similar to the regular `summarize` command except that it is for missing values. A missing value will have a code of `.`, `.a`, `.b`, etc. Observations with these codes are tabulated in the columns labeled `Obs=.` and `Obs>.`. Remember that a missing value is recorded in a Stata dataset as an extremely high value. Within `mi`, a missing-value code, `.` (dot), has a special meaning. It denotes the missing values eligible for imputation. If you have a set of missing values that should not be imputed, you should record them as extended missing values, that is, as `.a`, `.b`, etc. The column labeled `Obs<.` contains the number of observations that are not missing. For example, our dependent variable has 300 missing values we want to impute, no missing values we do not want to impute (`.a`, `.b`, etc.), and scores on 1,393 observations. Notice that we listed all our variables in the command, but neither `not_smsa` nor `south` appear in the table. This is because they have no missing values.

Some datasets use the extended missing-value codes `.a`, `.b`, `.c`, etc. One of these extended missing-value codes might be assigned for people who answer "Don't know". If you want to impute missing values for any of the extended missing-value codes, you will want to recode it to a system missing value of dot (`.`) before you perform the multiple imputation. For example, if you used `.a` for "Don't know" responses on age and want to include these responses when you do the multiple imputation, you should type `recode agem (.a = .)` prior to performing multiple imputation.

Next we type the `misstable patterns` command. This command can produce a lot of output when there are many different patterns. Here are the patterns that each variable has for at least 2% of the total N.

```
. misstable patterns ln_wagem gradem agem ttl_expm tenurem not_smsa south blackm
    Missing-value patterns
      (1 means complete)
```

	Pattern					
Percent	1	2	3	4	5	6
51%	1	1	1	1	1	1
8	1	1	1	1	1	0
7	1	1	0	1	1	1
6	1	1	1	0	1	1
5	1	1	1	1	0	1
4	1	0	1	1	1	1
4	0	1	1	1	1	1
3	1	1	1	1	0	0
2	1	0	1	1	1	0

```
      (output omitted)
```

```
    100%
```

```
Variables are  (1) blackm  (2) gradem  (3) agem  (4) tenurem  (5) ttl_expm
               (6) ln_wagem
```

As noted in the results, a 1 indicates that the value is present. Thus 51% of the sample have a value on all the variables. If we did a listwise deletion, we would have lost 49% of our cases! Below this row are different patterns. The most common pattern is to have data for all but the sixth variable, which we see from the bottom of the table is `ln_wagem`. Eight percent of the participants are in this pattern. This table is not especially useful here because there are no dominant patterns of missingness.

Next we will generate a dummy variable for each of our variables that has missing values. We want the dummy variable to be coded 0 if the variable is observed and 1 if the variable has a missing value. We will use the `misstable summarize` command again, but this time we include the `generate(miss_)` option. This option generates the dummy variables and adds the prefix `miss_` to each variable name. For example, `agem` is a variable we want to impute, and `miss_agem` will be a dummy variable coded 1 if the person has a missing value on `agem` and 0 if the person has an observed value. We use the `quietly` prefix because we already have seen the standard `misstable summarize` output. We also use `describe miss_*` to review the changes. Here are the commands and results:

```
. quietly misstable summarize ln_wagem gradem agem ttl_expm tenurem not_smsa
> south blackm, generate(miss_)
. describe miss_*
```

Variable name	Storage type	Display format	Value label	Variable label
miss_ln_wagem	byte	%8.0g		(ln_wagem>=.)
miss_gradem	byte	%8.0g		(gradem>=.)
miss_agem	byte	%8.0g		(agem>=.)
miss_ttl_expm	byte	%8.0g		(ttl_expm>=.)
miss_tenurem	byte	%8.0g		(tenurem>=.)
miss_blackm	byte	%8.0g		(blackm>=.)

The `generate()` option is nice because it not only generates the dummy variables, but also it adds a variable label to each of the generated variables to remind us what has been done.

We can treat each of these dummy variables as a dependent variable and do a logistic regression to locate possible auxiliary variables. We do not have any candidates for auxiliary variables in our dataset. Can you think of some candidates we should have included? For instance, gender would be an auxiliary variable. Here we show the six logistic regression commands, recognizing that, ideally, we should have included additional variables that are not part of our model but may help explain missingness. If your data happen to have variables with very few missing values, the `logit` command will have estimation problems and will drop one or more variables and cases. You might simply ignore those results because there are few missing values on those variables. You are looking for the results of the logistic regressions for variables that have several missing values, say, 5% or more.

```
. logit miss_ln_wagem gradem agem ttl_expm tenurem not_smsa south blackm
> if ln_wagem <= .
. logit miss_gradem ln_wagem agem ttl_expm tenurem not_smsa south blackm
> if gradem <= .
. logit miss_agem ln_wagem gradem ttl_expm tenurem not_smsa south blackm
> if agem <= .
. logit miss_ttl_expm ln_wagem gradem agem tenurem not_smsa south blackm
> if ttl_expm <= .
. logit miss_tenurem ln_wagem gradem agem ttl_expm not_smsa south blackm
> if tenurem <= .
. logit miss_blackm ln_wagem gradem agem ttl_expm tenurem not_smsa south
> if blackm <= .
```

A quick way to evaluate potential auxiliary variables, as described in chapter 13, is to simply correlate each dummy variable with possible auxiliary variables as described in the previous chapter. Using the same candidates that we did with the logistic regression, we could run

```
pwcorr miss_ln_wagem miss_gradem miss_agem miss_ttl_expm miss_tenurem    ///
    miss_blackm ln_wagem gradem agem ttl_expm tenurem blackm not_smsa    ///
    south, obs sig
```

Any significant correlation between any of the dummy variables and any of the possible test variables would be a candidate to include as a missing variable.

We are not interested in predicting the indicator variables if the person has an extended missing value such as .a, .b, etc. We ensure the avoidance of predicting these variables by using the if condition to drop any case that has an extended missing value such as .a. This works because these extended missing values are recorded in the Stata dataset as a larger value than the value assigned to the . (dot). Any variable that is statistically significant in these logistic regressions should be included in the imputation step. In our example, these are already included because they are all variables used in the analysis stage.

14.6.2 Setup and multiple-imputation stage

Next we tell Stata how to arrange the imputed datasets; that is, we choose a multiple-imputation storage style. We could store the datasets in a wide format, using the wide style, where we have new variable names for each imputed dataset and they go to the right. Or we could store the datasets in a long format, where the datasets are stacked. Using the long style, we have our initial dataset, labeled 0. Below that, we have a dataset labeled 1; below that is a dataset labeled 2; and so on. We will use this long style in this example.

You could imagine how the stacked datasets could get very, very long. If we imputed 100 datasets on a base sample of 10,000 observations, we would need 1,000,000 records. Stata has a way of minimizing the storage issues with this approach by including only the records that have imputed values in each of the subsequent sets. In our example, we would have all our records in the first set, labeled 0. In the second and subsequent sets, we would only have cases for the 49% of the participants who had missing values. This would cut the number of records in our file in half. The style containing the complete sets is flong (full and long), which is the style we will use; the style that only has the cases with missing values is mlong (marginal and long). If you run out of memory space, you could change from the flong to the mlong style. Stata has other storage styles described in the *Stata Multiple-Imputation Reference Manual*.

To prepare our data for multiple imputation, we need to run three commands:

```
. mi set flong
. mi register imputed ln_wagem gradem agem ttl_expm tenurem blackm
. mi register regular not_smsa south
```

The mi set flong command tells Stata how to arrange our multiple datasets. The mi register imputed command registers all the variables that have missing values and need to be imputed. The mi register regular command registers all the variables that have no missing values or for which we do not want to impute values.

We are now ready to create the multiple completed datasets. Here we use the `mi impute` command to obtain imputations and the `rseed()` option to set a seed at some arbitrary value so that the results can be duplicated. You can enter any value in `rseed()`; I use 2121 in this example.

```
. mi impute mvn ln_wagem gradem agem ttl_expm tenurem blackm, add(20) rseed(2121)
Performing EM optimization:
  observed log likelihood = -5347.0692 at iteration 12

Performing MCMC data augmentation ...

Multivariate imputation              Imputations =        20
Multivariate normal regression             added =        20
Imputed: m=1 through m=20                 updated =         0

Prior: uniform                         Iterations =      2000
                                          burn-in =       100
                                          between =       100
```

Variable	Complete	Observations per *m* Incomplete	Imputed	Total
ln_wagem	1393	300	300	1693
gradem	1545	148	148	1693
agem	1528	165	165	1693
ttl_expm	1487	206	206	1693
tenurem	1493	200	200	1693
blackm	1594	99	99	1693

```
(Complete + Incomplete = Total; Imputed is the minimum across m
of the number of filled-in observations.)
```

The `mi impute mvn` command specifies that we are using the multivariate normal model to impute missing values. It would be good to check that the variables are reasonably normal. With a large sample, violations of this assumed normality may not be too serious. We specified the `add(20)` option to generate 20 datasets in addition to the initial dataset that has missing values. Each of the 20 datasets will be complete; each will have no missing values. The imputed values will vary from one of these datasets to the next.

Why did we impute 20 complete datasets? Much of the literature, especially the early applications, uses relatively few imputed datasets, often picking $m = 5$. Early software was much harder to use than Stata is, so this might have been one motivation for a small m. The theory behind multiple imputation as presented by Rubin (1987) was based on an infinite number of imputed, complete datasets. However, high relative efficiency for even small m has been documented when the assumptions are appropriate. Rubin (1987) and van Buuren, Boshuizen, and Knook (1999) report that $m = 5$ can produce 95% relative efficiency when half the values are missing, given that the MAR assumption is justified. However, others have shown cases where a much larger value of m is needed (Kenward and Carpenter 2007). The *Stata Multiple-Imputation Reference Manual* recommends an m of at least 20. Because of the ease with which Stata can implement multiple imputations, you should adhere to this recommendation and may experiment with even larger values of m. If you obtain comparable results with 10,

20, 40, and 60 imputed datasets, this is reassuring. The multiple imputation and the analysis take a bit longer with more imputations, but with modern computers, there is no reason to limit the number to 5. The current example took 8 seconds for the imputation stage and 1 second for the analysis stage (described later) using $m = 20$, compared with 42 seconds and 5 seconds when estimated using $m = 100$. This was using a not-so-new Windows computer with five other programs running in the background. There is rapidly decreasing marginal utility to making m even larger. However, the cost of computation time is fairly small for making m large.

Along with the creation of our 20 new complete datasets, the `mi set` command created three new variables at the bottom of the list of variables in our Variables window. `_mi_id` is a new ID variable. It ranges from 1 for our first case to 1,693 for our last case. If you do a tabulation of it, you will see that each ID value has a frequency of 21; that is, 1 for each of our 20 imputed datasets and 1 for our original dataset. Our new data file now has 35,553 observations. The `_mi_miss` variable is simply an indicator variable coded 0 if there are no missing values and 1 if there are any in the original data. It contains a missing value for all records in imputed data. As we saw before, 51.09% of the observations had no missing values. The `_mi_m` variable identifies datasets and ranges from 0 to 20. All 1,693 cases in the first imputed dataset have `_mi_m = 1`; all 1,693 cases in the second imputed dataset have `_mi_m = 2`; and so on. Original records have `_mi_m = 0`.

The `mi impute mvn` command uses data augmentation, an iterative imputation method, to fill in missing values. Thus it is important to check the convergence of data augmentation after imputation; however, a discussion of this step is beyond the scope of this book. For details, you can refer to *Convergence of the MCMC method* in [MI] **mi impute mvn**.

14.6.3   The analysis stage

Now we are ready to run our 20 regressions and pool the results. We use the prefix command `mi estimate:` in front of the regression command. Stata then knows to do the 20 regressions and pool the results. We have added the option `dftable` to the `mi estimate` prefix command to see coefficient-specific degrees of freedom. You might want to run this without the `dftable` option to obtain confidence intervals. Here are the command and results:

```
. mi estimate, dftable: regress ln_wagem gradem agem ttl_expm tenurem not_smsa
> south blackm
```

Multiple-imputation estimates   Imputations   =   20
Linear regression   Number of obs   =   1,693
                                                  Average RVI   =   0.4091
                                                  Largest FMI   =   0.4344
                                                  Complete DF   =   1685
DF adjustment: Small sample   DF: min   =   95.58
                                                           avg   =   229.31
                                                           max   =   670.94
Model F test: Equal FMI   F(7,   771.9) =   69.45
Within VCE type: OLS   Prob > F   =   0.0000

ln_wagem	Coefficient	Std. err.	t	P>|t|	df	% increase std. err.
gradem	.0765953	.0066448	11.53	0.000	95.6	31.69
agem	.0208913	.0039398	5.30	0.000	163.2	20.92
ttl_expm	.0144492	.0099197	1.46	0.148	110.3	28.25
tenurem	.060269	.0089321	6.75	0.000	154.1	21.84
not_smsa	-.1148061	.0256842	-4.47	0.000	151.3	22.15
south	-.0833896	.0211312	-3.95	0.000	670.9	6.86
blackm	-.0293377	.025407	-1.15	0.249	222.0	16.64
_cons	.1247307	.0993645	1.26	0.210	267.1	14.51

These results look similar to what we get with the regress command on one dataset, but some information is additional and some information is missing. On the right, we have the number of imputations, 20; the number of observations after imputations, 1,693; and what the degrees of freedom would have been if there were no missing values, 1,685. We have a different number of degrees of freedom for different variables, ranging from 95.6 to 670.9. These numbers are estimated using complex formulas described in the *Stata Multiple-Imputation Reference Manual*. The calculated degrees of freedom depends on the number of imputations and, loosely speaking, the rates of missing values for different variables, because both of these factors influence our inference. If you repeat this analysis using more imputations, you will have more information for estimating the parameters and will gain additional degrees of freedom. For example, repeating this analysis with 100 imputations rather than 20 increases the average degrees of freedom from the 229.3 reported here to 661.6 degrees of freedom. The dftable option gives us the specific degrees of freedom for each of the predictors. Although having more imputations will increase the degrees of freedom, this does not necessarily result in a higher level of statistical significance.

There is an overall F test of the model, $F(7, 771.9) = 69.45$, $p < 0.001$, and you will notice an adjustment for the degrees of freedom. In a separate analysis using 100 imputations, the $F(7, 1417.6) = 72.08$, $p < 0.001$. In both cases, the model is highly significant. We could report the significance for each of the variables. For instance, we could say that each additional year of tenure on a job increases the natural log of income by 0.06, $t(154.1) = 6.75$, $p < 0.001$. In writing a report, you should explain that the degrees of freedom has been adjusted based on the number of imputations and fractions of information about parameter estimates lost because of missing values.

The `Average RVI = 0.4091` line is an estimate of the average relative inflation in variance of the estimates, that is, in the squared standard error, that is caused by the missing values. Ideally, this would be close to zero. The obtained value of 0.4091 is relatively high because we had missing values for almost half the participants. `mi estimate` explicitly recognizes this inflation, which increases the standard errors, thus reducing the t values and increasing the probabilities. This increase in the standard errors is conservative and an example of how this approach is not cheating or taking advantage of made-up new data.

14.6.4　For those who want an R^2 and standardized βs

Stata's `mi estimate` command does not pool the R^2 that is obtained for each of the 20 solutions. It also does not pool the standardized beta weights, βs. Rubin's rule (1987) for pooling may not apply to pooling the R^2s and the βs—both parameter estimates are not normally distributed because of the upper limit of 1.0 (although there are rare cases where βs can exceed 1). However, the values of these coefficients in social-science research rarely approach these limits, and a simple average may be satisfactory. Because the sampling distribution of the R^2 and βs may have a substantial negative skew, a better solution is to first transform the values by using an inverse hyperbolic-tangent transformation. Then the final estimate is transformed back by using the hyperbolic tangent. This approach was originally recommended in Fisher's tests of correlations and is sometimes labeled a z transformation. This approach is recommended by Harel (2009).

Fortunately, there is a community-contributed command, `mibeta`, that was written by Yulia Marchenko. You can find and install this command by typing `search mibeta`. Let's say that we want to estimate how much variance in `ln_wage` our set of predictors explains. We need a pooled estimate of R^2. We might also be interested in the standardized β for education. We can use the `mibeta` command to obtain these estimates.

```
. mibeta ln_wagem gradem agem ttl_expm tenurem not_smsa south blackm, fisherz
> miopts(vartable)
```

Multiple-imputation estimates   Imputations   =   20
Linear regression

Variance information

| | Imputation variance | | | | | Relative |
	Within	Between	Total	RVI	FMI	efficiency
gradem	.000025	.000018	.000044	.734106	.433913	.978765
agem	.000011	4.7e-06	.000016	.46211	.323137	.9841
ttl_expm	.00006	.000037	.000098	.644875	.401654	.980313
tenurem	.000054	.000025	.00008	.484594	.333845	.983582
not_smsa	.000442	.000207	.00066	.491946	.337276	.983416
south	.000391	.000053	.000447	.141827	.125629	.993758
blackm	.000474	.000163	.000646	.360586	.270397	.98666
_cons	.00753	.002232	.009873	.311198	.241821	.988053

Note: FMIs are based on Rubin's large-sample degrees of freedom.

Multiple-imputation estimates   Imputations   =   20
Linear regression   Number of obs   =   1,693
                                           Average RVI   =   0.4091
                                           Largest FMI   =   0.4339
                                           Complete DF   =   1685
DF adjustment: Small sample   DF: min   =   95.58
                                                   avg   =   229.31
                                                   max   =   670.94
Model F test: Equal FMI   F(7, 771.9)   =   69.45
Within VCE type: OLS   Prob > F   =   0.0000

ln_wagem	Coefficient	Std. err.	t	P>|t|	[95% conf. interval]	
gradem	.0765953	.0066448	11.53	0.000	.0634046	.0897859
agem	.0208913	.0039398	5.30	0.000	.0131118	.0286708
ttl_expm	.0144492	.0099197	1.46	0.148	-.0052086	.0341071
tenurem	.060269	.0089321	6.75	0.000	.0426237	.0779142
not_smsa	-.1148061	.0256842	-4.47	0.000	.165552	-.0640601
south	-.0033896	.0211312	-3.95	0.000	-.1248809	-.0418982
blackm	-.0293377	.025407	-1.15	0.249	-.0794075	.0207322
_cons	.1247307	.0993645	1.26	0.210	-.0709066	.320368

Standardized coefficients and R-squared
Summary statistics over 20 imputations

	mean*	min	p25	median	p75	max
gradem	.3219557	.278	.3141422	.3265982	.3345306	.357
agem	.1447876	.119	.1349936	.1457571	.1505709	.18
ttl_expm	.0518086	.0164	.0312976	.0544998	.0635064	.0976
tenurem	.2181023	.186	.2039858	.2191592	.2309489	.254
not_smsa	-.11595	-.138	-.1297013	-.1127403	-.1085154	-.0906
south	-.0931871	-.11	-.0977573	-.0940692	-.088983	-.0757
blackm	-.0294481	-.0565	-.0372899	-.0265284	-.0208183	-.0119
R-square	.2918254	.271	.286382	.2930947	.3000547	.309
Adj R-square	.2888821	.267	.2834174	.290158	.297147	.306

* based on Fisher's z transformation

Notice that we have included two options. The `fisherz` option implements the z transformation to help normalize the sampling distribution. The `miopts(vartable)` option implements an option from the `mi estimate` command's set of options. This option provides very helpful additional information that we discuss below. The mean $R^2 = 0.292$ and the mean standardized weight for `gradem` is 0.322. We should not treat these values as formal parameter estimates, but they give a sense of how much of the variance we can explain and the approximate standardized strength for the effect of education. To see if means are reasonable estimates, we can look at other summaries of the distribution of R^2 and the standardized β weights over imputed data as reported by `mibeta`.

From the results table labeled "Standardized coefficients and R-squared", we have some useful information to help us assess the quality of our estimates. We have seen that the β for `gradem` is 0.322. To the right of that in the table, we see that for over 20 regressions, the minimum value is 0.278, the 25th percentile is 0.314, the median is 0.327 (close to the mean, suggesting that the sampling distribution is symmetrical), the 75th percentile is 0.335, and the maximum value is 0.357. We can conclude that the estimate is quite stable across the 20 imputations. Even more useful is the top table in the results, which is labeled "Variance information". This information is available because we used the `miopts(vartable)` option. Perhaps the most useful information in this table is in the last column on the right, "Relative efficiency". For `gradem`, the relative efficiency is 0.979. This is how efficient our estimate is when using 20 imputed datasets, compared with what we would have obtained with use of an infinite number of imputed datasets. When this value is very close to 1.000, we can be confident that m is large enough. There is no convention as to how close this needs to be to 1.000, but a value of at least 0.98 is reasonable. In general, when the variance in an estimate from one dataset to another (between the datasets) is fairly large, increasing the value of m will be very beneficial. When there is little variance between datasets, there is little to gain by using a large value of m.

14.6.5 When impossible values are imputed: Binary variables, squares, and interactions

The MVN assumption assumes a multivariate normal distribution. As a consequence, we may have imputed values that are outside the possible range of a variable. Remember that a normal distribution can range from minus infinity to plus infinity, and this is not the case with any of our variables. Here is a summary of the 33,860 observations in our 20 completed datasets. Notice the restriction of if `_mi_m > 0` so that we do not include the original dataset in our summary results. The dataset included the original data where the value of `_mi_m` was 0 and we are only interested in the 20 created datasets; that is, `_mi_m` equals 1 to 20.

```
. summarize ln_wagem gradem agem ttl_expm tenurem not_smsa south blackm
> if _mi_m > 0
```

Variable	Obs	Mean	Std. dev.	Min	Max
ln_wagem	33,860	1.614246	.4375837	-.0769101	4.242752
gradem	33,860	12.15952	1.838568	0	19.27205
agem	33,860	22.81635	3.03105	12.32953	33.09295
ttl_expm	33,860	3.330754	1.569392	-1.422059	15.53846
tenurem	33,860	1.734753	1.582867	-3.253729	15.5
not_smsa	33,860	.2658004	.441765	0	1
south	33,860	.3951565	.4888915	0	1
blackm	33,860	.2627107	.4394428	-1.130642	1.804802

The scores for education, gradem, range from 0 to 19.272. In our original data, the range was 0 to 18. Because a normal distribution does not have a fixed upper or lower limit, we can understand how we might have an imputed value of slightly over the maximum. In our original data, agem ranged from 18 to 30, and here it ranged from 12.330 to 33.093. This change is a bit more worrisome because the study was intended to be limited to people ages 18 to 30. The minimum imputed value for tenurem is -3.254, which is confusing. A person cannot be on a job for less than 0 years. If we do a tabulation on tenurem, we see that these impossible negative values are rare, so the imputed values may not be too problematic. We might be more concerned about the blackm variable, an indicator variable coded as 1 if the person is black and 0 otherwise. A minimum value of -1.131 and a maximum value of 1.805 for blackm make no intuitive sense.

We know the cause of these "impossible" values. It is that the MVN solution does not limit the imputed values to be in a specified range as with tenurem or to only take on certain values as with blackm. There has been considerable controversy over how to handle the "impossible" values. One approach that was widely used in early applications of multiple imputation involved fixing the problem by restricting the range of continuous variables or by rounding to the nearest integer for binary variables. We could take all the negative values for tenurem and change them to 0. We could change the agem scores below 18 to 18 and those above 30 to 30. We could assign anybody who has a score on blackm that is greater than 0.5 a value of 1 and anybody who has a score of 0.5 or lower a value of 0. Intuitively, this is an appealing solution.

More recently, the choice of how to handle "impossible" values is to leave them alone. Although this may not seem intuitively reasonable, it may be the best solution. The imputation model and the analysis model need to be compatible or else the results will be biased. If the analysis stage, where we did the regressions, used different datasets (because of the rounding or truncating) than the one generated by the imputation model, then the results would be biased (Horton, Lipsitz, and Parzen 2003). Today, the recommended approach is to leave the imputed values as they are. Statisticians will continue to work on this problem, but usually the conclusions you draw will not change whether you make the adjustment or not.

Not illustrated here is what you do when you have an interaction term $(X_1 X_2)$ or squared variables (X^2). The recommended approach for these situations is to create the interactions or squared variables in the original dataset, before doing the multiple-imputation stage (von Hippel 2009). Because of the way the interactions and squared terms are imputed as distinct variables, the values of the imputed X^2 may not be equal to the value of the imputed X times itself. You might have something like an imputed $X = 10.3$ and an imputed $X^2 = 98.6$. Similarly, the values of the imputed $X_1 X_2$ may not equal the value of the imputed X_1 times the imputed X_2. It would be tempting to leave the interaction terms and squared terms out of the original dataset, do the imputation, and then compute them such that if an imputed $X = 10.3$, the X^2 will equal 106.09. X^2 will then be defined as a "passive" variable in Stata. This is not recommended; von Hippel has shown that doing this will introduce a bias. The best general advice is to impute everything and do nothing to change any imputed values for the analysis stage.

14.7 Summary

We have only touched the surface of Stata's multiple-imputation capabilities. The *Stata Multiple-Imputation Reference Manual* is well written and gives numerous examples for more specialized applications. I included this brief introduction to multiple imputation because it would serve most needs of researchers.

Professional journals are increasingly demanding that some sort of imputation be done so that all available data can be used in the analysis. Several simulations suggest that most of the modern approaches yield remarkably similar findings. We have discussed some issues, such as rounding imputed values for binary variables. There is an enormous amount of scientific investigation by statisticians into what is the optimal approach. It can be shown that there are situations where different strategies lead to very different parameter estimates and tests of significance. However, in most applications, one type of multiple imputation produces results that are similar to other types. We may be worrying about more subtle distinctions than is necessary. The multivariate normal approach outlined in this chapter should work for a wide range of situations; see, for example, Allison (2001).

I only illustrated the use of the `regress` command with the `mi estimate` prefix command. This one example can be used in a wide range of research applications. However, the `mi estimate` prefix command works with many Stata commands. Among those not covered in this book is `logit` used for logistic regression. The *Stata Multiple-Imputation Reference Manual* lists all estimation commands that work with the `mi estimate` prefix. These cover count models, ordinal models, categorical models, quantile regression models, specialized regression commands, descriptive statistics for means, proportions and ratios, many survey regression commands, and many panel-data regression commands.

Here is a checklist of what we need to do for multiple imputation:

1. Include in the imputation model all variables that will be used in the analysis model, including the dependent variable.

2. Include auxiliary variables that predict patterns of missingness.

3. Include additional variables that predict a person's score on a variable that has missing values.

4. Drop observations that have variables you do not want to impute because the item was deliberately skipped.

5. Avoid adding variables that have a lot of missing values themselves because including them may increase the uncertainty of your imputations and greatly reduce your degrees of freedom.

6. Explore patterns of missing values to see if there are certain variables or combinations of variables that explain the lion's share of missing values.

7. Although you should include all important variables in the imputation stage, including too many can create estimation problems due to multicollinearity.

8. Generate all interactions and squared variables in the original dataset before the imputation stage.

9. Impute a reasonable number of completed datasets, at least $m = 20$, and experiment with different numbers of imputed datasets.

10. Do not change the imputed values as you move to the analysis stage, even if they seem to be "impossible" values.

11. Use the `mibeta` command if you want pooled estimates of R^2 and the βs and also to obtain the relative efficiency of the value you have used for m.

Those who have been plagued by missing-data problems may think these procedures can change lead to gold. They cannot. These procedures should be used with caution, and the MAR assumption should be given serious consideration. Properly specified imputation models, however, can do better than any of the alternative ways of working with missing values.

14.8 Exercises

1. Describe a study in which the data are MCAR.

2. Describe a regression model using survey data in which the data are not MCAR but are instead MAR.

3. How can you have an important auxiliary variable that is not related to a person's score? Why is such a variable important to include when doing the imputations?

4. If you use $m = 10$, what statistical results would indicate that you need a much larger m?

5. A person says that when you get significant results by using multiple imputation, it is just because you made up data. Give an intuitive explanation of why this argument is wrong.

6. Why do you lose degrees of freedom when you do multiple imputations? When would you lose the most degrees of freedom?

7. Use the dataset we used in chapter 10, `ops2004.dta`. Using this dataset, we saw a multiple regression predicting a person's concern for the environment by using their education, income, involvement in the community, health problems, and how much they feel the environment impacts people's health. Answer each of the following:

   a. How much missing data are there? Which variables contain the biggest number of missing values?

   b. Past research has shown that males are less likely to complete all questions. Evaluate whether gender needs to be included as an auxiliary variable. Why is it a good idea to include gender as an auxiliary variable based on this analysis?

   c. Impute 20 datasets and include the auxiliary variable. How can you do this so that you get the same result if you run your do-file another time?

   d. Use the `mi estimate` prefix command to do the regression and compare this with the results reported in chapter 10.

   e. Why does income have far fewer degrees of freedom than do the other variables?

8. Repeat exercise 7, but use `mibeta` to obtain estimates for R^2 and for the βs.

15   An introduction to multilevel analysis

Multilevel models, often called mixed models or hierarchical linear models (HLM), involve nested data. These models are useful for two types of nested data. The first is for data with individuals nested within groups. Here each observation represents a different individual, but individuals can be divided into groups that are likely to have some similar characteristics. The second is for data with multiple observations on the same individual.

15.1   Questions and data for groups of individuals

Suppose you sampled 100 mothers from each of 20 counties in the United States. You might be interested in the educational aspirations that the mothers have for their children. Two levels of variables could predict the educational aspirations. First, there are individual-level characteristics such as each mother's own education and her household income. Your hypothesis might be that the greater the mother's income and education, the higher her educational aspirations for her children. Second, because your individuals are grouped in 20 counties, county-level characteristics might predict the mothers' educational expectations for their children. For example, each county's median income and expenditures on education might be important predictors. These county-level variables could influence mothers' educational aspirations independently of the mothers' own characteristics. Mothers from wealthy counties that invest heavily in education might have higher educational aspirations for their children regardless of the education and income of an individual mother.

Can you see a complication that arises when you have two-level data? The 100 mothers in each county will have differing values for educational aspirations, household income, education, and other (possibly even unobserved) variables, but their values for these variables will likely be more homogeneous than 100 randomly selected mothers from the entire country. We can also refer to the homogeneity as correlated data because the scores on individual-level variables are likely to be more highly correlated with the scores from individuals within the group than with the scores from individuals outside the group. For example, the mothers from a rural county may tend to have lower education and household income than mothers from suburban counties. For the county-level variables, all 100 mothers in a given county will have exactly the same score on median county education and expenditure on education. Linear regression using the `regress` command, discussed in chapters 9 and 10, assumes that observations are independent. Multilevel analysis can address the lack of independence of the observations when you are analyzing grouped data.

The *Stata Multilevel Mixed-Effects Reference Manual* provides several examples of multilevel analysis in this situation. A comprehensive two-volume book on these models by Rabe-Hesketh and Skrondal (2022) provides numerous examples. Note that the random-effects models for multilevel data that are demonstrated in this chapter assume you have quite a few groups at the higher level. Unless you have 20 to 30 groups at the higher level (county in this case), this type of analysis can be problematic and even 20 or 30 groups limit your power (Snijders and Bosker 2012).

15.2 Questions and data for a longitudinal multilevel application

Longitudinal data or panel data are the second type of data that multilevel models are appropriate for. With longitudinal data, the same individual's scores are collected at each wave of data collection, creating a panel of people. This is often called panel data because a single panel of people is measured at several time points. The scores are nested in the individual. Consider a six-month intervention designed to reduce the blood pressure of obese women through a physical activity program. You would want to measure each woman's blood pressure before the start of the intervention (time 0). Then you might measure it again at 2 months (time 2), at 4 months (time 4), and finally at 6 months (time 6) when the physical activity program concludes. You might even want to measure it after 12 months (time 12) to see whether the effects are long lasting. In this example, you have longitudinal data where the multiple measurements of a person's blood pressure are nested in the person. If you had five measures of blood pressure for each individual, they would not be identical, but they would surely be correlated and hence not independent. The longitudinal data could involve other than individual people as the unit of analysis. The analysis might involve a sample of 500 counties reporting their rate of people driving while intoxicated per 1,000 population each year from 2005 to 2016. The rates for the 11 years would be nested in the counties.

There are various approaches to analyzing longitudinal data of this nature. One option is to fit an appropriate structural equation model using Stata's structural equation modeling commands, `sem` and `gsem`. Structural equation modeling was discussed in chapter 13 and can be extended to cover this type of analysis (Acock 2013). In this chapter, we will use Stata's multilevel analysis command, `mixed`. The *Stata Multilevel Mixed-Effects Reference Manual* provides additional examples. It also covers additional multilevel commands for special circumstances such as when the outcome is a categorical or count variable.

15.3   Fixed-effects regression models

When we have longitudinal data or panel data, we can write our models using a subscript for the individual and a second subscript for time. We will use i for the individual and t for the time. We can express the fixed-effects model as

$$y_{it} = \beta_0 + \boldsymbol{\beta}\mathbf{x}_{it} + \mu_i + \eta_{it}$$

where

- β_0 is the intercept.

- $\mathbf{x}_{it}$ is the set of variables that are time varying, for example, month, wave, or year. In addition to the wave of data, these could be such factors that change over time such as percentage of peers who drink or whether you had a paid job at each wave. These are labeled time-varying covariates.

- $\boldsymbol{\beta}$ contains the coefficients on the time-varying covariates.

- μ_i are the individual-specific effects that are constant across repeated measurements. These effects may arise from individual-specific characteristics such as gender, race, or mother's education, but these variables are not included in the model and may not even be observable. This model allows for these effects, μ_i, to be correlated with the observed predictors ($\mathbf{x}_{it}$).

- η_{it} are the unobserved random errors (residuals) and vary across individuals and times.

The fixed-effects model estimates are widely used in economics because they can provide consistent estimates of $\boldsymbol{\beta}$ while controlling for the effects of the observed and unobserved time-invariant covariates (μ_i) that are correlated with $\mathbf{x}_{it}$ (Allison 2009). If the μ_i are independent of $\mathbf{x}_{it}$, then the random-effects model that we will discuss next can give consistent estimates. The random-effects estimator is also more efficient, meaning that you will typically obtain smaller standard errors.

Although fixed-effects models are not the focus of this chapter, they can easily be fit in Stata using the `xtreg` command with the `fe` option. You can find more details and examples in the `xtreg` entry of the *Stata Longitudinal-Data/Panel-Data Reference Manual*.

15.4   Random-effects regression models

A simple random-effects model can be expressed as

$$y_{it} = \beta_0 + \boldsymbol{\beta}\mathbf{x}_{it} + \boldsymbol{\gamma}\mathbf{z}_i + \mu_i + \eta_{it}$$

Notice a few differences from the fixed-effects model. We can now estimate coefficients, $\boldsymbol{\gamma}$, the effects of time-invariant covariates, $\mathbf{z}_i$, that we have measured. μ_i are the effects of unobserved time-invariant covariates and are assumed to be random and uncorrelated with observed covariates. Suppose your dataset includes a variable recording gender, a time-invariant, individual-specific variable. It would be a z covariate, and you would estimate its effect. On the other hand, if you do not have a gender variable, its effect would be incorporated in μ_i, and you would need to assume it was uncorrelated with any of the observed covariates.

We can divide this model into two parts. The fixed component, $\beta_0 + \boldsymbol{\beta}\mathbf{x}_{it} + \boldsymbol{\gamma}\mathbf{z}$, describes the overall relationship between our dependent variable and our independent variable. The random component, in this model, μ_i, represents the effects of the unobserved time-invariant variables. We also have an error term, η_{it}, that varies across both individuals and time. In more general terms, we can write the multilevel models that we will fit to longitudinal data as

$$\text{score} = \text{fixed part} + \text{random effects} + \text{error}$$

We can use the graph in the upper left of figure 15.1 to represent the fixed component for a random-effects model. This provides an estimate of the general trajectory for all individuals. Consider a study of how often people drink that runs from age 18 to age 28. At age 18, wave 0, we expect a person to report that he or she had 2 drinks in the last month. At age 22, wave 4, we expect a person to report that he or she had about 4 drinks, and at age 28, we expect a person to report that he or she had about 7 drinks. You may think a linear trend like this is unreasonable because you believe most people drink less in their late 20s than in their early 20s. This can be tested by including a quadratic term in the fixed portion of the model to allow for the deceleration. The coefficients estimated in the fixed portion of the model are often what are of most interest. However, the fixed portion describes the general trend—it certainly does not describe everyone because of a lot of variation between people in their trajectories.

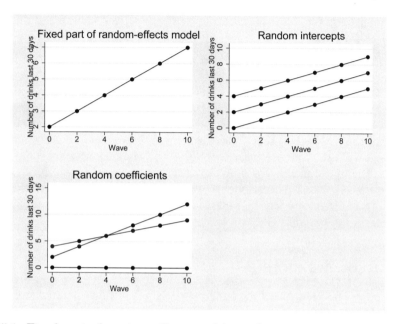

Figure 15.1. Fixed part of random-effects model, random intercepts, and random coefficients

We can consider two types of random effects with longitudinal analysis. The first is a random intercept and corresponds to the μ_i in the random-effects equation shown above. A model with random intercepts allows for individual-to-individual variations In the intercept. The graph in the upper right of figure 15.1 illustrates what we might find for a sample of 3 people. They all share the common slope estimated in the fixed portion of the model, and you see this in their three slopes being parallel. Each of their trajectories is increasing at the same rate. However, there is random variation in their intercepts. It makes sense that with a study of blood pressure, drinking behavior, and many other outcomes that you would expect people to vary widely in their initial level at (wave 0). When we fit a random-intercept model, we also recognize the individual variance around the estimate of the intercept, β_0, in the fixed portion of the model.

Many researchers doing longitudinal analysis want to allow for random intercepts in their model. The random-intercept growth-curve trajectory is often as far as researchers go, but there are clearly situations where we also need to incorporate a second random effect, a random slope. This is illustrated in the graph on the bottom left of figure 15.1. This is called a random-slope model or random-coefficients model because it incorporates random variation in both the intercept and the slope. It is easy to think of why this random-coefficients model might be important for studying growth curves in drinking behavior between age 18 and age 28. In spite of the overall upward trend reflected in the fixed portion of the model, we also expect many people to have an intercept of 0.0 and a slope of 0.0. These people did not drink when they were 18 and never started drinking. Other people may have a high intercept and a negative slope. Perhaps they had a serious drinking problem as an adolescent, but after intervention, they may not drink at all by the time they are 28.

Two types of predictors can be included in a random-effects model. Some variables are time invariant. The parents' drinking behavior during adolescence would be an example as well as the person's gender. Another type of predictor involves time-varying covariates. These variables change over the time frame of the study. Heavy peer drinking behavior when the person was an adolescent would be a time-invariant variable over the time frame of this study, but heavy peer drinking between ages 18 and 28 would be a time-varying covariate. The percentage of peers who were heavy drinkers at any given age might be an important time-varying predictor of spikes in the trajectory. This would be time varying because a person might have few peers who drank heavily at age 18, many who drank heavily at age 22, and a middle-range number who drank heavily at age 28. The score of the variable would vary over time.

15.5 An applied example

In this section, we provide a brief introduction to using multilevel analysis for longitudinal analysis by providing a detailed example. We use `longitudinal_mixed.dta`. This is a subset of the NLSY97 dataset that we have used before. This subset of variables includes youth who were 17 years old in 1997 and were asked the number of days they consumed alcohol in the last 30 days. They were asked the same question each of the following years. We will use their responses from 1998, 2000, 2002, 2004, 2006, and 2008. Thus we are looking at people as they aged from 18 in 1998 to 28 in 2008. There were a lot of data missing each year. If we relied on casewise deletion, we would analyze only the 181 people who provided an answer each and every year. However, almost half the people (46.3%) answered in 4 or more years. Using Stata's command for multilevel models, `mixed`, we will use all available data. Our working dataset also includes whether the person is a woman or a man, labeled `male`. This will be used as a time-invariant covariate.

15.5.1 Research questions

Can you think of research questions we can ask of these multilevel data?

- What happens to the number of days drinking as a person ages from 18 to 28?

- Is there a linear trend? Is there a quadratic trend?

- Are there spikes that cannot be described by a simple curve?

- Does the number of days go up and then level off or even go down as a person approaches 28?

- Do men drink more days a month than women?

- Is there an interaction between age and gender where the difference between the trajectories of women and men varies depending on their age?

We will cover only this single example of a multilevel longitudinal model. However, as you work through this, you should think of examples from your own field of study. What happens to weight in the 12 months following weight-loss surgery? What happens over five years? What happens to a person's salary from ages 25 to 35? From 45 to 60? How does the trajectory vary by gender? Race? Education? What happens to marital satisfaction over the first five years of marriage? What happens in the second five years? What happens to a person's political conservatism during his or her 20s, 40s, or 60s? Regardless of your field of study, multilevel longitudinal models are likely to be a very useful research tool.

15.5.2   Reshaping data to do multilevel analysis

First, we need to open the data and take a look at them. We type

```
. use http://www.stata-press.com/data/agis6r/longitudinal_mixed
```

Figure 15.2 shows a portion of the data in the Data Browser:

	id	male	drink98	drink00	drink02	drink04	drink06	drink08
63	283	Male	.	.	1	1	4	1
64	286	Female	.	10	10	5	1	0
65	289	Female	.	0	5	.	7	5
66	290	Female	2	0	2	2	4	3
67	292	Female	2	.	2	2	6	5
68	295	Female	0	4	.	2	6	1
69	297	Male	.	.	2	.	5	2
70	300	Female	1	0	9	2	1	2
71	302	Female	8	.	.	.	.	.
72	314	Male	.	.	1	3	5	5
73	325	Male	1	2	12	5	12	12

Figure 15.2. `longitudinal_mixed.dta` in the Data Browser

These data are in the wide format with one row for each observation and one column for each wave of data `id`, `male`, `drink98`, `drink00`, ..., `drink08`. Thus the person whose `id` number is 283 is a man who did not report the number of days he drank in 1998 or 2000 but did report drinking just 1 day a month in 2002 and 2004. He reported drinking 4 days a month in 2006 but was back down to 1 day a month in 2008. Compare this with person 325, who is also a man and reported his drinking behavior in every wave. Just looking at this tiny part of the dataset, we see that it seems likely there will be a significant individual-to-individual variation in the intercepts as well as the slopes. In this wide format, we have 1,771 observations (rows) and 8 variables (columns).

The multilevel commands in Stata require us to transform these data from wide format to long format. Before we reshape the data for multilevel analysis, it is simplest to keep only the variables you will use in the longitudinal analysis. We do this by using the `drop` or `keep` command discussed in section 3.7. We have already done this by eliminating all the other variables from the NLSY dataset. We must keep an identification variable (labeled `id` in this dataset) and any possible covariates you may want to consider as time-varying or time-invariant covariates.

Next, we need the longitudinal variable to have the same stem for each wave of data with a number at the end of the stem indicating the wave in which it was measured. The NLSY97 dataset already has the same stem, `drink`, for the variables, but "98" is bigger than "00", and this would make the numbering out of order. We want to change the numerical suffix to represent the time difference between the waves. We will use the `clonevar` command, which makes new variables identical to the original variables in all respects (values, variable labels, etc.) but uses numbers from 0 for `drink98` to 10 for `drink08`. Because the measurements are 2 years apart, we start the first wave as 0 and then increment this by 2 for each wave: 0, 2, 4, 6, 8, and 10. If the measurements were yearly, we would enter 0, 1, 2, 3, 4, and 5. If we had measurements at a base-line—3 months, 6 months, and 18 months—we might use 0, 3, 6, and 18 to accurately reflect the time differences. We will also drop the original variables because they are no longer needed:

```
clonevar drink0 = drink98
clonevar drink2 = drink00
clonevar drink4 = drink02
clonevar drink6 = drink04
clonevar drink8 = drink06
clonevar drink10 = drink08
drop drink98 drink00 drink02 drink04 drink06 drink08
```

Now we will use the `reshape` command that we used in section 9.8.

```
reshape long drink, i(id) j(wave)
```

We use `long` because we want to reshape the data from a wide format to a long format. Next we name the stem for our longitudinal variable, `drink`. After the comma, we indicate the identification variable by specifying `i(id)`. The `i` in the `i()` option indicates that we are entering the identification variable, and within the parentheses, we enter `id` because that is the name of the identification variable in this dataset. Finally, we enter `j(wave)`. The `j()` option requests that the new variable created be named `wave`, which will be 0 for 1998, 2 for 2000, and so on, based on the numerical suffix. The name `wave` is arbitrary. We could have used `year`, and in other applications, we might use `month`, `week`, or `hour`.

What to use for the suffix number?

In our example, we used 0, 2, 4, 6, 8, and 10 because the times were 2 years apart. If you had measurements at 0, 4, 8, 12, and 52 for a study where time measurements were in weeks, this would be fine for a linear growth curve. However, if you use a quadratic term, then you might have a problem because the product increases so quickly, 0, 16, 64, 144, and 2,704. With a more complex curve where you needed to cube the numbers, you would have 0, 64, 512, 1,728, and 140,608. This is likely to create estimation problems.

One solution is to use another measure of time. Instead of weeks, you might use months 0, 1, 2, 3, and 12 or even years 0, 4/52, 8/52, 12/52, and 1. If you do change how time is coded, you want to be careful how you interpret the coefficients; that is, remember whether a 1-unit change in time represents 1 week, 1 month, or $1/52 = 1.92\%$ of a year.

There will be a lot of rows when the data are in the long format. Where we had 1,771 rows in the wide format with 8 variables, in the long format, we have 6 rows for each case, yielding 10,626 rows of data, but our 8 variables are now just 4. Figure 15.3 is part of the data in the long format:

	id	wave	male	drink
373	283	0	Male	.
374	283	2	Male	.
375	283	4	Male	1
376	283	6	Male	1
377	283	8	Male	4
378	283	10	Male	1
379	206	0	Female	.
380	286	2	Female	10
381	286	4	Female	10
382	286	6	Female	5
383	286	8	Female	1
384	286	10	Female	0
385	289	0	Female	.
386	289	2	Female	0
387	289	4	Female	5
388	289	6	Female	.
389	289	8	Female	7
390	289	10	Female	5

Figure 15.3. Data shown in long format in the Data Browser

Study the person with `id` of 283 in this long format and compare him or her with how his or her data appeared in the wide format. In the long format, we have a row for each wave. Person 283 in wave 0 (1998) was a male and did not report how many days

he drank. The same is true in wave 2 (2000). In wave 4, he reported drinking 1 day in
the last month.

Going back and forth between wide and long formats

Reshaping data from wide to long and back to wide is a complex data management
process that Stata accomplishes with a short one-line command. Sometimes, when
you are doing a longitudinal analysis on a dataset, you have reshaped the data to
be in the long format, but you want to go back to the original wide format. Stata
keeps everything it did in the `reshape` command in memory, so to go back to a
wide format, type `reshape wide`. After doing some analysis in the wide format,
to get back to the long format, type `reshape long`. This is an example of the
remarkable data management capabilities of Stata compared with other software
packages.

15.6 A quick visualization of our data

Now that the data are in the long format, we will start our analysis by seeing if there is
an obvious visible trend. We will create a graph of the long-format data to do this. To
keep the graph simple, we restrict the number of individual trend lines in the graph. We
will create this graph only for those people who have `id` less than 100. You should pick
a range of the `id` variable to give you 10 to 20 individual trajectories. Our command to
produce figure 15.4 is

```
. twoway connected drink wave if id < 100, connect(L)
```

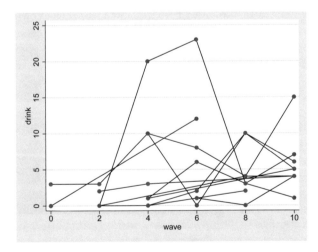

Figure 15.4. Selected individual growth trajectories between age 18 and age 28

From figure 15.4, it is hard to say what is happening. It looks as if there is a gradually increasing number of days a person drinks, so we expect a positive fixed-effects component for the slope. It also appears that the intercept (initial level at age 18) is not too far from 0. You might guess the intercept will be about 2, and the slope might be about 0.5. With just a few cases, these are wild guesses, but if we showed all the cases in this figure, it would be a huge mess and likely uninterpretable. Here are some things you might observe in this graph (what else can you see?):

- There are a lot of missing observations. The line starting at 0 has only observations at wave 0 and wave 6. Only two of these cases had observations at wave 0. We will not omit people unless they have no information.

- One case has a missing value for 1998, wave 0, a score of 0 at wave 2 when the person was 20, but then jumps up high when the person was 22 and 24 to drinking only to drop back down sharply.

- Some people seem to be consistently low and would have fairly flat trajectories (small intercept and small slope) in the random coefficients framework.

- Although we have only 2 observations for wave 0, using all the available data, we probably have variation in the intercept.

15.7 Random-intercept model

This section introduces three random-intercept models. The first model is for a linear trend, the second model is for a quadratic trend, and the third model is a free format where time is treated as a categorical variable. In section 15.8, we will show how to allow coefficients to vary across individuals, but first, we will introduce the random-intercept model.

15.7.1 Random intercept—linear model

Stata's `mixed` command is amazingly short for the complexity of what it is doing, but it does require careful attention to how it is written.

The first part of the `mixed` command shows the outcome variable, `drink`, and the list of predictors follow this. Here we have only one predictor, the `wave` variable. Although we have not included other time-varying covariates such as the percentage of peers who drank each year, those variables could be added after `wave`. We specify the predictor as `c.wave` because this is a continuous predictor representing the person's age.[1] So far, this command looks like most other commands we have covered, but we next encounter two vertical bars, | |, followed by `id:`. This tells Stata how much variance there is in the intercepts across people. We do not directly estimate separate intercepts for each of the

---

1. The `c.` term is not necessary here but will be needed when we add a quadratic term. Therefore, we include `c.` here for consistency.

1,554 people in our study who have some data reported, but we get an estimate of the variance of those 1,554 intercepts. If there is substantial variance in the intercepts, then a random-intercept model is justified. We should save the results so we can compare them with other models. We use the `estimates store` command to do this. Here is our command for the linear trend allowing for random effects with the results and the command to store the results for later use:

```
. mixed drink c.wave || id:

Performing EM optimization ...

Performing gradient-based optimization:
Iteration 0:   log likelihood = -17216.599
Iteration 1:   log likelihood = -17216.599

Computing standard errors ...

Mixed-effects ML regression                 Number of obs     =        5,474
Group variable: id                          Number of groups  =        1,554
                                            Obs per group:
                                                         min =            1
                                                         avg =          3.5
                                                         max =            6
                                            Wald chi2(1)      =       499.41
Log likelihood = -17216.599                 Prob > chi2       =       0.0000
```

drink	Coefficient	Std. err.	z	P>|z|	[95% conf. interval]	
wave	.4930213	.0220615	22.35	0.000	.4497815	.5362611
_cons	1.917751	.1677386	11.43	0.000	1.588989	2.246512

Random-effects parameters	Estimate	Std. err.	[95% conf. interval]	
id: Identity				
var(_cons)	10.05363	.6419645	8.870953	11.39398
var(Residual)	24.80612	.5520718	23.74734	25.9121

```
LR test vs. linear model: chibar2(01) = 568.55        Prob >= chibar2 = 0.0000
. estimates store linear
```

We have 5,474 observations in our dataset, and these are nested in 1,554 groups or people. The groups are the individuals; hence, we have 1,554 people in our analysis. The observations are up to 6 measurements for each individual, `drink0`, `drink2`, ..., `drink10`. We are using all the available data. Notice that although some individuals have the maximum of 6 waves of data, the average is just 3.5 waves, and some individuals have reported their drinking behavior for only the minimum of 1 wave.

The regression coefficients tell us the fixed component of our result. The intercept (`_cons`) is 1.918. We expect an 18-year-old to report drinking just under 2 days out of the last 30. For each one-year increase in wave, the person is expected to increase the number of days by 0.493 days. Both the intercept and the slope are highly significant. To interpret this, you need to remember that a wave is every two years, but a one-unit change in wave represents the change for just one year. So we would expect a 19-year-old (wave = 1) to drink about $1.918 + 0.493 \times 1 = 2.411$ days a month. We would expect a person who is 20 (wave = 2) to drink $1.918 + 0.493 \times 2 = 2.904$ days a month, and so on. Each year, we expect the number of days to increase by 0.493.

The estimated variance of the random intercept is var(_cons) = 10.054. Stata does not give us a simple test of significance for this. The technical problem with such a test is that there is a boundary problem because a variance cannot be less than 0.0. However, we can see from the 95% confidence interval on var(_cons) [8.871, 11.394] that there is variance in the intercepts. A simple way of interpreting var(_cons) is to convert it to a standard deviation and then put a 95% confidence interval for your sample around the intercept. The sd(_cons) = $\sqrt{10.054} = 3.17$. Hence, approximately 95% of the people in your sample will have an intercept between $1.918 \pm 1.96 \times 3.17$, that is, between -4.2952 and 8.131. Of course, the true lower limit is 0, so the confidence interval is 0 to 8.131. Substantively, this is a lot of variation in the intercept for this sample.

To visualize the random-effects model, we can use the `margins` command and the `marginsplot` command. `margins` produces estimated means at specific time points. `marginsplot` uses these estimated means to produce a graph of these results. We specify the waves (time points) for which we want the estimated means. The option `at(wave=(0(2)10))` yields 6 estimates for wave 0 to wave 10 in increments of 2. This produces estimates for years 0, 2, 4, 6, 8, and 10. Care is needed when reading the results, and you need to pay attention to the first part of the results where we see wave 0 is number 1, wave 2 is number 2, ..., and wave 10 is number 6.

```
. margins, at(wave=(0(2)10))

Adjusted predictions                              Number of obs = 5,474
Expression: Linear prediction, fixed portion, predict()
1._at: wave =  0
2._at: wave =  2
3._at: wave =  4
4._at: wave =  6
5._at: wave =  8
6._at: wave = 10
```

	Margin	Delta-method std. err.	z	P>|z|	[95% conf. interval]	
_at						
1	1.917751	.1677386	11.43	0.000	1.588989	2.246512
2	2.903793	.1369429	21.20	0.000	2.63539	3.172196
3	3.889836	.1151703	33.77	0.000	3.664106	4.115565
4	4.875878	.1080218	45.14	0.000	4.66416	5.087597
5	5.861921	.1181817	49.60	0.000	5.630289	6.093553
6	6.847963	.1419817	48.23	0.000	6.569684	7.126243

The `marginsplot` command produces a graph, which shows the estimated growth in drinking from just under two days in the last month to almost seven days. By default, the graph (figure 15.5) includes the confidence interval for the estimated means.

```
. marginsplot
```

Variables that uniquely identify margins: wave

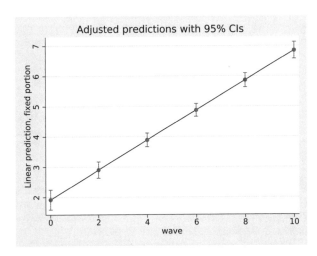

Figure 15.5. Fixed-effects results of days drinking last month between ages 18 and 28

15.7.2   Random-intercept model—quadratic term

We can explore two alternatives to the linear trend to fit these data. One is a quadratic. It seems likely that as a person's age moves beyond the early 20s, there may be a deceleration in the behavior. Thus we might predict a linear component reflecting an initial increase in drinking from 18 to say, 24 or 25, but then a negative quadratic component to bring the drinking down a bit after that age.

We could generate a new variable with the command `generate wavesquare = wave*wave`. Then we could use the command `mixed drink wave wavesquare || id:`. Instead, we will take advantage of Stata's notation for including squared terms. When we insert two hash marks (`##`) between two variable names, Stata interprets this as if we had entered a variable and a variable-squared. To save the results of the quadratic model, we type `estimates store` after the `mixed` command. Here are the commands and the results:

```
. mixed drink c.wave##c.wave || id:

Performing EM optimization ...

Performing gradient-based optimization:
Iteration 0:   log likelihood = -17201.188
Iteration 1:   log likelihood = -17201.188

Computing standard errors ...
```

Mixed-effects ML regression			Number of obs	=	5,474
Group variable: id			Number of groups	=	1,554
			Obs per group:		
			min =		1
			avg =		3.5
			max =		6
			Wald chi2(2)	=	535.19
Log likelihood = -17201.188			Prob > chi2	=	0.0000

drink	Coefficient	Std. err.	z	P>|z|	[95% conf. interval]	
wave	.9295978	.0813806	11.42	0.000	.7700948	1.089101
c.wave#c.wave	-.0405579	.0072885	-5.56	0.000	-.054843	-.0262727
_cons	1.173831	.2137214	5.49	0.000	.7549443	1.592717

Random-effects parameters	Estimate	Std. err.	[95% conf. interval]	
id: Identity				
var(_cons)	10.14196	.643112	8.956669	11.48412
var(Residual)	24.60029	.5475923	23.5501	25.6973

```
LR test vs. linear model: chibar2(01) = 581.20          Prob >= chibar2 = 0.0000
. estimates store quadratic
```

We still have 5,474 observations across the waves of the 1,554 people. All the parameter estimates are still significantly different from zero, but they have changed. The intercept, 1.174, is significant but considerably smaller than the 1.918 we had before. The linear component, 0.930, is not only significant, but much larger than the 0.493 we had before. This reflects how there is an early, fairly sharp increase in the number of days a person drank in the last month for the first few years after age 18. The quadratic coefficient, c.wave#c.wave, is −0.041 and is significant. We expected this would be negative. The coefficient looks small, but remember it is multiplied by wave-squared. To simplify the interpretation, you should look at a graph.

To obtain the estimated values based on the fixed portion of the model, we first type

```
. margins, at(wave=(0(2)10))
Adjusted predictions                                    Number of obs = 5,474
Expression: Linear prediction, fixed portion, predict()
1._at: wave =  0
2._at: wave =  2
3._at: wave =  4
4._at: wave =  6
5._at: wave =  8
6._at: wave = 10
```

	Margin	Delta-method std. err.	z	P>|z|	[95% conf. interval]	
_at						
1	1.173831	.2137214	5.49	0.000	.7549443	1.592717
2	2.870795	.1369328	20.96	0.000	2.602411	3.139178
3	4.243296	.1317906	32.20	0.000	3.984991	4.501601
4	5.291334	.1315462	40.22	0.000	5.033508	5.549159
5	6.014909	.1213646	49.56	0.000	5.777038	6.252779
6	6.41402	.1619082	39.62	0.000	6.096686	6.731355

We see that there is a bigger increase in the number of days at the start of the growth curve compared with the end. Comparing the estimated marginal means for the quadratic model, between wave 0 and wave 2, we see an increase of $2.871 - 1.174 = 1.697$ days. By contrast, between wave 8 and wave 10, there is an increase of only $6.414 - 6.015 = 0.399$ days.

We then use the `marginsplot` command to generate the graph shown in figure 15.6.

Figure 15.6. Adding a quadratic term to our model

Does our quadratic model fit better than our linear model? Because we saved the results of both models under the names `linear` for the linear model and `quadratic` for the quadratic model, we can run a likelihood-ratio chi-squared test to see whether there is a significant difference.

```
. lrtest linear quadratic
Likelihood-ratio test
Assumption: linear nested within quadratic
  LR chi2(1) =  30.82
  Prob > chi2 = 0.0000
```

The results are highly significant with a χ^2 with 1 degree of freedom $= 30.82$, $p < 0.001$. This means that our more complex model that added the quadratic term and hence used 1 degree of freedom fits the data significantly better than our linear growth trajectory.

Although there is a highly statistically significant improvement in the model fit, the likelihood-ratio chi-squared test is extremely sensitive to sample size, and we do have a large sample. Is there a practically significant difference in the model fit? A proportional reduction in error (PRE) measuring how much the residual (error) variance is reduced by adding the quadratic term may be useful. We will call the random-intercept linear model "Model 1" and the random-intercept quadratic model "Model 2".

$$\text{PRE} = \frac{\text{var(Residual)}\,\text{Model 1} - \text{var(Residual)}\,\text{Model 2}}{\text{var(Residual)}\,\text{Model 1}}$$
$$= \frac{24.806 - 24.600}{24.806}$$
$$= 0.008$$

From this, we can see that although the quadratic model represents a statistically significant improvement in the fit of the model, from a practical point of view, there is not a practically significant improvement in the fit with a PRE of less than 1%, which is 0.008. This PRE measure looks only at the change in the residual variance. It overlooks the issue of whether the level 2 variance increases or decreases. Alternative measures that include evaluation of level 2 variance in the PRE have been presented by Snijders and Bosker (2012) and Raudenbush and Bryk (2002). An application of these measures using Stata is presented by Rabe-Hesketh and Skrondal (2022, 148–151).

When you add a quadratic term, it is critical to interpret the results without going beyond the range of actual data you have. We can see how the number of days is beginning to level off, but it does not go down in the age range we have. We should not guess what happens if we had data for additional waves beyond age 28. When a quadratic model fits the data and does top out within the time span and then starts back down, it is possible to determine exactly when it tops out and starts to go down. We show how to apply this to the present example with the caution that the expected number of days per month a person drinks does not get fewer until you go outside the range of our data; hence, we do not have actual data to support what happens after age 28. The formula to determine the peak of the curve is peak $= -b/2a$, where b is the coefficient for the linear term, c.wave (0.9295978), and a is the coefficient for the quadratic term, c.wave#c.wave (-0.0405579). We can determine that the peak number of days per month a person drinks occurs at wave 11.46 by typing the following command:

```
. display -.9295978/(2*(-.0405579))
11.460132
```

The way we have labeled the suffix for drink, wave 11.46 would correspond to ages between 30 and 32 (see the top part of the margins command). Remember that because this is outside our time span, we would not normally report this based on our data.

15.7.3 Treating time as a categorical variable

So far, we have imposed two possible functional forms of the relationship between drinking and age, either a linear form or a quadratic form. As an alternative, we can avoid imposing a particular form on the relationship by estimating separate coefficients for each age, 18, 20, 22, 24, 26, and 28. To do this, we treat our continuous age variable as a factor variable using the i. prefix notation. If we fit the model by using the following command, we will not be imposing any assumption about the shape of the relationship. Here are our results:

```
. mixed drink i.wave || id:

Performing EM optimization ...

Performing gradient-based optimization:
Iteration 0:   log likelihood = -17198.516
Iteration 1:   log likelihood = -17198.515

Computing standard errors ...

Mixed-effects ML regression                     Number of obs     =      5,474
Group variable: id                              Number of groups  =      1,554
                                                Obs per group:
                                                              min =          1
                                                              avg =        3.5
                                                              max =          6
                                                Wald chi2(5)      =     541.66
Log likelihood = -17198.515                     Prob > chi2       =     0.0000
```

drink	Coefficient	Std. err.	z	P>|z|	[95% conf. interval]	
wave						
2	1.15965	.291726	3.98	0.000	.5878774	1.731422
4	3.014499	.2802921	10.75	0.000	2.465136	3.563861
6	3.864924	.2806947	13.77	0.000	3.314773	4.415075
8	4.718234	.273886	17.23	0.000	4.181427	5.25504
10	4.983518	.2749629	18.12	0.000	4.444601	5.522436
_cons	1.378645	.2414423	5.71	0.000	.9054266	1.851863

Random-effects parameters	Estimate	Std. err.	[95% conf. interval]	
id: Identity				
var(_cons)	10.17328	.6441161	8.986025	11.5174
var(Residual)	24.55744	.5467354	23.5089	25.65275

LR test vs. linear model: chibar2(01) = 584.11   Prob >= chibar2 = 0.0000

The value of the intercept, _cons = 1.379, is the expected value initially when the person was 18 years old. At wave 2, the person was 20 years old, and we expect him or her to have drunk $1.379 + 1.160 = 2.539$ days, which is substantially higher, $z = 3.98; p < 0.001$. At age 22, we expect the person to have drunk $1.379 + 3.014 = 4.393$ days, which is also highly significant. We will store these results by typing

```
. estimates store means
```

We can type the **margins** command to obtain the mean number of days a person drank at each age:

```
. margins, at(wave=(0(2)10))
Adjusted predictions                              Number of obs = 5,474
Expression: Linear prediction, fixed portion, predict()
1._at: wave =  0
2._at: wave =  2
3._at: wave =  4
4._at: wave =  6
5._at: wave =  8
6._at: wave = 10
```

	Margin	Delta-method std. err.	z	P>|z|	[95% conf. interval]	
_at						
1	1.378645	.2414423	5.71	0.000	.9054266	1.851863
2	2.538295	.206095	12.32	0.000	2.134356	2.942234
3	4.393144	.1851641	23.73	0.000	4.030229	4.756059
4	5.243569	.1835962	28.56	0.000	4.883727	5.603411
5	6.096879	.1716476	35.52	0.000	5.760455	6.433302
6	6.362163	.1729029	36.80	0.000	6.02328	6.701047

Examining these marginal means, we can see that they do not fall on a perfectly smooth line or a perfectly smooth curve, although the means appear to be consistent with the curve we obtained for the quadratic model. We can now use the **marginsplot** command to obtain figure 15.7:

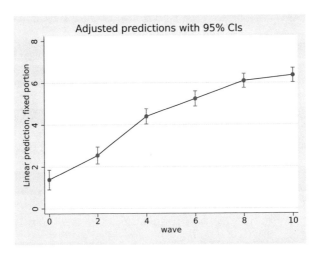

Figure 15.7. Treating age as a factor variable to fit means

This figure is fairly close to figure 15.6, where we had a smooth curve. The only apparent discrepancy is for ages 20 to 22, where it appears there is a big increase in the number of days, likely related to the age to drink legally in the United States being 21.

How does this model compare with the linear model? The quadratic model? We can run the likelihood-ratio test for each comparison.

```
. lrtest linear means
Likelihood-ratio test
Assumption: linear nested within means
 LR chi2(4) =  36.17
Prob > chi2 = 0.0000
. lrtest quadratic means
Likelihood-ratio test
Assumption: quadratic nested within means
 LR chi2(3) =   5.34
Prob > chi2 = 0.1482
```

These results show that the means model does significantly better than the linear model, $\chi^2(4) = 36.17, p < 0.001$, but it does not do significantly better than the quadratic model, $\chi^2(3) = 5.34, p = 0.148$. Using the PRE coefficient discussed in section 15.7.2, we can compare the random-intercept means model with the random-intercept linear model. The PRE $= (24.806 - 24.557)/24.806 = 0.01$. Thus although the difference between these models is statistically significant, the means model does not explain more than 1% of the residual variance. Given these comparisons, the simplest linear model would work well in the range of data we observe. If we had data over a longer age range and saw the drinking drop off at higher ages, then the quadratic model might be preferred.

15.8 Random-coefficients model

In the upper-right graph of figure 15.1, we showed how three observations might look over time if we were just interested in the random-intercept effect. In figure 15.4, we showed how a small subsample of people actually had very different patterns of drinking, with some starting low and staying low, some starting low and rapidly increasing, and some starting high and gradually decreasing. We fit the random-intercept model because it seemed reasonable to assume that individuals have different intercepts. In this section, we will introduce the random-coefficient model that has both a random intercept and a random slope as illustrated in the graph on the lower left of figure 15.1.

The random-coefficients model seems that it should help us fit the data better than the random-intercept model based on the few people we had in figure 15.4. We can fit this model treating age (`wave`) as a continuous variable with a linear relationship to drinking, having a quadratic allowing for the relationship to curve, and as a factor variable that allows the drinking behavior to go up and down without imposing a continuous functional form. To demonstrate how to fit the random-coefficient model, we will use the linear model. The difference here from our linear command is that after we specify the identification variable `|| id:`, we add `wave` to indicate to Stata that we want a random effect for the slope of `wave`.

We will allow for the random intercept and the random slope for wave to be correlated. What would a positive correlation mean? A positive correlation between the intercepts and slopes would imply that people who have a higher initial level, that is, who drink more often at age 18, will also have a steeper slope. If true, this would have policy implication for efforts to limit drinking. If the intercept and slope were positively correlated, then programs that reduce adolescent drinking would have important benefits—lowering the frequency of drinking in high school and thus lowering the drinking trajectory over the next 10 years.

The `mixed` command has a default that the random intercept and random slope are uncorrelated. This means the covariance matrix of the random effects is diagonal, with the covariance of the random intercept and random slope fixed at zero. Because we want to relax this assumption and allow them to be correlated, we add an option to the `mixed` command to implement this. Here are the command and results:

```
. mixed drink c.wave || id: wave, cov(unstructured)

Performing EM optimization ...

Performing gradient-based optimization:
  (output omitted )

Computing standard errors ...

Mixed-effects ML regression                 Number of obs     =       5,474
Group variable: id                          Number of groups  =       1,554

                                            Obs per group:
                                                          min =           1
                                                          avg =         3.5
                                                          max =           6

                                            Wald chi2(1)      =      350.87
Log likelihood = -17012.374                 Prob > chi2       =      0.0000
```

drink	Coefficient	Std. err.	z	P>|z|	[95% conf. interval]	
wave	.4493337	.0239881	18.73	0.000	.4023178	.4963496
_cons	2.239133	.1304158	17.17	0.000	1.983522	2.494743

Random-effects parameters	Estimate	Std. err.	[95% conf. interval]	
id: Unstructured				
var(wave)	.2401082	.0237827	.1977404	.2915537
var(_cons)	.3068283	.1602235	.1102565	.8538597
cov(wave,_cons)	.2714252	.061205	.1514657	.3913847
var(Residual)	21.31517	.4762878	20.40181	22.26942

```
LR test vs. linear model: chi2(3) = 977.00          Prob > chi2 = 0.0000
Note: LR test is conservative and provided only for reference.
```

This model has a fixed component and a random component. The fixed component tells us that the fixed intercept is 2.239 and the fixed slope is 0.449, both being highly significant. These represent the relationship between drink and wave. However, we now have four parameters in the random-effects section. The var(_cons) variable is familiar. It is the variance of the random intercepts, and because the 95% confidence interval is far from containing 0.0, it appears that a random intercept is needed. Now we also have a parameter estimate for var(wave), and its 95% confidence interval implies that there is variance in the slopes across individuals.

Do the random intercept and random slope covary? The random-effects parameter, cov(wave,_cons), is 0.2714, and its confidence interval is far from 0. This indicates that the intercept and slope are correlated. We could use our PRE measure to see whether the random-coefficient linear model accounts for proportionally more of the variance. We reduce our variance by PRE = $(24.806 - 21.043)/24.806 = 0.153$. Thus allowing for random slopes proportionally reduces our residual or error variance by 15.3%.

As an aid to visualize what the random-coefficient model is doing, we produce a prediction of each person's scores using the **predict** command. Then we produce a graph (figure 15.8) relating the newly predicted variable to wave overall using the **twoway lfit** command. Notice that I added an option to **twoway lfit** to make the line thick, lwidth(thick). Finally, I used multiple `twoway line` commands to display the trajectories of several individuals:

```
. predict yhat_drink, fitted
(1,302 missing values generated)

. twoway (lfit yhat_drink wave, lwidth(thick))
>         (line yhat_drink wave if id == 13)
>         (line yhat_drink wave if id == 61)
>         (line yhat_drink wave if id == 77)
>         (line yhat_drink wave if id == 82)
>         (line yhat_drink wave if id == 54)
>         (line yhat_drink wave if id == 125)
>         (line yhat_drink wave if id == 134)
>         (line yhat_drink wave if id == 138)
>         (line yhat_drink wave if id == 334)
>         (line yhat_drink wave if id == 364)
>         (line yhat_drink wave if id == 559)
>         (line yhat_drink wave if id == 715)
>         (line yhat_drink wave if id == 938), legend(off)
```

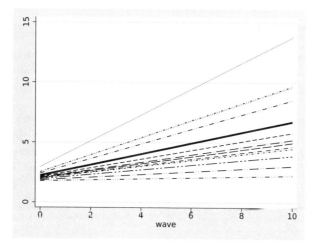

Figure 15.8. Plots of estimated days for several people based on the random-coefficient model

This graph provides fairly convincing evidence for people varying in both their intercepts and their slopes. Notice that `var(_cons) = 0.307` for this model is dramatically smaller than it was for the random-intercept model, where `var(_cons) = 10.054`. Looking at the figure, you can see that if we restricted all the slopes to be parallel, they would need to have much more variance in the intercepts. Because the random-coefficient model fits the data better and makes sense conceptually, the random-intercept model may have overestimated the variance in the intercept. These people did not differ as much in drinking behavior at age 18 as the random-intercept model implied.

Seeing the individual differences in the intercept and the big differences in the slopes raises the question of why do individuals vary this much. We have seen how you can incorporate time-varying covariates such as the percentage of peers who drink at each age as a covariate. In the next section, we will show how to use time-invariant covariates to account for the individual differences.

What would you do if you had another variable besides `wave` that varied, such as the percentage of peers who drank measured at each year, say, `peers`? Then you might type

```
mixed drink c.wave c.peers || id: wave, covariance(unstructured)
```

This command would produce a random intercept for each person, we would have a fixed component for the effect of `wave` and `peers`, and we would have a random slope for `wave` but not for `peers`. This would mean that each person could have a different intercept and trajectory over time but only a fixed component for peers. This and many other extensions of the `mixed` command, although beyond the scope of this introduction, are presented in the *Stata Multilevel Mixed-Effects Reference Manual*.

15.9   Including a time-invariant covariate

It has often been argued that the experiences you have before you are 18 years old have a significant effect on your trajectory after that. Can you think of time-invariant variables that would influence individual trajectories? Those who have a high frequency of church attendance as adolescents might have both a lower intercept and a flatter slope. People whose parents were heavy drinkers might have a different trajectory. We will consider just a single time-invariant covariate, `gender`, but the ideas we discuss are relevant to any such variables you feel would influence a person's trajectory. Gender is time invariant because it is constant for the duration of the time studied. For example, with very rare exceptions, a person's gender is constant between 18 and 28.

This can be done for any of the models we fit. To keep things as simple as possible we will just use the linear growth trajectory model. We will add `i.male`, treating gender as a factor variable. We will also include a random coefficient for the slope of `wave`.

```
. mixed drink c.wave i.male || id: wave

Performing EM optimization ...

Performing gradient-based optimization:
Iteration 0:   log likelihood = -17007.215
Iteration 1:   log likelihood = -17000.063
Iteration 2:   log likelihood = -17000.038
Iteration 3:   log likelihood = -17000.038

Computing standard errors ...

Mixed-effects ML regression                    Number of obs     =      5,474
Group variable: id                             Number of groups  =      1,554

                                               Obs per group:
                                                            min =          1
                                                            avg =        3.5
                                                            max =          6

                                               Wald chi2(2)      =     361.84
Log likelihood = -17000.038                    Prob > chi2       =     0.0000
```

drink	Coefficient	Std. err.	z	P>|z|	[95% conf. interval]	
wave	.4437515	.0245979	18.04	0.000	.3955405	.4919626
male						
Male	1.086603	.1913298	5.68	0.000	.7116039	1.461603
_cons	1.725033	.1636966	10.54	0.000	1.404194	2.045872

Random-effects parameters	Estimate	Std. err.	[95% conf. interval]	
id: Independent				
var(wave)	.2803658	.0190368	.2454305	.3202738
var(_cons)	1.286128	.5196101	.5826255	2.83909
var(Residual)	21.12014	.4929654	20.17571	22.10877

```
LR test vs. linear model: chi2(2) = 913.96           Prob > chi2 = 0.0000
Note: LR test is conservative and provided only for reference.
```

The slope of `wave` is 0.444, meaning that the fixed component for time is an increase of 0.444 days a month each year. The slope for `male` is 1.087, meaning that men are expected to drink just over 1 more day a month. There is variance for both the intercept and the slope of `wave`.

This model assumes that the gender gap of men drinking just over 1 more day per month than women is a constant difference between age 18 and age 28 because we did not include an interaction between `male` and `wave`. To visualize the effect of gender without any interaction, we can type `margins male, at(wave(0(2)8))`. The only difference between this `margins` command and the earlier ones is that we are doing it separately for women and men by placing the factor variable `male` before the comma. Then we type `marginsplot` to obtain figure 15.9.

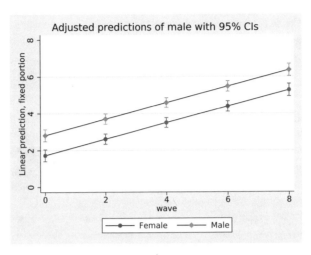

Figure 15.9. Gender differences in growth trajectories between 18 and 28 (assuming no interaction)

It is possible that the effect of gender varies by age, and the assumption that the lines are parallel may be unreasonable. Perhaps there is an increasing or a decreasing gender gap in the difference in drinking by men and women between ages 18 and 28. We can estimate this interaction effect as follows:

```
. mixed drink c.wave##i.male || id: wave
Performing EM optimization ...
Performing gradient-based optimization:
  (output omitted)
Computing standard errors ...
Mixed-effects ML regression               Number of obs     =       5,474
Group variable: id                        Number of groups  =       1,554
                                          Obs per group:
                                                      min =           1
                                                      avg =         3.5
                                                      max =           6
                                          Wald chi2(3)      =      385.04
Log likelihood =  -16989.76               Prob > chi2       =      0.0000
```

drink	Coefficient	Std. err.	z	P>|z|	[95% conf. interval]	
wave	.3328034	.0346532	9.60	0.000	.2648844	.4007224
male						
Male	.2408692	.2673299	0.90	0.368	-.2830877	.7648262
male#c.wave						
Male	.2227025	.0490476	4.54	0.000	.126571	.318834
_cons	2.137202	.187434	11.40	0.000	1.769838	2.504566

Random-effects parameters	Estimate	Std. err.	[95% conf. interval]	
id: Independent				
var(wave)	.2766611	.0188117	.2421422	.316101
var(_cons)	1.321935	.5187408	.6126179	2.85253
var(Residual)	21.06079	.4908944	20.1203	22.04524

```
LR test vs. linear model: chi2(2) = 915.56                     Prob > chi2 = 0.0000
Note: LR test is conservative and provided only for reference.
```

We see that `wave` has a significant effect, `male` does not, but the interaction of `male` with `wave` is significant. We need to be careful interpreting these results in the presence of a significant interaction. Remember from chapter 10 that the value of the intercept, `_cons` = 2.137, is the estimated days a person drank when all the variables are 0. That is, `wave` = 0, `male` = 0, and `wave` × `male` = 0. This would be the estimate for an 18-year-old woman of 2.137 days. The insignificant effect of `male` = 0.241 is the difference between men and women at `wave` = 0. An 18-year-old man is estimated to have drunk 2.137 + 0.241 = 2.378 days, and this is not significantly different from an 18-year-old woman.

What about the growth trend? The significant effect of `wave` is 0.333 days per year. This will be the growth trajectory for women because women are coded as 0 in the variable `male` and have a value of 0 for the interaction `male#wave`. Thus the results reduce to the estimated days being 2.137 + 0.333(`wave`) for women. The results reduce to the estimated days being (2.137+0.241)+(0.333+0.223)(`wave`) or 2.378+0.556(`wave`) for men. So we can see that men started slightly higher in our sample (2.378) and their trajectory increased significantly faster (0.556).

$$\text{Women: Est. days} = 2.137 + 0.333(\texttt{wave})$$
$$\text{Men: Est. days} = 2.378 + 0.556(\texttt{wave})$$

We can type `margins male, at(wave=(0(2)8))` and then `marginsplot` (see figure 15.10) to help us interpret this. We are interested in seeing separate trajectories for women and men given a significant interaction effect. These results are just like the earlier commands, except we add our factor variable (`male`) before the comma.

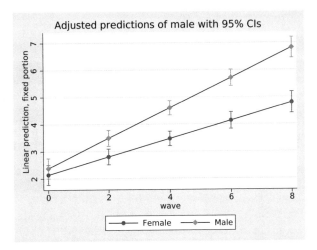

Figure 15.10. `marginsplot` for drinking over time by gender

This graph shows that men and women start drinking roughly the same number of days a month, both below 2.5 days. Over the next 10 years, the women show a gradual increase in drinking, but the men show a sharper increase that is significantly steeper than the increase for women.

We could add a quadratic term and even an interaction between gender and the quadratic by typing `mixed drink c.wave##c.wave##i.male || id: wave`. We will not show the output from this command. We type `margins male, at(wave=(0(2)8))` and `marginsplot` to obtain figure 15.11.

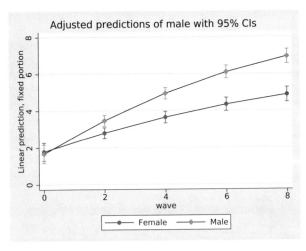

Figure 15.11. Growth trajectory for women and men allowing for an interaction effect

15.10 Summary

The `mixed` command offers many extensions to ordinary least-squares regression covered in chapter 10. We have shown how it can be used to study longitudinal and panel models, where each person has a series of scores. The random-effects models fit by the `mixed` command can estimate the effects of time-invariant covariates on the growth trajectory. Often the effects of such variables are a primary concern as illustrated by the role of gender in section 15.9.

We have covered two variations of random-effects multilevel longitudinal models. The random-intercept model is used when we are willing to assume that people have parallel growth curves but differ in their initial level. This assumes that the differences between individuals remain constant over the time frame of the data. These models allow each individual to have a potentially different intercept and estimate the variance in the intercept.

The second variation of random-effects multilevel longitudinal models we covered is random coefficients that allow the slope (trajectory) as well as the intercept to vary across individuals. Some people not only may start higher or lower than others but also may have very different trajectories. A common belief is that college freshmen women gain a number of pounds their freshmen year. The random-intercept model would fit the model allowing women to vary in their initial weight but assuming a fixed slope for the growth after that. The random-coefficient model would allow for variation in the women's initial weight as well as variation in their individual trajectories.

Perhaps the most important part of this chapter is the ability to include covariates to explain the individual trajectories. We have briefly mentioned how time-varying covariates can be added to both the random-intercept and the random-coefficient models. We provide an example of how a time-invariant variable, `gender`, influences both the intercept and the slope. Finally, we showed how the time-invariant variable can interact with time to produce a growing gender gap.

We have just touched the basics of the capabilities of the `mixed` command. The *Stata Multilevel Mixed-Effects Models Reference Manual* demonstrates many more options available in `mixed`, such as computing small-sample adjustments to test statistics and specifying autoregressive, exponential, and other structures for the residuals. You will also find many additional commands for special types of outcomes, such as counts or dichotomous outcomes.

15.11 Exercises

All the exercises use `longitudinal_exercise.dta`. This dataset has the weight of people measured each year from age 18 to age 28, `weight0–weight10`. It also includes a variable for each person's identification number, `id`; his or her gender, `male`; and his or her race or ethnicity, `race`. These data are from the National Longitudinal Survey 1997 (NLSY97) (Bureau of Labor Statistics, U.S. Department of Labor 2015), which was originally downloaded from the Inter-University Consortium for Political and Social Research (ICPSR). These data are in the wide format.

1. Print a listing of the first 15 lines of the data in the wide format. Convert the data to long format, creating a variable, `time`, representing years, and include the variables `male` and `race`. List the first 15 lines of the data in the long format. Explain the differences.

2. What happens to a person's weight between age 18 and age 28? Fit a linear model with a random intercept. Interpret the coefficients in the linear model. Interpret the random effect.

3. Fit and interpret a quadratic model. Fit a quadratic model with a random intercept. Interpret the coefficients in the quadratic model. Test whether the quadratic model does significantly better at fitting the data than the linear model in exercise 2.

4. Create a `marginsplot` of both the linear (exercise 2) and the quadratic (exercise 3) models. Interpret the curve in the quadratic model.

5. You heard that people put on the most weight from age 18 to age 22. Fit the model using a free format where you are estimating a separate coefficient for each year. Does this seem to support the idea you heard? What about age 20? Does this free model fit better than the linear model (exercise 2)? Does it fit better than the quadratic model (exercise 3)? Which of the three models makes the most sense?

6. Fit a multilevel longitudinal model that includes the `race` variable in the fixed portion of the model. (Run a frequency distribution for `race` to see how it is coded.) Next, fit a model in which there is an interaction between `race` and `time`. Produce a `marginsplot` showing `race` differences with the trajectory for weight that includes the interaction. Interpret all the coefficients in the model with the interaction. Interpret the `marginsplot`.

16 Item response theory (IRT)

In chapter 12, we introduced measurement methods based on classical measurement theory. We covered summated scales and focused on Likert-type scales. These methods rely on summing or averaging scores on a set of items. When you compute the sum or mean, each item has equal weight, $1 \times \text{item}_1 + 1 \times \text{item}_2 + \cdots + 1 \times \text{item}_k$. In addition to Likert-type scales, other summated scales are often based on items with binary responses—yes or no items or correct or wrong items.

An alternative approach to measurement is known as item response theory (IRT). This approach has a long history (Lord 1952; Rasch 1960). The roots of IRT are carefully documented by Bock (1997). It has become popular with computer adaptive testing. Instead of focusing on computer adaptive testing, we will introduce IRT models as an alternative to summative measures. We will consider how IRT models can be used to measure attitudes, values, opinions, and beliefs.

There are two conceptually distinct approaches, IRT and Rasch modeling. Stata's set of IRT commands was designed from the framework of IRT. As you work through this chapter, some of the key conceptual differences will become apparent. IRT modelers recognize that a Rasch model can be fit using a corresponding IRT model. This misses the point that they have different theoretical bases. Rasch modeling begins with the model and makes the data fit the model, dropping items that do not fit the Rasch model.

This chapter begins by comparing IRT measures to summated scales because summated scales are so widely used in social, behavioral, and health sciences. We then introduce IRT models for binary items. Finally, we extend the IRT model to provide an alternative to summing Likert-type measures where there are multiple, ordinal response categories such as "Strongly agree", "Agree", "Disagree", and "Strongly disagree".

Fitting IRT models has typically required specialized packages that were somewhat complicated to use. Stata includes a set of commands that makes IRT measurement easy to implement.

16.1 How are IRT measures of variables different from summated scales?

The idea behind summated scales is to draw a series of items that represents the domain of the attitude, value, or belief being measured. Some studies can use a large number of items, say, 20, 30, or more to represent the full range of the domain. By contrast, with the wide use of large-scale surveys, especially when analyzing secondary data, we are limited to just a few items to measure each of the variables. Because of space restrictions, there are often five or fewer items to measure an opinion, value, attitude, or belief.

Likert-type scales, as an example of summated scales, rely heavily on the alpha reliability coefficient, α, where an $\alpha \geq 0.80$ is a gold standard that a scale is reliable. Remember from the box at the end of section 12.3.3 that α depends only on the number of items and the average correlation of the items. When you have a large number of items, some of the items may not be highly correlated, and alpha will still be large enough. With a scale that has just a few items, the items need to be substantially correlated with one another.[1] If you have five very similar items, then they will be

---

1. Nunnally and Bernstein (1994, 305) note "... it is desirable to mix easy and difficult items even if it sacrifices a slight amount of reliability". This is reasonable for scales with many items, but when there are only a few items, any items that are much easier or much more difficult than the others will substantially lower the α.

highly correlated and hence have an acceptable α. This means that the items will be similar to each other and tap only a small portion of the true domain of the concept you are measuring.

Similar items are only differentiating people across a narrow range of the true distribution of the variable. Consider the continuum below, where we have five similar items that measure happiness. I have labeled these hypothetical items i1 to i5. There are also four people, John, Taylor, Assad, and Afra, who are placed along the continuum where their true score on happiness lies.

Although the individuals vary across the range of the continuum, the items are bunched together in the middle of the first continuum of happiness. They will do a good job differentiating a person in your sample who is slightly below average or slightly above average on happiness from others, for example, differentiating Taylor and Assad from each other and differentiating Taylor from Afra, who is very happy. They cannot differentiate between Assad and Afra. Because the items are similar in difficulty, they are likely to be highly correlated, and the α is likely strong. Many summated scales that have high reliability with just a few items also have similar means for the items. This is evidence that they are all tapping the same small part of the continuum.

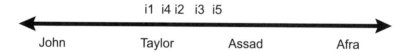

When using IRT to create a scale, we prefer to pick items that vary greatly in difficulty (location on the continuum) as a way to differentiate people across the continuum. The item locations might look like those on the continuum below:

A summated scale created from these items may not have a strong alpha because they are likely less highly correlated with each other. Remember that the goal of an IRT scale is not to produce similar items. The advantage of the IRT scale is that it provides information that can differentiate people across a much greater range of true scores.

Why is this greater differentiation important? If you are using a person's attitude to predict some behavior, then identifying those people with more extreme attitudes will help you make a better prediction.

The best uses of IRT are when you are developing a computer adaptive measure or developing a new scale. However, IRT can be used to evaluate and modify existing measures. Evaluating existing measures developed as summated scales that contain just a few items is somewhat problematic because they often lack good items at the very negative or very positive location on the continuum.

- IRT can be used to evaluate the psychometric properties of an existing scale, each item in a scale, and in the case of Likert-type items, even each of the response options.

- IRT can be used to shorten a scale by dropping items that are of redundant difficulty. These items will inflate α but do not help differentiate people. This is very important when you can include only a few items in your final instrument to measure the variable.

- IRT can be used to identify parts of the distribution that your items do not measure. IRT can show you where your scale would benefit by an additional item that is both more difficult and answered positively by just a few people or easy and answered positively by most people.

- IRT can be used to develop a pool of items where a few of them are given to the participants. This computer adaptive testing is used in tests such as driver's license tests or SAT tests. People may get their own subset of items.

16.2   Overview of three IRT models for dichotomous items

Many measures use simple yes or no, agree or disagree, or correct or incorrect response options. For example, when researchers measure children, it is often useful to simplify the response options this way because children may not differentiate between "Strongly agree" and "Agree" or "Strongly disagree" and "Disagree". This is relevant to other populations where people do not make fine distinctions or find making them frustrating and end up skipping items. It could also be argued that the distinction between "Agree" and "Strongly agree" or "Disagree" and "Strongly disagree" sometimes reflects personality differences rather than true differences in the attitude or belief. However, the dichotomous response items do miss the added information possible when these additional distinctions are appropriate.

IRT models vary in how many parameters are estimated. A one-parameter model is based solely on item difficulty. You select items that have a range of difficulty from very easy to very difficult. A two-parameter IRT model is based on both item difficulty and item discrimination. A three-parameter model is based on item difficulty and item discrimination and adds a guessing parameter.

16.2.1   The one-parameter logistic (1PL) model

The one-parameter logistic (1PL) IRT model (often called a Rasch model) differentiates items based solely on item difficulty. This can be illustrated intuitively by measuring how high a person can jump. You could set the bar for the first jump at just 2 feet, then 3 feet, 4 feet, 5 feet, and finally 6 feet. John might make the 2-foot jump about half the time but have very little chance of jumping any higher. Taylor might be able to make the 2-foot jump most of the time, make the 3-foot jump about half the time, and rarely jump over a higher bar height. Assad might be able to jump over the 2-foot height almost always, usually over the 3-foot height, and about half the time over the 4-foot height. On a very good day, Assad might make the 5-foot jump, but there is almost no chance of him jumping any higher. Camila might jump over the 2-foot and 3-foot bar even when she is feeling terrible. She might jump over the 4-foot and 5-foot height most of the time and even jump over the 6-foot height about half the time.

Compare this with having them jump over bars set at 3.1 feet, 3.2 feet, 3.3 feet, 3.4 feet, and 3.5 feet; these jumps have similar difficulty and would give more consistent results with each other and hence have a higher α. However, these similar jumps would not tell us that Assad can jump higher than Taylor or that Camila is amazing.

The high jump measures how high a person can jump almost ideally. I say "almost ideally" because the performance might vary depending on the elevation, wind speed, etc. Performance will also vary depending on the individual's physical health, injuries, and experience. There is a single parameter, difficulty, for each jump. If you jump over a 6-foot bar, there is a high probability that you could jump over any bar of a lesser height. The item characteristic curves (ICCs) for the 2-foot, 3-foot, 4-foot, 5-foot, and 6-foot jumps might look like those plotted in figure 16.1. The ICCs show the probability of succeeding at a jump of each height across a range of true jumping abilities.

Figure 16.1. Item characteristic curves and item difficulties for a 1PL model of jumping ability

The horizontal axis "Theta" (θ) represents a person's true latent jumping ability, which has been standardized to follow a standard normal distribution. The graph shows values from -4 to 4, although it is unlikely to find someone with values near those extremes. The vertical axis is a probability of a successful jump. You could think of this scale of jumping ability as a normal z-score distribution. A person who has extremely limited jumping ability, say, a $\theta = -2.0$, would have a very low probability of jumping over any of the bar heights. Draw a vertical line up from $\theta = -2.0$ (see the vertical line in figure 16.1). If -2.0 were a person's true jumping ability, he or she would have a small probability of succeeding at the 2-foot jump ($\text{Pr} \approx 0.2$) and almost no chance of making any of the higher jumps. A person with a higher true score, say, 0.0, would have a very high probability of jumping over a 2-foot bar and just over a 50/50 chance of jumping over the 3-foot bar. As a final example, a person with extremely high jumping ability, say, $\theta = 2.0$, would almost certainly jump over all the bar heights.

The 1PL model fits the difficulty of each item. The difficulty represents the value of the latent ability for which an individual would have a 0.5 probability of success. In figure 16.1, vertical lines represent the difficulties. The difficulty for the 2-foot jump is -1.36, and the difficulty for the 5-foot jump is 0.76. If May's jumping ability is $\theta = -1.36$, she would have a 0.5 probability of jumping over the 2-foot bar. If instead, she had a jumping ability of $\theta = 0.76$, she would have a 0.5 probability of jumping over the 5-foot bar and a probability of almost 1 of jumping over the 2-foot bar.

16.2.2 The two-parameter logistic (2PL) model

The second parameter, discrimination, is added in the 2PL IRT model. We will illustrate this with a dataset from the *Stata Item Response Theory Reference Manual* (that is, type use https://www.stata-press.com/data/r17/masc1). We have selected four items that have variable names q1, q2, q5, and q7. These variables are dichotomous correct or incorrect items measuring mathematical ability. Using the 2PL IRT model, we can see that the items vary not only in their difficulty but also in their discrimination (see figure 16.2).

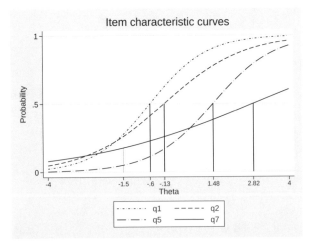

Figure 16.2. Item characteristic curves for a 2PL model

Items with steeper slopes have better discrimination, and items with flatter slopes have worse discrimination. Technically, discrimination is the slope (tangent) of the curve when the probability of success is 0.5. Better discrimination is preferred when trying to differentiate between two individuals' ability levels. Item q7 has a very high difficulty score of 2.82 but a relatively flat slope and hence fairly poor discrimination. This means that a number of people answered this item positively even though their true score on the latent variable was much lower than 2.82. The discrimination for q7 is just 0.36. Item q5 was less difficult, 1.48, but it was relatively more discriminating (steeper slope, discrimination = 0.99).

The curves for q7 and q5 even cross over. Consider Galina, who has a true mathematical ability of $\theta = -1.5$. She has a higher probability of answering item q7 positively ($\Pr \approx 0.17$) than she has of answering q5 positively ($\Pr \approx 0.05$) even though the 2PL IRT model tells us q7 is a much more difficult item than q5.

In many applications, a 1PL (Rasch) model is all you want or need. When we are measuring opinions, attitudes, values, and beliefs, researchers often add the second parameter to allow some items to differentiate more sharply or distinctly and other items to differentiate less sharply or distinctly. Advocates of Rasch intentionally select items that differ in difficulty but have the same discrimination. They instead identify and reconsider the use of items that do not fit well in the 1PL model (Bond et al. 2021). With the 2PL model, the discrimination parameter is incorporated into the model to provide improved fit of the data to the model. Rasch modelers contend that adding items that have different discrimination power is like adding apples and oranges and that you lose the true linear quality of a fundamental measure like a ruler. Rasch modelers advocate that their models can provide linear information. This requires a special interpretation of interval level measurement as explained by Salzberger (2010).

From an IRT perspective, the 2PL model adjusts for differences in discrimination when estimating the relationship between the items and the latent score, and this is important to obtain optimal fit to your data. Fitting the 2PL model requires a larger sample because of the additional parameter. The best choice of either a 1PL or a 2PL IRT model likely depends on the underlying ability being measured and cost or reward of parsimony versus model fit.

16.2.3   The three-parameter logistic (3PL) model

A 3PL model has an adjustment for guessing. If you think of a multiple-choice test, you would expect to answer some items correctly if you just picked option A for each item. Some items may be easier to guess correct than others. The 3PL model assumes that the estimated guessing parameter is a constant for all people. It is likely that where guessing is a factor, some people will be much better than others, and this will not be reflected in a constant guessing parameter. We will not cover this option, but it is described in the *Stata Item Response Reference Manual*. The 3PL model is not often used when measuring opinions, attitudes, values, and beliefs. There is a possible four-parameter model representing "carelessness" or an upper limit on the probability of a success. Difficult to fit, this is not a commonly used IRT model and is not available in Stata.

16.3   Fitting the 1PL model using Stata

To demonstrate a 1PL model, we have selected items from a study of the effects of unemployment on self-confidence. The study was completed by Price et al. (2004) using a survey in Baltimore and Detroit (1996–1998) and obtained from the Inter-University Consortium for Social and Political Research (ICPSR). We picked five items that asked participants about their confidence after they lost their job. For demonstrating how to fit models for dichotomous items, we have dichotomized what were originally Likert-type items that had response options of "Not at all", "A little", "Somewhat", or "A lot". Three items were negatively stated, and two were positively stated. We dichotomized the items, so only the most confident response was coded "High confidence". Because we selected only five of the original items and then modified their coding, the results reported here are shown only to illustrate how to fit an IRT model and should not be compared with the findings in the original study. We are using these data for illustrative purposes only. Here are the five items and how we coded or reverse coded them (a 1 is the highly confident response, and a 0 is the less confident response).

- Item 2: I am insecure about my abilities ("Not at all" is a highly confident response coded 1).

- Item 4: I am uncertain about the future ("Not at all" is a highly confident response coded 1).

- Item 5: I feel rejected ("Not at all" is a highly confident response coded 1).

- Item 7: I am confident ("A lot" is a highly confident response coded 1).

- Item 10: I am motivated ("A lot" is a highly confident response coded 1).

Here are frequency distributions for each of the items:

```
. use http://www.stata-press.com/data/agis6r/attitude
(PREVENTING DEPRESSION IN COUPLES FACING JOB LOSS, 1996-1998: [BALTIMORE, MD])
. fre dn2 dn4 dn5 dn7 dn10
```

dn2 — RECODE of n2 (INSECURE ABOUT ABILITIES)

		Freq.	Percent	Valid	Cum.
Valid	0 Low confidence	811	54.54	54.98	54.98
	1 High confidence	664	44.65	45.02	100.00
	Total	1475	99.19	100.00	
Missing	.	12	0.81		
Total		1487	100.00		

dn4 — RECODE of n4 (UNCERTAIN ABOUT FUTURE)

		Freq.	Percent	Valid	Cum.
Valid	0 Low confidence	1219	81.98	82.70	82.70
	1 High confidence	255	17.15	17.30	100.00
	Total	1474	99.13	100.00	
Missing	.	13	0.87		
Total		1487	100.00		

dn5 — RECODE of n5 (FEEL REJECTED)

		Freq.	Percent	Valid	Cum.
Valid	0 Low confidence	509	34.23	34.56	34.56
	1 High confidence	964	64.83	65.44	100.00
	Total	1473	99.06	100.00	
Missing	.	14	0.94		
Total		1487	100.00		

dn7 — RECODE of n7 (CONFIDENT)

		Freq.	Percent	Valid	Cum.
Valid	0 Low confidence	635	42.70	43.11	43.11
	1 High confidence	838	56.36	56.89	100.00
	Total	1473	99.06	100.00	
Missing	.	14	0.94		
Total		1487	100.00		

dn10 — RECODE of n10 (MOTIVATED)

		Freq.	Percent	Valid	Cum.
Valid	0 Low confidence	940	63.21	63.73	63.73
	1 High confidence	535	35.98	36.27	100.00
	Total	1475	99.19	100.00	
Missing	.	12	0.81		
Total		1487	100.00		

In classical measurement theory, the proportion of individuals giving a positive response is used as an indication of item difficulty. Notice how the items differ in their difficulty as reflected by the proportion giving a positive response. Item **dn5** asks whether they feel rejected, and 65.4% of those answering the question gave the highly confident response, "Not at all". By contrast, item **dn4** asks whether they are uncertain about the future, and only 17.3% report a highly confident response, "Not at all". We can examine each item, and the higher the proportion giving a confident response, the less difficult a measure of confidence the item is. Items for which relatively few people give a positive response provide the most difficult test of their confidence. Because these items vary in difficulty, we expect correlations to be low. If the proportion correct for a pair of items were 0.1 and 0.8, the maximum correlation possible would be small.

16.3.1 The estimation

The command to fit this model is as follows:

```
. irt 1pl dn2 dn4 dn5 dn7 dn10

Fitting fixed-effects model:

Iteration 0:    log likelihood = -4621.5209
Iteration 1:    log likelihood =  -4616.607
Iteration 2:    log likelihood = -4616.6057
Iteration 3:    log likelihood = -4616.6057

Fitting full model:

Iteration 0:    log likelihood = -4196.8333
Iteration 1:    log likelihood = -3993.0408
Iteration 2:    log likelihood =  -3989.611
Iteration 3:    log likelihood = -3989.5915
Iteration 4:    log likelihood = -3989.5915

One-parameter logistic model                Number of obs = 1,479
Log likelihood = -3989.5915
```

		Coefficient	Std. err.	z	P>|z|	[95% conf. interval]	
	Discrim	2.059114	.0765293	26.91	0.000	1.909119	2.209108
dn2							
	Diff	.1709084	.0425518	4.02	0.000	.0875085	.2543084
dn4							
	Diff	1.234974	.056633	21.81	0.000	1.123975	1.345972
dn5							
	Diff	-.512255	.0454498	-11.27	0.000	-.6013349	-.423175
dn7							
	Diff	-.2193236	.0430899	-5.09	0.000	-.3037781	-.134869
dn10							
	Diff	.4660937	.0442333	10.54	0.000	.3793981	.5527892

We also run the `estat report` postestimation command, sorting items based on their difficulty parameter, with the `byparm` and `sort(b)` options because this simplifies the presentation of results. Here are our command and results:

```
. estat report, byparm sort(b)
One-parameter logistic model                    Number of obs = 1,479
Log likelihood = -3989.5915
```

	Coefficient	Std. err.	z	P>|z|	[95% conf. interval]	
Discrim	2.059114	.0765293	26.91	0.000	1.909119	2.209108
Diff						
dn5	-.512255	.0454498	-11.27	0.000	-.6013349	-.423175
dn7	-.2193236	.0430899	-5.09	0.000	-.3037781	-.134869
dn2	.1709084	.0425518	4.02	0.000	.0875085	.2543084
dn10	.4660937	.0442333	10.54	0.000	.3793981	.5527892
dn4	1.234974	.056633	21.81	0.000	1.123975	1.345972

These results show we have 1,479 observations. The discrimination parameter is labeled `Discrim` and is 2.06. The assumption is that the five items share a common discrimination parameter. The difficulty of each item is labeled `Diff`. For example, the difficulty of item `dn4` is 1.23, our most difficult item, and the difficulty of `dn5` is -0.51, our least difficult item.

Would more items be helpful? Could we drop any of these items? It might be nice to add at least one item that was more difficult than any of these to get the ideal range of difficulty. It would clearly make sense to add an easy item, that is, one that has a negative difficulty. This would provide information about those who have had their confidence shattered by job loss. We might say as a rule of thumb that it would be nice to have items covering a fairly large range of difficulties, perhaps from -1.5 to 1.5 or -2.0 to 2.0, or perhaps even more extreme values if we could find items at those extremes. This would allow us to have reliable information for people who were very low or very high on the attitude we are measuring. It would not make sense to drop any of the items because none of them are redundant. If we had difficulty scores for two or more items that were very close together, then we would have redundant items and could drop one of them. If you apply an IRT model to widely used summated scales that have a large number of items, you will often find that there are multiple redundant items but few items at one or both of the extremes. The redundant items make the α's for the summated scales look good but do not provide reliable information to differentiate people along the full range of the attitude continuum. When large-scale surveys require you to include just a few items, eliminating redundant items is a good way to go.

To obtain a visual appreciation of how these items vary in difficulty, we can generate an ICC graph. The postestimation command for this is `irtgraph icc`. We include the `blocation` option to show where the probability of getting the positive answer is 0.50. This location marks the difficulty of the curve for each item.

In this chapter, I show the basic commands needed to create the graphs of the IRT models. However, the displayed graphs have been enhanced with options to ease readability. Here is the basic command to create the ICC graph:

```
. irtgraph icc, blocation
```

Figure 16.3 shows the resulting graph:

Figure 16.3. Item characteristic curves for 1PL model of confidence after loss of job

What item has the most difficulty? Looking at figure 16.3, we see that item **dn4** (uncertainty about the future) would have a probability only of 0.50 of endorsement if the person had a $\theta = 1.23$. This would suggest such a response would be positive only if the person had fairly high confidence after being laid off. Perhaps such a person is confident because he or she got an interview for a great new job just before taking the survey.

16.3.2   How important is each of the items?

We can graph the item information function (IIF) for each item. This reflects how much information each item provides and at what part of the continuum it offers the most information. The command to produce the IIF graph and the graph (figure 16.4) itself are shown below.

```
. irtgraph iif
```

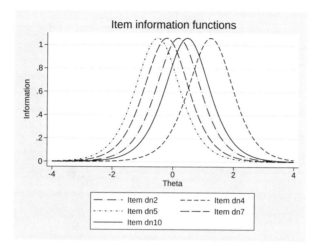

Figure 16.4. Item information function graph

This graph shows how much information each item provides. Whereas classical summated scales rely on measures such as item-total correlation for evaluating the usefulness of individual items, IRT models allow us to evaluate the information provided by each item. Consider our most difficult item, **dn4**, which concerns certainty about the future. It provides the most information around its difficulty level, $\theta = 1.23$ (height shows where the item provides the most information value). Item **dn4** does not help us discriminate people who are a lot more extreme than this, say, $\theta > 2.0$. Not many people would be that extreme, so this may be okay. Still, an even more difficult item than **dn4** would strengthen the scale's ability to identify the very most confident people who recently loss their job. Item **dn4** provides almost no information to discriminate between people who have low levels of confidence, but this is not a problem because we have other items to provide that information, for example, **dn5** and **dn7**.

Because we are using a 1PL model, the height and shape of each curve must be identical. This graph shows that none of our items are redundant. The height of the curve represents where the item provides the most information on the continuum. The tightness of the curve is an indication of how discriminating the item is. Information functions for highly discriminating items are tall and narrow. Our set of items appears useful for distinguishing individuals in the part of the continuum from slightly low confidence, **dn5**, to somewhat high confidence, **dn4**, where the items provide the most information. The figure shows that we have reliable information over a range of the continuum even though it is hard to look at this graph without wanting to add one more item that had a higher difficulty level and especially one with a lower difficulty value so that we would have reliable information from very low to very high confidence. A scale created from these five items would have limited ability to identify people with extremely low confidence after losing their jobs.

16.3.3   An overall evaluation of our scale

We can combine the information from the IIF for each item into a test information function that gives us an overall idea of how well our scale is doing. The graph of the test information function appears in figure 16.5. We want to know what part of the total distribution we can measure. It is important to see the standard error for the test information function so that we know how well we can represent each part of the overall continuum on confidence after job loss. In our command below, the **se** option provides standard errors and is used to reflect confidence or a lack of confidence in the total information provided by our set of items. This graph reflects the overall reliability in terms of the information we have for assessing the true latent variable, confidence after job loss.

```
. irtgraph tif, se
```

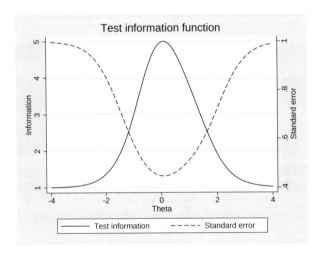

Figure 16.5. Overall test information function and standard error for the set of five items

This figure shows that we have a lot of information to differentiate people who have an average amount of confidence (reflected in the height of the solid line). However, as you move above or below $\theta = 0.0$, our confidence drops off. Indeed, there is almost no reliable information about scores below $\theta = -1$, and the standard error approaches the scale's information. (Notice that the scale for the standard error is given on the right-hand side of the graph, while the scale for the information function is given on the left-hand side.)

Missing values using IRT models

Our data have a small number of missing values. A total of 1,487 people were asked this set of items about confidence. Eight of these people did not answer any of the five items, and we cannot say anything about their level of confidence without additional information. When we did our IRT analysis, Stata used all available observations when estimating the equation for each item, and we have $N = 1479$ (that is, $1487-8$) people who answered at least one of the items.

Alternatively, we could have used listwise deletion. With this approach, we would analyze only the 1,458 people who answered all 5 items. To impose this restriction, we would use the IRT command `irt 1pl dn2 dn4 dn5 dn7 dn10, listwise`. This would work for all the IRT commands presented in this chapter. Listwise deletion will give biased estimates unless the missing values are missing completely at random. Listwise deletion ignores information from those people who skipped any of the items.

16.3.4   Estimating the latent score

Where summated scales use the mean score or total score, IRT models estimate the latent score by predicting θ for each person based on the fitted model. We can estimate the latent score of each person by typing

```
. predict rasch_score, latent
(option ebmeans assumed)
(using 7 quadrature points)

. summarize rasch_score
```

Variable	Obs	Mean	Std. dev.	Min	Max
rasch_score	1,487	.0007206	.8425341	−1.206341	1.504424

The `predict` command produces empirical Bayes means estimates of the latent variable, confidence after job loss. The mean value of the estimated θ is approximately $M = 0.0$, with an SD $= 0.84$ and a range from -1.21 to $+1.50$. The variable `rasch_score` would be used as your measure of confidence after job loss based on this model. We saw from the information function graphs that this score has limited reliability at the bottom of this range.

So what do we gain from running a 1PL model? For this 1PL model, the estimated latent variable is highly correlated with a simple summated score, but this is not surprising because the observed summated score is a sufficient statistic for θ when fitting the 1PL model. Before you say that Rasch modeling is much ado about nothing, think about what we gain. Rasch modeling lets us know what parts of the attitude, belief, or value continuum we are measuring well (have strong information) and what parts we are measuring without much reliability. IRT provides a set of tools for developing a scale that represents the full range of a continuum. Because most standard summated-type scales fail on this account, converting them to an IRT score will not often make a lot of difference. It is still worthwhile to do an IRT analysis of an existing scale. The analysis will provide a systematic method to find where more items are needed (usually at the extremes in difficulty) and where we have redundant items that add a burden on our participants but add scant independent information. By adding a few items on the extreme, we can tap a greater part of the continuum. By dropping redundant items, we reduce the length of the scale without much loss of information.

Some researchers are reluctant to use an IRT score for a variable in their analyses because they would like a different mean or standard deviation. For example, you might want to rescale the estimated θ to have an $M = 100$ and an SD $= 15$. If we call Y the new score and X the estimated IRT score, we could use

$$Y_i = M_{\text{new}} + (X_i - M_{\text{IRT}}) \times (\text{SD}_{\text{new}} / \text{SD}_{\text{IRT}})$$

If you have an estimated IRT score of -1.4 with $M = 0$ and SD $= 1$, then the rescaled value would be

$$Y_i = 100 + (-1.4 - 0) \times (15/1) = 79$$

This rescaling formula can also be applied to any of the estimated scores in the models presented below.

16.4 Fitting a 2PL IRT model

Before we fit a 2PL model for these items, you might want to run a quick test of significance to see whether the 2PL model fits the data significantly better than a 1PL model. There is little sense in fitting a more complicated 2PL model unless it fits the data better. We will present the results of the 2PL model in section 16.4.1, but at this point, we can perform a likelihood-ratio chi-squared test to see whether allowing the second parameter makes a significant difference in how well we fit the data. We fit the 1PL model, store the estimates, fit the 2PL model, and then perform the likelihood-ratio test to compare the fit of the two models. Here are the commands:

```
irt 1pl dn2 dn4 dn5 dn7 dn10
estimates store rasch
irt 2pl dn2 dn4 dn5 dn7 dn10
lrtest rasch
```

The `estimates store` command saves the results of the 1PL model and assigns them the name `rasch`, but any name would work. After fitting the 2PL model—note the only difference in the commands for the two models is that we replace `1pl` with `2pl`—we run the likelihood-ratio test by typing `lrtest rasch`. This compares the then current solution for the 2PL model with the stored results for the 1PL model that we had named `rasch`. We will not show the intermediate results, but here is the result of the `lrtest` command:

```
. lrtest rasch
Likelihood-ratio test
Assumption: rasch nested within .
 LR chi2(4) =   23.15
Prob > chi2 = 0.0001
```

The $\chi^2(4) = 23.15$ is statistically significant, $\Pr < 0.001$. This χ^2 has 4 degrees of freedom because we are now estimating 4 additional discrimination values (5 discrimination values rather than 1). Because the more complicated 2PL IRT model improves the fit, we can say that there is a statistically significant difference in how discriminating the five items are. If the χ^2 had not been significant, this would be evidence to stay with the 1PL model.

The likelihood-ratio chi-squared test is sensitive to sample size. Because we have a large sample, it is possible that even small and inconsequential differences in discrimination of the different items will yield a statistically significant χ^2. On the other hand, when developing a new measure, we often have a small sample, say, $N = 100$, and there could be substantial differences in the discrimination of items even though the χ^2 was not significant. Thus the chi-squared test is only one piece of information. With a significant χ^2 and if the 2PL results (not shown here) had very different discrimination estimates for the five items, a Rasch modeler would insist on modifying the items so that a single discrimination coefficient could be estimated, while others would prefer to fit the 2PL model that better fits the data using this set of items.

16.4.1 Fitting the 2PL model

Extending our 1PL model to an IRT model with two parameters is straightforward. The command is the same, except we replace 1pl with 2pl:

```
. irt 2pl dn2 dn4 dn5 dn7 dn10

Fitting fixed-effects model:

Iteration 0:    log likelihood = -4621.5209
Iteration 1:    log likelihood =  -4616.607
Iteration 2:    log likelihood = -4616.6057
Iteration 3:    log likelihood = -4616.6057

Fitting full model:

Iteration 0:    log likelihood = -4199.6255
Iteration 1:    log likelihood = -3986.9392
Iteration 2:    log likelihood = -3978.2722
Iteration 3:    log likelihood = -3978.0158
Iteration 4:    log likelihood = -3978.0153
Iteration 5:    log likelihood = -3978.0153

Two-parameter logistic model                     Number of obs = 1,479
Log likelihood = -3978.0153
```

	Coefficient	Std. err.	z	P>|z|	[95% conf. interval]	
dn2						
Discrim	2.961973	.305367	9.70	0.000	2.363465	3.560482
Diff	.1506225	.037865	3.98	0.000	.0764085	.2248365
dn4						
Discrim	1.641559	.1580974	10.38	0.000	1.331694	1.951424
Diff	1.367027	.0893992	15.29	0.000	1.191808	1.542246
dn5						
Discrim	2.103759	.1797506	11.70	0.000	1.751454	2.456063
Diff	-.5095228	.0473406	-10.76	0.000	-.6023087	-.4167368
dn7						
Discrim	2.104367	.1766265	11.91	0.000	1.758185	2.450548
Diff	-.2204127	.0430737	-5.12	0.000	-.3048356	-.1359898
dn10						
Discrim	1.713951	.1422667	12.05	0.000	1.435113	1.992788
Diff	.4987321	.0510842	9.76	0.000	.398609	.5988553

These results are similar to those for the 1PL model result, except now we have a different discrimination value for each item. Table 16.1 shows the comparison.

Table 16.1. Comparison of 1PL and 2PL model results

Item	1PL Difficulty	2PL Difficulty	1PL Discrimination	2PL Discrimination
dn2	0.171	0.151	2.059	2.962
dn4	1.235	1.367	2.059	1.642
dn5	−0.512	−0.510	2.059	2.104
dn7	−0.219	−0.220	2.059	2.104
dn10	0.466	0.499	2.059	1.714

Figure 16.6 shows the item characteristic curves for our five items:

```
. irtgraph icc
```

Figure 16.6. Item characteristic curves for 2PL model of confidence

Item **dn2** has a difficulty of 0.151 and a steep discrimination value of 2.96. Item **dn2** clearly separates people who are a bit below $\theta = 0.151$ from those who are a bit above this value. Compare this with item **dn4**, which has a difficulty of 1.367. This item is much more difficult but also less discriminating. This means that more people respond positively to **dn4** even if their true latent score is quite a bit lower than 1.367. Also, a good number of people will have a negative response to **dn4** even though their true latent score is quite a bit greater than $\theta = 1.367$. With the 1PL model, we assumed all the discrimination values were an identical 2.06. Because the 2PL does significantly better based on the likelihood-ratio chi-squared test and because there appears to be considerable difference in how much the items discriminate, we should consider using the 2PL model or modifying the items so that their discrimination power is more consistent.

We can get more information about the discrimination ability of the items by looking at the IIF graph for each item. We do this below by typing the following, which produces figure 16.7:

```
. irtgraph iif
```

Figure 16.7. Item information functions for the 2PL model

This graph shows how much information each item provides. Whereas classical summated scales rely on measures such as item-total correlation for evaluating the usefulness of individual items, IRT models allow us to evaluate the information provided by each item. Consider our most difficult item, **dn4**, which concerns certainty about the future. It provides the most information around its difficulty level, $\theta = 1.23$ (height shows where the item provides the most information value). Item **dn4** does not help us discriminate people who are a lot more extreme than this, say, $\theta > 2.0$. Not many people would be that extreme, so this may be okay. Still, an even more difficult item than **dn4** would strengthen the scale's ability to identify the very most confident people who recently loss their job. Item **dn4** provides almost no information to discriminate between people who have low levels of confidence, but this is not a problem because we have other items to provide that information, for example, **dn5** and **dn7**.

Because we are using a 1PL model, the height and shape of each curve must be identical. This graph shows that none of our items are redundant. The height of the curve represents where the item provides the most information on the continuum. The tightness of the curve is an indication of how discriminating the item is. Information functions for highly discriminating items are tall and narrow. Our set of items appears useful for distinguishing individuals in the part of the continuum from slightly low confidence, **dn5**, to somewhat high confidence, **dn4**, where the items provide the most information. The figure shows that we have reliable information over a range of the continuum even though it is hard to look at this graph without wanting to add one more item that had a higher difficulty

It is useful to compare this with the information function graph for the 1PL model where we forced the same discrimination value on all five items. Clearly, **dn2** provides a lot of information to differentiate people near the center of the scale. This is reflected by the height of the curve and the steepness of the slope in the neighborhood of their difficulty value. Item **dn4** provides some information for the people who have more confidence, but the information is considerably less information than **dn2** provides for the center of the distribution. Notice that **dn5** and **dn7** provide information for people who are fairly low on confidence, but we have little information for people who are very low on confidence.

Finally, we can graph the test information function (figure 16.8) to get a picture of how reliable our scale is.

```
. irtgraph tif, se
```

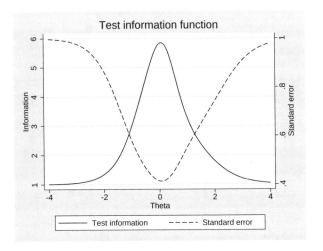

Figure 16.8. Test information function for 2PL model

If we compare the test information that our five items offer using the 2PL model, we can see that this model provides even more information near the center of the continuum than the 1PL model did. Notice that the curve for this test information function peaks about 6, while the curve for the test information function for the 1PL model peaks about 5.

We can estimate the confidence after job loss by typing

```
. predict irt_score, latent
(option ebmeans assumed)
(using 7 quadrature points)
```

The descriptive statistics for the 2PL predictions stored in `irt_score` and the 1PL predictions stored in `rasch_score` are quite similar:

```
. summarize rasch_score irt_score
```

Variable	Obs	Mean	Std. dev.	Min	Max
rasch_score	1,487	.0007206	.8425341	−1.206341	1.504424
irt_score	1,487	.0006717	.8443658	−1.202996	1.469786

By using the `correlate` command, we can see that the two scores are correlated at $r = 0.99$. There is considerable debate in the technical IRT literature on the most appropriate approach. Because of the measurement clarity of the 1PL model, I would prefer it to the 2PL model if it were reasonable to assume a single discrimination value. However, as in our example, the 2PL model did significantly better based on the chi-squared test, and the items had substantially different discrimination scores, as clearly shown in the IIF graph in figure 16.7.

16.5   The graded response model—IRT for Likert-type items

By design, Likert-type items have more than two response categories. These items are widely used in measurement of attitudes, values, and beliefs. Using additional ordered response categories beyond agree or disagree may help extend the range of the measurement to include both ends of the continuum.

Here is an example of a Likert-type item, including the item's stem and responses:

Global warming is real.

1. Strongly agree

2. Agree

3. Disagree

4. Strongly disagree

A graded response model fits the probability that an individual with a given value of θ chooses response k or higher. This is done separately for each item. Thus we get a difficulty value for each response option on each item rather than just one difficulty for each item. The difficulty corresponding to response k of item i represents the θ value, where individuals have a 50% chance of selecting response k or higher on this item.

When you create a Likert-type scale by summing items coded in this manner, the differences between codes of 1 and 2 are treated as the same as between 2 and 3 or 3 and 4. We simply add or average the scores. However, for some items, a response of 3 (Disagree) may be much more difficult than a response of 2 (Agree), but a response of 4 (Strongly disagree) may not be much more difficult than a response of 3 (Disagree). Equally, with a Likert-type scale, we assume that a 1 on the first item has the same difficulty as a 1 on the second item, and so on. These assumptions are difficult to defend, which makes the classical measurement practice of summing the scores questionable.

In using a graded response model, we are extending the 2PL IRT model.[2] Each item will have its own estimated difficulty scores for each response, and each item will have its own discrimination score.

16.5.1   The data

The original items measuring confidence after job loss were dichotomized for the earlier analysis we did using the 1PL and 2PL models. However, the actual items had four responses. We have reversed-coded the first three of the items so that a code of 4 reflects the greatest confidence. For example, on item n5 (feel rejected), a person who

---

2. The corresponding extension of the 1PL model to a Likert-type scale is called the partial credit model. You would fit it by using irt pcm n2 n4 n5 n7 n10, where pcm has a difficulty for each response but a single discrimination score across all items.

answered "Not at all" would be coded as a 4. For item n10 (motivated), a person who
answered "A lot" would be coded as a 4. Here is a frequency distribution of our items,
showing the original responses:

```
. fre n2 n4 n5 n7 n10
```

n2 — INSECURE ABOUT ABILITIES

		Freq.	Percent	Valid	Cum.
Valid	1 A lot	75	5.04	5.08	5.08
	2 Somewhat	306	20.58	20.75	25.83
	3 A little	430	28.92	29.15	54.98
	4 Not at all	664	44.65	45.02	100.00
	Total	1475	99.19	100.00	
Missing	.	12	0.81		
Total		1487	100.00		

n4 — UNCERTAIN ABOUT FUTURE

		Freq.	Percent	Valid	Cum.
Valid	1 A lot	234	15.74	15.88	15.88
	2 Somewhat	501	33.69	33.99	49.86
	3 A little	484	32.55	32.84	82.70
	4 Not at all	255	17.15	17.30	100.00
	Total	1474	99.13	100.00	
Missing	.	13	0.87		
Total		1487	100.00		

n5 — FEEL REJECTED

		Freq.	Percent	Valid	Cum.
Valid	1 A lot	50	3.36	3.39	3.39
	2 Somewhat	148	9.95	10.05	13.44
	3 A little	311	20.91	21.11	34.56
	4 Not at all	964	64.83	65.44	100.00
	Total	1473	99.06	100.00	
Missing	.	14	0.94		
Total		1487	100.00		

n7 — CONFIDENT

		Freq.	Percent	Valid	Cum.
Valid	1 NOT AT ALL	31	2.08	2.10	2.10
	2 A LITTLE	125	8.41	8.49	10.59
	3 SOMEWHAT	479	32.21	32.52	43.11
	4 A LOT	838	56.36	56.89	100.00
	Total	1473	99.06	100.00	
Missing	.	14	0.94		
Total		1487	100.00		

n10 — MOTIVATED

		Freq.	Percent	Valid	Cum.
Valid	1 NOT AT ALL	64	4.30	4.34	4.34
	2 A LITTLE	259	17.42	17.56	21.90
	3 SOMEWHAT	617	41.49	41.83	63.73
	4 A LOT	535	35.98	36.27	100.00
	Total	1475	99.19	100.00	
Missing	.	12	0.81		
Total		1487	100.00		

16.5.2 Fitting our graded response model

We use the `irt grm` command to fit a graded response model for an ordinal scale. The command and its results are as follows:

```
. irt grm n2 n4 n5 n7 n10
```
  (*output omitted*)

```
Graded response model                      Number of obs = 1,479
Log likelihood = -7471.3661
```

	Coefficient	Std. err.	z	P>|z|	[95% conf. interval]	
n2						
Discrim	2.179148	.1362609	15.99	0.000	1.912082	2.446214
Diff						
>=2	-2.103581	.0972377			-2.294164	-1.912999
>=3	-.861577	.0497801			-.9591442	-.7640098
=4	.1356028	.0420148			.0532553	.2179503
n4						
Discrim	1.609505	.0986348	16.32	0.000	1.416184	1.802826
Diff						
>=2	-1.463049	.0791114			-1.618104	-1.307993
>=3	-.0121909	.0466419			-.1036074	.0792256
=4	1.368935	.0762028			1.21958	1.51829
n5						
Discrim	2.585076	.1924925	13.43	0.000	2.207798	2.962354
Diff						
>=2	-2.209929	.1028444			-2.4115	-2.008357
>=3	-1.342604	.0612457			-1.462643	-1.222564
=4	-.4911488	.0411847			-.5718693	-.4104284
n7						
Discrim	1.470344	.099162	14.83	0.000	1.27599	1.664698
Diff						
>=2	-3.262259	.2031714			-3.660467	-2.86405
>=3	-1.953588	.1079976			-2.16526	-1.741917
=4	-.2813937	.0502735			-.379928	-.1828594

n10						
Discrim	1.372692	.0879344	15.61	0.000	1.200344	1.54504
Diff						
>=2	-2.826451	.1638261			-3.147544	-2.505357
>=3	-1.259156	.077168			-1.410402	-1.107909
=4	.5437429	.0581496			.4297719	.657714

Interpreting the difficulty may be initially confusing. Let's consider item **n2** (insecurity about abilities). A person with a θ of -2.10 has a 50% chance of picking response 1, "A lot" of insecurity, rather than >=2, that is, responses 2, 3, or 4. A person with a $\theta = -0.86$ has a 50% chance of picking responses 1 or 2 rather than responses 3 or 4. A person with a $\theta = 0.14$ has a 50% chance of picking responses 1, 2, or 3 rather than option 4. Alternatively, this person has a 50% chance of picking option 4, "Not at all" insecure. Although Likert-type scales treat all differences (1 versus 2; 2 versus 3; 3 versus 4) as equal when they are added, the graded response models allow for differences to vary. Consider item **n10**. As we go up in response difficulty from >=2 to >=3 to =4, we see that the differences in difficulty are not equal.

With a graded response model, a particular response means something quite different for some items. Consider the most confident response to items **n2**, **n4**, and **n5**. For each item, a response of 4, "Not at all", would be treated equally by a summated Likert-type scale. For item **n2**, a response of 4, "Not at all", has a difficulty of $\theta = 0.14$, close to the middle of the scale for the true latent variable of confidence after job loss. For item **n4**, a response of 4 has a $\theta = 1.37$, indicating relatively high difficulty. Only people who were quite confident after they lost a job would be likely to give this response. If we look at item **n5**, the θ for a response of 4 is just $\theta = -0.49$. Even a person with a fairly low confidence would be likely to give the most positive response to this item. For a Likert-type scale, a 4 is a 4 is a 4. For a graded response model, a 0.14 is not a 1.37 is not a -0.49. This added sensitivity is an important advantage of a graded response model over traditional summated scoring systems for Likert-type items.

With binary data, we produced an item characteristic curve for all the items. For the graded response model, we run this for each item, one at a time. We call this the boundary characteristics curve because it plots the boundary for each response. Figure 16.9 shows the boundary characteristic curve for item **n4**.

```
. irtgraph icc n4, blocation
```

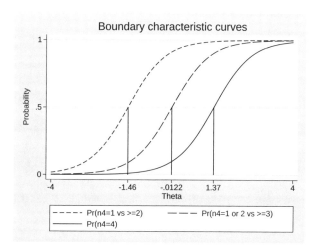

Figure 16.9. Boundary characteristic curves for item **n4** (uncertainty about the future)

We can see that the four responses cover a substantial part of the potential range in confidence after job loss. This greater range is one advantage of using Likert-type responses rather than dichotomous responses. Just as we stressed on having items that covered a range of the latent variable, now we want our responses for the set of items to cover a wide range. Examining the results of our **irt grm n2 n4 n5 n7 n10** command, we can see that the items do a good job covering the negative part of the continuum where confidence is low, but we do not have item or response combinations that do an equally good job of differentiating extremely high positive levels of confidence.

We can get a good idea of how much information each of our items is providing by examining an IIF graph for our items (see figure 16.10).

```
. irtgraph iif
```

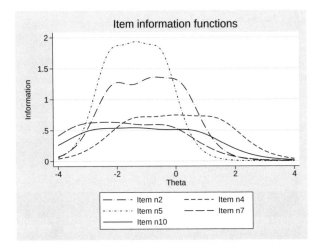

Figure 16.10. Item information function graph for graded response IRT set of items

From this graph, we can see that we have a lot of information to cover the distribution from very low confidence up to the middle of the true range of confidence. We have much less information for tapping the people who are extremely confident. Item **n5** appears to provide us the most information. Item **n4** appears to provide the most information about those who are very confident. Another item, perhaps one more challenging than **n4**, might strengthen this scale.

Although the IIF graph is helpful for evaluating items and seeing where an additional item would be beneficial, an overall evaluation of the reliability or information value of our scale would be useful. Figure 16.11 repeats the IIF graph but adds a vertical line at $\theta = 0$. How much reliable information do we have for a person who has a score of 0.0? Going up the vertical line, we see that we get about 0.5 from each of items **n7** and **n10**. We also get about 0.7 from item **n4**. We get about 1.2 from item **n5** and about 1.3 from item **n2**. If we did the same thing for a person who has very high confidence, say, $\theta = 2.0$, we would have a lot less reliable information.

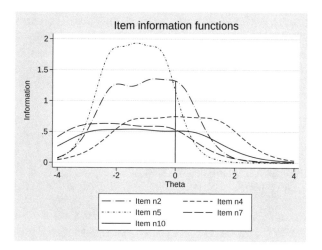

Figure 16.11. Item information functions with vertical line at $\theta = 0$

We can use the test information function graph to get a better picture of how much reliable information we have for each part of the continuum from extremely low to extremely high confidence after job loss. This is shown in figure 16.12.

```
. irtgraph tif, se
```

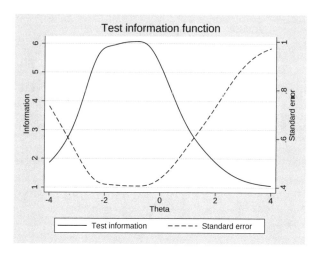

Figure 16.12. Test information function graph for graded response IRT set of items

The test information function graph shows that our set of items provides a lot of information to measure those whose confidence is challenged by their job loss but provides limited information to differentiate between those people who are the most confident after their job loss. Although the standard error goes up quickly as θ moves away from zero, notice that the scale of the standard error (on the right side of the figure) is very different from the scale of the information function. The standard error equals $1/\sqrt{\text{Information}}$. Thus, at a point on θ, say, -2, where there is a lot of information, the standard error will be small, and the reliability will be strong. At a different point on θ where there is little information, such as 2, there is little information in the measure; hence, the standard error is large and the reliability is poor.

16.5.3 Estimating a person's score

We can estimate confidence after job loss using the command `predict confidence, latent`, where confidence is an arbitrary name for our predicted value of confidence after job loss. This new variable can then be used in subsequent analyses.

16.6 Reliability of the fitted IRT model

Classical measurement theory reports a single number, such as the value of the θ coefficient, to represent the reliability of a scale. Most IRT measures do not report a measure of reliability. Instead, the test information function graph with the standard error of the function shows you exactly where your measure has a high reliability and where it does not. This is an important difference because IRT analysis of a measure shows us that the reliability of the information provided varies, sometimes widely for one part of the scale compared with another part. Although reliability coefficients are rarely reported with IRT measures, there is literature on reliability measures for IRT (Thissen 2000).

Imagine a measure to qualify people for certification as a Stata expert. You would be interested in certifying only those people who had a high true score on the measure. If your measure had a test information function similar to the one in figure 16.12, then you would have a terrible certification tool. It would lack reliability precisely for those with high values of α. The fact that it had better reliability to distinguish between a person who had little expertise from a person who had even less expertise, that is, a negative θ, would not be helpful. With IRT, it is important to know how reliable our information is for specific values of θ. With computer-adapted IRT measures, each person may get a different set of questions, and he or she may keep receiving questions until obtaining a specified information function value, but with paper-and-pencil measures where there are a fixed, small number of items, reliability may vary dramatically across the range of θ.

In IRT models, we have focused on evaluating reliability based on the information the test provides at different points across the continuum of the concept being measured. We conceptualize reliability as the consistency with which a measure can distinguish between two people who have different true scores on the concept being measured. Importantly, this consistency varies from one point to another on the continuum based on the size of the information function. We have seen from the test information function graphs for the 1PL and 2PL models that both provided good reliability information at the middle of the confidence continuum but not at either end and especially not at the low end for those who are least confident after a job loss. We have seen how the graded response model provides reliable information over a wider range than the 1PL and 2PL models and especially how it did better at the lower end.

Thissen (2000) shows that we can represent this fitted model reliability in terms of the test information function as

$$\rho = 1 - \sigma_e^2$$

When Stata fits the IRT model, it fixes the mean of θ at 0.0 and the variance at 1.0. This is necessary to identify the model and is the same method used in the structural equation modeling approach to IRT. Thus the formula for reliability is actually the variance of the fitted model, 1.0, minus the error variance, σ_e^2. The difference between 1.0 and the error variance is the portion of the variance that is reliable.

The difficulty with this formula is that the error variance is not constant across the range of θ. At some points on the scale, there is very little error variance; at other points, there is a lot. The error variance is small when there is a lot of information and larger when there is less information. In fact, the error variance can be defined as $1/I$, where I is the information. For example, if the test information were 10, at some point on the scale, the error variance would be $1/10 = 0.1$. In figure 16.12, the test information function is approximately 6 for negative values of θ down to about -2.0. Thus, for this part of the scale, the error variance would be $1/6 = 0.167$, and the reliability would be a respectable $1 - 0.167 = 0.833$. At other points along the scale, the reliability will not be very good. For example, for a θ a bit below $+2.0$, the $I \approx 2$ and the error variance is $1/2 = 0.50$. Thus at that area of the scale, the reliability is only $1 - 0.50 = 0.50$—far from adequate. If we want to have a measure of reliability for different parts of the scale, ρ_i, we can calculate the fitted model reliability at specific values of θ as

$$\rho_i = 1 - \sigma_{e_i}^2 = 1 - (1/I_i)$$

This formula defines the reliability of the measure at different points, i, along the θ continuum. Stata does not provide these values automatically, but using the `data()` option of the `irtgraph tif` command allows us to obtain the test information at the levels of θ used to produce the graph. This works for any of the IRT models we have covered. We can apply this to our 2PL model using the following code:

```
irt 2pl dn2 dn4 dn5 dn7 dn10
irtgraph tif, se data(tif_2pl, replace) n(5) range(-2 2) nodraw
use tif_2pl, clear
generate rel_irt_2pl = 1 - (1/tif)
```

The results of these commands are not shown here, but we explain the commands and the results you will receive as you type the commands and follow the next few paragraphs.

After typing the `irt` command for the 2PL model, we produce the test information graph by using the command `irtgraph tif`. When we do this, the values of the test information, I, and the standard errors are not stored after the graph is produced. We add the `data()` option to create a dataset containing this information. This new dataset

contains both the test information and its standard error. We named this new dataset
`tif_2pl` in this example. By default, Stata uses 300 data points along the range of θ
from -4 to 4 to make a smooth graph of the total information function. We specify
`n(5)` and `range(-2 2)` to compute the test information at only the 5 points we are
interested in, -2, -1, 0, 1, and 2. We specify the `nodraw` option because we are using
only 5 values of θ, and we do not need to see the graph.

Open the dataset we just created by typing the `use` command. Stop here, and open
the Data Browser to see what `tif_2pl.dta` looks like. It contains our 5 values of θ,
the test information function for each value, and the standard error for values of θ at
-2, -1, 0, 1, and 2. Finally, we generate the reliability for each value of θ with the
`generate` command, which is based on our formula of one minus the error variance.
Now open the Data Browser and you will see the following:

	theta	tif	tif_se	rel_irt_2pl
1	-2	1.3416645	.8633324	.2546572
2	-1	2.9790856	.57937334	.6643266
3	0	5.8268036	.41427126	.8283793
4	1	3.3000745	.55047567	.6969765
5	2	1.812977	.74268362	.448421

Figure 16.13. Data Browser of `tif_2pl.dta`

These results show that around the neutral position, $\theta = 0$, our reliability of the 2PL
response IRT is quite strong, $\rho_0 = 0.828$. However, as we move in either direction along
the continuum (more than average or less than average confidence after job loss), the
reliability decreases alarmingly. At $\theta = 1.0$ and $\theta = -1.0$, the reliability is weak with
$\rho_1 = 0.697$ and $\rho_{-1} = 0.664$. Beyond this point, our reliability is very poor; at $\theta = 2$,
$\rho_2 = 0.448$, and at $\theta = -2$, $\rho_{-2} = 0.255$. We could report this as shown in table 16.2:

Table 16.2. Reliability for five values of θ from a 2PL model fit

θ	Reliability
-2	0.255
-1	0.664
0	0.828
1	0.697
2	0.448

The variability of reliability is remarkable. This illustrates why we should not rely
on a single measure of reliability. Remember that if the reliability is $\rho_{-2} = 0.255$, then
almost 75% of the variance in the measure of people who have very low confidence,
$\theta = -2.0$, is not reliable. A Likert-type scale where we would use the graded response

IRT model provides a lot more information than the 2PL model because the 2PL model has just two responses providing information for each item. The same reliability analysis can be applied to the graded response model. Having multiple responses for each item offers considerably more information and hence more reliability across a broader range of the continuum. The reliabilities for the graded response model are $\rho_{-2} = 0.829$, $\rho_{-1} = 0.835$, $\rho_0 = 0.810$, $\rho_1 = 0.677$, and $\rho_2 = 0.465$.

This approach to evaluating reliability can be applied to measures that rely on cut scores to determine who passes some standard, for example, the cut score for the bar exam, a driver's license, readiness for the first grade, or admission to graduate school. When a measure is used this way, the reliability over much of the continuum is not an issue. The reliability in the neighborhood of the cut score is the critical point. We would want a high reliability at that point. However, in developing measures of attitudes, beliefs, and values, we likely want reliability to be high across a broad range of the underlying dimension being measured.

16.7   Using the Stata menu system

So far, we have shown how to use the Stata commands to fit IRT (Rasch) models. You can also reproduce these results using Stata's menu system. You can access the menu by selecting Statistics ▷ IRT (item response theory) from the main Stata menu. This opens the *Item response theory (IRT) models* Control Panel shown in figure 16.14. On the left, you can select to create a new model (the Model tab), modify how the results are reported (the Report tab), construct any of the graphs we have shown in this chapter (the Graph tab), perform a test of differential item functioning (the DIF tab), or close a log if you had opened one for the set of commands (the Finish tab). Let's see how these work to run our 1PL model of confidence after job loss. We first return to our original attitude data.

```
. use http://www.stata-press.com/data/agis6r/attitude, clear
(PREVENTING DEPRESSION IN COUPLES FACING JOB LOSS, 1996-1998: [BALTIMORE, MD])
```

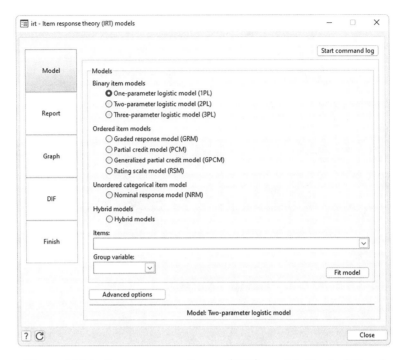

Figure 16.14. *Item response theory (IRT) models* Control Panel

Select the Model tab, and then select *One-parameter logistic model (1PL)* under *Binary item models*. Type the names of the *Items*: `dn2 dn4 dn5 dn7 dn10`. You need only to click on the Fit model button for Stata to produce the output in your Results window.

Before you click on Fit model, you might explore some of the advanced options. If we click on Advanced options in the lower left of the dialog box, we obtain access to many options, including some we have not covered (see figure 16.15). In the *Advanced options* dialog box, we can select *Drop observations with any missing items* on the Model tab. Doing this will give us listwise deletion. On the by/if/in tab, we could fit the model for a specified subset of the data, such as women or men. The Weights tab allows the use of weighted data. The SE/Robust tab provides several options for estimating standard errors, such as *Clustered robust* for a clustered sample and *Bootstrap* estimates. The *Clustered robust* estimator would be important if you had a clustered sample, such as 50 students from each of 20 schools, where `school` would be your cluster variable. The Report tab allows us to control the information reported. Once you have selected whatever options you want, click on OK, which returns you to the main IRT Control Panel, where you can then click on Fit model.

Figure 16.15. Main tab of the Advanced options dialog box for IRT

After we click on **Fit model** and obtain our numerical estimates, we can click on the **Report** tab on the left of the control panel and change the way the results are presented. We could click on *Sort by parameter b (difficulty)* to reproduce the results we reported when we used the commands directly. Clicking on the **Graph** tab shows us the graphing options we have previously covered. In figure 16.16, we have clicked on *Item characteristic curves (ICCs)* and *Add vertical lines for estimated item difficulties*. We want this for all the items, so to the right of *All items*, we would click on **Submit**. The **Add options** button gives you some flexibility on the appearance of the graph. You may want to use the Graph Editor to polish the appearance of the figure.

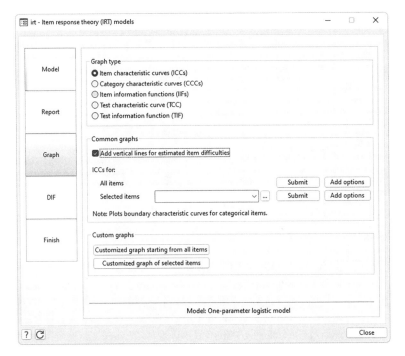

Figure 16.16. **Graph** tab for the IRT Control Panel

This is a very well-designed user interface for IRT, and you should be able to reproduce all the results in this chapter using the various options. The Control Panel would also be useful to try IRT features that go beyond what we have covered in this chapter.

16.8   Extensions of IRT

What we have done in this chapter is important if you are making a scale using either binary or Likert-type items. However, IRT offers many extensions to what we have covered here. Many of these are covered in the *Stata Item Response Theory Reference Manual*. Like most Stata documentation, this reference manual provides a variety of examples using meaningful data and includes straightforward interpretations of the results.

We have not covered the partial credit model. It is similar to the graded response model, except it assumes all the item responses shared the same discrimination parameter. Thus the partial credit model is an extension of the 1PL model to ordinal response categories such as Likert-type items. IRT is also possible when you have nominal categories such as a person's religious identification using the nominal response model. Stata even has a hybrid model that allows you to specify different models for subsets of items that have varying levels of measurement. For instance, using the `irt hybrid` command, you can fit a model where some binary items are forced to have a single discrimination parameter, other binary items have different discrimination values, and some items have nominal categories. Of special interest, you may want to examine Stata's differential item function (DIF) commands, `difmh` and `diflogistic`. These commands can be used to see whether particular items are biased against certain groups such as women, minorities, elderly, or low income. Differential item functioning has been used in important contributions to creating unbiased tests. It can also be used to explore group differences. For example, you might use the DIF commands to compare women and men or economic groups on how they respond to different aspects of marital satisfaction such as emotional support or financial stability. The DIF commands are covered in the *Stata Item Response Theory Reference Manual* along with excellent examples of their use. The `diflogistic` command can test whether each item favors one group over the other and do this for different values of θ.

16.9   Exercises

1. Open `irt_exercises.dta`. There are five items related to supporting the federal government spending more on certain things: environment, health, cities, education, and race equality. The items are coded with a 0 for spending either the right amount or too much or a 1 for spending too little. You decide that a liberal person would be more likely to want the government to spend more on all of these and hence respond that the federal government is spending too little. Run a frequency distribution, and look only at this result. How do the items vary in their difficulty? What items are the most difficult to endorse (that is, coded as 1 for spending too little), and what are the least difficult?

2. Using `irt_exercises.dta`, run a 1PL model. How do the items vary in difficulty compared with what you said when you did the frequency distributions for exercise 1? Produce an ICC graph and interpret the result. In the ICC graph, add the `range(-2 2)` option to spread out the difficulties. Add the `blocation` option to show the difficulty of each item. Remember that options go after the comma in the command line.

3. Using `irt_exercises.dta`, assess the reliability of these items as a scale of "Pro Big Government". First, run alpha on these five items as you would in a summated scale. Give examples of items that would likely improve alpha but not provide much additional information. Second, run reliability based on the test information from the 1PL model, and estimate the reliability of the measure at θ values of -2, -1, 0, 1, and 2. Compare the results for alpha with those for the reliability based on information. What does the IRT-based reliabilities tell you that the alpha reliability did not tell you? What type of items should you add to improve reliability?

4. Using `irt_exercises.dta`, run a 2PL IRT model. Produce an ICC graph and interpret the result. In the ICC graph, add the `range(-2 2)` option to restrict the range of θ in the graph. Add the `blocation` option to show the difficulty of

each item. Compare the discrimination coefficients for the 2PL model with the single discrimination coefficient for the 1PL model. Does this model fit the data significantly better than a 1PL Rasch model?

5. You are interested in evaluating a seven-item measure of negative peer influence for adolescents. Open `nlsy97_selected_variables.dta`. The items we will use are `pdrink97`, `psport97`, `pgang97`, `pcoll97`, `pvol97`, `pdrug97`, and `pcut97`. Students were asked what percentage of their friends drank, played sports, were gang members, planned to go to college, volunteered, used drugs, or cut classes. The students picked from 5 responses coded as 1–5. The responses were 1 if 0%–20% of their peers do the activity, 2 if 20%–39%, 3 if 40%–59%, 4 if 60%–79%, and 5 if 80%–100%. Four of these items are coded so that a higher score is more negative (`pdrink97`, `pgang97`, `pdrug97`, and `pcut97`). Three are coded so that a higher score is less negative (`psport97`, `pcoll97`, and `pvol97`). Reverse code `psport97`, `pcoll97`, and `pvol97`, and label them `rev_psport97`, `rev_pcoll97`, and `rev_pvol97` so that a high score means the influence is more negative for all seven items.

   a. Fit a graded response IRT model. Provide a detailed interpretation of the coefficients for `pdrink97` and `rev_psport97`.

   b. Produce an IIF graph for `pdrink97` and `rev_psport97`. Interpret and compare the information function for these two items. Include the discrimination function in your interpretation. Why does `rev_psport97` provide so little information for measuring negative peer influence? Could you have predicted that the graphs would look so different by comparing the discrimination coefficients for the items?

   c. Produce an IIF graph for all items. Which items provide the most information? Which items provide the least?

   d. Estimate the reliability of the measure for θ values of -2, -1, 0, 1, and 2. Where is your reliability strong? Where is it weak? If you wanted to strengthen the part of the scale where reliability is weak, what kind of items should you add?

   e. Drop the three reverse coded positive items, `rev_psport97`, `rev_pcoll97`, and `rev_pvol97`, and redo the analysis using just the four remaining items. How does reliability change?

   f. Fit the seven-item model, and predict the latent score for each person. Fit the four-item model, and predict the latent score for each model. What is the correlation between these two estimated scores? Show this relationship with a scattergram.

A What's next?

A.1 Introduction to the appendix

The goal I had in writing this book was to help you learn how to use Stata, including creating a dataset, managing the dataset, changing variables, creating graphs and tables, and doing basic data analysis. There is much more to learn about each of these topics, as well as about entirely new topics. At this point, you are ready to pursue these more advanced resources.

The purpose of this concluding chapter is to give you some guidance on what material is most useful as you develop greater expertise using Stata. What will give you a quick start? What requires a lot of statistical background? What are the most accessible resources? A word of caution as we start: new supporting resources appear regularly, so the suggestions here are current only at the time this book is published.

A.2 Resources

Many resources can help you expand your knowledge of Stata. More importantly, many of these resources are absolutely free and can be obtained over the Internet, including some online "movies" about specialized Stata techniques. Other resources include books about Stata and online courses.

A.2.1   Web resources

Stata maintains a webpage on resources for learning Stata at https://www.stata.com/
links/resources-for-learning-stata/, and this is an excellent place to start your resource
search. This webpage shows you links to a wide variety of sources that can help you
learn Stata and extend your knowledge of Stata.

We have installed a few commands from a webpage at Boston College. You can
check out the full list of available commands at https://ideas.repec.org/s/boc/bocode.
html. This site is often referred to by Stata users as the "SSC" (Statistical Software
Components Archive). This is the largest collection of community-contributed Stata
commands and is maintained by Christopher F. Baum. For example, go down the list
of commands for 2005, and find a command called `optifact`. This webpage has a brief
description of the command, and when you click on the link, it takes you to a more
detailed description. From there, you can click on the name of the author, Paul Millar,
to get a list of papers he has written about this procedure. All of these commands are
made available at no cost, and collectively, they represent a considerable extension of
the basic capabilities of Stata itself. To install a package from the SSC, simply type
`ssc install` *filename*, for example, `ssc install optifact`. The highly developed,
user-driven extensibility of Stata is a feature that sets it above competing statistical
analysis software.

The downloads of commands from the Statistical Software Components website have
increased dramatically over the last 10 years. Figure A.1 shows the number of downloads
and the number of abstracts that have been viewed. In 2000, there were fewer than
5,000 files downloaded, and in 2021, there were more than 106,000 files downloaded.
The Statistical Software Components archive is an extraordinary resource for all Stata
users.

Figure A.1. Growth of downloads of files from Statistical Software Components (source: https://logec.repec.org/scripts/seriesstat.pf?item=repec:boc:bocode)

Stata also has a Facebook page and a Twitter resource. You can find these at https://www.facebook.com/StataCorp and https://twitter.com/stata, respectively. In addition, there is a very valuable Stata Blog at https://blog.stata.com. The Stata Blog has entries that show you how to get the most out of Stata and features new and improved capabilities. You can receive automatic updates of this blog by subscribing to the RSS feed.

There is a Statalist Forum; see https://www.statalist.org. You can browse a long list of questions people have asked and the answers provided by other Stata users. You can register to join this forum and then you can ask your own questions. Many experts in the Stata community are members of this forum and provide excellent answers to questions. As a manner of professional courtesy, you should use the `search` command for information on any commands that you do not understand and also consult the Stata manuals before posting a question to the Statalist Forum.

Stata is a completely web-aware package, and web-based resources are constantly expanding. If you enter the command `search` followed by a keyword, Stata will search the web for relevant information. You might try it with a keyword, such as `search missing`, if you were concerned about having a lot of missing values in your dataset. Stata will give you a list of relevant resources followed by a list of commands you can install that will help you work with missing values.

We have discussed only a few of the available resources on the web. By the time you have checked these out, you will see more resources for your special interests and needs. Fortunately, many of these webpages have links to other webpages.

A.2.2   Books about Stata

Stata has a collection of reference manuals containing over 17,000 pages of information that includes details about each command, detailed examples, calculation formulas, and references to other literature. These reference manuals are available as PDFs that can be accessed from within Stata. The reference manuals are also available from the Stata website at https://www.stata.com/features/documentation/. All reference manuals are available as PDF files and installed when you install Stata. These manuals are an excellent resource, and many of the examples should be understandable now that you have finished this book. The examples for each command typically begin with a fairly simple problem, and subsequent examples deal with more complex applications of the command.

The *Stata Journal* is a peer-reviewed, indexed journal on Stata, which is published quarterly. The editors are Nicholas J. Cox and Stephen P. Jenkins. It includes articles on commands people have written that you might want to install; tutorials on how to do different tasks using Stata; articles on statistical analysis and interpretation, data management, and graphics; and book reviews. You can find out more about it at https://www.stata-journal.com.

Several excellent books about Stata have been published by Stata Press. *Data Analysis Using Stata* by Ulrich Kohler and Frauke Kreuter (2012; see https://www.stata-press.com/books/data-analysis-using-stata/) builds on what I have done in *A Gentle Introduction to Stata* and covers some more-advanced data-analysis techniques. It goes much further than I did on programming Stata.

You have seen how graph commands are the longest and most complicated. The *Stata Graphics Reference Manual* is competently written, but many find it hard to follow. Remember, if a picture is worth a thousand words, it takes a lot of words to tell a computer how to make a good picture of your data. *A Visual Guide to Stata Graphics* by Michael Mitchell (2022; see https://www.stata-press.com/books/visual-guide-to-stata-graphics/), who was previously associated with the UCLA Stata Portal, shows a few graphs on each page. You scan the book until you see something similar to what you want to do. Next to the figure, you find the Stata command that produced the graph. This does not make use of the dialog system, but you can use his examples to enhance the graphs you make using the dialogs.

The Workflow of Data Analysis Using Stata by J. Scott Long (2009; see https://www.stata-press.com/books/workflow-data-analysis-stata/) is the next book you should read if you are going to create datasets and manage them. It provides sage advice from a senior scholar and expert Stata user on how to manage complex datasets. A person who masters these skills is worth his or her weight in gold to a research team. Long will take you far beyond what I have covered in this book. A great complement to *The Workflow of Data Analysis Using Stata* is another Stata Press book by Michael Mitchell called *Data Management Using Stata: A Practical Handbook* (2020; see https://www.stata-press.com/books/data-management-using-stata/).

Regression Models for Categorical Dependent Variables Using Stata by J. Scott Long and Jeremy Freese (2014; see https://www.stata-press.com/books/regression-models-categorical-dependent-variables/) builds on chapter 13 (logistic regression), providing extensions to multinomial regression, ordered regression, Poisson regression, and zero-inflated models. It is extremely accessible given the complexity of the topic. One of the most important areas of development in Stata is multilevel analysis. Although this extends beyond the scope of my book, this type of analysis is an important extension to what I did cover.

Microeconometrics Using Stata by A. Colin Cameron and Pravin K. Trivedi (2022) is also published by Stata Press and is available at https://www.stata-press.com/books/microeconometrics-stata/. If you are going to do more-advanced statistics than we covered in this book, Cameron and Trivedi provide a remarkably accessible guide to a wide range of procedures and show you how to use them with Stata do-files. Full understanding of econometrics requires considerable advanced background in mathematics, but most of the topics Cameron and Trivedi discuss can be understood and applied with a minimum of mathematics. Even though the statistical concepts are advanced, the elegance of Stata makes the application of them quite straightforward. You do not need to be an economist to use this book because most of what is covered is as applicable to political science, sociology, criminal justice, and human development as it is to economics.

A special strength of Stata is that users can write their own commands. An advanced user who finds himself or herself doing some combination of actions by using several commands can decide to write one command that combines these commands. Another user might write a new command to add features to an existing Stata command. For most statistical software packages, this would be a major challenge, but it is much easier to do in Stata. *An Introduction to Stata Programming* by Christopher F. Baum (2016; see https://www.stata-press.com/books/introduction-stata-programming/), who in addition to maintaining the Statistical Software Components website, assists you in writing your own commands.

A specialized topic we have not covered involves working with complex samples. Stata has strong capabilities for this type of analysis. Many national surveys use stratified or cluster sample designs and deliberately oversample certain groups that would otherwise have too few observations for analysis. If you need to use such a survey for your research, you should contact the group that designed the survey and get their recommendations on how to manage the sample design. You will need to learn how to implement their advice in Stata. The *Stata Survey Data Reference Manual* provides detailed coverage of working with complex samples.

If you are fitting complex, multilevel, or longitudinal models, Stata has an abundant collection of panel-data (longitudinal-data) commands that are described in the

Stata Longitudinal-Data/Panel-Data Reference Manual. For an example of a multi-level model, you might have individuals nested in families that are nested in communities. With such data, all individuals in a given family would have the same score on family variables, such as household income. Also, all families in a given community would have the same score on community-level variables, for example, community crime rate or unemployment rate. The resulting lack of statistical independence requires more-complex procedures than we have covered in this book. *Multilevel and Longitudinal Modeling Using Stata* by Sophia Rabe-Hesketh and Anders Skrondal (2022; see https://www.stata-press.com/books/multilevel-longitudinal-modeling-stata/) is a truly remarkable treatment of this advanced topic. Although this is an extremely advanced and innovative treatment of the topic, they use great examples from published research. They show you step by step how to apply Stata to properly analyze the data.

No scientific field can advance without establishing the best possible ways to measure variables. Many areas of science have progressed dramatically as the direct result of improvements in measurement. *A Course in Item Response Theory and Modeling with Stata* by Tenko Raykov and George A. Marcoulides (2018; see https://www.stata-press.com/books/course-item-response-theory-modeling-stata/), who have long careers working to advance measurement, shows one way that behavioral, social, and health sciences can improve our measures. This book is highly recommended to those who found my chapter "Item response theory (IRT)" useful.

Consult the Stata Bookstore, https://www.stata.com/bookstore/books-on-stata/, to see a list of all the available books about using Stata. These include books on many special topics.

A.2.3   Short courses

Stata offers on-site, web-based, and classroom training sessions. On-site training is useful for Stata users of all levels, whether your site is new to Stata or needs an in-depth look at a specific feature of Stata. On-site training is taught at your facility by expert StataCorp personnel. If you are interested in arranging on-site training, see https://www.stata.com/training/onsite-training/ for additional details.

Classroom training courses are taught by various members of the StataCorp staff at sites around the country. Courses range from learning to use Stata effectively to learning to use Stata for subject-specific topics, like multilevel/mixed models and multiple imputation. Web-based training courses offer the same content as classroom training, but the attendees can participate from their own home or office. To view the list of available courses, dates, and other details, see https://www.stata.com/training/classroom-and-web/.

Stata also provides NetCourses to help you learn to use Stata more effectively. These courses include two that are designed to introduce you to data management, analysis, and programming with Stata, and a third, more advanced programming course. You can enroll in a regularly scheduled NetCourse or in NetCourseNow, which allows you to take the course at your own pace. These courses may be a little too advanced for a true beginner, but those who have completed this book will find them useful, as will those who have expertise in a competing statistical package. These courses are useful if you already know the statistical content and if you are switching to Stata from some other package such as SYSTAT, SAS, or IBM SPSS Statistics. Now that you have completed this book, you might want to pursue these NetCourses. You will be given weekly readings and assignments, and you will have a web location where you can ask for clarification and interact with other students. For more information, consult the Stata NetCourse website at https://www.stata.com/netcourse/.

Many individual instructors provide supporting documentation for their own students, and they have placed it on the web where anybody has access to it. One such instructor is Richard Williams, a professor of Sociology at Notre Dame, who has data and programs that cover a one-year graduate course in social statistics; see https://www3.nd.edu/~rwilliam/stats/StataHighlights.html. Williams' page is especially useful for people who have used IBM SPSS Statistics but are switching to Stata.

A.2.4   Acquiring data

So you want to use Stata. Where can you get data? National funding organizations that support social-science research expect researchers to make the data they collect available to others. This is a professional and ethical obligation that researchers have. As a result, you can acquire many national datasets at little or no cost. When you read an article that uses a dataset, you can do a web search on the name of the dataset with a search engine, such as Google. For example, I used a subset of variables from NLSY97 (National Longitudinal Survey of Youth, 1997). Enter NLSY97 in your search bar, and it will show you a link to a home page for the U.S. Department of Labor (https://www.bls.gov/nls/nlsy97.htm). Here you can download the documentation and data for all waves of this panel survey. They even provide an extraction-software program that will help you select variables and generate a Stata dataset. There is no charge to do this, unless you want a hard copy of documentation (and even that charge is minimal). Not all datasets are free, but the cost is usually minimal.

There are several clearinghouses that archive datasets. One of the best is the Inter-University Consortium for Political and Social Research (ICPSR), located at the University of Michigan. Many universities pay an annual fee for membership in this organization. If you are affiliated with an organization that is a member, your organization has a set of numbers that identifies each computer on its network, and this range of numbers is recorded at ICPSR. If you are eligible, go to the ICPSR webpage (https://www.icpsr.umich.edu). Enter a keyword and do a search. You might enter "recidivism", for example. This will give you a list of all the surveys that involve recidivism or include questions about it. You can then download the dataset and documentation.

When working with national datasets, you can run into some limitations in Stata. One possible limitation is the number of variables you can have in a dataset. With

Stata/BE, you are limited to 2,048 variables, and with Stata/SE, you are limited to 32,767 variables. Both of these numbers sound huge for any study, but some large datasets can exceed these numbers. Stata/MP allows up to 120,000 variables.

A.2.5 Learning from the postestimation methods

The Stata idea that you "type a little and get a little" is the key to their commands being so brief. The commands produce the critical results that most people need. Other software tries to include many extensions that are of interest in some cases but not most. This makes the commands much more complex than those in Stata. A command that fits comfortably in one line of Stata code might take 5–10 lines of code in other programs, perhaps many more. Other software often produces a huge amount of output, most of which you might not want. With Stata, you get only the output you want. Stata has many postestimation options that provide a wide variety of specialized output. The appropriate options vary depending on the command you are running. Suppose you have just run a regression command and are looking at the results. You wonder what postestimation options are available to you. Select Statistics ▷ Postestimation immediately after performing the regression. This opens the following dialog box, where I have expanded the Diagnostic and analytic plots menu.

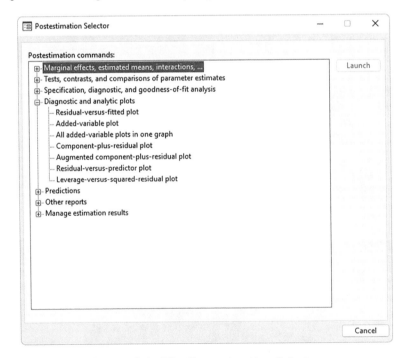

Figure A.2. The Postestimation Selector

As you explore the available postestimation commands, you will find many options
that go beyond the scope of this book. All of these are described in the Stata *Reference*
manuals. The manuals also give examples of how to use and interpret the commands.
A brief instructional video on the Postestimation Selector is provided at https://www.
stata.com/videos14/postestimation/.

A.3   Summary

At the beginning of this book, I assumed that you had no experience using a computer
program to create and manage data or to do data analysis and graphics. If you already
had experience using another software program and had a strong statistical background,
my gentle approach may have been a bit too slow at times. I deliberately made few
assumptions about your background and decided to build from the simplest applications
to the more complex.

You may encounter specialized topics in your statistics books that I have not em-
phasized here. Having gone through this book, you may be able to figure out what to
do on your own. Suppose that you need to do what is called a path analysis. You might
see an example like figure A.3.

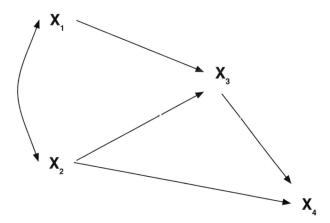

Figure A.3. A path model

Studying this figure, you see that X_3 depends on X_1 and X_2 and that X_4 depends on
X_2 and X_3. Because we see a curved line with an arrowhead on both ends linking X_1
and X_2, we acknowledge that we cannot regress X_2 on X_1 or vice versa because the
relationship is that they are just correlated. We are not assuming X_1 causes X_2 or that
X_2 causes X_1, just that they are correlated.

Your statistics book tells you that the path coefficients are standardized βs. You might guess that we could fit this model using

```
. correlate X1 X2
. regress X3 X1 X2, beta
. regress X4 X2 X3, beta
```

The correlation would go on the curved line. The standardized βs would go on the straight lines. You would also want to report both R^2 values. One problem you might have is that if there are different Ns for each variable because of missing values, you would want to do one of the following two things: 1) eliminate anybody who is missing values on any of the variables before doing the analysis, 2) use sem with method(mlmv) as discussed in chapter 13 to use full-information maximum likelihood estimation, or 3) use multiple imputation, as discussed in chapter 14, to use all available data.

This example is included here to show you that you have learned a lot and you should be ready to attack specialized statistical questions. Now you can reflect on what you have learned. We covered creating graphs, charts, tables, statistical inferences for one or two variables, analyses of variance, correlations, regressions, multiple regressions, and logistic regressions; entering data; labeling variables and values; managing datasets; generating new variables; and recoding variables. This is a lot of material. At this point, you know enough to do your own study or to manage a study for a research team. Although this book has been designed more for learning Stata than as a reference manual, the extended index can help you use it in the future as a reference manual.

You now have a valuable set of skills! Congratulations!

Glossary of acronyms

1PL	one-parameter logistic
ANCOVA	analysis of covariance
ANOVA	analysis of variance
ASE	asymptotic standard error
BMI	body mass index
CV	coefficient of relative variation
CVR	content validity ratio
DIF	differential item function
FIML	full-information maximum likelihood
GNP	gross national product
HLM	hierarchical linear models
ICC	intraclass correlation coefficient
ICC	item characteristic curve
ICPSR	Inter-University Consortium for Political and Social Research
IRT	item response theory
LR	likelihood ratio
MAR	missing at random
MCAR	missing completely at random
MLMV	maximum likelihood assuming missing values
MVN	multivariate normal regression
NLS	National Longitudinal Survey
NLSY97	National Longitudinal Survey of Youth, 1997
OLS	ordinary least squares
OR	odds ratio
PCA	principal component analysis
PCF	principal component factor
PF	principal factor
PRE	proportional reduction in error
RVI	relative increase in the variance
SD	standard deviation
SEM	structural equation modeling
SMCL	Stata Markup and Control Language
SSC	Statistical Software Components
VIF	variance inflation factor

Glossary of mathematical and statistical symbols

α	alpha reliability
β	beta weight
χ^2	chi-squared
V	Cramér's V
η^2	eta-squared
G	geometric mean
H	harmonic mean
ρ_i	intraclass reliability
κ	kappa reliability
M	mean
$\overline{X}$	mean
Mdn	median
ϕ	phi
ρ	Spearman's rho
R^2	R-squared

References

Acock, A. C. 2012. What to do about missing values. In *APA Handbook of Research Methods in Psychology, Volume 3: Data Analysis and Research Publication*, ed. H. Cooper, P. M. Camic, D. L. Long, A. T. Panter, D. Rindskopf, and K. J. Sher, 27–50. Washington, DC: APA.

———. 2013. *Discovering Structural Equation Modeling Using Stata*. Rev. ed. College Station, TX: Stata Press.

Acock, A. C., and D. H. Demo. 1994. *Family Diversity and Well-Being*. Thousand Oaks, CA: Sage.

Agresti, A. 2018. *Statistical Methods for the Social Sciences*. 5th ed. Boston: Pearson.

Allison, P. D. 2001. *Missing Data*. Thousand Oaks, CA: Sage.

———. 2009. *Fixed Effects Regression Models*. Newbury Park, CA: Sage.

Altman, D. G. 1991. *Practical Statistics for Medical Research*. London: Chapman & Hall/CRC.

Baum, C. F. 2016. *An Introduction to Stata Programming*. 2nd ed. College Station, TX: Stata Press.

Bock, R. D. 1997. A brief history of item theory response. *Educational Measurement: Issues and Practice* 16: 21–33. https://doi.org/10.1111/j.1745-3992.1997.tb00605.x.

Bond, T. G., Z. Yan, and M. Heene. 2021. *Applying the Rasch Model: Fundamental Measurement in the Human Sciences*. 4th ed. New York: Routledge.

Buis, M. L. 2010. hangroot: Stata module to create a hanging rootogram comparing an empirical distribution to the best fitting theoretical distribution. Statistical Software Components, Department of Economics, Boston College. https://ideas.repec.org/c/boc/bocode/s456886.html.

Bureau of Labor Statistics. 2005. NLSY97 Questionnaires and Codebooks. https://www.bls.gov/nls/quex/y97quexcbks.htm.

Bureau of Labor Statistics, U.S. Department of Labor. 2015. National Longitudinal Survey of Youth 1997 cohort, 1997–2013 (rounds 1–16). Produced by the National Opinion Research Center, the University of Chicago and distributed by the Center for Human Resource Research, The Ohio State University. Columbus, OH.

Cameron, A. C., and P. K. Trivedi. 2022. *Microeconometrics Using Stata*. 2nd ed. College Station, TX: Stata Press.

Carlin, J. B., J. C. Galati, and P. Royston. 2008. A new framework for managing and analyzing multiply imputed data in Stata. *Stata Journal* 8: 49–67. https://doi.org/10.1177/1536867X0800800104.

Cohen, J. 1988. *Statistical Power Analysis for the Behavioral Sciences*. 2nd ed. Hillsdale, NJ: Erlbaum.

Cox, N. J. 2014. egenmore: Stata modules to extend the generate function. Statistical Software Components, Department of Economics, Boston College. https://ideas.repec.org/c/boc/bocode/s386401.html.

Dattalo, P. 2008. *Determining Sample Size: Balancing Power, Precision, and Practicality*. New York: Oxford.

Day, R. D., and A. C. Acock. 2013. Marital well-being and religiousness as mediated by relational virtue and equality. *Journal of Marriage and Family* 75: 164–177. https://doi.org/10.1111/j.1741-3737.2012.01033.x.

Graham, J. W., A. E. Olchowski, and T. D. Gilreath. 2007. How many imputations are really needed? Some practical clarifications of multiple imputation theory. *Prevention Science* 8: 206–213. https://doi.org/10.1007/s11121-007-0070-9.

Greenland, S., S. J. Senn, K. J. Rothman, J. B. Carlin, C. Poole, S. N. Goodman, and D. G. Altman. 2016. Statistical tests, P values, confidence intervals, and power: A guide to misinterpretations. *European Journal of Epidemiology* 31: 337–350. https://doi.org/10.1007/s10654-016-0149-3.

Harel, O. 2009. The estimation of R^2 and adjusted R^2 in incomplete data sets using multiple imputation. *Journal of Applied Statistics* 36: 1109–1118. https://doi.org/10.1080/02664760802553000.

Hilbe, J. 2008. oddsrisk: Stata module to convert logistic odds ratios to risk ratios. Statistical Software Components, Department of Economics, Boston College. https://ideas.repec.org/c/boc/bocode/s456897.html.

Horton, N. J., S. R. Lipsitz, and M. Parzen. 2003. A potential for bias when rounding in multiple imputation. *American Statistician* 57: 229–232. https://doi.org/10.1198/0003130032314.

Jann, B. 2013. fre: Stata module to display one-way frequency table. Statistical Software Components, Department of Economics, Boston College. https://ideas.repec.org/c/boc/bocode/s456835.html.

———. 2014. center: Stata module to center (or standardize) variables. Statistical Software Components, Department of Economics, Boston College. https://ideas.repec.org/c/boc/bocode/s444102.html.

Kenward, M. G., and J. R. Carpenter. 2007. Multiple imputation: Current perspectives. *Statistical Methods in Medical Research* 16: 199–218. https://doi.org/10.1177/0962280206075304.

Kohler, U., and F. Kreuter. 2012. *Data Analysis Using Stata*. 3rd ed. College Station, TX: Stata Press.

Landis, J. R., and G. G. Koch. 1977. The measurement of observer agreement for categorical data. *Biometrics* 33: 159–174. https://doi.org/10.2307/2529310.

Lawshe, C. H. 1975. A quantitative approach to content validity. *Personnel Psychology* 28: 563–575. https://doi.org/10.1111/j.1744-6570.1975.tb01393.x.

Long, J. S. 2009. *The Workflow of Data Analysis Using Stata*. College Station, TX: Stata Press.

Long, J. S., and J. Freese. 2014. *Regression Models for Categorical Dependent Variables Using Stata*. 3rd ed. College Station, TX: Stata Press.

Lord, F. M. 1952. *A Theory of Test Scores*. Iowa City, IA: Psychometric Society.

McFadden, D. 1974. Conditional logit analysis of qualitative choice behavior. In *Frontiers in Econometrics*, ed. P. Zerembka, 105–142. New York: Academic Press.

Mitchell, M. N. 2020. *Data Management Using Stata: A Practical Handbook*. 2nd ed. College Station, TX: Stata Press.

———. 2022. *A Visual Guide to Stata Graphics*. 4th ed. College Station, TX: Stata Press.

Nunnally, J. C., and I. H. Bernstein. 1994. *Psychometric Theory*. 3rd ed. New York: McGraw–Hill.

Price, R. H., A. D. Vinokur, G. W. Howe, and R. D. Caplan. 2004. Preventing depression in couples facing job loss, 1996–1998 (ICPSR 3567). Ann Arbor, MI. Inter-university Consortium for Political and Social Research. https://doi.org/10.3886/ICPSR03567.v1.

Rabe-Hesketh, S., and A. Skrondal. 2022. *Multilevel and Longitudinal Modeling Using Stata*. 4th ed. College Station, TX: Stata Press.

Rasch, G. 1960. *Probabilistic Models for Some Intelligence and Attainment Tests*. Copenhagen: Danish Institute of Educational Research.

Raudenbush, S. W., and A. S. Bryk. 2002. *Hierarchical Linear Models: Applications and Data Analysis Methods*. 2nd ed. Thousand Oaks, CA: Sage.

Raykov, T., and G. A. Marcoulides. 2018. *A Course in Item Response Theory and Modeling with Stata*. College Station, TX: Stata Press.

Royston, P. 2004. Multiple imputation of missing values. *Stata Journal* 4: 227–241. https://doi.org/10.1177/1536867X0400400301.

―――. 2009. Multiple imputation of missing values: Further update of ice, with an emphasis on categorical variables. *Stata Journal* 9: 466–477. https://doi.org/10.1177/1536867X0900900308.

Royston, P., J. B. Carlin, and I. R. White. 2009. Multiple imputation of missing values: New features for mim. *Stata Journal* 9: 252–264. https://doi.org/10.1177/1536867X0900900205.

Rubin, D. B. 1987. *Multiple Imputation for Nonresponse in Surveys.* New York: Wiley.

Salzberger, T. 2010. Does the Rasch model convert an ordinal scale into an interval scale? *Rasch Measurement Transactions* 24: 1273–1275.

Schafer, J. L. 1997. *Analysis of Incomplete Multivariate Data.* Boca Raton, FL: Chapman & Hall/CRC.

Shultz, K. S., D. J. Whitney, and M. J. Zickar. 2021. *Measurement Theory in Action: Case Studies and Exercises.* 3rd ed. New York: Routledge.

Smith, T. W., P. Marsden, M. Hout, and J. Kim. 2015. General Social Surveys, 1972–2014 [machine-readable data file]. Principal Investigator, Tom W. Smith; Co-Principal Investigator, Peter V. Marsden; Co-Principal Investigator, Michael Hout; Sponsored by National Science Foundation. NORC ed. Chicago: NORC at the University of Chiago [producer]; Storrs, CT: The Roper Center for Public Opinion Research, University of Connecticut [distributor].

Snijders, T. A. B., and R. J. Bosker. 2012. *Multilevel Analysis: An Introduction to Basic and Advanced Multilevel Modeling.* 2nd ed. London: Sage.

Stepner, M. 2013. binscatter: Stata module to generate binned statterplots. Statistical Software Components, Department of Economics, Boston College. https://ideas.repec.org/c/boc/bocode/s457709.html.

Thissen, D. 2000. Reliability and measurement precision. In *Computerized Adaptive Testing: A Primer,* ed. H. Wainer, 159–184. London: Lawrence Erlbaum.

Utts, J. M. 2014. *Seeing Through Statistics.* 4th ed. Belmont, CA: Brooks/Cole.

van Buuren, S., H. C. Boshuizen, and D. L. Knook. 1999. Multiple imputation of missing blood pressure covariates in survival analysis. *Statistics in Medicine* 18: 681–694. https://doi.org/10.1002/(SICI)1097-0258(19990330)18:6%3C681::AID-SIM71%3E3.0.CO;2-R.

von Hippel, P. T. 2009. How to impute interactions, squares, and other transformed variables. *Sociological Methodology* 39: 265–291. https://doi.org/10.1111/j.1467-9531.2009.01215.x.

Wang, Z. 1999. lrdrop1: Stata module to calculate likelihood-ratio test after dropping one term. Statistical Software Components, Department of Economics, Boston College. https://ideas.repec.org/c/boc/bocode/s400901.html.

Wasserstein, R. L., and N. A. Lazar. 2016. The ASA statement on p-values: Context, process, and purpose. *American Statistician* 70: 129–133. https://doi.org/10.1080/00031305.2016.1154108.

Williams, R. 2012. Using the margins command to estimate and interpret adjusted predictions and marginal effects. *Stata Journal* 12: 308–331. https://doi.org/10.1177/1536867X1201200209.

Author index

Subject index